Lecture Notes in Computer Science　8461

Commenced Publication in 1973
Founding and Former Series Editors:
Gerhard Goos, Juris Hartmanis, and Jan van Leeuwen

Erika Ábrahám   Catuscia Palamidessi (Eds.)

Formal Techniques for Distributed Objects, Components, and Systems

34th IFIP WG 6.1 International Conference, FORTE 2014
Held as Part of the 9th International Federated Conference
on Distributed Computing Techniques, DisCoTec 2014
Berlin, Germany, June 3-5, 2014
Proceedings

 Springer

Volume Editors

Erika Ábrahám
RWTH Aachen University, Informatik 2
Ahornstraße 55, 52074 Aachen, Germany
E-mail: abraham@informatik.rwth-aachen.de

Catuscia Palamidessi
Inria, Bâtiment Alan Turing, Campus de l'École Polytechnique
1, Rue Honoré d'Estienne d'Orves, 91120 Palaiseau, France
E-mail: catuscia@lix.polytechnique.fr

ISSN 0302-9743   e-ISSN 1611-3349
ISBN 978-3-662-43612-7   e-ISBN 978-3-662-43613-4
DOI 10.1007/978-3-662-43613-4
Springer Heidelberg New York Dordrecht London

Library of Congress Control Number: 2014939037

LNCS Sublibrary: SL 2 – Programming and Software Engineering

Typesetting: Camera-ready by author, data conversion by Scientific Publishing Services, Chennai, India

Printed on acid-free paper

Springer is part of Springer Science+Business Media (www.springer.com)

Foreword

In 2014, the 9th International Federated Conference on Distributed Computing Techniques (DisCoTec) took place in Berlin, Germany, during June 3–5. It was hosted and organized by the Technische Universität Berlin. The DisCoTec series, one of the major events sponsored by the International Federation for Information Processing (IFIP), included three conferences:

- COORDINATION 2014, the 16th International Conference on Coordination Models and Languages

- DAIS 2014, the 14th IFIP WG 6.1 International Conference on Distributed Applications and Interoperable Systems

- FORTE 2014, the 34th IFIP WG 6.1 International Conference on Formal Techniques for Distributed Objects, Components and Systems

Together, these conferences cover the complete spectrum of distributed computing subjects ranging from theoretical foundations over formal specification techniques to systems research issues.

Each day of the federated event began with a plenary speaker nominated by one of the conferences. The three invited speakers were:

- Frank Leymann (University of Stuttgart, Germany)

- Maarten van Steen (VU University Amsterdam, The Netherlands)

- Joachim Parrow (Uppsala University, Sweden)

There were also three satellite events, taking place on June 6–7:

1. The 5th International Workshop on *Interactions between Computer Science and Biology* (CS2BIO) with keynote lectures by Marco Pettini (Université de la Mediterranée, France) and Vincent Danos (University of Edinburgh, UK) and a tutorial by Jeffrey Johnson (Open University, UK)

2. The 7th Workshop on *Interaction and Concurrency Experience* (ICE) with keynote lectures by Kim Larsen (Aalborg University, Denmark) and Pavol Cerny (University of Colorado Boulder, USA)

3. The First International Workshop on *Meta Models for Process Languages* (MeMo) with keynote lectures by Joachim Parrow (Uppsala University, Sweden) and Marino Miculan (Università degli Studi di Udine, Italy)

This program offered an interesting and stimulating event for the participants. Sincere thanks go the chairs and members of the Program Committees of the involved conferences and workshops for their highly appreciated effort. Moreover, organizing DisCoTec 2014 was only possible thanks to the dedicated work of the Organizing Committee from TU Berlin, including Margit Russ, Kirstin Peters (also Publicity and Workshop Chair), and Christoph Wagner. Finally, many thanks go to IFIP WG 6.1 for providing the umbrella for this event, to EATCS and TU Berlin for their support and sponsorship, and to EasyChair for providing the refereeing infrastructure.

June 2014   Uwe Nestmann

Preface

This volume contains the proceedings of FORTE 2014, the 34th IFIP WG 6.1 International Conference on Formal Techniques for Distributed Objects, Components and Systems. FORTE 2014 took place June 3–5, 2014, as part of DisCoTec 2014, the 9th International Federated Conference on Distributed Computing Techniques. After 1996 in Kaiserslautern and 2003 in Berlin, this year the conference returned to Germany, in the heart of Europe, to the exciting, multi-faceted city of Berlin.

FORTE—since 2014 the heir to the original FORTE series, FMOODS series and joint FMOODS/FORTE conference series—is a forum for fundamental research on theory, models, tools, and applications for distributed systems, supporting the advance of science and technologies in this area. The conference encourages contributions that combine theory and practice and that exploit formal methods and theoretical foundations to present novel solutions to problems arising from the development of distributed systems. FORTE covers distributed computing models and formal specification, testing and verification methods. The application domains include all kinds of application-level distributed systems, telecommunication services, Internet, embedded and real-time systems, cyber-physical systems and sensor networks, as well as networking and communication security and reliability.

We received 55 abstracts, out of which 50 full papers were submitted for review. Each submission was reviewed by at least four Program Committee members. Based on the reviews and a thorough (electronic) discussion by the Program Committee, we selected 18 papers for presentation at the conference and for publication in this volume.

Joachim Parrow (Uppsala University, Sweden) was the keynote speaker of FORTE 2014. He is well-known in our community for his fundamental contribution to concurrency theory. In particular, he is one of the founding fathers of the π-calculus, and of the Fusion calculus. His team in Uppsala is the developer and the maintainer of the Mobility Workbench, a tool for manipulating and analyzing mobile concurrent systems. In his keynote speech, Joachim Parrow presented his recent work on the use of interactive theorem provers to validate frameworks of formalisms.

We would like to thank all who contributed to making FORTE 2014 a successful event in a constructive atmosphere: first of all the authors for submitting the results of their research to FORTE; the Program Committee and the additional reviewers for the reviews, efficient discussions, and a fair selection process; our invited speaker for enriching the program with his inspiring talk; the FORTE Steering Committee for taking care of the general needs and interests of the series; and of course the attendees of the event for their interest in the presentations and for the numerous constructive discussions. We benefited greatly from the EasyChair conference management system, which we used to handle the submission, review, discussion, and proceedings preparation processes. We would also like to express our thank to the International Federation for Information Processing (IFIP), the European Association for Theoretical Computer Science (EATCS) and the Technische Universität Berlin for their great support. Last but not least, we are grateful to the DisCoTec General Chair Uwe Nestmann and all members of his local organization team at the University of Berlin for taking care of all the organizational issues.

June 2014   Erika Ábrahám
                                                                  Catuscia Palamidessi

Organization

Program Committee

Erika Ábrahám (Co-chair)	RWTH Aachen University, Germany
Myrto Arapinis	University of Edinbourgh, UK
Paul C. Attie	American University of Beirut, Lebanon
Dirk Beyer	University of Passau, Germany
Michele Boreale	University of Florence, Italy
Johannes Borgström	Uppsala University, Sweden
Roberto Bruni	University of Pisa, Italy
Pedro R. D'Argenio	Universidad Nacional de Córdoba, Argentina
Frank S. de Boer	LIACS/CWI, The Netherlands
Yuxin Deng	Shanghai Jiaotong University, China
Yliès Falcone	University of Grenoble, France
Daniele Gorla	Sapienza Università di Roma, Italy
Susanne Graf	CNRS/VERIMAG, France
Rachid Guerraoui	EPFL, Switzerland
Klaus Havelund	NASA/JPL, USA
Axel Legay	IRISA/Inria at Rennes, France
Jay Ligatti	University of of South Florida, USA
Alberto Lluch Lafuente	IMT Lucca, Italy
Antonia Lopes	University of Lisbon, Portugal
Sjouke Mauw	University of Luxembourg, Luxembourg
Annabelle McIver	Macquarie University, Australia
Sebastian A. Mödersheim	Technical University of Denmark, Denmark
Peter Csaba Ölveczky	University of Oslo, Norway
Catuscia Palamidessi (Co-chair)	Inria Saclay, France
Doron Peled	Bar Ilan University, Israel
Anna Philippou	University of Cyprus, Cyprus
Sanjiva Prasad	Indian Institute of Technology Delhi, India
Sophie Quinton	Inria, France
Ana Sokolova	University of Salzburg, Austria
Heike Wehrheim	University of Paderborn, Germany

Additional Reviewers

Åman Pohjola, Johannes	Alvim, Mario S.	Arun-Kumar, S.
Aigner, Martin	Andric, Marina	Baldan, Paolo
Akshay, S.	Armstrong, Alasdair	Beggiato, Alessandro
Albright, Yan	Aronis, Stavros	Bensalem, Saddek

Blech, Jan Olaf
Bordenabe, Nicolás E.
Bracciali, Andrea
Bucchiarone, Antonio
Budde, Carlos Esteban
Calzavara, Stefano
Carbone, Marco
Chakraborty, Supratik
Chatzikokolakis, Kostas
Chothia, Tom
Combaz, Jacques
Dang, Thao
de Gouw, Stijn
Defrancisco, Richard
Doko, Marko
Fahrenberg, Uli
Feng, Xinyu
Ferguson, Danielle
Fernandez, Jean-Claude
Gadducci, Fabio
Gebler, Daniel
Giachino, Elena
van Glabbeek, Rob
Guanciale, Roberto
Haas, Andreas

Hüttel, Hans
Isenberg, Tobias
Jakobs, Marie-Christine
Jonker, Hugo
Juhlin, Cory
Kirsch, Christoph
Kordy, Barbara
Lanese, Ivan
Lippautz, Michael
Lodaya, Kamal
Long, Huan
Loreti, Michele
Löwe, Stefan
Mari, Federico
Mauro, Jacopo
Melgratti, Hernán
Mizera, Andrzej
Monti, Raúl E.
Mukund, Madhavan
Neykova, Rumyana
Nielson, Flemming
Nobakht, Behrooz
Nyman, Ulrik
Padovani, Luca
Pang, Jun

Parker, David
Pattinson, Dirk
Pelozo, Silvia
Probst, Christian W.
Rabehaja, Tahiry
Ramalingam, Ganesan
Ray, Donald
Regis, Germán
Sebastio, Stefano
Serbanescu, Vlad Nicolae
Steenken, Dominik
Suresh, S.P.
Tiezzi, Francesco
Timm, Nils
Toninho, Bernardo
Torres Vieira, Hugo
Traonouez, Louis Marie
Trujillo, Rolando
Tschantz, Michael Carl
Vafeiadis, Viktor
Vandin, Andrea
Vasconcelos, Vasco T.
Weber, Tjark

Steering Committee

Chair

Jean-Bernard Stefani   Inria, France

Elected Members

Frank S. de Boer   LIACS/CWI, The Netherlands
Einar Broch Johnsen   University of Oslo, Norway
Heike Wehrheim   University of Paderborn, Germany

Rotating Members

2011–2014 Roberto Bruni   University of Pisa, Italy
2011–2014 Juergen Dingel   Queens's University, Canada
2012–2015 Holger Giese   University of Potsdam, Germany
2012–2015 Grigore Rosu   University of Illinois at Urbana-Champaign,
                                 USA
2013–2016 Dirk Beyer   University of Passau, Germany
2013–2016 Michele Boreale   University of Florence, Italy

Table of Contents

Bisimulation, Abstraction and Reduction

Type Checking Liveness
for Collaborative Processes
with Bounded and Unbounded Recursion*

Søren Debois[1], Thomas Hildebrandt[1], Tijs Slaats[1,2], and Nobuko Yoshida[3]

[1] IT University of Copenhagen, Copenhagen, Denmark
{debois,hilde,tslaats}@itu.dk
[2] Exformatics A/S, Copenhagen, Denmark
[3] Imperial College London, London, UK
yoshida@doc.ic.ac.uk

Abstract. We present the first session typing system guaranteeing response liveness properties for possibly non-terminating communicating processes. The types augment the branch and select types of the standard binary session types with a set of required responses, indicating that whenever a particular label is selected, a set of other labels, its responses, must eventually also be selected. We prove that these extended types are strictly more expressive than standard session types. We provide a type system for a process calculus similar to a subset of collaborative BPMN processes with internal (data-based) and external (event-based) branching, message passing, bounded and unbounded looping. We prove that this type system is sound, i.e., it guarantees request-response liveness for dead-lock free processes. We exemplify the use of the calculus and type system on a concrete example of an infinite state system.

1 Introduction

Session types were originally introduced as typing systems for particular π-calculi, modelling the interleaved execution of two-party protocols. A well-typed process is guaranteed freedom from race-conditions as well as communication compatibility, usually referred to as session fidelity [15,26,24]. Session types have subsequently been studied intensely, with much work on applications, typically to programming languages, e.g., [11,17,14,20]. A number of generalisations of the theory has been proposed, notably to multi-party session types [16]. Multi-party session types have a close resemblance to choreographies as found in standards for business process modelling languages such as BPMN [21] and WS-CDL, and has been argued in theory to be able to provide typed BPMN processes [8].

Behavioral types usually furnish *safety* guarantees, notably progress and lock-freedom [3,1,5,10,25]. In contrast, in this paper we extend binary session types

---

* Work supported in part by the Computational Artifacts project (VELUX 33295, 2014-2017), by the Danish Agency for Science, Technology and Innovation, by EPSRC EP/K034413/1, EP/K011715/1 and EP/L00058X/1, and by the ICT COST Action 1201 STSM.

E. Ábrahám and C. Palamidessi (Eds.), FORTE 2014, LNCS 8461, pp. 1–16, 2014.

to allow specification of *liveness*—the property of a process eventually "doing something good". Liveness properties are usually verified by model-checking techniques [6,2,4], requiring a state-space exploration. In the present paper we show that a fundamental class of liveness properties, so-called *request-response* properties, can be dealt with by type rules, that is, without resorting to states-pace exploration. As a consequence, we can deal statically with infinite state systems as exemplified below. Also, liveness properties specified in types can be understood and used as interface specifications and for compositional reasoning.

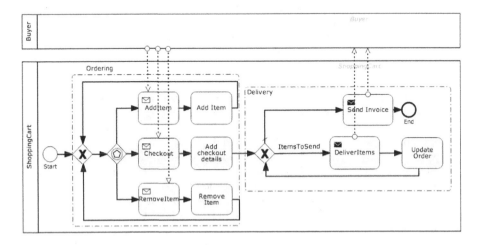

Fig. 1. A Potentially Non-live Shopping Cart BPMN Process

As an example, the above diagram contains two pools: The Buyer and the ShoppingCart. Only the latter specifies a process, which has two parts: Ordering and Delivery. Ordering is a loop starting with an event-based gateway, branching on the message received by the customer. If it is AddItem or RemoveItem, the appropriate item is added or removed from the order, whereafter the loop repeats. If it is Checkout, the loop is exited, and the Delivery phase commences. This phase is again a loop, delivering the ordered items and then sending the invoice to the buyer.

A buyer who wants to communicate *safely* with the Shopping Cart, must follow the protocol described above, and in particular must be able to receive an unbounded number of items before receiving the invoice. Writing $\mathsf{AI}, \mathsf{RI}, \mathsf{CO}, \mathsf{DI}$, and SI for the actions "Add Items", "Remove Items", "Checkout", "Deliver Items" and "Send Invoice"; we can describe this protocol with a session type:

$$\mu t.\&\{\mathsf{AI}.?.t, \mathsf{RI}.?.t, \mathsf{CO}.?.\mu t'. \oplus \{\mathsf{DI}.!.t', \mathsf{SI}.!.\mathsf{end}\}\} \ .$$

This session type can be regarded as a *behavioral* interface, specifying that the process first expects to receive either an AI (AddItem), RI (RemoveItem) or a CO (CheckOut) event. The two first events must be followed by a message (indicated by "?"), which in the implementation provides the item to be added or removed, after which the protocol returns to the initial state. The checkout event is followed by a message (again indicated by a "?") after which the protocol enters a new loop, either sending a DI (DeliverItem) event followed by a message (indicated by a "!") and repeating, or sending an SI (SendInvoice) event followed by a message (the invoice) and ending.

However, standard session types can not specify the very relevant *liveness* property, that a CheckOut event is *eventually* followed by an invoice event. This is an example of a so-called *response* property: an action (the request) must be followed by a particular response. In this paper we conservatively extend binary session types to specify such response properties, and we show that this extension is strictly more expressive than standard session types. We do so by annotating the checkout selection in the type with the required response:

$$\mu t.\&\{\mathsf{AI}.?.t, \mathsf{RI}.?.t, \mathsf{CO}[\{\mathsf{SI}\}].?.\mu t'. \oplus \{\mathsf{DI}.!.t', \mathsf{SI}.!.\mathsf{end}\}\}\ .$$

Intuitively: "if CO is selected, then subsequently also SI must be selected."

Determining from the flow graph alone if this response property is guaranteed is in general not possible: Data values dictate whether the second loop terminates. However, we can remove this data-dependency by replacing the loop with a bounded iteration. In BPMN this can be realised by a Sequential Multiple Instance Sub-process, which sequentially executes a (run-time determined) number of instances of a sub-process. With this, we may re-define Delivery as in Fig. 2, yielding a re-defined Shopping Cart process which has the response property.

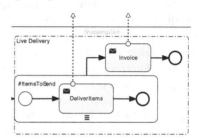

Fig. 2. Live delivery with MI Sub-Process

In general, we need also be able to check processes where responses are requested within (potentially) infinite loops. The type system we present gives such guarantees, essentially by collecting all requested responses in a forward analysis, exploiting that potentially infinite loops can guarantee a particular response only if every path through the loop can; and that order (request-response vs response-request) is in this case irrelevant. We prove that, if the system is lock free, then the typing system indeed guarantees that all requested responses are eventually fulfilled. Lock-freedom is needed because, as is well known, collaborative processes with interleaved sessions may introduce dependency locks. Lock-freedom is well-studied for both π-calculus, e.g., [18], and binary session types [3,1,5,10,25], or may alternatively be achieved by resorting to global types [16].

In summary, our contributions are as follows.

- We extend binary session types with a notion of *required response*.
- We prove that this extension induces a strictly more expressive language class than standard session types.

- We give a typing system conservatively extending standard binary session types which gives the further guarantee that a lock-free well-typed process will, in any execution, provide all its required responses.
- We exemplify the use of these extended types to guarantee both safety and liveness properties for a non-trivial, infinite state collaborative process, which exhibits both possibly infinite looping and bounded iteration.

Related work. There is a vast amount of work on verification of collaborative processes. Most of the work take a model-checking approach, where the system under verification is represented as a kind of automaton or Petri Nets. An example that explicitly addresses collaborative business processes is [23], which however does not cover liveness properties. Live Sequence Charts (LSCs) [6] is a conservative extension of Message Sequence Charts allowing to distinguish possible (may) from required (must) behaviour, and thus the specification of liveness properties. LSCs can be mapped to symbolic timed automata [2] but relies as all model-checking approaches on abstraction techniques for reducing a large or even infinite state space to a tractable size. Here the work in [4] is interesting for the fact that the model-checking can be split on components. The work in [19] allows for model-checking of ML programs by a translation to higher-order recursion schemes. Interestingly, the model-checking problem is reduced to a type-checking problem, but rely on a technique for generation of a specific type system for the property of interest. In contrast, our approach is based on a single type system directly applicable for the process language at hand, where the (less general) liveness and safety properties of interest are specified as the type to be checked and can also be used as interface descriptions of processes. The fair subtyping of [22], the only work on session types addressing liveness we are aware of, details a liveness-preserving subtyping-relation for a session types-like CCS calculus. Here liveness is taken to mean the ability to always eventually output a special name, whereas in the present work, we consider the specification of fine-grained request-response liveness properties—*"if* something happens, something else must happen".

Overview of this paper. In Sec. 2 we define our calculus and its LTS-semantics. In Sec. 3 we extend binary session types with specification of response liveness properties, give transition semantics for types, and sketch a proof that the extended types induce a strictly larger class of languages than does standard types. In Sec. 4 we define exactly how types induce a notion of liveness on processes. In Sec. 5 we give our extended typing rules for sessions with responses and state its subject reduction result. In Sec. 6 we prove that the extended typing rules guarantees liveness for lock-free processes. Finally, in Sec. 7 we conclude. For want of space, this paper omits details and proofs; for these, refer to [7].

2   Process Terms and Semantics

Processes communicate only via named communication (session) channels by synchronizing send and receive actions or synchronizing select and branch events (as in standard session typed π-calculus). The session typing rules presented in the next section guarantees that there is always at most one active send and receive action for a given channel. To distinguish dual ends of communication channels, we employ *polarised names* [13,26]: If c is a channel name, c^+ and c^- are the dual ends of the channel c. We call these *polarised channel names*, with "+" and "-" polarities. If k is a polarised channel name, we write $\bar{k}$ for its dual, e.g., $\overline{c^+} = c^-$. In general c ranges over channel names; p over polarities $+, -$; k, h over polarised channel names; x over data variables; i over recursion variables (explained below); v over data values including numbers, strings and booleans; e over data expressions; and finally X, Y over process variables.

$$P ::= k!\langle e\rangle.P \mid k?(x).P \mid k!l.P \mid k?\{l_i.P_i\}_{i\in I} \mid \mathbf{0} \mid P|Q$$
$$\mid \operatorname{rec} X.P \mid (\operatorname{rec}^e X(i).P; Q) \mid X[\tilde{k}] \mid \text{if } e \text{ then } P \text{ else } Q$$

The first four process constructors are for taking part in a communication. These are standard for session typed π-calculi, except that for simplicity of presentation, we only allow data to be sent (see Section 7). The process $k!\langle e\rangle.P$ sends data v over channel k when $e \Downarrow v$, and proceeds as P. Dually, $k?(x).P$ receives a data value over channel k and substitutes it for the x binding in P. A *branch* process $k?\{l_i.P_i\}_{i\in I}$ offers a choice between labels l_i, proceeding to P_i if the i'th label is chosen. The process $\mathbf{0}$ is the standard inactive process (termination), and $P \mid Q$ is the parallel composition of processes P and Q.

Recursion comes in two forms: a general, potentially non-terminating recursion $\operatorname{rec} X.P$, where X binds in P; and a primitive recursion, guaranteed to terminate, with syntax $(\operatorname{rec}^e X(i).P; Q)$. The latter process, when $e \Downarrow n + 1$, executes $P\{n/i\}$ and repeats, and when $e \Downarrow 0$, evolves to Q. By convention in $(\operatorname{rec}^e X(i).P; Q)$ neither of $\mathbf{0}$, $\operatorname{rec} Y.P'$, $(\operatorname{rec}^{e'} Y(i).P'; P'')$ and $P' \mid P''$ occurs as subterms of P. These conventions ensure that the process $(\operatorname{rec}^e X(i).P; Q)$ will eventually terminate the loop and execute Q. Process variables $X[\tilde{k}]$ mention the channel names $\tilde{k}$ active at unfolding time for technical reasons.

We define the free polarised names $\mathsf{fn}(P)$ of P as usual, with $\mathsf{fn}(X[\tilde{k}]) = \tilde{k}$; substitution of process variables from $X[\tilde{k}]\{P/X\} = P$; and finally value substitution $P\{v/x\}$ in the obvious way, e.g., $k!\langle e\rangle.P\{v/x\} = k!\langle e\{v/x\}\rangle.(P\{v/x\})$. Variable substitution can never affect channels.

Example 2.1. We now show how to model the example BPMN process given in the introduction. To illustrate the possibility of type checking infinite state systems, we use a persistent data object represented by a process $\mathrm{DATA}(o)$ communicating on a session channel o.

$$\mathrm{DATA}(o) = \operatorname{rec} X.\ o^+?(x).\ \operatorname{rec} Y.\ o^+?\begin{cases} \mathsf{read}.\ o^+!\langle x\rangle.\ Y[o^+] \\ \mathsf{write}.\ X[o^+] \\ \mathsf{quit}.\ \mathbf{0} \end{cases}$$

After having received its initial value, this process repeatedly accepts commands read and write on the session channel o for respectively reading and writing its value, or the command quit for discarding the data object.

To make examples more readable, we employ the following shorthands. We write $\mathsf{init}(o, v).P$ for $o^-!\langle v\rangle.P$, which initializes the data object; we write $\mathsf{free}\, o.P$

for o^-!quit.P, the process which terminates the data object session; we write read $o(x).P$ for o^-!read. o^-?$(x).P$, the process which loads the value of the data object o into the process-local variable x; and finally, we write $o := e.P$ for o^-!write.o^-!$\langle e \rangle.P$, the process which sets the value of the data-object o.

The shopping cart process can then be modelled as

$$P(Q) = \text{DATA}(o) \mid \text{init}(o, \epsilon). \ \text{rec } X.k \begin{cases} \text{AI. } k?(x). \ \text{read } o(y). \ o := add(y,x). \ X[ko^-] \\ \text{RI. } k?(x). \ \text{read } o(y). \ o := rem(y,x). \ X[ko^-] \\ \text{CO. } k?(x). \ \text{read } o(y). \ o := add(y,x). \ Q \end{cases}$$

Here k is the session channel shared with the customer and o is the session channel for communicating with the data object modelling order data. We assume our expression language has suitable operators "add" and "rem", adding and removing items from the order. Finally, the process Q is a stand-in for either the (non live) delivery part of the BPMN process in Fig. 1 or the live delivery part shown in Fig. 2. The non-live delivery loop can be represented by the process

$$D_0 = \text{rec } Y. \ \text{read } o(y). \ \text{if } n(y) > 0 \begin{array}{l} \text{then } k!\text{DI. } k!\langle next(y) \rangle. \ o := update(y). \ Y[ko^-] \\ \text{else } k!\text{SI. } k!\langle inv(y) \rangle. \ \text{free } o.\mathbf{0} \end{array}$$

where $n(y)$ is the integer expression computing from the order y the number of items to send, $next(y)$, $update(y)$ and $inv(y)$ are, respectively, the next item(s) to be sent; an update of the order to mark that these items have indeed been sent; and the invoice for the order. Whether this process terminates depends on the data operations. Using instead bounded iteration, live delivery becomes:

$$D = \text{read } o(y). \ (\text{rec}^{n(y)} \ Y(i).$$
$$k!\text{DI.read } o(y). \ k!\langle pickitem(y,i) \rangle.Y[ko^-];$$
$$k!\text{SI. read } o(y). \ k!\langle inv(y) \rangle. \ \text{free } o.\mathbf{0})$$

(The second line is the body of the loop; the third line is the continuation.) Here $pickitem(y, i)$ is the expression extracting the ith item from the order y. $\quad\square$

Transition Semantics. We give a labelled transition semantics in Fig. 3. We assume a total evaluation relation $e \Downarrow v$; note the absence of a structural congruence. We assume τ is neither a channel nor a polarised channel. Define subj$(k!v) = $ subj$(k?v) = $ subj$(k\&l) = $ subj$(k\oplus l) = k$ and subj$(\tau) = $ subj$(\tau : l) = \tau$, and $\bar{\tau} = \tau$. We use these rules along with symmetric rules for [3-PARL] and [3-COM1/2]. Compared to standard CCS or π semantics, there are two significant changes: (1) In the [3-PARL], a transition λ of P is *not* preserved by parallel if the co-channel of the subject of λ is in P'; and (2) in prefix rules, the co-name of the subject cannot appear in the continuation. We impose (1) because if the co-channel of the subject of λ is in P', then $P \mid P'$ does not offer synchronisation on λ to its environment; the synchronisation is offered only to P'. E.g., the process $P = c^+!\langle v \rangle.Q \mid c^-?(x).R$ does not have a transition

$$[\text{3-Out}] \quad \frac{e \Downarrow v}{k!\langle e \rangle.P \xrightarrow{k!v} P} \quad \overline{k} \notin \mathsf{fn}(P) \qquad [\text{3-In}] \quad \frac{}{k?(x).P \xrightarrow{k?v} P\{v/x\}} \quad \overline{k} \notin \mathsf{fn}(P)$$

$$[\text{3-Sel}] \quad \frac{}{k!l.P \xrightarrow{k \oplus l} P} \quad \overline{k} \notin \mathsf{fn}(P) \qquad [\text{3-Bra}] \quad \frac{}{k?\{l_i.P_i\}_{i \in I} \xrightarrow{k \& l_i} P_i} \quad \overline{k} \notin \mathsf{fn}(P)$$

$$[\text{3-ParL}] \quad \frac{P \xrightarrow{\lambda} Q}{P \mid P' \xrightarrow{\lambda} Q \mid P'} \quad \mathsf{subj}(\lambda) \notin \mathsf{fn}(P')$$

$$[\text{3-Com1}] \quad \frac{P \xrightarrow{\overline{k}!v} P' \quad Q \xrightarrow{k?v} Q'}{P \mid Q \xrightarrow{\tau} P' \mid Q'} \qquad [\text{3-Com2}] \quad \frac{P \xrightarrow{\overline{k} \oplus l} P' \quad Q \xrightarrow{k \& l} Q'}{P \mid Q \xrightarrow{\tau:l} P' \mid Q'}$$

$$[\text{3-Rec}] \quad \frac{P\{\mathrm{rec}\,X.P/X\} \xrightarrow{\lambda} Q}{\mathrm{rec}\,X.P \xrightarrow{\lambda} Q} \qquad [\text{3-Prec0}] \quad \frac{e \Downarrow 0 \quad Q \xrightarrow{\lambda} R}{(\mathrm{rec}^e\,X(i).P; Q) \xrightarrow{\lambda} R}$$

$$[\text{3-PrecN}] \quad \frac{e \Downarrow n+1 \quad P\{n/i\}\{(\mathrm{rec}^n\,X(i).P; Q)/X\} \xrightarrow{\lambda} R}{(\mathrm{rec}^e\,X(i).P; Q) \xrightarrow{\lambda} R}$$

$$[\text{3-CondT}] \quad \frac{e \Downarrow \mathsf{true} \quad P \xrightarrow{\lambda} P'}{\mathsf{if}\ e\ \mathsf{then}\ P\ \mathsf{else}\ Q \xrightarrow{\lambda} P'} \qquad [\text{3-CondF}] \quad \frac{e \Downarrow \mathsf{false} \quad Q \xrightarrow{\lambda} Q'}{\mathsf{if}\ e\ \mathsf{then}\ P\ \mathsf{else}\ Q \xrightarrow{\lambda} Q'}$$

Fig. 3. Transition semantics for terms

$c^+!\langle v \rangle.Q \mid c^-?(x).R \xrightarrow{c^+!v} Q \mid c^-?(x).R$. If it had such a transition, no environment U able to receive on c^- could be put in parallel with P and form a well-typed process, since both U and $c^-?(d).R$ would then contain the name c^- free. The reason for (2) is similar: If a process $k!\langle e \rangle.P \xrightarrow{k!v} P$, and P contains $\overline{k}$, again no well-typed environment for that process can contain $\overline{k}$.

3   Session Types with Responses

In this section, we generalise binary session types to *session types with responses*. In addition to providing the standard communication safety properties, these also allow us to specify response liveness properties.

Compared to standard session types, we do not consider delegation (name passing). Firstly, as illustrated by our example calculus, the types are already expressive enough to cover a non-trivial subset of collaborative processes. Secondly, as we show in the end of the section, session types with responses are already strictly more expressive than standard session types with respect to the languages they can express. Thus, as we also address in Sec. 7, admitting delegation and answering the open question about how response obligations can be safely exchanged with the environment, is an interesting direction for future work which is beyond the scope of the present paper.

We first define request/response liveness in the abstract. In general, we shall take it to be the property that "a request is eventually followed by a response".

Definition 3.1. *A* request/response structure *is a tuple* $(A, R, \mathsf{req}, \mathsf{res})$ *where A is a set of actions, R is a set of responses, and* $\mathsf{req} : A \to R$ *and* $\mathsf{res} : A \to R$ *are maps defining the set of responses requested respectively performed by an action.*

Notation. We write ϵ for the empty string, we let ϕ, ψ range over finite strings, and we let α, β, γ range over finite or infinite sequences. We write sequence concatenation by juxtaposition, i.e., $\phi\alpha$.

Definition 3.2. *Suppose* $(A, R, \mathsf{req}, \mathsf{res})$ *is a request/response structure and α a sequence over A. Then the* responses $\mathsf{res}(\alpha)$ *of α is defined by* $\mathsf{res}(\alpha) = \cup\{\mathsf{res}(a) \mid \exists\varphi, \beta.\ \alpha = \varphi a\beta\}$. *Moreover, α is* live *iff* $\alpha = \phi a \beta \implies \mathsf{req}(a) \subseteq \mathsf{res}(\beta)$.

Definition 3.3 (LTS with requests/responses). *Let* $(S, L, \to)$ *be an LTS. When the set of labels L is the set of actions of a request/response structure, we say that $(S, L, \to)$ is an* LTS with requests/responses, *and that a transition sequence of this LTS is* live *when its underlying sequence of labels is.*

Next, syntax of types. Let l range over labels and L sets of labels.

$$S, T ::= \ \&\{l_i[L_i].T_i\}_{i \in I} \mid \oplus\{l_i[L_i].T_i\}_{i \in I} \mid\ !.T \mid\ ?.T \mid \mu t.T \mid t \mid \mathsf{end}$$

By convention, the l_i in each $\&\{l_i[L_i].T_i\}_{i \in I}$ resp. $\oplus\{l_i[L_i].T_i\}_{i \in I}$ are distinct.

A session type is a (possibly infinite) tree of actions permitted for one partner of a two-party communication. The type $\&\{l_i[L_i].T_i\}_{i \in I}$, called *branch*, is the type of *offering* a choice between different continuations. If the partner chooses the label l_i, the session proceeds as T_i. Compared to standard session types, making the choice l_i also requests a subsequent response on every label mentioned in the set of labels L_i; we formalise this in the notion of *responsive trace* below. Dual to branch is *select* $\oplus\{l_i[L_i].T_i\}_{i \in I}$: the type of *making* a choice between different continuations. Like branch, making a choice l_i requests every label in L_i as future responses. The type $!.T$ and $?.T$ are the types of sending and receiving data values. As mentioned above, channels cannot be communicated. Also, we have deliberately omitted types of values (e.g. integers, strings, booleans) being sent, since this can be trivially added and we want to focus on the behavioural aspects of the types. Finally, session types with responses include recursive types. We take the equi-recursive view, identifying a type T and its unfolding into a potentially infinite tree. We define the central notion of *duality* between types as the symmetric relation induced coinductively by the following rules.

$$\frac{}{\mathsf{end} \bowtie \mathsf{end}} \qquad \frac{T \bowtie T'}{!.T \bowtie\ ?.T'} \qquad \frac{T_i \bowtie T_i' \quad J \subseteq I}{\&\{l_i[L_i].T_i\}_{i \in I} \bowtie \oplus\{l_j[L_j'].T_j'\}_{j \in J}} \tag{1}$$

The first rule says that dual processes agree on when communication ends; the second that if a process sends a message, its dual must receive; and the third says that if one process offers a branch, its dual must choose among the offered choices. However, required responses do not need to match: the two participants in a session need not agree on the notion of liveness for the collaborative session.

Example 3.4. Recall from Ex. 2.1 the processes $DATA(o)$ encoding data-object and $P(D)$ encoding the (live) shopping-cart process. The former treats the channel o as $T_D = \mu t.?.\mu s.\&\{\text{read}.!.s, \text{write}.t, \text{quit}.\text{end}\}$. The latter treats its channel k to the buyer as $T_P = \mu t.\&\{\text{Al}.?.t, \text{Rl}.?.t, \text{CO}[\{\text{Sl}\}].?.\mu t'. \oplus \{\text{Dl}.!.t', \text{Sl}.!.\text{end}\}\}$. To illustrate both responses in unbounded recursion and duality of disparate responses, note that the $P(D)$ actually treats its data object channel o^- according to the type $T_E = \mu t.!.\mu s. \oplus \{\text{read}.?.s, \text{write}[\{\text{read}\}].t, \text{quit}.\text{end}\}$, i.e., every write is eventually followed by a read. However, $T_D \bowtie T_E$: the types T_E and T_D are nonetheless dual. □

Having defined the syntax of session types with responses, we proceed to give their semantics. The meaning of a session type is the possible sequences of communication actions it allows, requiring that pending responses eventually be done. Formally, we equip session types with a labeled transition semantics in Fig. 4. We emphasise that under the equi-recursive view of session types, the transition system of a recursive type T may in general be infinite.

Type transition labels: $\rho ::= \;!\;|\;?\;|\;\&l[L]\;|\;\oplus l[L]$
Type transition label duality: $!\bowtie ?$ and $\&l[L] \bowtie \oplus l[L']$

$$[4\text{-Out}] \quad \frac{}{!.T \xrightarrow{!} T} \qquad \frac{}{?.T \xrightarrow{?} T} \quad [4\text{-In}]$$

$$[4\text{-Bra}] \quad \frac{i \in I}{\&\{l_i[L_i].T_i\}_{i\in I} \xrightarrow{\&l_i[L_i]} T_i} \qquad \frac{i \in I}{\oplus\{l_i[L_i].T_i\}_{i\in I} \xrightarrow{\oplus l_i[L_i]} T_i} \quad [4\text{-Sel}]$$

Fig. 4. Transitions of types (1)

Taking actions A to be the set of labels ranged over by ρ, and recalling that $\mathcal{L}$ is our universe of labels for branch/select, we obtain a request/response structure $(A, \mathcal{P}(\mathcal{L}), \text{req}, \text{res})$ with the latter two operators defined as follows.

$$\text{res}(!) = \text{res}(?) = \emptyset \quad \text{res}(\&l[L]) = \text{res}(\oplus l[L]) = \{l\}$$
$$\text{req}(!) = \text{req}(?) = \emptyset \quad \text{req}(\&l[L]) = \text{req}(\oplus l[L]) = L$$

Selecting a label l performs the response l; pending responses L associated with that label are conversely requested. The LTS of Fig. 4 is thus one with responses, and we may speak of its transition sequences being live or not.

Definition 3.5. *Let T be a type. We define:*

1. *The traces $\text{tr}(T) = \{(\rho_i)_{i\in I} \mid (T_i, \rho_i)_{i\in I} \text{ transition sequence of } T \}$*
2. *The responsive traces $\text{tr}_R(T) = \{\alpha \in \text{tr}(T) \mid \alpha \text{ live }\}$.*

That is, in responsive traces any request is followed by a response.

Definition 3.6. *A type* T *is a* standard *session type if it requests no responses, that is, every occurrence of* L *in it is has* $L = \emptyset$. *Define* $\mathsf{sel}(\rho) = l$ *when* $\rho = \&l[L]$ *or* $\rho = \oplus l[L]$, *otherwise* ϵ; *lift* $\mathsf{sel}(-)$ *to sequences by union. We then define:*

1. *The* selection traces $\mathsf{str}(T) = \{\mathsf{sel}(\alpha) \mid \alpha \in \mathsf{tr}(T)\}$
2. *The* responsive selection traces $\mathsf{str}_R(T) = \{\mathsf{sel}(\alpha) \mid \alpha \in \mathsf{tr}_R(T)\}$.
3. *The* language of standard session types
   $\mathcal{T} = \{\alpha \mid \alpha \in \mathsf{str}(T), T \text{ is a standard session type}\}$.
4. *The* language of responsive session types
   $\mathcal{R} = \{\alpha \mid \alpha \in \mathsf{str}_R(T), T \text{ is a session type with responses}\}$.

That is, we compare standard session types and session types of responses by considering the sequences of branch/select labels they admit. This follows recent work on multi-party session types and automata [8,9].

Example 3.7. The type T_P of Example 3.4 has (amongst others) the two selection traces: $t = $ AI CO DI DI SI and $u = $ AI CO DI DI DI $\cdots$. Of these, only t is responsive; u is not, since it never selects SI as required by its CO action. That is, $t, u \in \mathsf{str}(T_P)$ and $t \in \mathsf{str}_R(T_P)$, but $u \notin \mathsf{str}_R(T_P)$. □

Theorem 3.8. *The language of session types with responses* $\mathcal{R}$ *is strictly more expressive than that of standard session types* $\mathcal{T}$; *that is,* $\mathcal{T} \subset \mathcal{R}$.

Proof (sketch). The non-strict inclusion is immediate by definition; it remains to prove it strict. For this consider the session type with responses $T = \mu t. \oplus \{a[b].t; b[a].t\}$, which has as responsive traces all strings with both infinitely many as and bs. We can find every sequence a^n as a *prefix* of such a trace. But, (by regularity) any *standard* session type that has all a^n as finite traces must also have the trace a^ω, which is not a responsive trace of T, and thus the responsive traces of T can not be expressed as the traces of a standard session type.

4   Session Typing

Recall that the standard typing system [15,26] for session types has judgements $\Theta \vdash_{\mathsf{std}} P \triangleright \Delta$. We use this typing system without restating it; refer to either [15,26] or the full version of this paper [7]. In this judgement, Θ takes process variables to session type environments; in turn, a *session typing environment* Δ is a finite partial map from channels to types. We write Δ, Δ' for the union of Δ and Δ', defined when their domains are disjoint. We say Δ is *completed* if $\Delta(T) = \mathsf{end}$ when defined; it is *balanced* if $k : T, \overline{k} : U \in \Delta$ implies $T \bowtie U$.

We generalise transitions of types (Fig. 4) to session typing environments in Fig. 5, with transitions $\delta ::= \tau \mid \tau : l, L \mid k : \rho$. We define $\mathsf{subj}(k : \rho) = k$ and $\mathsf{subj}(\tau : l, L) = \mathsf{subj}(\tau) = \tau$. We lift $\mathsf{sel}(-), \mathsf{req}(-)$, and $\mathsf{res}(-)$ to actions δ in the obvious way, e.g., $\mathsf{req}(\tau : l, L) = L$. The type environment transition is thus an LTS with responses, and we may speak of its transition sequences being live.

$$[\text{5-Lift}] \quad \frac{T \xrightarrow{\rho} T'}{k : T \xrightarrow{k:\rho} k : T'} \qquad [\text{5-Par}] \quad \frac{\Delta \xrightarrow{\delta} \Delta'}{\Delta, \Delta'' \xrightarrow{\delta} \Delta', \Delta''}$$

$$[\text{5-Com1}] \quad \frac{\Delta_1 \xrightarrow{k:!} \Delta_1' \quad \Delta_2 \xrightarrow{\overline{k}:?} \Delta_2'}{\Delta_1, \Delta_2 \xrightarrow{\tau} \Delta_1', \Delta_2'} \qquad [\text{5-Com2}] \quad \frac{\Delta_1 \xrightarrow{k:\oplus l[L]} \Delta_1' \quad \Delta_2 \xrightarrow{\overline{k}:\& l[L']} \Delta_2'}{\Delta_1, \Delta_2 \xrightarrow{\tau:l, L \cup L'} \Delta_1', \Delta_2'}$$

Fig. 5. Transitions of types (2)

Definition 4.1. *We define a binary relation on type transition labels δ and transition labels λ, written $\delta \simeq \lambda$, as follows. $\tau \simeq \tau$, $k : \& l[L] \simeq k \& l$, $k : ! \simeq k!v$, $\tau : l, L \simeq \tau : l$, $k : \oplus l[L] \simeq k \oplus l$, $k : ? \simeq k?x$.*

Theorem 4.2. *If $\Gamma \vdash_{\text{std}} P \triangleright \Delta$ and $P \xrightarrow{\lambda} Q$, then there exists $\delta \simeq \lambda$ s.t. $\Delta \xrightarrow{\delta} \Delta'$ and $\Gamma \vdash_{\text{std}} Q \triangleright \Delta'$.*

Definition 4.3. *The typed transition system is the transition system which has states $\Gamma \vdash_{\text{std}} P \triangleright \Delta$ and transitions $\Gamma \vdash_{\text{std}} P \triangleright \Delta \xrightarrow{\lambda, \delta} \Gamma \vdash_{\text{std}} P' \triangleright \Delta'$ whenever there exist transitions $P \xrightarrow{\lambda} P'$ and $\Delta \xrightarrow{\delta} \Delta'$ with $\delta \simeq \lambda$.*

We can now say what it means for a process to be live (relying on the definition of maximal transition sequences given in Def. 6.2 below).

Definition 4.4 (Live process). *A well-typed process $\Theta \vdash_{\text{std}} P \triangleright \Delta$ is live wrt. Θ, Δ iff for any maximal transition sequence $(P_i, \lambda_i)_i$ of P there exists a live type transition sequence $(\Delta_i, \delta_i)_i$ of Δ s.t. $((P_i, \Delta_i), (\lambda_i, \delta_i))_i$ is a typed transition sequence of $\Theta \vdash_{\text{std}} P \triangleright \Delta$.*

Example 4.5. Wrt. the standard session typing system, *both* of the processes $P(D_0)$ and $P(D)$ of Example 2.1 are typable wrt. the types we postulated for them in Example 3.4. Specifically, we have $\cdot \vdash_{\text{std}} P(D_0) \triangleright k : T_P, o^+ : T_D, o^- : \overline{T_D}$ and similarly for $P(D)$. The judgement means that the process $P(D)$ treats k according to T_P and the (two ends of) the data object according to T_D and its syntactic dual $\overline{T_D}$. The standard session typing system of course does not act on our liveness annotations, and so does not care that $P(D_0)$ is not live.

5 Typing System for Liveness

We now give our extended typing system for session types with responses. The central judgement will be $\Gamma; L \vdash P \triangleright \Delta$, with the intended meaning that "with process variables Γ and pending responses L, the process P conforms to Δ." We shall see in the next section that a well-typed lock-free P is live and will eventually perform every response in L. We need:

1. *Session typing environments* Δ defined at the start of Section 4.
2. *Response environments* L are simply sets of branch/select labels.
3. *Process variable environments* Γ are finite partial maps from process variables X to tuples (L, L, Δ) or (L, Δ). We write these (A, I, Δ) for (A)ccumulated selections and request (I)nvariant. We define $(\Gamma + L)(X) = (A \cup L, I, \Delta)$ when $\Gamma(X) = (A, I, \Delta)$ and $\Gamma(X)$ otherwise, writing $\Gamma + l$ instead of $\Gamma + \{l\}$.

Our typing system is in Fig. 6. The rules [6-BRA]/[6-SEL] types branch/select.

$$[\text{6-Out}] \quad \frac{\Gamma; L \vdash P \triangleright \Delta, k : T}{\Gamma; L \vdash k!\langle e \rangle.P \triangleright \Delta, k : !.T} \qquad [\text{6-In}] \quad \frac{\Gamma; L \vdash P \triangleright \Delta, k : T}{\Gamma; L \vdash k?(x).P \triangleright \Delta, k : ?.T}$$

$$[\text{6-Bra}] \quad \frac{\forall i \in I : \quad \Gamma + l_i; (L \setminus l_i) \cup L_i \vdash P_i \triangleright \Delta, k : T_i}{\Gamma; L \vdash k?\{l_i.P_i\}_{i \in I} \triangleright \Delta, k : \&\{l_i[L_i].T_i\}_{i \in I}}$$

$$[\text{6-Sel}] \quad \frac{\Gamma + l_j; (L \setminus l_j) \cup L_j \vdash P \triangleright \Delta, k : T_j}{\Gamma; L \vdash k!l_j.P \triangleright \Delta, k : \oplus\{l_i[L_i].T_i\}_{i \in I}} \quad (j \in I)$$

$$[\text{6-Par}] \quad \frac{\Gamma; L_1 \vdash P_1 \triangleright \Delta_1 \qquad \Gamma; L_2 \vdash P_2 \triangleright \Delta_2}{\Gamma; L_1 \cup L_2 \vdash P_1 \mid P_2 \triangleright \Delta_1, \Delta_2} \qquad [\text{6-Inact}] \quad \frac{\Delta \text{ completed}}{\Gamma; \emptyset \vdash \mathbf{0} \triangleright \Delta}$$

$$[\text{6-Var}] \quad \frac{L \subseteq I \subseteq A \qquad \mathsf{dom}(\Delta) = \tilde{k}}{\Gamma, X : (A, I, \Delta); L \vdash X[\tilde{k}] \triangleright \Delta} \qquad [\text{6-VarP}] \quad \frac{L \subseteq L' \qquad \mathsf{dom}(\Delta) = \tilde{k}}{\Gamma, X : (L', \Delta); L \vdash X[\tilde{k}] \triangleright \Delta}$$

$$[\text{6-RecP}] \quad \frac{\Gamma, X : (L', \Delta); L' \vdash P \triangleright \Delta \qquad \Gamma; L' \vdash Q \triangleright \Delta \qquad L \subseteq L'}{\Gamma; L \vdash (\mathsf{rec}^e\ X(i).P; Q) \triangleright \Delta}$$

$$[\text{6-Rec}] \quad \frac{\Gamma, X : (\emptyset, I, \Delta); I \vdash P \triangleright \Delta \quad L \subseteq I}{\Gamma; L \vdash \mathsf{rec}\,X.P \triangleright \Delta} \qquad [\text{6-Cond}] \quad \frac{\Gamma; L \vdash P \triangleright \Delta \quad \Gamma; L \vdash Q \triangleright \Delta}{\Gamma; L \vdash \mathsf{if}\ e\ \mathsf{then}\ P\ \mathsf{else}\ Q \triangleright \Delta}$$

Fig. 6. Typing System

To type $k!l.P$ wrt. $k : \oplus l[L'].T$, P must do every response in L'. For this we maintain an environment L of pending responses. In the hypothesis, when typing P, we add to this the new pending responses L'. But selecting l performs the response l, so altogether, to support pending responses L in the conclusion, we must have pending responses $L \setminus \{l\} \cup L'$ in the hypothesis. Branching is similar.

For finite processes, liveness is ensured if the inactive process can be typed with the empty request environment. For infinite processes there is no point at which we can insist on having no pending responses. Consider $\mathsf{rec}\,X.\ k!a.\ k!b.\ X[k]$, typeable under $k : \mu t. \oplus \{a[b].t; b[a].t\}$. This process has the single transition sequence $P \xrightarrow{k \oplus a} k!b.P \xrightarrow{k \oplus b} P \xrightarrow{k \oplus a} \cdots$. At each state but the initial one either b or a is pending. Yet the process is live: *any response requested in the body of the recursion is also discharged in the body*, although not in order. Since infinite behaviour arises as of unfolding of recursion, responses are ensured if the body of every recursion discharges the requests of that body, even if out of order.

For general recursion, [6-REC] and [6-VAR], we thus find for each recursion a set of responses, such that at most that set is requested in its body and that it reponds with at least that set. In the process variable environment Γ we record this response invariant for each variable, along with a tally of the responses performed since the start of the recursion. The tally is updated by the rules [6-SEL]/[6-BRA] for select and branch. The rule for process variable [6-VAR] typing then checks that the tally includes the invariant, and that the invariant includes every currently pending response.

Definition 5.1. *We define* std(Γ), *the* standard *process variable environment of Γ by* std(Γ)(X) = Δ *when* $\Gamma(X) = (A, I, \Delta)$ *or* $\Gamma(X) = \Delta$.

Theorem 5.2. *If* $\Gamma; L \vdash P \triangleright \Delta$ *then also* std(Γ) $\vdash_{std} P \triangleright \Delta$.

Theorem 5.3 (Subject reduction). *Suppose that* $\cdot; L \vdash P \triangleright \Delta$ *with and* $P \xrightarrow{\lambda} Q$. *Then there exists a type transition* $\Delta \xrightarrow{\delta} \Delta'$ *with* $\delta \simeq \lambda$, *such that* $\cdot; (L \setminus \text{res}(\delta)) \cup \text{req}(\delta) \vdash Q \triangleright \Delta'$. *Moreover, if* Δ *balanced then also* Δ' *balanced.*

Example 5.4. With the system of Figure 6, the process $P(D)$ is typable wrt. the types given Example 3.4. The process $P(D_0)$ on the other hand is not: We have $\cdot; \emptyset \vdash P(D) \triangleright k : T_P, o^+ : T_D, o^- : \overline{T_D}$, but the same does *not* hold for $P(D_0)$. We also exemplify a typing judgment with non-trivial guaranteed responses. The process D, the order-fulfillment part of $P(D)$, can in fact be typed

$$\cdot; \{SI\} \vdash D \triangleright k : \mu t'. \oplus \{DI.!.t', SI.!.\text{end}\}, o^- : \overline{T_D}$$

Note the left-most $\{SI\}$, indicating intuitively that this process will eventually select SI in *any* execution. The process D has this property essentially because it is implemented by bounded recursion.   □

6   Liveness

We now prove that a lock-free process well-typed under our liveness typing system is indeed live as defined in Def. 4.4. To define lock-freedom and fairness, we must track occurrences of prefixes across transitions. This is straightforward in the absence of a structural congruence; refer to [12] for a formal treatment. Our notion of lock-freedom is derived from [18].

Definition 6.1. *A prefix M is a process on one of the forms* $k!\langle e \rangle.P$, $k?(x).P$, $k?\{l_i.P_i\}$, *or* $k!l.P$. *An occurence of a prefix M in a process P is a path in the abstract syntax tree of P to a subterm on the form M (see [12] for details). An occurrence of a prefix P in M where $P \xrightarrow{\lambda} Q$ is preserved by the latter if M has the same occurrence in Q; executed otherwise. It is enabled if it is executed by some transition, and top-level if it is not nested in another prefix.*

Definition 6.2. *An infinite transition sequence* $s = (P_i, \lambda_i)_{i \in \mathbb{N}}$ *is* fair *iff whenever a prefix* M *occurs enabled in* P_n *then some* $m \geq n$ *has* $P_m \xrightarrow{\lambda_m} P_{m+1}$ *executing that occurence. A transition sequence* s *is* terminated *iff it has length* n *and* $P_n \not\rightarrow$. *It is* maximal *iff it is finite and terminated or infinite and fair. A maximal transition sequence* (P_i, λ_i) *is* lock-free *iff whenever there is a top-level occurence of a prefix* M *in* P_i, *then there exists some* $j \geq i$ *s.t.* $P_j \xrightarrow{\lambda_j} P_{j+1}$ *executes that occurrence. A process is* lock-free *iff all its transition sequences are.*

Definition 6.3. *For a process transition label* λ, *define* $\mathsf{sel}(\lambda)$ *by* $\mathsf{sel}(k!v) = \mathsf{sel}(k?v) = \mathsf{sel}(\tau) = \emptyset$ *and* $\mathsf{sel}(k \& l) = \mathsf{sel}(k \oplus l) = \mathsf{sel}(\tau : l) = l$. *Given a trace* α *we lift* $\mathsf{sel}(-)$ *pointwise, that is,* $\mathsf{sel}(\alpha) = \{\mathsf{sel}(\lambda) \mid \alpha = \phi\lambda\alpha'\}$.

Proposition 6.4. *Suppose* $\cdot ; L \vdash P \triangleright \Delta$ *with* P *lock-free, and let* $s = (P_i, \alpha_i)_i$ *be a maximal transition sequence of* P. *Then* $L \subseteq \mathsf{sel}(\alpha)$.

Example 6.5. We saw in Example 5.4 that the process D of Example 2.1 is typable $\cdot ; \{\mathsf{SI}\} \vdash D \triangleright \cdots$. By Proposition 6.4 above, noting that D is clearly lock-free, every maximal transition sequence of D must eventually select SI.

Theorem 6.6. *Suppose* $\cdot ; L \vdash P \triangleright \Delta$ *with* P *lock-free. Then* P *is live for* $\cdot, \Delta$.

Example 6.7. We saw in Example 5.4 that $P(D)$ is typable as $\cdot ; \emptyset \vdash P(D) \triangleright k : T_P, o^+ : T_D, o^- : \overline{T_D}$. Noting $P(D)$ lock-free, by the above Theorem it is live, and so will uphold the liveness guarantee in T_P: if CO is selected, then eventually also SI is selected. Or in the intuition of the example: If the buyer performs "Checkout", he is guaranteed to subsequently receive an invoice.

7   Conclusion and Future Work

We introduced a conservative generalization of binary session types to *session types with responses*, which allows to specify response liveness properties. We showed that session types with responses are strictly more expressive (wrt. the classes of behaviours they can express) than standard binary session types. We provided a typing system for a process calculus similar to a non-trivial subset of collaborative BPMN processes with possibly infinite loops and bounded iteration and proved that lock-free, well typed processes are live.

We have identified several interesting directions for future work: Firstly, the present techniques could be lifted to multi-party session types, which guarantees lock-freedom. Secondly, investigate more general liveness properties. Thirdly, channel passing is presently omitted for simplicity of presentation and not needed for our expressiveness result (Theorem 3.8). Introducing it, raises the question of wether one can delegate the responsibility for doing responses or not? If *not*, then channel passing does not affect the liveness properties of a lock-free process, and so is not really interesting for the present paper. If one *could*, it must be ensured that responses are not forever delegated without ever being fulfilled, which is an interesting challenge for future work. We hope to leverage existing techniques for the π-calculus, e.g., [18]. Finally, and more speculatively, we plan to investigate relations to fair subtyping [22] and Live Sequence Charts [6].

References

1. Bettini, L., Coppo, M., D'Antoni, L., De Luca, M., Dezani-Ciancaglini, M., Yoshida, N.: Global progress in dynamically interleaved multiparty sessions. In: van Breugel, F., Chechik, M. (eds.) CONCUR 2008. LNCS, vol. 5201, pp. 418–433. Springer, Heidelberg (2008)
2. Brill, M., Damm, W., Klose, J., Westphal, B., Wittke, H.: Live sequence charts: An introduction to lines, arrows, and strange boxes in the context of formal verification. In: Ehrig, H., Damm, W., Desel, J., Große-Rhode, M., Reif, W., Schnieder, E., Westkämper, E. (eds.) INT 2004. LNCS, vol. 3147, pp. 374–399. Springer, Heidelberg (2004)
3. Carbone, M., Debois, S.: A graphical approach to progress for structured communication in web services. In: ICE, pp. 13–27 (2010)
4. Cheung, S.-C., Giannakopoulou, D., Kramer, J.: Verification of liveness properties using compositional reachability analysis. In: Jazayeri, M. (ed.) ESEC 1997 and ESEC-FSE 1997. LNCS, vol. 1301, pp. 227–243. Springer, Heidelberg (1997)
5. Coppo, M., Dezani-Ciancaglini, M., Padovani, L., Yoshida, N.: Inference of global progress properties for dynamically interleaved multiparty sessions. In: De Nicola, R., Julien, C. (eds.) COORDINATION 2013. LNCS, vol. 7890, pp. 45–59. Springer, Heidelberg (2013)
6. Damm, W., Harel, D.: Lscs: Breathing life into message sequence charts. Formal Methods in System Design 19, 45–80 (2001)
7. Debois, S., Hildebrandt, T., Slaats, T., Yoshida, N.: Type checking liveness for collaborative processes with bounded and unbounded recursion (full version), http://www.itu.dk/~hilde/liveness-full.pdf
8. Deniélou, P.-M., Yoshida, N.: Multiparty session types meet communicating automata. In: Seidl, H. (ed.) Programming Languages and Systems. LNCS, vol. 7211, pp. 194–213. Springer, Heidelberg (2012)
9. Deniélou, P.-M., Yoshida, N.: Multiparty compatibility in communicating automata: Characterisation and synthesis of global session types. In: Fomin, F.V., Freivalds, R., Kwiatkowska, M., Peleg, D. (eds.) ICALP 2013, Part II. LNCS, vol. 7966, pp. 174–186. Springer, Heidelberg (2013)
10. Dezani-Ciancaglini, M., de'Liguoro, U., Yoshida, N.: On progress for structured communications. In: Barthe, G., Fournet, C. (eds.) TGC 2007. LNCS, vol. 4912, pp. 257–275. Springer, Heidelberg (2008)
11. Dezani-Ciancaglini, M., Drossopoulou, S., Mostrous, D., Yoshida, N.: Objects and session types. Inf. Comput. 207, 595–641 (2009)
12. Fossati, L., Honda, K., Yoshida, N.: Intensional and extensional characterisation of global progress in the π-calculus. In: Koutny, M., Ulidowski, I. (eds.) CONCUR 2012. LNCS, vol. 7454, pp. 287–301. Springer, Heidelberg (2012)
13. Gay, S.J., Hole, M.: Subtyping for session types in the pi calculus. Acta Inf. 42, 191–225 (2005)
14. Honda, K., Mukhamedov, A., Brown, G., Chen, T.-C., Yoshida, N.: Scribbling interactions with a formal foundation. In: Natarajan, R., Ojo, A. (eds.) ICDCIT 2011. LNCS, vol. 6536, pp. 55–75. Springer, Heidelberg (2011)
15. Honda, K., Vasconcelos, V.T., Kubo, M.: Language primitives and type discipline for structured communication-based programming. In: Hankin, C. (ed.) ESOP 1998. LNCS, vol. 1381, pp. 122–138. Springer, Heidelberg (1998)
16. Honda, K., Yoshida, N., Carbone, M.: Multiparty asynchronous session types. In: POPL, pp. 273–284 (2008)

17. Hu, R., Yoshida, N., Honda, K.: Session-based distributed programming in Java. In: Vitek, J. (ed.) ECOOP 2008. LNCS, vol. 5142, pp. 516–541. Springer, Heidelberg (2008)
18. Kobayashi, N.: A type system for lock-free processes. I&C 177, 122–159 (2002)
19. Kobayashi, N., Ong, C.-H.L.: A type system equivalent to the modal mu-calculus model checking of higher-order recursion schemes. In: LICS, pp. 179–188 (2009)
20. Mostrous, D., Vasconcelos, V.T.: Session typing for a featherweight Erlang. In: De Meuter, W., Roman, G.-C. (eds.) COORDINATION 2011. LNCS, vol. 6721, pp. 95–109. Springer, Heidelberg (2011)
21. Object Management Group BPMN Technical Committee, Business Process Model and Notation, v2.0, Webpage (2011), http://www.omg.org/spec/BPMN/2.0/PDF
22. Padovani, L.: Fair subtyping for open session types. In: Fomin, F.V., Freivalds, R., Kwiatkowska, M., Peleg, D. (eds.) ICALP 2013, Part II. LNCS, vol. 7966, pp. 373–384. Springer, Heidelberg (2013)
23. Roa, J., Chiotti, O., Villarreal, P.: A verification method for collaborative business processes. In: Daniel, F., Barkaoui, K., Dustdar, S. (eds.) BPM Workshops 2011, Part I. LNBIP, vol. 99, pp. 293–305. Springer, Heidelberg (2012)
24. Vasconcelos, V.: Fundamentals of session types. I&C 217, 52–70 (2012)
25. Torres Vieira, H., Thudichum Vasconcelos, V.: Typing progress in communication-centred systems. In: De Nicola, R., Julien, C. (eds.) COORDINATION 2013. LNCS, vol. 7890, pp. 236–250. Springer, Heidelberg (2013)
26. Yoshida, N., Vasconcelos, V.T.: Language primitives and type discipline for structured communication-based programming revisited: Two systems for higher-order session communication. ENTCS 171, 73–93 (2007)

Property Specification Made Easy: Harnessing the Power of Model Checking in UML Designs

Daniela Remenska[1,3], Tim A.C. Willemse[2],
Jeff Templon[3], Kees Verstoep[1], and Henri Bal[1]

[1] Dept. of Computer Science, VU University Amsterdam, The Netherlands
[2] Dept. of Computer Science, TU Eindhoven, The Netherlands
[3] NIKHEF, Amsterdam, The Netherlands

Abstract. Developing correct concurrent software is challenging. Design errors can result in deadlocks, race conditions and livelocks, and discovering these is difficult. A serious obstacle for an industrial uptake of rigorous analysis techniques such as model checking is the learning curve associated to the languages — typically temporal logics — used for specifying the application-specific properties to be checked. To bring the process of correctly eliciting functional properties closer to software engineers, we introduce PASS, a Property ASSistant wizard as part of a UML-based front-end to the mCRL2 toolset. PASS instantiates pattern templates using three notations: a natural language summary, a μ-calculus formula and a UML sequence diagram depicting the desired behavior. Most approaches to date have focused on LTL, which is a state-based formalism. Conversely, μ-calculus is event-based, making it a good match for sequence diagrams, where communication between components is depicted. We revisit a case study from the Grid domain, using PASS to obtain the formula and monitor for checking the property.

1 Introduction

A challenge during the development of concurrent systems is detecting design errors, as such errors can cause deadlocks, livelocks, race conditions, starvation, etc. The sheer number of different executions and the inherent non-determinism in concurrent systems make complete testing of such software infeasible. Instead, more rigorous formal analysis techniques like model checking are required, which exhaustively analyze the behaviors of (an abstraction of) the system. Toolsets such as SPIN, nuSMV, CADP and mCRL2 offer such analysis techniques. Despite the research effort, these tools are still not widely accepted in industry. One problem is the learning curve associated with becoming proficient in the underlying mathematical formalisms that must be used for describing models in these toolsets.

Bridging the gap between industry-adopted methodologies based on UML software designs and the aforementioned tools and languages, in [1] we devised a methodology for automatically verifying UML sequence and activity diagrams. Our prototype uses the mCRL2 language [2] and toolset as its backend, without users having to leave the UML domain, except when specifying application-specific properties.

E. Ábrahám and C. Palamidessi (Eds.), FORTE 2014, LNCS 8461, pp. 17–32, 2014.

While the mCRL2 toolset can automatically discover deadlocks and search for specific events, its model checking facilities require users to specify their application-specific properties in a data-enriched extension of the modal μ-calculus [3]. A downside is that it is not very accessible and requires a high degree of mathematical maturity. As already simpler languages such as Linear Temporal Logic (LTL) and Computational Tree Logic (CTL) are not widespread in industry, the μ-calculus stands little chance of being embraced by the industry. In fact, most requirements are written in natural language, and often contain ambiguities which make it difficult even for experienced practitioners to capture them accurately in any temporal logic. There are subtle but crucial details which are often overlooked and need to be carefully considered in order to distill the right formula.

In an attempt to ease the use of temporal logic, in [4], a pattern-based classification was developed for capturing requirements and generating input to model checking tools. The authors observed that almost all (> 500) properties they surveyed can be mapped into one of several property patterns. Each pattern is a high-level, formalism-independent abstraction and captures a commonly occurring requirement. Their hierarchical taxonomy is based on the idea that each pattern has a *scope*, which defines the extent of program execution over which the pattern must hold, and a *behavior*, which describes the intent of the pattern. The pattern system identifies 5 scopes and 11 behavior variations that can be combined to create 55 different property templates. Examples of scopes are: *globally*, and *after* an event or state occurs; examples of behavior classification are: *absence* (an event or state should never occur during an execution) and *response* (an event or state must be followed by another event or state).

Although the patterns website [5] contains a collection of mappings for different target formalisms such as LTL and CTL, in practice practitioners have to fully understand the solutions before they can select and apply the appropriate ones. To mitigate this problem, several conversational tools [6–8] have been proposed for elucidating properties, based on the patterns. These tools guide users in selecting the appropriate pattern and optionally produce a formula in some target temporal logic. Alternative approaches [9–15] tackle the property specification problem by proposing new graphical notations for specifying properties. As far as we have been able to trace, all approaches deal with state-based logics. Such logics conceptually do not match the typical event-based UML sequence diagrams and activity diagrams, in which events represent methods calls or asynchronous communication between distributed components.

The contribution of our work is a simplification of the process of specifying functional requirements for event-based systems. We introduce PASS, a Property ASSistant which is a tool that guides and facilitates deriving system properties. Our starting point was the pattern system [4], which we extended with over 50 useful property templates. The pattern templates instantiated with PASS have three notations: a natural language summary, a μ-calculus formula and a UML sequence diagram depicting desired behaviors. We utilized mCRL2's rich data extensions of the μ-calculus to express complex data-dependent properties. Lastly, we automatically generate monitors which can be used for property-driven on-the-fly state space exploration using the standard exploration facilities of mCRL2. Our monitors are essentially sequence diagrams, acting as observers of message exchanges.

We deliberately chose to develop PASS as an Eclipse plug-in, as our strong motivation was to stay within an existing UML development environment, rather than use an external helper tool for this. We are convinced that this increases the tool accessibility by allowing software engineers to remain focused in the realm of UML designs. In addition, a tight connection between elements of the design and instances of the property template is kept, such that, if the design is changed, these changes can be easily propagated in the property template placeholders. To this end, we use the standard MDT-UML2 [16] Eclipse modeling API. We revisit a case study we did previously in [1], this time using PASS to obtain the formula and monitor for checking the property.

Structure. In Section 2 we survey related approaches, and outline their advantages and shortcomings. Section 3 introduces mCRL2, μ-calculus and UML sequence diagrams. We describe our approach in Section 4. In Section 5 we apply PASS on a case study from the Grid domain, and we conclude in Section 6.

2   Related Work

PROPEL [6] is a tool that guides users in selecting the appropriate template from the patterns classification. PROPEL adds new patterns covering subtle aspects not addressed by the patterns classification of [4] (such as considering the effect of multiple occurrences of a cause in a pattern); at the same time it omits patterns such as the universality, bounded existence and chain patterns. The resulting templates are represented using "disciplined natural language" and finite state automata rather than temporal logic expressions. Similar to PROPEL, the tools SPIDER [7] and Prospec [8] extend the original patterns but add compositionality. SPIDER is no longer maintained and available; the latest version of Prospec that we found and tested (Fig. 1 left) produces formulas in Future Interval Logic, not LTL as stated in [8].

Approaches that use a graphical notation for specifying properties come closest to the realm of modeling the system behavior. In [10], formulas are represented as acyclic graphs of states and temporal operators as nodes. Technically, the underlying LTL formalism is hidden from the user but the notation still closely resembles the formalism. As such, it is not very accessible. Another tool, called the TimeLine Editor [11] permits formalizing specific requirements using timeline diagrams. For instance, response formulas are depicted in timeline diagrams by specifying temporal relations among events and constraints. These diagrams are then automatically converted into Büchi automata, amenable to model checking with SPIN. Unfortunately the tool is no longer available. The CHARMY approach [9] presents a scenario-based visual language called Property Sequence Charts (PSC). Properties in this language are relations on a set of exchanged system messages. The language borrows concepts from UML 2.0 Sequence Diagrams and the tool uses the toolset SPIN as a backend for model checking generated Büchi automata [17]. The PSC notation uses textual restrictions for past and future events, placed as circles directly on message arrows (Fig. 1 right). A drawback of PSC is that it does not support asynchronous communication, which is omnipresent in concurrent systems. Furthermore, CHARMY is a standalone framework for architectural descriptions, not inter-operable with UML tools. As such, its use in industrial contexts is limited.

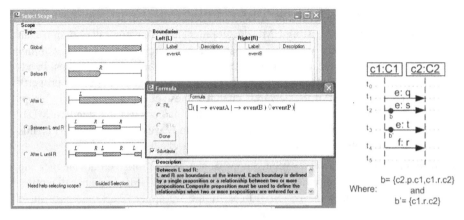

Fig. 1. Left: Prospec tool; right: CHARMY PSC graphical notation

Among the UML-based tools are HUGO/RT [12] and vUML [13]. HUGO/RT is a tool for model checking UML 2.0 interactions against a model composed of message-exchanging state machines. The interactions represent the desired properties, and are translated together with the system model into Büchi automata for model checking with SPIN. The version we tested supports no asynchronous messages nor combined fragments. vUML [13] is, like HUGO/RT, essentially a tool for automating verifications of UML state machines. Properties must be specified in terms of undesired scenarios. The verification is based on the ability to reach error states. This is inconvenient, as users must specify these manually. Live Sequence Charts (LSC) are also used [14, 15] as a graphical formalism for expressing behavioral properties. They can distinguish between possible (cold) and mandatory (hot) behaviors. For both, Büchi automata and LTL formulas are generated automatically from the diagrams. UML 2.0 sequence diagrams borrow many concepts from LSC, by introducing the *assert* and *negate* fragments capturing mandatory and forbidden behavior. However, LSCs lack many UML features.

3   Preliminaries

3.1   Brief Introduction to mCRL2 and μ-Calculus

mCRL2 is a language and accompanying toolset for specifying and analyzing concurrent systems. Our choice for using the mCRL2 language is motivated by its rich set of abstract data types as first-class citizens, as well as its powerful toolset for analyzing, simulating, and visualizing specifications. The fragment of the mCRL2 syntax that is most commonly used is given by the following BNF grammar:

$$p ::= a(d_1, \ldots, d_n) \mid \tau \mid \delta \mid p + p \mid p \cdot p \mid p \| p \mid \sum_{d:D} p \mid c \to p \diamond q$$

Actions are the basic ingredients for models. They represent some observable atomic event. An action a of a process may have a number of data arguments $d_1, \ldots, d_n$.

The action τ denotes an internal step, which cannot be observed from the external world. Non-deterministic choice between two processes is denoted by the "+" operator. Processes can be composed sequentially and in parallel by means of "$\cdot$" and "$||$". The sum operator $\sum_{d:D} p$ denotes choice among processes parameterized by variable d. The behavior of the conditional process $c \rightarrow p \diamond q$ depends on the value of the boolean expression c: if it evaluates to true, process p is chosen and otherwise process q is chosen. This allows for modeling systems whose behavior is data-dependent. There are a number of built-in data types in mCRL2, such as integers, reals, booleans, lists, and sets. Furthermore, by a **sort** definition one can define a new data type. Recursive process equations can be declared by **proc**.

The semantics associated with the mCRL2 syntax is a Labeled Transition System (LTS) that has multi-action labeled transitions, which can carry data parameters. The language used by the mCRL2 toolset for model checking specific properties is an extension of the modal μ-calculus [18]. This formalism stands out from most modal and temporal logic formalisms with respect to its expressive power. Temporal logics like LTL, CTL and CTL* all have translations [19] into μ-calculus, witnessing its generality. This expressiveness comes at a cost: very complex formulas with no intuitive and apparent interpretation can be coined. The syntax of mCRL2's modal μ-calculus formulas we are concerned with in this paper is defined by the following grammar:

$$\phi ::= b \mid \phi \wedge \phi \mid \phi \vee \phi \mid \forall d{:}D.\ \phi \mid \exists d{:}D.\ \phi \mid [\rho]\phi \mid \langle\rho\rangle\phi \mid \mu Z.\ \phi(Z) \mid \nu Z.\ \phi(Z)$$
$$\rho ::= \alpha \mid nil \mid \rho \cdot \rho \mid \rho^* \mid \rho^+$$
$$\alpha ::= a(d_1, \ldots, d_n) \mid b \mid \neg\alpha \mid \alpha \cap \alpha \mid \alpha \cup \alpha \mid \bigcap d{:}D.\ \alpha \mid \bigcup d{:}D.\ \alpha$$

Properties are expressed by state formulas ϕ, which contain Boolean data terms b that evaluate to true or false and which can contain data variables, the standard logical connectives *and* ($\wedge$) and *or* ($\vee$), the modal operators *must* ($[\_]\_$) and *may* ($\langle\_\rangle\_$), and the least and greatest fixpoint operators μ and ν. In addition to these, mCRL2's extensions add universal and existential quantifiers $\forall$ and $\exists$.

The modal operators take regular expressions ρ for describing words of actions, built up from the empty word nil, individual actions described by an action formula α, word concatenation $\rho \cdot \rho$ and (arbitrary) iteration of words ρ^* and ρ^+. Action formulas describe sets of actions; these sets are built up from the empty set of actions (in case Boolean expression b evaluates to false), the set of all possible actions (in case Boolean expression b evaluates to true), individual actions $a(d_1, \ldots, d_n)$, action complementation and finite and possibly infinite intersection $\cap$ and union $\cup$. A state of an LTS (described by an mCRL2 process) satisfies $\langle\rho\rangle\phi$ iff from that state, there is at least one transition sequence matching ρ, leading to a state satisfying ϕ; $[\rho]\phi$ is satisfied by a state iff all transition sequences matching ρ starting in that state lead to states satisfying ϕ. For instance, $[\neg(\bigcup n{:}Nat.\ read(n + n))]false$ states that a process should not execute any actions other than read actions with even-valued natural numbers. Note that $[a]\phi$ is trivially satisfied in states with no "a"-transitions.

In mCRL2, verification of μ-calculus formulas is conducted using tooling that operates on systems of fixpoint equations over first-order logic expressions. This sometimes requires too much overhead to serve as a basis for lightweight bug-hunting, as it can be difficult to interpret the counterexamples that are obtained from these equation systems in terms of the original mCRL2 process. Observers, or monitors (à la Büchi) defined in

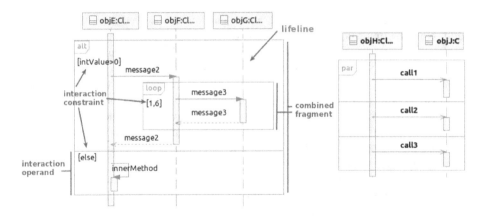

Fig. 2. Sequence diagrams with combined fragments

the mCRL2 model itself, can sometimes be used to bypass the problem. However, not all μ-calculus formulas are amenable to such a conversion, as we will see in Section 4.2.

3.2 UML Sequence Diagrams

Sequence diagrams model the interaction among a set of components, with emphasis on the sequence of *messages* exchanged over time. Graphically, they have two dimensions: the objects participating in the scenarios are placed horizontally, while time flows in the vertical dimension. The participants are shown as rectangular boxes, with the vertical lines emanating from them known as *lifelines*. Each message sent between the lifelines defines a specific communication, synchronous or asynchronous. Messages are shown as horizontal arrows from the lifeline of the sender to the lifeline of the receiver instance.

Sequence diagrams have been considerably extended in UML 2.x to allow expressing of complex control flows such as branching, iterations, and referring to existing inter-actions. **Combined fragments** are used for this purpose. The specification supports different fragment types, with operators such as *alt, opt, loop, break, par*. They are visualized as rectangles with a keyword indicating the type. Each combined fragment consists of one or more interaction operands. Depending on the type of the fragment, constraints can guard each of the interaction operands. Combined fragments can be nested with an arbitrary nesting depth, to capture complex workflows. Figure 2 shows how some of them can be used.

There are also two less-known combined fragments: *assert* and *neg*. Their use in practice is limited, because their semantics described in the UML 2.0 superstructure specification [20] are rather vague and confusing. By default, sequence diagrams without the use of these two operators only reflect possible behavior, while *assert* and *neg* alter the way a trace can be classified as valid or invalid. The specification characterizes the semantics of a sequence diagram as a pair of valid and invalid traces, where a trace is a sequence of events or messages. The potential problems with the UML 2.0 assertion and negation are explained in [21]. In summary, the specification aims at depicting of re-quired and forbidden behaviors. However, as [21] points out, stating that "the sequences of the operand of the assertion are the only valid continuations. All other continuations result in an invalid trace" suggests that the invalid set of traces for an *assert* fragment is its complement, i.e., the set of all other possible traces. Conversely, the standard also declares that the invalid set of traces are associated only with the use of a *neg* fragment, which is contradictory. For this reason, we also believe that these two operators should rather be considered as modalities. We restrict their usage to single events in property specifications, and assign the following semantics: *neg* is considered a set-complement operator for the event captured by the fragment, while *assert* specifies that an event must occur. In addition, we disallow nestings between these two fragments. We find that this does not limit the expressiveness of property specifications in practice.

4   The Approach

4.1   The Rationale

To describe our proposal to a correct and straightforward property elucidation, we outline the motivations behind the choices we made, and how they differ from existing related approaches.

While we follow on the idea of using a guiding questionnaire to incrementally refine various aspects of a requirement, we find the resulting artifacts (LTL formulas or graphical representations of finite state machines) from using the available ones (discussed in Section 2) not yet suitable for practical application in our context. For one, the practitioner must manually define the events to be associated with the placeholders when instantiating the template. To avoid potential errors, as well as reduce effort in specifications, we want to ideally stay in the same IDE used for modeling the system, and select only existing events that represent valid communication between components. In addition, we can already obtain mCRL2 models from UML designs comprising sequence diagrams [1]. In our experience, visual scenarios are the most suitable and commonly used means to specify the dynamics of a system. We believe that such a visual depiction of a scenario, more than finite state machines, improves the practitioner's understanding of the requirement as well. This is why we chose sequence diagrams as a property specification artifact too.

Most of the invented notations used by existing scenario approaches can fit well in UML 2.0 sequence diagrams. Profiles are a standard way to extend UML for expressing concepts not included in the official metamodel. In short, UML profiles consist of *stereotypes* that can be applied to any UML model, like classes, associations, or messages. We used this mechanism to apply the restrictions on the usage of *neg* and *assert*, as well as to distinguish between events presenting interval bounds and regular ones, from the patterns. As an example, Fig. 3a depicts the *precedence chain* pattern (with a *between-Q-and-R* scope), with the stereotypes applied to messages Q and R. The pattern expresses that event P must precede the chain of events S, T, always when the system execution is in the scope between events Q and R. We find this a much more intuitive scenario representation than the CHARMY/PSC one (Fig. 3b), for the same pattern. Notice that we do not have to specify constraints on past unwanted events, as they are automatically reflected in the μ-calculus formula, as long as there is a distinction between interval-marking messages, regular, mandatory, and forbidden ones.

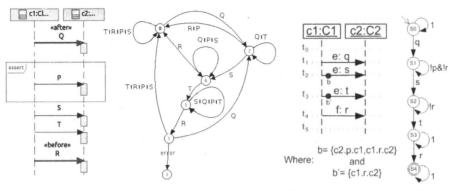

(a) Sequence Diagram with monitor   (b) PSC with Büchi automaton [9]

Fig. 3. Scenarios for the precedence chain pattern

Also, the CHARMY/PSC notation presents the scenario in a negative form, using "f:" to explicitly mark an error message.

Furthermore, most visual scenario approaches cover the (state-based) LTL mappings and extensions of the pattern system. Event-based temporal logics have not received much attention. Even though the original pattern system does not cover μ-calculus, such mappings [22] have been developed by the CADP team. These are adequate for action- or event-based systems, making them a good match for sequence diagrams, where communication between components is depicted. LTL logic is interpreted over Kripke structures, where the states are labeled with elementary propositions that hold in each state, while μ-calculus is interpreted over LTS-es, in which the transitions are labeled with actions that represent state changes. Even though both are complementary representations of the more general finite state automata, conversions between them are not practical, as they usually lead to a significant state space increase. For example, the fact that a lock has been acquired or released can be naturally expressed by actions. Since state-based temporal logics lack this mechanism, an alternative is to introduce a variable to indicate the status of the lock, i.e., expose the state information. With such properties, LTS representations are more intuitive, and easier to query using event-based logics.

Given that communication among components proceeds via actions (or events) which can represent synchronous or asynchronous communication, property specification can be defined over sequences of actions that are data-dependent. Fortunately, μ-calculus is rich enough to express both state and action formulas, and provides means for quantification over data, which many formalisms lack. With our approach, a practitioner can use a wild-card "*" to express that the property should be evaluated for all values that message parameters can carry. This allows us to use patterns which would otherwise make sense only for state-based formalisms. For example, the *universality* pattern is used to describe a portion of the system's execution which contains only states/events that have a desired property. Checking if a certain event is executed in every step of the system execution is not useful most of the time, so we adapted it in the context of μ-calculus.

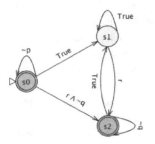

Fig. 4. A Büchi automaton

Fig. 5. Launching PASS from the Eclipse Project Explorer

Finally, for the purpose of on-the-fly verification, we provide an automatically generated mCRL2 monitor which corresponds to the property formula. We interpret a sequence diagram as an observer of the message exchanges in the system. This helps in avoiding generation of those parts of the state space for which it is certain that they do not compose with the property monitor. In addition, although mCRL2 offers direct model checking with μ-calculus and can provide feedback when the property fails to hold, this feedback is not at the level of the mCRL2 process specification. Using the monitor, the counter-example will be provided at the UML level.

Although any mature visual UML modeling tool can be used, we chose IBM's Rational Software Architect (RSA) environment. One of the advantages is that RSA is built on top of Eclipse, making it relatively easy to extend the functionality. To this end, PASS is developed as an Eclipse plug-in, using the lightweight UML profile, and as such is available (Fig. 5) to any Eclipse-based UML tool.

4.2 Transforming a μ-Calculus Formula into a Monitor Process

A general model checking mechanism used with tools like SPIN is to construct a Büchi automaton for an LTL formula, which accepts exactly those executions that violate the property. A product of the model state space (typically a Kripke structure) and the Büchi automaton is then composed, and checked for emptiness. Although syntactically Büchi is similar to the finite-state monitor for which we aim, the difference lies in the acceptance conditions: a monitor accepts only finite runs of the system, while Büchi can trap infinite executions through detection of cycles, but potentially needs the entire state space generated in the process. Runtime verification does not store the entire state space of a model, so it cannot detect such cycles. In addition, to expose state information, transitions in Fig. 4 are labeled with elementary propositions rather than actions (notice the $\wedge$ operator). As such, we cannot use existing tools for constructing Büchi automata with our approach.

Not every property can be monitored at runtime when only a finite run has been observed so far. Monitorable properties are those for which a violation occurs along a finite execution. This problem has been studied [23], and it is known that the class of monitorable properties is strictly larger than that of *safety* properties. However, an exact categorization of monitorable properties is missing. In particular, the definition of *liveness* requires that any finite system execution must be extendable to an infinite one that satisfies the property. By defining an end-scope of a property, we can also assert violations to *existence* patterns, which are typically in the *liveness* category. Such runtime monitor can also assert *universality* and *absence* patterns with or without scope combinations. We found that we are able to construct a monitor for about 50% of the property patterns.

We translate a core fragment of the μ-calculus to mCRL2 processes which can subsequently serve as observer processes for monitorable properties. The idea behind the translation is that a violation of a property of the form $[\alpha]\phi$ is witnessed by an action that matches the action formula α. A monitor for such a formula synchronizes with precisely those actions matching α. This generalizes to sequences of actions matching words described by some ρ for formulas of the form $[\rho]\phi$. Without loss of generality, we restrict to the following grammar:

$$\phi ::= b \mid \forall d{:}D.\phi \mid [\rho]\phi \mid \phi \wedge \phi$$
$$\rho ::= \alpha \mid nil \mid \rho \cdot \rho \mid \rho + \rho \mid \rho^* \mid \rho^+$$
$$\alpha ::= a(d_1, \ldots, d_n) \mid \neg\alpha \mid b \mid \alpha \cap \alpha \mid \alpha \cup \alpha \mid \bigcap d{:}D.\, \alpha \mid \bigcup d{:}D.\, \alpha$$

Before we present the translation, we convert the formulas in guarded form. That is, we remove every occurrence of ρ^* and nil using the following rules:

$$[nil]\phi = \phi \qquad\qquad [\rho^*]\phi = [nil]\phi \wedge [\rho^+]\phi \tag{1}$$

The function TrS takes two arguments (a formula and a list of typed variables) and produces a process. It is defined inductively as follows:

$$\mathsf{TrS}_l(b) \qquad\quad = (\neg b \to error) \tag{2}$$
$$\mathsf{TrS}_l(\forall d : D.\phi_1) = \sum d{:}D.\mathsf{TrS}_{l\,+\!+[d:D]}(\phi_1) \tag{3}$$
$$\mathsf{TrS}_l(\phi_1 \wedge \phi_2) \;\; = \mathsf{TrS}_l(\phi_1) + \mathsf{TrS}_l(\phi_2) \tag{4}$$
$$\mathsf{TrS}_l([\rho]\phi_1) \qquad = \mathsf{TrR}_l(\rho) \cdot \mathsf{TrS}_l(\phi) \tag{5}$$

where TrR takes a regular expression (and a list of typed variables) and produces a process or a condition:

$$\mathsf{TrR}_l(\alpha) \qquad = \bigoplus_{a \in Act} \left(\sum d_a{:}D_a.\, \mathsf{Cond}_l(a(d_a), \alpha) \to a(d_a) \right) \tag{6}$$
$$\mathsf{TrR}_l(\rho_1 \cdot \rho_2) = \mathsf{TrR}_l(\rho_1) \cdot \mathsf{TrR}_l(\rho_2) \tag{7}$$
$$\mathsf{TrR}_l(\rho_1 + \rho_2) = \mathsf{TrR}_l(\rho_1) + \mathsf{TrR}_l(\rho_2) \tag{8}$$
$$\mathsf{TrR}_l(\rho^+) \qquad = X(l) \qquad where\ X(l) = \mathsf{TrR}_l(\rho) \cdot X(l)\ is\ a\ recursive\ process \tag{9}$$

where $\bigoplus$ is a finite summation over all action names $a \in Act$ of the mCRL2 process and where Cond takes an action and an action formula and produces a condition that describes when the action is among the set of actions described by the action formula:

$$\mathsf{Cond}_l(a(d_a), a'(e)) \qquad = \begin{cases} d_a = e & \text{if } a = a' \\ false & \text{otherwise} \end{cases} \tag{10}$$
$$\mathsf{Cond}_l(a(d_a), b) \qquad\;\; = b \tag{11}$$
$$\mathsf{Cond}_l(a(d_a), \neg\alpha) \qquad = \neg\mathsf{Cond}_l(a(d_a), \alpha) \tag{12}$$
$$\mathsf{Cond}_l(a(d_a), \alpha_1 \cap \alpha_2) = \mathsf{Cond}_l(a(d_a), \alpha_1) \wedge \mathsf{Cond}_l(a(d_a), \alpha_2) \tag{13}$$
$$\mathsf{Cond}_l(a(d_a), \alpha_1 \cup \alpha_2) = \mathsf{Cond}_l(a(d_a), \alpha_1) \vee \mathsf{Cond}_l(a(d_a), \alpha_2) \tag{14}$$
$$\mathsf{Cond}_l(a(d_a), \textstyle\bigcup d{:}D.\, \alpha) = \exists d{:}D.\, \mathsf{Cond}_l(a(d_a), \alpha) \tag{15}$$
$$\mathsf{Cond}_l(a(d_a), \textstyle\bigcap d{:}D.\, \alpha) = \forall d{:}D.\, \mathsf{Cond}_l(a(d_a), \alpha) \tag{16}$$

```
proc Monitor = Mon_"[true*.Q.(not (P or R))*.S]false";
% Applying rule (5):
proc Mon_"[true*.Q.(not (P or R))*.S]false" = Mon_"true*.Q.(not (P or R))*.S". Mon_"false";
% Applying rule (2):
proc Mon_"false" = error;
% Applying rule (7):
proc Mon_"true*.Q.(not(P or R))*.S" = Mon_"true*". Mon_"not(P or R)*". Mon_"S";
...
% Applying rule (6):
proc Mon_"not(P or R)" = (satisfy(action_1, not(P or R))) -> action_1
  + (satisfy(action_2, not(P or R))) -> action_2;
...
  + (satisfy(action_n, not(P or R))) -> action_n;
....
% Applying rule (12):
satisfy(action, not(actionFormula)) = !satisfy(action, actionFormula);
% Applying rule (14):
satisfy(action, or(actionFormula_1, actionFormula_2)) =
        satisfy(action, actionFormula_1) || satisfy(action, actionFormula_2);
% Applying rule (10):
satisfy(action, actionFormula) = (action == actionFormula);
```

Fig. 6. Transforming a μ-calculus formula into a monitor

An mCRL2 process p violates formula ϕ iff the synchronous parallel composition of processes p and $TrS_{[]}(\phi)$ can reach a state in which action $error$ is enabled.

Using the above translation, Fig. 3a shows monitor visualization next to the sequence diagram for the precedence chain pattern. Such a monitor can be placed in parallel with the system model, to perform runtime verification. Clearly, in the "worst" case, if the model is correct with respect to the property, all relevant model states will be traversed. In practice however, refutation can be found quickly after a limited exploration. A sketch of such a translation applied on a model with actions $action\_1$, $action\_2,\ldots,action\_n$ is shown in Fig. 6. Intuitively, the monitor process will step through those exact actions that the original system takes. If a sequence of steps refuting the formula is completed, the monitor will execute the "error" action as a last step, indicating that a counter-example trace has been found. More examples of monitors along with references to the applied transformation rules in each step, can be found at [24].

5   Case Study: DIRAC's Executor Framework Revisited

DIRAC [25] is the grid framework used to support production activities of the LHCb experiment at CERN. All major LHCb tasks, such as raw data transfer from the experiment's detector to the grid storage, data processing, and user analysis, are covered by DIRAC. Jobs submitted via its interface undergo several processing steps between the moment they are submitted, to the point when they execute on the grid.

The crucial Workload Management components responsible for orchestrating this process are the *ExecutorDispatcher* and the *Executors*. Executors process any task sent to them by the ExecutorDispatcher, each one being responsible for a different step in the handling of tasks (such as resolving the job's input data). The ExecutorDispatcher takes care of persisting the state of the tasks and distributing them amongst the Executors, based on the task requirements. It maintains a queue of tasks waiting to be processed, and other internal data structures to keep track of the distribution of tasks among the Executors. During testing, developers experienced certain problems: occasionally, tasks submitted in the system would not get dispatched, despite the fact that their responsible Executors were idle at the moment. The root cause of this problem could not be identified by testing with different workload scenarios, nor by analysis of the generated logs. In [1] we manually formulated this problem as the following safety property:

```
[true* .
synch_call(1,ExecutorQueues,_queues,pushTask(JobPath,taskId,false)).true*.
!(synch_call(1,ExecutorQueues,_queues,popTask([JobPath])))*.
synch_reply(1,ExecutorDispatcher,_eDispatch,
_sendTaskToExecutor_return(OK,0))]false,
```

meaning that a task pushed in the queue must be processed, i.e., removed from the queue before the ExecutorDispatcher declares that there are no more tasks for processing. Explicit model checking was not feasible in this case due to the model size (50 concurrent processes), so we resorted to writing a standard monitoring process set to run in parallel with the original model. With a depth-first traversal in mCRL2, we effectively discovered a trace [1] violating the property within minutes, and used our tool to import and automatically visualize the counter-example as a sequence diagram in RSA. Since the bug was reported and fixed, we wanted to check if the problem still persists after the fix, this time using PASS to elicit the property.

5.1 PASS: The Property ASSistant

To cope with the ambiguity of system requirements, PASS guides the practitioner via a series of questions to distinguish the types of scope and behavior as a relation between multiple events. By answering these questions, one is led to consider some subtle aspects of the property, which are typically overlooked when manually specifying the requirement in temporal logic. The last part of the property (i.e. "before the ExecutorDispatcher declares that there are no more tasks for processing") is easily recognized as a scope restriction, which the user can choose by selecting the appropriate answer from the Scope Question Tree wizard page. This results in a *Before-R* scope restriction, where the actual communication can be selected by double-clicking the end-event placeholder (Fig. 7). This presents the user with a popup window with all the possible message exchanges in the model, so he can choose the actual message, in this case the reply message $\_sendTaskToExecutor$. As already pointed out in [6], a closer examination of the patterns classification reveals some aspects which are not considered, and may lead to variants in the original scope and behavior definitions. For example, the definition of the *Before-R* scope requires that the event R necessarily occurs. This means, if R does not occur until the end of the run, the intent or behavior of the property could be violated, yet the property as a whole would not be violated unless R happens. In practice however, it is useful to introduce an *Until-R* variant for cases where the end-delimiter may not occur until the end of the system execution. This is captured by the last question in Fig. 7. Similar considerations have led to new variants of the *After-Q-Until-R* and *After-Q-Before-R* patterns. For instance, whether subsequent occurrences of Q should be ignored, or should effectively reset the beginning of the interval in which the behavior is considered, are reflected in the questionnaire.

It is easy to elicit the behavior requirement as a *response* pattern ("a task *pushed* in the queue must be processed, i.e., *removed* from the queue"). The actual events of interest in this case are *pushTask* and *popTask*. Again, an extension of the pattern system

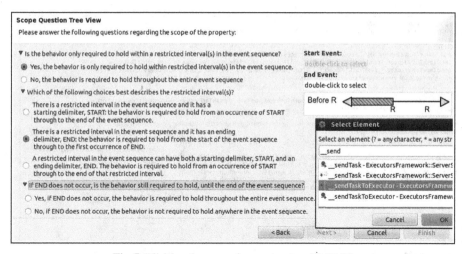

Fig. 7. Eliciting the scope for a property with PASS

allows for the user to decide whether the first event (the cause) must necessarily occur in the first place. The Behavior Question Tree part of the wizard is shown in Fig. 8. Adding 4 scope and 2 behavior variations have led to more than 100 ((5+**4**)∗(11+**2**)) unique patterns to be chosen from.

At the end of the questionnaire, the user is presented (Fig. 9) with a summary of the requested property, which can be reviewed before making the final decision. A μ-calculus formula pertaining to the property is presented, along with the possibility to assign concrete parameter values that messages carry. Since the property should be evaluated for all possible values of the taskId's domain, a wildcard "∗" can be used

Behavior Question Tree View

Please answer the following questions regarding the behavior of the property:

▼ How many events of primary interest are there in this behavior?
   ○ One event.
   ◉ Two events.
   ○ Three events.

▼ Which of the following best describes how A and B interact?
   ◉ If A occurs, B is required to occur subsequently

   ○ B is not allowed to occur until after A occurs.

▼ Is A required to occur?

   ○ Yes, A is required to occur.

   ◉ No, A is not required to occur.

Event A:
pushTask
Event B:
popTask
Event C:
double-click to select
Exceptional event X:
double-click to select

[< Back]   [Next >]   [Cancel]   [Finish]

Fig. 8. Eliciting the behavior for a property with PASS

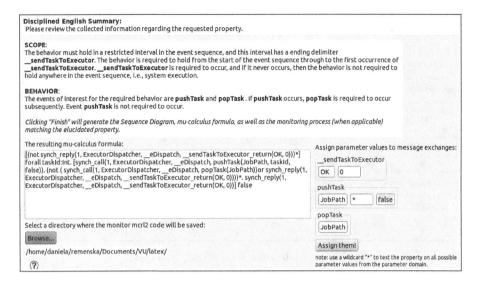

Fig. 9. Summary of the elicited property with PASS

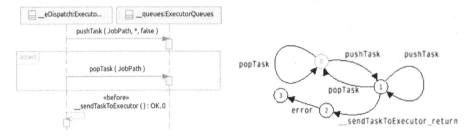

Fig. 10. A sequence diagram for the property   **Fig. 11.** A monitor for the property

(as shown in the second parameter of *pushTask*). This assignment results in a formula with a *forall* quantifier. In addition, a sequence diagram (Fig. 10) and a monitor process in mCRL2 (visualized in Fig. 11 without the data, for clarity) are generated, to be used in the final model checking phase. It is worth noticing that our original manually constructed formula was not entirely correct, and as such could potentially produce spurious counter-examples. The general pattern template obtained with PASS is:

```
[( not R)*. P. (not (S or R))*. R] false
```

while the original one was a more restrictive formula of the following form:

```
[true*. P. (not S)*. R] false
```

Using the generated monitor, we performed runtime verification on the corrected model. We linearized the model with the mCRL2 toolset, and used LTSmin's symbolic reachability tool [26] for efficient state space exploration. LTSmin is language-independent, and can be used as an mCRL2 model checking back-end. Taking less than 20 minutes, the symbolic state space explorer finished the traversal (2.85 million states) without discovering an *error* step, effectively concluding that the property holds. The PASS tool, along with the patterns extensions, the model and the monitor of this case study, is available at [24]. While outside of the current scope, a Java Web Start version of the tool is available for users who want to elicit a property for existing mCRL2 models created manually and independently of any UML environment.

6   Conclusions and Future Work

In an effort to automate more aspects of formal verification of distributed systems, we introduced PASS, a Property ASSistant that brings the process of correctly specifying functional properties closer to software engineers. Through a series of questions, the practitioner can consider subtle aspects about a property which are often overlooked. Motivated by the wish to stay within an existing UML development environment, rather than use an external helper tool, PASS was developed as an Eclipse plug-in, thus keeping a strong relationship between the model elements and the property template ones. Our approach to specifying properties is based on the pattern system [4], which we extended with useful pattern variations for the event-based μ-calculus formalism. Besides offering a natural language summary of the elicited property, a μ-calculus formula and a UML sequence diagram are provided, depicting the desired behavior. In addition, PASS automatically generates monitors to be used for efficient property-driven runtime verification using the mCRL2 toolset. We believe that automating the property specification process, while keeping practitioners in their familiar environment, should lead to more active adoption of methods for formal analysis of designs. We revisited a case study from the grid domain, and discovered that despite a reasonably good understanding of μ-calculus, our previously manually defined property was in fact not fully correct. Using the monitor, we performed runtime verification, which in the end resorted to full exploration of the state space, and did not disprove the property.

Besides instantiating pattern templates, part of our ongoing work is to define a methodology that would allow the experienced practitioner to directly write sequence diagrams expressing requirements, based on which a μ-calculus formula and a monitor would be provided.

References

1. Remenska, D., Templon, J., Willemse, T.A.C., Homburg, P., Verstoep, K., Casajus, A., Bal, H.: From UML to Process Algebra and Back: An Automated Approach to Model-Checking Software Design Artifacts of Concurrent Systems. In: Brat, G., Rungta, N., Venet, A. (eds.) NFM 2013. LNCS, vol. 7871, pp. 244–260. Springer, Heidelberg (2013)
2. Groote, J., et al.: The Formal Specification Language mCRL2. In: Proc. MMOSS 2006 (2006)
3. Groote, J.F., Willemse, T.A.C.: Model-checking processes with data. In: Science of Computer Programming (2005)
4. Dwyer, M.B., et al.: Patterns in property specifications for finite-state verification. In: Proc. ICSE 1999 (1999)

5. Dwyer, M.B., et al.: Property Specification Patterns,
   `http://patterns.projects.cis.ksu.edu`
6. Smith, R.L., et al.: Propel: an approach supporting property elucidation. In: Proc. ISCE 2002 (2002)
7. Konrad, S., Cheng, B.H.: Facilitating the construction of specification pattern-based properties. In: Proc. RE 2005. IEEE (2005)
8. Mondragon, O., Gates, A.Q., Roach, S.: Prospec: Support for Elicitation and Formal Specification of Software Properties. In: Proc. of Runtime Verification Workshop. ENTCS (2004)
9. Autili, M., Inverardi, P., Pelliccione, P.: Graphical scenarios for specifying temporal properties: an automated approach. Automated Software Eng. (2007)
10. Lee, I., Sokolsky, O.: A Graphical Property Specification Language. In: Proc. of 2nd IEEE Workshop on High-Assurance Systems Engineering (1997)
11. Smith, M.H., et al.: Events and Constraints: A Graphical Editor for Capturing Logic Requirements of Programs. In: Proc. RE 2001 (2001)
12. Knapp, A., Wuttke, J.: Model checking of UML 2.0 interactions. In: Kühne, T. (ed.) MoDELS 2006. LNCS, vol. 4364, pp. 42–51. Springer, Heidelberg (2007)
13. Lilius, J., Paltor, I.P.: vUML: a Tool for Verifying UML Models. In: Proc. ASE 1999 (1999)
14. Kugler, H.-J., Harel, D., Pnueli, A., Lu, Y., Bontemps, Y.: Temporal logic for scenario-based specifications. In: Halbwachs, N., Zuck, L.D. (eds.) TACAS 2005. LNCS, vol. 3440, pp. 445–460. Springer, Heidelberg (2005)
15. Baresi, L., Ghezzi, C., Zanolin, L.: Modeling and Validation of Publish/Subscribe Architectures. In: Testing Commercial-off-the-Shelf Components and Systems. Springer, Heidelberg
16. The Eclipse Foundation: Eclipse Modeling MDT-UML2 component,
    `http://www.eclipse.org/uml2/`
17. Giannakopoulou, D., Havelund, K.: Automata-Based Verification of Temporal Properties on Running Programs. In: Proc. ASE 2001 (2001)
18. Emerson, E.A.: Model checking and the Mu-calculus. In: DIMACS Series in Discrete Mathematics. American Mathematical Society (1997)
19. Cranen, S., Groote, J.F., Reniers, M.: A linear translation from CTL* to the first-order modal μ-calculus. Theoretical Computer Science (28) (2011)
20. OMG: UML2.4 Superstructure Spec.,
    `http://www.omg.org/spec/UML/2.4/Superstructure`
21. Harel, D., Maoz, S.: Assert and negate revisited: Modal semantics for UML sequence diagrams. Software & Systems Modeling 7 (2008)
22. Mateescu, R.: Property Pattern Mappings for Regular Alternation-Free μ-Calculus,
    `http://www.inrialpes.fr/vasy/cadp/resources/`
    `evaluator/rafmc.html`
23. Bauer, A.: Monitorability of omega-regular languages. CoRR abs/1006.3638 (2010)
24. Remenska, D., Willemse, T.A.C.: PASS: Property ASSistant tool for Eclipse,
    `https://github.com/remenska/PASS`
25. Tsaregorodtsev, A., et al.: DIRAC: A Community Grid Solution. In: Proc. CHEP 2007. IOP Publishing (2007)
26. Blom, S., van de Pol, J.: Symbolic Reachability for Process Algebras with Recursive Data Types. In: Fitzgerald, J.S., Haxthausen, A.E., Yenigun, H. (eds.) ICTAC 2008. LNCS, vol. 5160, pp. 81–95. Springer, Heidelberg (2008)

Formal Specification and Verification of CRDTs

Peter Zeller, Annette Bieniusa, and Arnd Poetzsch-Heffter

University of Kaiserslautern, Germany
{p_zeller,bieniusa,poetzsch}@cs.uni-kl.de

Abstract. *Convergent Replicated Data Types* (CRDTs) can be used as basic building blocks for storing and managing replicated data in a distributed system. They provide high availability and performance, and they guarantee eventual consistency. In this paper, we develop a formal framework for the analysis and verification of CRDTs. We investigate and compare the three currently used specification techniques for CRDTs and formalize them based on an abstract model for managing replicated data in distributed systems. We show how CRDT implementations can be expressed in our framework and present a general strategy for verifying CRDTs. Finally, we report on our experiences in using the framework for the verification of important existing CRDT implementations. The framework and the proofs were developed within the interactive theorem prover Isabelle/HOL.

Keywords: CRDT, formal verification, eventual consistency.

1 Introduction

Global computing systems and worldwide applications often require *data replication*, that is, the data is not only stored at one computing node, but at several nodes. There are a number of reasons for replication. To realize reliable services, high availability and fault-tolerance might be important. A centralized storage system might not provide enough throughput for allowing millions of users to access the data. Furthermore, systems often serve clients from different regions in the world; Geo-replication helps to keep the latency low. Last but not least, mobile clients might not be connected all the time, but should provide certain offline functionality using a local store that is synchronized with the global state when the connection is reestablished.

The CAP theorem[6] tells us that distributed systems cannot guarantee high availability, partition tolerance, and strong consistency at the same time. In this paper, we investigate techniques that aim at high availability and partition tolerance by providing a weaker form of consistency, called *eventual consistency*[14,15,11,5].

In an eventually consistent system, the different replicas do not have to provide the same view of the data at all times. Operations manipulating the data are first applied to a subset of the replicas. At some suitable later point in time, the updates are communicated to the other replicas. Only after all updates are

E. Ábrahám and C. Palamidessi (Eds.), FORTE 2014, LNCS 8461, pp. 33–48, 2014.

delivered to all replicas the data has to be consistent again. This means in particular that the replicas have to be able to merge concurrent updates into a consistent view. It usually depends on the application how a merge operation should behave. The idea of replicated data types is to package a behavior given by operations and a way to handle concurrent updates, so that they can be reused in many situations.

Convergent replicated data types (CRDTs)[12] are a special class of replicated data types where concurrent updates are handled by merging the resulting states. The basic setting is that there is a number of replicas of the data type. Operations are executed on a single replica and the different replicas conceptually exchange their whole states with each other according to some protocol. The state of a replica is also called the *payload*. To guarantee convergence, there needs to be a partial order on the payloads and a merge operation computing the least upper bound, such that the payloads form a semilattice. All operations which change the payload have to increase the payload with respect to the partial order. This setup ensures that replicas which have seen the same set of updates also have the same state and thus return the same value. This property is called Strong Eventual Consistency (SEC)[13].

A simple example of a CRDT is a counter. A counter provides update operations to increment or decrement the value and a query function to read the value. It is usually implemented by keeping the number of increments and the number of decrements for each replica in a map from replica-IDs to positive integers. Each replica only increments its own increment- and decrement-counts and states are merged by taking the component-wise maximum. It is easy to prove that this computes a least upper bound. The value of the counter can be determined by summing up all increment counts in the map and subtracting the sum of the decrement counts. Separating increment- and decrement-counts ensures, that the updates are increasing operations. Having a count for every replica instead of a single counter ensures that no updates are lost due to concurrent writes.

Contributions. In general, CRDT implementations can be quite sophisticated and complex, in particular in the way they handle concurrent updates. Therefore it is important to provide high-level behavioral specifications for the users and techniques to verify CRDT implementations w.r.t. their specifications. Towards this challenge, the paper makes the following contributions:

- A framework in Isabelle/HOL [10] that supports the formal verification of CRDTs. The framework in particular provides a system model that is parametric w.r.t. the CRDT to be analyzed and support for verification.
- We analyzed, clarified, and formalized different specification and abstract implementation techniques for CRDTs (Sections 3, 4 and 6).
- We successfully verified a number of CRDTs described in the literature with our framework.

We present the system model in Section 2; describe our specification technique in Section 3, the implementation technique in Section 4 and the verification aspects in Section 5. In Section 6 we discuss an alternative specification technique. Finally, we consider related work, summarize the results, and give an outlook on future work in Sections 7 and 8

2   System Model

We developed a formal system model that supports an arbitrary but fixed number of replicas and is parametric in the CRDT to be analyzed, i.e., it can be instantiated with different CRDTs. A CRDT is parameterized by four type parameters and described by four components:

- **pl**, the type of the payload (i.e. the state at each replica)
- **ua**, the type for the update arguments (a sum type of all update operations)
- **qa**, the type for the query arguments (a sum type of all query operations)
- **r**, the sum type for the possible return values of the queries

- **init** :: pl, the initial payload for all replicas
- **update** :: $ua \Rightarrow replicaId \Rightarrow pl \Rightarrow pl$, the function expressing how an update operation modifies the payload at a given replica, where $replicaId$ denotes the node on which the update is performed first
- **merge** :: $pl \Rightarrow pl \Rightarrow pl$, the function merging payloads
- **query** :: $qa \Rightarrow pl \Rightarrow r$, the function expressing the results of querying a payload

Table 1. System Model

System state:
$version :: replicaId \rightarrow \mathbb{N}$
$payloadHistory :: (version \times payload) \ set$
$systemState :: (replicaId \rightarrow payload) \times (replicaId \rightarrow version) \times payloadHistory$
Operations and traces:
$Operation := Update(replicaId, args) \quad \mid \quad Merge(replicaId, version, payload)$
$Trace := Trace; Operation \quad \mid \quad []$
Operational semantics:

$$s_{init} = (\lambda r.\ init_{crdt},\ \lambda r.\ v_0,\ \emptyset) \qquad \frac{}{s \xrightarrow{[]} s} \qquad \frac{s \xrightarrow{as} s' \quad s' \xrightarrow{a} s''}{s \xrightarrow{as;a} s''}$$

$$(update) \quad \frac{v' = vs(r)(r+\!=\!1) \quad pl' = update_{crdt}(a, r, pls(r))}{(pls, vs, ph) \xrightarrow{Update(r,a)} (pls(r := pl'),\ vs(r := v'),\ ph \cup \{(v', pl')\})}$$

$$(merge) \quad \frac{(v, pl) \in ph \quad v' = vs(r) \sqcup v \quad pl' = merge_{crdt}(pls(r), pl)}{(pls, vs, ph) \xrightarrow{Merge(r,v,pl)} (pls(r := pl'),\ vs(r := v'),\ ph \cup \{(v', pl')\})}$$

Given a CRDT ($init_{crdt}$, $update_{crdt}$, $merge_{crdt}$, $query_{crdt}$), the system model describes the labeled transition relation $s \xrightarrow{tr} s'$ expressing that executing trace tr in state s leads to state s' (cf. Table 1) where a trace is a sequence of operations and an operation is either the application of an update or a merge (queries need not be considered, as they do not modify the state). The state of the system consists of three components:

– For each replica r, its current payload.
– For each replica r, its current version vector[8]. The *version vector* or short *version* is a mapping from replica-IDs to natural numbers. If the version of r has m as entry for key k, the payload of r has merged the first m operations applied to replica k into its payload.
– The set of all version-payload pairs that have been seen during execution so far. This set is called the *payload history* and is used to make sure that a merge operation can only be applied to version-payload pairs that appeared earlier in the execution.

Initially, the payload of each replica is $init_{crdt}$, the version vector of each replica is the all-zero vector, and the payload history is the empty set. There are two kind of transition steps:

– An *update* operation $Update(r, a)$ applies an update function of the CRDT (determined by the arguments a) to the current payload of r and modifies the state accordingly; in particular, the rth component of the version vector of r is incremented by one.
– A *merge* operation $Merge(r, v, pl)$ is executed as follows: The new version v' is calculated by taking the least upper bound of the old version vector $vs(r)$ and the merged version vector v. Similarly, the new payload pl' is the least upper bound operation on payloads, which is specific to the respective CRDT, and implemented by the $merge_{crdt}$ function.

Discussion. The system model focuses on simple operational behavior. Other aspects, such as timestamps, were intentionally left out because they would make the system model more complicated than needed for most CRDTs. Only a few CRDTs like the Last-Writer-Wins-Register depend on timestamps. Also, often timestamps are only used to provide some total order on operations, and lexicographic ordering of the version vectors also suffices to provide such an order.

3   Specification

In this section we present and formalize a technique for specifying the behavior of CRDTs based on the system model presented in the previous section.

A specification should tell users the result value of any query operation, when a trace of operations performed in the system is given. A trace gives a total order on the operations performed in the system, but for operations performed independently on different replicas this order does not influence the result. Therefore, we would like to abstract from this total order. Furthermore, the traces include explicit merge operations, but from a user's perspective this merge operations are implicit. Thus, it should not be important, how updates were delivered to a replica. The result of an operation should only depend on those operations that are visible when the operation is about to be performed. Hence, the trace can be actually deconstructed into a partially ordered set of update operations, where the partial order is the visibility relation, which we denote by $\prec$ in the following.

The specification technique that we formalize here supports the sketched abstractions and explains the result of an operation only depending on the visible update history. It follows the ideas from Bouajjani et al.[4], and Burckhardt et al.[5], but is specifically tailored to CRDTs, allowing for some simplifications. In the case of CRDTs, the visibility relation is a partial order. All operations at one replica are ordered by time and a merge makes all operations, which are visible to the source of the merge, visible at the destination of the merge.

Formalization. In our formalization we represent the visibility relation using version vectors. The advantage of this is that they are easy to handle in the operational semantics and also when working with Isabelle/HOL. The properties of a partial order like transitivity and antisymmetry are already given by the structure and do not have to be specified additionally. The version vector at each replica can be directly derived from a given trace. It also uniquely identifies every operation, and we can encode the whole history of updates with the visibility relation as a set of update operations, represented by (*version, replicaId, args*) triples. We call this structure the **update history** and denote it by H in the following. The visibility relation $\prec$ on update operations is simply derived from the order on the version vectors.

A specification is formalized as a function *spec*, which takes the update history visible at a given replica and the arguments of a query and returns the result of the query. A specification is **valid** if for every reachable state and all queries a, the specification yields the same result as the application of the query to the current state:

$$\forall_{tr,pls,vs,a,r.}\ s_{init} \xrightarrow{tr} (pls, vs, \_) \ \Rightarrow\ spec(H(tr, vs(r)), a) = query_{crdt}(a, pls(r))$$

Here, the term $H(tr, vs(r))$ calculates the update history from the trace tr while only taking the operations before the version $vs(r)$ into account.

Examples. Table 2 shows specifications for several CRDTs from the literature[12]. The **Counter** is a data type providing an update-operation to increment or decrement the value of the Counter and a query-operation $Get()$ which returns the current value of the counter. The argument to the update is a single integer value. We specify the return value of a $Get()$ operation on a counter by taking all update operations e from the update history H and then summing up their update arguments. The **Grow-Set** is a set which only allows adding elements. An element is in the set, when there exists an operation adding the element. The **Two-Phase-Set** also allows to remove elements from the set, with

Table 2. Specifications of CRDTs

Counter:	$spec(H, Get()) = \sum_{e \in H.} args(e)$
Grow-Set:	$spec(H, Contains(x)) = \exists_{e \in H}. args(e) = Add(x)$
Two-Phase-Set:	$spec(H, Contains(x)) = \exists_{e \in H}. args(e) = Add(x) \wedge$ $\neg(\exists e \in H.\ args(e) = Remove(x))$
Two-Phase-Set (guarded remove):	$spec(H, Contains(x)) = \exists_{e \in H}. args(e) = Add(x) \wedge$ $\neg(\exists_{e \in H}. args(e) = Remove(x) \wedge (\exists_{f \in H}. args(f) = Add(x) \wedge f \prec e))$
Observed-Remove-Set:	$spec(H, Contains(x)) = \exists_{a \in H}. args(a) = Add(x) \wedge$ $\neg(\exists_{r \in H}. a \prec r \wedge args(r) = Remove(x))$
Multi-Value-Register:	$spec(H, Get()) = \{x \mid \exists_{e \in H}. args(e) = Set(x) \wedge \neg(\exists_{f \in H}. e \prec f)\}$

the limitation that an element cannot be added again once it was removed. An element is in the set, if there is an operation adding the element and no operation removing it. This specification allows removing an element before it was added to the set, which might not be desired. The **Two-Phase-Set with the guarded remove operation**, ignores remove operations, when the respective element is not yet in the set. For this data type, an element is in the set, when there exists an operation adding the element, and there is no operation which removes the element and which happened after an add operation of the same element. The **Observed-Remove-Set** is a set, where an element can be added and removed arbitrarily often. A remove operation only affects the add operations which have been observed, i.e. which happened before the remove operation. We specify that the query $Contains(x)$ returns true, if and only if there exists an update operation a adding x to the set and there exists no update operation r which happened after a and removes x from the set. The final example is the **Multi-Value-Register**. It has a $Set(x)$ operation to set the register to a single value. The $Get()$ query returns a set containing the values of the last concurrent Set operations. More precisely, it returns all values x so that there exists an operation $Set(x)$, for which no later update operation exists.

Properties and Discussion. It is not possible to describe non-converging data types with this technique. Since the specified return value of a query only depends on the visible update history and the arguments, two replicas which have seen the same set of updates will also return the same result.

One problem with this specification technique is that in general a specification can reference all operations from the past. The state of a replica is basically determined by the complete update history, which can be quite large and not very abstract. Therefore it is hard to reason about the effects of operations when programming with the data types or when verifying properties about systems using them, where one usually wants to reason about the effect of a single method in a modular way.

Also, the example of the Two-Phase-Set with a guarded remove operation shows that small changes to the behavior of one update operation can make the whole specification more complex. We would like such a change to only affect the specification of the remove operation. Thus, the question is whether we can specify CRDTs avoiding these problems. We present and discuss an alternative specification technique in Section 6. It is also possible to use abstract implementations as a form of specification, as detailed in the next section.

4 Implementations

To implement a CRDT in our framework one has to define the type of the payload and the four fields of the CRDT record ($init_{crdt}$, $update_{crdt}$, $merge_{crdt}$, $query_{crdt}$) as defined in the system model. Technically, the implementation can be any Isabelle function with a matching type.

To keep the examples short, we introduced a *uid*-function, which generates a new unique identifier. This can easily be implemented in our system model by adding a counter to the payload of the data type. A unique identifier can then be obtained by taking a pair (*replicaId, counter*) and incrementing the counter. It is also possible to use the version vector as a unique identifier for an update operation, which can make the verification easier, as the payload is then directly related to the update history.

Table 3. Abstract and optimized implementation of a Counter CRDT

Abstract Counter:	$s :: (id \times int)set = \{\}$ $\mathbf{update}(x, r, s) = s \cup \{(uid(), x)\}$ $\mathbf{merge}(s, s') = s \cup s'$ $\mathbf{query}(Get(), s) = \sum_{(id,x) \in s} x$
Optimized Counter:	$s :: (replicaId \to int) \times (replicaId \to int) = (\lambda r.\, 0, \lambda r.\, 0)$ $\mathbf{update}(x, r, (p, n)) = \mathbf{if}\ x \geq 0\ \mathbf{then}\ (p(r := p(r) + x), n)$ $\qquad\qquad\qquad\qquad\quad \mathbf{else}\ (p, n(r := n(r) - x))$ $\mathbf{merge}((p, n), (p', n')) = (\lambda r.\, max(p(r), p'(r)), \lambda r.\, max(n(r), n'(r)))$ $\mathbf{query}(Get(), (p, n)) = \sum_r p(r) - \sum_r n(r)$

Table 3 shows two implementations of the Counter CRDT. The first implementation is an abstract one, in which the payload is a set of all update arguments tagged with a unique identifier. The query can then be answered by summing up all the update arguments in the set. This implementation is very inefficient, but easy to understand. The second implementation is closer to Counter implementations found in real systems. Here, the payload consists of two mappings from replicaIds to integers. The first map (p) sums up all the positive update operations per replica and the second map (n) sums up all the negative ones. While this is still one of the easier CRDTs, it is not trivial to see, that the optimized implementation is valid with respect to its specification. We will come

Table 4. State-based specifications of CRDTs

Grow-Set:	$s ::'\ a\ set = \{\}$
	$\mathbf{update}(Add(x), r, s) = s \cup \{x\}$
	$\mathbf{merge}(s, s') = s \cup s'$
	$\mathbf{query}(Contains(x), s) = x \in s$
Two-Phase-Set:	$s ::'\ a \Rightarrow \{init = 0, in = 1, out = 2\} = (\lambda x.\ init)$
	$\mathbf{update}(Add(x), r, s) = (\mathbf{if}\ s(x) = init\ \mathbf{then}\ s(x := in)\ \mathbf{else}\ s)$
	$\mathbf{update}(Rem(x), r, s) = s(x := out)$
	$\mathbf{merge}(s, s') = (\lambda x.\ max(s(x), s'(x)))$
	$\mathbf{query}(Contains(x), s) = (s(x) = in)$
Two-Phase-Set (guarded remove):	Same as above, but with different remove operation:
	$\mathbf{update}(Rem(x), r, s) = (\mathbf{if}\ s(x) = in\ \mathbf{then}\ s(x := out)\ \mathbf{else}\ s)$
Observed-Remove-Set:	$s.e :: (id \times'\ a)set = \{\}, s.t :: id\ set = \{\}$
	$\mathbf{update}(Add(x), r, s) = s(e := s.e \cup \{(uid(), x)\})$
	$\mathbf{update}(Rem(x), r, s) = s(t := s.t \cup \{id | \exists_x.(id, x) \in s.e\})$
	$\mathbf{merge}(s, s') = (e = s.e \cup s'.e,\ t = s.t \cup s'.t)$
	$\mathbf{query}(Contains(x), s) = \exists_{id}.(x, id) \in s.e \wedge id \notin s.t$
Multi-Value-Register:	$s.e :: (id \times'\ a)set = \{\}, s.t :: id\ set = \{\}$
	$\mathbf{update}(Set(x), r, s) = s(e := \{(uid(), x)\},$
	$\qquad\qquad\qquad\qquad\quad t := s.t \cup \{id | \exists_x.(id, x) \in s.e\})$
	$\mathbf{merge}(s, s') = (e = s.e \cup s'.e,\ t = s.t \cup s'.t)$
	$\mathbf{query}(Get(), s) = \{x | \exists_{id}.(x, id) \in s.e \wedge id \notin s.t\}$

back to this example in Section 5 and show how the correctness can be proven using our framework.

Table 4 shows abstract implementations of the other CRDTs introduced in Section 3. The Grow-Set can be implemented using a normal set where the merge is simply the union of two sets. The payload of the Two-Phase-Set can be described by assigning one out of three possible states to each element. In a new, empty set all elements are in the *init* state. Once an element is added, it goes to the *in* state, and when it is removed it goes to the *out* state. The merge simply takes the maximum state for each element with respect to the order *init* < *in* < *out*. The last two CRDTs in Table 4 have a very similar implementation. This is not very surprising, as the *Set* operation of the register is basically an operation, that first removes all elements from the set and then adds a single new element. In both cases the payload consists of a set of elements tagged with an unique identifier and a set of tombstones, that contains all unique identifiers of the removed elements. The unique identifier makes sure, that the remove operation only affects previous add-operations, as it is demanded by the specification.

Relation to Specifications. All CRDT implementations can be specified by the specification technique described in Section 3, when the merge operation computes a least upper bound with respect to a semilattice and the update operations are increasing with respect to the order on the semilattice. This is possible, as the state can be reconstructed from a given update history, when the implementation is known. Because the merge operation of a CRDT computes a least upper bound, it is straight-forward to extend it to a merge function, which merges a set of payloads. Then a function to calculate the state can be defined recursively in terms of previous versions: If there is an update at the top of the history, apply the update operation to the merge of all previous versions. If there is no update operation at the top, just take the merge of all previous versions. This terminates, when the set of all previous versions only consists of the initial state.

The converse is also true: each specification given in this form describes a CRDT. A specification can be turned into an inefficient implementation by storing the visible update history in the payload of the data type. The update history is just a growing set which can be merged using the union of sets, thus forming a semilattice.

5   Verification

In our work on verification of CRDTs we considered two properties. The first property is the convergence of a CRDT, meaning that two replicas, which have received the same set of updates, should return the same results for any given query. This property is common to all CRDTs and does not require any further specification. The second property is the behavior of a CRDT, i.e. we want to prove, that a specification as presented in Section 3 is valid for a given implementation. As we discussed earlier, this is a strictly stronger property, but it requires a specification for each data type.

Section 5.1 covers the verification of the convergence property, in Section 5.2 we present a technique for verifying the behavior, and in Section 5.3 we evaluate our experience in using Isabelle/HOL for the verification of CRDTs with the presented techniques.

5.1   Verification of Convergence

The convergence property can be verified by proving that the payload of the CRDT forms a semilattice, such that the merge-operation computes a least upper bound and the update-operations increase the payload with respect to the order on the semilattice.[12]

However, only very simple data types form a semilattice in the classical mathematical sense. Often the semilattice properties only hold for a subset of the payloads. For some states which are theoretically representable by the payload type, but are never reached in an actual execution, the semilattice properties sometimes do not hold. In theory it could even be the case that there are two reachable states for which the merge operation does not yield the correct result, but where the two states can never be reached in the same execution. However, for the examples we considered it was always sufficient to restrict the payload to exclude some of the unreachable states. Technically, this was done by giving

Table 5. Verifying convergence of CRDTs

(refl)	$Inv(H, pl) \Rightarrow pl \leq_{crdt} pl$
(trans)	$Inv(H_1, pl_1) \wedge Inv(H_2, pl_2) \wedge Inv(H_3, pl_3) \wedge$ $\quad pl_1 \leq_{crdt} pl_2 \wedge pl_2 \leq_{crdt} pl_3 \Rightarrow pl_1 \leq_{crdt} pl_3$
(antisym)	$Inv(H_1, pl_1) \wedge Inv(H_2, pl_2) \wedge pl_1 \leq_{crdt} pl_2 \leq_{crdt} pl1 \Rightarrow pl_1 = pl_2$
(commute)	$Inv(H_1, pl_1) \wedge Inv(H_2, pl_2) \Rightarrow merge_{crdt}(pl_1, pl_2) = merge_{crdt}(pl_2, pl_1)$
(upper bound)	$Inv(H_1, pl_1) \wedge Inv(H_2, pl_2) \Rightarrow pl_1 \leq_{crdt} merge_{crdt}(pl_1, pl_2)$
(least upper bound)	$Inv(H_1, pl_1) \wedge Inv(H_2, pl_2) \wedge Inv(H_3, pl_3) \wedge$ $\quad pl_1 \leq_{crdt} pl_3 \wedge pl_2 \leq_{crdt} pl_3 \Rightarrow merge_{crdt}(pl_1, pl_2) \leq pl_3$
(monotonic updates)	$Inv(H, pl) \Rightarrow pl \leq_{crdt} update_{crdt}(args, r, pl)$

an invariant Inv over the update history H and the payload pl. The same type of invariant will also be used for the verification of behavioral properties in the next section. In the examples we considered, it was not necessary to use the update history H in the invariant. An overview of the sufficient conditions for convergence, which we used, is given in Table 5. The order on the payloads is denoted by $\leq_{crdt}$.

In order to verify these conditions for the Counter CRDT, we have to define the order on the payloads. Here we can simply compare the mappings for each replicaId: $(p, n) \leq (p', n') \leftrightarrow \forall_r \ p(r) \leq p'(r) \wedge n(r) \leq n'(r)$. An invariant is not required for this example and the proof of the semilattice conditions can be done mainly automatically by Isabelle/HOL. In fact, for all the easier examples, it was possible to do the majority of the proofs with the automated methods provided by Isabelle/HOL (sledgehammer, auto, . . .).

5.2   Verification of Behavior

For the verification of behavioral properties we have developed a small framework, which simplifies the verification and provides two general strategies for verifying a CRDT. The first strategy basically is an induction over the traces. The idea of the second strategy is to show that a CRDT behaves equivalently to another CRDT which has already been verified. In this paper we only present the first strategy.

When using this strategy, one has to provide an invariant between the payloads and the visible update history. It then has to be shown that the invariant implies the specification, that the invariant holds for the initial payload with the empty update history, and that the invariant is maintained by update- and merge-operations. Table 6 shows the four subgoals.

For both operations our framework provides basic properties about **valid update histories** (predicate *valid*), which hold for all CRDTs. Because we used version vectors for representing the visibility relation, it is not necessary to specify the partial order properties of the relation, but instead it is necessary

Table 6. Verifying behavior of CRDTs

The invariant must hold initially:

$Inv(\{\}, initial_{crdt})$

Merges must preserve the invariant:

$\forall_{H_1, H_2, pl_1, pl_2} \ valid(H_1) \wedge valid(H_2) \wedge Inv(H_1, pl_1) \wedge Inv(H_2, pl_2)$
$\qquad \wedge consistent(H_1, H_2) \Rightarrow Inv(H_1 \cup H_2, merge_{crdt}(pl_1, pl_2))$

Updates must preserve the invariant:

$\forall_{H, pl, r, v, args} \ valid(H) \wedge Inv(H, pl) \wedge v = sup_v(H)$
$\qquad \Rightarrow Inv(H \cup \{(v(r := v(r) + 1), r, args)\}, update_{crdt}(args, r, pl))$

The invariant must imply the specification:

$\forall_{H, pl, qa} \ valid(H) \wedge Inv(H, pl) \Rightarrow query_{crdt}(qa, pl) = spec(H, qa)$

---

to specify constraints for the version vectors. The most important property is that the updates on one replica form a total order where the local component of the version vector is always increased by one and the other components increase monotonically. Other properties describe the causality between version vectors in more detail and can be found in [16].

In the case of an update operation one has to show that the invariant is maintained when adding a new update to the top of the update history, meaning that all other updates are visible to the new update. In a real execution this is usually not the case, but the framework can still do this abstraction step, because updates which are not visible do not influence the new update.

In the case of a merge operation one can assume that the invariant holds for two *compatible* update histories with two corresponding payloads, and then has to show that the invariant also holds for the union of the two update histories with the merged payload. Two update histories are *compatible*, when for each replica, the sequence of updates on that replica in one update history is a prefix of the sequence of updates in the other update history.

To verify the counter example we used the following invariant: $Inv(H, (p, n)) \leftrightarrow \forall_r \ p(r) = \sum\{x | \exists_v \ (v, r, x) \in H \wedge x \geq 0\} \wedge n(r) = \sum\{-x | \exists_v \ (v, r, x) \in H \wedge x < 0\}$. For proving, that a merge-operation preserves the invariant, we have to use the property of *compatible* histories. From this property we get, that for any replica r, we either have $\{x | \exists_v \ (v, r, x) \in H \wedge x \geq 0\} \subseteq \{x | \exists_v \ (v, r, x) \in H' \wedge x \geq 0\}$ or the other way around. This combined with the fact, that all elements are positive, ensures that calculating the maximum yields the correct result. The other parts of the verification, namely update-operations, the initial state and the connection between the invariant and the specification, are rather trivial on paper, whereas in Isabelle the latter requires some work in transforming the sums.

5.3   Evaluation

We used the interactive theorem prover Isabelle/HOL[10] for the verification of several important CRDTs. To this end, we manually translated the pseudo-code implementations from the literature[12,2] into Isabelle functions, and then verified those implementations. The verified CRDTs are the Increment-Only-Counter, PN-Counter, Grow-Set, Two-Phase-Set, a simple and an optimized OR-Set implementation, and a Multi-Value-Register. The theory files are available on GitHub[1].

For the simple data types, the semilattice properties were mostly automatically proved by Isabelle/HOL. For the more complicated data types, like the optimized OR-Set or the similarly implemented MV-register, a suitable invariant had to be found and verified first, which required more manual work in the proofs.

Verifying the behavior of the data types was a more difficult task. Finding a suitable invariant has to be done manually, and the invariant has to be chosen such that it is easy to work with it in Isabelle/HOL. Proving that the invariant is maintained also requires many manual steps, as it usually requires some data transformations which can not be handled automatically by Isabelle/HOL.

We found two small problems, while verifying the CRDTs mentioned above:

- When trying to verify an implementation of the OR-set based on figure 2 in [3], we found a small problem in our translation of this implementation to Isabelle. In the original description the remove-operation computes the set R of entries to be removed with the formula $R = \{(e, n) | \exists n : (e, n) \in E\}$. When this expression is translated to Isabelle code in a direct way, one obtains an equation like $R = \{(e, n).\ \exists n.(e, n) \in E\}$. Then R will always contain all possible entries, because in Isabelle e and n are new variables, and e does not reference the parameter of the function as intended. This problem can be easily fixed, and was not a real issue in the original description, but rather a mistake made in the translation to Isabelle, which happened because of the different semantics of the pseudo-code used in the original description and Isabelle.

- We discovered another small problem with the MV-Register presented in specification 10 from [12]. This MV-register is slightly different from the one described in the previous sections, as its assign operation allows to assign multiple values to the register in one step. The problem is in the assign function. When the assigned list of elements is empty, the payload will also be empty after the operation. This is a problem, because all information about the current version is lost. It thus violates the requirement that updates monotonically increase the payload and it can lead to inconsistent replicas. As an example consider the following sequence of operations executed on replica 1: $\{(\bot, [0, 0])\} \xrightarrow{Assign(\{a\})} \{(a, [1, 0])\} \xrightarrow{Assign(\{b\})} \{(b, [2, 0])\} \xrightarrow{Assign(\{\})} \{\}$ $\xrightarrow{Assign(\{c\})} \{(c, [1, 0])\}$. Furthermore assume that replica 2 first merges the

---

[1] https://github.com/SyncFree/isabelle_crdt_verification

payload $\{(b, [2,0])\}$ and then the payload $\{(c, [1,0])\}$. Then all updates have been delivered to both replicas, but the payload of replica 1 is $\{(c, [1,0])\}$ and the payload of replica 2 is $\{(b, [2,0])\}$. This problem can be easily fixed by disallowing the assignment of an empty set or by storing the current version in an extra field of the payload.

6 Alternative Specifications

We have already seen two specification techniques: specifications based on the complete update history, and abstract implementations, which are a kind of state-based specifications. Another specification technique was sketched in [1]. In this section we discuss and formalize the technique.

The technique is a state-based one, and uses the notation of pre- and post-conditions to specify the effect of operations on the state. Using the technique of pre- and post-conditions, a sequential specification can be given as a set of Hoare-triples. The Hoare-triple $\{P\}op\{Q\}$ requires that Q should hold after operation op whenever P was true before executing the operation.

For example, the increment operation of a counter can be specified by the triple $\{val() = i\}\ inc(x)\ \{val() = i + x\}$ and similarly a set is specified using triples like $\{true\}\ add(e)\ \{contains(e)\}$. Such a sequential specification is applicable to replicated data types if there is no interaction with other replicas between the pre- and post-condition.

In such cases, the replicated counter and the Observed-Remove-Set behave exactly as their corresponding sequential data type. For the Two-Phase-Set this is not true, since an add-operation does not guarantee that the element is in the set afterwards. There are examples like the Multi-Value-Register, where no corresponding and meaningful sequential data type exists, but for replicated data types which try to mimic sequential data types, it is a desirable property to maintain the sequential semantics in time spans where there are no concurrent operations, i.e. where the visibility relation describes a sequence.

In [1] those sequential specifications are combined with concurrent specifications, that describe the effect of executing operations concurrently. The concurrent specification is written in a similar style as the sequential specification. Instead of only a single operation it considers several operations of the following form executed in parallel: $\{P\}op_1 \parallel op_2 \parallel \cdots \parallel op_n\{Q\}$. The informal meaning is that if P holds in a state s, then executing all operations on s independently and then merging the resulting states should yield a state where Q holds.

Formally, we define a triple $\{P\}op_1 \parallel op_2 \parallel \cdots \parallel op_n\{Q\}$ to be valid, if the following condition is met:

$$\forall_{tr,pls,vs,ph,pls',vs',ph',r1,\ldots,r_n,op_1,op_n} : s_{init} \xrightarrow{tr} (pls, vs, ph)$$
$$\wedge (pls, vs, ph) \xrightarrow{Update(r_1,op_1);\ldots;Update(r_n,op_n)} (pls', vs', ph')$$
$$\wedge \forall_{i\in\{1,\ldots,n\}}\ pls(r_i) = pls(r_1)$$
$$\wedge P(pls(r_1)) \Rightarrow Q(merge_{crdt}(pls'(r_1), \ldots, pls'(r_n)))$$

If we reach a state (pls, vs, ph) where the payload on the replicas r_1 to r_n are equal and satisfy the pre-condition P, then executing each operation op_i on replica r_i yields a state (pls', vs', ph') where the post-condition Q holds for the merged payload of replicas r_1 to r_n.

Obviously, one can only specify a subset of all possible executions using this specification techniques. The advantages of this technique is that it is more modular and thus better composable than the technique introduced in Section 3, and that it is easier to see the sequential semantics of the data type. Also, there is the principle of permutation equivalence[1], which can be applied to this technique very easily, and is a good design guideline for designing new CRDTs.

7   Related Work

Burckhardt et al.[5] worked on verifying the behavioral properties of CRDTs. Their techniques are very similar to ours, but they have not used a tool to check their proofs. Their formal system model is more general than ours, as it supports timestamps and visibility relations which are not partial orders.

Bouajjani et al.[4] present a specification technique which is based on the history of updates with the visibility relation. They obtain a more flexible system model by allowing the partial order to be completely different for different operations. This allows them to cover a wide selection of optimistic replication systems, in particular ones that use speculative execution. In contrast to our work, they use an algorithmic approach to reduce the verification problem to model-checking and reachability.

The only other work we are aware of which uses a theorem prover to verify CRDTs is by Christopher Meiklejohn. Using the interactive theorem prover Coq, the semilattice properties of the increase-only-counter and the PN-counter CRDTs[9] are verified. Unlike our work, the behavioral properties of CRDTs are not considered and the verification is not based on a formal system model.

8   Conclusion and Future Work

In this paper, we have presented a formal framework for the analysis and verification of CRDTs. As the case studies have shown, it is feasible to verify CRDTs with Isabelle/HOL. The problem found in the MV-register during verification shows that it is easy to miss some corner case when designing a CRDT. The verified CRDTs were given in pseudo-code and then translated to Isabelle, which is a very high level language. Real implementations of the same CRDTs will probably be more complex, and thus the chance of introducing bugs might be even higher. But also the amount of work required for verifying a real implementation is higher.

It is an open question if more research into the automated verification and testing of CRDTs is required. This depends on how applications will use CRDTs in the future. For sequential data types, it is often sufficient to have lists, sets, and maps for managing data, as can be seen in commonly used data formats like

XML or JSON. In the case of CRDTs, more data types are required, because different applications require different conflict resolution behavior. This could be very application specific. For example, an application could require a set where add-operations win over remove-operations, but when a remove-operation is performed by an administrator of the system, then that operation should win. If every application needs its own CRDTs, then automatic tools to auto-generate correct code might be a good idea.

In future work, we want to extend the specification techniques presented in this paper for reasoning about applications using CRDTs. Such large-scale distributed applications are usually long-running and should be stable, but are difficult to maintain. It is therefore of special interest to have a stable and correct code base.

Acknowledgement. This research is supported in part by European FP7 project 609 551 SyncFree.

References

1. Bieniusa, A., Zawirski, M., Preguiça, N.M., Shapiro, M., Baquero, C., Balegas, V., Duarte, S.: Brief announcement: Semantics of eventually consistent replicated sets. In: Aguilera, M.K. (ed.) DISC 2012. LNCS, vol. 7611, pp. 441–442. Springer, Heidelberg (2012)
2. Bieniusa, A., Zawirski, M., Preguiça, N.M., Shapiro, M., Baquero, C., Balegas, V., Duarte, S.: An optimized conflict-free replicated set. CoRR, abs/1210.3368 (2012)
3. Bieniusa, A., Zawirski, M., Preguiça, N.M., Shapiro, M., Baquero, C., Balegas, V., Duarte, S.: An optimized conflict-free replicated set. CoRR, abs/1210.3368 (2012)
4. Bouajjani, A., Enea, C., Hamza, J.: Verifying eventual consistency of optimistic replication systems. In: Jagannathan, Sewell (eds.) [7], pp. 285–296
5. Burckhardt, S., Gotsman, A., Yang, H., Zawirski, M.: Replicated data types: specification, verification, optimality. In: Jagannathan, Sewell (eds.) [7], pp. 271–284
6. Gilbert, S., Lynch, N.A.: Brewer's conjecture and the feasibility of consistent, available, partition-tolerant web services. SIGACT News 33(2), 51–59 (2002)
7. Jagannathan, S., Sewell, P. (eds.): The 41st Annual ACM SIGPLAN-SIGACT Symposium on Principles of Programming Languages, POPL 2014, San Diego, CA, USA, January 20-21. ACM (2014)
8. Lamport, L.: Time, clocks, and the ordering of events in a distributed system. Commun. ACM 21(7), 558–565 (1978)
9. Meiklejohn, C.: Distributed data structures with Coq, http://christophermeiklejohn.com/coq/2013/06/11/distributed-data-structures.html (June 2013)
10. Nipkow, T., Paulson, L.C., Wenzel, M.T.: Isabelle/HOL. LNCS, vol. 2283. Springer, Heidelberg (2002)
11. Saito, Y., Shapiro, M.: Optimistic replication. ACM Comput. Surv. 37(1), 42–81 (2005)

12. Shapiro, M., Preguiça, N., Baquero, C., Zawirski, M.: A comprehensive study of Convergent and Commutative Replicated Data Types. Rapport de Recherche RR-7506, INRIA (January 2011)
13. Shapiro, M., Preguiça, N.M., Baquero, C., Zawirski, M.: Conflict-free replicated data types. In: Défago, X., Petit, F., Villain, V. (eds.) SSS 2011. LNCS, vol. 6976, pp. 386–400. Springer, Heidelberg (2011)
14. Terry, D.B., Theimer, M., Petersen, K., Demers, A.J., Spreitzer, M., Hauser, C.: Managing update conflicts in bayou, a weakly connected replicated storage system. In: SOSP, pp. 172–183 (1995)
15. Vogels, W.: Eventually consistent. ACM Queue 6(6), 14–19 (2008)
16. Zeller, P.: Specification and Verification of Convergent Replicated Data Types. Master's thesis, TU Kaiserslautern, Germany (2013)

Actor- and Task-Selection Strategies for Pruning Redundant State-Exploration in Testing

Elvira Albert, Puri Arenas, and Miguel Gómez-Zamalloa

DSIC, Complutense University of Madrid, Spain

Abstract. Testing concurrent systems requires exploring all possible non-deterministic interleavings that the concurrent execution may have. This is because any of the interleavings may reveal the erroneous behaviour. In testing of actor systems, we can distinguish two sources of non-determinism: (1) *actor-selection*, the order in which actors are explored and (2) *task-selection*, the order in which the tasks within each actor are explored. This paper provides new strategies and heuristics for pruning redundant state-exploration when testing actor systems by reducing the amount of unnecessary non-determinism. First, we propose a method and heuristics for actor-selection based on tracking the amount and the type of interactions among actors. Second, we can avoid further redundant interleavings in task-selection by taking into account the access to the *shared-memory* that the tasks make.

1 Introduction

Concurrent programs are becoming increasingly important as multicore and networked computing systems are omnipresent. Writing correct concurrent programs is harder than writing sequential ones, because with concurrency come additional hazards not present in sequential programs such as race conditions, data races, deadlocks, and livelocks. Therefore, software validation techniques urge especially in the context of concurrent programming. Testing is the most widely-used methodology for software validation. However, due to the non-deterministic interleavings of processes, traditional testing for concurrent programs is not as effective as for sequential programs. Systematic and exhaustive exploration of all interleavings is typically too time-consuming and often computationally intractable (see, e.g., [16] and its references).

We consider actor systems [1,9], a model of concurrent programming that has been gaining popularity and that it is being used in many systems (such as ActorFoundry, Asynchronous Agents, Charm++, E, ABS, Erlang, and Scala). Actor programs consist of computing entities called actors, each with its own local state and thread of control, that communicate by exchanging messages asynchronously. An actor configuration consists of the local state of the actors and a set of pending *tasks*. In response to receiving a message, an actor can update its local state, send messages, or create new actors. At each step in the computation of an actor system, firstly an actor and secondly a process of its pending tasks are scheduled. As actors do not share their states, in testing

E. Ábrahám and C. Palamidessi (Eds.), FORTE 2014, LNCS 8461, pp. 49–65, 2014.

one can assume [13] that the evaluation of all statements of a task takes place serially (without interleaving with any other task) until it releases the processor (gets to a return instruction). At this point, we must consider two levels of non-determinism: (1) *actor-selection*, the selection of which actor executes, and (2) *task-selection*, the selection of the task within the selected actor. Such non-determinism might result in different configurations, and they all need to be explored as only some specific interleavings/configurations may reveal the bugs.

A naïve exploration of the search space to reach all possible system configurations does not scale. The challenge is in avoiding the exploration of redundant states which lead to the same configuration. Partial-order reduction (POR) [6,8] is a general theory that helps mitigate the state-space explosion problem by exploring the subset of all possible interleavings which lead to a different configuration. A concrete algorithm (called DPOR) was proposed by Flanagan and Godefroid [7] which maintains for each configuration a backtrack set, which is updated during the execution of the program when it realises that a non-deterministic choice must be tried. Recently, TransDPOR [16] extends DPOR to take advantage of the transitive dependency relations in actor systems to explore fewer configurations than DPOR. As noticed in [12,16], their effectiveness highly depend on the actor selection order. Our work enhances these approaches with novel strategies and heuristics to further prune redundant state exploration, and that can be easily integrated within the aforementioned algorithms. Our main contributions can be summarized as follows:

1. We introduce a strategy for actor-selection which is based on the number and on the type of interactions among actors. Our strategy tries to find a *stable actor*, i.e., an actor to which no other actor will post tasks.
2. When temporal stability of any actor cannot be proven, we propose to use heuristics that assign a weight to the tasks according to the error that the actor-selection strategy may make when proving stability w.r.t. them.
3. We introduce a task-selection function which selects tasks based on the access to the shared memory that they make. When tasks access disjoint parts of the shared memory, we avoid non-determinism reordering among tasks.
4. We have implemented our actor-selection and task-selection strategies in aPET [2], a Test Case Generation tool for concurrent objects. Our experiments demonstrate the impact and effectiveness of our strategies.

The rest of the paper is organized as follows. Section 2 presents the syntax and semantics of the actor language we use to develop our technique. In Sec. 3, we present a state-of-the-art algorithm for testing actor systems which captures the essence of the algorithm in [16] but adapted to our setting. Section 4 introduces our proposal to establish the order in which actors are selected. In Sec. 5, we present our approach to reduce redundant state exploration in the task selection strategy. Our implementation and experimental evaluation is presented in Sec. 6. Finally, Section 7 overviews related work and concludes.

2   The Actor Model

We consider a distributed message-passing programming model in which each actor represents a processor which is equipped with a procedure stack and an unordered buffer of pending tasks. Initially all actors are idle. When an idle actor's task buffer is non-empty, some task is removed, and the task is executed to completion. Each task besides accessing its own actor's global storage, can post tasks to the buffers of any actor, including its own. When a task does complete, its processor becomes idle, chooses a next pending task to remove, and so on.

2.1   Syntax and Semantics

Actors are materialized in the language syntax by means of objects. An actor sends a message to another actor x by means of an asynchronous method call, written $x \ ! \ m(\bar{z})$, being $\bar{z}$ parameters of the message or call. In response to a received message, an actor then spawns the corresponding method with the received parameters $\bar{z}$. The number of actors does not have to be known a priori, thus in the language actors can be dynamically created using the instruction **new**. Tasks from different actors execute in parallel. The grammar below describes the syntax of our programs.

$$M ::= \textbf{void} \ m(\bar{T} \ \bar{x})\{s; \}$$
$$s \ ::= s \ ; \ s \mid x = e \mid x = \text{this}.f \mid \text{this}.f = y \mid \textbf{if} \ b \ \textbf{then} \ s \ \textbf{else} \ s \mid$$
$$\textbf{while} \ b \ \textbf{do} \ s \mid x = \textbf{new} \ C \mid x \ ! \ m(\bar{z}) \mid \textbf{return}$$

where x, y, z denote variables names, f a field name and s an instruction. For any entity A, the notation $\bar{A}$ is used as a shorthand for $A_1, ..., A_n$. We use the special actor identifier this to denote the current actor. For the sake of generality, the syntax of expressions e, boolean conditions b and types T is not specified. As in the object-oriented paradigm, a class denotes a type of actors including their behavior, and it is defined as a set of fields and methods. In the following, given an actor a, we denote by $class(a)$ the class to which the actor belongs. $Fields(C)$ stands for the set of fields defined in class C. We assume that there are no fields with the same name and different type. As usual in the actor model [16], we assume that methods do not return values, but rather that their computation modify the actor state. The language is deliberately simple to explain the contributions of the paper in a clearer way and in the same setting as [16]. However, both our techniques and our implementation also work in an extended language with tasks synchronization using future variables [5].

An *actor* is a term $act(a, t, h, \mathcal{Q})$ where a is the actor identifier, t is the identifier of the *active task* that holds the actor's lock or $\perp$ if the actor's lock is free, h is its local heap and $\mathcal{Q}$ is the set of tasks in the actor. A *task* is a term $tsk(t, m, l, s)$ where t is a unique task identifier, m is the method name executing in the task, l is a mapping from local variables to their values, and s is the sequence of instructions to be executed or ϵ if the task has terminated. A *state* or

$$(\text{MSTEP}) \ \frac{selectActor(S) = act(a, \bot, h, \mathcal{Q}), \mathcal{Q} \neq \emptyset, selectTask(a) = t, S \overset{a \cdot t}{\leadsto}{}^{*} S'}{S \xrightarrow{a \cdot t} S'}$$

$$(\text{SETFIELD}) \ \frac{t = tsk(t, m, l, \mathsf{this}.f = y; s)}{act(a, t, h, \mathcal{Q} \cup \{t\}) \leadsto act(a, t, h[f \mapsto l(y)], \mathcal{Q} \cup \{tsk(t, m, l, s)\})}$$

$$(\text{GETFIELD}) \ \frac{t = tsk(t, m, l, x = \mathsf{this}.f; s)}{act(a, t, h, \mathcal{Q} \cup \{t\}) \leadsto act(a, t, h, \mathcal{Q} \cup \{tsk(t, m, l[x \mapsto h(f)], s)\})}$$

$$(\text{NEWACTOR}) \ \frac{t = tsk(t, m, l, x = \mathsf{new} \ D; s), \mathsf{fresh}(a'), h' = newheap(D), l' = l[x \rightarrow a']}{act(a, t, h, \mathcal{Q} \cup \{t\}) \leadsto act(a, t, h, \mathcal{Q} \cup \{tsk(t, m, l', s)\}) \cdot act(a', \bot, h', \{\})}$$

$$(\text{ASYNC}) \ \frac{t = tsk(t, m, l, x \ ! \ m_1(\bar{z}); s), l(x) = a_1, \ \mathsf{fresh}(t_1), \ l_1 = buildLocals(\bar{z}, m_1, l)}{act(a, t, h, \mathcal{Q} \cup \{t\}) \cdot act(a_1, \_, \_, \mathcal{Q}') \leadsto}$$
$$act(a, t, h, \mathcal{Q} \cup \{tsk(t, m, l, s)\}) \cdot act(a_1, \_, \_, \mathcal{Q}' \cup \{tsk(t_1, m_1, l_1, body(m_1))\})$$

$$(\text{RETURN}) \ \frac{t = tsk(t, m, l, \mathsf{return}; s)}{act(a, t, h, \mathcal{Q} \cup \{t\}) \leadsto act(a, \bot, h, \mathcal{Q})}$$

Fig. 1. Summarized Semantics for Distributed and Concurrent Execution

configuration S has the form $a_0 \cdot a_1 \cdots a_n$, where $a_i \equiv act(a_i, t_i, h_i, \mathcal{Q}_i)$. The execution of a program from a method m starts from an initial state $S_0 = \{act(0, 0, \bot, \{tsk(0, m, l, body(m))\}$. Here, l maps parameters to their initial values (null in case of reference variables), $body(m)$ is the sequence of instructions in method m, and $\bot$ stands for the empty heap.

Fig. 1 presents the semantics of the actor model. As actors do not share their states, the semantics can be presented as a macro-step semantics [13] (defined by means of the transition "$\longrightarrow$") in which the evaluation of all statements of a task takes place serially (without interleaving with any other task) until it gets to a **return** instruction. In this case, we apply rule MSTEP to select an available task from an actor, namely we apply the function $selectActor(S)$ to select non-deterministically one *active* actor in the state (i.e., an actor with a non-empty queue) and $selectTask(a)$ to select non-deterministically one task of a's queue. The transition $\leadsto$ defines the evaluation within a given actor. We sometimes label transitions with $a \cdot t$, the name of the actor a and task t selected (in rule MSTEP) or evaluated in the step (in the transition $\leadsto$). The rules GETFIELD and SETFIELD read and write resp. an actor's field. The notation $h[f \mapsto l(y)]$ (resp. $l[x \mapsto h(f)]$) stands for the result of storing $l(y)$ in the field f (resp. $h(f)$ in variable x). The remaining sequential instructions are standard and thus omitted. In NEWACTOR, an active task t in actor a creates an actor a' of class D which is introduced to the state with a free lock. Here $h' = newheap(D)$ stands for a default initialization on the fields of class D. ASYNC spawns a new task (the initial state is created by $buildLocals$) with a fresh task identifier t_1. We assume $a \neq a_1$, but the case $a = a_1$ is analogous, the new task t_1 is added to $\mathcal{Q}$ of a. In what follows, a *derivation* or *execution* $E \equiv S_0 \longrightarrow \cdots \longrightarrow S_n$ is a sequence of macro-steps (applications of rule MSTEP). The derivation is *complete* if S_0 is the initial state and all actors in S_n are of the form $act(a, \bot, h, \{\})$. Since the execution is non-deterministic, multiple derivations are possible from a state. Given a state S, $exec(S)$ denotes the set of all possible derivations starting at S.

3   A State-of-the-Art Testing Algorithm

This section presents a state-of-the-art algorithm for testing actor systems – which captures the essence of the algorithm DPOR in [7] and its extension TransDPOR [16]– but it is recasted to our setting. The main difference with [7,16] is that we use functions $selectActor$ and $selectTask$ that will be redefined later with concrete strategies to reduce *redundant* state exploration.

To define the notion of redundancy, we rely in the standard definition of partial order adapted to our macro-step semantics. An execution $E = S_0 \xrightarrow{a_1 \cdot t_1} \cdots \xrightarrow{a_n \cdot t_n} S_n$ defines a *partial order* [7] between the tasks of an actor. We write $t_i < t_j$, if t_i, t_j belong to the same actor a and t_i is selected before t_j in E. Given S, we say that $E_1, E_2 \in exec(S)$ are *equivalent* if they have the same partial order for all actors.

Definition 1 (redundant state exploration). *Two complete executions are redundant if they have the same partial order.*

The algorithm DPOR [7], and its extension TransDPOR [16], achieve an enormous reduction of the search space. Function *Explore* in Fig. 2 illustrates the construction of the search tree that these algorithms make. It receives as parameter a derivation E, which starts from the initial state. We use $last(E)$ to denote the last state in the derivation, $next(S, a \cdot t)$ to denote the step $S \xrightarrow{a \cdot t} S'$ and $E \cdot next(S, a \cdot t)$ to denote the new derivation $E \xrightarrow{a \cdot t} S'$. Intuitively, each node (i.e., state) in the search tree is evaluated with a backtracking set *back*, which is used to store those actors that must be explored from this node. The backtracking set *back* in the initial state is empty. The crux of the algorithm is that, instead of considering all actors, the *back* set is dynamically updated by means of function $updateBackSets(E, S)$ with the actors that need to be explored. In particular, an actor is added to *back* only if during the execution the algorithm

```
1:  procedure Explore(E)
2:      S = last(E);
3:      updateBackSets(E, S);
4:      a = selectActor(S);
5:      if a! = ε then
6:          back(S) = {a};
7:          done(S) = ∅;
8:          while ∃(a∈back(S)\done(S)) do
9:              done(S) = done(S) ∪ {a};
10:             for all t ∈ selectTask(a) do
11:                 Explore(E · next(S, a · t));
```

Fig. 2. A state-of-the-art algorithm for testing

```
{    /* main Block */                      class Worker₁ {
    Reg rg = new Reg;                          void q(Reg rg) {
    Worker₁ wk1 = new Worker₁();                   rg ! m(); // m
    Worker₂ wk2 = new Worker₂();                   return;
    rg ! p();    //p                           }
    wk1 ! q(rg); // q                      }
    wk2 ! h(rg); // h
}
                                           class Worker₂ {
class Reg {                                     void h(Reg rg) {
    int f=1;  int g=1;                             rg ! t(); // t
    void p() {this.f++; return;}                   return;
    void m() {this.g*2; return;}               }
    void t() {this.g++; return;}           }
}
```

Fig. 3. Running Example

realizes that it was *needed*. Intuitively, it is *needed* when, during the execution, a new task t of an actor a previously explored, occurs. Therefore, we must try different reorderings between the tasks since according to Def. 1 they might not be redundant. In this case, the back set of the last state S in which a was used to give a derivation step might need to be updated. As a simple example, consider a state S in which an actor a with a unique task t_1 is selected. Now, assume that when the execution proceeds, a new task t_2 of a is spawned by the execution of a task t' of an actor a' and that t' was in S. This means that it is required to consider also first the execution of t_2 and, next the execution of t_1, since it represents a different partial order between the tasks of a. This is accomplished by adding a' to the back set of S, which allows exploring the execution in which a' is selected before a at S, and thus considering the partial order $t_2 < t_1$. The formal definition of *updateBackSets* (and its optimization with *freeze* flags to avoid further redundancy) can be found at [16]. Function *selectActor* at line 4 selects non-deterministically an active actor in S (or returns ϵ if there is none). The *back* set is initialized with the selected actor. The while loop at line 8 picks up an actor in the *back* set that has not been evaluated before (checked in *done* set) and explores all its tasks (lines 10-11).

Example 1. Consider the program in Fig. 3 borrowed from [16] and extended with field accesses to later explain the concepts in Sec. 5. It consists of 3 classes, one *registry* Reg and two *workers* Worker₁ and Worker₂, together with a *main* block from which the execution starts. In Fig. 4 we show the search tree built by executing $Explore(E_0)$, where $E_0 = S_{ini} \xrightarrow{main} S_0$, and S_{ini} is the initial state from the main block. The branches in the tree show the macro-steps performed labeled with the task selected at the step (the object identifier is omitted). We distinguish three types of edges: dotted edges are introduced by the **for** loop at line 10 in Fig. 4, dashed edges are eliminated by the improvement of [16], and normal edges are introduced by the **while** loop at line 8. After executing the main block,

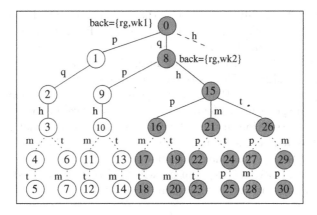

Fig. 4. Execution Tree

there are three actors S_0={rg, wk1, wk2} in node 0 and their queues of pending tasks are $\mathcal{Q}_{rg}$={p()}, $\mathcal{Q}_{wk1}$={q(rg)} and $\mathcal{Q}_{wk2}$={h(rg)} resp. Let us focus on the execution $E_2 = S_0 \xrightarrow{p} S_1 \xrightarrow{q} S_2$. The recursive call $Explore(E_2)$ updates the back set of S_0 because a new task m() of rg (previously explored) occurs. Since this task has been produced by the execution of wk1 ! q(rg) and task q(rg) is in S_0, then $back(S_0) = \{$rg, wk1$\}$. The derivation continues and task wk2 ! h(rg) is selected. The execution of $E_3=E_2 \xrightarrow{h} S_3$ introduces t() in the queue of rg. The recursive call $Explore(E_3)$ updates the back set of node 0 by introducing wk2 in $back(S_0)$ since it is the responsible of introducing t() on rg (dashed line in node 0). This branch, which generates 14 more (redundant) executions, can be avoided by introducing a "freeze" flag as done in [16], an optimization that we adopt but which is no relevant to explain our contributions. In S_3, the unique active actor rg is selected, and its tasks explored. The execution continues in a similar way and other nodes are added to the back sets. For instance, the back set of node 8 is updated with wk2 from node 10.

4 Actor-Selection Based on Stability Criteria

This section introduces our method to establish the order in which actors are selected based on their *stability* levels. In Sec. 4.1 we first motivate the problem. Afterwards, Sec. 4.2 introduces the notion of *temporarily stable actor* and sufficient conditions to ensure it dynamically during testing. Finally, Section 4.3 presents heuristics based on the stability level of actors.

4.1 Motivation

In Algorithm 2, function *selectActor* selects non-deterministically an active actor in the state. As noticed in [12], the pruning that can be achieved using the testing algorithm in Sec. 3 is highly dependent on the order in which tasks are considered for processing. Consider the execution tree in Fig. 4. By inspecting the branches associated to the terminal nodes, we can see that the induced partial order $p<m<t$ occurs in the executions ending in $5, 12, 18$, $p<t<m$ in those ending in $7, 14, 20$, $m<p<t$ ending in 23, $m<t<p$ ending in node 25, $t<p<m$ ending in 28, and $t < m < p$ ending in 30. Hence, it is enough to consider the coloured subtree since the remaining executions (ending in $5, 7, 12, 14$) have the same partial order than some other execution in the coloured tree. Our work is motivated by the observation that if *selectActor* first selects an actor to which no other actors will post tasks, then we can avoid redundant computations. In particular, if *selectActor* selects wk1, the exploration will lead to the coloured search tree, which does not make any redundant state-exploration.

4.2   The Notion of Temporal Stability

The notion of temporal stability will allow us to guide the selection of actors so that the search space can be pruned further and redundant computations avoided. An actor is *stable* if there is no other actor different from it that introduces tasks in its queue. Basically, this means that the actor is autonomous since its execution does not depend on any other actor. In general, it is quite unlikely that an actor is stable in a whole execution. However, if we consider the tasks that have been spawned in a given state, it is often the case that we can find an actor that is temporarily stable w.r.t. the actors in that state.

Definition 2 (temporarily stable actor). $act(a, t, h, \mathcal{Q})$ *is temporarily stable in S iff, for any E starting from S and for any subtrace* $S \xrightarrow{*} S' \in E$ *in which the actor a is not selected, we have* $act(a, t, h, \mathcal{Q}) \in S'$.

The intuition of the definition is that an actor's queue cannot be modified by the execution of other actors (which are different from itself). E.g., actor rg in Ex. 1 is not temporarily stable in S_0 because the derivation $S_0 \xrightarrow{p} S_1 \xrightarrow{q} S_2$ introduces the task m() in the queue of rg.

Lemma 1. *Let a be a temporarily stable actor in a state S. For any execution E generated by Explore(S) such that selectActor(S)=a, we have back(S)={a}.*

The intuition of the lemma is that if *selectActor* returns a temporarily stable actor a, it is ensured that, from that state, there will be only a branch in the search tree (that corresponds to the selection of a), i.e., no other actors will be added to *back* during its exploration using the testing algorithm *Explore*.

   Our goal is to come up with sufficient conditions that ensure actors stability and that can be computed during dynamic execution. To this end, given a method m_1 of class A_1, we define $Ch(A_1::m_1)$ as the set of all chains of method calls of the form $A_1::m_1 \rightarrow A_2::m_2 \rightarrow \cdots \rightarrow A_k::m_k$, with $k \geq 2$, such that $A_i::m_i \neq A_j::m_j$, $2 \leq i \leq k-1$, $i \neq j$ and there exists a call within $body(A_i::m_i)$ to method $A_{i+1}::m_{i+1}$, $1 \leq i < k$. This captures all paths $A_2::m_2 \rightarrow A_{k-1}::m_{k-1}$, without cycles, that go from $A_1::m_1$ to $A_k::m_k$. The set $Ch(A_1::m_1)$ can be computed statically for all methods.

Theorem 1 (sufficient conditions for temporal stability). *We say that* $act(a,t,h,\mathcal{Q}) \in S$, $class(a)=A_n$ *is temporarily stable in* S, *if for every* $act(a',t',$ $h',\mathcal{Q}') \in S$, $a \neq a'$, $class(a')=A_1$, *and for every* $tsk(\_,m_1,l,s) \in \mathcal{Q}'$, *one of the following conditions holds:*

1. *There is no chain* $A_1::m_1 \to \cdots \to A_n::m_n \in Ch(A_1::m_1)$; *or*
2. *For all chains* $A_1::m_1 \to \cdots \to A_n::m_n \in Ch(A_1::m_1)$, $l(x) \neq a$ *holds, for all* $x \in dom(l)$, $h'(f) \neq a$ *for all* $f \in Fields(A_1)$, *and for all* $act(a'',\_,h'',\_) \in S$ *with* $class(a'')=A_i$, $2 \leq i \leq n-1$, *then* $h''(f) \neq a$, *for all* $f \in Fields(A_i)$.

Intuitively, the theorem above ensures that a' cannot modify the queue of a. This is because (1) there is no transitive call from m_1 to any method of class A_n to which object a belongs, or (2) there are transitive calls from m_1 to some method of class A_n, but no reference to actor a can be found along the chain of objects that will lead to the potential call (that will post a task on actor a). In order to be sound, we check the second condition on all objects in the state whose type matches that of the methods considered in the chain of calls. The following example illustrates why seeking the reference in intermediate objects is required in condition (2).

Example 2. Consider $S=act(a_1,\_,h_1,\mathcal{Q}_1) \cdot act(a_2,\_,h_2,\emptyset) \cdot act(a_3,\_,h_3,\mathcal{Q}_3)$, of classes A, B and C resp., with $\mathcal{Q}_3=\{tsk(t_3, m, l_3, \{y!p(); \mathsf{return};\})\}$, $l_3(y) = a_2$, $body(B :: p) = \{x = \mathsf{this}.f; x!q(); \mathsf{return};\}$, and $h_2(f) = a_1$. Then, even if a_3 does not have a reference to a_1, it is able to introduce the call $q()$ to $\mathcal{Q}_1$. This is because from m there is a call to $p()$ and from there to $f!q()$ with $h_2(f) = a_1$. Thus actor a_1 is not temporarily stable.

Th. 1 allows us to define *selectActor* in Fig. 2 such that it returns an actor a in S which is temporarily stable. If such actor does not exist, then it returns randomly an active object in S.

Example 3. Consider Ex. 1. At node 0 the actor rg is not temporarily stable because in the queue of wk1 there is a call q(rg) (i.e., actor rg can be reachable from q), and in the body of method q there is also a call to method m() of class Reg (i.e., rg can possibly be modified by wk1). However, actors wk1 and wk2 are temporarily stable at node 0. Thus we can select any of these actors to start the exploration. In Fig. 4, actor wk1 has been selected, resulting in the coloured subtree. Similarly, in node 8, rg is not temporarily stable but wk2 it is.

4.3   Heuristics Based on Stability Level

When we are not able to prove that there is a stable actor, then we can use heuristics to determine which actor must be explored first. In particular, we refine the definition of function *selectActor* so that it computes *stability levels* for the actors and selects the actor with highest stability level. Our heuristics tries to weight the loss of precision of the sufficient conditions in Th. 1 in the following way: (1) k_a: this is the value assigned by the heuristics to the case in

which an object is not stable due to a direct call from another object that has
a reference to it, (2) k_b: it corresponds to the case in which stability is lost by
a transitive (indirect) call from another object that has a reference to it, (3)
k_c: this is the case in which the object that breaks its stability does not have
a reference to it (instead some intermediate object will have it). It is clear that
the heuristics must assign values such that $k_a > k_b > k_c$. This is because the
most likely scenario in which the sufficient conditions detect an unfeasible non-
stability is (3) since the loss of precision can be large when we seek references
to the object within all other objects of the intermediate types in the call chain.
The first scenario (1) is more likely to happen since we have both the reference
and the direct call. Scenario (2) is somewhere in the middle.

Thus, we define the stability level of $a \in class(A_n)$ w.r.t. a $tsk(t, m_1, l, \_)$ of an
actor $act(a', \_, h', \_) \in S$ breaking its stability ($a \neq a'$, $class(a')=A_1$) and a chain
$Ch = A_1{::}m_1 \to^* A_n{::}m_n$, denoted as $st(a, t, Ch, S)$, as follows:

(a) If $l(x)=a$, for some $x \in dom(l)$ or $h'(f)=a$, for some $f \in Fields(A_1)$ and
    $n=2$, then $st(a, t, Ch, S)=k_a$.
(b) If $l(x)=a$, for some $x \in dom(l)$ or $h'(f)=a$, for some $f \in Fields(A_1)$ and
    $n > 2$, then $st(a, t, Ch, S)=k_b$.
(c) Otherwise, i.e., $l(x) \neq a$, for all $x \in dom(l)$ and $h'(f) \neq a$, for all $f \in$
    $Fields(A_1)$, then $st(a, t, Ch, S)=k_c$.

The *stability level of an actor* $a \in S$, $class(a)=A_n$, w.r.t. a task $tsk(t, m_1, l, \_)$
from $act(a', \_, h', \_) \in S$, $class(a')=A_1$, denoted as $st(a, t, S)$, is defined as
$\sum st(a, t, Ch, S)$ such that $Ch = A_1{::}m_1 \to^* A_n{::}m_n \in Ch(A_1{::}m_1)$.

Definition 3 (stability level of an actor). *Let a be a non temporarily stable
actor in a state S. The stability level of a in S, denoted as $st(a, S)$, is defined
as $\sum st(a, t, S)$ such that $t \in Q'$, $act(a', t, h', Q') \in S$, $a \neq a'$.*

Given a state $S = a_1 \cdot \ldots \cdot a_n$, the above definition allows us to define the function
selectActor(S) in Fig. 2 such that, in case of finding an active actor, it returns
a temporarily stable actor a if it exists, and otherwise it returns a_i, where a_i
satisfies $st(a_i, S) \geq st(a_j, S)$, for all $1 \leq i, j \leq n$, $i \neq j$.

Example 4. Let us consider the program in Fig. 5, borrowed from [16], which
computes the nth element in the Fibonacci sequence in a distributed fashion.
The computation starts with the execution of a task fib(3) on actor a_1, which
in turn generates two actors a_2 and a_3 with $Q_{a_2} = \{\text{fib}(2)\}$ and $Q_{a_3} = \{\text{fib}(1)\}$.
Both a_2 and a_3 are clearly temporarily stable since there is no reference pointing
to them. Let us select a_2 and therefore execute its task fib(2). This generates
two more actors a_4 and a_5 with $Q_{a_4} = \{\text{fib}(1)\}$ and $Q_{a_5} = \{\text{fib}(0)\}$. Again a_4
and a_5 are clearly temporarily stable. After selecting successively a_3, a_4 and a_5
we reach a state S, where a_3, a_4 and a_5 have an empty queue, $Q_{a_1} = \{\text{res}(1)\}$,
and $Q_{a_2} = \{\text{res}(1), \text{res}(0)\}$. At this point, our sufficient condition for temporal
stability is not able to determine a stable actor. Namely, a_1 is clearly non-stable
since the execution of task res on a_2 can, and will, eventually launch a task res

```
class Fib {
    Fib parent;
    Int n = 0;
    Int r = 0;
    Fib(Fib p){
        parent = p;
    }
    void fib(Int v) {
        if (v <= 1) then parent!res(v);
        else {
            Fib child1 = new Fib(this);
            child1!fib(v-1);
            Fib child2 = new Fib(this);
            child2!fib(v-2);
        }
        return;
    }
}

    void res(Int v) {
        if (n == 0) then {
            n++;
            r = v;
        }
        else {
            r = r + v;
            if (parent ≠ null) then parent!res(r);
        }
        return;
    }
}

{// Main block
    Fib a1 = new Fib(null);
    a1!fib(3);
}
```

Fig. 5. Distributed Fibonacci

on it. However, a_2 is stable, but we cannot determine it syntactically since there is a call chain $Fib::res \rightarrow Fib::res \rightarrow Fib::res$ (i.e. we can reach from $Fib::res$ to $Fib::res$ through $Fib::res$), which forces us to look for a reference to a_2 within all actors of type Fib (cond. 2 of Th. 1). That includes a_4 and a_5 whose parent field points to a_2. Interestingly, our heuristics assigns a much lower non-stability factor to a_2 than to a_1, making it being selected first. Specifically, $st(a_2, S) = k_c$ whereas $st(a_1, S) = 2 * k_a + 2 * k_c$. The latter is because we find 4 tasks that break the stability, 2 of them fulfill condition (a) and the two others condition (c). A wrong selection of a_1 would cause a backtracking at S which produces the exploration of redundant executions. In this concrete example, 8 executions would be explored, whereas with our right selection we explore 4.

We have defined a heuristics which according to our experiments works very well in practice. However, there are other factors to be taken into account to define other heuristics. For instance, it is relevant to consider if the calls appear within conditional instructions (and thus they may finally not hold). This can be easily detected from the control flow graph of the program, where we can define the "depth" of the calls according to the number of conditions that need to be checked to perform the call. In the absence of a stable object, it is also sensible to select the object that is breaking most stabilities, since once it is explored, those objects whose stability it was breaking might become stable.

5   Task Selection Based on Shared-Memory Access

In the section, we present our approach to reduce redundant state exploration within task selection. In Sec. 5.1, we first motivate the problem and characterize the notion of task independence. In Sec. 5.2 we provide sufficient conditions to ensure it. Finally, Sec. 5.3 presents our task selection function.

5.1   Motivation

Let us observe that there can be executions with different partial-orders which lead to the same state, which according to a stronger notion of redundancy could be considered as redundant executions. Consider node 15 in the search tree of Fig. 4. At this point, only tasks of actor rg are available. The derivations ending in nodes 18, 23, 25 result in the same state (namely fields of object rg are f=2, g=3) and the derivations to nodes 20, 28 and 30 also result in the same state (f=2, g=4). The reason for this redundancy is that the execution of p is independent from the executions of m and t because they access disjoint areas of the shared memory. However tasks m and t are not independent and the order in which they are executed affects the final result.

Definition 4. *Tasks t_1 and t_2 are independent, written $indep(t_1, t_2)$, if for any complete execution $S_0 \longrightarrow \cdots \longrightarrow S_n$ with $t_1 < t_2$, there exists another execution $S_0 \longrightarrow \cdots \longrightarrow S_n$ with $t_2 < t_1$.*

Observe that according to Def. 1, the above two derivations are not redundant (as they have a different partial order). However, they are redundant because they lead to the same state, which is a stronger notion of redundancy.

5.2   The Notion of Task Independence

The notion of independence between tasks is well-known in concurrent programming [3]. Basically, tasks t and t' are independent if t does not write in the shared locations that t' accesses, and viceversa. The following definition provides a syntactic way of ensuring task independence by checking the fields that are read and written. Let $act(a, \_, \_, \mathcal{Q}) \in S$ and $tsk(t, m, \_, s) \in \mathcal{Q}$. We define the set $W(t)$ as $\{f \mid \text{this.} f = y \in s\}$. Similarly, the set $R(t)$ is defined as $\{f \mid x = \text{this.} f \in s\}$. The following theorem is an immediate consequence of the definition of independent task above. We denote by $indep(t_1, t_2)$ that t_1 and t_2 are independent.

Theorem 2 (sufficient condition for tasks independence). *Given a state S, an actor $act(a, \_, \_, \mathcal{Q}) \in S$ and two tasks $t_1, t_2 \in \mathcal{Q}$. If $R(t_1) \cap W(t_2) = \emptyset$, $R(t_2) \cap W(t_1) = \emptyset$ and $W(t_1) \cap W(t_2) = \emptyset$, then $indep(t_1, t_2)$ holds.*

Note that since the actor state is local, i.e., fields cannot be accessed from other actors. Thus, all accesses to the heap are on the actor this.

```
9:    for all t ∈ selectTask(a) do
10:      unmark(a); mark(t, a);
11:      Explore(E · next(S, a · t))
```

Fig. 6. Refining Algorithm 2 with Task Selection

5.3   A Task-Selection Function Based on Task-Independence

We now introduce in Alg. 2 a task selection function which avoids unnecessary reorderings among independent tasks. To this end, we introduce marks in the tasks such that the elements in the queues have the form $\langle t, flag \rangle$, where t is a task and *mark* is a boolean flag which indicates if the task can be selected. Furthermore, we treat queues as lists and assume that its elements appear in the order in which they were added to the queue during execution. In order to implement task independence in Alg. 2, we replace lines 10 and 11 of Alg. 2 by those in Fig. 6 where we have that: (1) function $selectTask(a)$ returns the list of unmarked tasks in the queue $\mathcal{Q}$ of a, i.e, those tasks of the form $\langle t, false \rangle$; (2) procedure $unmark(a)$ traverses $\mathcal{Q}$ and changes the flag *mark* to *false*; and (3) procedure $mark(t, a)$ sets the flag *mark* to *true* for all tasks which are independent with t and occur in $\mathcal{Q}$ after t.

Intuitively the task selection process works as follows. Given $act(a, \_, \_, \mathcal{Q}) \in S$, $\mathcal{Q}$ contains a list $[t_1, \ldots, t_n]$ of tasks. These tasks are selected one by one traversing $\mathcal{Q}$ (line 10 of Alg, 2). This means that if t_i is selected by $selectTask(a)$ and t_i is independent from t_j, then $i < j$, i.e., the task t_i is selected before t_j. Furthermore, procedure $mark(t_i, a)$ puts the flag *mark* of t_j to *true*. Thus, in the following step in which actor a is selected, task t_j cannot be chosen, i.e., the *direct* order $t_i < t_j$ is pruned. By direct order, we mean that t_j is selected immediately after t_i. However, when t_j is selected from S, as it occurs after t_i, then t_i will not be marked. This branch will capture the direct order $t_j < t_i$. Since both orders generate equivalent states, no solution is missed.

Example 5. Consider the execution tree in Fig. 4, and the subtree from node 15 in Fig. 7, where $\bar{t}$ denotes that the flag *mark* of t is *true*. At this point, all tasks in rg have the flag *mark* set to *false*. Thus $selectTask(\mathsf{rg})$ returns the list $[p, m, t]$. Procedure *unmark* does nothing. The execution of $mark(p, \mathsf{rg})$ then sets the flag *mark* of m and t to *true* since $indep(p, m)$ and $indep(p, t)$. This branch is therefore cut at node 16 ($selectTask(\mathsf{rg})$ returns the empty list). Afterwards, the selection of m from node 15 does not mark any task. However, when selecting p from node 21, procedure $mark(p, \mathsf{rg})$ sets the flag of t to *true* since we have the independence relation $indep(p, t)$. Hence at node 22 the branch is cut ($selectActor(\mathsf{rg})$ returns the empty list). Similarly, at node 27 the branch is cut because of $indep(p, m)$. The only derivations are those ending in nodes 25 and 30 which correspond to the order of tasks $m < t < p$ and $t < m < p$, resp.

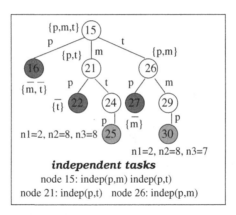

Fig. 7. Pruning due to task-selection

6   Implementation and Experimental Evaluation

We have implemented and integrated all the techniques presented in the paper within the tool aPET [2], a test case generator for ABS programs which is available at http://costa.ls.fi.upm.es/apet. ABS [10] is a concurrent, object-oriented, language based on the *concurrent objects* model, an extension of the actors model which includes *future variables* and synchronization operations. Handling those features within our techniques does not pose any technical complication. This section reports on experimental results which aim at demonstrating the applicability, effectiveness and impact of the proposed techniques during testing. The experiments have been performed using as benchmarks: (i) a set of classical actor programs borrowed from [12,13,16] and rewritten in ABS from ActorFoundry, and, (ii) some ABS models of typical concurrent systems. Specifically, *QSort* is a distributed version of the Quicksort algorithm, *Fib* is an extension of the example at Fig. 5, *PI*, computes an approximation of π distributively, *PSort* is a modified version of the sorting algorithm used in the dCUTE study [13], *RegSim* is a server registration simulation, *DHT* is a distributed hash table, *Mail* is an email client-server simulation, and *BB* is a classical producer-consumer. All sources are available at the above website. For each benchmark, we consider two different tests with different input parameters. Table 1 shows the results obtained for each test. After the name, the first (resp. second) set of columns show the result with (resp. without) our task selection function. For each run, we measure: the number of finished executions (column *Execs*); the total time taken and number of states generated by the whole exploration (columns *Time* and *States*); and the number of states at which no stable actor is found and the heuristics is used for actor selection (column *H*). Times are in milliseconds and are obtained on an Intel(R) Core(TM) i5-2300 CPU at 2.8GHz with 8GB of RAM, running Linux Kernel 2.6.38.

Table 1. Experimental evaluation

Test	No task sel. reduction				With task. sel. reduct.				Speedup	
	Execs	Time	States	H	Execs	Time	States	H	Execs	Time
QSort(5)	16	14	72	23	16	15	72	23	1.0x	1.0x
QSort(6)	32	29	146	55	32	29	146	55	1.0x	1.0x
Fib(5)	16	17	72	23	16	15	72	23	1.0x	1.0x
Fib(7)	4096	5425	16760	6495	4096	5432	16760	6495	1.0x	1.0x
Pi(3)	6	10	38	3	6	10	38	3	1.0x	1.0x
Pi(5)	120	65	932	5	120	66	932	5	1.0x	1.0x
PSort(4,1)	288	70	1294	144	288	71	1294	144	1.0x	1.0x
PSort(4,2)	5760	1389	25829	2880	288	71	1304	144	20.0x	19.6x
RegSim(6,1)	10080	804	27415	0	720	135	3923	0	14.0x	6.0x
RegSim(4,2)	11520	860	31576	0	384	70	2132	0	30.0x	12.3x
DHT(a)	1152	132	3905	0	36	5	141	0	32.0x	26.4x
DHT(b)	480	97	2304	0	12	4	85	0	40.0x	24.2x
Mail(2,2)	2648	553	11377	0	460	119	2270	0	5.8x	4.6x
Mail(2,3)	1665500	>200s	5109783	0	27880	4022	94222	0	>60x	>50x
BB(3,1)	155520	23907	475205	0	4320	674	13214	0	36.0x	35.5x
BB(4,2)	1099008	165114	3028298	0	45792	6938	126192	0	24.0x	23.8x

A relevant point to note, which is not shown in the table, is that no back-tracking due to actor selection is performed at any state of any test. The number of executions is therefore induced by the non-determinism at task selection. In most states, overall in 99.9% of them, our sufficient condition for temporal stability is able to determine a stable actor (compare column H against *States*). Interestingly, at all states where no stable actor can be found, the heuristics for temporal stability guides the execution towards selections of actors which are indeed temporarily stable. This demonstrates that, even though our sufficient condition for stability and heuristics are syntactic, they are very effective in practice since they are computed dynamically on every state. Another important point to observe is the huge pruning of redundant executions which our task selection function is able to achieve for most benchmarks. Last two columns show the gain of the task selection function in number of executions and time. In most benchmarks, the speedup ranges from one to two orders of magnitude (the more complex the programs the bigger the speedup). There is however no reduction in the first three benchmarks. This is because they only generate actors of the same type, and at most two kinds of tasks, usually recursive, which are dependent. This is also the main reason of the loss of precision of our sufficient condition for temporal stability for these benchmarks (namely, cond. 2 of Th. 1 needs to consider all actors in the state).

There are two more benchmarks, *Chameneos* and *Shortpath*, also borrowed from [16], that have been used in our evaluation. We do not provide concrete data for them in the table since they cannot be handled yet by our current implementation. In *Chameneos* the heuristics needs to be used at many states in order to select an actor. The heuristics of Sec. 4.3 enriched to take into account calls affected by conditional instructions (as described at the end of Sec. 4) would always be able to select actors which are indeed temporarily stable. The *ShortPath* benchmark poses new challenges. It builds a cyclic graph of actors, all of the same type, which interact through a recursive task. An intelligent actor selection heuristics able to prune redundant executions in this case would require detecting tasks which execute their base case. This could be done by computing *constrained call-chains*, and checking dynamically that the constraints hold in order to sum-up the effect of the call-chain when computing the non-stability factor.

7   Related Work and Conclusions

We have proposed novel techniques to further reduce state-exploration in testing actor systems which have been proven experimentally to be both efficient and effective. Whereas in [12, 16] the optimal redundancy reduction can only be accomplished by trying out different selection strategies, our heuristics is able to generate the most intelligent strategy on the fly. Additionally, our task selection reduction has been shown to be able to reduce the exploration in up to two orders of magnitude. Our techniques can be used in combination with the testing algorithms proposed in [7, 16]. In particular, the method in [16] makes a blind selection on the actor which is chosen for execution first. While in some cases, such selection is irrelevant, it is known that the pruning that can be achieved is highly dependent on the order in which tasks are considered for processing (see [12]). Sleep sets, as defined in [8], can be used as well to guide actor-selection by relying on different criteria than ours (in particular, they use a notion of independence different from ours). However, we have not found practical ways of computing them, while we can syntactically detect stable actors by some inspections in the state. Also, we define actor selection strategies based on the stability level of actors. The accuracy of such strategies can be improved by means of static analysis. In particular, points-to analysis [15] can be useful in Th. 2 to detect more accurately if there is a reference to an object from another one and also to know from which object a method is invoked. Another novelty of our approach to reduce useless state-exploration is to consider the access to the shared memory that tasks make. This allows us to avoid non-deterministic task-selection among independent tasks. A strong aspect of our work is that it can be used in symbolic execution [4, 11] directly. In symbolic execution, it is even more crucial to reduce state-exploration, since we already have non-deterministic choices due to branching in the program and due to aliasing of reference variables. In aPET, we use our method to prune the state-exploration of useless interleavings in the context of symbolic execution of actor programs. Recently, the project Setak [14] has developed a new testing framework for actor programs. Differently to us, where everything is automatic, part of the testing is doing manually, and programmers may specify the order of tasks during the execution of a test.

Acknowledgements. This work was funded partially by the EU project FP7-ICT-610582 ENVISAGE: Engineering Virtualized Services (http://www. envisage-project.eu) and by the Spanish projects TIN2008-05624 and TIN2012-38137.

References

1. Agha, G.A.: Actors: A Model of Concurrent Computation in Distributed Systems. MIT Press, Cambridge (1986)
2. Albert, E., Arenas, P., Gómez-Zamalloa, M., Wong, P.Y.H.: aPET: A Test Case Generation Tool for Concurrent Objects. In: Proc. of ESEC/FSE 2013, pp. 595–598. ACM (2013)
3. Andrews, G.R.: Concurrent Programming: Principles and Practice. Benjamin/Cummings (1991)
4. Clarke, L.A.: A System to Generate Test Data and Symbolically Execute Programs. IEEE Transactions on Software Engineering 2(3), 215–222 (1976)
5. de Boer, F.S., Clarke, D., Johnsen, E.B.: A Complete Guide to the Future. In: De Nicola, R. (ed.) ESOP 2007. LNCS, vol. 4421, pp. 316–330. Springer, Heidelberg (2007)
6. Esparza, J.: Model checking using net unfoldings. Sci. Comput. Program. 23(2-3), 151–195 (1994)
7. Flanagan, C.: Patrice Godefroid. Dynamic Partial-Order Reduction for Model Checking Software. In: Proc. of POPL 2005, pp. 110–121. ACM (2005)
8. Godefroid, P.: Using Partial Orders to Improve Automatic Verification Methods. In: Larsen, K.G., Skou, A. (eds.) CAV 1991. LNCS, vol. 575, pp. 176–185. Springer, Heidelberg (1992)
9. Haller, P., Odersky, M.: Scala actors: Unifying Thread-Based and Event-Based Programming. Theor. Comput. Sci. 410(2-3), 202–220 (2009)
10. Johnsen, E.B., Hähnle, R., Schäfer, J., Schlatte, R., Steffen, M.: ABS: A Core Language for Abstract Behavioral Specification. In: Aichernig, B.K., de Boer, F.S., Bonsangue, M.M. (eds.) FMCO 2010. LNCS, vol. 6957, pp. 142–164. Springer, Heidelberg (2011)
11. King, J.C.: Symbolic Execution and Program Testing. Commun. ACM 19(7), 385–394 (1976)
12. Lauterburg, S., Karmani, R.K., Marinov, D., Agha, G.: Evaluating Ordering Heuristics for Dynamic Partial-Order Reduction Techniques. In: Rosenblum, D.S., Taentzer, G. (eds.) FASE 2010. LNCS, vol. 6013, pp. 308–322. Springer, Heidelberg (2010)
13. Sen, K., Agha, G.: Automated Systematic Testing of Open Distributed Programs. In: Baresi, L., Heckel, R. (eds.) FASE 2006. LNCS, vol. 3922, pp. 339–356. Springer, Heidelberg (2006)
14. Setak, A.: Framework for Stepwise Deterministic Testing of Akka Actors, http://mir.cs.illinois.edu/setak
15. Steensgaard, B.: Points-to Analysis in almost Linear Time. In: Proc. of POPL 1991, pp. 32–41. ACM Press (1996)
16. Tasharofi, S., Karmani, R.K., Lauterburg, S., Legay, A., Marinov, D., Agha, G.: TransDPOR: A Novel Dynamic Partial-Order Reduction Technique for Testing Actor Programs. In: Giese, H., Rosu, G. (eds.) FMOODS/FORTE 2012. LNCS, vol. 7273, pp. 219–234. Springer, Heidelberg (2012)

Efficient and Generalized Decentralized Monitoring
of Regular Languages

Yliès Falcone, Tom Cornebize, and Jean-Claude Fernandez

Univ. Grenoble Alpes, LIG, VERIMAG, 38000 Grenoble, France

Abstract. This paper proposes an efficient and generalized decentralized monitoring algorithm allowing to detect satisfaction or violation of any regular specification by local monitors alone in a system without central observation point. Our algorithm does not assume any form of synchronization between system events and communication of monitors, uses state machines as underlying mechanism for efficiency, and tries to keep the number and size of messages exchanged between monitors to a minimum. We provide a full implementation of the algorithm with an open-source benchmark to evaluate its efficiency in terms of number, size of exchanged messages, and delay induced by communication between monitors. Experimental results demonstrate the effectiveness of our algorithm which outperforms the previous most general one along several (new) monitoring metrics.

1 Introduction

Monitoring is a verification technique based on runtime information. From a practical perspective, a decision procedure, the so-called *monitor*, analyzes a sequence of events (or a trace) from the system under scrutiny, and emits verdicts w.r.t. satisfaction or violation of a specification formalized by a property. Being lightweight is an important feature of monitoring frameworks because the performance of the system should be disturbed in a minimal way. When the monitor collects events from a monolithic system, we refer to this as *centralized monitoring*.

Modern systems are in essence distributed: they consist of several computation units (referred to as components in the sequel), possibly interacting together, and evolving independently. Monitoring distributed systems is a long-standing problem. The main challenge is to design algorithms that allow to i) efficiently monitor computation units of a system, ii) let local monitors recompute a global state of the system with minimal communication, and iii) monitor against rich specifications. Existing monitoring frameworks usually assume the existence of a central observation point in the system to which components have to send events to determine verdicts; as seen for instance in [1, 2]. In that case, from a theoretical perspective, monitoring reduces to the centralized case. A more challenging situation occurs when such central observation point cannot be introduced or used in the system. Introducing a central observation point implies to modify the architecture of the system, which is unrealistic in many application domains mainly for economic reasons. Using a central observation point (i.e., one of the components) is also undesirable because it induces i) more communication, ii) unbalanced overhead between components, and iii) more risks of total failure in case of failure of a component. When no such central observation point exists in the system, we refer to this as

E. Ábrahám and C. Palamidessi (Eds.), FORTE 2014, LNCS 8461, pp. 66–83, 2014.

decentralized monitoring. In the decentralized setting, monitors emit verdicts with incomplete information: local monitors read local traces, i.e., incomplete versions of the global trace, and have to communicate with each other to build up a global verdict.

Related Work. Several approaches exist for monitoring distributed systems. A temporal logic, MTTL, for expressing properties of asynchronous multi-threaded systems was presented in [3]. Its monitoring procedure takes as input a *safety* formula and a partially-ordered execution of a parallel asynchronous system. MTTL augments linear temporal logic (LTL) [4] with modalities related to the distributed/multi-threaded nature of the system. Several works like [5] target physically distributed systems and address the monitoring problem of partially-ordered traces, and introduce abstractions to deal with the combinatorial explosion of these traces. Close to our work is an approach to monitoring violations of invariants in distributed systems using knowledge [6]. Model-checking the system allows to pre-calculate the states where a violation can be reported by a process alone. When communication (i.e., more knowledge) is needed between processes, synchronizations are added. Both [6] and our approach try to minimize the communication induced by the distributed nature of the system but [6] i) requires the property to be stable (and considers only invariants) and ii) uses a Petri net model to compute synchronization points. We do not assume any model of the system, i.e., we consider it as a black box. Decentralized monitoring is also related to diagnosis of discrete-event systems which has the objective of detecting the occurrence of a fault after a finite number of steps, see for instance [7, 8]. There are two main differences between monitoring and diagnosis. In diagnosis, a specification with normal and faulty behavior is an input to the problem. Also, when considering observability of distributed systems, diagnosis assumes a central observation point which may not have full access to information. On the contrary, decentralized monitoring does not assume a central observation point, but that local monitors have access to all local information. Similarly, decentralized observation [9] uses a central observation point in a system that collects verdicts from local observers that have limited memory to store local traces. Note, neither diagnosis nor observability considers minimizing the communication overhead.

In [10], we proposed a decentralized monitoring algorithm for (all) LTL formulas. The main novelties were to i) avoid the need for a central observation point in the system and ii) try to reduce the communication induced by monitoring by minimizing the number of messages exchanged between monitors. The approach in [10] uses LTL specifications "off-the-shelf" by allowing the user to abstract away from the system architecture and conceive the system as monolithic. The algorithm relied on a decentralized version of *progression* [11]: at any time, each monitor carries a temporarily extended goal (aka an "obligation") which represents the formula to be satisfied according to the monitor that carries it. The monitor rewrites its obligation according to local observations and goals received from other monitors. According to the propositions referred in the obtained formula, it might communicate its local obligation to other monitors. Our approach relied on the perfect synchrony hypothesis (i.e., neither computation nor communication takes time) where communication relied on a synchronous bus. This hypothesis is reasonable for certain critical embedded systems e.g., in the automotive domain (cf. [10] for more arguments along this line). Moreover, it has been recently shown that this approach does not only "work on paper" but can be implemented when finding a suitable sampling time such that the perfect synchrony hypothesis holds [12].

Nevertheless, to facilitate the application of [10] in more real scenarios, several directions of improvement can be considered. First, it is assumed in [10] i) that at each time instant, monitors receive an event from the system and can communicate with each others, and ii) that communication does not take time. Second, the approach used LTL formulas to represent the local state of the monitor and progression (i.e., formula rewriting) each time a new event is received. A downside of progression, is the continuous growth of the size of local obligations with the length of trace; thus imposing a heavy overhead after 100 events. Finally, while [10] minimizes communication in terms of number of messages (i.e., obligations), it neglects their (continuously growing) size, with the risk of oversizing the communication device, in practice.

Originality. In this paper, we propose to overcome the aforementioned drawbacks of [10] and make important generalization steps for its applicability. First, instead of input specifications as LTL formulas we consider ("off-the-shelf") finite-state automata and can thus handle all regular languages instead of only counter-free ones. Thanks to the finite-word semantics of automata, we avoid the monitorability issues induced by the infinite-word semantics of LTL [13–15]. Interestingly, algorithms using an automata-based structure are more runtime efficient than those using rewriting (in terms of consumption of time and memory). While our algorithm generally doubles the number of exchanged messages, it reduces the size of messages, the execution time and memory consumption of local monitors by several orders of magnitude. Note, our algorithm is generic: by modifying some of its parameters, one can influence the aforementioned monitoring metrics. Second, in practice, communication and reception of events might not occur at the same rate or the communication device might become unavailable during monitoring. Our algorithm allows desynchronization between the reception of events from the system and communication between monitors but also arbitrarily long periods of absence of communication, provided that a global clock exists in the system. Our algorithm is fully implemented in an open-source benchmark. Our experimental results demonstrate that our algorithm i) leads to a more lightweight implementation, and ii) outperforms the one in [10] along several (new) monitoring metrics.

Overview of the Decentralized Monitoring Algorithm. Let $\mathcal{C} = \{C_1, \dots, C_n\}$ be the set of system components. Let L be a regular language formalizing a requirement over the system global behavior, i.e., L does not take into account the system structure. Let $\tau_i = \tau_i(0) \cdots \tau_i(t)$ be the local behavioral trace on component C_i at time $t \in \mathbb{N}$. Further, let $\tau = \tau_1(0) \cup \dots \cup \tau_n(0) \cdot \tau_1(1) \cup \dots \cup \tau_n(1) \cdots \tau_1(t) \cup \dots \cup \tau_n(t)$ be the global behavioral trace, at time $t \in \mathbb{N}$, obtained by merging local traces. (An hypothesis of our framework is the existence of a global clock in the system.) From L, one can construct a *centralized monitor* for L, i.e., a decision procedure having access to the global trace τ and emitting verdict $\top$ (resp. $\bot$) whenever τ is a good (resp. bad) prefix for L, i.e., whenever $\tau \cdot \Sigma^* \subseteq L$ (resp. $\tau \cdot \Sigma^* \subseteq (\Sigma^* \setminus L)$). Then, from a centralized monitor, we define its *decentralized version*, i.e., a monitor keeping track of possible evaluations of a centralized monitor when dealing with partial information about the global trace. A copy of the decentralized monitor is attached to each component. Our decentralized monitoring algorithm orchestrates message-based communication between monitors. Monitors exchange information about their received events or their evaluation of the current global state. Communication is assumed to be reliable (no message losses) but is not synchronized with the production of events on the system: when a monitor sends a message, there is no special assumption about the arrival time, except that it is finite.

The decentralized monitoring algorithm evaluates the global trace τ by reading each local trace τ_i of C_i, in separation. In particular, it exhibits the following properties.

- If a local monitor yields the verdict $\bot$ (resp. $\top$) on some component C_i by observing τ_i, it implies that $\tau \cdot \Sigma^* \subseteq \Sigma^* \setminus L$ (resp. $\tau \cdot \Sigma^* \subseteq L$) holds. That is, a locally observed violation (resp. satisfaction) is, in fact, a global violation (resp. satisfaction).
- If the monitored global trace τ is such that $\tau \cdot \Sigma^* \subseteq \Sigma^* \setminus L$ (resp. $\tau \cdot \Sigma^* \subseteq L$), at some time t, one of the local monitors on some component C_i yields $\bot$ (resp. $\top$), at some time $t' \geq t$ because of some latency induced by decentralized monitoring, whatever is the global trace between t and t'.

Paper Organization. The rest of this paper is organized as follows. Section 2 introduces some preliminaries and notations. Section 3 proposes a generic (centralized) monitoring framework, compatible with frameworks that synthesize monitors in the form of finite-state machines. Section 4 shows how to decentralize a monitor. In Sec. 5, we present how decentralized monitors communicate with each other to obtain a verdict in a decentralized manner. Section 6 describes the relation between centralized and decentralized monitoring. Section 7 presents our benchmark, DECENTMON2, used to evaluate an implementation of our monitoring algorithm. Section 8 presents some perspectives.

2   Preliminaries and Notations

For $i, j \in \mathbb{N}$, the (underlying set associated to the) interval of integers from i to j is denoted by $[i; j]$. The set of finite sequences over a finite set E is noted E^*.

We consider that the global system consists of a set of components $\{C_1, \ldots, C_n\}$, with $n \in \mathbb{N} \setminus \{0\}$. Each component emits events synchronously and has a local monitor attached to it. An event local to component C_i is built over a set of atomic propositions $AP_i, i \in [1; n]$, i.e., the local set of events is $\Sigma_i = 2^{AP_i}$. The set of all atomic propositions is $AP = \cup_{i \in [1;n]} AP_i$. Atomic propositions are local to components by requiring that $\{AP_i \mid i \in [1; n]\}$ is a partition of AP. (Note, this hypothesis simplifies the presentation of the results in the paper but is not an actual limitation of our framework.) The set of all local events in the system is $\cup_{i \in [1;n]} \Sigma_i$, where Σ_i is visible to the monitor at component $C_i, i \in [1; n]$. The global specification refers to events in $\Sigma = 2^{AP}$ and is given by a regular language $L \subseteq \Sigma^*$. Note that the specification does not take into account the architecture of the system and may refer to events involving atomic propositions from several components (i.e., $\Sigma \neq \cup_{i \in [1;n]} \Sigma_i$ in the decentralized case whereas $\Sigma = \cup_{i \in [1;n]} \Sigma_i$ in the centralized one or when there is only one component). We assume that the (regular) language to be monitored is recognized by a deterministic finite-state automaton $(Q, \Sigma, q_{\text{init}}, \delta, F)$ where Q is the set of states, $q_{\text{init}} \in Q$ the initial state, δ the transition function, and $F \subseteq Q$ the set of accepting states.

Over time, for $i \in [1; n]$, the monitor attached to C_i receives a trace $\tau_i \in (2^{AP_i})^*$, a sequence of local events, representing the behavior of C_i. The global behavior of the system is given by a global trace $\tau = (\tau_1, \tau_2, \ldots, \tau_n)$. The global trace is a sequence of pair-wise union of the local events in components traces, each of which at time t is of length $t + 1$ i.e., $\tau = \tau(0) \cdots \tau(t)$, where for $i < t$, $\tau(i)$ is the (i+1)-th element of τ. The sub-sequence $\tau[i; j]$ is the sequence containing the (i+1)-th to the (j+1)-th elements. The substitution of the element at index t in a sequence τ by e is noted $\tau[t|e]$.

3   Centralized Monitoring of (Propositional) Regular Languages

In this section we propose a general framework for centralized monitoring of regular languages. The framework is compatible with the existing monitoring frameworks that synthesize monitors as finite-state machines for propositional regular languages.

In the centralized case, the monitor is a central observation point. Generally speaking, the purpose of the monitor is to determine whether the observed sequence forms a good or a bad prefix of the language being monitored. For this purpose, the monitor emits verdicts in some truth-domain $\mathbb{B}$ s.t. $\{\bot, \top\} \subset \mathbb{B}$ where $\top$ and $\bot$ are two "definitive values" used respectively when a validation (good prefix) and violation (bad prefix) of the language has been found, respectively.

Definition 1 (Good and bad prefixes [16]). *The sets of good and bad prefixes of a language $L \subseteq \Sigma^*$ are defined as:*

$$\mathrm{good}(L) = \{\tau \in \Sigma^* \mid \tau \cdot \Sigma^* \subseteq L\}, \qquad \mathrm{bad}(L) = \{\tau \in \Sigma^* \mid \tau \cdot \Sigma^* \subseteq (\Sigma^* \setminus L)\}.$$

Using good and bad prefixes, we can define the centralized semantic relation $\models_C$ for traces, using, for instance, the truth-domain $\mathbb{B} \stackrel{\mathrm{def}}{=} \{\bot, ?, \top\}$, where the truth-value ? indicates that no verdict has been found yet. Given $\tau \in \Sigma^*$, we say that $\tau \models_C L = \top$ (resp. $\bot$) whenever $\tau \in \mathrm{good}(L)$ (resp. $\mathrm{bad}(L)$) and $\tau \models_C L = ?$ otherwise.

Definition 2 (Centralized Monitor). *A centralized monitor is a tuple $(Q, \Sigma, q_0, \delta,$ verdict) where Q is the set of states, $\Sigma = 2^{AP}$ the alphabet of events, q_0 the initial state, $\delta : Q \times \Sigma \to Q$ the complete transition function, and verdict : $Q \to \mathbb{B}$ is a function that associates a truth-value to each state.*

A monitor is a Moore automaton, processing events from its alphabet, and emitting a verdict upon receiving each event. Monitor-synthesis algorithms ensure that i) for any $\tau \in \Sigma^*$, verdict$(\delta(q_0, \tau)) = \top/\bot$ iff $\tau \in \mathrm{good}/\mathrm{bad}(L)$, where δ is extended to sequences in the natural way; ii) for any $q \in Q$, if verdict$(q) \in \{\top, \bot\}$ then $\forall \sigma \in \Sigma : \delta(q, \sigma) = q$. A centralized monitor is a decision procedure w.r.t. the centralized semantics relation $\models_C$.

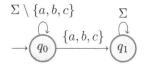

Fig. 1. Transitions of CM_1

Remark 1 (Truth-domains). More involved truth-domains with refined truth-values (e.g., the ones used in [16, 15]) can be used in our framework without any particular difficulty.

Example 1 (Centralized Monitor). Consider $AP^1 = \{a, b, c\}$ and L_1 the language of words over 2^{AP^1} that contain at least one occurrence of the event $\{a, b, c\}$. The monitor CM_1 of this language has its transition function δ_1 depicted in Fig. 1. Moreover, verdict$(q_0) = ?$ and verdict$(q_1) = \top$. Consider $\tau_1 = \emptyset \cdot \{a, b\} \cdot \{a, b, c\} \cdot \{a\}$, we have $\emptyset \cdot \{a, b\} \cdot \{a, b, c\} \in \mathrm{good}(L_1)$ and $\tau_1 \in \mathrm{good}(L_1)$.

4   Decentralizing a Monitor

Let us now use the previous example to see what would happen when using a centralized monitor on a local component where only a subset of AP can be observed. Let us consider a simple architecture with three components C_A, C_B, C_C respectively with sets of atomic propositions $AP_A^1 = \{a\}, AP_B^1 = \{b\}, AP_C^1 = \{c\}$. If we use a central monitor on, say C_A, no event (in $2^{AP_A^1}$) could allow the monitor to reach q_1. Monitors should thus take into account what could *possibly* happen on other components. Given an observation on a local component, a decentralized monitor computes the *set of states that are possible* with this observation, and refines (i.e., eliminate possible states) when communicating with other monitors (as we shall see in Sec. 5).

Given a centralized monitor, we define its decentralized version as follows.

Definition 3 (Decentralized Monitor). *Given a centralized monitor* $(Q, \Sigma, q_0, \delta,$ verdict), *the associated decentralized monitor is a 5-tuple* $(2^Q \setminus \{\emptyset\}, (2^{[1;n]} \setminus \{\emptyset\}) \times \Sigma, \{q_0\}, \Delta_\delta, \text{verdict}_D)$ *where:*

- $(2^{[1;n]} \setminus \{\emptyset\}) \times \Sigma$ *is the alphabet,*
- $\Delta_\delta : (2^Q \setminus \{\emptyset\}) \times (2^{[1;n]} \setminus \{\emptyset\}) \times \Sigma \to (2^Q \setminus \{\emptyset\})$ *is the decentralized transition function defined as:*
$$\Delta_\delta(\mathcal{Q}, s, \sigma) = \{q' \in Q \mid \exists \sigma' \in \Sigma, \exists q \in \mathcal{Q} : \sigma = \sigma' \cap \bigcup_{j \in s} AP_j \wedge q' = \delta(q, \sigma')\},$$
- $\text{verdict}_D : (2^Q \setminus \{\emptyset\}) \to \mathbb{B}$ *is the decentralized verdict function, s.t.:*

$$\text{verdict}_D(\mathcal{Q}) = \begin{cases} b \; \textit{if } \exists b \in \mathbb{B} : \{\text{verdict}(q) \mid q \in \mathcal{Q}\} = \{b\}, \\ ? \; \textit{otherwise,} \end{cases}$$

for any $\mathcal{Q} \in 2^Q \setminus \{\emptyset\}$.

Intuitively, a decentralized monitor "estimates" the global state that would be obtained by a centralized monitor observing the events produced on all components. The estimation of the global state is modeled by a set of possible states (of the centralized monitor) given the (local) information received so far. When a decentralized monitor receives an event (s, σ), it is informed that the union of the atomic propositions that occurred on the components indexed in the set s is σ. The transition function is s.t. if the estimated global state is $\mathcal{Q} \in 2^Q \setminus \{\emptyset\}$ and it receives (s, σ) as event, then the estimated global state changes to $\Delta_\delta(\mathcal{Q}, s, \sigma)$ which contains all states s.t. one can find a transition in δ from a state in $\mathcal{Q}$ labeled with a global event σ' compatible with σ. In other words, if the actual global state belongs to $\mathcal{Q}$, and the union of events that happen on components indexed in s is σ, then the actual global state belongs to $\Delta_\delta(\mathcal{Q}, s, \sigma)$ which is the set of states that can be reached from a state in $\mathcal{Q}$ with all possible global events (obtained by any observation that could happen on components indexed in $[1; n] \setminus s$). Regarding verdicts, a decentralized monitor emits the same verdict as a centralized one when the current state contains states of the centralized monitor that evaluate on the same verdict.

Example 2 (Decentralized Monitor). Let us consider again the architecture and language L_1 of Example 1. Consider what happens initially on any of the components executing DM_1, the decentralized version of CM_1, see Fig. 2. Initially, the estimated global state is $\{q_0\}$. Suppose the monitor is informed that $\{a\}$ occurred on component

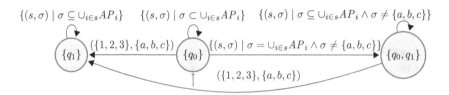

Fig. 2. Transitions of DM_1

C_A (of index 1), then it will change its estimated global state to $\Delta_{\delta_1}(\{q_0\}, \{1\}, \{a\}) = \{q_0, q_1\}$. Intuitively, this transition can be understood as follows. Knowing that $\{a\}$ occurred on C_A, the other possible global events are $\{a, b\}$, $\{a, c\}$, and $\{a, b, c\}$, as the monitor does not have information on what happened on C_B and C_C. In CM_1, from state q_0 and these events, states q_0 and q_1 can be reached. Note, the only way to reach $\{q_1\}$ in DM_1, i.e., to know that the global state is q_1 (and is unique), DM_1 has to know that the union of events that occurred on components indexed in $\{1, 2, 3\}$ is $\{a, b, c\}$.

As illustrated by the example, a decentralized monitor does not depend on the component on which it executes. Its transitions can occur on any component, as it receives an event together with the identifier of components on which such an event occurred. However, a decentralized monitor shall communicate with other decentralized monitors.

5   Communication and Decision Making

Our aim is now to define how a collection of decentralized monitors, analyzing a given distributed trace, should communicate with each other to obtain a verdict in a decentralized manner. The verdict indicates whether the trace, when interpreted as a global trace, is a good or a bad prefix of the language.

5.1   Preliminaries: Local Memory, Clocks, and Communication

Monitor Local Memory. The local memory of a monitor is a partial function mem : $\mathbb{N} \rightarrow \Sigma \times (2^{[1;n]} \setminus \{\emptyset\})$, purposed to record the "local knowledge" w.r.t. (past instants of) the global (actual) trace produced by the system. If mem$(t) = (\sigma_t, s_t)$, it means that the monitor knows that the set of all atomic propositions received by the components in s_t is σ_t. Moreover, if $\sigma \in \Sigma$ is the global event at time t and mem$(t) = (\sigma_t, s_t)$, then $\sigma \cap (\bigcup_{i \in s_t} AP_i) = \sigma_t$. In next section, we will see how after communicating, local monitors can discard elements from their memory.

As a local monitor memorizes the observed local events, it may inform other monitors of the content of its memory via messages. When a monitor receives a memory chunk from another monitor, it merges it with its local memory. For this purpose, for two memories mem and mem$'$, we define the merged memory mem $\sqcup$ mem$'$:

$$(\text{mem} \sqcup \text{mem}')(t) = \begin{cases} \text{mem}(t) \cup \text{mem}'(t) & \text{if } t \in \text{dom}(\text{mem}) \cap \text{dom}(\text{mem}'), \\ \text{mem}'(t) & \text{if } t \in \text{dom}(\text{mem}') \setminus \text{dom}(\text{mem}), \\ \text{mem}(t) & \text{otherwise,} \end{cases}$$

where the union $(\sigma, s) \cup (\sigma', s')$ between two memory elements (σ, s) and (σ', s') is defined as $(\sigma \cup \sigma', s \cup s')$. For instance, consider mem $= \{0 \mapsto (\{b\}, \{1, 2\}), 1 \mapsto (\{a, b\}, \{1, 2\}), 2 \mapsto (\emptyset, \{2\})\}$ and mem$' = \{1 \mapsto (\{c\}, \{3\}), 2 \mapsto (\{c\}, \{3\})\}$, we have mem $\sqcup$ mem$' = \{0 \mapsto (\{b\}, \{1, 2\}), 1 \mapsto (\{a, b, c\}, \{1, 2, 3\}), 2 \mapsto (\{c\}, \{2, 3\})\}$.

Monitor Local Clocks. Each local monitor carries two local (discrete) clocks t and t_{last}. The purpose of t is simply to store the time instant of the last received event from the local component. The purpose of t_{last} is to store the time instant for which it knows the global state of the system. Indeed, the decentralized monitoring algorithm presented in next section will ensure that, on each monitor M_i, for a global trace τ:

- the last event σ emitted by the local component was at time $t : \sigma = \tau(t)$.
- the current state is the state corresponding to $t_{last} : q = \delta(q_0, \tau[0; t_{last} - 1])$;

How Monitors Communicate. As mentioned before, local monitors are required to communicate with each other to share collected information (from their local observation or other monitors). To ensure that communication between monitors aggregates correctly information over time, we suppose having two functions leader_mon and choose_mon that can be defined e.g., according to the architecture and possibly changing over time.

The function choose_mon $: [1; n] \rightarrow [1; n]$ indicates for each monitor, the monitor it should communicate with. Local monitors are referred to by their indexes. For information to aggregate correctly, we require choose_mon to be bijective, and such that $\forall i \in [1; n], \forall k \in [1; n - 1] :$ choose_mon$^k(i) \neq i$ where choose_mon$^k(i) = \underbrace{\text{choose\_mon}(\ldots(\text{choose\_mon}(i))\ldots)}_{k \text{ times}}$. One can consider for instance choose_mon$(i) = (i \mod n) + 1$. Note: these requirements are not limitations of our framework but rather guidelines for configuring the communication of our monitors where the architecture is such that a bidirectional direct communication exists between any two components. The proposed algorithms can be easily adapted to any other architecture, provided that a bidirectional communication path exists between any two components (which otherwise would limit the interest of decentralized monitoring).

The function leader_mon $: [1; n] \rightarrow \{true, false\}$ indicates whether the monitor on the component of the given index is a leader. When receiving new events from the system, only leader monitors can send the local events received from their components. The number of leader monitors influences communication metrics of the monitoring algorithm (see Sec. 7). Using a function makes the algorithm generic and allows leader monitors to change over time.

5.2 Decentralized Monitoring Algorithm

Let us now present the main algorithm for decentralized monitoring. The algorithm is executed independently on each component until there is no event to read and the local monitor has determined the global state, which is given by the condition $t_{last} > t$ (the time instant corresponding to the last known global state is greater than the time instant of the last received event from the local component).

At an abstract level, the algorithm is an execution engine using a decentralized monitor as per Definition 3. It computes the locally estimated global state of the system by aggregating information from events read locally and partial traces received from other monitors. It stores in q the last known global state of the system at time t_{last}, and in t the time instant of the last event received from the system. The main steps of the algorithm can be summarized as follows:

Algorithm DM (*Decentralized Monitoring*).   Let L be the monitored language and q_0 the initial state of its associated centralized monitor. Initialize variables q to q_0, t_{last} to 0, and t to -1. Then, repeat the following steps until the end of the trace and $t_{last} > t$.

DM1. [Wait] for something from the outside: either an event σ from the system or a message from another monitor (a pair $(q', t_{new}) \in Q \times \mathbb{N}$ or a partial memory m).

DM2. [Update] If an event (resp. a trace) is received from a component (resp. another monitor), update memory and t. If a state is received, update the known global state.

DM3. [Compute new state] Using the transition function of the decentralized monitor (Definition 3) and the local memory between t_{last} and t, compute the set of possible states. If the set of possible states is a singleton, q and t_{last} are updated.

DM4. [Evaluate and return] If a definitive verdict ($\top$ or $\bot$) is found, return it (and inform other monitors).

DM5. [Prepare communication] Prepare a message to be sent. If a state is received or a new state has been computed (i.e., if q and t_{last} have been modified), append it to the message together with t_{last}. If there are events that occurred after the last found state ($t \geq t_{last}$), append them to the message, provided that the monitor is a leader (leader_mon$(i) = true$) or these events come from another monitor.

DM6. [Communicate] If there is a non-empty message to be sent, then send it to the associated monitor (as determined by function choose_mon(i)).

At a concrete level, the abstract algorithm is realized in Algorithms 1, 2, and 3. These algorithms execute in the same memory space, and variables are global. The receive function (Algorithm 1) realizes steps **DM1** and **DM2** where i) events and messages from other monitors are received, and, ii) the memory and current state are updated. The receive function is called by the main loop (Algorithm 3) and blocks the execution until an input is received. It can receive three possible inputs (and any combination of them): an event σ from the component (then it updates mem and t), a state q' from another monitor (then it updates q and t_{last} if it does not have fresher information), a partial memory m from another monitor (then it updates mem), or both a state and a partial memory. The function also keeps track of whether a state or a partial memory was received using two Booleans rcv_state and rcv_mem. The update_state function (Algorithm 2) realizes step **DM3** by implementing the transition function Δ_δ of the decentralized monitor using at the same time the local memory mem for efficiency reasons. Variable q keeps track of the last know global state (at time t_{last}. Variable $\mathcal{Q}$ is a temporary variable that keeps track of the set of possible states. Variable upd_state is set to $true$ if the execution of update_state function allows to update the last know global state. The main loop (Algorithm 3) realizes steps **DM4**, **DM5**, and **DM6** where the message is built. Step **DM4** is realized by lines 8 to 11, where, if a new global state is known (either computed with update_state or received in a message), then it is checked if the associated verdict is definitive. The new state together with t_{last} are added to the message. Then, when there are some local events to be shared ($t_{\text{last}} \leq t$), if the monitor received a partial memory or the monitor is a leader (line 12), the partial memory from t_{last} to t (i.e., $\text{mem}(t_{\text{last}}, t)$) and the value of t_{last} are added to the message (line 13). Finally (lines 14-15), the (non-empty) message is sent to the monitor of index choose_mon(i).

Remark 2 (Domain of mem*).* At any moment, the only used elements of mem are those between t_{last} and t. Thus, after each step of the algorithm, elements before t_{last} can be discarded. Thus, $\text{dom}(\text{mem}) = [t_{\text{last}}; t]$ is of bounded size under certain conditions discussed in Sec. 6.

The following example illustrates the decentralized monitoring algorithm. Local monitors keep in memory only the events occurring at time instants within $[t_{\text{last}}; t]$.

---

1 $(rcv\_mem, rcv\_state) \longleftarrow$
   $(false, false)$
2 **when** *an event $\sigma \in \Sigma_i$ is received from component*:
3 $\quad$ $t \longleftarrow t + 1$
4 $\quad$ $\text{mem} \longleftarrow \text{mem} \sqcup [t \mapsto (\sigma, \{i\})]$
5 **when** *a state $q' \in Q$ is received with time t_{new}*:
6 $\quad$ **if** $t_{\text{new}} > t_{\text{last}}$ **then**
7 $\quad\quad$ $(q, t_{\text{last}}) \longleftarrow (q', t_{\text{new}})$
8 $\quad\quad$ $rcv\_state \longleftarrow true$
9 **when** *a partial memory $m \in \mathbb{N} \to \Sigma \times (2^{[1;n]} \setminus \{\emptyset\})$ is received*:
10 $\quad$ $\text{mem} \longleftarrow \text{mem} \sqcup m$
11 $\quad$ $rcv\_mem \longleftarrow true$

Algorithm 1. function receive

---

1 $\mathcal{Q} \longleftarrow \{q\}$
2 $upd\_state \longleftarrow false$
3 **for** t' *from* t_{last} **to** t **do**
4 $\quad$ $(\sigma, s) \longleftarrow \text{mem}(t')$
5 $\quad$ $\mathcal{Q} \longleftarrow \Delta_\delta(\mathcal{Q}, s, \sigma)$
6 $\quad$ **if** $\exists q' \in Q : \mathcal{Q} = \{q'\}$ **then**
7 $\quad\quad$ $(q, t_{\text{last}}) \longleftarrow (q', t' + 1)$
8 $\quad\quad$ $upd\_state \longleftarrow true$

Algorithm 2. function update_state

Example 3 (Decentralized Monitoring). Let us go back to the monitoring of the specification introduced in Example 1 and see how this specification is monitored with Algorithms 1, 2, and 3. Table 1 shows how the situation evolves on all three monitors when monitoring the global trace $\emptyset \cdot \{a, b\} \cdot \{a, b, c\} \cdot \{a\}$. As mentioned earlier, the sequence of states of the centralized monitor is $q_0 \cdot q_0 \cdot q_1 \cdot q_1$, and the verdict associated to this trace is $\top$, obtained after the third event. For this example, leader_mon(i) = (i = 1) and choose_mon(i) = ($i \mod 3$) + 1. For simplicity, in this example, communication between monitors and events from the system occur at the same rate. Cells are colored in grey when a communication occurs between monitors or an event is read from a component. On each monitor, between any two communications or event receptions, the local memory is represented on two lines: first the values of t_{last}, t, and q the last determined global state, and second the memory content.

- Initially, on each monitor, $t = -1$ (no event received), $t_{\text{last}} = 0$ (the time instant of the last known state), the last know global state is q_0, and the memory is empty.
- When the global event $\emptyset$ occurs, each monitor $M_i, i \in [1; 3]$ receives the corresponding local event and records in its memory: $\{0 \mapsto (\emptyset, \{i\})\}$. According to update_state, all monitors are able to determine that the global state is (still) q_0, and they update t to 1 and t_{last} to 1 and discards the information about the local received event in memory. Then, each monitor M_i sends the information about its computed state to monitor $M_{\text{choose\_mon}(i)}$. Upon the reception of their message, there is no change in the state of local monitors: the values of t and t_{last} remain the same, and the memory remains empty (the information about the event received at $t = 0$ was discarded because the monitors were able to compute the global state at $t = 0$).
- The remaining steps execute similarly until all monitors return $\text{verdict}(q_1) = \top$.

---

1 $(t_{\text{last}}, t) \longleftarrow (0, -1)$
2 $(q, \mathcal{Q}) \longleftarrow (q_0, \{q_0\})$
3 mem $\longleftarrow \{\}$
4 **repeat until** *the end of the trace and* $t_{\text{last}} > t$**:**
5 $\quad$ initialize *message*
6 $\quad$ receive()
7 $\quad$ update_state()
8 $\quad$ **if** *upd_state* $\vee$ *rcv_state* **then**
9 $\quad\quad$ **if** $\text{verdict}(q) \in \{\top, \bot\}$ **then**
10 $\quad\quad\quad$ **return** $\text{verdict}(q)$
11 $\quad\quad$ add (q, t_{last}) to *message*
12 $\quad$ **if** $t_{\text{last}} \leq t \wedge (rcv\_mem \vee \text{leader\_mon}(i))$ **then**
13 $\quad\quad$ add $(\text{mem}(t_{\text{last}}, t), t_{\text{last}})$ to *message*
14 $\quad$ **if** *message is not empty* **then**
15 $\quad\quad$ send *message* to $M_{\text{choose\_mon}(i)}$
16 **return** $\text{verdict}(q)$

Algorithm 3. Decentralized monitoring algorithm executing on C_i (main loop)

Remark 3 (Optimizations). Further optimizations can be taken into account in the algorithm. For instance, using a history of sent messages, monitors can remove information from some messages addressed to another monitor, if they already sent this information in a previous message. Further studies are needed to explore the trade-off between local memory consumption vs the size of exchanged messages in the system.

Table 1. Decentralized monitoring of L_1 on 3 components

Monitor 1			Monitor 2			Monitor 3		
$t_{last}=0$	$t=-1$	$q=q_0$	$t_{last}=0$	$t=-1$	$q=q_0$	$t_{last}=0$	$t=-1$	$q=q_0$
{}			{}			{}		
Read event $\emptyset$			Read event $\emptyset$			Read event $\emptyset$		
$t_{last}=1$	$t=0$	$q=q_0$	$t_{last}=1$	$t=0$	$q=q_0$	$t_{last}=1$	$t=0$	$q=q_0$
$\emptyset$			$\emptyset$			$\emptyset$		
Send to M_2 $(q_0,1)$			Send to M_3 $(q_0,1)$			Send to M_1 $(q_0,1)$		
$t_{last}=1$	$t=0$	$q=q_0$	$t_{last}=1$	$t=0$	$q=q_0$	$t_{last}=1$	$t=0$	$q=q_0$
$\emptyset$			$\emptyset$			$\emptyset$		
Read event $\{a\}$			Read event $\{b\}$			Read event $\emptyset$		
$t_{last}=1$	$t=1$	$q=q_0$	$t_{last}=1$	$t=1$	$q=q_0$	$t_{last}=2$	$t=1$	$q=q_0$
$\{1 \mapsto (\{a\},\{1\})\}$			$\{1 \mapsto (\{b\},\{2\})\}$			$\emptyset$		
Send to M_2 $((\{a\},\{1\}),1)$			Send to M_3 $((\{b\},\{2\}),1)$			Send to M_1 $(q_0,2)$		
$t_{last}=2$	$t=1$	$q=q_0$	$t_{last}=1$	$t=1$	$q=q_0$	$t_{last}=2$	$t=1$	$q=q_0$
$\emptyset$			$\{1 \mapsto (\{a,b\},\{1,2\})\}$			$\emptyset$		
Read event $\{a\}$			Read event $\{b\}$			Read event $\{c\}$		
$t_{last}=2$	$t=2$	$q=q_0$	$t_{last}=1$	$t=2$	$q=q_0$	$t_{last}=2$	$t=2$	$q=q_0$
$\{2 \mapsto (\{a\},\{1\})\}$			$\{1 \mapsto (\{a,b\},\{1,2\}),$ $2 \mapsto (\{b\},\{2\})\}$			$\{2 \mapsto (\{c\},\{3\})\}$		
Send to M_2 $(q_0,2),((\{a\},\{1\}),2)$			Send to M_3 $((\{a,b\},\{1,2\}),(\{b\},\{2\}),1)$			Send to M_1 $((\{c\},\{3\}),2)$		
$t_{last}=2$	$t=2$	$q=q_0$	$t_{last}=2$	$t=2$	$q=q_0$	$t_{last}=2$	$t=2$	$q=q_0$
$\{2 \mapsto (\{a,c\},\{1,3\})\}$			$\{2 \mapsto (\{a,b\},\{1,2\})\}$			$\{2 \mapsto (\{b,c\},\{2,3\})\}$		
Read event $\{a\}$			Read event $\emptyset$			Read event $\emptyset$		
$t_{last}=2$	$t=3$	$q=q_0$	$t_{last}=2$	$t=3$	$q=q_0$	$t_{last}=2$	$t=3$	$q=q_0$
$\{2 \mapsto (\{a,c\},\{1,3\}),$ $3 \mapsto (\{a\},\{1\})\}$			$\{2 \mapsto (\{a,b\},\{1,2\}),$ $3 \mapsto (\emptyset,\{2\})\}$			$\{2 \mapsto (\{b,c\},\{2,3\}),$ $3 \mapsto (\emptyset,\{3\})\}$		
Send to M_2 $((\{a,c\},\{1,3\}),(\{a\},\{1\}),2)$			Send to M_3 $(q_0,2),$ $((\{a,b\},\{1,2\}),(\emptyset,\{2\}),2)$			Send to M_1 $((\{b,c\},\{2,3\}),(\emptyset,\{3\}),2)$		
$t_{last}=4$	$t=3$	$q=q_0$	$t_{last}=4$	$t=3$	$q=q_1$	$t_{last}=4$	$t=3$	$q=q_0$
$\emptyset$			$\emptyset$			$\emptyset$		
Return verdict$(q_1) = \top$			Return verdict$(q_1) = \top$			Return verdict$(q_1) = \top$		

6   Semantics and Properties of Decentralized Monitoring

In this section, we discuss further the semantics induced by the decentralized monitoring algorithm and its properties.

Definition 4 (Semantics of Decentralized Monitoring). *Let* $\mathcal{C} = \{C_1, \ldots, C_n\}$ *be the set of system components,* $L \subseteq (2^{AP})^*$ *be a regular language, and* $\mathcal{M} = \{M_1, \ldots, M_n\}$ *be the set of component monitors. Further, let* $\tau = \tau_1(0) \cup \ldots \cup \tau_n(0) \cdot \tau_1(1) \cup \ldots \cup \tau_n(1) \cdots \tau_1(t) \cup \ldots \cup \tau_n(t)$ *be the global behavioral trace, at time* $t \in \mathbb{N}$. *If some component* C_i, *with* $i \leq n$, M_i *has a local state* $\mathcal{Q}$ *s.t.* verdict$_D(\mathcal{Q}) = \top$ *(resp.* $\bot$*), then* $\tau \models_D L = \top$ *(resp.* $\bot$*). Otherwise,* $\tau \models_D L = ?$.

By $\models_D$ we denote the satisfaction relation on finite traces in the decentralized setting to differentiate it from the centralized one. Obviously, $\models_C$ and $\models_D$ both yield values from the same truth-domain. However, the semantics are not equivalent, since the current state of the decentralized monitor can contain several states of the centralized one, when a local component has not enough information to determine a verdict. This feature was illustrated in Example 3 where at $t = 2$, the global trace is $\emptyset \cdot \{a, b\} \cdot \{a, b, c\}$, which is a good prefix of the monitored language, only reported at $t = 4$ by Monitor 2.

The precise relation between the centralized and decentralized semantics is given by the two following theorems.

Theorem 1 (Soundness). *Let* $L \subseteq \Sigma^*$ *and* $\tau \in \Sigma^*$, *then* $\tau \models_D L = \top/\bot \Rightarrow \tau \models_C L = \top/\bot$, *and* $\tau \models_C L = ? \Rightarrow \tau \models_D L = ?$.

Soundness states that i) all definitive verdicts found by the decentralized monitoring algorithm are actual verdicts that would be found by a centralized monitor, having access to the global trace, and ii) decentralized monitors do not find more definitive verdicts ($\top$ or $\bot$) than the centralized one.

Theorem 2 (Completeness). *Let* $L \subseteq \Sigma^*$ *and* $\tau \in \Sigma^*$, *then* $\tau \models_C L = \top/\bot \Rightarrow \exists \tau' \in \Sigma^* : \tau \cdot \tau' \models_D L = \top/\bot$.

Completeness states that all verdicts found by the centralized algorithm for some global trace τ will be eventually found by the decentralized algorithm on a continuation $\tau \cdot \tau'$. Generally, when the rate of communication between monitors (compared to the reception of events) is unknown or when not all monitors are leaders, it is not possible to determine the maximal length of τ'. When monitors communicate at the same rate as monitors receive events and all monitors are leaders (i.e., they can send message spontaneously – leader_mon$(i) = true$, for any $i \in [1; n]$), then, as was the case in [10], we can bound the maximal length of τ' by n (the number of components in the system), which also represents the maximal delay, induced by decentralized monitoring.

Theorem 3 (Completeness with bounded delay). *Let* $L \subseteq \Sigma^*$ *and* $\tau \in \Sigma^*$, *if monitors receive events and communicate at the same rate and if all monitors are leaders, then* $\tau \models_C L = \top/\bot \Rightarrow \exists \tau' \in \Sigma^* : |\tau'| \leq n \wedge \tau \cdot \tau' \models_D L = \top/\bot$.

7   Implementation and Experimental Results

We present DECENTMON2 a new benchmark tool used to evaluate decentralized monitoring (Sec. 7.1) using specifications given as LTL formulas (Sec. 7.2) and specifications patterns (Sec. 7.3). Then, we draw conclusions from our experiments (Sec. 7.4). Further experimental results are available at [17].

7.1   DECENTMON2: A Benchmark for Generalized Decentralized Monitoring

DECENTMON2 is an benchmark dedicated to decentralized monitoring. DECENTMON2 consists of: a completely redeveloped version of DECENTMON [10], an implementation of the decentralized monitoring algorithm presented in Sec. 5.2, a trace generator, and an LTL-formula generator. DECENTMON2 consists of 1,300 LLOC, written in the functional programming language OCaml. It can be freely downloaded and run from [17].

The system takes as input multiple traces (that can be automatically generated), corresponding to the behavior of a distributed system, and a specification given by a deterministic finite-state automaton. Then the specification is monitored against the traces in two different modes: a) by merging the traces to a single, global trace and then using a "centralized monitor" for the specifica-

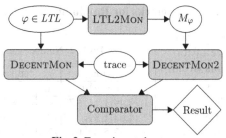

Fig. 3. Experimental setup

tion (i.e., all components send their respective events to the central monitor who makes the decisions regarding the trace), b) by using the decentralized version introduced in [10], and c) by using the decentralized approach introduced in this paper (i.e., each trace is read by a local monitor in the two last cases). To favor the centralized case, monitors send their events only if they differ from the previous one, which decreases the number of exchanged messages. We have evaluated the three different monitoring approaches (i.e., centralized vs. LTL-decentralized vs generalized-decentralized) using several set-ups described in the remainder of this section. To compare monitoring metrics obtained with the decentralized algorithm in [10] and the one in this paper, we used LTL2MON [18], to convert LTL formulas into automata-based (centralized) monitors. For our comparison purposes, we used results on common LTL formulas and traces using the experimental setup depicted in Fig. 3. For each of the metric mentioned in the following sections, ratios are obtained by dividing the value obtained in the decentralized case over the value obtained in the centralized case.

To compare with the decentralized monitoring algorithm obtained in [10], the emission of events occurs at the same rate as the communication between monitors. Recall that it was assumed in [10] whereas our monitoring algorithm allows different ratios.

Each line of the following arrays is obtained by conducting 1,000 tests, each with a fresh trace of 1,000 events and specification. We use the same architecture as in the running example. Note that benchmarks with different architectures and rates of communication/event-emission were also conducted, and are available from [17].

For the following monitoring metrics, we measure the size of the elements exchanged by monitors as follows. Suppose we monitor an LTL formula φ over AP with an automaton defined over the alphabet $\Sigma = 2^{AP}$ with set of states Q: each event is of size $\lceil \log_2 |\Sigma| \rceil$, each state is of size $\lceil \log_2 |Q| \rceil$, each time unit t is of size $\lceil \log_2(t) \rceil$, each formula is of size $n \times \lceil \log_2(|AP| + |Op|) \rceil$ where n is the number of symbols in the formula, AP is the set of atomic propositions of the formula and $Op = \{\top, \bot, \vee, \wedge, \neg, \Rightarrow, \Leftrightarrow, \mathbf{X}, \mathbf{F}, \mathbf{G}, \mathbf{U}, \mathbf{R}, \mathbf{W}, \overline{\mathbf{X}}, \#, (,)\}$ is the set of symbols in formulas handled by DECENTMON. Then in the following tables, the following metrics are used: #msg., the total number of exchanged messages, |msg.|, the total size of exchanged messages (in bits), |trace| the size of the prefix of the trace needed to obtain a verdict, delay, the number of additional events needed by the decentralized algorithm to reach a verdict compared to the centralized one, |mem|, the memory in bits needed for the structures (i.e., formulas for [10], partial function mem plus state for our algorithm).

7.2 Benchmarks for Randomly Generated formulas

For each size of formula (from 1 to 6), DECENT-MON2 randomly generated 1,000 formulas in the architecture described in Example 1. How the three monitoring approaches compared on these formulas can be seen in Tables 2 and 3. The first column of these tables shows the size of the monitored LTL formulas. Note, our system measures formula size in terms of operator entailment[1] inside it (state formulas excluded), e.g., $\mathbf{F}a \wedge \mathbf{G}(b \wedge c)$ is of size 2.

Table 2. Number and size of messages - random formulas

$|\varphi|$	#msg.			|msg.|			#msg. ratio		|msg.| ratio	
	cm	dm1	dm2	cm	dm1	dm2	dm1/cm	dm2/cm	dm1/cm	dm2/cm
1	3.49	1.13	3.73	10.4	87.2	23.8	0.32	1.06	8.31	2.27
2	4.04	1.89	5.4	12.1	316	39.2	0.46	1.33	26.0	3.23
3	9.33	5.34	16.9	27.9	3,220	166	0.57	1.37	115	4.5
4	25.1	12.6	35.9	75.3	8,430	350	0.5	1.27	112	4.16
5	39.7	21.9	71.0	119	36,500	775	0.55	1.33	306	4.86
6	90.9	47.3	116	272	284,000	1,180	0.52	1.23	1,040	4.21

For example, the last line in Table 2 says that we monitored 1,000 randomly generated LTL formulas of size 6. On average, monitors using the centralized algorithm, the decentralized algorithm using LTL formulas, and the decentralized algorithm using automata, exchanged 90.9, 47.3, 116 messages, had messages of size 272 bits, 284,000 bits, 1180 bits, respectively. The last two pairs of columns show the ratios of the previous metrics obtained in the decentralized cases over the centralized one. For instance, the last line in Table 2 says that the decentralized algorithm with LTL formulas induced 0.52 times the number of messages of the centralized algorithm, whereas the decentralized algorithm with automata induced 1.23 times the number of messages. Message ratios and metrics in Table 3 read similarly.

Table 3. Trace length, delay, and memory size - random formulas

$|\varphi|$	|trace|			delay		|mem|	
	cm	dm1	dm2	dm1	dm2	dm1	dm2
1	1.33	1.66	2.61	0.32	1.28	44.2	7.93
2	1.67	2.15	3.2	0.48	1.53	156	9.72
3	5.21	5.79	8.8	0.58	1.6	458	10.4
4	15.7	16.4	19.3	0.7	1.66	1,100	11.3
5	25.5	26.4	36.3	0.82	1.79	2630	12.4
6	59.4	60.2	63.2	0.76	1.66	5,830	12.0

7.3 Benchmarks for Patterns of Formulas

We also conducted benchmarks with more realistic specifications, obtained from specification patterns [19]. Actual formulas underlying the patterns are available at [20, 17]. We generated formulas as follows. For each pattern, we randomly select one of its associated formulas. Such a formula is "parametrized" by some atomic propositions. To obtain randomly generated formula, using the distributed alphabet, we randomly instantiate atomic propositions.

---

[1] Experiments show that operator entailment is more representative of how difficult it is to progress it in a decentralized manner. formulas of size above 6 are not realistic in practice.

Table 4. Number and size of messages - specification patterns

$|\varphi|$	#msg.			|msg.|		#msg. ratio		|msg.| ratio	
	cm	dm1	dm2	cm	dm1	dm2	dm1/cm	dm2/cm	dm1/cm	dm2/cm
abs	7.33	4.46	17.9	22	2,050	194	0.6	2.44	93.6	8.85
exis	43.9	19.7	64.2	131	10,200	663	0.45	1.46	77.6	5.03
bexis	65.3	31.6	379	19.6	1,170,000	5,450	0.48	2.17	5,970	10.4
univ	10.3	5.92	30.9	31	2,750	379	0.57	2.98	88.6	12.2
prec	77.6	25.4	68.1	232	8,710	648	0.32	1.29	37.4	4.11
resp	959	425	1,070	2,870	337,000	9,760	0.44	1.12	117	3.39
precc	7.68	4.81	18.9	23.	5,180	218	0.62	2.47	225	9.53
respc	643	381	732	1,920	719,000	6,680	0.59	1.13	372	3.46
consc	490	201	469	1,470	337,000	4,260	0.41	1.13	229	3.43

Results are reported in Tables 4 and 5 for each kind of patterns (absence, existence, bounded existence, universal, precedence, response, precedence chain, response chain, constrained chain), we generated again 1,000 formulas, monitored over the same architecture as used in Example 1.

7.4   Conclusions from the Experiments and Discussion

The number and size of exchanged messages when monitoring with the decentralized algorithm using automata are in the same order of magnitude (and most often lower) as when monitoring with the centralized algorithm. Comparing the decentralized monitoring algorithms, the number of messages when using LTL formulas is always lower but the size of messages is much bigger in that case (sometimes by orders of magnitude). Delays are always greater when using automata but they remain in the same order of magnitude. Please also note that we have conducted

Table 5. Trace length, delay, and memory size - specification patterns

$|\varphi|$	|trace|		delay		|mem|	
	cm	dm1	dm2	dm1	dm2	dm1	dm2
abs	3.89	4.55	5.66	0.66	1.77	496	12.4
exis	28.2	28.9	29.9	0.65	1.68	376	11.7
bexis	42.6	43.1	116	0.581	1.56	28,200	14.4
univ	5.96	6.73	7.76	0.76	1.79	498	13.0
prec	50.8	51.6	35.5	0.81	1.66	663	11.5
resp	638	639	639	0.32	0.7	1,540	8.61
precc	4.11	4.82	5.72	0.7	1.64	1,200	11.6
respc	427	428	428	0.59	1.16	4,650	10.7
consc	325	325	326	0.6	1.35	2,720	10.8

benchmarks where our algorithm uses only one leader monitor, which tends to augment the delay (whereas in the algorithm using LTL formulas monitors are not constrained) - see the discussion below. Regarding the size of memory, the algorithm using automata is always more efficient by several orders of magnitude when the size of formulas grows.

Efficiency of Implementation. Another interesting feature of our algorithm is its usability in implementation. We measured the execution time (in seconds) and real memory consumption of the two (reasonably optimized) implementations of benchmarks (in the same programming language), see Table 6 where |msg.| is in kb and |mem| in MB.

We only report the results when monitoring formulas of type bounded existence, over the same alphabet as before, with a trace of 10,000 events. For other kinds of formulas, the trend is similar. As expected, progression is

Table 6. Performance of implementations

	#msg.	|msg.|	|mem|	time
DECENTMON	367	21,667	157,845	4.724
DECENTMON2	3,258	59	18	0.064

certainly more costly and thus less appropriate for monitoring. Moreover, the size of messages (and hence the size of formulas) monitors have to handle becomes unmanageable quite rapidly.

Influence of the Number of Leaders. We also made some experiments (omitted for space reasons) regarding the influence of the number of leader monitors. It turns out that, as the number of leaders augments in the system, the number of messages augments, whereas the delay induced by decentralized monitoring reduces. For instance, by allowing all monitors to communicate spontaneously (i.e., with leader_mon$(i) = true$ for any $i \in [1; n]$), we observed that, for several patterns of formulas, i) a shorter average delay and less memory consumption by a factor of 1.5, and ii) the total size of messages was, in average, multiplied by 1.7 while their number was multiplied by 2 (thus the average size of messages decreased).

8 Future Work

Experiments in Sec. 7 indicate that some parameters of our monitoring algorithm such as the frequency of communication, the number of leader monitors, and the communication architecture, influence monitoring metrics. Our experiments allowed to sketch some empiric laws but a deeper understanding of the influence of each of these parameters is certainly needed to optimize decentralized monitoring on specific architectures.

Another line of research is related to security in decentralized monitoring, when for instance monitoring security-related properties, or when the property involves atomic propositions with confidential information. Decentralized monitoring imposes local monitors to communicate, for instance over some network. Exchanged messages contain information about the observation or state of monitors w.r.t. the property of interest. Some confidentiality issues may arise. Thus, an interesting question is to determine how and to what extent monitors could encode their local observation, transmit the encoded information, so that the message is of benefit to the recipient (in terms of gained information), but not to an external observer.

Communication is constrained by the choose_mon function to e.g., reflect architectural constraints. We will determine how to optimize the definition of the choose_mon function according to the monitored language, the memory content, or the current state of local monitors so as to minimize the size and number of exchanged messages.

Another extension is to augment local monitors with enforcement primitives [21] to correct violations. For this purpose, monitors can use their estimated global state and release events only when the (estimated) states are associated to a "good" verdict.

References

1. Falcone, Y., Jaber, M., Nguyen, T.H., Bozga, M., Bensalem, S.: Runtime verification of component-based systems. In: Barthe, G., Pardo, A., Schneider, G. (eds.) SEFM 2011. LNCS, vol. 7041, pp. 204–220. Springer, Heidelberg (2011)
2. Zhou, W., Sokolsky, O., Loo, B.T., Lee, I.: *dMaC*: Distributed monitoring and checking. In: Bensalem, S., Peled, D.A. (eds.) RV 2009. LNCS, vol. 5779, pp. 184–201. Springer, Heidelberg (2009)
3. Sen, K., Vardhan, A., Agha, G., Rosu, G.: Decentralized runtime analysis of multithreaded applications. In: 20th Parallel and Distributed Processing Symp. IEEE (2006)
4. Pnueli, A.: The temporal logic of programs. In: 18th Annual Symp. on Foundations of Computer Science, pp. 46–57 (1977)
5. Genon, A., Massart, T., Meuter, C.: Monitoring distributed controllers: When an efficient LTL algorithm on sequences is needed to model-check traces. In: Misra, J., Nipkow, T., Sekerinski, E. (eds.) FM 2006. LNCS, vol. 4085, pp. 557–572. Springer, Heidelberg (2006)
6. Graf, S., Peled, D., Quinton, S.: Monitoring distributed systems using knowledge. In: Bruni, R., Dingel, J. (eds.) FMOODS/FORTE 2011. LNCS, vol. 6722, pp. 183–197. Springer, Heidelberg (2011)
7. Wang, Y., Yoo, T.S., Lafortune, S.: New results on decentralized diagnosis of discrete event systems. In: 42nd Ann. Allerton Conf. on Comm., Control, and Computing (2004)
8. Cassez, F.: The complexity of codiagnosability for discrete event and timed systems. In: Bouajjani, A., Chin, W.-N. (eds.) ATVA 2010. LNCS, vol. 6252, pp. 82–96. Springer, Heidelberg (2010)
9. Tripakis, S.: Decentralized observation problems. In: 44th IEEE Conf. Decision and Control, pp. 6–11. IEEE (2005)
10. Bauer, A.K., Falcone, Y.: Decentralised LTL monitoring. In: Giannakopoulou, D., Méry, D. (eds.) FM 2012. LNCS, vol. 7436, pp. 85–100. Springer, Heidelberg (2012)
11. Bacchus, F., Kabanza, F.: Planning for temporally extended goals. Annals of Mathematics and Artificial Intelligence 22, 5–27 (1998)
12. Bartocci, E.: Sampling-based decentralized monitoring for networked embedded systems. In: 3rd Int. Work. on Hybrid Autonomous Systems. EPTCS, vol. 124, pp. 85–99 (2013)
13. Bauer, A., Leucker, M., Schallhart, C.: Monitoring of real-time properties. In: Arun-Kumar, S., Garg, N. (eds.) FSTTCS 2006. LNCS, vol. 4337, pp. 260–272. Springer, Heidelberg (2006)
14. Falcone, Y., Fernandez, J.-C., Mounier, L.: Runtime verification of safety-progress properties. In: Bensalem, S., Peled, D.A. (eds.) RV 2009. LNCS, vol. 5779, pp. 40–59. Springer, Heidelberg (2009)
15. Falcone, Y., Fernandez, J.C., Mounier, L.: What can you verify and enforce at runtime? Software Tools for Technology Transfert 14, 349–382 (2012)
16. Bauer, A., Leucker, M., Schallhart, C.: Runtime verification for LTL and TLTL. ACM Trans. Softw. Eng. Methodol. 20, 14 (2011)
17. Cornebize, T., Falcone, Y.: DecentMon2 (2013), http://decentmon2.forge.imag.fr
18. Bauer, A.K.: LTL2MON (2009), http://ltl3tools.sourceforge.net
19. Dwyer, M.B., Avrunin, G.S., Corbett, J.C.: Patterns in property specifications for finite-state verification. In: Intl. Conf. on Software Engineering (ICSE), pp. 411–420. ACM (1999)
20. Alavi, H., Avrunin, G., Corbett, J., Dillon, L., Dwyer, M., Pasareanu, C.: Specification patterns website (2011), http://patterns.projects.cis.ksu.edu/
21. Falcone, Y., Mounier, L., Fernandez, J.C., Richier, J.L.: Runtime enforcement monitors: composition, synthesis, and enforcement abilities. Formal Methods in System Design 38, 223–262 (2011)

A Model-Based Certification Framework for the EnergyBus Standard

Alexander Graf-Brill[1], Holger Hermanns[1], and Hubert Garavel[2,3,4]

[1] Saarland University — Computer Science
66123 Saarbrücken, Germany
{grafbrill,hermanns}@cs.uni-saarland.de
http://depend.cs.uni-saarland.de
[2] Inria
[3] Univ. Grenoble Alpes, LIG, 38000 Grenoble, France
[4] CNRS, LIG, 38000 Grenoble, France
hubert.garavel@inria.fr
http://convecs.inria.fr

Abstract. The EnergyBus is an upcoming industrial standard for electric power transmission and management, based on the CANopen field bus. This paper reviews the particularities of the EnergyBus architecture and reports on the application of formal methods and protocol engineering tools to build a model-based conformance testing framework that is considered to become part of the certification process for EnergyBus-compliant products.

1 Introduction

Light Electric Vehicles (LEVs) are booming in many countries: In the Netherlands for instance, a traditionally bike-affine country, the last year has seen LEV sales outnumber ordinary bike sales with respect to total revenue. Many different OEMs and unit suppliers, including for instance Bosch and Panasonic, but also fleet operators such as Deutsche Bahn are active in this new market, and the annual market growth, especially for *pedelecs* – pedal assisted electric vehicles – is predicted to be at least 20% for the coming years. Bike vendors throughout Europe are feeling this trend and they react by turning into LEV vendors. When doing so, one of the first problems they face is the multitude of plugs and sockets in use to connect battery packs and chargers. Different OEMs partly use the same plug type, but with different pin interpretation. Cellphone users may know this problem, but in the LEV context this problem is safety critical, because the battery capacities are much larger, and charging them in the wrong way may make them catch fire.

The EnergyBus association[1] is a consortium assembling all major industrial players (and Saarland University); their intention is not limited to interoperability between chargers and batteries, but broader, namely to ensure

---

[1] http://www.energybus.org

interoperability between all electric LEV components so that one eventually can freely combine battery pack, motor, charger, and even the dashboard, as long as all devices are EnergyBus-compliant. At the core of this initiative is a universal plug integrating a CAN-Bus with switchable power lines. The initiative has caught further momentum by broadening its scope to stationary smart power micro-grids [1], making it a full-fledged standardisation effort for *Energy Management Systems* (EMS).

To make the devices interoperate requires however more than standardised plugs and sockets. A protocol stack is needed, which orchestrates the exchange of messages and guarantees safe interoperation. LEV and CAN-bus experts are progressing fast on the design and standardisation of this protocol stack; version 1.0 of the EnergyBus standard was released on March 2011 and updated with version 1.0.6 in August 2012 [2]. Version 2.0 is about to be published and serves as the starting point for the recent work of the IEC/ISO/TC69/JPT61851-3 standardisation commision. This work raises many challenging issues: Are these protocols correct? Do their implementations (originating from multiple device manufacturers) conform to the EnergyBus standard?

The authors had the unique opportunity to closely follow and interact with the standardisation activities, applying state-of-the-art protocol engineering methods and tools to the EnergyBus specifications under design. To formally describe the EnergyBus protocol, we used the *LOTOS New Technology* (LNT) language [3], a successor of the LOTOS [4] and E-LOTOS [5] ISO/IEC international standards for the formal specification of communication protocols and distributed systems. We used the LOTOS and LNT compilers and verification tools of the CADP toolbox[2] [6]. Based on the TGV [7] model-based test generator, we developed a tool platform for the automatised conformance testing [8] of EnergyBus/CANopen implementations against the formal specification. The platform is ready to be used as a mandatory step in a certification process which is to be rolled out by the EnergyBus association as soon as first prototype devices become available seeking the EnergyBus-compliance label. This can be a door opener for formal methods research in a much broader context than model-based testing, and in an industrial area with rapidly growing societal and economic impact. To prepare for that, this paper gives a detailed and precise account of the EnergyBus architecture, together with a discussion of the formal modelling and testing activities performed.

The paper is organised as follows. Section 2 briefly recalls the principles of the CANopen field bus and Section 3 presents the main features of the EnergyBus. Section 4 reports about the formal specification work done for the EnergyBus and Section 5 describes the model-based framework set up to check the conformance of EnergyBus implementations. Section 6 discusses related work and Section 7 concludes the paper and draws perspectives about future work.

---

[2] http://cadp.inria.fr

2   CANopen

The communication backbone of the EnergyBus is the CANopen field bus protocol [9]. The latter was developed from 1993 to 1995 in the ESPRIT project ASPIC under chairmanship of Bosch and is a widely adopted field bus protocol in the automation area. The standard is administrated by the "CAN in Automation" (CiA) association[3], which manages and supports standardisation of CAN-related applications. CANopen in turn is based on the *Controller Area Network* (CAN) bus protocol but it is designed in such a way that other protocols can replace the two lowest (in the sense of the ISO/OSI model) layers.

CANopen, in its original form, is a very robust Carrier Sensing Media Access protocol with Bit Arbitration (CSMA/BA). In the CAN philosophy, every communication task has its own dedicated message name — the function code — which is combined with the node-id to form the *Communication Object Identifier* (COB-id).

The network itself is built up by several nodes sharing a CAN line, which is accessed in an equal bit-rate setting and with uniquely assigned node-ids. CANopen adds several protocols for different communication tasks and a local interface object for on-top applications — the *Object Dictionary* (OD). This is basically a two-dimensional array structure with predefined interpretations of the different entries. The directory entries are used to exchange data values between the application and the CANopen network, and to store configuration parameters for the various CANopen protocols.

Some CANopen protocols are relevant for the discussion that follows. The *Network Management* (NMT) protocol enables a dedicated master node to manage the basic operation status of other nodes in the network: such "slave" nodes can be started, stopped, reset, or brought to operational state.

The *Service Data Object* (SDO) protocol is mainly used for setting up and configuring the devices inside a network. This is a client/server protocol between two nodes. Each two nodes use a fixed pair of COB-ids for their communication, a so-called SDO Channel.

Contrary to SDO, the role of the *Process Data Object* (PDO) protocol is the periodic transmission of status information or application data, and event notification.

Error control service is supported by the *Heartbeat protocol*, in which each node periodically sends its current NMT state to the network. A time-out of these messages is used to signal the "loss" of the node to every listening node.

Emergency messages (EMCY) are used to report the occurrences of internal device errors to the network participants.

The so-called *Layers Setting Services* (LSS) [10] provide basic configuration mechanisms to assign node-ids and to adjust the communication baud rate of single network nodes. These services are orthogonal to the other CANopen protocols and are especially applied to unconfigured devices, for which identification is derived from the device unique "virtual type" label.

---

[3] http://www.can-cia.org

3 EnergyBus

The EnergyBus Standard [2] aims at a common standard for electric devices in the context of Energy Management Systems (EMS). This includes the definition of a connector family, on the one hand, and appropriate communication protocols, on the other hand. The central and innovative role of the EnergyBus is the transmission and management of electrical power. So the purpose of its protocol suite is not just to transmit data, but in particular to manage the safe electricity access and distribution inside an EnergyBus network.

The development of the EnergyBus protocols is in the hands of the EnergyBus e.V. and its members. Conceptually, it extends the underlying CANopen architecture with several components, and the EnergyBus protocols are developed in terms of *CANopen application profiles* endorsed by the CiA association [2]. Among these, the 'Pedelec Profile 1" (PP1) is very detailed and targets a predominant business context.

3.1 Power Lines and EnergyBus Devices

An EnergyBus network contains one or several power lines, which may be of two kinds: the *main power lines*, which carry either DC (ranging from 12 to 250 V) or AC (from 85 to 265 V), and the *auxiliary power line*, which carries low-voltage DC (between 9 and 12 V) and is always powered. The type of the network can be restricted by application profiles, such as the PP1, which has a single main power line and an auxiliary power line (12 V).

CANopen devices are physical entities implementing CANopen specifications. EnergyBus devices are CANopen devices that also implement EnergyBus specifications. *Active devices* are connected to the main power lines, while *passive devices* are only connected to auxiliary power lines. Since malfunctioning of the main lines can be lethal, the proper functioning of active devices is crucial for electrical safety. Yet, passive devices are important too — even if they are low powered, and even if low- and high-voltage lines are strictly separated — because passive devices behaving incorrectly may interfere with active ones and put the network at risk.

3.2 Virtual Devices

The EnergyBus specification adopts the concept of a Virtual Device from the CANopen standard. Each EnergyBus device supports one Object Dictionary, several communication services, and can implement several Virtual Devices. The roles of almost all functional elements operating in an EnergyBus network are defined in terms of Virtual Devices.

A Virtual Device is usually characterised by: (1) its behaviour, usually specified as a combination of textual definitions and *Finite-State Automata* (FSAs); (2) by dedicated OD entries, namely, electric or physical parameters possibly influencing the flow of energy; and (3) by its communication settings, such as PDO definitions [11]. Each instance of a Virtual Device is assigned a set of these

PDOs together with distinct COB-ids to uniquely identify a PDO's sender. Virtual devices include:

- *General Application Objects*, which store the list of all implemented Virtual Devices, their nominal voltage and current ranges, their status and control word entries, temperatures, and so on. Each EnergyBus device must implement this Virtual Device exactly once.
- *Battery Packs* are the simplest kind of power supply in the EnergyBus. In general, they are accumulators and so have the capability of being recharged inside the EnergyBus. Moreover, Battery Packs can be removed from the network.
- *Voltage Converters* change the voltage of electrical power sources. There are different kinds of Voltage Converters offering different operation modi, the most prominent one being — at least in the LEV and pedelec setting — the *External Charger Station*.
- *Motor Control Unit* (MCU) are Virtual Devices specifying specific status values and control capabilities of motor equipments and providing protocol interfaces to them.
- The *Human Machine Interface* (HMI) is a dashboard that displays information to the user. It can be used to start/stop and configure the network, to turn on/off the lights, to choose support profiles for the motor, etc.
- The most important Virtual Device is the *EnergyBus Controller* detailed out in the next subsection.

3.3 EnergyBus Controller

The *EnergyBus Controller* (EBC) is responsible for managing the distribution of electric power. In general, several EBCs can coexist in an EnergyBus network, but to avoid interferences, there is always exactly one EBC active, which has the fixed node-id "1", implying highest priority — all the other EBCs being basically turned off. The active EBC has the authority to turn on/off the entire EnergyBus and to control its attached devices.

The EBC is supposed to ensure electrical safety of the network, especially protection against over/under voltage or current, and achieves this by limiting the power flows according to parameters collected as characteristic and actual values from the devices attached. To do so, the EBC sets appropriate limits to other devices and dynamically adjusts these limits according to the actual settings of the system. Nevertheless, every device is ultimately responsible for its own safety and must protect itself from damage by disconnecting itself from power lines if necessary.

The EBC functionality requires the device hosting the EBC to provide the CANopen NMT master functionality to control the communication behaviour, and LSS master functionality to initialise and configure the devices as network nodes. The EBC controls the internal state and monitors the Heartbeat of every connected device. It maintains SDO channel connections to all slave devices for controllability reasons. Each Virtual Device (except the EBC itself) maintains an SDO server channel to the EBC and no client channels.

3.4 Subtask Protocols

Besides the general task to safely distribute electric power throughout the network, there are special situations in which the EnergyBus uses specific smaller protocols, e.g. for charging Battery Packs, updating the devices' software, diagnostics, energy saving via sleep mode functionality, etc.

4 Formal Modelling of the EnergyBus

A formal specification is a pre-requisite for modern protocol engineering approaches; the present section reports about the specification activities carried out for the EnergyBus.

4.1 CANopen and EnergyBus Specification Documents

As mentioned in Section 3, the EnergyBus is defined on top of CANopen, and EnergyBus devices are CANopen devices, which inherit features from CANopen and extend them with additional ones. Thus, a formal specification of the EnergyBus requires to model certain CANopen features (e.g., NMT, LSS, OD), although not in full detail.

The CANopen and EnergyBus specifications are given informally, as a combination of text, protocol flow charts, and FSAs — the latter being used to summarise the behaviour of devices as seen by other devices. Master devices are entitled to modify the current states of slave devices by sending special messages. The CANopen specifications are stable, whereas all EnergyBus protocols (except perhaps the Boot Loader protocol) have been evolving quickly.

The basic CANopen standard is defined in [9] (about 150 pages). CANopen associates to each device several data structures (e.g., the OD) and various services, among which the NMT, PDO, SDO, EMCY, and (optional) LSS. There are additional services of CANopen, each represented by its own set of protocols, being enabled and disabled according to the current state of the NMT FSAs.

Concerning the NMT: The behaviour of each NMT slave node in the network can be seen as a 6-state FSA. Textual explanations are provided for each of these states: *Initialising, Reset Application*, and *Reset Communication* describe initialisation stages, whereas *Pre-Operational, Operational*, and *Stopped* represent communication configurations. The NMT service enables the NMT master node to manipulate the NMT FSAs of the NMT slave nodes. The corresponding NMT protocols are provided in textual form and sequence diagrams.

Concerning the LSS: While being optional in CANopen, this service turns mandatory in an EnergyBus network. It is defined in [10] (about 60 pages) as an FSA with four states, and several corresponding protocols.

The EnergyBus standard is defined as a collection of 14 documents [2], 11 of which describe particular types of Virtual Devices, giving for each device its specific OD entries and specifying its behaviour as one or several FSAs. The EnergyBus standard brings various extensions to CANopen, among which the

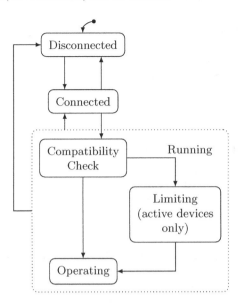

Fig. 1. EnergyBus Energy Management System FSA

Energy Management System (EMS) and its *Boot Loader* and *Sleep Mode* protocols, each being defined by a specific FSA.

Concerning the EMS: This service is at the core of the EnergyBus; the basic behaviour and interaction capabilities of an EnergyBus Device, as seen by the EBC, is represented by the EMS FSA depicted on Fig. 1. A device is in the *Disconnected* state when not connected to the EnergyBus, possibly powered by an external source. A device is in the *Connected* state when the connector is plugged, i.e., when it is connected to the CAN network and when the EnergyBus can be used as an auxiliary power supply. The three states labelled *Running* describe the successful connection to the CANopen/EnergyBus network. Devices in state *Compatibility Check* are examined to check the compatibility of their electric/electronic characteristic values to those of already connected devices. If the device is connected to the main power lines of the EnergyBus, its variable power settings are being adjusted in state *Limiting*. Finally, devices in state *Operating* can execute their running application. The EBC controls the EMS FSA of the connected EnergyBus devices via SDO writes to the *control word* entry of their Object Directories.

4.2   Formal Specification of the EnergyBus in LNT

To formally model the EnergyBus, we chose the LNT specification language [3], which is the most recent descendent in the family of LOTOS [4] and E-LOTOS [5] languages. In a nutshell, LNT combines functional languages — to describe data types and functions operating on typed values — and process calculi — to describe concurrent agents that execute in parallel, synchronise using rendezvous, and communicate via message passing. As usual with process calculi, the operational semantics of LNT is defined in terms of *Labeled Transition Systems* (LTSs) and *Structural Operational Semantics* (SOS) rules. A translator from LNT to LOTOS exists, thus enabling LNT specifications to be compiled, executed, and verified using the CADP toolbox [6].

As mentioned above, our formal specification is based on the CANopen and EnergyBus standards. For the latter, we took into account about 400 pages of documentation, out of which approximately 300 pages describe OD entries. The modelling process took six months, with several iterations to follow the EnergyBus specification updates and to introduce abstractions in the models.

Our LNT model [12, Appendix C] is divided into several parts, each representing a single aspect (e.g., a specific service) of the CANopen/EnergyBus specifications. Each part is split into a header file containing the type and channel definitions, and a file containing the process definitions. These files are assembled together by means of *cpp* preprocessor directives (e.g., #include, #ifdef, etc.) to produce a model having about 1700 lines of LNT code and 200 lines of comments. Table 1 provides data concerning the different parts, the second column providing best-effort estimations, as information about a given component being often distributed across multiple documents.

Table 1. Size of informal and formal specifications

Component	Documentation (pages)	LNT code (lines)
NMT	8	260
Heartbeat	6	200
EMCY/Error	4	145
LSS	62	360
EMS	3	440
PDO	45	60
SDO	25	30
OD/Variables	300	70

The FSAs are directly translated to LNT code by implementing their states as LNT enumerated types and their corresponding actions as LNT processes. The different FSAs are intended to run in parallel, loosely coupled to each other. They synchronise and communicate using a mixed approach that combines message passing and shared variables. There is also a master/slave hierarchy between FSAs; for instance, all services must monitor the current state of the NMT by consulting the corresponding variable's value. LNT was found sufficiently expressive to describe this particular model of coordination. Like most process calculi, LNT does not support shared variables as a primitive communication paradigm, but it is easy to model them as additional parallel processes.

A straightforward modelling of the OD in LNT would consist of a two-dimensional array structure hosting different types of data; yet, this would certainly cause an explosion in the number of states and transitions in the underlying LTS. We therefore chose a refined modelling approach by only modelling relevant OD entries, and by "specialising" our LNT code depending on the specific nature of each OD entry: (1) *global constants* common to all devices are modelled as LNT constant functions; (2) *local constants* specific to a particular device are modelled as parameters of the LNT process(es) corresponding to this device; (3) *local variables* internal to a given device are modelled as LNT local variables; and (4) *global variables* shared between several devices are modelled, as explained above, using dedicated LNT processes with communication gates to read and write these variables and, if needed, an additional channel that notifies all "listeners" of any value update.

We also specialised the translation of PDOs and SDOs into LNT, and only modelled their useful aspects, which saved much modelling effort compared to producing fully-detailed generic process models for them. Each defined PDO [11] is represented by its own LNT process, parameterised by the PDO's COB-id and the actual names of the corresponding variables. SDOs are not represented as LNT processes, but as pairs of read/write operations affecting specific variables.

4.3   Results and Discussion

As it is often the case, formal modelling revealed problems in textual specification documents. For instance, it uncovered ambiguities in a former version of the LSS on how to take the NMT initialisation process into account; also, the Sleep Mode protocol exhibited gaps [12, Appendix B] preventing its formalization. There have been several iterations with the industrial partners to solve issues raised by confusing and non-consistent naming, and mismatches between natural language and logics.

The LNT specification developed for the EnergyBus standard was mechanically checked using the LNT2LOTOS, CÆSAR.ADT, and CÆSAR compilers provided by the CADP toolbox [6]. These tools enabled to fix various mistakes, such as undefined identifiers and typing errors. This is a significant enhancement compared to most protocol standards, which are "only" checked by human reviewers.

An automated search for deadlocks was performed. More stringent analyses could have been done using the powerful verification capabilities of CADP (equivalence checking, model checking, etc.), but we decided to focus our work on conformance testing.

5   Conformance Testing for the EnergyBus

The goal of conformance testing is to examine whether the functional behaviour a given implementation — referred to as the *Implementation Under Test* (IUT) — conforms to a (hopefully formal) specification, which defines the expected correct behaviour. In the case of certification, there are usually several implementations from various manufacturers to be compared against the same specification, which thus plays the role of an authoritative, central reference and avoids divergence between implementations.

5.1 Model-Based Testing

For the EnergyBus, we used a *model-based testing* approach in which physical CANopen/EnergyBus devices are the IUTs, and the LNT specification is the reference.

In this approach, each IUT is considered as a black box (i.e., each device is only accessible via its CAN/CANopen interface, without extra means to probe its internal state). The functional behaviour of the IUT is checked by applying a suite of *test cases* derived from the LNT specification. *Test generation* (i.e., the production of test cases) is, to a large extent, automated: taking as input the LNT specification and a set of high-level scenarios (called *test purposes*) provided by a human, a large number of detailed low-level test cases are produced automatically — thus, avoiding the frequent risk of introducing mistakes in test cases. *Test execution*, i.e., the application of test cases to the IUT — namely, sending inputs to the IUT, observing the outputs of the IUT, and comparing them to the correct outputs predicted by the LNT specification — runs automatically without human intervention.

The general model-based testing framework presented in [13] and especially [8] is the theoretical basis for this work. For test generation, we chose to use the TGV tool [7], partly because it is directly applicable to LNT specifications. We now briefly mention how to instantiate the general framework in this particular case.

Concerning the *formal domain* for LNT specifications, we use *Input Output Labeled Transition Systems* (IOLTS), i.e., LTSs whose actions are divided into three classes: inputs, outputs, or internal (τ). As the LNT compiler only produces LTSs, the user must provide a criterion to distinguish between inputs and outputs.

Concerning the *test assumption*, we assume an IOLTS where in every state every input action is enabled, which exactly models the IUT behaviour. Thus, we are able to formally reason about a relation between the specification and the IUT.

The *implementation relation* presented in [8] is **input/output conformance** (**ioco**), which requires that the implementation, after executing some trace, is allowed to perform only those output actions permitted in the "matching" states (i.e., states reached after this same trace) of the specification.

For the EnergyBus, we must use the **ioco**$_U$ implementation relation [14], which is slightly weaker than **ioco** and ranges over so-called "underspecified" traces. The reason is that we perform black box testing of the IUT through its CAN/CANopen interface, modelled as a test context $C[\_]$: thus, the IUT is a composition of the EnergyBus device with $C[\_]$, while the specification is a composition of the device LNT model with $C[\_]$. By using **ioco**$_U$, we avoid forbidden behaviour due to unspecified interaction between the IUT and $C[\_]$, thus preserving the *soundness* of testing.

The *test purposes* given to the TGV tool are finite IOLTSs (specified in LNT by the user and automatically translated into IOLTSs by the LNT compiler) that describe "interesting" scenarios, i.e., paths of the EnergyBus specification that shall be considered for testing. Test purposes can be seen as high-level goals that restrict the set of possible test cases.

TGV generates so-called *test graphs*, which are finite IOLTSs. In these graphs, each execution path starting from the initial state corresponds to a *test case*, i.e., a sequence of inputs sent to the IUT and outputs received from the IUT. Test graphs are prepared to accept every output, even if erroneous, from the IUT. A test case terminates when reaching a state labelled with a *test verdict*, which is either *pass* if the path is legal according to the specification, or *fail* if the last output of the path is unexpected, or *inconclusive* when the path leaves the area of the specification defined by the test purpose when generating the test case.

5.2   Test Platform Architecture

We implemented this model-based testing approach in a hardware/software platform, the architecture of which is depicted on Figure 2.

The left-hand side of the figure represents *test generation*. The two main inputs of the TGV tool are the LNT specification of EnergyBus and the test purpose(s) given in LNT. Using the LNT and LOTOS compilers of CADP, these LNT files are translated into LTSs accessible via the dedicated OPEN/CÆSAR API [15]. Additional information about the list of input and output actions enables to turn these LTSs into IOLTSs. TGV produces as output test graph(s) encoded in the BCG format of CADP.

The right-hand side of the figure represents *test execution*. It operates on a test graph generated by TGV and a physical EnergyBus device, which is accessed through its CANopen interface. The latter is provided by emtas[4], an SME developping industrial CANopen solutions. The execution engine returns whether the device complies with the test graph(s).

The test execution software (nearly 3100 lines of C code) is logically split into modules performing different tasks. The *Explorer* module uses the BCG library of CADP to traverse the test graph. In this graph, the *Partitioner* and *IO-Chooser* modules select a test case on the fly, using a uniform random generator to choose one among several enabled transitions. The *Adapter* module provides software and hardware interface based on an industrial CANopen stack. The *Instantiator* module replaces abstract data values by concrete ones in transition actions, so as to provide the *Driver* with parameters used in the *Adapter* functions. Finally, the *Driver* module connects both worlds, checks test verdicts, and emits test results.

Although TGV can also extract test cases from test graphs, we do not use this feature and stop TGV right after test graph generation, thus avoiding the non-deterministic choices between inputs and outputs made by TGV. This way, we fit better with the theory of [8] and our test cases can handle the situation — likely to happen in a multi-layer communication protocol — where a particular action takes non-negligible time and is interrupted by an output of the IUT.

---

[4] http://www.emtas.de

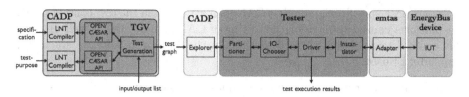

Fig. 2. Tool architecture

5.3 Abstractions

When modelling real-world examples, one often faces the state-space explosion problem. Initially, the implicit LTS representation and on-the-fly algorithms provided by CADP's OPEN/CÆSAR framework [15] (upon which TGV is built) have been sufficient to handle the complexity of our models. But adding the LSS and PDO protocols in full led to state-space explosion arising from data types, such as 8-byte message data.

To overcome the issue, we applied various abstraction techniques to appropriate areas of our model. The most effective approach was *data abstraction* [16]: data ranges for LSS addresses, and other identifying parameter values were reduced to either two-value domains (e.g., *own_id* and *wrong_id* with binary tests for equality) or three-value domains (e.g. *smaller_id*, *own_id*, and *bigger_id* with accordingly abstracted order relations). Data abstraction was also applied to energy management components. Such abstraction is perfectly compatible with the intended behaviour, which checks whether a given variable is above or below certain thresholds (absolute measurements) or compares it against its previous value (relative measurements). From a conformance testing point of view, such abstractions can be seen as a simple application of action refinement [17], transferring the complexity from the LNT model to the adapter component.

5.4 Results and Discussion

Discussions with EnergyBus developers were distilled into test purposes covering realistic scenarios, such as the initialisation of unconfigured nodes via combinations of LSS communications, or the boot-up procedure of configured nodes, including the transmission of its PDOs with dynamic and static variable values. These test purposes are of manageable size (about 80 lines of LNT code on average) and generate complex test graphs (e.g., 600 states and 1100 transitions each) that would be difficult to produce manually.

These test purposes provide the initial database for setting up a model-based certification process for EnergyBus-compliance. Since no EnergyBus devices are thus far available on the market, we emulated them with C code, using the same software stack and hardware as the adapter component, bridged by a CAN connection. This provides us with a fully automatic way to exercise, debug and tune the testing platform itself, and to prepare for the arrival of the first prototype devices to be certified.

As our LNT specification models CANopen aspects (via the test context $C[\_]$), our platform can be applied for the testing of CANopen devices as well. In fact, this enabled us to detect three deviations in the CANopen software stack [12, Appendix E] used.

1. missing counter value data in SYNC message reception;
2. missing state change in the LSS FSA during configuration process by slave devices;
3. wrong behaviour of unconfigured slaves in the LSS Fastscan protocol (not confirmed yet).

Notably, deviation (1) was not signalled by a *fail* test verdict, but by a time-out of test execution followed by a manual inspection of the test results log file. This is due to the fact that IOLTSs do not model quantitative time: the LNT specification allowed to stay in the current quiescent state, from which a sequence of internal actions could lead to the expected output; this could have been avoided in a timed setting.

6   Related Work

Model-based conformance testing [13] [8] is an established technology supported by various tools, such as TGV [7] [18], TorX [19], and Uppaal-Tron [20] that generate tests for real-time systems. Model-based testing has been discussed for automotive [21] and fieldbus [22] settings, though without focussing on formal conformance testing or product certification. Formal verification was performed for TTP [23]. Deep investigations of CAN and FlexRay efficiency [24] and timing [25] have been carried out. The specific aspects of the electric vehicle domain have been detailed out in [26]. Formal models for smart energy systems have been discussed in [27]. To the best of our knowledge, the combination of formal modelling, model-based testing, and component certification has not been discussed so far in the literature, for sure not in the context of mobile energy management.

7   Conclusion and Future Work

Energy management networks are rapidly gaining importance for small- and medium-scale applications, including electric vehicles, caravans, combinations of solar panels and storage devices, etc. Our work pushes forward formal specification and model-based testing approaches via the EnergyBus standard. Harvesting a close interaction of the authors in the standardisation activities, state-of-the-art protocol engineering technology has been used to model and check EnergyBus specifications, in parallel to setting up a testing framework ready-to-use for device compliance certification. Apart from preparing for certification, our concrete contributions are threefold:

1. We produced a formal specification [12, Appendix C] in LNT of the key aspects of the EnergyBus, including the required CANopen features. This specification, which has been submitted to the EnergyBus association, provides a readable and compact model that can be used as a basis for future corporate work and automated analyses.
2. This specification work and the computer analysis of the formal specifications have revealed various ambiguities and inconsistencies [12, Appendix B] in the EnergyBus description.
3. A model-based platform for the conformance testing of EnergyBus/CANopen implementations against our formal specification has been developed. We detected three inconsistencies [12, Appendix E] in an industrial CANopen implementation; two of them have been acknowleged as defects and the confirmation for the third one is pending.

Thus, there is already a clear return on the investment in developing formal specifications. Our work shows that model-based testing approaches are applicable — if not directly out of the box, at least without too much stretching, i.e., using simple abstraction techniques. The LNT language, which had not been used priorly for field bus protocols, has shown to be a beginner-friendly notation and provided a formal basis for discussing with the EnergyBus experts. Furthermore the CADP tools (especially the LNT translator) benefited from the EnergyBus modelling feedback.

Our work is to some extent driving as well as driven by the evolution of the EnergyBus forthcoming standard. A current focus is on the subtask protocols (see Section 3.4), including the Charging Protocol. The testing platform will be connected to EnergyBus device prototypes as soon as they are available. The EnergyBus association considers a strict certification process for any device asking for the EnergyBus-compliance label: model-based testing has the potential to become a mandatory step in this process, as a supplement to conventional integration testing already used by the CiA association. To the best of our knowledge, this would then be the first time that applied formal methods are an integral and mandatory step in the introduction of a new industrial standard. It also can be seen as a spearhead for deeper modelling and analysis activities, especially with respect to real-time and power flow properties. This asks for timed and hybrid automata models, together with effective model checking techniques. As a whole, the greater LEV domain appears as a very promising arena for applied formal methods.

Acknowledgments. This work has been performed under the aegis of the Alexander-von-Humboldt foundation, partly in the framework of the German transregional DFG project AVACS[5] and of the European IST FP7 projects SENSATION[6] and MEALS[7]. It benefited from scientific exchanges with

---

[5] http://www.avacs.org

[6] http://sensation-project.eu

[7] http://meals-project.eu

EnergyBus e.V, with the CAN in Automation association, and with the em-tas company. Ackowledgements are due to Dr. Wendelin Serwe for his advices on the best way of using the TGV tool, and to the anonymous reviewers for their comments about the present paper.

References

1. Vetter, M., Rohr, L., Ortiz, B., Schies, A., Schwunk, S., Wachtel, J.: Dezentrale netzgekoppelte PV-Batteriesysteme. In: VDI-Konferenz Elektrische Energiespe-icher – Stationäre Anwendungen und Industriebatterien, pp. 101–112 (2011)
2. CAN in Automation International Users and Manufacturers Group e.V., EnergyBus e. V.: CiA 454 Work Draft Application profile for energy management systems – Document series 1 to 14, v. 1.0.6 (2012)
3. Champelovier, D., Clerc, X., Garavel, H., Guerte, Y., Lang, F., McKinty, C., Powazny, V., Serwe, W., Smeding, G.: Reference Manual of the LOTOS NT to LOTOS Translator (Version 5.8). Technical report, INRIA/VASY and INRIA/CONVECS (2013)
4. ISO/IEC: LOTOS — A Formal Description Technique Based on the Temporal Ordering of Observational Behaviour. International Standard 8807 (1989)
5. ISO/IEC: Enhancements to LOTOS (E-LOTOS). International Standard 15437:2001 (2001)
6. Garavel, H., Lang, F., Mateescu, R., Serwe, W.: CADP 2011: A Toolbox for the Construction and Analysis of Distributed Processes. Software Tools for Technology Transfer (STTT) 15, 89–107 (2013)
7. Jard, C., Jéron, T.: TGV: Theory, Principles, and Algorithms. Software Tools for Technology Transfer (STTT) 7, 297–315 (2005)
8. Tretmans, J.: Model-based Testing with Labelled Transition Systems. In: Hierons, R.M., Bowen, J.P., Harman, M. (eds.) FORTEST. LNCS, vol. 4949, pp. 1–38. Springer, Heidelberg (2008)
9. CAN in Automation International Users and Manufacturers Group e.V.: CiA 301 CANopen Application Layer and Communication Profile, v. 4.2.0 (2011)
10. CAN in Automation International Users and Manufacturers Group e.V.: CiA 305 Layer setting services (LSS) and protocols, v. 3.0.0 (2013)
11. CAN in Automation International Users and Manufacturers Group e.V., Energy-Bus e. V.: CiA 454 Work Draft Application profile for energy management systems – Part 3: PDO communication, v. 1.0.2 (2012)
12. Graf-Brill, A.: Model-based Testing Approaches for the EnergyBus. Reports of SFB/TR 14 AVACS 96, SFB/TR 14 AVACS (2014) ISSN: 1860–9821, http://www.avacs.org
13. Broy, M., Jonsson, B., Katoen, J.-P., Leucker, M., Pretschner, A. (eds.): Model-Based Testing of Reactive Systems. LNCS, vol. 3472. Springer, Heidelberg (2005)
14. van der Bijl, M., Rensink, A., Tretmans, J.: Compositional Testing with ioco. In: Petrenko, A., Ulrich, A. (eds.) FATES 2003. LNCS, vol. 2931, pp. 86–100. Springer, Heidelberg (2004)
15. Garavel, H.: OPEN/CÆSAR: An Open Software Architecture for Verification, Simulation, and Testing. In: Steffen, B. (ed.) TACAS 1998. LNCS, vol. 1384, pp. 68–84. Springer, Heidelberg (1998)

16. Prenninger, W., Pretschner, A.: Abstractions for Model-Based Testing – Proceedings of the International Workshop on Test and Analysis of Component Based Systems (TACoS 2004). Electronic Notes in Theoretical Computer Science 116, 59–71 (2005)
17. van der Bijl, H.M., Rensink, A., Tretmans, G.J.: Atomic Action Refinement in Model Based Testing. Technical Report TR-CTIT-07-64, Centre for Telematics and Information Technology University of Twente, Enschede (2007)
18. Garavel, H., Viho, C., Zendri, M.: System Design of a CC-NUMA Multiprocessor Architecture Using Formal Specification, Model Checking, Co-simulation, and Test Generation. Software Tools for Technology Transfer (STTT) 3, 314–331 (2001)
19. Tretmans, J., Brinksma, E.: TorX: Automated Model Based Testing – Côte de Resyste (2003)
20. Hessel, A., Larsen, K., Mikucionis, M., Nielsen, B., Pettersson, P., Skou, A.: Testing Real-Time Systems Using UPPAAL. In: Hierons, R.M., Bowen, J.P., Harman, M. (eds.) FORTEST. LNCS, vol. 4949, pp. 77–117. Springer, Heidelberg (2008)
21. Bringmann, E., Krämer, A.: Model-Based Testing of Automotive Systems. In: ICST, pp. 485–493. IEEE Computer Society (2008)
22. Gerke, M., Ehlers, R., Finkbeiner, B., Peter, H.J.: Model Checking the FlexRay Physical Layer Protocol. In: Kowalewski, S., Roveri, M. (eds.) FMICS 2010. LNCS, vol. 6371, pp. 132–147. Springer, Heidelberg (2010)
23. Rushby, J.: An Overview of Formal Verification for the Time-Triggered Architecture. In: Damm, W., Olderog, E.-R. (eds.) FTRTFT 2002. LNCS, vol. 2469, pp. 83–106. Springer, Heidelberg (2002)
24. Milbredt, P., Vermeulen, B., Tabanoglu, G., Lukasiewycz, M.: Switched FlexRay: Increasing the Effective Bandwidth and Safety of FlexRay Networks. In: Emerging Technologies and Factory Automation (ETFA), pp. 1–8. IEEE (2010)
25. Krause, J., Hintze, E., Magnus, S., Diedrich, C.: Model Based Specification, Verification, and Test Generation for a Safety Fieldbus Profile. In: Ortmeier, F., Daniel, P. (eds.) SAFECOMP 2012. LNCS, vol. 7612, pp. 87–98. Springer, Heidelberg (2012)
26. Goswami, D., Lukasiewycz, M., Kauer, M., Steinhorst, S., Masrur, A., Chakraborty, S., Ramesh, S.: Model-based Development and Verification of Control Software for Electric Vehicles. In: Proceedings of the 50th Annual Design Automation Conference (DAC 2013), Austin, Texas, USA, pp. 96:1–96:9. ACM (2013)
27. Hartmanns, A., Hermanns, H.: Modelling and Decentralised Runtime Control of Self-stabilising Power Micro Grids. In: Margaria, T., Steffen, B. (eds.) ISoLA 2012, Part I. LNCS, vol. 7609, pp. 420–439. Springer, Heidelberg (2012)

Effectiveness for Input Output Conformance Simulation iocos⋆

Carlos Gregorio-Rodríguez, Luis Llana, and Rafael Martínez-Torres

Departamento Sistemas Informáticos y Computación
Universidad Complutense de Madrid, Spain
cgr@sip.ucm.es, llana@ucm.es, rmartine@fdi.ucm.es

Abstract. In this paper we continue the study of the input-output conformance simulation (iocos). In particular, we focus on implementation aspects to show that iocos is indeed an interesting semantic relation for formal methods. We address two complementary issues: a) In the context of model based testing (MBT) we present an online, also called on-the-fly, testing algorithm that checks whether an implementation conforms a given specification. Online testing combines test generation and execution and avoids the generation of the complete test suite for the specification. We prove both soundness and completeness of the online algorithm with respect to the iocos relation. b) In the context of formal verification and model checking minimisation a key issue is to efficiently compute the considered semantic relations; we show how the coinductive flavour of our conformance relation iocos makes it appropriate to be cast into an instance of the Generalised Coarsest Partition Problem (GCPP) and thus it can be efficiently computed.

Keywords: Model Based Testing, Online Testing, Simulation Algorithm, Input Output Conformance Simulation, Model Checking Minimisation, Verification, Generalised Coarsest Partition Problem, Formal Methods.

1 Introduction

In a recent paper [12] we introduced the input-output conformance simulation relation (iocos) that refines the classic Tretman's ioco. The work by Tretmans [25] has settled a solid and widespread framework in the Model Based Testing (MBT) community: it offers both offline and online [9] testing algorithms; and there are several model-based test generation tools (e.g. [26,3]) that implement the ioco-testing theory.

From a theoretical point of view, some interesting particularities of the ioco-framework are: behaviours are modelled as labelled transition systems (LTS); quiescent states (see [24]) are considered; implementations should be input-enabled; and the ioco relation is a trace-based semantics, and thus a linear semantics [27].

⋆ Research partially supported by the Spanish MEC projects TIN2009-14312-C02-01 and TIN2012-36812-C02-01.

E. Ábrahám and C. Palamidessi (Eds.), FORTE 2014, LNCS 8461, pp. 100–116, 2014.
© IFIP International Federation for Information Processing 2014

Our iocos approach shares LTS as models, quiescence, and much of the conformance philosophy, while considering a wider behaviour domain not imposing, but allowing, implementations to be input enabled. The substantial difference is that the conformance relation is an input-output simulation (iocos) —a branching semantics [27]— with greater discriminatory power than ioco (see Theorem 1 below). In [12] we presented an offline algorithm that starting from a formal model of the specification produced a test suite to be checked against the possible implementations. We proved the resulting test suite to be sound and exhaustive for the given specification with respect to iocos.

In this paper we present an alternative approach to offline testing that avoids the generation of the whole test suite. When time or space requirements are considered, a more suitable testing approach is the so called online testing. Online testing considers a concrete implementation to be checked against the specification. It combines test generation from the specification model and test execution against the implementation. In this approach only a single step of a test is generated from the model and executed in the implementation; the results of this execution are taken into account to generate the next step in the test, that is again checked against the implementation. In order to show the applicability of our conformance relation, in this paper we define an online testing algorithm for iocos that we prove to be sound and complete.

An essential point of our conformance relation is that it is simulation-based. Simulation is an important notion pervading many fields in computer science (model checking, concurrency theory, formal verification...). It is an active area of research both theoretical (e.g. [2,8,17,10]) and practical (e.g. [5,22]). Regarding practical implementation applications for iocos, it is particularly interesting its use in model checking minimisation ([6,14]) as a technique to overcome the state explosion problem.

The quest for efficient algorithms[1] to compute this relation has been an area of active research in the last years (e.g.[11,5,22]). In [22] you can find an excellent review of the state of the art for simulation algorithms. One of the most outstanding algorithms is the one presented in [11], and subsequently corrected in [28]. It is one of the fastest algorithms and quasi-optimal in space. This algorithm exploits the representation of the simulation problem as a Generalised Coarsest Partition Problem (GCPP). We show in this paper how the conformance relation iocos can be cast into an instance of the GCPP. Therefore it can be efficiently computed using the algorithm in [28].

The paper is organised as follows: in Section 2 we present the essential notation, definitions and results of the iocos-theory used in the rest of the paper. In Section 3, definition and behaviour of our online testing algorithm are explained and we discuss other related online testing algorithms in the literature. Section 4 is devoted to prove that iocos is indeed a relation that can be

---

[1] As a general overview, we could say that while deciding trace inclusion on finite-state processes is PSPACE-hard [23], the simulation preorder is decidable in polynomial time. Actually, simulation preorder is the coarsest preorder included in trace inclusion with this property.

efficiently computed. We use the technique of system transformation to adequate iocos to the problem definition in [11]. Then we prove that this transformation holds all requirements to be computed as a GCPP. Finally in Section 5 we make a summary and advance some future research lines. In order to meet the space requirements, there is an appendix containing the more technical proofs of the paper. This appendix will be available on-line in case of acceptance of the paper.

2   Preliminaries

This section presents the notation used in the paper and reviews the formal framework of the iocos theory introduced in [12,16].

We consider two disjoint finite sets of actions: inputs I, initiated by the environment and annotated with a question mark, $a?, b?, c? \in I$; and outputs O, initiated by the system, and annotated with an exclamation mark, $o!, u!, t! \in O$. In many cases we want to name actions in a general sense, inputs and outputs indistinctly. We will consider the set $L = I \cup O$ and we will omit the exclamation or question marks when naming generic actions, $x, y, z \in L$.

A state with no output actions cannot autonomously proceed, such a state is called *quiescent*. Quiescence is an essential component of the ioco theory. For the sake of simplicity and without lost of generality (see for instance [25,24]), we directly introduce the event of quiescence as a special action denoted by $\delta! \in O$ into the definition of our models.

Definition 1. A *labelled transition system with inputs and outputs* is a 4-tuple $(S, I, O, \rightarrow)$ such that

- S is a set of states or behaviours.
- I and O are disjoint sets of input and output actions respectively. Output action include the quiescence symbol $\delta! \in O$. We define $L = I \cup O$.
- $\rightarrow \subseteq S \times L \times S$. As usual we write $p \xrightarrow{x} q$ instead of $(p, x, q) \in \rightarrow$ and $p \xrightarrow{x}$, for $x \in L$, if there exists $q \in S$ such that $p \xrightarrow{x} q$. Analogously, we will write $p \xrightarrow{x} \!\!\!\!/\,$, for $x \in L$, if there is no q such that $p \xrightarrow{x} q$.
  In order to allow only coherent quiescent systems the set of transitions $\rightarrow$ should also satisfy:
  - if $p \xrightarrow{\delta!} p'$ then $p = p'$. A quiescent transition is always reflexive.
  - if $p \xrightarrow{o!} \!\!\!\!/\,$ for any $o! \in O \backslash \{\delta!\}$, then $p \xrightarrow{\delta!} p$. A state with no (regular) outputs is quiescent.
  - if there is $o! \in O \backslash \{\delta!\}$ such that $p \xrightarrow{o!}$, then $p \xrightarrow{\delta!} \!\!\!\!/\,$. A quiescent state performs no other output action.
- A system is *input-enabled* if at any $s \in S$ for every $a? \in I$ we have $s \xrightarrow{a?}$.   □

We denote the set of labelled transition systems with inputs and outputs just as *LTS*. In general we use $p, q, p', q' \dots$ for states or behaviours, but also i, i', s and s' when we want to emphasise the concrete role of a behaviours as implementation or specification. We consider implementations and specifications, or, more generally, behaviours under study, as states of the same *LTS*.

A trace is a finite sequence of symbols of L. We will normally use the symbol σ to denote traces, that is, $\sigma \in L^*$. The empty trace is denoted by ϵ and we juxtapose, $\sigma_1\sigma_2$, to indicate concatenation of traces. The transition relation of labelled transition systems can naturally be extended using traces instead of single actions, $p \xrightarrow{\sigma} q$. Next we introduce some definitions and notation frequently used in the paper.

Definition 2. Let $(S, I, O, \rightarrow) \in LTS$, and $p \in S$, we define:

1. p after $\sigma = \{p' \mid p' \in S, p \xrightarrow{\sigma} p'\}$, the set of states after the trace σ.
2. $\mathsf{outs}(p) = \{o! \mid o! \in O, p \xrightarrow{o!}\}$, the outputs of a state p (it may include $\delta!$).
3. $\mathsf{ins}(p) = \{a? \mid a? \in I, p \xrightarrow{a?}\}$, the set of inputs of a state p. □

A behaviour is deterministic when for any $x \in L$, if $p \xrightarrow{x} p_1$ and $p \xrightarrow{x} p_2$ then $p_1 = p_2$; or equivalently the set p after σ is always empty or a singleton. While some models prevent non determinism we assume and allow all kinds of non-deterministic behaviour both in specifications and implementations.

Next we recall the simulation-based formal definition of iocos.

Definition 3. Let $(S, I, O, \rightarrow) \in LTS$, we say that a relation $R \subseteq S \times S$ is a iocos-relation if and only if for any $(p, q) \in R$ the following conditions hold:

1. $\mathsf{ins}(q) \subseteq \mathsf{ins}(p)$
2. $\forall a? \in \mathsf{ins}(q)$ if $p \xrightarrow{a?} p'$ then $\exists q' \in S$ such that $q \xrightarrow{a?} q' \wedge (p', q') \in R$.
3. $\forall o! \in \mathsf{outs}(p)$ if $p \xrightarrow{o!} p'$ then $\exists q' \in S$ such that $q \xrightarrow{o!} q' \wedge (p', q') \in R$.

We define the *input-output conformance simulation* (iocos) as the union of all iocos-relations (the biggest iocos-relation). □

Additional details on iocos rationale and examples appear in [12], where it is also proved that iocos is a strictly finer relation than ioco.

Theorem 1. [12] Let $(S, I, O, \rightarrow) \in LTS$; then iocos $\subseteq$ ioco. That is, for any $p, q \in S$, whenever we have p iocos q it is also true that p ioco q. □

3   An Online Testing Algorithm for **iocos**

The main goal of this section is to prove iocos as a suitable conformance relation to be used in online testing. As usual, the online testing algorithm merges test generation and execution into a single interactive process. In order to understand the notation and some ideas and key concepts behind Algorithm 1, next we recall the iocos theory of testing: test definition and test execution.

Definition 4. A *test* is a syntactical term defined by the following BNF:

$$T = \textbf{✗} \mid \textbf{✓} \mid T_1 \oplus T_2 \mid T_1 + T_2 \mid x; T \qquad \text{where } x \in L$$

We denote the set of tests as $\mathcal{T}$. □

As usual in MBT, the environments we want to model should be able to respond at any moment to any possible output of the implementation under test. That is, tests like $a?; T_{a?}$ will not be accepted as *valid* tests, but should be completed into tests like $a?; T_{a?} + \sum_{o! \in O} o!; T_{o!}$. For the sake of simplicity we use $\sum_{i \in \{1,...,n\}} T_i$ as a shortcut for $T_1 + \cdots + T_n$.

Particularly interesting is that we consider two kind of choices in the tests: the one corresponding to the $+$ operator, with conjunctive semantics, and the $\oplus$ operator with a disjunctive meaning. To define how tests interacts with behaviours and what is the result of the execution of that experiment, we follow Abramsky's ideas in [1] and use a predicate to define the outcomes of the interaction between a test and the behaviour or implementation being tested.

Definition 5. Let $(S, I, O, \rightarrow) \in LTS$, $s \in S$, $a? \in I$, and $o! \in O$, we inductively define the predicate pass $\subseteq S \times \mathcal{T}$ as follows:

$$
\begin{aligned}
&s \text{ pass } \boldsymbol{\mathsf{X}} = \mathit{false} \\
&s \text{ pass } \boldsymbol{\checkmark} = \mathit{true} \\
&s \text{ pass } o!; T_{o!} = \begin{cases} \mathit{true} & \text{if } o! \notin \text{outs}(s) \\ \bigwedge \{s' \text{ pass } T_{o!} | s \xrightarrow{o!} s'\} & \text{otherwise} \end{cases} \\
&s \text{ pass } a?; T_{a?} = \begin{cases} \mathit{false} & \text{if } a? \notin \text{ins}(s) \\ \bigwedge \{s' \text{ pass } T_{a?} | s \xrightarrow{a?} s'\} & \text{otherwise} \end{cases} \\
&s \text{ pass } T_1 + T_2 = s \text{ pass } T_1 \wedge s \text{ pass } T_2 \\
&s \text{ pass } T_1 \oplus T_2 = s \text{ pass } T_1 \vee s \text{ pass } T_2
\end{aligned}
$$

□

For the sake of convenience the pass predicate is inductively defined over the whole set of tests, with a simpler structural formulation, while at the end we will only be interested in valid tests.

In [12] we defined an algorithm (Definition 6 below) that starting from a given specification s produced a test suite $\mathcal{T}(s)$ of valid tests that characterised the specification with respect to the iocos conformance relation as stated in Theorem 2 below.

Definition 6. Let $(S, I, O, \rightarrow) \in LTS$ and $p \in S$. We denote with $\mathcal{T}(p)$ the set of valid tests from p by applying a finite number of recursive applications of one of the following non-deterministic choices:

1. $T = \boldsymbol{\checkmark} \in \mathcal{T}(p)$.
2. If $a? \in \text{ins}(p)$, then $T \in \mathcal{T}(p)$ where

$$
T = a?; \bigoplus \{T_{p_{a?}} \mid p \xrightarrow{a?} p_{a?}\} + \sum_{\substack{o! \in \text{outs}(p)}} o!; \bigoplus \{T_{p_{o!}} \mid p \xrightarrow{o!} p_{o!}\} + \sum_{\substack{o! \in O \\ o! \notin \text{outs}(p)}} o!; \boldsymbol{\mathsf{X}}
$$

3. If $\text{ins}(p) = \varnothing$ then $T \in \mathcal{T}(p)$ where

$$
T = \sum_{\substack{o! \in \text{outs}(p)}} o!; \bigoplus \{T_{p_{o!}} \mid p \xrightarrow{o!} p_{o!}\} + \sum_{\substack{o! \in O \\ o! \notin \text{outs}(p)}} o!; \boldsymbol{\mathsf{X}}
$$

In all cases the tests T_p are chosen non-deterministically from the set $\mathcal{T}(p)$, $T_\delta(p) = \checkmark$ if $p \xrightarrow{\delta!}$, and $T_{\delta!}(p) = \textbf{\textit{X}}$ otherwise. $\square$

Theorem 2. [12](***Completeness***) Let $(S, I, O, \rightarrow) \in LTS$ and $p, q \in S$, $T \in \mathcal{T}(p)$: q pass T iff q iocos p. $\square$

Online Algorithm. Offline generation of test leads to a massive test suite.[2] This is not surprising given that the test suite should be able to prove and disprove the conformance with any *possible* implementation. Online testing, on the contrary, considers a concrete implementation under test (IUT) and, therefore, the testing process can be guided by the mutual interaction.

The online testing algorithm for iocos is defined in Algorithm 1. This algorithm somehow merges the test generation and execution (Definition 5 and 6), and it considers only the necessary continuations by taking into account the current state of the specification and the last response from the implementation.

Algorithm 1 starts with a specification, an IUT, and a desired number of iterations (parameters s, IUT and $maxIter$ in function TE). The testing process will continue until a $\textbf{\textit{X}}$ verdict is found, indicating IUT does not conform s, or until the number of iterations has been reached without a faulty behaviour found in IUT.

According to Definition 5 the testing process will yield a $\textbf{\textit{X}}$ verdict on these cases: a mandatory input is rejected by IUT or an unexpected output by IUT is registered by the tester. In Algorithm 1, the first situation is solved in the first conditional inside the first **case** statements in function TE_{REC} (lines 16 and 17). Let us note that to check the enabled actions in IUT (line 16), is equivalent to check condition 1 in Definition 3 (iocos).

Otherwise, if the action that the test chooses to offer is actually enabled in the IUT, the stimulus is sent to the implementation (line 18) and then condition 2 in Definition 3 (iocos) should be tested: at least one of the descendant tests must be passed by the current state of the implementation, otherwise the final return statement outside the loop will propagate the $\textbf{\textit{X}}$ verdict. The *copy* clause (line 19) —theoretically essential, see [1,21]— is used to check every descendant test against the same state of the implementation. For software artifacts, and even embedded systems that can be easily replicated, this is indeed a feasible operation.

In a similar way, if we focus on output actions, conditional in lines 28 and 29 detects unexpected outputs from the implementation. Otherwise, if an output received from the IUT is acceptable, the algorithm has to proceed and check condition 3 in Definition 3 (iocos) as described previously.

Algorithm 1 is non-deterministic and the three cases in the **choice** statement (line 13) are arbitrarily chosen in every run of the function TE_{REC}. The *reset* case introduces the possibility of breadth exploration of the IUT, while the other two choices produce a (one step) deep exploration.

---

[2] Of course, there is a very interesting line of research in MBT that tries to reduce the size of the test suite while keeping a *good* coverage.

Algorithm 1. Online Testing Algorithm for iocos

1: **function** TE($s, iut, maxIter$)
2:     $continue \leftarrow \checkmark$
3:     $numIter \leftarrow maxIter$
4:     **while** $numIter > 0 \wedge continue == \checkmark$ **do**
5:         $continue, numIter \leftarrow TE\_REC(s, iut, numIter)$
6:         **if** $continue == \checkmark$ **then**
7:             reset iut
8:     **return** $continue$
9: **function** TE$_{REC}$($s, iut, numIter$)
10:     **if** $numIter = 0$ **then**
11:         **return** $\checkmark, numIter$
12:     **else**
13:         **choice**
14:             **case** *action* **do**   ▷ Offers an input to the implementation
15:                 choice $a \in ins(s)$
16:                 **if** $a?$ is not enabled in iut **then**
17:                     **return** $\checkmark\!\!\!\!\times, numIter$
18:                 send $a?$ to iut
19:                 $iut_0 \leftarrow copy(iut)$
20:                 **for** $s' \in s$ after $a?$ **do**
21:                     $iut \leftarrow copy(iut_0)$
22:                     $continue, numIter \leftarrow$ TE$_{REC}(s', iut, numIter - 1)$
23:                     **if** $continue == \checkmark$ **then**
24:                         **return** $\checkmark, numIter$
25:                 **return** $\times, numIter$
26:             **case** *wait* **do**   ▷ Waits for an output from the implementation
27:                 wait $o!$ from iut
28:                 **if** s after $o! = \varnothing$ **then**
29:                     **return** $\times, T$
30:                 $iut_0 \leftarrow copy(iut)$
31:                 **for** $s' \in s$ after $o!$ **do**
32:                     $iut \leftarrow copy(iut_0)$
33:                     $continue, numIter \leftarrow$ TE$_{REC}(s', iut, numIter - 1)$
34:                     **if** $continue == \checkmark$ **then**
35:                         **return** $\checkmark, numIter$
36:                 **return** $\times, numIter$
37:             **case** *reset* **do**   ▷ Resets implementation and restart
38:                 **return** $\checkmark, maxIter$
39:

There are in the literature of MBT two essential works we can relate Algorithm 1 with. In [9] de Vries and Tretmans presented an online algorithm for ioco that is non-deterministic and even termination is one of the non-deterministic choices. In [15] Larsen et al. describe an online algorithm for an ioco-based conformance relation extended with real time and considering a concrete environment, namely rtioco$_e$. Algorithm 1 is more similar in form to that on [15] and share with it the *reset* clause and the explicit use of the number of iterations. We do not consider explicit environments but the most general possible environment.[3] As in [9,15], quiescence detection can be implemented with a timeout.

In [29] you can find a practical online testing algorithm that is implemented in the MBT tool developed at Microsoft Research called Spec Explorer. The framework and the approach are somehow different: they use interface automaton as the specification model and assume the implementation to be in the domain of the specifications. In this work soundness and completeness are not even mentioned.

Soundness and Completeness. The rest of this section is devoted to prove that Algorithm 1 is indeed sound and complete.

In [9] correctness of the online algorithm for ioco is stated under fairness assumptions (*weather conditions* [19]) in the non-deterministic choices. In [15] online algorithm for rtioco$_e$ is proved to be sound and complete assuming the classic *test hypothesis*,[4] fairness in the randomisation of algorithm choices, and deterministic IUT.

In our model, we allow both implementations and specifications to behave non-deterministically and, as usual, we assume fairness in the non-deterministic choices and the *test hypothesis* ([9,15]). Test hypothesis assumes that any IUT can be modelled in the domain of *LTS*.

Theorem 3. Let $(S, I, O, \rightarrow)$ be a *LTS*, let $i, s \in S$, and $n \in \mathbb{N}$. If the function call $\mathrm{TE}(s, i, n)$ in Algorithm 1 returns a ✗, then i iocos̸ s.

Proof. The proof proceed by induction on the parameter n of $\mathrm{TE}(s, i, n)$, following the ideas commented in the algorithm explanation.   □

Asserting completeness implies that, for any faulty implementation of a given specification s, the online testing process in Algorithm 1 should eventually yield a ✗ result, that is, the algorithm should drive the computation through a test passed by the specification and failed by the implementation. Let us note that a key point to prove the completeness is to assure that all states in the specification and implementation should be inspected. This is where the fairness requirement is needed: every infinitely often eligible action is eventually executed. To ensure this possibility one of the choices of the algorithm is to reset the IUT and to

---

[3] To introduce environments might lead to a reduction of the search-space because this additional knowledge can be used to further restrict the testing process.

[4] The behaviour of IUT can be described in the model domain. Only the existence is assumed, not a concrete and known instance.

restart the algorithm (lines 37 and 38). Moreover, assuming the fairness hypothesis also implies that the number of times required to ensure that all states have been checked is not known a priori. So the number of iterations appearing in Proposition 1 and Theorem 1 cannot be determined at the beginning of the execution.

Proposition 1. Let $(S, I, O, \rightarrow)$ be a LTS, let $i, s \in S$, and let $T \in \mathcal{T}(s)$ be a test such that s pass T and i pa$\cancel{ss}$ T. Then there exist $n, n' \in \mathbb{N}$ such that $\mathrm{TE_{REC}}(s, i, n)$ returns $\cancel{\checkmark}$, n'.

Proof. We make the proof by induction on the depth of T. The case base is when $T = \checkmark$ that is trivial since i pass T. According to Definition 6, there are two cases. We are going to consider the test

$$T = a?; \bigoplus \{T_{s_{a?}} \mid s \xrightarrow{a?} s_{a?}\} + \sum_{o! \in \mathsf{outs}(s)} o!; \bigoplus \{T_{s_{o!}} \mid s \xrightarrow{o!} s_{o!}\} + \sum_{\substack{o! \in O \\ o! \notin \mathsf{outs}(s)}} o!; \cancel{\checkmark}$$

The other case is simpler than this one. Since i pa$\cancel{ss}$$T$, there are three possibilities to make the test fail:

1. i pa$\cancel{ss}$ $a?; \bigoplus \{T_{s_{a?}} \mid s \xrightarrow{a?} s_{a?}\}$. Since we are assuming the *fairness hypothesis*, by choosing an arbitrary high n the choice in line 15 of the algorithm will eventually choose the action $a?$. If $a?$ is not enabled in i, then the algorithm returns $\cancel{\checkmark}$ in line 17. Otherwise the algorithm sends $a?$ to the implementation. Again, by the *fairness hypothesis* the implementation, eventually will go to a state i' such that i' pa$\cancel{ss}$ $\bigoplus \{T_{s_{a?}} \mid s \xrightarrow{a?} s_{a?}\}$. Let us name $n_{i'}$ the number of iterations needed to reach this state. On the other hand, since s pass T, s' pass $\bigoplus \{T_{s_{a?}} \mid s \xrightarrow{a?} s_{a?}\}$ for any $s' \in s$ after $a?$. So by induction hypothesis for any $s' \in s$ after $a?$ there exist $n_{s'} \in \mathbb{N}$ such that $\mathrm{TE_{REC}}(s', i, n_{s'})$ returns $\cancel{\checkmark}$. So by choosing $n_0 \geq= n_{i'} + \sum_{s' \in s \text{after} a?} n_{s'}$, there exists n' such that the $\mathrm{TE_{REC}}(s, i, n_0)$ returns $\cancel{\checkmark}$, n'.

2. i pa$\cancel{ss}$ $\sum_{o! \in \mathsf{outs}(s)} o!; \bigoplus \{T_{s_{o!}} \mid s \xrightarrow{o!} s_{o!}\}$. In this case there is $o! \in \mathsf{outs}(s)$ such that i produces output $o!$ and goes to an state i' such that i pa$\cancel{ss}$$\bigoplus \{T_{s_{o!}} \mid s \xrightarrow{o!} s_{o!}\}$. By the *fairness hypothesis* the implementation will eventually produce that output and will go to state i'. Let us name $n_{i'}$ the number of iterations needed to reach this state. On the other hand, s' pass $\bigoplus \{T_{s_{o!}} \mid s \xrightarrow{o!} s_{o!}\}$ for any $s' \in s$ after $o!$. So by induction hypothesis for any $s' \in s$ after $o!$ there exist $n_{s'} \in \mathbb{N}$ such that $\mathrm{TE_{REC}}(s', i, n_{s'})$ returns $\cancel{\checkmark}$. So by choosing $n_0 \geq= n_{i'} + \sum_{s' \in s \text{after} o!} n_{s'}$, there exists n' such that the $\mathrm{TE_{REC}}(s, i, n_0)$ returns $\cancel{\checkmark}$, n'.

3. i pa$\cancel{ss}$$\sum_{\substack{o! \in O \\ o! \notin \mathsf{outs}(s)}} o!; \cancel{\checkmark}$. In this case there is $o! \in O$ such that i produces output $o!$. By the *fairness hypothesis* the implementation will produce this output an the algorithm will return $\cancel{\checkmark}$ in line 29.   □

Since the main function of the algorithm just makes calls to the recursive algorithm as a corollary we get the following result:

Theorem 4. Let $(S, I, O, \rightarrow)$ be a *LTS*, let $i, s \in S$. If $i \text{ iocos̲ } s$ then there exist $n \in \mathbb{N}$ such that the function call $\text{TE}(s, i, n)$ in Algorithm 1 returns ✗. □

4 iocos̲ as a Generalised Coarsest Partition Problem

Milner in [18] introduced the preorder relation called simulation. Simulation equivalence strongly preserves ACTL*, and also strongly preserves LTL and ACTL as sublogics of ACTL* [6]. Both ACTL and LTL are widely used for model checking in practice.

Simulation is a close relative of the well known bisimulation equivalence [20]. Bisimulation equivalence can be fast computed by reducing it to the problem of determining the coarsest partition of a set stable with respect to a given relation [13]. An equivalent result for computing simulation as a generalised coarsest partition problem (GCPP) was given in [11] and corrected in [28]. This algorithm keeps a very good time complexity while its space complexity can be considered minimal.

Although iocos̲ definition is simulation-like, it has particularities inherited from the classic requirements for the conformance relations when dealing with inputs and outputs, and even the use of input-output actions is not symmetric in the definition. Therefore, the applicability of simulation algorithms to compute iocos̲is not straightforward.

We will show in this section that fortunately we can compute iocos̲ by using any algorithm that solves the GCPP. To achieve this goal, first we will show how to transform the LTS into graphs and partitions as defined in [11,28]. Then we will define the relation g-iocos̲ (graph-iocos̲) in the transformed LTS that will be equivalent to iocos̲. Finally, we will formally prove that the transformed LTS holds the conditions of the GCPP.

4.1 Transforming an LTS into a Graph

The GCPP in [11] is defined in terms of graphs. These graphs have no labels in the edges. The objective is to transform an *LTS* into a graph without actions and without loosing information. The idea to achieve this is to *encode* the action associated to a transition into the states of the graph. So the states of the associated graph of an *LTS* will be pairs: the first component of the pair refers to a state of the *LTS* whereas the second component is the action needed to reach this state.

One of the details that we have to deal with to transform iocos̲ into a simulation is that in Definition 3 (iocos̲) the implementation is allowed to introduce unspecified behaviour. We do not need to take into account those states reached by implementation when input actions are not present in the specification. To overcome this situation, in the transformed system, we need to represent these states by adding a sort of new *magic state*, that we denote by the symbol ∗. Such a state has the next property: *every possible implementation* will fulfil it. Moreover, in the transformation we will embed the transition action symbol into the state itself. Exceptionally, and just for the sake of uniformity, a new action symbol $(\cdot)$ is used for states with no incoming transitions.

Definition 7. Let $\mathcal{L} = (S, I, O, \rightarrow)$ be a labelled transition system. We define its transformed graph as $\mathbb{T}(\mathcal{L}) = (N, \Rightarrow)$ where $N = (S \cup \{*\}) \times (L \cup \{\cdot\})$ and $\Rightarrow$ is defined by the following rules.

$$\frac{s \xrightarrow{y} s'}{(s, x) \Rightarrow (s', y)}, \quad \frac{s \xrightarrow{a?}}{(s, x) \Rightarrow (*, a?)}, \quad \frac{}{(*, x) \Rightarrow (*, y)}, \quad \frac{s, s' \in S}{x, y \in L \cup \{\cdot\}, \ a? \in I}$$

The nodes of N will be denoted by the letters n, n_1, n_2, etc. Since these nodes come from states of the original labelled transition system, we annotate the arcs of the graph with the action of the target node for readability reasons. In this way will write $n_1 \xRightarrow{x} n_2$ whenever $n_1 \Rightarrow n_2$ and there is $s_2 \in S$ such that $n_2 = (s_2, x)$.

Following the same rationale we adapt the definition of the function ins: $\mathsf{ins}(*, x) = \varnothing$ and $\mathsf{ins}(s, x) = \mathsf{ins}(s)$ if $s \in S$. □

Definition 8. Let $(N, \Rightarrow)$ be the transformed graph of an $\mathcal{L} \in LTS$, a relation $R \subseteq N \times N$ is g-iocos simulation iff for any $n_1, n_2 \in N$, $(n_1, n_2) \in R$ the following conditions hold:

1. $n_1 = (s_1, x)$, $n_2 = (s_2, y)$ and $x = y$.
2. $\mathsf{ins}(n_2) \subseteq \mathsf{ins}(n_1)$
3. for all $a \in L$, if $n_1 \xRightarrow{a} n_1'$ then exists n_2' such that $n_2 \xRightarrow{a} n_2'$ and $n_1' R n_2'$.

For $n_1, n_2 \in N$, we say that n_1 g-iocos n_2 if there exists a g-iocos simulation R such that $(n_1, n_2) \in R$. □

At a first glance, g-iocos is defined as a *kind* of ready simulation preorder [4]. Next, we show that computing g-iocos over graphs is equivalent to compute iocos on LTS. Proposition 2 describes how to transform a concrete iocos-simulation into a g-iocos-simulation, while Proposition 3 presents the reciprocal transformation. Finally, Theorem 5 is a corollary of the previous results showing iocos and g-iocos to be two different formulations for the same semantics in two different domains.

Proposition 2. Let $\mathcal{L} = (S, I, O, \rightarrow)$, let $\mathbb{T}(\mathcal{L}) = (N, \Rightarrow)$ be its transformed graph, let R be iocos relation $R \subseteq S \times S$, and let $R' \subseteq N \times N$ defined as

$$R' = \{((i, a), (s, a)|(i, s) \in R, \forall a \in L \cup \{\cdot\}\} \cup \{(i, a)(*, a)| \ a \in L \cup \{\cdot\}, i \in S \cup \{*\}\}$$

Then R' is a g-iocos simulation.

Proof. Let us take $(n_1, n_2) \in R'$ and check that R' holds the statements of Definition 8.

$n_2 = (*, a)$. i.e., we are in the second subset of R'. Trivially we have $\mathsf{ins}(n_1) \supseteq \varnothing = \mathsf{ins}(n_2)$ (statement 2 of Definition 8). As $(*, x) \Rightarrow (*, y)$ for any $x, y \in L$ and $(n_1', (*, a)) \in R'$ for any n_1', then statement 3 of Definition 8 holds.

$n_1 = (*, a)$. As R' is defined, $n_2 = (*, a)$, and it is solved as in the previous case. $n_1 \neq (*, a)$ **and** $n_2 \neq (*, a)$. Let us assume that $n_1 = (i, a)$ and $n_2 = (s, a)$. Since R is an iocos simulation, we obtain $\mathsf{ins}(n_1) = \mathsf{ins}((i, a)) = \mathsf{ins}(i) \supseteq \mathsf{ins}(s) = \mathsf{ins}((s, a)) = \mathsf{ins}(n_2)$ (statement 2 of Definition 8).

Now let us take action $x \in L$ such that $n_1 \xLongrightarrow{x} n_1'$. If $x \in O$ then we obtain that there exist i' such that $i \xrightarrow{x} i'$ and $n_1' = (i', x)$. Since R is a iocos simulation, then there exists s' such that $s \xrightarrow{a} s'$ and $(s, s') \in R$. Again, by the construction of the transitions $n_2 = (s, a) \xLongrightarrow{x} (s', x) = n_2'$ and $(n_1', n_2') \in R'$ by definition of R'.

If $x \in I$ there are two possibilities: either $x \notin \mathsf{ins}(i)$ or $x \in \mathsf{ins}(i)$. In the first case we have $(i, a) \xrightarrow{x} (*, a) = n_1'$ by the way transitions are defined. Since R is an iocos simulation $\mathsf{ins}(s) \subseteq \mathsf{ins}(i)$ and therefore $x \notin \mathsf{ins}(s)$. Then $n_2 = (s, a) \xLongrightarrow{x} (*, x) = n_2'$ and $(n_1', n_2') \in R'$. In the second case there exists i' such that $i \xrightarrow{x} i'$. If $x \in \mathsf{ins}(s)$, since R is an iocos simulation there exists s' such that $s \xrightarrow{x} s'$ and and $(s, s') \in R$. By the construction of the transitions $n_2 = (s, a) \xLongrightarrow{x} (s', x) = n_2'$ and $(n_1', n_2') \in R'$ by definition of R'. If $x \notin \mathsf{ins}(s)$, then $(s, a) \xrightarrow{x} (*, x) = n_2'$. Then $(n_1', n_2') \in R'$ by definition of R' $\qquad\square$

Proposition 3. Let $\mathcal{L} = (S, I, O, \to)$ be a labelled transition system, let $\mathbb{T}(\mathcal{L}) = (N, \Rightarrow)$ be its transformed graph, let $R' \subseteq N \times N$ be a g-iocos relation, and let $R \subseteq S \times S$ defined as $R = \{(i, s) | \exists a \in L \cup \{\cdot\}.\ ((i, a), (s, a)) \in R' \wedge i, s \in S\}$. Then R is a iocos simulation.

Proof. Let $(i, s) \in R$. By construction of R, there exists $a \in L$ and $n_1 = (i, a)$ and $n_2 = (s, a)$ such that $(n_1, n_2) \in R'$. Since R' is a g-iocos simulation, we have $\mathsf{ins}(i) = \mathsf{ins}((i, a)) = \mathsf{ins}(n_1) \supseteq \mathsf{ins}(n_2) = \mathsf{ins}((s, a)) = \mathsf{ins}(s)$ according to the statement 1 of the definition of iocos. Now let us check the other two conditions:

- Let us consider $b? \in \mathsf{ins}(s)$ such $i \xrightarrow{b?} i'$, so $(i, a) \xLongrightarrow{b?} (i', b?)$. Since R' is a g-iocos simulation there exists $n_2' = (s', b?)$ such that $n_2 \xLongrightarrow{b?} n_2$. Since $b? \in \mathsf{ins}(s)$, $s' \neq *$, so $s' \in S$. Finally, by definition of, R we obtain $(i', s') \in R$.
- The case when $o! \in \mathsf{outs}(i)$ and $i \xrightarrow{o!} i'$ is similar to the previous one, but in this case $s' \neq *$ because $o! \notin I$. $\qquad\square$

Finally, we obtain the theorem that relates iocos and g-iocos. This theorem is a corollary of the previous Proposition 2 and 3.

Theorem 5. Let $\mathcal{L} = (S, I, O, \to)$ be a labelled transition system and $\mathbb{T}(\mathcal{L}) = (N, \Rightarrow)$ its transformed graph. Then, for any $s_1, s_2 \in S$, we have $(s_1, s_2) \in \mathsf{iocos}$ if and only if $((s_1, x), (s_2, x)) \in \mathsf{g\text{-}iocos}\ \forall x \in L$. $\qquad\square$

4.2   g-iocos as a GCPP Problem

To conclude this section we will show that g-iocos can be seen as an instance of the GCPP. In order to make the paper self-contained, we are going to reproduce in condensed form definitions from [11].

Definition 9. Let $\mathcal{L} = (S, I, O, \rightarrow)$ be a labelled transition system and $\mathbb{T}(\mathcal{L}) = (N, \Rightarrow)$ its transformed graph.

1. A *partition pair* is a tuple $\langle \mathcal{S}, \precsim \rangle$ such that $\mathcal{S} = \{\alpha, \beta, \dots\}$ is a partition of N and $\precsim$ is a reflexive and acyclic relation on $\mathcal{S}$.
2. Let $\mathcal{S}$ be a partition and let $n \in N$, we write $[n]_{\mathcal{S}}$ as the unique element of $\mathcal{S}$ that contains n.
3. Let $\alpha, \beta \in \mathcal{S}$, we write $\alpha \Rightarrow_{\exists} \beta$ iff $\exists a \in \alpha$ such that $a \Rightarrow g$ for some $b \in \beta$. We write $\alpha \Rightarrow_{\forall} \beta$ iff $\forall a \in \alpha$ we have $a \Rightarrow b$ for some $b \in \beta$.
4. We say that $\langle \mathcal{S}, \precsim \rangle$ is *stable* with respect to $\Rightarrow$ iff

$$\forall \alpha, \beta, \gamma \in \mathcal{S} \quad \text{if } (\alpha, \beta) \in \precsim \wedge \alpha \Rightarrow_{\exists} \gamma \text{ then } \exists \epsilon \in \mathcal{S} : \ (\gamma, \epsilon) \in \precsim \wedge \beta \Rightarrow_{\forall} \epsilon$$

5. Let $\langle S_1, \precsim_1 \rangle$ and $\langle S_2, \precsim_2 \rangle$ be partition pairs. We say that $\langle S_1, \precsim_1 \rangle$ is a refinement of $\langle S_2, \precsim_2 \rangle$, written $\langle S_1, \precsim_1 \rangle \sqsubseteq \langle S_2, \precsim_2 \rangle$, if S_1 is finer than S_2, i.e., $(\forall \alpha \in S_1 \exists \alpha' \in S_2 : \ \alpha \subseteq \alpha')$ and $\precsim_1 \subseteq \precsim_2 (S_1)$ where $\precsim_2 (S_1)$ is the induced relation on S_1 by $\precsim_2$: $(\alpha, \beta) \in \precsim_2 (S_1)$ iff there exist $\alpha', \beta' \in S_2$ such that $\alpha \subseteq \alpha'$, $\beta \subseteq \beta'$ and $(\alpha', \beta') \in \precsim_2$.
6. Let us consider a pair $\langle S, \precsim \rangle$, the Generalised Coarsest Partition Problem (GCPP) for $\langle S, \precsim \rangle$ consists in finding a partition pair $\langle S_0, \precsim_0 \rangle$ such that: a) $\langle S_0, \precsim_0 \rangle \sqsubseteq \langle S \precsim \rangle$, b) $\langle S_0, \precsim_0 \rangle$ is stable respect to $\Rightarrow$, and c) $\langle S_0, \precsim_0 \rangle$ is maximal fitting a) and b). □

Now we are ready to set up our key concepts in order to embed iocos computation into GCPP problem via a g-iocos reduction.

Definition 10. Let $\mathcal{L} = (S, I, O, \rightarrow)$ be a labelled transition system and $\mathbb{T}(\mathcal{L}) = (N, \Rightarrow)$ its transformed graph. We write $\equiv_{\text{g-iocos}}$ for the kernel of g-iocos, that is $(a, b) \in \equiv_{\text{g-iocos}}$ iff $(a, b) \in$ g-iocos and $(b, a) \in$ g-iocos.

Since $\equiv_{\text{g-iocos}}$ is an equivalence relation, it induces the partition $N/ \equiv_{\text{g-iocos}}$. In this partition we can define $\precsim_{\text{g-iocos}}$ as the natural relation induced by g-iocos in $N/ \equiv_{\text{g-iocos}}$, namely, for $n_1, n_2 \in N$, $([n_1]_{\text{g-iocos}}, [n_2]_{\text{g-iocos}}) \in \precsim_{\text{g-iocos}}$ iff $(n_1, n_2) \in$ g-iocos. □

Let us note, that $\precsim_{\text{g-iocos}}$ is reflexive and acyclic in $N/ \equiv_{\text{g-iocos}}$, so $\langle N/ \equiv_{\text{g-iocos}}, \precsim_{\text{g-iocos}} \rangle$ is a partition pair. So, the rest of this section is devoted to prove that the partition $\langle N/ \equiv_{\text{g-iocos}}, \precsim_{\text{g-iocos}} \rangle$ can be solved with any algorithm that solves the GCPP. In order to do it we need to define an initial partition pair $\langle \Omega, \preccurlyeq \rangle$ such that $\langle N/ \equiv_{\text{g-iocos}}, \precsim_{\text{g-iocos}} \rangle \sqsubseteq \langle \Omega, \preccurlyeq \rangle$.

Definition 11. Let $\mathcal{L} = (S, I, O, \rightarrow)$ be a labelled transition system and $\mathbb{T}(\mathcal{L}) = (N, \Rightarrow)$ its transformed graph.

- We define the partition $\Omega = \{\alpha_1, \alpha_2, \dots \alpha_n\} \subseteq \mathcal{P}(N)$ as follows: $(n_1, n_2) \in \alpha_i$ if and only if $n_1 = (s_1, x)$, $n_2 = (s_2, y)$, $\text{ins}(s_2) = \text{ins}(s_1)$ and $x = y$.
- We define the relation $\preccurlyeq \subseteq \Omega \times \Omega$ as $[n_1]_{\Omega} \preccurlyeq [n_2]_{\Omega}$ iff $n_1 = (s_1, x)$, $n_2 = (s_2, y)$, $\text{ins}(s_2) \subseteq \text{ins}(s_1)$ and $x = y$. □

Lemma 1. Let $\mathcal{L} = (S, I, O, \to)$ be a labelled transition system and its transformed graph $\mathbb{T}(\mathcal{L}) = (N, \Rightarrow)$. Then $\langle N/\equiv_{\text{g-iocos̲}}, \precsim_{\text{g-iocos̲}} \rangle \sqsubseteq \langle \Omega, \preccurlyeq \rangle$.

Proof. This lemma is immediate because of the definition of **g-iocos̲**-simulation, kernel $\equiv_{\text{g-iocos̲}}$ and the induced partition pair $\langle N/\equiv_{\text{g-iocos̲}}, \precsim_{\text{g-iocos̲}} \rangle$. $\square$

Lemma 2. Let $\mathcal{L} = (S, I, O, \to)$ be a labelled transition system and its transformed graph, $\mathbb{T}(\mathcal{L}) = (N, \Rightarrow)$, then the partition pair $\langle N/\equiv_{\text{g-iocos̲}}, \precsim_{\text{g-iocos̲}} \rangle$ is stable with respect to $\Rightarrow$.

Proof. Let us consider equivalence classes $[n_1]_{\text{g-iocos̲}}, [n_2]_{\text{g-iocos̲}}, \gamma \in N/\equiv_{\text{g-iocos̲}}$ such that $([n_1]_{\text{g-iocos̲}}, [n_2]_{\text{g-iocos̲}}) \in \precsim_{\text{g-iocos̲}}$ and $[n_1]_{\text{g-iocos̲}} \Rightarrow_\exists \gamma$. Then there exists $n_1' \in \gamma$ and $x \in L$ such that $n_1 \xrightarrow{x} n_1'$. As $(n_1, n_2) \in$ **g-iocos̲** there exists n_2' such that $n_2 \xRightarrow{x} n_2'$ and $([n_1']_{\text{g-iocos̲}}, [n_2']_{\text{g-iocos̲}}) \in \precsim_{\text{g-iocos̲}}$. Let us consider n_2' a *maximal* element with respect to **g-iocos̲**, i.e, for any n_i' such that $(n_1, n_i') \in$ **g-iocos̲** we have $(n_i', n_2') \in$ **g-iocos̲** .

Next we will prove that $[n_2] \Rightarrow_\forall [n_2']$. Let us consider $n_3 \in [n_2]$. Since they belong to the same $\equiv_{\text{g-iocos̲}}$ class, the equivalence kernel makes true $(n_2, n_3) \in$ **g-iocos̲** . Therefore there exists n_3' such that $n_3 \xRightarrow{x} n_3'$ and $(n_2', n_3') \in$ **g-iocos̲**. Again, $(n_3, n_2) \in$ **g-iocos̲**, there exists n_2'' such that $n_2 \xRightarrow{x} n_2''$ and $(n_3', n_2'') \in$ **g-iocos̲**. Since **g-iocos̲** is transitive we obtain $(n_2', n_2'') \in$ **g-iocos̲**. Since n_2' was a maximal element then $n_2' = n_2''$ and then $n_3' \in [n_2']$. $\square$

We also need to show that $\langle N/\equiv_{\text{g-iocos̲}}, \precsim_{\text{g-iocos̲}} \rangle$ is maximal with respect to the points a) and b) of the GCPP. In order to do it, first let us note that any partition pair $\langle S, \precsim \rangle$ induces a natural relation in N that we will denote by $\precsim (N)$.

Definition 12. Let $\mathcal{L} = (S, I, O, \to)$ be a labelled transition system and $\mathbb{T}(\mathcal{L}) = (N, \Rightarrow)$ its transformed graph, and let $\langle S, \precsim \rangle$ be a partition pair. We define the relation $\precsim (N) \subseteq N \times N$ as $(n_1, n_2) \in \precsim (N)$ iff $([n_1]_S, [n_2]_S) \in \precsim$. $\square$

Second, if $\langle S, \precsim \rangle$ satisfies the points a) and b) of the GCPP for the partition pair $\langle \Omega, \preccurlyeq \rangle$, then the following lemma states that $\precsim (N)$ is a **g-iocos̲**-simulation.

Lemma 3. Let $\mathcal{L} = (S, I, O, \to)$ be a labelled transition system and $\mathbb{T}(\mathcal{L}) = (N, \Rightarrow)$ its transformed graph, and let $\langle S, \precsim \rangle$ be a refinement of $\langle \Omega, \preccurlyeq \rangle$ such that is stable with respect to $\Rightarrow$. Then $\precsim (N)$ is a **g-iocos̲**-simulation.

Proof. Let us consider $(n_1, n_2) \in N(\precsim)$. Since $\langle S, \precsim \rangle$ is a refinement of $\langle \Omega, \preccurlyeq \rangle$, we obtain $([n_1]_\Omega, [n_2]_\Omega) \in \preccurlyeq$. Then n_1 has the form (s_1, x), and n_2 has the form (s_2, y) with $x = y$ and $\text{ins}(n_2) \subseteq \text{ins}(n_1)$, hence fulfilling 1 of Definition 8.

Now let us consider $x \in L$ and $n_1' \in N$ such that $n_1 \xRightarrow{x} n_1'$. By rewriting all those elements at *coarse level* in S we obtain $([n_1]_S, [n_2]_S) \in \precsim$ and $[n_1]_S \Rightarrow_\exists [n_1']_S$. Since $\langle S, \precsim \rangle$ is stable there exists $\delta \in S$ such that $[n_2]_S \Rightarrow_\forall \delta$ and $([n_1']_S, \delta) \in \precsim$. At *discrete level* that means there exists $n_2' \in \delta$ such that $n_2 \Rightarrow n_2'$. Since $\langle S, \precsim \rangle$ is a refinement of $\langle \Omega, \preccurlyeq \rangle$, we obtain $([n_1']_\Omega, [n_2']_\Omega) \in \preccurlyeq$. Since $n_1 \xRightarrow{x} n_1'$, then n_1' has the form (s_1', x) (see transformation rules in Definition 7). By the definition of Ω (Definition 11), then n_2' has also the form (s_2', x). Therefore $n_2 \xRightarrow{x} n_2'$. $\square$

Now Since g-iocos̲ is the maximal g-iocos̲-simulation, we obtain that $\precsim (N) \subseteq$ g-iocos̲. From this fact is easy to prove the following lemma.

Lemma 4. Let $G = (N, \Rightarrow)$ be the transformed graph of an *LTS* and let $\langle S, \precsim \rangle$ be a partition pair such that $\precsim (N)$ is a g-iocos̲-simulation. Then $\langle S, \precsim \rangle \sqsubseteq \langle N_{\equiv_{\text{g-iocos̲}}}, \precsim_{\text{g-iocos̲}} \rangle$.

Proof. First let us consider $\alpha \in S$ and $a, b \in \alpha$. Since $\precsim$ is reflexive we obtain $(\alpha, \alpha) \in \precsim$ and therefore $(a, b) \in \precsim (N)$ and $(b, a) \in \precsim (N)$. Now considering that $\precsim (N) \subseteq$ g-iocos̲ we obtain $(a, b) \in \equiv_{\text{g-iocos̲}}$. Therefore all elements of α are in the same equivalence class in $N/\equiv_{\text{g-iocos̲}}$, so S is a refinement of $N/\equiv_{\text{g-iocos̲}}$. Now let us consider $\alpha, \beta \in \precsim$, let us consider $a, b \in N$ such that $[a]_S = \alpha$ and $[b]_S = \beta$. Since $\precsim (N) \subseteq$ g-iocos̲, we obtain $(a, b) \in$ g-iocos̲ and $([a]_{\text{g-iocos̲}}, [b]_{\text{g-iocos̲}}) \in \precsim_{\text{g-iocos̲}}$. Since $[a]_S \subseteq [a]_{\text{g-iocos̲}}$ and $[b]_S \subseteq [b]_{\text{g-iocos̲}}$, we obtain $([a]_S, [b]_S) \in \precsim_{\text{g-iocos̲}} (S)$.   □

Finally, we obtain the main theorem of this section.

Theorem 6. Let $\mathcal{L} = (S, I, O, \rightarrow)$ be a labelled transition system and $\mathbb{T}(\mathcal{L}) = (N, \Rightarrow)$ its transformed graph, then $\langle N_{\equiv_{\text{g-iocos̲}}}, \precsim_{\text{g-iocos̲}} \rangle$ is the solution of the GCPP for the partition pair $\langle \Omega, \preccurlyeq \rangle$.

Proof. The points a) and b) of the GCPP follows from Lemmas 1, and 2. The maximality follows from Lemmas 3 and 4.   □

5   Conclusions and Future Work

In this paper we have defined an online algorithm that allows to check if a certain implementation iocos̲-conforms a given specification by interacting with it and without computing any a priori set of tests. Under fairly standard hypothesis —even weaker than in other models— we prove the algorithm to be sound and complete.

We plan to introduce test selection criteria and coverage in the iocos̲-theory. This technique is mainly used in offline testing but we think that implementations of the online algorithm we have presented can also benefit from them to further restrict the search tree.

Since iocos̲ is a branching semantics, it is essential in the online algorithm to make use of the *copy* clause (see for instance [1] for a more elaborated discussion). While this copy capability will exclude some systems to being tested with iocos̲ —essentially unique systems that cannot be replicated— for a vast number of applications, for instance to check software products, it could definitely be a feasible operation. The implementation of our online algorithm is currently under development using cluster computing techniques.

In this paper we have also proved that the conformance relation iocos̲, in spite of its particularities and asymmetry with input and output actions, can be solved with the GCPP. Actually, we are adapting the mCRL2 toolset [7], that implements one of the best solution to the GCPP [28], to compute iocos̲ and the minimised LTS for a give specification. This technique, frequently used in model checking, allows to reduce the size of the models and therefore the state explosion in any further testing process. Moreover, we plan to investigate the logic preservation properties of iocos that would allow to perform model checking of the intended model specifications and integrate MBT and model checking in the same theory.

Finally, once the ground model has proved to be useful, we plan to improve the expressiveness introducing a syntax language and integrating internal τ actions.

References

1. Abramsky, S.: Observational equivalence as a testing equivalence. Theoretical Computer Science 53(3), 225–241 (1987)
2. Aceto, L., de Frutos Escrig, D., Gregorio-Rodrguez, C., Ingolfsdottir, A.: Axiomatizing weak simulation semantics over BCCSP. Theoretical Computer Science (March 26, 2013) (to appear)
3. Belinfante, A.: Jtorx: A tool for on-line model-driven test derivation and execution. In: Esparza, J., Majumdar, R. (eds.) TACAS 2010. LNCS, vol. 6015, pp. 266–270. Springer, Heidelberg (2010)
4. Bloom, B., Istrail, S., Meyer, A.R.: Bisimulation can't be traced. Journal of the ACM 42(1), 232–268 (1995)
5. Bulychev, P., Chatain, T., David, A., Larsen, K.G.: Efficient on-the-fly algorithm for checking alternating timed simulation. In: Ouaknine, J., Vaandrager, F.W. (eds.) FORMATS 2009. LNCS, vol. 5813, pp. 73–87. Springer, Heidelberg (2009)
6. Bustan, D., Grumberg, O.: Simulation-based minimization. ACM Trans. Comput. Logic 4(2), 181–206 (2003)
7. Cranen, S., Groote, J.F., Keiren, J.J.A., Stappers, F.P.M., de Vink, E.P., Wesselink, W., Willemse, T.A.C.: An overview of the mcrl2 toolset and its recent advances. In: Piterman, N., Smolka, S.A. (eds.) TACAS 2013 (ETAPS 2013). LNCS, vol. 7795, pp. 199–213. Springer, Heidelberg (2013)
8. de Frutos-Escrig, D., Gregorio-Rodríguez, C., Palomino, M., Romero-Hernández, D.: Unifying the linear time-branching time spectrum of process semantics. Logical Methods in Computer Science 9(2:11), 1–74 (2013)
9. de Vries, R.G., Tretmans, J.: On-the-fly conformance testing using spin. STTT 2(4), 382–393 (2000)
10. Fábregas, I., de Frutos Escrig, D., Palomino, M.: Logics for contravariant simulations. In: Hatcliff, J., Zucca, E. (eds.) FMOODS 2010, Part II. LNCS, vol. 6117, pp. 224–231. Springer, Heidelberg (2010)
11. Gentilini, R., Piazza, C., Policriti, A.: From bisimulation to simulation: Coarsest partition problems. J. Autom. Reasoning 31(1), 73–103 (2003)
12. Gregorio-Rodríguez, C., Llana, L., Martínez-Torres, R.: Input-output conformance simulation (iocos) for model based testing. In: Beyer, D., Boreale, M. (eds.) FMOODS/FORTE 2013. LNCS, vol. 7892, pp. 114–129. Springer, Heidelberg (2013)
13. Kanellakis, P.C., Smolka, S.A.: CCS expressions, finite state processes, and three problems of equivalence. Information and Computation 86(1), 43–68 (1990)
14. Katoen, J.-P., Kemna, T., Zapreev, I., Jansen, D.N.: Bisimulation minimisation mostly speeds up probabilistic model checking. In: Grumberg, O., Huth, M. (eds.) TACAS 2007. LNCS, vol. 4424, pp. 87–101. Springer, Heidelberg (2007)

15. Larsen, K.G., Mikucionis, M., Nielsen, B.: Online testing of real-time systems using UPPAAL. In: Grabowski, J., Nielsen, B. (eds.) FATES 2004. LNCS, vol. 3395, pp. 79–94. Springer, Heidelberg (2005)
16. Llana, L., Martínez-Torres, R.: Ioco as a simulation. In: Counsell, S., Núñez, M. (eds.) SEFM 2013. LNCS, vol. 8368, pp. 125–134. Springer, Heidelberg (2014)
17. Lüttgen, G., Vogler, W.: Ready simulation for concurrency: It's logical? Information and Computation 208(7), 845–867 (2010)
18. Milner, R.: An algebraic definition of simulation between programs. In: Proceedings 2nd Joint Conference on Artificial Intelligence, pp. 481–489. BCS (1971), Report No. CS-205, Computer Science Department, Stanford University
19. Milner, R.: A Calculus of Communication Systems. LNCS, vol. 92. Springer, Heidelberg (1980)
20. Milner, R.: Communication and Concurrency. Prentice Hall (1989)
21. Rabanal, P., Rodríguez, I., Rubio, F.: Testing restorable systems: formal definition and heuristic solution based on river formation dynamics. Formal Aspects of Computing 25(5), 743–768 (2013)
22. Ranzato, F.: A More Efficient Simulation Algorithm on Kripke Structures. In: Chatterjee, K., Sgall, J. (eds.) MFCS 2013. LNCS, vol. 8087, pp. 753–764. Springer, Heidelberg (2013)
23. Stockmeyer, L.J., Meyer, A.R.: Word problems requiring exponential time: Preliminary report. In: Aho, A.V., Borodin, A., Constable, R.L., Floyd, R.W., Harrison, M.A., Karp, R.M., Strong, H.R. (eds.) STOC, pp. 1–9. ACM (1973)
24. Stokkink, G., Timmer, M., Stoelinga, M.: Talking quiescence: a rigorous theory that supports parallel composition, action hiding and determinisation. In: Petrenko, A.K., Schlingloff, H. (eds.) MBT. EPTCS, vol. 80, pp. 73–87 (2012)
25. Tretmans, J.: Model based testing with labelled transition systems. In: Hierons, R.M., Bowen, J.P., Harman, M. (eds.) FORTEST. LNCS, vol. 4949, pp. 1–38. Springer, Heidelberg (2008)
26. Tretmans, J., Brinksma, E.: Torx: Automated model-based testing. In: Hartman, A., Dussa-Ziegler, K. (eds.) First European Conference on Model-Driven Software Engineering, pp. 31–43 (December 2003)
27. van Glabbeek, R.J.: The Linear Time – Branching Time Spectrum I: The Semantics of Concrete, Sequential Processes. In: Handbook of Process Algebra, pp. 3–99. Elsevier (2001)
28. van Glabbeek, R.J., Ploeger, B.: Correcting a space-efficient simulation algorithm. In: Gupta, A., Malik, S. (eds.) CAV 2008. LNCS, vol. 5123, pp. 517–529. Springer, Heidelberg (2008)
29. Veanes, M., Campbell, C., Schulte, W., Tillmann, N.: Online testing with model programs. In: Wermelinger, M., Gall, H. (eds.) ESEC/SIGSOFT FSE, pp. 273–282. ACM (2005)

A Program Logic for Verifying Secure Routing Protocols

Chen Chen[1], Limin Jia[2], Hao Xu[1], Cheng Luo[1],
Wenchao Zhou[3], and Boon Thau Loo[1]

[1] University of Pennsylvania, Philadelphia, USA
{chenche,haoxu,boonloo}@cis.upenn.edu
[2] Carnegie Mellon University, Pittsburgh, USA
liminjia@cmu.edu
[3] Georgetown University, Washington, USA
wzhou@cs.georgetown.edu

Abstract. The Internet, as it stands today, is highly vulnerable to attacks. However, little has been done to understand and verify the formal security guarantees of proposed secure inter-domain routing protocols, such as Secure BGP (S-BGP). In this paper, we develop a sound program logic for SANDLog—a declarative specification language for secure routing protocols—for verifying properties of these protocols. We prove invariant properties of SANDLog programs that run in an adversarial environment. As a step towards automated verification, we implement a verification condition generator (VCGen) to automatically extract proof obligations. VCGen is integrated into a compiler for SANDLog that can generate executable protocol implementations; and thus, both verification and empirical evaluation of secure routing protocols can be carried out in this unified framework. To validate our framework, we (1) encoded several proposed secure routing mechanisms in SANDLog, (2) verified variants of path authenticity properties by manually discharging the generated verification conditions in Coq, and (3) generated executable code based on SANDLog specification and ran the code in simulation.

1 Introduction

In recent years, we have witnessed an explosion of services provided over the Internet. These services are increasingly transferring customers' private information over the network and being used in mission-critical tasks. Central to ensuring the reliability and security of these services is a secure and efficient Internet routing infrastructure. Unfortunately, the Internet infrastructure, as it stands today, is highly vulnerable to attacks. The Internet runs *Border Gateway Protocol* (BGP), where routers are grouped into Autonomous Systems (*ASes*) administrated by Internet Service Providers (*ISPs*). Individual ASes exchange route advertisements with neighboring ASes using the *path-vector* protocol. Each originating AS first sends a route advertisement (containing a single AS number) for the IP prefixes it owns. Whenever an AS receives a route advertisement, it

E. Ábrahám and C. Palamidessi (Eds.), FORTE 2014, LNCS 8461, pp. 117–132, 2014.

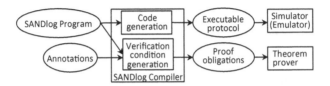

Fig. 1. Architecture of a unified framework for implementing and verifying secure routing protocols. The round objects represent the inputs and outputs of the framework, which are either code or proofs. The rectangular objects are software components of the framework.

adds itself to the AS *path*, and advertises the best route to its neighbors based on its routing policies. Since these route advertisements are not authenticated, ASes can advertise non-existent routes or claim to own IP prefixes that they do not. These faults may lead to long periods of interruption of the Internet; best epitomized by recent high-profile attacks [10,24].

In response to these vulnerabilities, several new Internet routing architectures and protocols for a more secure Internet have been proposed. These range from security extensions of BGP (Secure-BGP (S-BGP) [19], ps-BGP [28], so-BGP [30]), to "clean-slate" Internet architectural redesigns such as SCION [31] and ICING [22]. However, *none* of the proposals formally analyzed their security properties. These protocols are implemented from scratch, evaluated primarily experimentally, and their security properties shown via informal reasoning.

Existing protocol analysis tools [7,12,14] are rarely used in analyzing routing protocols because routing protocols are considerably more complicated than cryptographic protocols: they often compute local states, are recursive, and their security properties need to be shown to hold on arbitrary network topologies. As the number of models is infinite, model-checking-based tools, in general, cannot be used to prove the protocol secure.

To overcome the above limitations, we develop a novel proof methodology to verify these protocols. We augment prior work on declarative networking (NDLog) [21] with cryptographic libraries to provide compact encoding of secure routing protocols. We call this extension SANDLog (*Secure and Authenticated Network DataLog*). It has been shown that such a Datalog-like language can be used for implementing a variety of network protocols [21]. We develop a program logic for reasoning about SANDLog programs that run in an adversarial environment. Based on the program logic, we implement a verification condition generator (VCGen), which takes as inputs the SANDLog program and user-provided annotations, and outputs intermediary proof obligations as lemma statements in Coq's syntax. Proofs for these lemmas are later completed manually. VCGen is integrated into the SANDLog compiler, which augments the declarative networking engine RapidNet [26] to handle cryptographic functions. The compiler is able to translate SANDLog specification into executable code, which is amenable to implementation and evaluation. Both verification and empirical evaluation of secure routing protocols can be carried out in this unified framework (Figure 1).

We summarize our technical contributions:

1. We define a program logic for verifying SANDLog programs in the presence of adversaries (Section 3). We prove that our logic is sound.
2. We implement VCGen for automatically generating proof obligations and integrate VCGen into a compiler for SANDLog (Section 4).
3. We encode S-BGP and SCION in SANDLog, verify path authenticity properties of these protocols, and run them in simulation (Section 5).

Due to space constraints, we omit many details, which can be found in our companion technical report [9].

2   SANDLog

We introduce the syntax and operational semantics of SANDLog, which extends the *Network Datalog* (NDLog) [21] with a library for cryptographic functions. The complete definitions can be found in our TR.

2.1   Syntax

SANDLog's syntax is summarized below. A SANDLog program is composed of a set of rules, each of which consists of a rule head and a rule body. A rule head is a tuple. A rule body consists of a list of body elements which are either tuples or atoms. Atoms include assignments and inequality constraints. The binary operator *bop* denotes inequality relations. Each SANDLog rule specifies that if all the tuples in the body are derivable and all the constraints specified by the atoms in the body are satisfied, then the head tuple is derivable. These features are shared between NDLog [21] and SANDLog. Unique to SANDLog, are the cryptographic functions denoted f_c, implemented as a library. This library includes commonly used functions such as signature generation and verification.

Crypt func	f_c	::=	f_sign_asym $\mid$ f_verify_asym $\cdots$
Atom	a	::=	$x := t \mid t_1 \; bop \; t_2$
Terms	t	::=	$x \mid c \mid \iota \mid f(t) \mid f_c(t)$
Body Elem	B	::=	$p(agB) \mid a$
Arg List	ags	::=	$\cdot \mid ags, x \mid ags, c$
Rule Body	$body$	::=	$\cdot \mid body, B$
Body Args	agB	::=	$@\iota, ags$
Rule	r	::=	$p(agH) :- body$
Head Args	agH	::=	$agB \mid @\iota, ags, F_{agg}\langle x \rangle, ags$
Program	$prog(\iota)$	::=	$r_1, \cdots, r_k$

To support distributed execution, SANDLog assumes that each node has a unique identifier denoted ι. A SANDLog program *prog* is parametrized over the identifier of the node it runs on. A location specifier, written $@\iota$, specifies where a tuple resides and is the first argument of a tuple. We require all body tuples to reside on the same node as the program. A rule head can specify a location different from its body tuples. When such a rule is executed, the derived head tuple is sent to the specified remote node. Finally, SANDLog supports aggregation functions (denoted $F_{agg}\langle x \rangle$), such as max and min, in the rule head.

An Example Program. The following program can be used to compute the best path between each pair of nodes in a network. s is the location parameter of the program, representing the ID of the node where the program is executing. Each node stores three kinds of tuples: $link(@s, d, c)$ means that there is a direct link from s to d with cost c; $path(@s, d, c, p)$ means that p is a path from s to d with cost c; and $bestPath(@s, d, c, p)$ states that p is the lowest-cost path between s and d.

$sp1$ $path(@s, d, c, p) :\!- link(@s, d, c), p := [s, d]$.
$sp2$ $path(@z, d, c, p) :\!- link(@s, z, c1), path(@s, d, c2, p1), c := c1 + c2, p := z :: p1$.
$sp3$ $bestPath(@s, d, min\langle c \rangle, p) :\!- path(@s, d, c, p)$.

Rule $sp1$ computes all one-hop paths based on direct links. Rule $sp2$ expresses that if there is a link from s to z of cost $c1$ and a path from s to d of cost $c2$, then there is a path from z to d with cost $c1+c2$ (for simplicity, we assume links are symmetric, i.e. if there is a link from s to d with cost c, then a link from d to s with the same cost c also exists). Finally, rule $sp3$ aggregates all paths with the same pair of source and destination (s and d) to compute the best path. The arguments that appear before the aggregation denotes the group-by keys.

2.2   Operational Semantics

The operational semantics of SANDLog adopts a distributed execution model. Each node runs a designated program, and maintains a database of derived tuples in its local state. Nodes can communicate with each other by sending tuples over the network. The evaluation of the SANDLog programs follows the PSN algorithm [20], and maintains the database incrementally. The semantics introduced here is similar to that of NDLog except that we make explicit, which tuples are derived, which are received, and which are sent over the network. This addition is crucial to specifying and proving protocol properties. The constructs needed for defining the operational semantics of SANDLog are presented below.

Table	$\Psi ::= \cdot \mid \Psi, (n, P)$	*Network Queue*	$\mathcal{Q} ::= \mathcal{U}$
Update	$u ::= -P \mid +P$	*Local State*	$\mathcal{S} ::= (\iota, \Psi, \mathcal{U}, prog(\iota))$
Update List	$\mathcal{U} ::= [u_1, \cdots, u_n]$	*Configuration*	$\mathcal{C} ::= \mathcal{Q} \triangleright \mathcal{S}_1, \cdots, \mathcal{S}_n$

We write P to denote tuples. The database for storing all derived tuples on a node is denoted Ψ. Because there could be multiple derivations of the same tuple, we associate each tuple with a reference count n, recording the number of valid derivations for that tuple. An update is either an insertion of a tuple, denoted $+P$, or a deletion of a tuple, denoted $-P$. We write $\mathcal{U}$ to denote a list of updates. A node's local state, denoted $\mathcal{S}$, consists of the node's identifier ι, the database Ψ, a list of unprocessed updates $\mathcal{U}$, and the program $prog$ that ι runs. A configuration of the network, written $\mathcal{C}$, is composed of a network update queue $\mathcal{Q}$, and the set of the local states of all the nodes in the network. The queue $\mathcal{Q}$ models the update messages sent across the network.

Figure 2 presents an example scenario of executing the shortest-path program shown in Section 2.1. The network consists of three nodes, A, B and C, connected

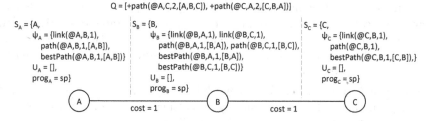

Fig. 2. An Example Scenario

by two links with cost 1. In the current state, all three nodes are aware of their direct neighbors, i.e., link tuples are in their databases Ψ_A, Ψ_B and Ψ_C. They have constructed paths to their neighbors (i.e., the corresponding path and bestPath tuples are stored). In addition, node B has applied *sp2* and generated updates +path(@A,C,2,[A,B,C]) and +path(@C,A,2,[C,B,A]), which are currently queued and waiting to be delivered to their destinations (node A and C respectively).

Top-Level Transitions. The small-step operational semantics of a node is denoted $S \hookrightarrow S', \mathcal{U}$. From state S, a node takes a step to a new state S' and generates a set of updates $\mathcal{U}$ for other nodes in the network. The small-step operational semantics of the entire system is denoted $\mathcal{C} \xrightarrow{\tau} \mathcal{C}'$, where τ is the time of the transition step. A trace $\mathcal{T}$ is a sequence of transitions: $\xrightarrow{\tau_0} \mathcal{C}_1 \xrightarrow{\tau_1} \mathcal{C}_2 \cdots \xrightarrow{\tau_n} \mathcal{C}_{n+1}$, where the time points on the trace are monotonically increasing ($\tau_0 < \tau_1 < \cdots < \tau_n$). We assume that the effects of a transition take place at time τ_i (reflected in $\mathcal{C}_{i+1}$). Figure 3 defines the rules for system state transition.

Rule NodeStep states that the system takes a step when one node takes a step. As a result, the updates generated by node i are appended to the end of the network queue. We use ∘ to denote the list append operation. Rule Dequeue applies when a node receives updates from the network. We write $\mathcal{Q}_1 \oplus \mathcal{Q}_2$ to denote a merge of two lists. Any node can dequeue updates sent to it and append those updates to the update list in its local state. Here, we overload the ∘ operator, and write $S \circ \mathcal{Q}$ to denote a new state, which is the same as S, except that the update list is the result of appending $\mathcal{Q}$ to the update list in S.

We omit the detailed rules for state transitions within a node. Instead, we explain it through examples. At a high-level, those rules either fire base rules—rules that do not have a rule body—at initialization; or computes new updates based on the program and the first update in the update list. Continue the example scenario, node A dequeues +path(@A,C,2,[A,B,C]), and puts it into the unprocessed update list $\mathcal{U}_A$ (rule Dequeue). Node A then fires all rules that are triggered

$$\boxed{\mathcal{C} \to \mathcal{C}'}$$

$$\frac{S_i \hookrightarrow S_i', \mathcal{U} \qquad \forall j \in [1, n] \wedge j \neq i, \ S_j' = S_j}{\mathcal{Q} \triangleright S_1, \cdots S_n \to \mathcal{Q} \circ \mathcal{U} \triangleright S_1', \cdots S_n'} \text{ NodeStep}$$

$$\frac{\mathcal{Q} = \mathcal{Q}' \oplus \mathcal{Q}_1 \cdots \oplus \mathcal{Q}_n \qquad \forall j \in [1, n] \qquad S_j' = S_j \circ \mathcal{Q}_j}{\mathcal{Q} \triangleright S_1, \cdots S_n \to \mathcal{Q}' \triangleright S_1', \cdots S_n'} \text{ Dequeue}$$

Fig. 3. Operational Semantics

by the update, and generates new updates $\mathcal{U}_{in}$ and $\mathcal{U}_{ext}$ ($\mathcal{U}_{in}$ and $\mathcal{U}_{ext}$ denote updates to local (internal) states and remote (external) states respectively.) In the resulting state, the local state of node A is updated: path(@A,C,2,[A,B,C]) is inserted into Ψ_A, and $\mathcal{U}_A$ now includes $\mathcal{U}_{in}$. The network queue is updated to include $\mathcal{U}_{ext}$ (rule NODESTEP).

Incremental Maintenance. Following the strategy proposed in [20], the local database is maintained incrementally by processing updates one at a time. The rules are rewritten into Δ *rules*, which can efficiently generate all the updates triggered by one update. For any given rule r that contains k body tuples, k Δ rules of the following form are generated, one for each $i \in [1, k]$.

$$\Delta p(agH) :- p_1^{\nu}(agB_1), ..., p_{i-1}^{\nu}(agB_{i-1}), \Delta p_i(agB_i),$$
$$p_{i+1}(agB_{i+1}), ..., p_k(agB_k), a_1, ..., a_m$$

Δp_i in the body denotes the update currently being considered. Δp in the head denotes new updates that are generated as the result of firing this rule. Here p^{ν} denotes the set of tuples whose name is p and includes the current update being considered. p is drawn only from the set of tuples that does not include the current update. For example, the Δ rules for *sp2* are:

sp2a Δpath(@z,d,c,p) :- Δlink(@$s,z,c1$), path(@$s,d,c2,p1$), $c := c1 + c2, p := z::p1$.
sp2b Δpath(@z,d,c,p) :- link$^{\nu}$(@$s,z,c1$), Δpath(@$s,d,c2,p1$), $c := c1 + c2, p := z::p1$.

Rules *sp2a* and *sp2b* are Δ rules triggered by updates of the link and path relation respectively. For instance, when node A processes +path(@A,C,2,[A,B,C]), only rule *sp2b* is fired. In this step, path$^{\nu}$ includes the tuple path(@A,C,2,[A,B,C]), while path does not. On the other hand, link$^{\nu}$ and link denote the same set of tuples, because the update is a path tuple, and thus does not affect tuples with a different name.

Rule Firing. Here we explain through examples how they work. Informally, a Δ rule is fired if instantiations of its body tuples are present in the derived tuples and available updates. The resulting rule head will be put into the update lists, depending on whether it needs to be sent to another node, or consumed locally.

We revisit the example in Figure 2. Upon receiving +path(@A,C,2,[A,B,C]), A will trigger Δ rule *sp2b* and generate a new update +path(@B,C,3,[B,A,B,C]), which will be included in $\mathcal{U}_{ext}$ as it is destined to a remote node B. The Δ rule for *sp3* will also be triggered and will generate a new update +bestPath(@A,C,2,[A,B,C]), which will be included in $\mathcal{U}_{in}$. After evaluating the Δ rules triggered by the update +path(@A,C,2,[A,B,C]), we have $\mathcal{U}_{in} = \{$+bestPath(@A,C,2,[A,B,C])$\}$ and $\mathcal{U}_{ext} = \{$+path(@B,C,3,[B,A,B,C])$\}$. In addition, bestpath$_{agg}$, the auxiliary relation that maintains all candidate tuples for bestpath, is also updated to reflect that a new candidate tuple has been generated. It now includes bestpath$_{agg}$(@A,C,2,[A,B,C]).

Discussion. The semantics introduced here will not terminate for programs with a cyclic derivation of the same tuple, even though set-based semantics will. Most routing protocols do not have such issue (e.g., cycle detection is well-adopted in routing protocols). Our prior work [23] has proposed improvements to solve this issue. It is a straightforward extension to the current semantics and is not crucial for demonstrating the soundness of the program logic we develop.

The operational semantics is correct if the results are the same as one where all rules reside in one node and a global fixed point is computed at each round. The proof of correctness is out of the scope of this paper. We are working on correctness definitions and proofs for variants of PSN algorithms. Our initial results for a simpler language can be found in [23]. SANDLog additionally allows aggregates, which are not included in [23]. The soundness of our logic only depends on the specific evaluation strategy implemented by the compiler, and is orthogonal to the correctness of the operational semantics. Updates to the operational semantics is likely to come in some form of additional bookkeeping in the representation of tuples, which we believe will not affect the overall structure of the program logic; as these metadata are irrelevant to the logic.

3   A Program Logic for SANDLog

Inspired by program logics for reasoning about cryptographic protocols [12,15], we define a program logic for SANDLog. The properties we are interested in are safety properties, which should hold throughout the execution of SANDLog programs that interact with attackers.

Attacker Model. We assume *connectivity-bound* network attackers, a variant of the Dolev-Yao network attacker model. An attacker can send and receive messages to and from its neighbors. We assume a symbolic model of the cryptographic functions: an attacker can operate cryptographic functions to which it has the correct keys, such as encryption, decryption, and signature generation. This model does not allow an attacker to eavesdrop or intercept packets. This makes sense in the application domain that we consider, as attackers are malicious nodes in the network that participate in the routing protocol exchange. All the links we consider represent dedicated physical cables that connect neighboring nodes, which are hard to eavesdrop without physical intrusion.

This attacker model manifests in the formal system in two places: (1) the network is modeled as connected nodes, some of which run the SANDLog program that encodes the prescribed protocol and others are malicious and run arbitrary SANDLog programs; (2) assumptions about cryptographic functions are admitted as axioms in proofs.

Syntax. We use first-order logic formulas, denoted φ, as property specifications. The atoms, denoted A, include predicates and term inequalities.

$$\textit{Atoms } A ::= P(t)@(\iota, \tau) \mid \mathsf{send}(\iota, \mathsf{tp}(P, \iota', t))@\tau \mid \mathsf{recv}(\iota, \mathsf{tp}(P, t))@\tau$$
$$\mid \mathsf{honest}(\iota, prog(\iota), \tau) \mid t_1 \; bop \; t_2$$

Predicate $P(t)@(\iota, \tau)$ means that tuple $P(t)$ is derivable at time τ by node ι. The first element in t is a location identifier ι', which may be different from ι. When a tuple $P(\iota', ...)$ is derived at node ι, it is sent to ι'. This *send* action is captured by predicate $\mathsf{send}(\iota, \mathsf{tp}(P, \iota', t))@\tau$. Predicate $\mathsf{recv}(\iota, \mathsf{tp}(P, t))@\tau$ denotes that node ι has received a tuple $P(t)$ at time τ. $\mathsf{honest}(\iota, prog(\iota), \tau)$ means that node ι starts to run program $prog(\iota)$ at time τ. Since predicates take time points as an argument, we are effectively encoding linear temporal logic (LTL) in

$$\boxed{\Sigma; \Gamma \vdash prog(i) : \{i, t_b, t_e\}.\varphi(i, t_b, t_e)}$$

$\forall p \in hdOf(prog),\ \varphi_p$ is closed under trace extension
$\forall r \in rlOf(prog),\ r = h(\boldsymbol{v}) :\!- p_1(\boldsymbol{s}_1), ..., p_m(\boldsymbol{s}_m), q_1(\boldsymbol{u}_1), ..., q_n(\boldsymbol{u}_n), a_1, ..., a_k$
$\quad \Sigma; \Gamma \vdash \forall i, \forall t, \forall \boldsymbol{y}$

$$\frac{\bigwedge_{j\in[1,k]}[a_j] \wedge \bigwedge_{j\in[1,m]} (p_j(\boldsymbol{s}_j)@(i,t) \wedge \varphi_{p_j}(i,t,\boldsymbol{s}_j)) \wedge \bigwedge_{j\in[1,n]} \mathsf{recv}(i, \mathsf{tp}(q_j, \boldsymbol{u}_j))@t}{\Sigma; \Gamma \vdash prog(i) : \{i, y_b, y_e\}. \bigwedge_{p\in hdOf(prog)} \forall t, \forall \boldsymbol{x}, y_b \leqslant t < y_e \wedge p(\boldsymbol{x})@(i,t) \supset \varphi_p(i,t,\boldsymbol{x})}$$

where $\supset \varphi_h(i,t,\boldsymbol{v})$ ⟶ where $\boldsymbol{y} = fv(r)$ ⟶ INV

$$\boxed{\Sigma; \Gamma \vdash \varphi} \quad \frac{\Sigma; \Gamma \vdash prog(i) : \{i, y_b, y_e\}.\varphi(i, y_b, y_e) \quad \Sigma; \Gamma \vdash \mathsf{honest}(\iota, prog(\iota), t)}{\Sigma; \Gamma \vdash \forall t', t' > t, \varphi(\iota, t, t')} \ \text{HONEST}$$

Fig. 4. Selected Rules in Program Logic

first-order logic [18]. Using these atoms and first-order logic connectives, we can specify security properties such as route authenticity (see Section 5 for details).

Logical Judgments. The logical judgments use two contexts: context Σ contains all the free variables and Γ contains logical assumptions.

(1) $\Sigma; \Gamma \vdash \varphi$ ⟶ (2) $\Sigma; \Gamma \vdash prog(i) : \{i, y_b, y_e\}.\varphi(i, y_b, y_e)$

Judgment (1) states that φ is provable given the assumptions in Γ. Judgment (2) is an assertion about SANDLog programs. We write $\varphi(\boldsymbol{x})$ when $\boldsymbol{x}$ are free in φ. $\varphi(\boldsymbol{t})$ denotes the resulting formula of substituting $\boldsymbol{t}$ for $\boldsymbol{x}$ in $\varphi(\boldsymbol{x})$. Recall that $prog$ is parametrized over the identifier of the node it runs on. The assertion of an invariant property for such a program is parametrized over not only the node ID i, but also the starting point of executing the program (y_b) and a later time point y_e. Judgment (2) states that any trace $\mathcal{T}$ *containing* the execution of program $prog$ by a node ι, starting at time τ_b, satisfies $\varphi(\iota, \tau_b, \tau_e)$ for any time point τ_e later than τ_b. Intuitively, the trace contains several threads running concurrently, only one of them runs the program and the other threads can be malicious. Since τ_e is any time after τ_b (the time $prog$ starts), φ is an invariant property of $prog$. For example, $\varphi(i, y_b, y_e)$ could specify that whenever i derives a path tuple, every link in the path must have existed in the past.

Inference Rules. The inference rules of our program logic include all standard first-order logic ones (e.g. Modus ponens), omitted for brevity. We explain two key rules (Figure 4) in our proof system.

Rule INV derives an invariant property of a program $prog$. The invariant property states that if a tuple p is derived by this program, then some property φ_p must be true; formally: $\forall t, \forall \boldsymbol{x}, y_b \leqslant t < y_e \wedge p(\boldsymbol{x})@(i,t) \supset \varphi_p(i,t,\boldsymbol{x})$, where p is the tuple name of a rule head of $prog$, and $\varphi_p(i,t,\boldsymbol{x})$ is an invariant property associated with $p(\boldsymbol{x})$. For example, p can be path, and $\varphi_p(i,t,\boldsymbol{x})$ be that every link in argument *path* must have existed in the past. Rule INV states that the invariant of the program is the conjunction of all the invariants of the tuples it derives.

We require that the invariants φ_p be closed under trace extension (the first premise of INV). Formally: $\mathcal{T} \vDash \varphi(\iota, t, \boldsymbol{s})$ and $\mathcal{T}$ is a prefix of $\mathcal{T}'$ then $\mathcal{T}' \vDash \varphi(\iota, t, \boldsymbol{s})$.

For instance, the property that node ι has received a tuple P before time t is closed under trace extension; the property that node ι never sends P to the network is not closed under trace extension. This restriction has not affected our case studies: the invariants used in verification only assert what happened in the past, or facts independent of time (e.g., arithmetic constraints).

Intuitively, the premises of INV need to establish that (1) when p is a base tuple—its derivation is independent of any other tuples—φ holds; and (2) when p is derived using other tuples, φ holds. The last (second) premise of INV does precisely that. It checks every rule in $prog$ and proves that the body tuples and the invariants associated with the body tuples together imply the invariant of the head tuple. For example, for $sp1$, to show that the invariant associated with path is true, we can use the fact that there is a link tuple, that the invariant associated with that link tuple is true, and that the constraint $p = [s, d]$ is true. This is sound because we are inducting over the derivation tree of the head tuple.

This premise looks complicated because the body tuples need to be treated differently depending on whether they are derived locally, received from the network, or constraints. For each rule r in $prog$, we assume that the body of r is arranged so that the first m tuples are derived by $prog$, the next n tuples are received from the network, and constraints constitute the rest of the body. The right-hand-side of the implication of the last (second) premise is the invariant associated with tuple h. A rule head is only derivable when all of its body tuples are derivable and constraints satisfied. For tuples that are derived earlier by $prog$ (denoted p_j), we can safely assume that their invariants hold at time t. All received tuples (q_j) should have been received prior to rule firing. Finally, the atoms (constraints, denoted a_j) should be true. Here, $[x := f(t)]$ rewrites the assignment statement into an equality check $x = f(t)$. The left-hand-side of that implication is a conjunction of formulas denoting the above conditions. When r only has a rule head, this premise is reduced to the right-hand-side of that implication, which is what case (1) mentioned above.

The last (second) premise of INV can be automatically generated given a SANDLog program and all the corresponding φ_ps. In Section 4, we detail the implementation of the verification condition generator for Coq.

The HONEST rule proves properties of the entire system based on invariants of a SANDLog program. If $\varphi(i, y_b, y_e)$ is the invariant of $prog$, and a node ι runs the program $prog$ at time t_b, then any trace containing the execution of this program satisfies $\varphi(\iota, t_b, t_e)$, where t_e is a time point after t_b. SANDLog programs never terminate: after the last instruction, the program enters a stuck state.

Soundness. We prove the soundness of our logic with regard to the trace semantics. First, we define the semantics for our logic and judgments in Figure 5. Formulas are interpreted on a trace $\mathcal{T}$. We elide the rules for first-order logic connectives. A tuple $P(t)$ is derivable by node ι at time τ, if $P(t)$ is either an internal update or an external update generated at a time point τ' no later than τ. A node ι sends out a tuple $P(\iota', t)$ if that tuple was derived by node ι. Because ι' is different from ι, it is sent over the network. A *received tuple* is one that comes from the network (obtained using DEQUEUE). Finally, an honest node ι

$\mathcal{T} \models P(t)@(\iota, \tau)$ iff $\exists \tau' \leqslant \tau$, $\mathcal{C}$ is the configuration on $\mathcal{T}$ prior to time τ',
$(\iota, \Psi, \mathcal{U}, prog(\iota)) \in \mathcal{C}$, at time τ', $(\iota, \Psi, \mathcal{U}, prog(\iota)) \hookrightarrow (\iota, \Psi', \mathcal{U}' \circ \mathcal{U}_{in}, prog(\iota)), \mathcal{U}_e$,
and either $P(t) \in \mathcal{U}_{in}$ or $P(t) \in \mathcal{U}_e$

$\mathcal{T} \models \mathsf{send}(\iota, \mathsf{tp}(P, \iota', t))@\tau$ iff $\mathcal{C}$ is the configuration on $\mathcal{T}$ prior to time τ,
$(\iota, \Psi, \mathcal{U}, prog(\iota)) \in \mathcal{C}$, at time τ, $(\iota, \Psi, \mathcal{U}, prog(\iota)) \hookrightarrow \mathcal{S}', \mathcal{U}_e$ and $P(@\iota', t) \in \mathcal{U}_e$

$\mathcal{T} \models \mathsf{recv}(\iota, \mathsf{tp}(P, t))@\tau$ iff $\exists \tau' \leqslant \tau$, $\mathcal{C} \xrightarrow{\tau'} \mathcal{C}' \in \mathcal{T}$,
$\mathcal{Q}$ is the network queue in $\mathcal{C}$, $P(t) \in \mathcal{Q}$, $(\iota, \Psi, \mathcal{U}, prog(\iota)) \in \mathcal{C}'$ and $P(t) \in \mathcal{U}$

$\mathcal{T} \models \mathsf{honest}(\iota, prog(\iota), \tau)$ iff at time τ, node ι's local state is $(\iota, [], [], prog(\iota))$

$\Gamma \models prog(i) : \{i, y_b, y_e\}.\varphi(i, y_b, y_e)$ iff Given any trace $\mathcal{T}$ such that $\mathcal{T} \models \Gamma$,
and at time τ_b, node ι's local state is $(\iota, [], [], prog(\iota))$
given any time point τ_e such that $\tau_e \geqslant \tau_b$, it is the case that $\mathcal{T} \models \varphi(\iota, \tau_b, \tau_e)$

Fig. 5. Trace-based semantics

runs *prog* at time τ and the local state of ι at time τ is the initial state with an empty table and update queue.

The semantics of invariant assertion states that if a trace $\mathcal{T}$ contains the execution of *prog* by node ι (formally defined as the node running *prog* is one of the nodes in the configuration $\mathcal{C}$), then given any time point τ_e after τ_b, the trace $\mathcal{T}$ satisfies $\varphi(\iota, \tau_b, \tau_e)$. This definition allows *prog* to run concurrently with other programs, some of which may be controlled by the adversary.

The program logic is proven to be sound with regard to the trace semantics.

Theorem 1 (Soundness) *1. If $\Sigma; \Gamma \vdash \varphi$, then for all grounding substitution σ for Σ, given any trace $\mathcal{T}$, $\mathcal{T} \models \Gamma\sigma$ implies $\mathcal{T} \models \varphi\sigma$;*

2. If $\Sigma; \Gamma \vdash prog(i) : \{i, y_b, y_e\}.\varphi(i, y_b, y_e)$, then for all grounding substitution σ for Σ, $\Gamma\sigma \models (prog)\sigma(i) : \{i, y_b, y_e\}.(\varphi(i, y_b, y_e))\sigma$.

4   Verification Condition Generator

As a step towards automated verification, we implement a verification condition generator (VCGen) to automatically extract proof obligations from a SANDLog program. VCGen is implemented in C++ and fully integrated to RapidNet [26], a declarative networking engine for compiling SANDLog programs. We target Coq, but other interactive theorem provers such as Isabelle HOL are possible.

More concretely, VCGen generates lemmas corresponding to the last premise of rule INV. It takes as inputs: the abstract syntax tree of a SANDLog program *sp*, and type annotations *tp*. The generated Coq file contains the following: (1) definitions for types, predicates, and functions; (2) lemmas for rules in the SANDLog program; and (3) axioms based on HONEST rule.

Definition. Predicates and functions are declared before they are used. Each predicate (tuple) *p* in the SANDLog program corresponds to a predicate of the same name in the Coq file, with two additional arguments: a location specifier and a time point. For example, the generated declaration of the *link* tuple link(@*node*, *node*) is the following

```
Variable link: node → node → node → time → Prop.
```

link(@n, n')	there is a link between n and n'.
route(@n, d, c, p, sl)	p is a path to d with cost c.
	sl is the signature list associated with p.
prefix(@n, d)	n owns prefix (IP addresses) d.
bestRoute(@n, d, c, p, sl)	p is the best path to d with cost c.
	sl is the signature list associated with p.
verifyPath(@n, n', d, p, sl,	a path p to d needs verifying against signature list sl.
$pOrig, sOrig$)	p is a sub-path of $pOrig$, and s is a sub-list of $sOrig$.
signature(@n, m, s)	n creates a signature s of message m with private key.
advertisement(@n', n, d, p, sl)	n advertises path p to neighbor n' with signature list sl.

Fig. 6. Tuples for $prog_{sbgp}$

For each user-defined function, a data constructor of the same name is generated, unless it corresponds to a Coq's built-in operator (e.g. list operations). The function takes a time point as an additional argument.

Lemmas. For each rule in a SANDLog program, VCGen generates a lemma in the form of the last premise in inference rule Inv (Figure 4). Rule $sp1$ of example program in Section 2.1, for instance, corresponds to the following lemma:

> Lemma r1: forall(s:node)(d:node)(c:nat)(p:list node)(t:time),
>
>   link s d c s t → p = cons (s (cons d nil)) → p-path s t s d c p t.

Here, *cons* is Coq's built-in list appending operation. and *p-path* is the invariant associated with predicate *path*.

Axioms. For each invariant φ_p of a rule head p, VCGen produces an axiom of the form: $\forall i, t, \boldsymbol{x}, \mathsf{Honest}(i) \supset p(\boldsymbol{x})@(i, t) \supset \varphi_p(i, \boldsymbol{x})$. These axioms are conclusions of the HONEST rule after invariants are verified. Soundness of these axioms is backed by Theorem 1. Since we always assume that the program starts at time $-\infty$, the condition that $t > -\infty$ is always true, thus omitted.

5 Case Studies

We investigate two secure routing protocols: S-BGP and SCION. Due to space constraints, we present in detail the verification of one property of S-BGP. All SANDLog specifications and Coq proofs can be found online at http://netdb.cis.upenn.edu/forte2014/.

Encoding. Secure Border Gateway Protocol (S-BGP) provides security guarantees such as origin authenticity and route authenticity over BGP through PKI and signature-based attestations. Our SANDLog encoding includes all necessary details of S-BGP's route attestation mechanisms. S-BGP requires that each node sign the route information it advertises to its neighbor, which includes the path, the destination prefix (IP address), and the identifier of the intended neighbor. Along with the advertisement, a node sends its own signature as well as all signatures signed by previous nodes on the subpaths. Upon receiving an advertisement, a node verifies all signatures.

Key tuples generated at each node executing $prog_{sbgp}$ are listed in Figure 6. Here n is the parameter representing the identifier of the node that runs $prog_{sbgp}$. All tuples except advertisement are stored at node n. An advertisement tuple encodes a route advertisement that, once generated, is sent over the network to one of n's neighbors. We summarize $prog_{sbgp}$ encoding in Table 1.

Empirical Evaluation. We use RapidNet [26] to generate low-level implementation from SANDLog encoding of S-BGP and SCION. We validate the low-level implementation in the ns-3 simulator [1]. Our experiments are performed on a synthetically generated topology consisting of 40 nodes, where each node runs the generated implementation of the SANDLog program. The observed execution traces and communication patterns match the expected protocol behavior. We also confirm that the implementation defends against known attacks such as adversely advertising non-existent routes.

Property Specification. We focus on route authenticity, encoded as φ_{auth1} below. It holds on any execution trace of a network where some nodes run S-BGP, and those who do not are considered malicious.

$$\varphi_{auth1} = \forall n, m, t, d, p, sl,$$
$$\mathsf{Honest}(n) \wedge \mathsf{advertisement}(m, n, d, p, sl)@(n, t) \supset \mathsf{goodPath}(t, p, d)$$

Formula φ_{auth1} asserts a property $\mathsf{goodPath}(t, p, d)$ on any advertisement tuple generated by an honest node n. $\mathsf{goodPath}(t, p, d)$ defined below asserts that all links in path p reaching the destination IP prefix d must have existed at a time point no later than t. This means that every pair of adjacent nodes n and m in path p had in their databases: tuple `link(@n, m)` and `link(@m, n)` respectively.

$$\frac{\mathsf{Honest}(n) \supset \exists t', t' \leqslant t \wedge \mathsf{prefix}(n, d)@(n, t')}{\mathsf{goodPath}(t, n :: nil, d)}$$

$$\frac{\mathsf{Honest}(n) \supset \exists t', t' \leqslant t \wedge \mathsf{link}(n, n')@(n, t') \quad \mathsf{goodPath}(t, n :: nil, d)}{\mathsf{goodPath}(t, n' :: n :: nil, d)}$$

$$\frac{\mathsf{Honest}(n) \supset \exists t', t' \leqslant t \wedge \mathsf{link}(n, n')@(n, t') \wedge \exists t'', t'' \leqslant t \wedge \mathsf{link}(n, n'')@(n, t'')}{\mathsf{goodPath}(t, n :: n'' :: p'', d)}$$
$$\frac{}{\mathsf{goodPath}(t, n' :: n :: n'' :: p'', d)}$$

The base case is when p has only one node, and we require that d be one of the prefixes owned by n (i.e., the prefix tuple is derivable). When p has two

Table 1. Summary of $prog_{sbgp}$ encoding

Rule	Summary	Head Tuple
r1:	Generate a route for prefix of own.	route($@n, d, c, p, sl$)
r2:	Generate a best route for destination.	bestRoute($@n, d, c, p, sl$)
r3:	Receive advertisement from neighbor.	verifyPath($@n, n', d, p, sl, pOrig, sOrig$)
r4:	Recursively verify signature list.	verifyPath($@n, n', d, p, sl, pOrig, sOrig$)
r5:	Generate a route for verified path.	route($@n, d, c, p, sl$)
r6:	Generate a signature for new route.	signature($@n, m, s$)
r7:	Send route advertisement to neighbors.	advertisement($@n', n, d, p, sl$)

nodes n' and n, we require that the link from n to n' exist from n's perspective, assuming that n is honest. The last case checks that both links (from n to n' and from n to n'') exist from n's perspective, assuming n is honest. In the last two rules, we also recursively check that the subpath also satisfies goodPath. By varying the definition of goodPath, we can specify different properties such as one that requires each subpath be authorized by the sender. φ_{auth1} is a general topology-independent security property.

Verification. To use the authenticity property of the signatures, we include the following axiom A_{sig} in the logical context Γ. This axiom states that if s is verified by the public key of n', and the node n' is honest, then n' must have generated a signature tuple. Predicate verify$(m, s, k)@(n, t)$, generated by VCGen when function f_verify in SANDLog returns true, means that node n verifies at time t that s is a valid signature of message m according to key k.

$$A_{sig} = \forall m, s, k, n, n', t, \text{verify}(m, s, k)@(n, t) \land \text{publicKeys}(n, n', k)@(n, t) \land$$
$$\text{Honest}(n') \supset \exists t', t' < t \land \text{signature}(n', m, s)@(n', t')$$

We first prove that $prog_{sbgp}$ has an invariant property φ_I:

(a) $\cdot; \cdot \vdash prog_{sbgp}(n) : \{i, y_b, y_e\}.\varphi_I(i, y_b, y_e)$

with $\varphi_I(i, y_b, y_e) = \bigwedge_{p \in hdOf(prog_{sbgp})} \forall t\, \boldsymbol{x}, y_b \leqslant t < y_e \land p(\boldsymbol{x})@(i, t) \supset \varphi_p(i, t, \boldsymbol{x}).$

Here, every φ_p in φ_I denotes the invariant property associated with each head tuple in $prog_{sbgp}$, and needs to be specified by the user. For instance, the invariant associated with the advertisement tuple is denoted $\varphi_{advertisement}$:

$$\varphi_{advertisement}(i, t, n', n, d, p, sl) = \text{goodPath}(t, p, d).$$

The proof of (a) is carried out in Coq; we manually discharged all lemmas generated by VCGen. Next, applying the HONEST rule to (a), we can deduce $\varphi = \forall n\, t, \text{Honest}(n) \supset \varphi_I(n, t, -\infty)$. φ is injected into the assumptions (Γ) by VCGen, and is safe to be used in subsequent proof steps. Finally, $\varphi \supset \varphi_{auth1}$ is also proven in Coq by applying standard first-order logic rules.

We explain interesting steps of proving (a). Similar to verifying (a), using INV, HONEST and keeping the only clause related to signature, we derive the following:

(a$_2$) $\cdot; \cdot \vdash \forall n, \forall t, \text{Honest}(n) \land \text{signature}(n, m, s)@(n, t) \supset$
$$\exists n', d, m = d :: n' :: p \land \varphi_{link2}(p, n, d, n', t)$$

Formula $\varphi_{link2}(p, n, d, n', t)$ states that n is the first node on the path p, the link from n to the next node on p exists, and the link between n and the receiving node n' also exists. This matches the non-recursive conditions in the definition of goodPath.

$\varphi_{link2}(p, n, d, n', t) = \text{link}(n, n')@(n, t) \land$
$$\exists p', p = n :: p' \land (p' = \text{nil} \supset \text{prefix}(n, d)@(n, t))$$
$$\land \forall p'', m', p' = m' :: p'' \supset \text{link}(n, m')@(n, t)$$

Now (a$_2$) has connected an honest node's signature to the existence of links related to it. Combining (a$_2$) and A_{sig}, each time a signature sig of a node n is properly verified in $prog_{sbgp}$, the invariant link2 (link tuples existed) holds under the assumption that n is honest.

Defining the invariant for tuple verifyPath is technically challenging. The direction in which we check the signature list is different from the direction in which the route is created. The invariant needs to convey that part of a path has been verified, and part of it still needs to be verified. The solution is to use implication to state that if the path to be verified satisfies goodPath, then the entire path satisfies goodPath.

6 Related Work

Cryptographic Protocol Analysis. Analyzing cryptographic protocols [12,27,17,25,14,6,4,15] has been an active area of research. Compared to cryptographic protocols, secure routing protocols have to deal with arbitrary network topologies and the protocols are more complicated: they may access local storage and commonly include recursive computations. Most model-checking techniques are ineffective in the presence of those complications.

Verification of Trace Properties. A closely related body of work is logic for verifying trace properties of programs (protocols) that run concurrently with adversaries [12,15]. We are inspired by their program logic that requires the asserted properties of a program to hold even when that program runs concurrently with adversarial programs. One of our contributions is a general program logic for a declarative language SANDLog, which differs significantly from an ordinary imperative language. The program logic and semantics developed here apply to other declarative languages that use bottom-up evaluation strategy.

Wang et al. [29] have developed a proof system for proving correctness properties of networking protocols specified in NDLog. Built on proof-theoretic semantics of Datalog, they automatically translate NDLog programs into equivalent first-order logic axioms. Those axioms state that all the body tuples are derivable if and only if the head tuple is derivable. One main difference is that unlike theirs, we made explicit in our semantics, the trace associated with the distributed execution of a SANDLog program. Another important difference is that we verify invariants associated with each derived tuple in the presence of attackers, which are not present in their system. Therefore, their system cannot be directly used to verify the security properties of secure routing protocols.

Networking Protocol Verification. Recently, several papers have investigated the verification of route authenticity properties on specific wireless routing protocols for mobile networks [2,3,11]. They have showed that identifying attacks on route authenticity can be reduced to constraint solving, and that the security analysis of a specific route authenticity property that depends on the topologies of network instances can be reduced to checking these properties on several four-node topologies. In our own prior work [8], we have verified route authenticity properties on variants of S-BGP using a combination of manual proofs and an automated tool, Proverif [7]. The modeling and analysis in these works are specific to the protocols and the route authenticity properties. Some of the properties that we verify in our case study are similar. However, we propose a general framework for leveraging a declarative programming language for verification and empirical evaluation of routing protocols. The program logic proposed here can be used to verify generic safety properties of SANDLog programs.

There has been a large body of work on verifying the correctness of various network protocol design and implementations using proof-based and model-checking techniques [5,16,13,29]. The program logic presented here is customized to proving safety properties of SANDLog programs, and may not be expressive enough to verify complex correctness properties. However, the operational semantics for SANDLog can be used as the semantic model for verifying protocols encoded in SANDLog using other techniques.

7 Conclusion and Future Work

We have designed a program logic for verifying secure routing protocols specified in the declarative language SANDLog. We have integrated verification into a unified framework for formal analysis and empirical evaluation of secure routing protocols. As future work, we plan to expand our use cases, for example, to investigate mechanisms for securing the data (packet forwarding) plane [22]. In addition, as an alternative to Coq, we are also exploring the use of automated first-order logic theorem provers to automate our proofs.

Acknowledgments. The authors wish to thank the anonymous reviewers for their useful suggestions. Our work is supported by NSF CNS-1218066, NSF CNS-1117052, NSF CNS-1018061, NSF CNS-0845552, NSFITR-1138996, NSF CNS-1115706, AFOSR Young Investigator award FA9550-12-1-0327 and NSF ITR-1138996.

References

1. ns 3 project: Network Simulator 3, http://www.nsnam.org/
2. Arnaud, M., Cortier, V., Delaune, S.: Modeling and verifying ad hoc routing protocols. In: Proceedings of CSF (2010)
3. Arnaud, M., Cortier, V., Delaune, S.: Deciding security for protocols with recursive tests. In: Bjørner, N., Sofronie-Stokkermans, V. (eds.) CADE 2011. LNCS, vol. 6803, pp. 49–63. Springer, Heidelberg (2011)
4. Bau, J., Mitchell, J.: A security evaluation of DNSSEC with NSEC3. In: Proceedings of NDSS (2010)
5. Bhargavan, K., Obradovic, D., Gunter, C.A.: Formal verification of standards for distance vector routing protocols. J. ACM 49(4) (2002)
6. Blanchet, B.: Automatic verification of correspondences for security protocols. J. Comput. Secur. 17(4) (December 2009)
7. Blanchet, B., Smyth, B.: Proverif 1.86: Automatic cryptographic protocol verifier, user manual and tutorial, http://www.proverif.ens.fr/manual.pdf
8. Chen, C., Jia, L., Loo, B.T., Zhou, W.: Reduction-based security analysis of internet routing protocols. In: WRiPE (2012)
9. Chen, C., Jia, L., Xu, H., Luo, C., Zhou, W., Loo, B.T.: A program logic for verifying secure routing protocols. Tech. rep., CIS Dept. University of Pennsylvania (February 2014), http://netdb.cis.upenn.edu/forte2014

10. CNET: How pakistan knocked youtube offline,
    `http://news.cnet.com/8301-10784_3-9878655-7.html`
11. Cortier, V., Degrieck, J., Delaune, S.: Analysing routing protocols: Four nodes topologies are sufficient. In: Degano, P., Guttman, J.D. (eds.) POST. LNCS, vol. 7215, pp. 30–50. Springer, Heidelberg (2012)
12. Datta, A., Derek, A., Mitchell, J.C., Roy, A.: Protocol Composition Logic (PCL). Electronic Notes in Theoretical Computer Science 172, 311–358 (2007)
13. Engler, D., Musuvathi, M.: Model-checking large network protocol implementations. In: Proceedings of NSDI (2004)
14. Escobar, S., Meadows, C., Meseguer, J.: A rewriting-based inference system for the NRL protocol analyzer: grammar generation. In: Proceedings of FMSE (2005)
15. Garg, D., Franklin, J., Kaynar, D., Datta, A.: Compositional system security with interface-confined adversaries. ENTCS 265, 49–71 (2010)
16. Goodloe, A., Gunter, C.A., Stehr, M.O.: Formal prototyping in early stages of protocol design. In: Proceedings of ACM WITS (2005)
17. He, C., Sundararajan, M., Datta, A., Derek, A., Mitchell, J.C.: A modular correctness proof of IEEE 802.11i and TLS. In: Proceedings of CCS (2005)
18. Kamp, H.W.: Tense Logic and the Theory of Linear Order. Phd thesis, Computer Science Department, University of California at Los Angeles, USA (1968)
19. Kent, S., Lynn, C., Mikkelson, J., Seo, K.: Secure border gateway protocol (S-BGP). IEEE Journal on Selected Areas in Communications 18, 103–116 (2000)
20. Loo, B.T., Condie, T., Garofalakis, M., Gay, D.E., Hellerstein, J.M., Maniatis, P., Ramakrishnan, R., Roscoe, T., Stoica, I.: Declarative Networking: Language, Execution and Optimization. In: SIGMOD (2006)
21. Loo, B.T., Condie, T., Garofalakis, M., Gay, D.E., Hellerstein, J.M., Maniatis, P., Ramakrishnan, R., Roscoe, T., Stoica, I.: Declarative networking. Communications of the ACM (2009)
22. Naous, J., Walfish, M., Nicolosi, A., Mazieres, D., Miller, M., Seehra, A.: Verifying and enforcing network paths with ICING. In: Proceedings of CoNEXT (2011)
23. Nigam, V., Jia, L., Loo, B.T., Scedrov, A.: Maintaining distributed logic programs incrementally. In: Proceedings of PPDP (2011)
24. One Hundred Eleventh Congress: 2010 report to congress of the u.s.-china economic and security review commission (2010),
    `http://www.uscc.gov/annual_report/2010/annual_report_full_10.pdf`
25. Paulson, L.C.: Mechanized proofs for a recursive authentication protocol. In: Proceedings of CSFW (1997)
26. RapidNet: A Declarative Toolkit for Rapid Network Simulation and Experimentation, `http://netdb.cis.upenn.edu/rapidnet/`
27. Roy, A., Datta, A., Derek, A., Mitchell, J.C., Seifert, J.-P.: Secrecy analysis in protocol composition logic. In: Okada, M., Satoh, I. (eds.) ASIAN 2006. LNCS, vol. 4435, pp. 197–213. Springer, Heidelberg (2007)
28. Wan, T., Kranakis, E., Oorschot, P.C.: Pretty secure BGP (psBGP). In: Proceedings of NDSS (2005)
29. Wang, A., Basu, P., Loo, B.T., Sokolsky, O.: Declarative network verification. In: Gill, A., Swift, T. (eds.) PADL 2009. LNCS, vol. 5418, pp. 61–75. Springer, Heidelberg (2008)
30. White, R.: Securing bgp through secure origin BGP (soBGP). The Internet Protocol Journal 6(3), 15–22 (2003)
31. Zhang, X., Hsiao, H.C., Hasker, G., Chan, H., Perrig, A., Andersen, D.G.: Scion: Scalability, control, and isolation on next-generation networks. In: Proceedings of IEEE S&P (2011)

Verifying Security Policies Using Host Attributes

Cornelius Diekmann[1], Stephan-A. Posselt[1], Heiko Niedermayer[1],
Holger Kinkelin[1], Oliver Hanka[2], and Georg Carle[1]

[1] Technische Universität München, München, Germany
surname@net.in.tum.de
[2] Airbus Group Innovations, München, Germany
first_name.surname@eads.net

Abstract. For the formal verification of a network security policy, it is
crucial to express the verification goals. These formal goals, called security invariants, should be easy to express for the end user. Focusing on
access control and information flow security strategies, this work discov-
ers and proves universal insights about security invariants. This enables
secure and convenient auto-completion of host attribute configurations.
We demonstrate our results in a civil aviation scenario. All results are
machine-verified with the Isabelle/HOL theorem prover.

1 Introduction

A distributed system, from a networking point of view, is essentially a set of
interconnected hosts. Its connectivity structure comprises an important aspect
of its overall attack surface, which can be dramatically decreased by giving each
host only the necessary access rights. Hence, it is common to protect networks
using firewalls and other forms of enforcing network level access policies. However, raw sets of such policy rules e.g., firewall rules, ACLs, or access control
matrices, scale quadratically with the number of hosts and "controlling complexity is a core problem in information security" [15]. A case study, conducted in
this paper, reveals that even a policy with only 10 entities may cause difficulties
for experienced administrators. Expressive policy languages can help to reduce
the complexity. However, the question whether a policy fulfills certain security
invariants and how to express these often remains.

Fig. 1. Formal objects: Security invariant and security policy

Using an attribute-based [21] approach, we model simple, static, positive security policies with expressive, Mandatory Access Control (MAC) security invariants. The formal objects, illustrated in Fig. 1, are carefully constructed for
their use-case. The policy is simply a graph, which can for example be extracted
from or translated to firewall rules. The security invariants are split into the

E. Ábrahám and C. Palamidessi (Eds.), FORTE 2014, LNCS 8461, pp. 133–148, 2014.
© IFIP International Federation for Information Processing 2014

formal semantics, accessible to formal analysis, and scenario-specific knowledge, easily configurable by the end user. This model landscape enables verification of security policies. Primarily, we contribute the following universal insights for constructing security invariants.

1. Both provably *secure* and *permissive* default values for host attributes can be found. This auto completion decreases the user's configuration effort.
2. The security strategy, information flow or access control, determines whether a security violation occurs at the sender's or at the receiver's side.
3. A violated invariant can always be repaired by tightening the policy *if and only if* the invariant holds for the deny-all policy.

We formally introduce the underlying model in Sect. 2. Then we present three examples of security invariant templates in Sect. 3 and conduct a formal analysis in Sect. 4. Our implementation and a case study are presented in Sections 5 and 6. Related work is described in Sect. 7. We conclude in Sect. 8.

2   Formal Model

We formalized all our theory in the Isabelle/HOL theorem prover [20]. To stay focused, we omit all proofs in this document but point the reader to the complete formal proofs by roman reference marks. For example, when the paper states 'foo[iv]', the machine-verified proof for the claim 'foo' can be found by following the corresponding endnote. Note that standards such as Common Criteria [7] require formal verification for their highest *Evaluation Assurance Level* (EAL7) and the Isabelle/HOL theorem prover is suitable for this purpose [7, §A.5]. Therefore, our approach is not only suitable for verification, but also a first step towards certification.

Retaining network terminology, we will use the term *host* for any entity which may appear in a policy[1], e.g., collections of IP addresses, names, or even roles. A *security policy* is "a specific statement of what is and is not allowed" [5]. Narrowing its scope to network level access control, a security policy is a set of rules which state the allowed communication relationships between hosts. It can be represented as a directed graph.

Definition 1 (Security Policy). *A security policy is a directed graph $G = (V, E)$, where the hosts V are a set of type $\mathcal{V}$ and the allowed flows E are a set of type $\mathcal{V} \times \mathcal{V}$. The type of G is abbreviated by $\mathcal{G} = (\mathcal{V} \text{ set}) \times ((\mathcal{V} \times \mathcal{V}) \text{ set})$.*

A policy defines rules (*"how?"*). It does not justify the intention behind these rules (*"why?"*). To reflect the *why?*-question, we note that depending on a concrete scenario, hosts may have varying security-relevant attributes. We model a host attribute of arbitrary type Ψ and establish a total mapping from the hosts

---

[1] In contrast to common policy terminology, we do not differentiate between subjects and targets (objects) as they are usually indistinguishable on the network layer and a host may act as both.

V to their scenario-specific attribute. Security invariants can be constructed by combining a *host mapping* with a *security invariant template*. Latter two are defined together because the same Ψ is needed for a related host mapping and security invariant template. Different Ψ may appear across several security invariants.

Definition 2 (Host Mapping and Security Invariant Template). *For scenario-specific attributes of type Ψ, a host mapping P is a total function which maps a host to an attribute. P is of type $V \Rightarrow \Psi$.*

A security invariant template m is a predicate[2] $m(\mathcal{G}, (V \Rightarrow \Psi))$, defining the formal semantics of a security invariant. Its first argument is a security policy, its second argument a host attribute mapping. The predicate $m(G, P)$ returns true iff the security policy G fulfills the security invariant specified by m and P.

Example 1. Label-based information flow security can be modeled with a simplified version of the Bell LaPadula model [2,3]. Labels, more precisely *security clearances*, are host attributes $\Psi = \{unclassified, confidential, secret, topsecret\}$. The Bell LaPadula's no read-up and no write-down rules can be summarized by requiring that the security clearance of a receiver r should be greater-equal than the security clearance of the sender s, for all $(s, r) \in E$. With a total order '$\leq$' on Ψ, the security invariant template can be defined as $m((V, E), P) \equiv \forall (s, r) \in E.\ P(s) \leq P(r)$.

Let the scenario-specific knowledge be that database $db_1 \in V$ is *confidential* and all other hosts are *unclassified*. Using lambda calculus, the total function P can be defined as ($\lambda h.$ **if** $h = db_1$ **then** *confidential* **else** *unclassified*). Hence $P(db_1) = confidential$. For any policy G, the predicate $m(G, P)$ holds if db_1 does not leak confidential information (i.e. there is no non-reflexive outgoing edge from db_1).

Security invariants formalize security goals. A template contributes the formal semantics. A host mapping contains the scenario-specific knowledge. This makes the scenario-independent semantics available for formal reasoning by treating P and G as unknowns. Even reasoning with arbitrary security invariants is possible by additionally treating m as unknown.

With this modeling approach, the end user needs not to be bothered with the formalization of m, but only needs to specify G and P. In the course of this paper, we present a convenient method for specifying P.

Security Strategies and Monotonicity. In IT security, one distinguishes between two main classes of security strategies: *Access Control Strategies* (ACS) and *Information Flow Strategies* (IFS) [12, §6.1.4]. An IFS focuses on confidentiality and an ACS on integrity or controlled access. We require that m is in one of these classes[3].

---

[2] A predicate is a total, Boolean-valued function.

[3] By limiting m to IFS or ACS, we emphasize that availability is not in the scope of this work. Availability requires reasoning on a lower abstraction level, for example, to incorporate network hardware failure. Availability invariants could be expressed similarly, but would require inverse monotonicity (see below).

The two security strategies have one thing in common: they prohibit illegal actions. From an integrity and confidentiality point of view, prohibiting more never has a negative side effect. Removing edges from the policy cannot create new accesses and hence cannot introduce new access control violations. Similarly, for an IFS, by statically prohibiting flows in the network, no new direct information leaks nor new side channels can be created. In brief, prohibiting more does not harm security. From this, it follows that if a policy (V, E) fulfills its security invariant, for a stricter policy rule set $E' \subseteq E$, the policy (V, E') must also fulfill the security invariant. We call this property *monotonicity*.

Composition of Security Invariants. Usually, there is more than one security invariant for a given scenario. However, composition and modularity is often a non-trivial problem. For example, access control lists that are individually secure can introduce security breaches under composition [13]. Also, information flow security of individually secure processes, systems, and networks may be subverted by composition [19]. This is known as the *composition problem* [2].

With the formalization in this paper, composability and modularity are enabled by design. For a fixed policy G with k security invariants, let m_i be the security invariant template and P_i the host mapping, for $i \in \{1 \ldots k\}$. The predicate $m_i(G, P_i)$ holds if and only if the security invariant i holds for the policy G. With this modularity, composition of all security invariants is straightforward[i]: all security invariants must be fulfilled. The monotonicity guarantees that having more security invariants provides greater or equal security.

$$m_1(G, P_1) \wedge \cdots \wedge m_k(G, P_k)$$

3   Examples of Security Invariant Templates

In this section, we present three examples of security invariant templates. Our implementation currently features more than ten templates and grows. All can be inspected in the published theory files. Common networking scenarios such as subnets, non-interference invariants, or access control lists are available. With the following templates, a larger case study is presented in Section 6.

Simplified Bell LaPadula with Trust. A simplified version of the Bell LaPadula model is already outlined in Example 1. In this paragraph, we extend this model with a notion of trust by adding a Boolean flag *trust* to the host attributes. For a host v, let $P(v).sc$ denote v's security clearance and $P(v).trust$ if v is trusted. A trusted host can receive information of any security clearance and may declassify it, i.e. distribute the information with its own security clearance. For example, a trusted host is allowed to receive any information and with the *unclassified* clearance, it is allowed to reveal it to anyone. The template is thus formalized as follows.

$$m\big((V, E), P\big) \equiv \forall (s, r) \in E. \begin{cases} True & \textbf{if} \;\; P(r).trust \\ P(s).sc \;\leq\; P(r).sc & \textbf{otherwise} \end{cases}$$

Domain Hierarchy. The domain hierarchy template mirrors hierarchical access control structures. It is best introduced by example. The tiny car company (cc) consists of the two sub-departments engineering (e) and sales (s). The engineering department itself consists of the brakes (br) and the wheels (wh) department. This tree-like organizational structure is illustrated in Fig. 2a. We denote a position by the fully qualified domain name, e.g., $wh.e.cc$ uniquely identifies the wheels department. Let '⊑' denote the '*is below or at the same hierarchy level*' relation, e.g., $wh.e.cc ⊑ wh.e.cc$, $wh.e.cc ⊑ e.cc$, and $wh.e.cc ⊑ cc$. However, $wh.e.cc ⋢ br.e.cc$ and $br.e.cc ⋢ wh.e.cc$. The '⊑' relation denotes a partial order[ii]. The company's command structures are strictly hierarchical, i.e. commands are either exchanged in the same department or travel from higher departments to their sub-departments. Formally, the receiver's level ⊑ sender's level. For a host v, let $P(v).level$ map to the fully qualified domain name of v's department. For example in Fig. 2b, $P(Bob).level = e.cc$.

As in many real-world applications of a mathematical model, exceptions exist. Those are depicted by exclamation marks in Fig. 2b. For example, Bob as head of engineering is in a trusted position. This means he can operate as if he were in the position of Alice. This implies that he can communicate on par with Alice, which also implies that he might send commands to the sales department. We model such exceptions by assigning each host a trust level. This trust level specifies up to which position in the hierarchy this host may act. For example, Bob in $e.cc$ with a trust level of 1 can act as if he were in cc, which means he has the same command power as Alice. Let $P(v).trust$ map to v's trust level. We implement a function $chop(level : DomainName, trust : \mathbb{N}) \Rightarrow DomainName$ which chops off $trust$ sub-domains from a domain name, e.g., $chop(br.e.cc, 1) = e.cc$. With this, the security invariant template can be formalized as follows.

$$m((V, E), P) \equiv \forall (s, r) \in E. \ P(r).level \sqsubseteq chop\big(P(s).level, \ P(s).trust\big)$$

Security Gateway. Hosts may belong to a certain domain. Sometimes, a pattern where intra-domain communication between domain members must be approved by a central instance is required. As an example, let several virtual machines belong to the same domain and a secure hypervisor manage intra-domain communication. As another example, inter-device communication of

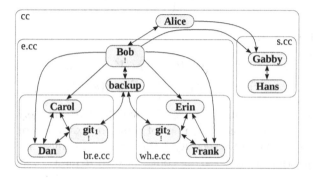

Fig. 2a (top): Organizational structure of **cc**

Fig. 2b (left): Policy and host mapping of **cc**

slave devices in the same domain is controlled by a central master device. We call such a central instance 'security gateway' and present a template for this architecture. Four host roles are distinguished: A security gateway (sgw), a security gateway accessible from the outside ($sgwa$), a domain member ($memb$), and a default value that reflects 'none of these roles' ($default$). The following table implements the access control restrictions. The role of the sender (snd), role of the receiver (rcv), the result (rslt), and an explanation are given.

snd	rcv	rslt	explanation
sgw	*	✓	Can send to the world.
$sgwa$	*	✓	— " —
$memb$	sgw	✓	Can contact its security gateway.
$memb$	$sgwa$	✓	— " —
$memb$	$memb$	✗	Must not communicate directly. May communicate via $sgw(a)$.
$memb$	$default$	✓	No restrictions for direct access to outside world. Outgoing accesses are not within the invariant's scope.
$default$	sgw	✗	Not accessible from outside.
$default$	$sgwa$	✓	Accessible from outside.
$default$	$memb$	✗	Protected from outside world.
$default$	$default$	✓	No restrictions.

This template is minimalistic in that it only restricts accesses to members (from other members or the outside world), whereas accesses from members to the outside world are unrestricted. It can be implemented by a simple table lookup. In-host communication is allowed by adding $s \neq r$.

$$m\big((V, E), P\big) \equiv \forall(s,r) \in E, \ s \neq r. \ \texttt{table}\big(P(s), \ P(r)\big)$$

4   Generic Semantic Analysis of Security Invariants

Offending Flows. Since m is monotonic, if an IFS or ACS security invariant is violated, there must be some flows in G that are responsible for the violation. By removing them, the security invariant should be fulfilled (if possible). We call a minimal set of such flows the *offending flows*. Minimality is expressed by requiring that every single flow in the offending flows bears responsibility for the security invariant's violation.

Definition 3   (Set of Offending Flows)

$$set\_offending\_flows(G, P) = \big\{ F \subseteq E \mid \neg m(G, P) \ \wedge \ m\big((V, E \setminus F), P\big) \ \wedge$$
$$\forall(s,r) \in F. \ \neg m\big((V, (E \setminus F) \cup \{(s,r)\}), P\big) \big\}$$

Example 2. The definition does not require that the offending flows are uniquely defined. This is reflected in its type since it is a set of sets. For example, for $G = (\{v_1, v_2, v_3\}, \{(v_1, v_2), (v_2, v_3)\})$ and a security invariant that v_1 must not transitively access v_3, the invariant is violated: v_2 could forward requests. The set of offending flows is $\{\{(v_1, v_2)\}, \{(v_2, v_3)\}\}$. This ambiguity tells the end user that there are multiple options to fix a violated security invariant. The policy can be tightened by prohibiting one of the offending flows, e.g., $\{(v_1, v_2)\}$.

If $m(G, P)$ holds, the set of offending flows is always empty[iii]. Also, for every element in the set of offending flows, it is guaranteed that prohibiting these flows leads to a fulfilled security invariant[iv]. It is not guaranteed that the set of offending flows is always non-empty for a violated security invariant. Depending on m, it may be possible that no set of flows satisfies Def. 3. However, Theorem 1 proves[v] an important insight: a violated invariant can always be repaired by tightening the policy if and only if the invariant holds for the deny-all policy.

Theorem 1 (No Edges Validity). *For m monotonic, arbitrary V, E, and P, let $G = (V, E)$ and $G_{deny\text{-}all} = (V, \emptyset)$. If $\neg m(G, P)$ then*

$$m\big(G_{deny\text{-}all},\, P\big) \longleftrightarrow set\_offending\_flows(G,\, P) \neq \emptyset$$

We demand that all security invariants fulfill $m\big(G_{deny\text{-}all},\, P\big)$. This means that violations are always fixable.

We call a host responsible for a security violation the *offending host*. Given one offending flow, the violation either happens at the sender's or the receiver's side. The following difference between ACS and IFS invariant can be observed. If m is an ACS, the host that initiated the request provokes the violation by violating an access control restriction. If m is an IFS, the information leak only occurs when the information reaches the unintended receiver. This distinction is essential as it renders the upcoming Def. 5 and 6 provable.

Definition 4 (Offending Hosts). *For $F \in set\_offending\_flows(G, P)$*

$$offenders(F) = \begin{cases} \{\, s \mid (s, r) \in F \,\} & \textbf{if } ACS \\ \{\, r \mid (s, r) \in F \,\} & \textbf{if } IFS \end{cases}$$

Secure Auto Completion of Host Mappings. Since P is a *total* function $V \Rightarrow \Psi$, a host mapping for *every* element of V must be provided. However, an end user might only specify the *security-relevant* host attributes. Let $P_C \subseteq V \times \Psi$ be a finite, possibly incomplete host attribute mapping specified by the end user. For some $\bot \in \Psi$, the total function P can be constructed by $P(v) \equiv$ (**if** $(v, \psi) \in P_C$ **then** ψ **else** $\bot$). Intuitively, if no host attribute is specified by the user, $\bot$ acts as a default attribute.

Given the user specified all security-relevant attributes, we observe that the default attribute can never solve an existing security violation. Therefore, we conclude that for a given security invariant m, a value $\bot$ can securely be used as a default attribute if it cannot mask potential security risks. In other words, a default attribute $\bot$ is secure w.r.t. the given information P if for all offenders v, replacing v's attribute[4] by $\bot$, denoted by $P_{v \mapsto \bot}$, has the same amount of security-relevant information as the original P.

---

[4] $P_{v \mapsto \bot} \equiv (\lambda x.\ \textbf{if}\ x = v\ \textbf{then}\ \bot\ \textbf{else}\ P(x))$, an updated P which returns $\bot$ for v.

Definition 5 (**Secure Default Attribute**). *A* $\bot$ *is a secure default attribute iff for a fixed* m *and for arbitrary* G *and* P *that cause a security violation, replacing the host attribute of any offenders by* $\bot$ *must guarantee that no security-relevant information is masked.*

$$\forall\, G\; P.\; \forall\, F \in set\_offending\_flows\,(G, P).\;\; \forall v \in \textit{offenders}(F).\; \neg\, m\big(G, P_{v \mapsto \bot}\big)$$

Example 3. In the simple Bell LaPadula model, an IFS, let us assume information is leaked. The predicate 'information leaks' holds, no matter to which lower security clearance the information is leaked. In general, if there is an illegal flow, it is from a higher security clearance at the sender to a lower security clearance at the receiver. Replacing the security clearance of the receiver with the lowest security clearance, the information about the security violation is always preserved. Thus, *unclassified* is the secure default attribute[vi]. In summary, if all classified hosts are labeled correctly, treating the rest as unclassified prevents information leakage.

To elaborate on Def. 5, it can be restated as follows. It focuses on the available security-relevant information in the case of a security violation. The attribute of an offending host v bears no information, except for the fact that there is a violation. A secure default attribute $\bot$ cannot solve security violations. Hence $P(v)$ and $\bot$ are equal w.r.t. the security violation. Thus, P and $P_{v \mapsto \bot}$ must be equal w.r.t. the information about the security violation. Requiring this property for all policies, all possible security violations, all possible choices of offending flows, and all candidates of offending hosts, this definition justifies that $\bot$ never hides a security problem.

Example 4. Definition 5 can be specialized to the exemplary case in which a new host x is added to a policy G without updating the host mapping. Consulting an oracle, x's real host attribute is $P(x) = \psi$. In reality, the oracle is not available and x is mapped to $\bot$ because it is new and unknown. Let x be an attacker. With the oracle's ψ-attribute, x causes a security violation. We demand that the security violation is exposed even without the knowledge from the oracle. Definition 5 satisfies this demand: if x mapped by the oracle to ψ causes a security violation, x mapped to $\bot$ does not mask the security violation.

A 'deny-all' default attribute is easily proven secure. Definition 5 reads the following for this case: if an offender v does something that violates $m(G, P)$, then removing all of v's rights ($P_{v \mapsto deny\text{-}all}$), a violation must persist. Hence, designing whitelisting security invariant templates with a restrictive default attribute is simple. However, to add to the ease-of-use, more permissive default attributes are often desirable since they reduce the manual configuration effort. In particular, if a security invariant only concerns a subset of a policy's hosts, no restrictions should be imposed on the rest of the policy. This is also possible with Def. 5, but may require a comparably difficult proof.

Example 5. In Example 1, no matter how many hosts are added to the policy, it is sufficient to only specify that db_1 is *confidential*. This confidentiality is guaranteed while no restrictions are put on hosts that do not interact with db_1.

Definition 6 (Default Attribute Uniqueness). *A default attribute $\perp$ is called unique iff it is secure (Def. 5) and there is no $\perp' \neq \perp$ s.t. $\perp'$ is secure.*

We demand that all security invariants fulfill Def. 6. This means that there is only one unique secure default attribute $\perp$.

Example 6. In the simple Bell LaPadula model, since the security clearances form a total order, the lowest security clearance is uniquely defined.

With the experience of proving Def. 5 and 6 for default attributes for 18 invariant templates, the connection between offending host and security strategy was discovered. During our early research, we realized that a Boolean variable, fixed for m, indicating the offending host was necessary to make Def. 5 and 6 provable. A classification of the different invariants revealed the important connection.

Default Attributes of Section 3's Templates. In the Bell LaPadula with Trust template, the default attribute is $(unclassified, untrusted)$[vii]. In the Domain Hierarchy, it is[viii] a special value $\perp$ with a trust of zero and which is at the lowest point in the hierarchy, i.e. $\forall\, l.\ \perp \sqsubseteq l$. Finally, it is worth mentioning that the $\sqsubseteq$-relation forms a lattice[ix], which is a desirable structure for security classes [10]. In the Security Gateway, the default attribute is $default$[x].

All default attributes allow flows between each other. This greatly adds to the ease-of-use, since the scope of an invariant is limited only to the explicitly configured hosts. The unconcerned parts of a security policy are not negatively affected.

Unique and Efficient Offending Flows. All security invariant templates presented in Section 3 have a simple, common structure: a predicate is evaluated for all flows. Let $\Phi(\Psi, \Psi)$ be this predicate. Note that all invariants of this structure fulfill monotonicity[xi].

Since Def. 3 is defined over all subsets, the naive computational complexity of is in **NP**. This section shows that – with knowledge about a concrete security invariant template m – it can be computed in linear time. For Φ-structured invariants, the offending flows are always uniquely defined and can be described intuitively[xii]5.

Theorem 2 (Φ Set of Offending Flows). *If m is Φ-structured $m(G, P) \equiv \forall(s, r) \in E.\ \Phi(P(s),\ P(r))$, then*

$$set\_offending\_flows(G, P) = \begin{cases} \{\{(s,r) \in E \mid \neg\, \Phi(P(s), P(r))\}\} & \textbf{if } \neg\, m(G, P) \\ \emptyset & \textbf{if } m(G, P) \end{cases}$$

Example 7. For the Bell LaPadula model, if no security violation exists the set of offending flows is $\emptyset$, else $\{\{(s, r) \in E \mid P(s) > P(r)\}\}$[xiv].

---

5 The same holds for templates with a structure similar to the Security Gateway[xiii].

Policy Construction. A policy that fulfills all security invariants can be constructed by removing all offending flows from the allow-all policy $G_{all} = (V, V \times V)$. This approach is sound[xv] for arbitrary m and even complete[xvi] for Φ-structured security invariant templates.

Example 8. If completely contradictory security invariants are given, the resulting (maximum) policy is the deny-all policy $G_{deny\text{-}all} = (V, \emptyset)$.

5 Implementation

We built a tool called topoS with all the features presented in this paper. Its core reasoning logic consists of code generated by Isabelle/HOL. This guarantees the correctness of all results computed by topoS's core [16].

Computational Complexity. topoS performs linear in the number of security invariants and quadratic in the number of hosts for Φ-structured invariants. For scenarios with less than 100 hosts, it responds interactively in less than 10 seconds. A benchmark of the automated policy construction, the most expensive algorithm, is presented in Fig. 3. For $|V|$ hosts, $|V|^2/4$ flows were created. With reasonable memory consumption, policies with up to 250k flows can be processed in less than half an hour. topoS contains a lot of machine generated code that is not optimized for performance but correctness. However, the overall theoretical and practical performance is sufficient for real-world usage. During our work with Airbus Group, we never encountered any performance issues.

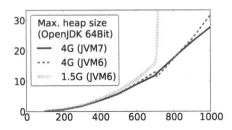

Fig. 3. Runtime of the policy construction algorithm for 100 Φ-structured invariants on an i7-2620M CPU (2.70GHz), Java Virtual Machine. X-axis: $|V|$, Y-axis: runtime in minutes.

Table 1. Statistics on Section 6's user-designed policies. Number of valid, violating, and missing flows. User experiences (top to bottom): Expert, Intermediate, Novice. Five participants each.

Section 6 User Case Study: Statistics		
Valid	Violations	Missing
16.0/15.8/1.7	1.0/3.2/4.4	5.0/5.6/2.1
14.0/14.0/1.4	1.0/1.6/1.9	7.0/7.4/1.0
12.0/10.6/5.7	4.0/6.6/4.9	11.0/11.2/6.2
median/arithmetic mean/std deviation		

6 Case Study: A Cabin Data Network

In this section, we present a slightly more complex scenario: a policy for a cabin data network for the general civil aviation. This example was chosen as security is very important in this domain and it provides a challenging interaction of different security invariants. It is a small imaginary toy example, developed in collaboration with Airbus Group. To make it self-contained and accessible to readers without aeronautical background knowledge, it does not obey aeronautical standards. However, the scenario is plausible, i.e. a real-world scenario may be similar. During our research, we also evaluated real world scenarios in this domain. With this experience, we try to present a small, simplified, self-contained, plausible toy scenario that, however, preserves many real world snares.

To estimate the scenario's complexity, we asked 15 network professionals to design its policy. On the one hand, as many use cases as possible should be fulfilled, on the other hand, no security violation must occur. Therefore, the task was to maximize the allowed flows without violating any security invariant. The results are illustrated in Table 1. Surprisingly, even expert network administrators made errors (both missing flows and security violations) when designing the policy.

A detailed scenario description, the host attribute mappings, and raw data are available in [11]. Using this reference, we also encourage the active reader to design the policy by oneself before it is revealed in Fig. 4b. The scenario is presented in the following compressed two paragraphs.

The network consists of the following hosts.

CC. The Cabin Core Server, a server that controls essential aircraft features, such as air conditioning and the wireless and wired telecommunication of the crew.

C1, C2. Two mobile devices for the crew to help them organize, e.g., communicate, make announcements.

Wifi. A wifi hotspot that allows passengers to access the Internet with their own devices. Explicitly listed as it might also be responsible for billing passenger's Internet access.

IFEsrv. The In-Flight Entertainment server with movies, Internet access, etc. Master of the IFE displays.

IFE1, IFE2. Two In-Flight Entertainment displays, mounted at the back of passenger seats. They provide movies and Internet access. Thin clients, everything is streamed from the IFE server.

P1, P2. Two passenger-owned devices, e.g., laptops, smartphones.

Sat. A satellite uplink to the Internet.

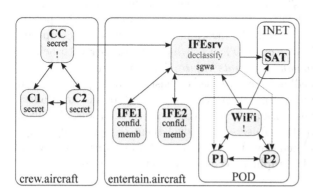

Fig. 4a (top): Security domains of the cabin data network

Fig. 4b (left): Cabin network policy and hosts' attributes

The following three security invariants are specified.

Security Invariant 1, Domain Hierarchy. Four different security domains exist in the aircraft, c.f. Fig. 4a. They separate the **crew** domain, the **entertainment** domain, the passenger-owned devices (**POD**) domain and the Internet (**INET**) domain.

In Fig. 4b, the host domain mapping is illustrated and trusted devices are marked with an exclamation mark.

The CC may send to the entertain domain, hence it is trusted. Possible use cases: Stewards coordinate food distribution; Announcement from the crew is send to the In-Flight Entertainment system (via CC) and distributed there to the IFE displays.

The Wifi is located in the **POD** domain to be reachable by PODs. It is trusted to send to the entertain domain. Possible use case: Passenger subscribes a film from the IFE server to her notebook or establishes connections to the Internet.

In the **INET** domain, the SAT is isolated to prevent accesses from the Internet into the aircraft.

Security Invariant 2, Security Gateway. The IFE displays are thin clients and strictly bound to their server. Peer to peer communication is prohibited. The Security Gateway model directly provides the respective access control restrictions.

Security Invariant 3, Bell LaPadula with Trust. Invariant 3 defines information flow restrictions by labeling confidential information sources. To protect the passenger's privacy when using the IFE displays, it is undesirable that the IFE displays communicate with anyone, except for the IFEsrv. Therefore, the IFE displays are marked as confidential (confid.). The IFEsrv is considered a central trusted device. To enable passengers to surf the Internet on the IFE displays by forwarding the packets to the Internet or forward announcements from the crew, it must be allowed to declassify any information to the default (i. e. unclassified) security clearance. Finally, the crew communication is considered more critical than the convenience features, therefore, CC, C1, and C2 are considered secret. As the IFEsrv is trusted, it can receive and forward announcements from the crew.

This case study illustrates that this complex scenario can be divided into three security invariants that can be represented with the help of the previously presented templates. Figure 4b also reveals that very few host attributes must be manually specified; the automatically added secure default attributes are not shown. All security invariants are fulfilled.

The automated policy construction yields the following results. The solid edges unified with the dashed edges[6] result in the uniquely defined policy with the maximum number of allowed flows. The solid lines were given by the policy, the dashed lines were calculated from the invariants. These 'diffs' are computed and visualized automatically by `topoS`. They provide the end user with helpful feedback regarding *'what do my invariants require?'* vs. *'what does my policy specify?'*. This results in a feedback loop we used extensively during our research to refine the policy and the invariants. It provides a 'feeling' for the invariants.

The main evaluation of this work are the formal correctness proofs. However, we also presented `topoS` to the 15 users and asked them to personally judge `topoS`'s utility. It was considered downright helpful and a majority would want to use it for similar tasks. The graphical feedback was also much appreciated.

7   Related Work

In a field study with 38 participants, Hamed and Al-Shaer discovered that "even expert administrators can make serious mistakes when configuring the network

---

[6] Unified with all reflexive edges, i.e. in-host communication.

security policy" [17]. Our user feedback session extends this finding as we discovered that even expert administrators can make serious mistakes when *designing* the network security policy.

In their inspiring work, Guttman and Herzog [15] describe a formal modeling approach for network security management. They suggest algorithms to verify whether configurations of firewalls and IPsec gateways fulfill certain security goals. These comparatively low-level security goals may state that a certain packet's path only passes certain areas or that packets between two networked hosts are protected by IPsec's ESP confidentiality header. This allows reasoning on a lower abstraction level at the cost of higher manual specification and configuration effort. Header space analysis [18] allows checking static network invariants such as no-forwarding-loops or traffic-isolation on the forwarding and middleboxes plane. It provides a common, protocol-agnostic framework and algebra on the packet header bits.

Firmato [1] was designed to ease management of firewalls. A firewall-independent entity relationship model is used to specify the security policy. With the help of a model compiler, such a model can be translated to firewall configurations. Ethane [6] is a link layer security architecture which evolved to the network operating system NOX [14]. They implement high-level security policies and propose a secure binding from host names to network addresses. In the long term, we consider topoS a valuable add-on on top of such systems for policy verification. For example, it could warn the administrator that a recent network policy change violates a security invariant, maybe defined years ago.

Expressive policy specification languages, such as Ponder [9], were proposed. Positive authorization policies (only a small aspect of Ponder) are roughly comparable to our policy graph. The authors note that e.g., negative authorization policies (deny-rules) can create conflicts. Policy constraints can be checked at compile time. In [4], a policy specification language (SPSL) with allow and deny policy rules is presented. With this, a conflict-free policy specification is constructed. Conflict-free Boolean formulas of this policy description and the policy implementation in the security mechanisms (router ACL entries) are checked for equality using a SAT solver. One unique feature covered is hidden service access paths, e.g., http might be prohibited in zone1 but zone1 can ssh to zone2 where http is allowed. [8] focuses on policies in dynamic systems and their analysis. These papers require specification of the verification goals and security goals and can thus benefit from our contributions.

This work's modeling concept is very similar to the Attribute Based Access Control (ABAC) model [21], though the underlying formal objects differ. ABAC distinguishes subjects, resources, and environments. Attributes may be assigned to each of these entities, similar to our host mappings. The ABAC policy model consists of positive rules which grant access based on the assigned attributes, comparably to security invariant templates. Therefore, our insights and contributions are also applicable to the ABAC model.

8   Conclusion

After more than 50k changed lines of formal theory, our simple, yet powerful, model landscape emerged. Representing policies as graphs makes them visualizable. Describing security invariants as total Boolean-valued functions is both expressive and accessible to formal analysis. Representing host mappings as partial configurations is end-user-friendly, transforming them to total functions makes them handy for the design of templates. With this simple model, we discovered important universal insights on security invariants. In particular, the transformation of host mappings and a simple sanity check which guarantees that security policy violations can always be resolved. This provides deep insights about how to express verification goals. The full formalization in the Isabelle/HOL theorem prover provides high confidence in the correctness.

Acknowledgments & Availability. We thank all the participants of our feedback session and the anonymous reviewers very much. A special thanks goes to our colleague Lothar Braun for his valuable feedback. Lars Hupel helped finalizing the paper. This work has been supported by the German Federal Ministry of Education and Research (BMBF) under support code 16BY1209F, project ANSII, and 16BP12304, EUREKA project SASER, and by the European Commission under the FP7 project EINS, grant number 288021.

Our Isabelle/HOL theory files and `topoS`'s Scala source code are available at `https://github.com/diekmann/topoS`

References

1. Bartal, Y., Mayer, A., Nissim, K., Wool, A.: Firmato: A novel firewall management toolkit. In: IEEE Symposium on Security and Privacy, pp. 17–31. IEEE (1999)
2. Bell, D.: Looking back at the Bell-La Padula model. In: Proceedings of the 21st Annual Computer Security Applications Conference, pp. 337–351 (December 2005)
3. Bell, D., LaPadula, L.: Secure computer systems: A mathematical model. MTR-2547, vol. II. The MITRE Corporation, Bedford (1973)
4. Bera, P., Ghosh, S., Dasgupta, P.: Policy based security analysis in enterprise networks: A formal approach. IEEE Transactions on Network and Service Management 7(4), 231–243 (2010)
5. Bishop, M.: What is computer security? IEEE Security & Privacy 1 (February 2003)
6. Casado, M., Freedman, M.J., Pettit, J., Luo, J., McKeown, N., Shenker, S.: Ethane: taking control of the enterprise. In: Proceedings of the 2007 Conference on Applications, Technologies, Architectures, and Protocols for Computer Communications, SIGCOMM 2007, pp. 1–12. ACM, New York (2007)
7. Common Criteria: Security assurance components. Common Criteria for Information Technology Security Evaluation CCMB-2012-09-003 (September 2012), `http://www.commoncriteriaportal.org/files/ccfiles/CCPART3V3.1R4.pdf`

8. Craven, R., Lobo, J., Ma, J., Russo, A., Lupu, E., Bandara, A.: Expressive policy analysis with enhanced system dynamicity. In: Proceedings of the 4th International Symposium on Information, Computer, and Communications Security, ASIACCS 2009, pp. 239–250. ACM, New York (2009)

9. Damianou, N., Dulay, N., Lupu, E., Sloman, M.: The ponder policy specification language. In: Sloman, M., Lobo, J., Lupu, E.C. (eds.) POLICY 2001. LNCS, vol. 1995, pp. 18–38. Springer, Heidelberg (2001)

10. Denning, D.E.: A lattice model of secure information flow. Communications of the ACM 19(5), 236–243 (1976)

11. Diekmann, C., Hanka, O., Posselt, S.-A., Schlatt, M.: Imaginary aircraft cabin data network (toy example) (July 2013),
http://www.net.in.tum.de/pub/diekmann/cabin_data_network.pdf

12. Eckert, C.: IT-Sicherheit: Konzepte-Verfahren-Protokolle, 8th edn. Oldenbourg Verlag (2013) ISBN 3486721380

13. Gong, L., Qian, X.: The complexity and composability of secure interoperation. In: Proceedings of 1994 IEEE Computer Society Symposium on Research in Security and Privacy, pp. 190–200 (1994)

14. Gude, N., Koponen, T., Pettit, J., Pfaff, B., Casado, M., McKeown, N., Shenker, S.: NOX: towards an operating system for networks. SIGCOMM Comput. Commun. Rev. 38(3), 105–110 (2008)

15. Guttman, J.D., Herzog, A.L.: Rigorous automated network security management. International Journal of Information Security 4, 29–48 (2005)

16. Haftmann, F., Nipkow, T.: Code generation via higher-order rewrite systems. In: Blume, M., Kobayashi, N., Vidal, G. (eds.) FLOPS 2010. LNCS, vol. 6009, pp. 103–117. Springer, Heidelberg (2010)

17. Hamed, H., Al-Shaer, E.: Taxonomy of conflicts in network security policies. IEEE Communications Magazine 44(3), 134–141 (2006)

18. Kazemian, P., Varghese, G., McKeown, N.: Header space analysis: static checking for networks. In: Networked Systems Design and Implementation, NSDI 2012. USENIX Association, Berkeley (2012)

19. McCullough, D.: A hookup theorem for multilevel security. IEEE Transactions on Software Engineering 16(6), 563–568 (1990)

20. Nipkow, T., Paulson, L.C., Wenzel, M.T.: Isabelle/HOL. LNCS, vol. 2283. Springer, Heidelberg (2002) (last updated 2013)

21. Yuan, E., Tong, J.: Attributed based access control (ABAC) for web services. In: IEEE International Conference on Web Services (2005)

Definitions, Lemmata, and Theorems

[i]all-security-requirements-fulfilled   [ii]instantiation   domainNameDept   ::   order
[iii]validmodel-imp-no-offending   [iv]remove-offending-flows-imp-model-valid   [v]valid-empty-edges-iff-exists-offending-flows   [vi]interpretation   BLPbasic: NetworkModel
[vii]interpretation   BLPtrusted: NetworkModel   [viii]interpretation   DomainHierarchyNG: NetworkModel   [ix]instantiation   domainName   ::   lattice   [x]interpretation
SecurityGatewayExtended-simplified: NetworkModel   [xi]monotonicity-eval-model-mono   [xii]ENF-offending-set   [xiii]ENFnr-offending-set   [xiv]BLP-offending-set
[xv]generate-valid-topology-sound   [xvi]generate-valid-topology-max-topo

Appendix

In this appendix, we provide the host attribute mappings of Section 6's case study.

Domain Hierarchy

CC	$\mapsto$	(level : *crew.aircraft*, trust : 1)
C1	$\mapsto$	(level : *crew.aircraft*, trust : 0)
C2	$\mapsto$	(level : *crew.aircraft*, trust : 0)
IFEsrv	$\mapsto$	(level : *entertain.aircraft*, trust : 0)
IFE1	$\mapsto$	(level : *entertain.aircraft*, trust : 0)
IFE2	$\mapsto$	(level : *entertain.aircraft*, trust : 0)
SAT	$\mapsto$	(level : *INET.entertain.aircraft*, trust : 0)
Wifi	$\mapsto$	(level : *POD.entertain.aircraft*, trust : 1)
P1	$\mapsto$	(level : *POD.entertain.aircraft*, trust : 0)
P2	$\mapsto$	(level : *POD.entertain.aircraft*, trust : 0)

Security Gateway

IFEsrv	$\mapsto$	*sgwa*
IFE1	$\mapsto$	*memb*
IFE2	$\mapsto$	*memb*

Simplified Bell LaPadula with Trust

CC	$\mapsto$	(sc : *secret*, trust : *False*)
C1	$\mapsto$	(sc : *secret*, trust : *False*)
C2	$\mapsto$	(sc : *secret* trust : *False*)
IFE1	$\mapsto$	(sc : *confidential*, trust : *False*)
IFE2	$\mapsto$	(sc : *confidential*, trust : *False*)
IFEsrv	$\mapsto$	(sc : *unclassified*, trust : *True*)

Denial-of-Service Security Attack
in the Continuous-Time World

Shuling Wang[1], Flemming Nielson[2], and Hanne Riis Nielson[2]

[1] State Key Laboratory of Computer Science, Institute of Software
Chinese Academy of Sciences, China
[2] DTU Informatics, Technical University of Denmark, Denmark

Abstract. Hybrid systems are integrations of discrete computation and continuous physical evolution. The physical components of such systems introduce
safety requirements, the achievement of which asks for the correct monitoring
and control from the discrete controllers. However, due to denial-of-service security attack, the expected information from the controllers is not received and
as a consequence the physical systems may fail to behave as expected. This paper proposes a formal framework for expressing denial-of-service security attack
in hybrid systems. As a virtue, a physical system is able to plan for reasonable
behavior in case the ideal control fails due to unreliable communication, in such
a way that the safety of the system upon denial-of-service is still guaranteed. In
the context of the modeling language, we develop an inference system for verifying safety of hybrid systems, without putting any assumptions on how the environments behave. Based on the inference system, we implement an interactive
theorem prover and have applied it to check an example taken from train control
system.

Keywords: Hybrid systems, Denial-of-service, Safety verification, Inference
system.

1   Introduction

Hybrid systems, also known as cyber-physical systems, are dynamic systems with interacting continuous-time physical systems and discrete controllers. The physical systems
evolve continuously with respect to time, such as aircrafts, or biological cell growth,
while the computer controllers, such as autopilots, or biological control circuits, monitor and control the behavior of the systems to meet the given design requirements. One
design requirement is safety, which includes time-critical constraints, or invariants etc.,
for the example of train control systems, the train should arrive at the stops on time, or
the train must always move with a velocity within a safe range.

However, due to the uncertainty in the environment, the potential errors in wireless
communications between the interacting components will make the safety of the system
very hard to guarantee. For the sake of safety, when the controllers fail to behave as
expected because of absence of expected communication and thus become unreliable,
the physical systems should provide feedback control, to achieve safety despite errors
in communication.

E. Ábrahám and C. Palamidessi (Eds.), FORTE 2014, LNCS 8461, pp. 149–165, 2014.

A Motivating Example. We illustrate our motivation by an example taken from train control system, that is depicted in Fig. 1. It consists of three inter-communicating components: Train, Driver and on board vital computer (VC). We assume that the train owns arbitrarily long movement authority, within which the train is allowed to move only, and must conform to a safety requirement, i.e. the velocity must be non-negative and cannot exceed a maximum limit. The train acts as a continuous plant, and moves with a given acceleration; both the driver and the VC act as controllers, in such a way that, either of them observes the velocity of the train periodically, and then according to the safety requirement, computes the new acceleration for the train to follow in the next period. According to the specification of the system, the message from the VC always takes high priority over the one from the driver.

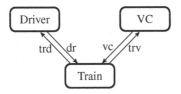

Fig. 1. The structure of train control example

However, the expected monitoring and control from VC or driver may fail due to denial-of-service security attack, e.g. if the driver falls asleep, or if the VC gets malfunction, and as a consequence, the train may get no response from any of them within a duration of time. The safety requirement of the train will then be violated very easily. This poses the problem of how to build a safe hybrid system in the presence of this sort of denial-of-service security attack from the environment.

The contribution of this paper includes the following aspects:

- a programming notation, for formally modeling hybrid systems and meanwhile being able to express denial-of-service due to unreliable communications, and an assertion language, for describing safety as annotations in such programs;
- a deductive inference system, for reasoning about whether the program satisfies the annotated safety property, and a subsequent interactive theorem prover.

As a direct application, we are able to build a safe system for the example such that:

(F1) the error configurations where neither driver nor VC is available are not reachable;
(F2) the velocity of the train keeps always in the safe range, although in the presence of denial-of-service attack from the driver or the VC.

Furthermore, when the behavior of the environments (i.e. driver and VC) is determined, e.g. by defining some constraints among the constants of the whole system, we can learn more precise behavior of the train.

In Section 2 and Section 3, we present the syntax and semantics for the formal modeling language. It is a combination of Hybrid CSP (HCSP) [5,20], a process algebra based modeling language for describing hybrid systems, and the binders from Quality Calculus [13], a process calculus that allows one to take measures in case of unreliable communications. With the introducing of binders, the modelling language is capable of programming a safe system that executes in an open environment that does not always live up to expectations.

In Section 4, we define an inference system for reasoning about HCSP with binders. For each construct P, the specification is of the form $\{\varphi\}\ P\ \{\psi, HF\}$, where φ and ψ are the pre-/post-condition recording the initial and terminating states of P respectively, and HF the history formula recording the whole execution history of P (thus able to specify global invariants). As a direct application, the (un-)reachability analysis can be performed by identifying the points corresponding to the error configurations by logical formulas and then checking the (un-)satisfiability of the formulas. In Section 5, we have applied a theorem prover we have implemented to verify properties (F1) and (F2) of the train control example. At last, we conclude the paper and address some future work.

Related Work.   There have been numerous work on formal modeling and verification of hybrid systems, e.g., [1,11,6,10,7], the most popular of which is *hybrid automata* [1,11,6]. For automata-based approaches, the verification of hybrid systems is reduced to computing reachable sets, which is conducted either by model-checking [1] or by the decision procedure of Tarski algebra [7]. However, hybrid automata, analogous to state machines, has little support for structured description; and meanwhile, the verification of it based on reachability computation is not scalable and only applicable to some specific linear hybrid systems, as it heavily depends on the decidability of the problems to be solved. Applying abstraction or (numeric) approximation [4,2,3] can improve the scalability, but as a pay we have to sacrifice the precision.

In contrast, deductive methods increasingly attract more attention in the verification of hybrid systems as it can scale up to complex systems. A differential-algebraic dynamic logic for hybrid programs [14] was proposed by extending dynamic logic with continuous statements, and has been applied for safety checking of European Train Control System [15]. However, the hybrid programs there can be considered as a textual encoding of hybrid automata, with no support for communication and concurrency. In [8,17], the Hoare logic is extended to hybrid systems modeled by Hybrid CSP [5,20], and then used for safety checking of Chinese Train Control System. But the logic lacks compositionality.

All the work mentioned above focus on safety without considering denial-of-service security attacks from the environment. Quality Calculus [13,12] for the first time proposed a programming notation for expressing denial-of-service in communication systems, but is currently limited to discrete time world.

2   Syntax

We first choose Hybrid CSP (HCSP) [5,20] as the modelling language for hybrid systems. HCSP inherits from CSP the explicit communication model and concurrency, thus is expressive enough for describing distributed components and the interactions between them. Moreover, it extends CSP with differential equations for representing continuous evolution, and provides several forms of interrupts to continuous evolution for realizing communication-based discrete control. On the other hand, Quality Calculus [13,12] is recently proposed to programming software components and their interactions in the presence of unreliable communications. With the help of *binders* specifying the success or failure of communications and then the communications to be performed before continuing, it becomes natural in Quality Calculus to plan for reasonable behavior in case the ideal behavior fails due to unreliable communication and thereby to increase the quality of the system.

In our approach, we will extend HCSP further with the notion of binders from Quality Calculus, for modelling hybrid systems in the presence of denial-of-service because of unreliable communications. The overall modelling language is given by the following syntax:

$$
\begin{aligned}
e \quad &::= c \mid x \mid f^k(e_1, ..., e_k) \\
b \quad &::= ch!e\{u_1\} \mid ch?x\{u_2\} \mid \&_q(b_1, \cdots, b_n) \\
P, Q ::= \text{ } &\text{skip} \mid x := e \mid b \mid \langle \mathcal{F}(\dot{s}, s) = 0 \& B \rangle \mid \langle \mathcal{F}(\dot{s}, s) = 0 \& B \rangle \rhd b \to Q \mid \\
&P \| Q \mid P; Q \mid \omega \to P \mid P^*
\end{aligned}
$$

Expressions e are used to construct data elements and consist of constants c, data variables x, and function application $f^k(e_1, ..., e_k)$.

Binders b specify the inputs and outputs to be performed before continuing. The output $ch!e\{u_1\}$ expects to send message e along channel ch, with u_1 being the acknowledgement in case the communication succeeds, and the dual input $ch?x\{u_2\}$ expects to receive a message from ch and assigns it to variable x, with u_2 being the acknowledgement similarly. We call both u_1 and u_2 *acknowledgment variables*, and assume in syntax that for each input or output statement, there exists a unique acknowledgement variable attached to it. In the sequel, we will use $\mathcal{V}$ and $\mathcal{A}$ to represent the set of data variables and acknowledgement variables respectively, and they are disjoint. For the general form $\&_q(b_1, \cdots, b_n)$, the quality predicate q specifies the sufficient communications among $b_1, \cdots, b_n$ for the following process to proceed. In syntax, q is a logical combination of quality predicates corresponding to $b_1, \cdots, b_n$ recursively (denoted by $q_1, \cdots, q_n$ respectively below). For example, the quality predicates for $ch!e\{u_1\}$ and $ch?x\{u_2\}$ are boolean formulas $u_1 = 1$ and $u_2 = 1$. There are two special forms of quality predicates, abbreviated as $\exists$ and $\forall$, with the definitions: $\forall \overset{\text{def}}{=} q_1 \wedge \cdots \wedge q_n$ and $\exists \overset{\text{def}}{=} q_1 \vee \cdots \vee q_n$. More forms of quality predicates can be found in [13].

Example 1. For the train example, define binder b_0 as $\&_\exists(\text{dr}?x_a\{u_a\}, \text{vc}?y_a\{w_a\})$, the quality predicate of which amounts to $u_a = 1 \vee w_a = 1$. It expresses that, the train is waiting for the acceleration from the driver and the VC, via dr and vc respectively, and as soon as one of the communications succeeds (i.e., when the quality predicate becomes true), the following process will be continued without waiting for the other. □

P, Q define processes. The skip and assignment $x := e$ are defined as usual, taking no time to complete. Binders b are explained above. The continuous evolution $\langle \mathcal{F}(\dot{s}, s) = 0 \& B \rangle$, where s represents a vector of continuous variables and $\dot{s}$ the corresponding first-order derivative of s, forces s to evolve according to the differential equations $\mathcal{F}$ as long as B, a boolean formula of s that defines the *domain of* s, holds, and terminates when B turns false. The communication interrupt $\langle \mathcal{F}(\dot{s}, s) = 0 \& B \rangle \rhd b \to Q$ behaves as

$\langle \mathcal{F}(\dot{s}, s) = 0 \& B \rangle$ first, and if b occurs before the continuous terminates, the continuous will be preempted and Q will be executed instead.

The rest of the constructs define compound processes. The parallel composition $P \| Q$ behaves as if P and Q run independently except that the communications along the common channels connecting P and Q are to be synchronized. In syntax, P and Q in parallel are restricted not to share variables, nor input or output channels. The sequential composition $P; Q$ behaves as P first, and if it terminates, as Q afterwards. The conditional $\omega \rightarrow P$ behaves as P if ω is true, otherwise terminates immediately. The condition ω can be used for checking the status of data variables or acknowledgement, thus in syntax, it is a boolean formula on data and acknowledgement variables (while for the above continuous evolution, B is a boolean formula on only data variables). The repetition P^* executes P for arbitrarily finite number of times.

It should be noticed that, with the addition of binders, it is able to derive a number of other known constructs of process calculi, e.g., internal and external choice [13].

Example 2. Following Example 1, the following model

$$t := 0; {}^1\langle \dot{s} = v, \dot{v} = a, \dot{t} = 1 \& t < T \rangle \trianglerighteq b_0{}^2 \rightarrow$$
$$(w_a = 1{}^3 \rightarrow a := y_a; w_a = 0 \wedge u_a = 1{}^4 \rightarrow a := x_a; \ w_a = 0 \wedge u_a = 0{}^5 \rightarrow \text{skip})$$

denoted by P_0, expresses that, the train moves with velocity v and acceleration a, and as soon as b_0 occurs within T time units, i.e. the train succeeds to receive a new acceleration from either the driver or the VC, then its acceleration a will be updated by case analysis. It can be seen that the acceleration from VC will be used in priority. For later reference we have annotated the program with labels (e.g. 1, 2, etc.).   □

3   Transition Semantics

We first introduce a variable *now* to record the global time during process execution, and then define the set $\mathcal{V}^+ = \mathcal{V} \cup \mathcal{A} \cup \{now\}$. A state, ranging over σ, σ', assigns a value to each variable in $\mathcal{V}^+$, and we will use Σ to represent the set of states. A flow, ranging over h, h', defined on a closed time interval $[r_1, r_2]$ with $0 \leq r_1 \leq r_2$, or an infinite interval $[r, \infty)$ with some $r \geq 0$, assigns a state in Σ to each point in the interval. Given a state σ, an expression e is evaluated to a value under σ, denoted by $\sigma(e)$ below.

Each transition relation has the form $(P, \sigma) \xrightarrow{\alpha} (P', \sigma', h)$, where P is a process, σ, σ' are states, h is a flow, and α is an event. It represents that starting from initial state σ, P evolves into P' and ends with state σ' and flow h, while performing event α. When the above transition takes no time, it produces a point flow, i.e. $\sigma(now) = \sigma'(now)$ and $h = \{\sigma(now) \mapsto \sigma'\}$, and we will call the transition *discrete* and write $(P, \sigma) \xrightarrow{\alpha} (P', \sigma')$ instead without losing any information. The label α represents events, which can be a discrete internal event, like skip, assignment, evaluation of boolean conditions, or termination of a continuous evolution etc., uniformly denoted by τ, or an external communication, like output $ch!c\{1\}$ or input $ch?c\{1\}$, or an internal communication $ch\dagger c\{1\}$, or a time delay d for some positive d. We call the events but the time delay *discrete events*, and will use β to range over them.

Table 1. The transition relations for binders and the auxiliary functions

$$(ch?x\{u\}, \sigma) \xrightarrow{ch?c\{1\}} (\epsilon, \sigma[x \mapsto c, u \mapsto 1])$$

$$(ch?x\{u\}, \sigma) \xrightarrow{d} (ch?x\{u\}, \sigma[now + d], h_d)$$

$$(ch!e\{u\}, \sigma) \xrightarrow{ch!\sigma(e)\{1\}} (\epsilon, \sigma[u \mapsto 1]) \quad (ch!e\{u\}, \sigma) \xrightarrow{d} (ch!e\{u\}, \sigma[now + d], h_d)$$

$$[\![q]\!](b_1, \cdots, b_n) = q[(b_1 \equiv \epsilon)/q_1, \cdots, (b_n \equiv \epsilon)/q_n]$$

$$\langle\!\langle()\rangle\!\rangle\sigma = \sigma \quad \langle\!\langle(\epsilon, b_2, \cdots, b_n)\rangle\!\rangle\sigma = \langle\!\langle(b_2, \cdots, b_n)\rangle\!\rangle\sigma$$

$$\langle\!\langle(ch?x\{u\}, b_2, \cdots, b_n)\rangle\!\rangle\sigma = \langle\!\langle(b_2, \cdots, b_n)\rangle\!\rangle(\sigma[u \mapsto 0])$$

$$\langle\!\langle(ch!e\{u\}, b_2, \cdots, b_n)\rangle\!\rangle\sigma = \langle\!\langle(b_2, \cdots, b_n)\rangle\!\rangle(\sigma[u \mapsto 0])$$

$$\langle\!\langle(\&_{q_k}(b_{k1}, \cdots, b_{km}), b_2, \cdots, b_n)\rangle\!\rangle\sigma = \langle\!\langle(b_{k1}, \cdots, b_{km}, b_2, \cdots, b_n)\rangle\!\rangle\sigma$$

$$\frac{[\![q]\!](b_1, \cdots, b_n) = false}{(\&_q(b_1, \cdots, b_n), \sigma) \xrightarrow{d} (\&_q(b_1, \cdots, b_n), \sigma[now + d], h_d)}$$

$$\frac{(b_i, \sigma) \xrightarrow{\beta} (b_i', \sigma')}{(\&_q(b_1, \cdots, b_i, \cdots, b_n), \sigma) \xrightarrow{\beta} (\&_q(b_1, \cdots, b_i', \cdots, b_n), \sigma')}$$

$$\frac{[\![q]\!](b_1, \cdots, b_n) = true \quad \langle\!\langle(b_1, \cdots, b_n)\rangle\!\rangle\sigma = \sigma'}{(\&_q(b_1, \cdots, b_n), \sigma) \xrightarrow{\tau} (\epsilon, \sigma')}$$

The transition relations for binders are defined in Table 1. The input $ch?x\{u\}$ may perform an external communication $ch?c\{1\}$, and as a result x will be bound to c and u set to 1, or it may keep waiting for d time. For the second case, a flow h_d over $[\sigma(now), \sigma(now) + d]$ is produced, satisfying that for any t in the domain, $h_d(t) = \sigma[now \mapsto t]$, i.e. no variable but the clock now in $\mathcal{V}^+$ is changed during the waiting period. Similarly, there are two rules for output $ch!e\{u\}$. Here $\sigma[now + d]$ is an abbreviation for $\sigma[now \mapsto \sigma(now) + d]$.

Before defining the semantics of general binders, we introduce two auxiliary functions. Assume $(b_1, \cdots, b_n)$ is an intermediate tuple of binders that occurs during execution (thus some of b_is might contain ϵ), q a quality predicate, and σ a state. The function $[\![q]\!](b_1, \cdots, b_n)$ defines the truth value of q under $(b_1, \cdots, b_n)$, which is calculated by replacing each sub-predicate q_i corresponding to b_i in q by $b_i \equiv \epsilon$ respectively; and function $\langle\!\langle(b_1, b_2, \cdots, b_n)\rangle\!\rangle\sigma$ returns a state that fully reflects the failure or success of binders $b_1, \cdots, b_n$, and can be constructed from σ by setting the acknowledgement variables corresponding to the failing inputs or outputs among $b_1, \cdots, b_n$ to be 0. Based on these definitions, binder $\&_q(b_1, \cdots, b_n)$ may keep waiting for d time, if q is false under $(b_1, \cdots, b_n)$, or perform a discrete event β that is enabled for some b_i, or perform a τ transition and terminate if q is true under $(b_1, \cdots, b_n)$. Notice that when q becomes true, the enabled discrete events can still be performed, as indicated by the second rule.

Example 3. Starting from σ_0, the execution of b_0 in Example 1 may lead to three possible states at termination:

- $\sigma_0[now + d, x_a \mapsto c_a, u_a \mapsto 1, w_a \mapsto 0]$, indicating that the train succeeds to receive c_a from the driver after d time units have passed, but fails for the VC;
- $\sigma_0[now + d, y_a \mapsto d_a, w_a \mapsto 1, u_a \mapsto 0]$, for the opposite case of the first;
- $\sigma_0[now + d, x_a \mapsto c_a, u_a \mapsto 1, y_a \mapsto d_a, w_a \mapsto 1]$, indicating that the train succeeds to receive messages from the driver as well as the VC after d time.   □

The transition relations for other processes are defined in Table 2. The rules for skip and assignment can be defined as usual. The idle rule represents that the process can stay at the terminating state ϵ for arbitrary d time units, with nothing changed but only the clock progress. For continuous evolution, for any $d > 0$, it evolves for d time units according to $\mathcal{F}$ if B evaluates to true within this period (the right end exclusive). A flow $h_{d,s}$ over $[\sigma(now), \sigma(now) + d]$ will then be produced, such that for any o in the domain, $h_{d,s}(o) = \sigma[now \mapsto o, s \mapsto S(o - \sigma(now))]$, where $S(t)$ is the solution as defined in the rule. Otherwise, the continuous evolution terminates at a point if B evaluates to false at the point, or if B evaluates to false at a positive open interval right to the point.

For communication interrupt, the process may evolve for d time units if both the continuous evolution and the binder can progress for d time units, and then reach the same state and flow as the continuous evolution does. It may perform a discrete event over b, and if the resulting binder b' is not ϵ, then the continuous evolution is kept, otherwise, the continuous evolution will be interrupted and Q will be followed to execute, and for both cases, will reach the same state and flow as the binder does. Finally, it may perform a τ event and terminate immediately if the continuous evolution terminates with a τ event but b not. Notice that the final state σ'' needs to be reconstructed from σ' by resetting the acknowledgement variables of those unsuccessful binders occurring in b to be 0.

Before defining the semantics of parallel composition, we need to introduce some notations. Two states σ_1 and σ_2 are *disjoint*, iff $\mathrm{dom}(\sigma_1) \cap \mathrm{dom}(\sigma_2) = \{now\}$ and $\sigma_1(now) = \sigma_2(now)$. For two disjoint states σ_1 and σ_2, $\sigma_1 \uplus \sigma_2$ is defined as a state over $\mathrm{dom}(\sigma_1) \cup \mathrm{dom}(\sigma_2)$, satisfying that $\sigma_1 \uplus \sigma_2(v)$ is $\sigma_1(v)$ if $v \in \mathrm{dom}(\sigma_1)$, otherwise $\sigma_2(v)$ if $v \in \mathrm{dom}(\sigma_2)$. We lift this definition to flows h_1 and h_2 satisfying $\mathrm{dom}(h_1) = \mathrm{dom}(h_2)$, and define $h_1 \uplus h_2$ to be a flow such that $h_1 \uplus h_2(t) = h_1(t) \uplus h_2(t)$. For $P \| Q$, assume σ_1 and σ_2 represent the initial states for P and Q respectively and are disjoint. The process will perform a communication along a common channel of P and Q, if P and Q get ready to synchronize with each other along the channel. Otherwise, it will perform a discrete event, that can be τ, an internal communication of P, or an external communication along some non-common channel of P and Q, if P can progress separately on this event (and the symmetric rule for Q is left out here). When neither internal communication nor τ event is enabled for $P \| Q$, it may evolve for d time units if both P and Q can evolve for d time units. Finally, the process will perform a τ event and terminate as soon as both the components terminate.

At last, the rules for conditional, sequential, and repetition are defined as usual.

Example 4. Starting from state σ_0, the execution of P_0 in Example 2 leads to the following cases (let v_0 denote $\sigma_0(v)$ below):

Table 2. The transition relations for processes

Skip, Assignment and Idle $(\text{skip}, \sigma) \xrightarrow{\tau} (\epsilon, \sigma)$

$$(x := e, \sigma) \xrightarrow{\tau} (\epsilon, \sigma[x \mapsto \sigma(e)]) \qquad (\epsilon, \sigma) \xrightarrow{d} (\epsilon, \sigma[now + d], h_d)$$

Continuous Evolution   For any $d > 0$,

$$\frac{S(t) \text{ is a solution of } \mathcal{F}(\dot{s}, s) = 0 \text{ over } [0, d] \text{ satisfying that } S(0) = \sigma(s)}{(\langle \mathcal{F}(\dot{s}, s) = 0 \& B \rangle, \sigma) \xrightarrow{d} (\langle \mathcal{F}(\dot{s}, s) = 0 \& B \rangle, \sigma[now + d, s \mapsto S(d)], h_{d,s})}$$

$$\frac{\begin{array}{c} (\sigma(B) = false) \text{ or } (\sigma(B) = true \wedge \exists \delta > 0. \\ (S(t) \text{ is a solution of } \mathcal{F}(\dot{s}, s) = 0 \text{ over } [0, \delta] \text{ satisfying that } S(0) = \sigma(s) \\ \text{and } \forall t \in (0, \delta).h_{\delta,s}(t + \sigma(now))(B) = false)) \end{array}}{(\langle \mathcal{F}(\dot{s}, s) = 0 \& B \rangle, \sigma) \xrightarrow{\tau} (\epsilon, \sigma)}$$

Communication Interrupt

$$\frac{(\langle \mathcal{F}(\dot{s}, s) = 0 \& B \rangle, \sigma) \xrightarrow{d} (\langle \mathcal{F}(\dot{s}, s) = 0 \& B \rangle, \sigma', h) \quad (b, \sigma) \xrightarrow{d} (b, \sigma'', h'')}{(\langle \mathcal{F}(\dot{s}, s) = 0 \& B \rangle \trianglerighteq b \to Q, \sigma) \xrightarrow{d} (\langle \mathcal{F}(\dot{s}, s) = 0 \& B \rangle \trianglerighteq b \to Q, \sigma', h)}$$

$$\frac{(b, \sigma) \xrightarrow{\beta} (b', \sigma') \quad b' \neq \epsilon}{(\langle \mathcal{F}(\dot{s}, s) = 0 \& B \rangle \trianglerighteq b \to Q, \sigma) \xrightarrow{\beta} (\langle \mathcal{F}(\dot{s}, s) = 0 \& B \rangle \trianglerighteq b' \to Q, \sigma')}$$

$$\frac{(b, \sigma) \xrightarrow{\beta} (\epsilon, \sigma')}{(\langle \mathcal{F}(\dot{s}, s) = 0 \& B \rangle \trianglerighteq b \to Q, \sigma) \xrightarrow{\beta} (Q, \sigma')}$$

$$\frac{(\langle \mathcal{F}(\dot{s}, s) = 0 \& B \rangle, \sigma) \xrightarrow{\tau} (\epsilon, \sigma') \quad \neg((b, \sigma) \xrightarrow{\tau} (\epsilon, -))}{b \equiv \&_q(b_1, \cdots, b_n) \quad \langle\!\langle (b_1, \cdots, b_n) \rangle\!\rangle \sigma' = \sigma''}{(\langle \mathcal{F}(\dot{s}, s) = 0 \& B \rangle \trianglerighteq b \to Q, \sigma) \xrightarrow{\tau} (\epsilon, \sigma'')}$$

Parallel Composition

$$\frac{(P, \sigma_1) \xrightarrow{ch?c\{1\}} (P', \sigma_1') \quad (Q, \sigma_2) \xrightarrow{ch!c\{1\}} (Q', \sigma_2')}{(P \parallel Q, \sigma_1 \uplus \sigma_2) \xrightarrow{ch\dagger c\{1\}} (P'\|Q', \sigma_1' \uplus \sigma_2')}$$

$$\frac{(P, \sigma_1) \xrightarrow{\beta} (P', \sigma_1') \quad \beta \in \{\tau, ch\dagger c\{1\}, ch?c\{1\}, ch!c\{1\} \mid}{ch \notin \mathbf{Chan}(P) \cap \mathbf{Chan}(Q)\} \quad \forall ch, c.(\neg((P, \sigma_1) \xrightarrow{ch?c\{1\}} \wedge (Q, \sigma_2) \xrightarrow{ch!c\{1\}})}{\wedge \neg((P, \sigma_1) \xrightarrow{ch!c\{1\}} \wedge (Q, \sigma_2) \xrightarrow{ch?c\{1\}}))}{(P \parallel Q, \sigma_1 \uplus \sigma_2) \xrightarrow{\beta} (P'\|Q, \sigma_1' \uplus \sigma_2)}$$

$$\frac{(P, \sigma_1) \xrightarrow{d} (P', \sigma_1', h_1) \quad (Q, \sigma_2) \xrightarrow{d} (Q', \sigma_2', h_2)}{\forall ch, c.\neg((P \parallel Q, \sigma_1 \uplus \sigma_2) \xrightarrow{ch\dagger c\{1\}}) \quad \neg((P \parallel Q, \sigma_1 \uplus \sigma_2) \xrightarrow{\tau})}{(P \parallel Q, \sigma_1 \uplus \sigma_2) \xrightarrow{d} (P'\|Q', \sigma_1' \uplus \sigma_2', h_1 \uplus h_2)}$$

$$(\epsilon\|\epsilon, \sigma) \xrightarrow{\tau} (\epsilon, \sigma)$$

Other Compound Constructs

$$\frac{\sigma(\omega) = true}{(\omega \to P, \sigma) \xrightarrow{\tau} (P, \sigma)} \qquad \frac{\sigma(\omega) = false}{(\omega \to P, \sigma) \xrightarrow{\tau} (\epsilon, \sigma)}$$

$$\frac{(P, \sigma) \xrightarrow{\alpha} (P', \sigma', h) \quad P' \neq \epsilon}{(P; Q, \sigma) \xrightarrow{\alpha} (P'; Q, \sigma', h)} \qquad \frac{(P, \sigma) \xrightarrow{\alpha} (\epsilon, \sigma', h)}{(P; Q, \sigma) \xrightarrow{\alpha} (Q, \sigma', h)}$$

$$\frac{(P, \sigma) \xrightarrow{\alpha} (P', \sigma', h) \quad P' \neq \epsilon}{(P^*, \sigma) \xrightarrow{\alpha} (P'; P^*, \sigma', h)} \qquad \frac{(P, \sigma) \xrightarrow{\alpha} (\epsilon, \sigma', h)}{(P^*, \sigma) \xrightarrow{\alpha} (P^*, \sigma', h)} \qquad (P^*, \sigma) \xrightarrow{\tau} (\epsilon, \sigma)$$

- P_0 terminates without the occurrence of b_0, the final state is $\sigma_0[now + T, t + T, v + aT, s + v_0 T + 0.5aT^2, u_a \mapsto 0, w_a \mapsto 0]$;
- b_0 occurs after d time units for some $d \leq T$, and as a result P_0 executes to location 2, with state $\sigma_0[now + d, t + d, v + ad, s + v_0 d + 0.5ad^2, u_a, w_a, x_a, y_a]$, where u_a, w_a, x_a and y_a have 3 possible evaluations as defined in Example 3, and then depending on the values of u_a and w_a, executes to location 3 or 4 respectively, and finally terminates after a corresponding acceleration update. □

Flow of a Process. Given two flows h_1 and h_2 defined on $[r_1, r_2]$ and $[r_2, r_3]$ (or $[r_2, \infty)$) respectively, we define the concatenation $h_1^\frown h_2$ as the flow defined on $[r_1, r_3]$ (or $[r_1, \infty)$) such that $h_1^\frown h_2(t)$ is equal to $h_1(t)$ if $t \in [r_1, r_2)$, otherwise $h_2(t)$. Given a process P and an initial state σ, if we have the following sequence of transitions:

$$(P, \sigma) \xrightarrow{\alpha_0} (P_1, \sigma_1, h_1) \quad (P_1, \sigma_1) \xrightarrow{\alpha_1} (P_2, \sigma_2, h_2)$$
$$\cdots \quad (P_{n-1}, \sigma_{n-1}) \xrightarrow{\alpha_{n-1}} (P_n, \sigma_n, h_n)$$

then we define $h_1^\frown \ldots ^\frown h_n$ as the *flow* from P to P_n with respect to the initial state σ, and furthermore, write $(P, \sigma) \xrightarrow{\alpha_0 \cdots \alpha_{n-1}} (P_n, \sigma_n, h_1^\frown \ldots ^\frown h_n)$ to represent the whole transition sequence (and for simplicity, the label sequence can be omitted sometimes). When P_n is ϵ, we call $h_1^\frown \ldots ^\frown h_n$ a *complete flow* of P with respect to σ.

4 Inference System

In this section, we define an inference system for reasoning about both discrete and continuous properties of HCSP with binders, which are considered for an isolated time point and a time interval respectively.

History Formulas. In order to describe the interval-related properties, we introduce history formulas, that are defined by duration calculus (DC) [19,18]. DC is a first-order interval-based real-time logic with one binary modality known as chop $^\frown$. History formulas HF are defined by the following subset of DC:

$$HF ::= \ell \circ T \mid \lceil S \rceil \mid HF_1 ^\frown HF_2 \mid \neg HF \mid HF_1 \vee HF_2$$

where ℓ is a temporal variable denoting the length of the considered interval, $\circ \in \{<, =\}$ is a relation, T a non-negative real, and S a first-order state formula over process variables. For simplicity, we will write $\lceil S \rceil^<$ as an abbreviation for $\lceil S \rceil \vee \ell = 0$.

HF can be interpreted over flows and intervals. We define the judgement $h, [a, b] \models HF$ to represent that HF holds under h and $[a, b]$, then we have

$$h, [a, b] \models \ell \circ T \text{ iff } (b - a) \circ T \qquad h, [a, b] \models \lceil S \rceil \text{ iff } \int_a^b h(t)(S) = b - a$$
$$h, [a, b] \models HF_1 ^\frown HF_2 \text{ iff } \exists c. a \leq c \leq b \wedge h, [a, c] \models HF_1 \wedge h, [c, b] \models HF_2$$

As defined above, ℓ indicates the length of the considered interval; $\lceil S \rceil$ asserts that S holds almost everywhere in the considered interval; and $HF_1^\frown HF_2$ asserts that the interval can be divided into two sub-intervals such that HF_1 holds for the first and HF_2 for the second. The first-order connectives $\neg$ and $\vee$ can be explained as usual.

All axioms and inference rules for DC presented in [18] can be applied here, such as

$$\text{True} \Leftrightarrow \ell \geq 0 \quad \lceil S \rceil^\frown \lceil S \rceil \Leftrightarrow \lceil S \rceil \quad HF^\frown \ell = 0 \Leftrightarrow HF$$
$$\lceil S_1 \rceil \Rightarrow \lceil S_2 \rceil \text{ if } S_1 \Rightarrow S_2 \text{ is valid in FOL}$$

Specification. The specification for process P takes form $\{\varphi\}\, P\, \{\psi, HF\}$, where the pre-/post-condition φ and ψ, defined by FOL, specify properties of variables that hold at the beginning and termination of the execution of P respectively, and the history formula HF, specifies properties of variables that hold throughout the execution interval of P. The specification of P is defined with no dependence on the behavior of its environment. The specification is *valid*, denoted by $\models \{\varphi\}\, P\, \{\psi, HF\}$, iff for any state σ, if $(P, \sigma) \to (\epsilon, \sigma', h)$, then $\sigma \models \varphi$ implies $\sigma' \models \psi$ and $h, [\sigma(now), \sigma'(now)] \models HF$.

Acknowledgement of Binders. In order to define the inference rules for binders b, we first define an auxiliary typing judgement $\vdash b \blacktriangleright \varphi$, where the first-order formula φ describes the acknowledgement corresponding to successful passing of b, and is defined without dependence on the precondition of b. We say $b \blacktriangleright \varphi$ *valid*, denoted by $\models b \blacktriangleright \varphi$, iff given any state σ, if $(b, \sigma) \to (\epsilon, \sigma', h)$, then $\sigma' \models \varphi$ holds.

The typing judgement for binders is defined as follows:

$$\vdash ch?x\{u\} \blacktriangleright u = 1 \qquad \vdash ch!e\{u\} \blacktriangleright u = 1 \qquad \frac{\vdash b_1 \blacktriangleright \varphi_1, \cdots, \vdash b_n \blacktriangleright \varphi_n}{\vdash \&_q(b_1, \cdots, b_n) \blacktriangleright [\![q]\!](\varphi_1, \cdots, \varphi_n)}$$

As indicated above, for input $ch?x\{u\}$, the successful passing of it gives rise to formula $u = 1$, and similarly for output $ch!e\{u\}$; for binder $\&_q(b_1, \cdots, b_n)$, it gives rise to formula $[\![q]\!](\varphi_1, \cdots, \varphi_n)$, which encodes the effect of quality predicate q to the sub-formulas $\varphi_1, \ldots, \varphi_n$ corresponding to $b_1, \ldots, b_n$ respectively.

Example 5. For binder b_0 in Example 1, we have $\vdash b_0 \blacktriangleright u_a = 1 \vee w_a = 1$, indicating that, if the location after b_0 is reachable, then at least one of the communications with the driver or the VC succeeds. □

4.1 Inference Rules

We first introduce an auxiliary function $mv(b)$, which given a binder b, returns the variables that may be modified by b. It can be defined directly by structural induction on b and we omit the details. The inference rules for deducing the specifications of all constructs are presented in Table 3.

Statements skip and assignment are defined as in classical Hoare Logic, plus $\ell = 0$ in the history formula, indicating that they both take zero time to complete. For each form of the binders b, the postcondition is the conjunction of the quantified precondition φ over variables in $mv(b)$ and the acknowledgement corresponding to the successful passing of b. The binders may occur without waiting any time, indicated by $\ell = 0$ as one disjunctive clause of each history formula. For both $ch?x\{u\}$ and $ch!e\{u\}$, if the waiting time is greater than 0, then φ will hold almost everywhere in the waiting interval

Table 3. An inference system for processes

$$\{\varphi\}\ \text{skip}\ \{\varphi, \ell = 0\} \quad \{\psi[e/x]\}\ x := e\ \{\psi, \ell = 0\}$$

$$\{\varphi\}\ ch?x\{u\}\ \{(\exists x, u.\varphi) \wedge u = 1, \lceil\varphi\rceil^<\} \quad \{\varphi\}\ ch!e\{u\}\ \{(\exists u.\varphi) \wedge u = 1, \lceil\varphi\rceil^<\}$$

$$\frac{\vdash \&_q(b_1, \cdots, b_n) \blacktriangleright \alpha}{\{\varphi\}\ \&_q(b_1, \cdots, b_n)\ \{(\exists mv(\&_q(b_1, \cdots, b_n)).\varphi) \wedge \alpha, \lceil\exists mv(\&_q(b_1, \cdots, b_n)).\varphi\rceil^<\}}$$

$$\{\varphi\}\ \langle\mathcal{F}(\dot{s}, s) = 0 \& B\rangle\ \{(\exists s.\varphi) \wedge cl(\neg B) \wedge cl(Inv), \lceil(\exists s.\varphi) \wedge B \wedge Inv\rceil^<\}$$

$$\frac{\vdash \&_q(b_1, \cdots, b_n) \blacktriangleright \alpha \quad \{(\exists mv(b).(\exists s.\varphi) \wedge cl(Inv)) \wedge \alpha\}\ Q\ \{\psi_1, h_1\}}{\{\varphi\}\langle\mathcal{F}(\dot{s}, s) = 0 \& B\rangle \trianglerighteq b \to Q\ \begin{cases}(\exists mv(b).(\exists s.\varphi) \wedge cl(\neg B) \wedge cl(Inv)) \vee \psi_1, \\ \lceil\exists mv(b).(\exists s.\varphi) \wedge B \wedge Inv\rceil^{<\frown}(\ell = 0 \vee h_1)\end{cases}}$$

$$\frac{\{\varphi\}\ P\ \{\psi_1, h_1\} \quad \{\varphi\}\ Q\ \{\psi_2, h_2\}}{\{\varphi\}\ P\|Q\ \{\psi_1 \wedge \psi_2, ((h_1^\frown\text{True}) \wedge h_2) \vee (h_1 \wedge (h_2^\frown\text{True}))\}}$$

$$\frac{\{\varphi\}\ P\ \{\psi_1, h_1\} \quad \{\psi_1\}\ Q\ \{\psi_2, h_2\}}{\{\varphi\}\ P; Q\ \{\psi_2, h_1^\frown h_2\}} \qquad \frac{\{\varphi \wedge \omega\}\ P\ \{\psi_1, h_1\}}{\{\varphi\}\ \omega \to P\ \{(\varphi \wedge \neg\omega) \vee \psi_1, \ell = 0 \vee h_1\}}$$

$$\frac{\{\varphi\}\ P\ \{\varphi, Inv\} \quad Inv^\frown Inv \Rightarrow Inv}{\{\varphi\}\ P^*\ \{\varphi, Inv \vee \ell = 0\}}$$

(the only possible exception is the right endpoint, at which the communication occurs and variables might be changed correspondingly). For $\&_q(b_1, \cdots, b_n)$, only the quantified φ over variables in $mv(b)$ is guaranteed to hold almost everywhere throughout the waiting interval, since some binders b_is that make q true might occur at sometime during the interval and as a consequence variables in φ might get changed.

For continuous evolution, the notion of differential invariants is used instead of explicit solutions. A *differential invariant* of $\langle\mathcal{F}(\dot{s}, s) = 0 \& B\rangle$ for given initial values of s is a first-order formula of s, which is satisfied by the initial values and also by all the values reachable by the trajectory of s defined by $\mathcal{F}$ within the domain B. A method on generating differential invariants for polynomial differential equations was proposed in [9]. Here we assume Inv is a differential invariant with respect to precondition φ for the continuous evolution (more details on using Inv are shown in the later example proof). For the postcondition, the quantified φ over the only modified variables s, the closure of $\neg B$, and the closure of Inv hold. The closure $cl(\cdot)$ extends the domain defined by the corresponding formula to include the boundary. For the history formula, the execution interval may be 0, or otherwise, the quantified φ over s, B and Inv holds almost everywhere throughout the interval.

For communication interrupt, if b fails to occur before the continuous evolution terminates, the effect of the whole statement is almost equivalent to the continuous evolution, except that some variables in b may get changed because of occurrences of some communications during the execution of the continuous evolution. Otherwise, if b succeeds within the termination of the continuous evolution, the continuous evolution will be interrupted and Q will start to execute from the interrupting point. At the interrupting point, the acknowledgement of b holds, and moreover, because s and variables in $mv(b)$ may have been modified, $\exists mv(b).((\exists s.\varphi) \wedge cl(Inv))$ holds (the closure here is to include the case when the interrupting point is exactly the termination point of the continuous evolution). For the second case, the postcondition is defined as the one for Q, and the history formula as the chop of the one for the continuous evolution before interruption and the one for Q afterwards. Finally, as indicated by the rule, the postcondition and history formula for the whole statement are defined as the disjunction of the above two cases.

The rule for $P\|Q$ is defined by conjunction, however, because P and Q may terminate at different time, the formula True is added to the end of the history formula with short time interval to make the two intervals equal. For $P; Q$, the history formula is defined by the concatenation of the ones of P and Q. The rule for $\omega \to P$ includes two cases depending on whether ω holds or not. At last, for P^*, we need to find the invariants, i.e. φ and Inv, for both the postcondition and history formula.

The general inference rules that are applicable to all constructs, like monotonicity, case analysis etc., can be defined as usual and are omitted here.

We have proved the following soundness theorem:

Theorem 1. *Given a process P, if $\{\varphi\}\ P\ \{\psi, HF\}$ can be deduced from the inference rules, then $\models \{\varphi\}\ P\ \{\psi, HF\}$.*

PROOF. The proof can be found at the report [16]. ☐

4.2 Application: Reachability Analysis

The inference system can be applied directly for reachability analysis. Given a labelled process S (a process annotated with integers denoting locations), a precondition φ and a location l in S, by applying the inference system, we can deduce a property ψ such that if S reaches l, ψ must hold at l, denoted by $\vdash S, l, \varphi \blacktriangleright \psi$. In another word, If $\vdash S, l, \varphi \blacktriangleright \psi$ and ψ is not satisfiable, then l will not be reachable in S with respect to φ. We have the following facts based on the structural induction of S:

- for any process P, $\vdash {}^l P, l, \varphi \blacktriangleright \varphi$ and $\vdash P^l, l, \varphi \blacktriangleright \psi$ provided $\{\varphi\}\ P\ \{\psi, -\}$;
- $\vdash \langle \mathcal{F}(\dot{s}, s) = 0 \& B \rangle \trianglerighteq {}^l b \to S', l, \varphi \blacktriangleright \varphi$. $\vdash \langle \mathcal{F}(\dot{s}, s) = 0 \& B \rangle \trianglerighteq b^l \to S', l, \varphi \blacktriangleright (\exists mv(b).(\exists s.\varphi) \land cl(Inv)) \land \alpha$ (denoted by φ'), if $\vdash b \blacktriangleright \alpha$ holds. $\vdash \langle \mathcal{F}(\dot{s}, s) = 0 \& B \rangle \trianglerighteq b \to S', l, \varphi \blacktriangleright \psi$ if $l \in S'$ and $\vdash S', l, \varphi' \blacktriangleright \psi$ hold;
- $\vdash S_1; S_2, l, \varphi \blacktriangleright \psi$ if $l \in S_1$ and $\vdash S_1, l, \varphi \blacktriangleright \psi$ hold. $\vdash S_1; S_2, l, \varphi \blacktriangleright \psi'$ if $l \in S_2$, $\{\varphi\}\ S_1\ \{\psi, -\}$ and $\vdash S_2, l, \psi \blacktriangleright \psi'$ hold;
- $\vdash \omega^l \to S', l, \varphi \blacktriangleright \varphi \land \omega$. $\vdash \omega \to S', l, \varphi \blacktriangleright \psi$ if $l \in S'$ and $\vdash S', l, \varphi \land \omega \blacktriangleright \psi$;
- $\vdash S'^*, l, \varphi \blacktriangleright \psi$, if $l \in S'$, $\vdash S', l, \varphi \blacktriangleright \psi$ and $\{\varphi\}\ S'\ \{\varphi, -\}$ hold.

Obviously, the monotonicity holds: if $\vdash S, l, \varphi \blacktriangleright \psi$ and $\psi \Rightarrow \psi'$, then $\vdash S, l, \varphi \blacktriangleright \psi'$.

Example 6. Consider P_0 in Example 2. Given precondition φ , we have $\vdash P_0, 1, \varphi \blacktriangleright (\exists t.\varphi) \land t = 0$, denoted by φ_1. Moreover, $\vdash P_0, 5, \varphi \blacktriangleright (\exists mv(b_0).(\exists s, v, t.\varphi_1) \land t \le T) \land (u_a = 1 \lor w_a = 1) \land (u_a = 0 \land w_a = 0)$, the formula is un-satisfiable, thus location 5 is not reachable. Other locations can be considered similarly. ☐

Implementation. We have mechanized the whole framework in Isabelle/HOL and implemented an interactive theorem prover for reasoning about hybrid systems modeled using HCSP with binders[1].

5 Train Control Example

We apply our approach to the train control system depicted in Fig. 1: firstly, we construct the formal model for the whole system, especially the train; secondly, prove for the train that it is safe against denial-of-service security attack with respect to properties (F1) and (F2); finally, explore the constraints that relate the constants of different components and learn more precise behavior of the train. Assume for the train that its acceleration ranges over $[-c, c]$ for some $c > 0$, and the maximum speed is v_{max}.

Table 4. The model of **train**

$$
\begin{aligned}
\mathsf{TR} = \mathsf{MV}(t_1, T_1) &\unrhd {}^0 \&_\exists (\mathsf{trd}!v\{u_v\}, \mathsf{trv}!v\{w_v\})^7 \\
&\to (u_v = 1 \wedge w_v = 1 \to (\mathsf{MV}(t_2, T_2) \unrhd \&_\exists (\mathsf{dr}?x_a\{u_a\}, \mathsf{vc}?y_a\{w_a\}) \to \\
&\quad (w_a = 1 \to (VA(v, y_a) \to a := y_a; \neg VA(v, y_a) \to \mathsf{SC}); \\
&\quad u_a = 1 \wedge w_a = 0 \to (VA(v, x_a) \to a := x_a; \neg VA(v, x_a) \to \mathsf{SC}); \\
&\quad u_a = 0 \wedge w_a = 0 \to {}^2\mathsf{skip}); t_2 \ge T_2 \to \mathsf{SC}; \\
&\quad u_v = 1 \wedge w_v = 0 \to (\mathsf{MV}(t_2, T_2) \unrhd \&_\exists (\mathsf{dr}?x_a\{u_a\}) \to \\
&\quad\quad (u_a = 1 \to (VA(v, x_a) \to a := x_a; \neg VA(v, x_a) \to \mathsf{SC}); \\
&\quad\quad u_a = 0 \to {}^3\mathsf{skip}); t_2 \ge T_2 \to \mathsf{SC}; \\
&\quad u_v = 0 \wedge w_v = 1 \to (\mathsf{MV}(t_2, T_2) \unrhd \&_\exists (\mathsf{vc}?y_a\{w_a\}) \to \\
&\quad\quad (w_a = 1 \to (VA(v, y_a) \to a := y_a; \neg VA(v, y_a) \to \mathsf{SC}); \\
&\quad\quad w_a = 0 \to {}^4\mathsf{skip}); t_2 \ge T_2 \to \mathsf{SC}; \\
&\quad u_v = 0 \wedge w_v = 0 \to {}^1\mathsf{skip}); t_1 \ge T_1 \to \mathsf{SC}; \\
\mathsf{MV} (t, T) &= t := 0; \langle \dot{s} = v, \dot{v} = a, \dot{t} = 1 \& t < T \rangle \\
\mathsf{SC} &= a := -c; \langle \dot{s} = v, \dot{v} = a \& v > 0 \rangle; a := 0
\end{aligned}
$$

Models. The model of the train is given in Table 4. There are two auxiliary processes: given a clock variable t and time T, MV (t, T) defines that the train moves with velocity v and acceleration a for up to T time units; and SC defines the feedback control of the train when the services from the driver or the VC fail: it performs an emergency brake by setting a to be $-c$, and as soon as v is reduced to 0, resets a to be 0, thus the train keeps still finally. The main process TR models the movement of a train. The train first moves for at most T_1 time units, during which it is always ready to send v to the driver as well as the VC along trd and trv respectively. If neither of them responses within T_1, indicated by $t_1 \ge T_1$, the self control is performed. Otherwise, if at least one communication occurs, the movement is interrupted and a sequence of case analysis is followed to execute.

The first case, indicated by $u_v = 1$ and $w_v = 1$, represents that the driver as well as the VC succeed to receive v. The train will wait for at most T_2 time units for the

---

[1] The prover, plus the models and proofs related to the train control example in next section, can be found at https://github.com/wangslyl/hcspwithbinders

Table 5. The models of **driver** and **VC**

$\mathsf{DR} = \mathsf{wait}\ T_3;\ ^5\&_\exists\mathsf{trd}?v_d\{u_v\};\ ^8u_v = 1$

$\quad \to (v_d \geq (v_{max} - cT_1 - cT_2)$

$\qquad \to []_{l\in[-c,0)}d_a := l;$

$\quad v_d < (cT_1 + cT_2) \to []_{l\in[0,c]}d_a := l;$

$\quad v_d \in [cT_1 + cT_2, v_{max} - cT_1 - cT_2)$

$\qquad \to []_{l\in[-c,c]}d_a := l;$

$\quad \&_\exists(\mathsf{dr}!d_a\{u_a\}, \mathsf{tick}?o\{u_c\}) \to$

$\qquad ^{12}(u_a = 1 \wedge u_c = 1 \to \mathsf{skip};$

$\qquad\quad u_a = 1 \wedge u_c = 0 \to \mathsf{tick}?o\{u_c\};$

$\qquad\quad u_a = 0 \wedge u_c = 1 \to \mathsf{skip};$

$\qquad\quad u_a = 0 \wedge u_c = 0 \to \mathsf{skip})$

$\quad ||\mathsf{CK});$

$\quad u_v = 0 \to \mathsf{skip}$

$\mathsf{CK} = \mathsf{wait}\ T_5;\ \mathsf{tick}!\checkmark$

$\mathsf{VC} = \mathsf{wait}\ T_4;\ ^6\&_\exists\mathsf{trv}?v_r\{w_v\};\ ^9w_v = 1$

$\quad \to (v_r \geq (v_{max} - cT_1 - cT_2)$

$\qquad \to r_a := -c;$

$\quad v_r < (cT_1 + cT_2) \to r_a := c;$

$\quad v_r \in [cT_1 + cT_2, v_{max} - cT_1 - cT_2)$

$\qquad \to []_{l\in[-c,c]}r_a := l;$

$\quad \&_\exists(\mathsf{vc}!r_a\{w_a\}, \mathsf{tick}?o\{w_c\}) \to$

$\qquad (w_a = 1 \wedge w_c = 1 \to \mathsf{skip};$

$\qquad\quad w_a = 1 \wedge w_c = 0 \to \mathsf{tick}?o\{w_c\};$

$\qquad\quad w_a = 0 \wedge w_c = 1 \to \mathsf{skip};$

$\qquad\quad w_a = 0 \wedge w_c = 0 \to \mathsf{skip})$

$\quad ||\mathsf{CK});$

$\quad w_v = 0 \to \mathsf{skip}$

new acceleration from the driver or the VC along dr and vc respectively, and during the waiting time, it continues to move with the original acceleration. The new acceleration is expected to satisfy a safety condition $VA(v, a)$:

$$(v > v_{max} - cT_1 - cT_2 \Rightarrow -c \leq a < 0) \wedge (v < cT_1 + cT_2 \Rightarrow c \geq a \geq 0)$$
$$\wedge(cT_1 + cT_2 \leq v \leq v_{max} - cT_1 - cT_2) \Rightarrow (-c \leq a \leq c)$$

which implies the boundaries for setting a to be positive or negative and is necessary for keeping the velocity always in $[0, v_{max}]$, otherwise, it will be rejected by the train. If both the driver and the VC fail to response within T_2, indicated by $t_2 \geq T_2$, the self control is performed. Otherwise, the following case analysis is taken: If the train receives a value (i.e. y_a) from VC, indicated by $w_a = 1$, then sets y_a to be the acceleration if it satisfies VA, otherwise, performs self control; if the train receives a value (i.e. x_a) from the driver but not from the VC, updates the acceleration similarly as above; if the train receives no value from both (in fact never reachable), the skip is performed.

The other three cases, indicated by $u_v = 1 \wedge w_v = 0$, $u_v = 0 \wedge w_v = 1$, and $u_v = 0 \wedge w_v = 0$, can be considered similarly.

One possible implementation for driver and VC is given in Table 5, in which process wait T_i for $i = 3, 4$ is an abbreviation for $t_i := 0; \langle t_i = 1 \& t_i < T_i \rangle$. In process DR, the driver asks the velocity of the train every T_3 time units, and as soon as it receives v_d, indicated by $u_v = 1$, it computes the new acceleration as follows: if v_d is almost reaching v_{max} (by the offset $cT_1 + cT_2$), then chooses a negative in $[-c, 0)$ randomly; if v_d is almost reaching 0, then chooses a non-negative in $[0, c]$ randomly; otherwise, chooses one in $[-c, c]$ randomly. The train then sends the value being chosen (i.e. d_a) to the train, and if it fails to reach the train within T_5 (i.e. the period of the clock), it will give up. The auxiliary process clock is introduced to prevent deadlock caused by the situation when the driver succeeds to receive velocity v_d from the train but fails to send acceleration d_a to the train within a reasonable time (i.e. T_5 here). VC and DR have very similar structure, except that VC has a different period T_4, and it will choose $-c$ or c as the acceleration for the first two critical cases mentioned above.

Finally, the train control system can be modeled as the parallel composition: $\mathsf{SYS} = \mathsf{TR}^* \| \mathsf{DR}^* \| \mathsf{VC}^* \| \mathsf{CK}^*$. By using $*$, each component will be executed repeatedly.

Proofs of Train. First of all, we define the precondition of TR^*, denoted by φ_0, to be $VA(v,a) \wedge 0 \leq v \leq v_{max} \wedge -c \leq a \leq c$, which indicates that in the initial state, v and a satisfy the safety condition and are both well-defined.

Secondly, we need to calculate the differential invariants for differential equations occurring in TR. Consider the equation in $\mathsf{MV}(t_1, T_1)$, the precondition of it with respect to φ_0, denoted by φ_1, can be simply calculated, which is $\varphi_0 \wedge t_1 = 0$, then by applying the method proposed in [9]:

$$\left(\begin{array}{l} (0 \leq t_1 \leq T_1) \wedge \\ (a < 0 \Rightarrow (v \geq cT_2 + (at_1 + cT_1)) \wedge (v \leq v_{max})) \\ \wedge (a \geq 0 \Rightarrow (v \leq v_{max} - cT_2 + (at_1 - cT_1)) \wedge (v \geq 0)) \end{array} \right)$$

denoted by Inv_1, constitutes a differential invariant of the continuous with respect to φ_1. It is a conjunction of three parts, indicating that: (1) t_1 is always in the range $[0, T_1]$; (2) if a is negative, v must be greater or equal than cT_2 plus a positive value (i.e. $at_1 + cT_1$), and meanwhile $v \leq v_{max}$; and (3) if a is positive, v must be less or equal than $v_{max} - cT_2$ plus a negative value (i.e. $at_1 - cT_1$), and meanwhile $v \geq 0$. This invariant is strong enough for guaranteeing $cT_2 \leq v \leq v_{max} - cT_2$ after the continuous escapes no matter what a is in $[-c, c]$. Similarly, we can calculate the invariant of the continuous occurring in $\mathsf{MV}(t_2, T_2)$, which is

$$\left(\begin{array}{l} (0 \leq t_2 \leq T_2) \wedge \\ (a < 0 \Rightarrow (v \geq 0 + (at_2 + cT_2)) \wedge (v \leq v_{max})) \\ \wedge (a \geq 0 \Rightarrow (v \leq v_{max} + (at_2 - cT_2)) \wedge (v \geq 0)) \end{array} \right)$$

denoted by Inv_2. This invariant is strong enough for guaranteeing $0 \leq v \leq v_{max}$ after the continuous escapes. Finally, the invariant of the differential equation of SC is $0 \leq v \leq v_{max}$, and we denote it by Inv_3.

Next, to prove (F1) and (F2), we can prove the following facts instead:

- Locations 1, 2, 3, 4 are not reachable for TR^*;
- Throughout the execution of TR^*, the invariant $0 \leq v \leq v_{max}$ always holds.

First we consider one loop of execution TR. For location 1, we can deduce that[2] $\vdash \mathsf{TR}, 1, \varphi_0 \blacktriangleright (\mathbf{u_v} \vee \mathbf{w_v}) \wedge (\neg \mathbf{u_v} \wedge \neg \mathbf{w_v})$, which is not satisfiable, thus location 1 is never reachable. Similarly, we can deduce that locations 2, 3, 4 are not reachable as well. Furthermore, by applying the inference system, we can deduce the specification $\{\varphi_0\}\ \mathsf{TR}\ \{\varphi_0, \lceil 0 \leq v \leq v_{max} \rceil^<\}$. After one loop of execution of the train, φ_0 still holds at termination. Thus, all the above reachability results obtained for TR still hold for TR^*, whose execution is equivalent to some finite number of executions of TR. Finally, plus that $\lceil 0 \leq v \leq v_{max} \rceil^<$ is idempotent over chop, we can deduce $\{\varphi_0\}\ \mathsf{TR}^*\ \{\varphi_0, \lceil 0 \leq v \leq v_{max} \rceil^<\}$, denoted by (**TrainSpec**), which implies that $0 \leq v \leq v_{max}$ is an invariant for the train.

---

[2] For simplicity, we use the boldface of an acknowledgment variable to represent the corresponding formula, e.g., $\mathbf{u_v}$ for $u_v = 1$.

By applying our interactive theorem prover, the fact (**TrainSpec**) is proved as a theorem, and the above reachability results can be implied from the lemmas proved for corresponding processes, according to the method introduced in Section 4.2.

We can see that, most of the proofs need to be performed in an interactive way, mainly because of the following reasons: firstly, we need to provide the differential invariants by ourselves during proof of continuous evolution; and secondly, we need to conduct the proof of DC formulas by telling which axiom or inference rule of DC should be applied. For the first problem, we will consider the integration of the prover to a differential invariant generator that can be implemented based on the method proposed in [9]. For the second, we will consider the decidability of DC and design algorithms for solving the decidable subsets, or as an alternative approach, consider translating DC formulas into HOL formulas in a semantic way and applying the existing automatic solvers for HOL instead. Both of these will be our future work.

Constraints of Constants. We can further analyze the behavior of the whole system SYS. By defining the constraints relating different constants, the behavior of communications between the three components can be determined. Consider the first loop of execution of each component, based on reachability analysis, we have the following facts: for locations 0, 5, 6, $t_1 = 0$, $t_3 = T_3$ and $t_4 = T_4$ hold respectively, and for locations 7, 8, 9, $t_1 \leq T_1$, $t_3 \geq T_3$ and $t_4 \geq T_4$ hold respectively. The synchronization points have four possibilities: $(7, 8)$, $(7, 9)$, $(7, 8, 9)$, or none. For the first case, i.e. the train succeeds to communicate with the driver but not with the VC, there must be $t_1 = t_3 < t_4$, and if $T_3 < T_4$ and $T_3 \leq T_1$ hold, this case will occur. The second one is exactly the contrary case. For the third case, there must be $t_1 = t_3 = t_4$, and if $T_3 = T_4 \leq T_1$ holds, this case will occur. Finally, if both $T_3 > T_1$ and $T_4 > T_1$ hold, the last case occurs, i.e., locations 7, 8 and 9 are not reachable, and thus the train fails to communicate with both the driver and the VC. Following this approach, more precise behavior of the communications of the train can be obtained.

6   Conclusion and Future Work

This paper proposes a formal modeling language, that is a combination of hybrid CSP and binders from quality calculus, for expressing denial-of-service due to unreliable communications in hybrid systems. With the linguistic support, it is able to build a safe hybrid system that behaves in a reasonable manner in the presence of denial-of-service security attack. The paper also develops an inference system for reasoning about such systems, with no dependence on the behavior of the environment, and furthermore implements an interactive theorem prover. We illustrate our approach by considering an example taken from train control system.

The investigation of our approach to more complex hybrid systems is one of our future work. Meanwhile, for facilitating practical applications, we will consider to achieve more support of automated reasoning in the theorem prover.

Acknowledgements. The research has been supported by NSFC-6110006 and NSFC-91118007, supported by the National Natural Science Foundation of China, and by IDEA4CPS, supported by the Danish Foundation for Basic Research.

References

1. Alur, R., Courcoubetis, C., Henzinger, T.A., Ho, P.: Hybrid automata: An algorithmic approach to the specification and verification of hybrid systems. In: Grossman, R.L., Ravn, A.P., Rischel, H., Nerode, A. (eds.) HS 1991 and HS 1992. LNCS, vol. 736, pp. 209–229. Springer, Heidelberg (1993)
2. Alur, R., Dang, T., Ivancic, F.: Predicate abstraction for reachability analysis of hybrid systems. ACM Transactions on Embedded Computing Systems 5(1), 152–199 (2006)
3. Asarin, E., Bournez, O., Dang, T., Maler, O.: Approximate reachability analysis of piecewise-linear dynamical systems. In: Lynch, N.A., Krogh, B.H. (eds.) HSCC 2000. LNCS, vol. 1790, pp. 20–31. Springer, Heidelberg (2000)
4. Clarke, E.M., Fehnker, A., Han, Z., Krogh, B.H., Ouaknine, J., Stursberg, O., Theobald, M.: Abstraction and counterexample-guided refinement in model checking of hybrid systems. Int. J. Found. Comput. Sci. 14(4), 583–604 (2003)
5. He, J.: From CSP to hybrid systems. In: A Classical Mind, pp. 171–189. Prentice Hall International (UK) Ltd. (1994)
6. Henzinger, T.A.: The theory of hybrid automata. In: LICS 1996, pp. 278–292 (1996)
7. Lafferrierre, G., Pappas, G.J., Yovine, S.: Symbolic reachability computation for families of linear vector fields. Journal of Symbolic Computation 11, 1–23 (2001)
8. Liu, J., Lv, J., Quan, Z., Zhan, N., Zhao, H., Zhou, C., Zou, L.: A calculus for hybrid CSP. In: Ueda, K. (ed.) APLAS 2010. LNCS, vol. 6461, pp. 1–15. Springer, Heidelberg (2010)
9. Liu, J., Zhan, N., Zhao, H.: Computing semi-algebraic invariants for polynomial dynamical systems. In: EMSOFT 2011, pp. 97–106. ACM (2011)
10. Lynch, N., Segala, R., Vaandrager, F., Weinberg, H.: Hybrid I/O automata. In: Alur, R., Sontag, E.D., Henzinger, T.A. (eds.) HS 1995. LNCS, vol. 1066, pp. 496–510. Springer, Heidelberg (1996)
11. Manna, Z., Pnueli, A.: Verifying hybrid systems. In: Grossman, R.L., Ravn, A.P., Rischel, H., Nerode, A. (eds.) HS 1991 and HS 1992. LNCS, vol. 736, pp. 4–35. Springer, Heidelberg (1993)
12. Nielson, H.R., Nielson, F.: Probabilistic analysis of the quality calculus. In: Beyer, D., Boreale, M. (eds.) FORTE 2013 and FMOODS 2013. LNCS, vol. 7892, pp. 258–272. Springer, Heidelberg (2013)
13. Nielson, H.R., Nielson, F., Vigo, R.: A calculus for quality. In: Păsăreanu, C.S., Salaün, G. (eds.) FACS 2012. LNCS, vol. 7684, pp. 188–204. Springer, Heidelberg (2013)
14. Platzer, A.: Differential-algebraic dynamic logic for differential-algebraic programs. J. Log. and Comput. 20(1), 309–352 (2010)
15. Platzer, A., Quesel, J.: European Train Control System: A case study in formal verification. In: Breitman, K., Cavalcanti, A. (eds.) ICFEM 2009. LNCS, vol. 5885, pp. 246–265. Springer, Heidelberg (2009)
16. Wang, S., Nielson, F., Riis Nielson, H.R.: A framework for hybrid systems with denial-of-service security attack. Technical Report ISCAS-SKLCS-14-06, Institute of Software, Chinese Academy of Sciences (2014)
17. Zhan, N., Wang, S., Zhao, H.: Formal modelling, analysis and verification of hybrid systems. In: Liu, Z., Woodcock, J., Zhu, H. (eds.) Unifying Theories of Programming and Formal Engineering Methods. LNCS, vol. 8050, pp. 207–281. Springer, Heidelberg (2013)
18. Zhou, C., Hansen, M.R.: Duration Calculus — A Formal Approach to Real-Time Systems. Monographs in Theoretical Computer Science. An EATCS Series. Springer, Heidelberg (2004)
19. Zhou, C., Hoare, C.A.R., Ravn, A.P.: A calculus of durations. Information Processing Letters 40(5), 269–276 (1991)
20. Zhou, C., Wang, J., Ravn, A.P.: A formal description of hybrid systems. In: Alur, R., Sontag, E.D., Henzinger, T.A. (eds.) HS 1995. LNCS, vol. 1066, pp. 511–530. Springer, Heidelberg (1996)

Quantitative Information Flow under Generic Leakage Functions and Adaptive Adversaries[*]

Michele Boreale[1],[**] and Francesca Pampaloni[2]

[1] Università di Firenze, Italy
michele.boreale@unifi.it
[2] IMT - Institute for Advanced Studies, Lucca, Italy

Abstract. We put forward a model of *action-based* randomization mechanisms to analyse quantitative information flow (QIF) under generic leakage functions, and under possibly adaptive adversaries. This model subsumes many of the QIF models proposed so far. Our main contributions include the following: (1) we identify mild general conditions on the leakage function under which it is possible to derive general and significant results on adaptive QIF; (2) we contrast the efficiency of adaptive and non-adaptive strategies, showing that the latter are as efficient as the former in terms of length up to an expansion factor bounded by the number of available actions; (3) we show that the maximum information leakage over strategies, given a finite time horizon, can be expressed in terms of a Bellman equation. This can be used to compute an optimal finite strategy recursively, by resorting to standard methods like backward induction.

Keywords: quantitative information flow, adaptive attackers, information theory.

1 Introduction

Quantitative Information Flow (QIF) is a well-established approach to confidentiality analysis: the basic idea is measuring how much information flows from sensitive to public data, relying on tools from Information Theory [11,3,10,21,4,5,20,6,7].

Two major issues that arise in QIF are: what measure one should adopt to quantify the leakage of confidential data, and the relationship between adaptive and non adaptive adversaries. Concerning the first issue, a long standing debate in the QIF community concerns the relative merits of leakage functions based on Shannon entropy (see e.g. [11,5]) and min-entropy (see e.g. [21,4]); other types of entropies are sometimes considered (see e.g. [17]). As a matter of fact, analytical results for each of these types of leakage functions have been so far worked out in a non-uniform, ad hoc fashion.

---

[*] Work partially supported by the EU project ASCENS under the FET open initiative in FP7.
[**] Corresponding author.
Michele Boreale, Università di Firenze, Dipartimento di Statistica, Informatica, Applicazioni (DiSIA), Viale Morgagni 65, I-50134 Firenze, Italy.

E. Ábrahám and C. Palamidessi (Eds.), FORTE 2014, LNCS 8461, pp. 166–181, 2014.
© IFIP International Federation for Information Processing 2014

Concerning the second issue, one sees that, with the notable exception of [17] which we discuss later on, QIF has so far been almost exclusively concerned with attackers that can only passively eavesdrop on the mechanism; or, at best, obtain answers in response to queries (or *actions*) submitted in a non-adaptive fashion [8]. Clearly, there are situations where this model is not adequate. To mention but two: chosen plaintext/ciphertext attacks against cryptographic hardware or software; adaptive querying of databases whose records contain both sensitive and non-sensitive fields.

In this paper, we tackle both issues outlined above. We: (a) put forward a general QIF model where the leakage function is built around a *generic uncertainty measure*; and, (b) derive several general results on the relationship between adaptive and non adaptive adversaries in this model. More in detail, we assume that, based on a secret piece of information $X \in \mathcal{X}$, the mechanism responds to a sequence of queries/actions $a_1, a_2, \ldots$ ($a_i \in Act$), adaptively submitted by an adversary, thus producing a sequence of answers/observations $Y \in \mathcal{Y}^*$. Responses to individual queries are in general probabilistic, either because of the presence of noise or by design. Moreover, the mechanism is stateless, thus answers are independent from one another. The adversary is assumed to know the distribution according to which X has been generated (the prior) and the input-output behaviour of the mechanism. An adaptive adversary can choose the next query based on past observations, according to a predefined strategy. Once a strategy and a prior have been fixed, they together induce a probability space over sequences of observations. Observing a specific sequence provides the adversary with information that modifies his belief about X, possibly reducing his uncertainty. We measure information leakage as the *average reduction in uncertainty*. We work with a generic measure of uncertainty, $U(\cdot)$. Formally, $U(\cdot)$ is just a real-valued function over the set of probability distributions on $\mathcal{X}$, which represent possible beliefs of the adversary. Just two properties are assumed of $U(\cdot)$: concavity and continuity. Note that leakage functions commonly employed in QIF, such as Shannon entropy, guessing entropy and error probability (the additive version of min-entropy) do fall in this category.

The other central theme of our study is the comparison between adaptive and the simpler non-adaptive strategies. All in all, our results indicate that, for even moderately powerful adversaries, there is no dramatic difference between the two, in terms of difficulty of analysis. A more precise account of our contributions follows.

1) We put forward a general model of adaptive QIF; we identify mild general conditions on the leakage function under which it is possible to derive general and significant results on adaptive QIF in this model.

2) We compare the difficulty of analyzing mechanisms under adaptive and non-adaptive adversaries. We first note that, for the class of mechanisms admitting a "concise" syntactic description - e.g. devices specified by a boolean circuit - the analysis problem is intractable (NP-hard), even if limited to very simple instances of the *non-adaptive* case. This essentially depends on the fact that such mechanisms can feature exponentially many actions in the syntactic size. In the general case, we show that non-adaptive finite strategies are as efficient as adaptive ones, up to an *expansion factor* in their length bounded by the number of distinct actions available. Practically, this indicates that, for mechanisms described in explicit form (e.g. by tables, like a DB) hence featuring an "affordable" number of actions available to the

adversary, it may be sufficient to assess resistance of the mechanism against non-adaptive strategies. This is important, because simple analytical results are available for such strategies [8].

3) We show that the maximum leakage is the same for both adaptive and non-adaptive adversaries, and only depends on an indistinguishability equivalence relation over the set of secrets.

4) We show that maximum information leakage over a finite horizon can be expressed in terms of a Bellman equation. This equation can be used to compute optimal finite strategies recursively. As an example, we show how to do that using Markov Decision Processes (MDP's) and backward induction.

Related Work. In [17], Köpf and Basin introduced an information-theoretic model of adaptive attackers for deterministic mechanisms. Their analysis is conducted essentially on the case of uniform prior distributions. Our model generalizes [17] in several respects: we consider probabilistic mechanisms, generic priors and generic uncertainty functions. More important than that, we contrast quantitatively the efficiency of adaptive and non-adaptive strategies, we characterize maximum leakage of infinite strategies, and we show how to express information leakage as a Bellman equation. The latter leads to search algorithms for optimal strategies that, when specialized to the deterministic case, are more time-efficient than the exhaustive search outlined in [17] (see Section 6).

Our previous paper [8] tackles multirun, non-adaptive adversaries, in the case of min-entropy leakage. In this simpler setting, a special case of the present framework, one manages to obtain simple analytical results, such as the exact convergence rate of the adversary's success probability as the number of observations goes to infinity.

[18,19] propose models to assess system security against classes of adversaries characterized by user-specified 'profiles'. While these models share some similarities with ours - in particular, they too employ MDP's to keep track of possible adversary strategies - their intent is quite different from ours: they are used to build and assess analysis tools, rather than to obtain analytical results. Also, the strategies they consider are tailored to worst-case adversary's utility, which, differently from our average-case measures, is not apt to express information leakage.

Alvim et al. [1] study information flow in interactive mechanisms, described as probabilistic automata where secrets and observables are seen as actions that alternate during execution. Information-theoretically, they characterize these mechanisms as channels with feedback, giving a Shannon-entropy based definition of leakage. Secret actions at each step depend on previous history, but it is not clear that this gives the adversary any ability to adaptively influence the next observation, in our sense.

Structure of the Paper. Section 2 introduces the model, illustrated with a few examples in Section 3. The subsequent three sections discuss the results outlined in (2), (3) and (4) above. Section 7 contains a few concluding remarks and some directions for further research. Due to lack of space, no detailed proof is given in this version of the paper.

2 Action-Based Randomization Mechanisms

2.1 Basic Definitions

Definition 1. An *action-based randomization mechanism*[1] is a 4-tuple $S = (X, Y, Act, \{M_a : a \in Act\})$ where (all sets finite and nonempty): X, Y and Act are respectively the sets of *secrets*, *observations* and *actions* (or *queries*) and for each $a \in Act$, M_a is a stochastic matrix of dimensions $|X| \times |Y|$.

For each action $a \in Act$, $x \in X$ and $y \in Y$, the element of row x and column y of M_a is denoted by $p_a(y|x)$. Note that for each x and a, row x of M_a defines a probability distribution over Y, denoted by $p_a(\cdot|x)$. A mechanism S is *deterministic* if each entry of each M_a is either 0 or 1. Note that to any deterministic mechanism there corresponds a function $f : X \times Act \to Y$ defined by $f(x, a) = y$, where $p_a(y|x) = 1$.

Definition 2 (Uncertainty). *Let $\mathcal{P}(X)$ be the set of all probability distributions on X. A function $U : \mathcal{P}(X) \to \mathbb{R}$ is an* uncertainty measure *if it is concave and continuous over $\mathcal{P}(X) \subseteq \mathbb{R}^{|X|}$.*

The role of concavity can be intuitively explained as follows. Suppose the secret is generated according to either a distribution p or to another distribution q, the choice depending from a coin toss, with head's probability λ. The coin toss introduces *extra randomness* in the generation process. Therefore, the overall uncertainty of the adversary about the secret, $U(\lambda \cdot p + (1 - \lambda) \cdot q)$, should be *no less* than the average uncertainty of the two original generation processes considered separately, that is $\lambda U(p) + (1 - \lambda)U(q)$. As a matter of fact, most uncertainty measures in QIF do satisfy concavity. Continuity is a technical requirement that comes into play only in Theorem 4.

Example 1. The following entropy functions, and variations thereof, are often considered in the quantitative security literature as measures of the difficulty or effort necessary to a passive adversary to identify a secret X, where X is a random variable over X distributed according to some $p(\cdot)$. All of them are easily proven to be uncertainty measures in our sense:

- *Shannon entropy*: $H(p) \triangleq - \sum_{x \in X} p(x) \log p(x)$, with $0 \log 0 = 0$ and log in base 2;
- *Error probability entropy*: $E(p) \triangleq 1 - \max_{x \in X} p(x)$;
- *Guessing entropy*: $G(p) \triangleq \sum_{i=1}^{n-1} i \cdot p(x_i)$ with $p(x_1) \geq p(x_2) \geq \ldots \geq p(x_n)$.

A *strategy* is a partial function $\sigma : Y^* \to Act$ such that $\mathrm{dom}(\sigma)$ is non-empty and prefix-closed. A strategy is *finite* if $\mathrm{dom}(\sigma)$ is finite. The *length* of a finite strategy is defined as $\max\{l \geq 0 : y^l \in \mathrm{dom}(\sigma)\} + 1$. For each $n \geq 0$ we will let $y^n, w^n, z^n, \ldots$ range over sequences in Y^n; given $y^n = (y_1, \ldots, y_n)$ and $0 \leq j \leq n$, we will let y^j denote the first j components of y^n, $(y_1, \ldots, y_j)$. Given a strategy σ and an integer $n \geq 0$, the *truncation* of σ at level n, denoted as $\sigma \backslash n$, is the finite strategy $\sigma_{|\cup_{0 \leq i \leq n} y^i}$. A finite strategy of length l is *complete* if $\mathrm{dom}(\sigma) = \cup_{0 \leq i \leq l-1} Y^i$. A strategy σ is *non-adaptive* if

---

[1] The term *information hiding system* is sometimes found to indicate randomization mechanisms. The former term, however, is also used with a different technical meaning in the literature on watermarking; so we prefer to avoid it here.

whenever y^n and w^n are two sequences of the same length then $\sigma(y^n) = \sigma(w^n)$ (that is, the decision of which action to play next only depends on the number of past actions); note that finite non-adaptive strategies are necessarily complete.

We note that strategies can be described as trees, with nodes labelled by actions and arc labelled by observations, in the obvious way. Any non-adaptive strategy also enjoys a simpler representation as a finite or infinite list of actions: we write $\sigma = [a_1, \ldots, a_i, \ldots]$ if $\sigma(y^{i-1}) = a_i$, for $i = 1, 2, \ldots$.

Example 2. Strategies $\sigma = [\varepsilon \mapsto a, y \mapsto b]$ and $\sigma' = [\varepsilon \mapsto a, y \mapsto b, y' \mapsto c, yy' \mapsto d]$ can be represented as in Fig. 1. Note that the tree's height is one less than the strategy's length.

2.2 Adaptive Quantitative Information Flow

Informally, we consider an adversary who repeatedly queries a mechanism, according to a predefined *finite* strategy. At some point, the strategy will terminate, and the adversary will have collected a sequence of observations $y^n = (y_1, \ldots, y_n)$. Note that both the length n and the probability of the individual observations y_i, hence of the whole y^n, will in general depend both on X and on the strategy played by the adversary. In other words, the distribution $p(\cdot)$ of X *and* the strategy σ together induce a probability distribution on a subset of all observation sequences: the

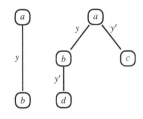

Fig. 1. Two strategy trees

ones that may arise as a result of a complete interaction with the mechanism, according to the played strategy.

Formally, let $p(\cdot)$ be any given probability distribution over X, which we will often refer to as the *prior*. For each finite strategy σ, we define a joint probability distribution $p_\sigma(\cdot)$ on $X \times \mathcal{Y}^*$, depending on σ and on $p(\cdot)$, as follows. We let $p_\sigma(x, \varepsilon) \overset{\triangle}{=} 0$ and, for each $j \geq 0$:

$$
p_\sigma(x, y_1, \ldots, y_j, y_{j+1}) \overset{\triangle}{=} \begin{cases} p(x) \cdot p_{a_1}(y_1|x) \cdot \cdots \cdot p_{a_j}(y_j|x) p_{a_{j+1}}(y_{j+1}|x) \\ \qquad\qquad\qquad \text{if } y^j \in \mathrm{dom}(\sigma), y^j y_{j+1} \notin \mathrm{dom}(\sigma) \\ 0 \qquad\qquad\quad \text{otherwise} \end{cases}
$$

where in the first case $a_i = \sigma(y^{i-1})$ for $i = 1, \ldots, j + 1$. In case $\sigma = [a]$, a single action strategy, we will often abbreviate $p_{[a]}(\cdot)$ as $p_a(\cdot)$. Note that the support of $p_\sigma(\cdot)$ is finite, in particular $\mathrm{supp}(p_\sigma) \subseteq X \times \{y^j y : j \geq 0, y^j \in \mathrm{dom}(\sigma), y^j y \notin \mathrm{dom}(\sigma)\}$.

Let (X, Y) be a pair of random variables with outcomes in $X \times \mathcal{Y}^*$, jointly distributed according to $p_\sigma(\cdot)$: here X represents the secret and Y represents the sequence of observations obtained upon termination of the strategy. We shall often use such shortened notations as: $p_\sigma(x|y^n)$ for $\Pr(X = x|Y = y^n)$, $p_\sigma(y^n)$ for $\Pr(Y = y^n)$, and so on. Explicit formulas for computing these quantities can be easily derived from the definition of $p_\sigma(\cdot)$ and using Bayes rule. We will normally keep the dependence of (X, Y) from $p(\cdot)$ and σ implicit. When different strategies are being considered at the same time and we want to stress that we are considering Y according to the distribution induced by a specific σ, we will write it as Y_σ.

Consider a prior $p(\cdot)$ and a *finite* strategy σ, and the corresponding pair of random variables (r.v.) (X, Y). We define the following quantities, expressing average uncertainty, conditional uncertainty and information gain about X, that may result from interaction according to strategy σ (by convention, we let here y^n range over sequences with $p_\sigma(y^n) > 0$):

$$U(X) \triangleq U(p)$$
$$U(X|Y) \triangleq \sum_{y^n} p_\sigma(y^n) U(p_\sigma(\cdot|y^n)) \tag{1}$$
$$I(X; Y) \triangleq U(X) - U(X|Y).$$

Note that, in the case of Shannon entropy, $I(X; Y)$ coincides with the familiar mutual information, traditionally measured in bits. In the case of error entropy, $I(X; Y)$ is what is called *additive leakage* in e.g. [4] and *advantage* in the cryptographic literature, see e.g. [13] and references therein.

In the rest of the paper, unless otherwise stated, we let $U(\cdot)$ be an arbitrary uncertainty function. The following fact about $I(X; Y)$ follows from $U(\cdot)$'s concavity and Jensen's inequality, plus routine calculations on probability distributions.

Lemma 1. $I(X; Y) \geq 0$. *Moreover* $I(X; Y) = 0$ *if* X *and* Y *are independent.*

Given the definitions in (1), adaptive QIF can be defined quite simply.

Definition 3 (QIF **under adaptive adversaries**). *Let S be a mechanism and $p(\cdot)$ be a prior over X.*

1. *For a* finite *strategy σ, let* $I_\sigma(S, p) \triangleq I(X; Y)$.
2. *For an* infinite *strategy σ, let* $I_\sigma(S, p) \triangleq \lim_{l \to \infty} I_{\sigma \backslash l}(S, p)$.
3. *(Maximum IF under $p(\cdot)$)* $I_\star(S, p) \triangleq \sup_\sigma I_\sigma(S, p)$.

Note that $l' \geq l$ implies $I_{\sigma \backslash l'}(S, p) \geq I_{\sigma \backslash l}(S, p)$, hence the limit in (2) always exists. Taking the distribution that achieves the maximum leakage, we can define an analog of channel capacity.

Definition 4 (Adaptive secrecy capacity). $C(S) \triangleq \sup_{p \in \mathcal{P}(X)} I_\star(S, p)$.

2.3 Attack Trees

It is sometimes useful to work with a pictorial representation of the adversary's attack steps, under a given strategy and prior. This can take the form of a tree, where each node represents an adversary's *belief* about the secret, that is, a probability distribution over X. The tree describes the possible evolutions of the belief, depending on the strategy and on the observations. We formally introduce such a representation below: it will be extensively used in the examples. Note that *attack* trees are different from *strategy* trees.

A *history* is a sequence $h \in (Act \times \mathcal{Y})^*$. Let $h = (a_1, y_1, \ldots, a_n, y_n)$ be such a history. Given a prior $p(\cdot)$, we define the *update of $p(\cdot)$ after h*, denoted by $p^h(\cdot)$, as the distribution on X defined by

$$p^h(x) \triangleq p_{\sigma_h}(x|y^n) \qquad (2)$$

where $\sigma_h = [a_1, \ldots, a_n]$, provided $p_{\sigma_h}(y^n) > 0$; otherwise $p^h(\cdot)$ is undefined.

The *attack tree* induced by a strategy σ and a prior $p(\cdot)$ is a tree with nodes labelled by probability distributions over X and arcs labelled with pairs (y, λ) of an observation and a probability. This tree is obtained from the strategy tree of σ as follows. First, note that, in a strategy tree, each node can be identified with the unique history from the root leading to it. Given the strategy tree for σ: (a) for each $y \in \mathcal{Y}$ and each node missing an outgoing y-labelled arc, attach a new y-labelled arc leading to a new node; (b) label each node of the resulting tree by $p^h(\cdot)$, where h is the history identifying the node, if $p^h(\cdot)$ is defined, otherwise remove the node and its descendants, as well as the incoming arc; (c) label each arc from a node h to a child hay in the resulting tree with $\lambda = p_a^h(y) \cdot$ to be parsed as $(p^h)_{[a]}(y)$. This is the probability of observing y under a prior $p^h(\cdot)$ when submitting action a.

The concept of attack tree is demonstrated by a few examples in the next section. Here, we just note the following easy to check facts. For each leaf h of the attack tree: (i) the leaf's label is $p^h(\cdot) = p_\sigma(\cdot|y^n)$, where y^n is the sequence of observations in h; (ii) if we let π_h be the product of the probabilities on the edges from the root to the leaf, then $\pi_h = p_\sigma(y^n)$. Moreover, (iii) each y^n s.t. $p_\sigma(y^n) > 0$ is found in the tree. As a consequence, for a *finite* strategy, taking (1) into account, the uncertainty of X given Y can be computed from the attack tree as:

$$U(X \mid Y) = \sum_{h \text{ a leaf}} \pi_h U(p^h) . \qquad (3)$$

3   Examples

We present a few instances of the framework introduced in the previous section. We emphasize that these examples are quite simple and only serve to illustrate our main definitions. In the rest of the paper, we shall use the following notation: we let $u\{x_1, \ldots, x_k\}$ denote the uniform distribution on $\{x_1, \ldots, x_k\}$.

Example 3. An attacker gets hold of the table shown in Fig. 2, which represents a fragment of a hospital's database. Each row of the table contains: a numerical id followed by the ZIP code, age, discharge date and disease of an individual that has been recently hospitalized. The table does not contain personal identifiable information. The attacker gets to know that a certain target individual, John Doe (JD), has been recently hospitalized. However, the attacker is ignorant of the corresponding id in the table and any information about JD, apart from his name. The attacker's task is to identify JD, i.e. to find JD's id in the table, thus learning his disease. The attacker is in

id	ZIP	Age	Date	Desease
1	z_1	65	d_2	Hearth disease
2	z_1	65	d_2	Flu
3	z_1	67	d_2	Short breath
4	z_1	68	d_1	Obesity
5	z_1	68	d_1	Hearth disease
6	z_3	66	d_2	Hearth disease
7	z_3	67	d_2	Obesity
8	z_3	31	d_2	Short breath
9	z_2	30	d_3	Hearth disease
10	z_2	31	d_3	Obesity

Fig. 2. Medical DB of Ex. 3

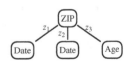

Fig. 3. Strategy tree of Ex. 3

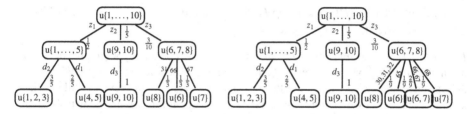

Fig. 4. The attack tree for Ex. 3

Fig. 5. The attack tree for Ex. 4. Leaves with the same label and their incoming arcs have been coalesced.

a position to ask a source, perhaps the hospital DB, queries concerning non sensitive information (ZIP code, age and discharge date) of any individual, including JD, and compare the answers with the table's entries.[2]

This situation can be modeled quite simply as an action-based mechanism S, as follows. We pose: $Act = \{ZIP, Age, Date\}$; $X = \{1, \ldots, 10\}$, the set of possible id's, and $\mathcal{Y} = \mathcal{Y}_{ZIP} \cup \mathcal{Y}_{Age} \cup \mathcal{Y}_{Date}$, where $\mathcal{Y}_{ZIP} = \{z_1, z_2, z_3\}$, $\mathcal{Y}_{Age} = \{30, 31, 65, 66, 67, 68\}$ and $\mathcal{Y}_{Date} = \{d_1, d_2, d_3\}$. The conditional probability matrices reflect the behaviour of the source when queried about ZIP code, age and discharge date of an individual. We assume that the source is truthful, hence answers will match the entries of the table. For example, $p_{Age}(y|1) = 1$ if $y = 65$ and 0 otherwise; $p_{ZIP}(y|2) = 1$ if $y = z_1$, 0 otherwise; and so on. Note that this defines a *deterministic* mechanism. Finally, since the attacker has no clues about JD's id, we set the prior to be the uniform distribution on X, $p(\cdot) = u\{1, \ldots, 10\}$.

Assume now that, for some reason - maybe for the sake of privacy - the number of queries to the source about an individual is limited to two. Fig. 3 displays a possible attacker's strategy σ, of length 2. Fig. 4 displays the corresponding attack tree, under the given prior. Note that the given strategy is not in any sense optimal. Assume we set $U(\cdot) = H(\cdot)$, Shannon entropy, as a measure of uncertainty. Using (3), we can compute $I_\sigma(S, p) = H(X) - H(X|Y) = \log 10 - \frac{3}{10}\log 3 - \frac{2}{5} \approx 2.45$ bits. With $U(\cdot) = E(\cdot)$, the error entropy, we have $I_\sigma(S, p) = E(X) - E(X|Y) = 0.5$.

Example 4 (noisy version). We consider a version of the previous mechanism where the public source queried by the attacker is not entirely truthful. In particular, for security reasons, whenever queried about age of an individual, the source adds a random offset $r \in \{-1, 0, +1\}$ to the real answer. The only difference from the previous example is that the conditional probability matrix $p_{Age}(\cdot|\cdot)$ is not deterministic anymore. For example, for $x = 1$, we have

$$p_{Age}(y|1) = \begin{cases} \frac{1}{3} & \text{if } y \in \{64, 65, 66\} \\ 0 & \text{otherwise} \end{cases}$$

(also note that we have to insert 29, 32, 64 and 69 as possible observations into $\mathcal{Y}_{Age}$). Fig. 5 shows the attack tree induced by the strategy σ of Fig. 3 and the uniform prior

---

[2] That this is unsafe is of course well-known from database security: the present example only serves the purpose of illustration.

in this case. If $U(\cdot) = H(\cdot)$ we obtain $I_\sigma(S, p) = \log 10 - \frac{3}{10} \log 3 - \frac{8}{15} \approx 2.31$ bits; if $U(\cdot) = E(\cdot)$, instead, $I_\sigma(S, p) = \frac{13}{30} \approx 0.43$.

Example 5 (cryptographic devices). We can abstractly model a cryptographic device as a function f taking pairs of a key and a message into observations, thus, $f : \mathcal{K} \times \mathcal{M} \to \mathcal{Y}$. Assume the attacker can choose the message $m \in \mathcal{M}$ fed to the device, while the key k is fixed and unknown to him. This clearly yields an action-based mechanism S where $\mathcal{X} = \mathcal{K}$, $Act = \mathcal{M}$ and $\mathcal{Y}$ are the observations. If we assume the observations noiseless, then the conditional probability matrices are defined by

$$p_m(y|k) = 1 \quad \text{iff} \quad f(k, m) = y.$$

We obtain therefore a deterministic mechanism. This is the way, for example, modular exponentiation is modeled in [17]. More realistically, the observations will be noisy, due e.g. to the presence of "algorithmic noise". For example, assume $\mathcal{Y} \subseteq \mathbb{N}$ is the set of possible Hamming weights of the ciphertexts (this is related to power analysis attacks, see e.g. [16]). Then we may set

$$p_m(y|k) = \Pr(f(k, m) + N = y)$$

where N is a random variable modelling noise. For example, in the model of DES S-Boxes considered in [8], $\mathcal{K} = \mathcal{M} = \{0, 1\}^6$, while $\mathcal{Y} = \{0, 1, 2, \ldots\}$ is the set of observations: the (noisy) Hamming weight of the outputs of the target S-Box. In this case, N is taken to be the cumulative weight of the seven S-Boxes other than the target one. It is sensible to assume this noise to be binomially distributed: $N \sim B(m, p)$, with $m = 28$ and $p = \frac{1}{2}$. See [8] for details.

4   Comparing Adaptive and Non-adaptive Strategies

Conceptually, we can classify systems into two categories, depending on the size of the set Act. Informally, the first category consists of systems with a huge - exponential, in the size of any reasonable syntactic description - number of actions. The second category consists of systems with an "affordable" number of actions. In the first category, we find, for instance, complex cryptographic hardware, possibly described via boolean circuits or other "succinct" notations (cf. the public key exponentiation algorithms considered in [17]). In the second category, we find systems explicitly described by tables, such as databases (Ex. 3 and 4) and S-Boxes (Ex.5).

4.1   Systems in Succinct Form

We argue that the analysis of such systems is in general an intractable problem, even if restricted to simple special instances of the *non-adaptive* case. We consider the problem of deciding if there is a finite strategy over a given time horizon yielding an information flow exceeding a given threshold. This decision problem is of course simpler than the problem of finding an optimal strategy over a finite time horizon: indeed, any algorithm for finding the optimal strategy can also be used to answer the first problem. We give some definitions.

Definition 5 (Systems in boolean forms). *Let t, u, v be nonnegative integers. We say a mechanism $\mathcal{S} = (\mathcal{X}, \mathcal{Y}, Act, \{M_a : a \in Act\})$ is in (t, u, v)-boolean form if $\mathcal{X} = \{0, 1\}^t$, $Act = \{0, 1\}^u$, $\mathcal{Y} = \{0, 1\}^v$ and there is a boolean function $f : \{0, 1\}^{t+u} \rightarrow \{0, 1\}^v$ such that for each $x \in \mathcal{X}, y \in \mathcal{Y}$ and $a \in Act, p_a(y|x) = 1$ iff $f(x, a) = y$. The size of $\mathcal{S}$ is defined as the syntactic size of the smallest boolean formula for f.*

It is not difficult to see that the class of boolean forms coincides, up to suitable encodings, with that of deterministic systems.

Definition 6 (Adaptive Bounding Problem in succinct form, ABPS). *Given a mechanism $\mathcal{S}$ in a (t, u, v)-boolean form, a prior distribution $p(\cdot), l \geq 1$ and $T \geq 0$, decide if there is a strategy σ of length $\leq l$ such that $I_\sigma(\mathcal{S}; p) > T$.*

In the following theorem, we shall assume, for simplicity, the following reasonable properties of $U(\cdot)$: if $p(\cdot)$ concentrates all the probability mass on a single element, and $q(\cdot)$ is the uniform distribution, then $0 = U(p) < U(q)$. A slight modification of the argument also works without this assumption. The theorem says that even length 1 (hence non-adaptive) strategies are difficult to assess.

Theorem 1. *Assume $U(\cdot)$ satisfies the above stated property. Then the ABPS is NP-hard, even if fixing $t = v = l = 1$, and $T = 0$.*

4.2 General Systems

The following results, which apply in general, are particularly interesting for systems with a moderate number of actions. The following theorem essentially says that, up to an expansion factor bounded by $|Act|$, non-adaptive strategies are as efficient as adaptive ones. Note that, for a strategy σ, the number of distinct actions that appear in σ is $|\text{range}(\sigma)|$.

Theorem 2. *For each finite strategy σ of length l it is possible to build a non-adaptive finite strategy σ' of length $|\text{range}(\sigma)| \times l$, such that $I_{\sigma'}(\mathcal{S}, p) \geq I_\sigma(\mathcal{S}, p)$.*

The intuition behind the construction of the strategy σ' is as follows. In any history induced by σ, each action can occur at most l times, and the order in which different actions appear in the history is not relevant as to the final belief that is obtained. For any history of σ to be simulated by an history of σ', it is therefore enough that the latter offers all actions offered by σ, each repeated l times. In deterministic systems, repetitions of the same action are not relevant, which leads to the following improved upper bound on the length of σ'.

Proposition 1. *If the mechanism $\mathcal{S}$ is deterministic, then the upper-bound in the previous theorem can be simplified to $|\text{range}(\sigma)|$.*

Example 6. We reconsider Ex. 3. For the adaptive strategy σ defined in Fig. 3, we have already shown that, for $U(\cdot) = H(\cdot)$, $I_\sigma(\mathcal{S}, p) \approx 2.45$. Consider now the non-adaptive strategy $\sigma' = [\text{ZIP}, \text{Date}, \text{Age}]$, which is just one action longer than σ. The corresponding attack tree is reported in Fig. 6: the final partition obtained with σ' is finer than the one obtained with σ. In fact, $I_{\sigma'}(\mathcal{S}, p) = \log 10 - \frac{2}{5} \approx 2.92 > I_\sigma(\mathcal{S}, p) \approx 2.45$.

The results discussed above are important from the point of view of the analysis. They entail that, for systems with a moderate number of actions, analyzing adaptive strategies is essentially equivalent to analyzing non-adaptive ones. The latter task can be much easier to accomplish. For example, results on asymptotic rate of convergence of non-adaptive strategies are available (e.g. [8, Th. IV.3]). They permit to analytically assess the resistance of a mechanism as the length of the considered strategies grows.

5   Maximum Leakage

In this section we show that the class of adaptive and non adaptive strategies induce the same maximum leakage. For truly probabilistic mechanisms, strategies achieving maximum leakage are in general infinite. A key notion is that of indistinguishability: an equivalence relation over X s.t. x and x' are indistinguishable if, no matter what strategy the adversary will play, he cannot tell them apart.

Definition 7 (Indistinguishability). *We define the following equivalence over X:*

$$x \equiv x' \quad \textit{iff for each finite } \sigma : \ p_\sigma(\cdot|x) = p_\sigma(\cdot|x').$$

Despite being based on a universal quantification over all finite strategies, indistinguishability is in fact quite easy to characterize, also computationally. For each $a \in Act$, consider the equivalence relation defined by $x \equiv_a x'$ iff $p_a(\cdot|x) = p_a(\cdot|x')$.

Lemma 2. $x \equiv x'$ *iff for each $a \in Act$, $p_a(\cdot|x) = p_a(\cdot|x')$. In other words, $\equiv$ is $\cap_{a \in Act} \equiv_a$.*

Now, consider $X/\equiv$, the set of equivalence classes of $\equiv$, and let c ranges over this set. Let $[X]$ be the r.v. whose outcome is the equivalence class of X according to $\equiv$. Note that $p(c) \stackrel{\triangle}{=} \Pr([X] = c) = \sum_{x \in c} p(x)$. We consistently extend our I-notation by defining

$$U(X\,|\,[X]) \stackrel{\triangle}{=} \sum_c p(c)U(p(\cdot\,|\,[X] = c)) \quad \text{and} \quad I(X\,;\,[X]) \stackrel{\triangle}{=} U(X) - U(X\,|\,[X]).$$

More explicitly, $p(\cdot|[X] = c)$ denotes the distribution over X that yields $p(x)/p(c)$ for $x \in c$ and 0 elsewhere; we will often abbreviate $p(\cdot|[X] = c)$ just as $p(\cdot|c)$. Note that $I(X\,;\,[X])$ expresses the information gain about X when the attacker gets to know the indistinguishability class of the secret. As expected, this is an upper-bound to the information that can be gained playing any strategy.

Theorem 3. $I_\star(S, p) \leq I(X\,;\,[X])$.

Proof. Fix any finite strategy σ and prior $p(\cdot)$. It is sufficient to prove that $U(X|Y) \geq U(X\,|\,[X])$. The proof exploits the concavity of U. First, we note that, for each x and y^j of nonzero probability we have (c below ranges over $X/\equiv$):

$$p_\sigma(x|y^j) = \sum_c \frac{p_\sigma(x, y^j, c)}{p_\sigma(y^j)} \ = \ \sum_c p_\sigma(c|y^j)p_\sigma(x|y^j, c). \tag{4}$$

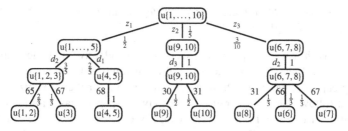

Fig. 6. The attack tree corresponding to the the non-adaptive strategy [ZIP, Date, Age] for Ex. 3

By (4), concavity of $U(\cdot)$ and Jensen's inequality

$$U(p(\cdot|y^j)) \geq \sum_c p_\sigma(c|y^j)U(p_\sigma(\cdot|y^j, c)).$$ (5)

Now, we can compute as follows (as usual, y^j below runs over sequences of nonzero probability):

$$U(X|Y) = \sum_{y^j} p_\sigma(y^j)U(p_\sigma(\cdot|y^j)) \geq \sum_{y^j,c} p_\sigma(y^j)p_\sigma(c|y^j)U(p_\sigma(\cdot|y^j, c))$$ (6)

$$= \sum_{y^j,c} p_\sigma(y^j)p_\sigma(c|y^j)U(p(\cdot|c)) = \sum_c (\sum_{y^j} p_\sigma(y^j, c))U(p(\cdot|c))$$ (7)

$$= \sum_c p(c)U(p(\cdot|c)) = U(X \,|\, [X])$$

where: (6) is justified by (5); and the first equality in (7) follows from the fact that, for each x, $p_\sigma(x|y^j, c) = p(x|c)$ (once the equivalence class of the secret is known, the observation y^j provides no further information about the secret).

As to the maximal achievable information, we start our discussion from deterministic mechanism.

Proposition 2. *Let S be deterministic. Let $\sigma = [a_1, \ldots, a_k]$ be a non-adaptive strategy that plays all actions in Act once. Then $I_\star(S, p) = I_\sigma(S, p)$.*

Hence, in the deterministic case, the maximal gain in information is obtained by a trivial brute-force strategy where all actions are played in any fixed order. It is instructive to observe such a strategy at work, under the form of an attack tree. The supports of the distributions that are at the same level constitute a partition of $\mathcal{X}$: more precisely, the partition at level i ($1 \leq i \leq k$) is given by the equivalence classes of the relation $\cap_{j=1}^i \equiv_{a_j}$. An example of this fact is illustrated by the attack tree in Fig. 6, relative to the non-adaptive strategy [ZIP, Date, Age] for the mechanism in Ex. 3. This fact had been already observed in [17] for the restricted model considered there. Indeed, one would obtain the model of [17] by stripping the probabilities off the tree in Fig. 6.

The general probabilistic case is slightly more complicated. Essentially, any non-adaptive strategy where each action is played infinitely often achieves the maximum information gain. The next theorem considers one such strategy.

Theorem 4. *There is a total, non-adaptive strategy σ s.t. $I_\sigma(S, p) = I(X; [X])$. Consequently, $I_\star(S, p) = I(X; [X])$.*

Of course, as shown in the preceding section, finite adaptive strategies can be more efficient in terms of length by a factor of $|Act|$ when compared with non-adaptive ones. Concerning capacity, we do not have a general formula for the maximizing distribution. In what follows, we limit our discussion to two important cases for $U(\cdot)$, Shannon entropy and error entropy. In both cases, capacity only depends on the number K of indistinguishability classes. For guessing entropy, we conjecture that $C(S) = \frac{K-1}{2}$, but at the moment a proof of this fact escapes us.

Theorem 5. *The following formulae holds, where $K = |X/ \equiv |$.*

- *For $U = H$ (Shannon entropy), $C(S) = \log K$.*
- *For $U = E$ (Error entropy), $C(S) = 1 - \frac{1}{K}$.*

Example 7. Consider the mechanism defined in Ex. 3. One has the following capacities: for $U(\cdot) = H(\cdot), C(S) = \log 8 = 3$, while for $U(\cdot) = E(\cdot), C(S) = \frac{7}{8} = 0.875$.

6 Computing Optimal Strategies

We show that, for finite strategies, $I_\sigma(S, p)$ can be expressed recursively as a Bellman equation. This allows for calculation of optimal finite strategies based on standard algorithms, such as backward induction.

6.1 A Bellman Equation

Let us introduce some terminology. For each y, the *y-derivative* of σ, denoted σ_y, is the function defined thus, for each $y^j \in \mathcal{Y}^*$: $\sigma_y(y^j) \triangleq \sigma(yy^j)$. Note that if σ has length $l > 1$, then σ_y is a strategy of height $\leq l - 1$. For $l = 1$, σ_y is the empty function. Recall that according to (2), for $h = ay$, we have[3]

$$p^{ay}(x) = p_a(x|y)$$

By convention, we let $I_\sigma(\cdots)$ denote 0 when σ is empty. Moreover, we write $I_{[a]}(\cdots)$ as $I_a(\cdots)$.

Lemma 3. *Let $p(\cdot)$ be any prior on X. Let σ be a strategy with $\sigma(\varepsilon) = a$. Then $I_\sigma(S; p) = I_a(S; p) + \sum_y p_a(y) I_{\sigma_y}(S; p^{ay})$.*

Let us say that a strategy σ of length l is *optimal* for S, $p(\cdot)$ and l if it maximizes $I_\sigma(S, p)$ among all strategies of length l.

---

[3] In terms of a given prior $p(\cdot)$ and of the matrices of S, this can be also expressed as: $p^{ay}(x) = \frac{p_a(y|x)p(x)}{\sum_{x'} p_a(y|x')p(x')}$.

Corollary 1 (Bellman-type equation for optimal strategies). *There is an optimal strategy $\sigma^\star$ of length l for S and $p(\cdot)$ that satisfies the following equation*

$$I_{\sigma^\star}(S; p) = \max_a \{ I_a(S; p) + \sum_{y:\, p_a(y)>0} p_a(y) I_{\sigma^\star_{a,y}}(S; p^{ay}) \} \qquad (8)$$

where $\sigma^\star_{a,y}$ is an optimal strategy of length $l - 1$ for S and $p^{ay}(\cdot)$.

Corollary 1 allows us to employ dynamic programming or backward induction to compute optimal finite strategies. We discuss this briefly in the next subsection.

6.2 Markov Decision Processes and Backward Induction

A mechanism S and a prior $p(\cdot)$ induce a *Markov Decision Process* (MDP), where all possible attack trees are represented at once. Backward induction amounts to recursively computing the most efficient attack tree out of this MDP, limited to a given length. More precisely, the MDP M induced by S and a prior $p(\cdot)$ is an in general infinite tree consisting of *decision* nodes and *probabilistic* nodes. Levels of

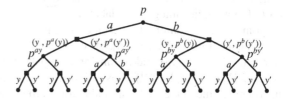

Fig. 7. The first few levels of a MDP induced by a prior $p(\cdot)$ and a mechanism with $Act = \{a, b\}$ and $\mathcal{Y} = \{y, y'\}$. Round nodes are decision nodes and squares nodes are probabilistic nodes. For the sake of space, labels of the last level of arcs and nodes are only partially shown.

decision nodes alternate with levels of probabilistic nodes, starting from the root which is a decision node. Decision nodes are labelled with probability distributions over X, edges outgoing decision nodes with actions, and edges outgoing probabilistic nodes with pairs (y, λ) of an observation and a real, in such a way that (again, we identify nodes with the corresponding history):

- a decision node corresponding to history h is labelled with $p^h(\cdot)$, if this is defined, otherwise the node and its descendants are removed, as well as the incoming edge;
- for any pair of consecutive edges leading from a decision node h to another decision node *hay*, for any $a \in Act$ and $y \in \mathcal{Y}$, the edge outgoing the probabilistic node is labelled with $(y, p^h_a(y))$.

Fig. 7 shows the first few levels of such a MDP.

In order to compute an optimal strategy of length $l \geq 1$ by backward induction, one initially prunes the tree at l-th decision level (the root is at level 0) and then assigns *rewards* to all leaves of the resulting tree. Moreover, each probabilistic node is assigned an *immediate gain*. Rewards are then gradually propagated from the leaves up to the root, as follows:

- each probabilistic node is assigned as a reward the sum of its immediate gain and the *average* reward of its children, average computed using the probabilities on the outgoing arcs;

– each decision node is assigned the *maximal* reward of its children; the arc leading to the maximizing child is marked or otherwise recorded.

Eventually, the root will be assigned the maximal achievable reward. Moreover, the paths of marked arcs starting from the root will define an optimal strategy of length l. We can apply this strategy to our problem, starting with assigning rewards 0 to each leaf node h, and immediate gain $I_a(S, p^h)$ to each a-child of any decision node h. The correctness of the resulting procedure is obvious in the light of Corollary 1.

In a crude implementation of the above outlined procedure, the number of decision nodes in the MDP will be bounded by $(|\mathcal{Y}| \times |Act|)^{l+1} - 1$ (probabilistic nodes can be dispensed with, at the cost of moving incoming action labels to outgoing arcs). Assuming that each distribution is stored in space $O(|\mathcal{X}|)$, the MDP can be built and stored in time and space $O(|\mathcal{X}| \times (|\mathcal{Y}| \times |Act|)^{l+1})$. This is also

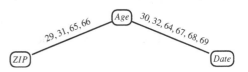

Fig. 8. A Shannon entropy optimal strategy for Ex. 4. Leaves with the same label and their incoming arcs have been coalesced.

the running time of the backward induction outlined above, assuming $U(\cdot)$ can be computed in time $O(|\mathcal{X}|)$ (some straightforward optimizations are possible here, but we will not dwell on this). By comparison, the running time of the exhaustive procedure outlined in [17, Th.1], for deterministic systems, runs in time $O(l \times |Act|^{r^l} \times |\mathcal{X}| \times \log |\mathcal{X}|)$, where r is the maximal number of classes in any relation $\equiv_a$; since r can be as large as $|\mathcal{Y}|$, this gives a worst-case running time of $O(l \times |Act|^{|\mathcal{Y}|^l} \times |\mathcal{X}| \times \log |\mathcal{X}|)$.

Example 8. Applying backward induction to the mechanism of Ex. 4 with $U(\cdot) = H(\cdot)$ and $l = 2$, one gets the optimal strategy σ shown in Fig. 8, with $I_\sigma(S, p) \approx 2.4$ bits.

In the general case, unfortunately, backward induction is quite memory-inefficient, even for a moderate number of observations or actions.

7 Conclusion and Further Work

We have proposed a general information-theoretic model for the analysis of confidentiality under adaptive attackers. Within this model, we have proven several results on the limits of such attackers, on the relations between adaptive and non-adaptive strategies, and on the problem of searching for optimal finite strategies.

There are several directions worth being pursued, starting from the present work. First, one would like to implement and experiment with the search algorithm described in Section 6. Adaptive querying of dataset, possibly specified via some query description language, might represent an ideal ground for evaluation of such algorithms. Second, one would like to investigate worst-case variations of the present framework: an interesting possibility is to devise an adaptive version of Differential Privacy [14,15] or one of its variants [9].

References

1. Alvim, M.S., Andrés, M.E., Palamidessi, C.: Information Flow in Interactive Systems. Journal of Computer Security (2011) (to appear)
2. Alvim, M.S., Chatzikokolakis, K., Palamidessi, C., Smith, G.: Measuring Information Leakage Using Generalized Gain Functions. In: IEEE 25th Computer Security Foundations Symposium 2012, pp. 265–279. IEEE Computer Society (2012)
3. Backes, M., Köpf, B.: Formally Bounding the Side-Channel Leakage in Unknown-Message Attacks. In: Jajodia, S., Lopez, J. (eds.) ESORICS 2008. LNCS, vol. 5283, pp. 517–532. Springer, Heidelberg (2008)
4. Braun, C., Chatzikokolakis, K., Palamidessi, C.: Quantitative Notions of Leakage for Onetry Attacks. In: Proc. of MFPS 2009. Electr. Notes Theor. Comput. Sci, vol. 249, pp. 75–91 (2009)
5. Boreale, M.: Quantifying information leakage in process calculi. Information and Computation 207(6), 699–725 (2009)
6. Boreale, M., Pampaloni, F., Paolini, M.: Asymptotic information leakage under one-try attacks. In: Hofmann, M. (ed.) FOSSACS 2011. LNCS, vol. 6604, pp. 396–410. Springer, Heidelberg (2011)
7. Boreale, M., Pampaloni, F., Paolini, M.: Quantitative information flow, with a view. In: Atluri, V., Diaz, C. (eds.) ESORICS 2011. LNCS, vol. 6879, pp. 588–606. Springer, Heidelberg (2011)
8. Boreale, M., Pampaloni, F.: Quantitative multirun security under active adversaries. In: Proc. of QEST 2012, pp. 158–167 (2012)
9. Boreale, M., Paolini, M.: Worst- and Average-Case Privacy Breaches in Randomization Mechanisms. In: Baeten, J.C.M., Ball, T., de Boer, F.S. (eds.) TCS 2012. LNCS, vol. 7604, pp. 72–86. Springer, Heidelberg (2012)
10. Chatzikokolakis, K., Palamidessi, C., Panangaden, P.: Anonimity Protocols as Noisy Channels. Information and Computation 206(2-4), 378–401 (2008)
11. Clark, D., Hunt, S., Malacaria, P.: Quantitative Analysis of the Leakage of Confidential Data. Electr. Notes Theor. Comput. Sci. 59(3) (2001)
12. Cover, T.M., Thomas, J.A.: Elements of Information Theory, 2/e. John Wiley & Sons (2006)
13. Dodis, Y., Smith, A.: Entropic Security and the Encryption of High Entropy Messages. In: Kilian, J. (ed.) TCC 2005. LNCS, vol. 3378, pp. 556–577. Springer, Heidelberg (2005)
14. Dwork, C.: Differential Privacy. In: Bugliesi, M., Preneel, B., Sassone, V., Wegener, I. (eds.) ICALP 2006. LNCS, vol. 4052, pp. 1–12. Springer, Heidelberg (2006)
15. Dwork, C., McSherry, F., Nissim, K., Smith, A.: Calibrating Noise to Sensitivity in Private Data Analysis. In: Halevi, S., Rabin, T. (eds.) TCC 2006. LNCS, vol. 3876, pp. 265–284. Springer, Heidelberg (2006)
16. Kelsey, J., Schneier, B., Wagner, D., Hall, C.: Side Channel Cryptanalysis of Product Ciphers. Journal of Computer Security 8(2/3) (2000)
17. Köpf, B., Basin, D.: An Information-Theoretic Model for Adaptive Side-Channel Attacks. In: ACM Conference on Computer and Communications Security 2007, pp. 286–296 (2007)
18. LeMay, E., Ford, M.D., Keefe, K., Sanders, W.H., Muehrcke, C.: Model-based Security Metrics using ADversary VIew Security Evaluation (ADVISE). In: Proc. of QEST 2011, pp. 191–200 (2011)
19. Ford, M.D., Buchholz, P., Sanders, W.H.: State-Based Analysis in ADVISE. In: Proc. of QEST 2012, pp. 148–157 (2012)
20. Köpf, B., Smith, G.: Vulnerability Bounds and Leakage Resilience of Blinded Cryptography under Timing Attacks. In: CSF 2010, pp. 44–56 (2010)
21. Smith, G.: On the Foundations of Quantitative Information Flow. In: de Alfaro, L. (ed.) FOSSACS 2009. LNCS, vol. 5504, pp. 288–302. Springer, Heidelberg (2009)

Uniform Protection for Multi-exposed Targets

Roberto Vigo, Flemming Nielson, and Hanne Riis Nielson

DTU Compute, Technical University of Denmark, Denmark
{rvig,fnie,hrni}@dtu.dk

Abstract. Ensuring that information is protected proportionately to its value is a major challenge in the development of robust distributed systems, where code complexity and technological constraints might allow reaching a key functionality along various paths. We propose a protection analysis over the Quality Calculus that computes the combinations of data required to reach a program point and relates them to a notion of cost. In this way, we can compare the security deployed on different paths that expose the same resource. The analysis is formalised in terms of flow logic, and is implemented as an optimisation problem encoded into Satisfiability Modulo Theories, allowing us to deal with complex cost structures. The usefulness of the approach is demonstrated on the study of password recovery systems.

Keywords: Security verification, distributed systems, protection analysis, security cost, Quality Calculus, Satisfiability Modulo Theories.

1 Introduction

Common sense tells that classified information has to be protected according to its value. This simple principle is at the heart of the concept of multi-level security and the basis for developing access control policies [1]. Nonetheless, despite its simplicity, this design criterion is often ignored in the realisation of complex systems, whether they be software, physical, or cyber-physical systems. On the one hand, code complexity and composition may inadvertently give rise to various paths leading to expose the very same piece of information; on the other hand, usability best practices may prescribe, and technological constraints may oblige, to offer multiple ways to access the same information. The question whether uniform security checks are performed on paths leading to the same resource is then crucial, and its answer far from being obvious.

The Quality Calculus has been introduced in [2] for attacking the problem of Denial-of-Service resorting to default data whenever actual data cannot be obtained due to unreliable communication. More in general, the calculus offers an elegant framework for reasoning about systems where the same functionality can be triggered in multiple ways, and thus enjoy a branching control flow. Taking a process algebraic point of view, suitable for describing software systems but also organisations or physical infrastructure, we develop a static analysis on a value-passing version of the calculus to attack the questions highlighted above.

E. Ábrahám and C. Palamidessi (Eds.), FORTE 2014, LNCS 8461, pp. 182–198, 2014.

Given a system P and a location l of interest, the *protection analysis* computes the information an adversary needs in order to drive P to l, considering all possible paths. This is achieved by translating P into a set of propositional formulae describing the dependency between information and reachability of locations: each satisfying assignment of such set of formulae describes a way in which l can be attained. Moreover, associating costs to literals of such formulae, different assignments can be ranked so as to compute the minimal cost for reaching l. In particular, we consider an attacker model where adversaries are *lucky*: initially having no knowledge, they can decide to *guess* some information on their way to l, incurring the corresponding cost.

Literals represent the knowledge of communication channels by the adversary. This approach proves useful as channels are abstract and flexible entities, which can model a great many cyber and physical scenarios. In particular, we assume that channels provide given degrees of security [3], and quantify their strength: in the cyber world, a secure channel is implemented by means of cryptography, the cost of guessing it being a function of some cryptographic keys (e.g. number of bits for some cryptosystems); in the physical world, a channel may represent a door, its cost quantifying the effort needed to open it (e.g. grams of dynamite). While the correctness of such channels is investigated in the realm of protocol verification, any system with a substantial need for security is likely to have standardised mechanisms to achieve various degrees of protection, and modelling them with secure channels is a coarse yet reasonable abstraction.

The ultimate goal of the framework is to check whether the protection ensured by the implementation, that is, the cheapest way for reaching l, is matching the specification requirements, formalised as a map from locations to desired confidentiality levels.

The novelty of the protection analysis is two-fold: first, the problem of quantifying security checks and comparing desired with actual protection is interesting *per se*; second, the quest for optimal attacks relies on arbitrary cost structures and objective functions, and is implemented via a reduction to Satisfiability Modulo Theories (SMT) that can be exploited in a great many different contexts. Whilst our SMT approach to optimisation is not entirely novel, non-linearly ordered and symbolic cost structures have not been explicitly addressed so far in connection to this technique.

The usefulness of the framework is demonstrated on the study of password recovery systems. We consider the *Microsoft account* system, where a challenge is sent to a previously registered e-mail or phone number, and the *Yahoo!Mail* system, which allows resetting a password upon answering previously selected questions. The results we present are obtained through an implementation of the analysis available at www.imm.dtu.dk/~rvig/quality-tool.html.

Outline. Section 2 introduces a motivating example developed throughout the paper. The calculus used to specify the example is presented in Sect. 3. In Sect. 4 the protection analysis is developed. The solution technique based on SMT is discussed in Sect. 5, where we also argue on the importance of complex cost sets. Section 6 concludes and sketches a line for future developments.

Related work. Our work is inspired by a successful strand of literature in protocol verification, where a protocol is translated into a set of first-order Horn clauses and resolution-based theorem proving is used to establish security properties [4,5], and by the flow logic approach to static analysis [6]. In particular, the translation from processes to propositional formulae is inspired by ProVerif [7] translation of protocols into first-order Horn clauses, but can be more formally understood as a flow logic where the carrier logic is not the usual Alternation-free Least Fixed Point Logic, since it cannot express optimisation problems.

In order to formalise the "need for protection" of a location we resort to confidentiality lattices, that are widely used for describing levels of security in access control policies. An excellent introductory reference is [1, chps. 6,7].

As for the solution technique we exploit, SMT is surveyed in [8], while [9,10] present two different approaches to solve optimisation problems via SMT. In particular, Nieuwenhuis and Oliveras [9] proposed to modify the DPLL(T) procedure inherent to SMT solvers so as to look for optimal assignments, while Cimatti et al. [10] developed the search for an optimal assignments on top of an SMT solver, as we do in Sect. 5. Nonetheless, both these works focus on numeric weights, which in our settings are represented with linearly ordered cost structures. Our more general notion of weight is modelled after Meadow's cost sets, formalised as monoids in [11].

Finally, another perspective on the technical developments underpinning the analysis points to computing *prime implicants* of a given formula [12], where in our case primality is sought with respect to the cost set.

2   Motivating Example

We demonstrate the flexibility and usefulness of the framework on the problem of password recovery. As defined in the Common Weakness Enumeration [13], "it is common for an application to have a mechanism that provides a means for a user to gain access to their account in the event they forget their password". It is then crucial to ensure that the protection to the account offered by the recovery mechanism is comparable to the protection provided by the password, otherwise we would have two paths leading to the same resource but performing a different amount of security checks. As noted by the Open Web Application Security Project [14]: "Weak password recovery processes allow stronger password authentication schemes to be bypassed. Non-existent password recovery processes are expensive to support or result in denial-of-service conditions." Below we encode such a system in the Value-Passing Quality Calculus.

$$\text{System} \triangleq (\nu\text{access})\,(\nu\text{ok})\,(\nu\text{pwd})\,(!(\text{Login}|\text{Recover}))$$

$$\text{Login} \triangleq {}^1\&_\forall(\text{id}?x_{id}, \text{pwd}?x_p).{}^2\text{access!ok}$$

$$\text{Recover} \triangleq {}^3\&_\forall(\text{id}?x'_{id}, \&_\exists(\text{mail}?x_m, \text{pin}?x_c)).$$
$${}^4\text{case } x_m \text{ of some}(y_m): {}^5\text{pwd!ok else}$$
$${}^6\text{case } x_c \text{ of some}(y_c): {}^7\text{pwd!ok else } 0$$

Process System is modelled after *Microsoft account* login mechanism, in charge of granting access to services such as mailboxes and technical forums. The main process is composed by two parallel sub-processes, running an unbounded number of times: the first one models the normal login procedure, while the second one abstracts the password recovery mechanisms.

According to process Login, in order to be granted access a user has to provide their own id and the corresponding password. This is mimicked by the two inputs expected by the *quality binder* at label 1, which are simultaneously active. The *quality guard* ∀ prescribes that both inputs have to be satisfied before proceeding, in any order. These inputs simulate two security checks: a party willing to authenticate into the system has to possess proper credentials, i.e., being able to communicate over id, pwd, and thus know such channels.

In the event the user forgot their password, the recovery mechanism comes into play. Microsoft offers two ways to recover a lost password: (*i*) a reset link is sent to an e-mail address previously registered by the user, or (*ii*) a 7-digit pin is sent to a phone number previously registered by the user. This behaviour is modelled by the quality binder at label 3 in process Recover. The binder is consumed as soon as the user has provided a valid id (e.g., an Outlook.com e-mail address), and proven their identity either through option (*i*) or option (*ii*). In the first case, the user needs to access a mailbox, simulated by an input on channel mail, while in the second case he or she has to provide the correct pin: the alternative is implemented by the existential guard ∃ instrumenting the inner quality binder. The case clauses at labels 4, 6 determine what combination of inputs triggered passing the binder. In both cases, the user gets a valid password for the account in question, simulated by the outputs at label 5 and 7, and hence will be able to fulfil the check enforced by process Login.

The key point of the example is that no matter how strong a user's password is, an attacker can always try to guess a 7-digit sequence[1]. In particular, the requirement for a password is having at least 8 characters and containing different cases, numbers, or symbols, which (almost) automatically makes a password stronger than the pin! In terms of confidentiality levels, this suggests that the desired security architecture is not necessarily met, as the protection offered by the three paths leading to authenticating, i.e. to label 2, might not be uniform, depending on the cost notion we resort to. While in this simple case such conclusion can be drawn after careful investigation of the system, there is a general need to develop automated techniques to cope with more complex scenarios. In the remainder of the paper we shall see how the protection analysis confirms our informal reasoning.

---

[1] As of Oct. 2013 there seemed to be no limit to the number of attempts one could try – we stopped our experiment at about 30. Some of our findings have been informally communicated in a number of situations and now we observe that they enforced both such limit and a daily threshold. While this mutation does make it more difficult to quantify the strength of the mechanism (cf. Sect. 5), it does not affect the relevance of the framework.

3   The Value-Passing Quality Calculus

In the following, we discuss the syntax and the intended semantics of the process calculus we use as specification language. It encodes a value-passing fragment of the Quality Calculus, from which in particular we inherit quality binders and the distinction between data and optional data, that allow modelling robust systems and give rise to branching control flows. As far as this paper is concerned, however, the reader can think of the calculus as a broadcast π-calculus enriched with quality binders. Such construct enhances succinctness, thus easing the task of specifying complex systems, but does not increase the expressiveness, hence the developments carry seamlessly to a variety of process calculi.

The formal semantics of the calculus is briefly commented upon in Appendix A, for it is instrumental to formulate the correctness statements but does not constitute a novelty per se.

Syntax and intended semantics. The Value-Passing Quality Calculus is displayed in Table 1. The calculus consists of four syntactic categories: processes P, input binders b, terms t, and expressions e. A process can be prefixed by a restriction, an input binder, an output $c!t$ of term t on channel c, or be the terminated process 0, the parallel composition of two processes, a replicated process, or a case clause.

An output $c!t$ broadcasts t to all processes ready to input over channel c; if there exists no such process, the output is consumed anyway (i.e., broadcasts are non-blocking actions).

An input binder can either be a simple input $c?x$ on channel c, or a *quality binder* $\&_q(b_1, \ldots, b_n)$, which is consumed as soon as enough sub-binders have been satisfied, as dictated by the quality guard q. A quality guard can be any Boolean predicate: we use the abbreviations $\forall$ and $\exists$ for the predicates specifying that all the sub-binders or at least one sub-binder have to be satisfied before proceeding, respectively, as we have seen in the example.

When a quality binder is consumed, some input variables occurring in its sub-binders might have not been bound to any value, if this is allowed by the quality guard. In order to record which inputs have been received and which have not, we always bind an input variable x to an expression e, which is some(c) if c is the name received by the input binding x, or none if the input is not received but we are continuing anyway. In this sense, we say that expressions represent *optional data*, while terms represent *data*, in the wake of programming languages like Standard ML. In order to insist on this distinction, variables x are used to mark places where expressions are expected, whereas variables y stand for terms.

The case clause in the syntax of processes is then used to inspect whether or not an input variable, bound to an expression, is indeed carrying data. The process case x of some(y) : P_1 else P_2 evolves into P_1 if x is bound to some(c), and in P_1 y is replaced by c; otherwise, if x is bound to none, P_2 is executed.

Observe that the adversary can always move into the scope of a restricted name by paying the corresponding cost, e.g. guessing pwd in the example. The standard semantics of restriction, according to which a new name c is only known within its scope, is encompassed by assigning c an infinite cost.

Table 1. The syntax of the Value-Passing Quality Calculus

$$P ::= 0 \mid (\nu c) \, P \mid P_1 | P_2 \mid {}^l b.P \mid {}^l c!t.P \mid \,!P \mid {}^l \text{case } x \text{ of some}(y) : P_1 \text{ else } P_2$$
$$b ::= c?x \mid \&_q(b_1, \cdots, b_n) \qquad\quad t ::= c \mid y \qquad\quad e ::= x \mid \text{some}(t) \mid \text{none}$$

As usual, in the following we consider closed processes (no free variable), and we make the simplifying assumption that processes are renamed apart so that names and variables are bound exactly once.

Table 1 defines a proper fragment of the original calculus, as it is not possible to check *what* is received by a given input. This simplification matches the spirit of the analysis, where the knowledge of channels corresponds to the capability of fulfilling the security checks that they represent.

Confidentiality labels. As argued in Sect. 1, different points in a system have to be protected according to the value of the information they process. This idea can be formalised introducing a simple, non-functional extension to the calculus, where a program point of interest is instrumented with a *unique* label $l \in \mathcal{L}$. This is the case of input binders, outputs, and case clauses in Table 1: we limit labels to be placed before these constructs since they represent proper actions. In the following, we will denote labels with the numerals $1, 2, \ldots$, thus taking $\mathcal{L} = \mathbb{N}$. We say that a label l is reached in an actual execution when the sub-process following l is ready to execute. Moreover, we assume to have a *confidentiality lattice* $(\Sigma = \{\sigma_1, \ldots, \sigma_n\}, \sqsubseteq_\Sigma)$, with greatest lower bound operator $\bigsqcap_\Sigma$, and a function $\gamma \colon \mathcal{L} \to \Sigma$ that maps labels into confidentiality levels. In particular, $\gamma(l_1) \sqsubseteq_\Sigma \gamma(l_2)$ denotes that the confidentiality (i.e., need for protection) of the program point indicated by l_2 is greater than or equal to the confidentiality of the program point indicated by l_1.

As an example of confidentiality lattice, consider the *military lattice* given by $\Sigma = \{\text{unclassified}, \text{confidential}, \text{secret}, \text{top-secret}\}$, with the ordering unclassified $\sqsubseteq_\Sigma$ confidential $\sqsubseteq_\Sigma$ secret $\sqsubseteq_\Sigma$ top-secret. More complex lattices, in particular non-linearly-ordered ones, are discussed in [1, chp. 7].

In our running example the intended security architecture prescribes $\gamma(2) = \gamma(5) = \gamma(7)$, as these three program points have the effect of authenticating a user into the system. We can thus rely on a simple security lattice unrestricted $\sqsubseteq_\Sigma$ restricted, where the higher element is assigned to labels $2, 5, 7$.

4   Protection Analysis

Given a process P, the protection analysis aims at estimating the amount of knowledge that a process Q has to possess in order for the execution of $P|Q$ to reach a given location l in P. Intuitively, P is running and communicating in a hostile environment, and Q represents an adversary that aims at reaching a protected location, for example authenticating into the system. We focus on formalisations of P such that l is not reached unless some interactions with the environment take place: the running example of Sect. 2 does not specify the user who is supposed to be logging in, so as to rule out the legal way to authenticating and focus on malicious behaviours.

We consider systems in which the communication takes place over secure channels, where the knowledge of a channel entails the capability of fulfilling the security checks governing the communication. The knowledge that an attacker Q needs to interact with P is thus defined as a set of such channels. Moreover, we can quantify this information by assigning costs to channels: in the case of IT systems, for instance, the degree of security provided by a channel is related to the strength of the cryptographic mechanisms it exploits, and in some cryptosystems be determined as the size of the cryptographic keys needed to communicate over the channel.

Let *Names* be the set of channels occurring in P. We assume to have a function cost : *Names* $\rightarrow \mathcal{K}$ that associates a cost $k \in \mathcal{K}$ to a channel c. Formally, we require $(\mathcal{K}, \oplus)$ to be a monoid equipped with a partial order $\sqsubseteq_\mathcal{K}$, such that $(\mathcal{K}, \sqsubseteq_\mathcal{K})$ is a lattice. Intuitively, the greater the protection a channel c ensures, the greater the effort required by Q in order to get access to the channel, and therefore the greater will be the value of cost(c) with respect to $\sqsubseteq_\mathcal{K}$. In the following, we will refer to $\mathcal{K}$ as the *cost set* of the analysis. We require $\oplus$ to be extensive, that is, the sum of two elements always dominates both the summands:

$$\forall k_1, k_2 \in \mathcal{K} \,.\, k_1 \sqsubseteq_\mathcal{K} (k_1 \oplus k_2) \wedge k_2 \sqsubseteq_\mathcal{K} (k_1 \oplus k_2) \tag{1}$$

Moreover, we assume that $\oplus$ is monotone and the least element $\bot \in \mathcal{K}$ is its identity element, that is, $\oplus$ is an upper bound operator of the lattice $(\mathcal{K}, \sqsubseteq_\mathcal{K})$, and therefore satisfies (1). As highlighted by Meadows [11], the monoid might not be commutative, as the order in which costs are paid might influence their combination. Whilst keeping this elegant generalisation, nonetheless we do not provide in practice any mechanism for re-determining costs dynamically, as the process is evaluated, nor do we discuss a context-sensitive notion of cost.

The outcome of the analysis is a map $\delta : \mathcal{L} \rightarrow \mathcal{P}(\mathcal{P}(\textit{Names}))$ from labels to sets of sets of names (channels), an element $\{c_1, \ldots, c_n\} \in \delta(l)$ denoting a set of channels whose total cost under-approximates the cost that Q incurs in order to enforce reaching l. Finally, $\delta(l)$ is computed such that all its elements have minimal costs with respect to the cost set.

An element of $\delta(l)$ is related to the confidentiality lattice $\Sigma = \{\sigma_1, \ldots, \sigma_n\}$ by means of a function $\alpha : \mathcal{P}(\textit{Names}) \rightarrow \Sigma$, compressing cost regions into confidentiality levels:

$$\alpha(\{c_1, \ldots, c_n\}) = \begin{cases} \sigma_1 & \text{if } \bigoplus_{i=1}^n \text{cost}(c_i) \in \{k_1^1, \ldots, k_1^{h_1}\} \\ \vdots \\ \sigma_m & \text{if } \bigoplus_{i=1}^n \text{cost}(c_i) \in \{k_m^1, \ldots, k_m^{h_m}\} \end{cases}$$

where α is a well-defined function if the sets of costs $\{k_i^1, \ldots, k_i^{h_i}\}$ are pairwise disjoint and their union is $\mathcal{K}$. Moreover, it is natural to require that α is monotone. A simple example in the cost set $(\mathbb{Z}, +)$ is given by the choice

$$\alpha(\{c_1,\dots,c_n\}) = \begin{cases} \text{low} & \text{if } \sum_{i=1}^{n} \text{cost}(c_i) \leq 1024 \\ \text{medium} & \text{if } 1024 < \sum_{i=1}^{n} \text{cost}(c_i) \leq 2048 \\ \text{high} & \text{if } 2048 < \sum_{i=1}^{n} \text{cost}(c_i) \end{cases}$$

where numbers could represent the length of cryptographic keys, and we state for instance that a program point is poorly protected if no more than 1024 bits are necessary to attain it (for a fixed cryptosystem).

Intuitively, the function γ is the specification expressing the target security architecture of a system with respect to a given confidentiality lattice, while the function δ captures (an under-approximation of) how this architecture has been realised in the implementation. The overall aim of the analysis, i.e., checking whether the deployed protection lives up to the required confidentiality, can thus be expressed by the property

$$\forall l \in \mathcal{L} \ . \ \gamma(l) \sqsubseteq_{\Sigma} \bigsqcap_{\mathcal{C} \in \delta(l)}{}_{\Sigma} \alpha(\mathcal{C})$$

A violation of this condition is referred to as a potential *inversion of protection*.

4.1   From Processes to Knowledge Constraints

The recursive function $[\![P]\!]$tt, defined in Table 2, translates a process P into a set of constraints of the form $\varphi \rightsquigarrow \bar{p}$, where φ is a propositional formula and $\bar{p}$ a positive literal. The intended semantics of a constraint implements a backward style of reasoning, according to which if Q knows p, i.e., $\bar{p} = $ tt, then it must be because it knows (enough information to satisfy) φ. As we shall see below, the consequent φ accounts for the checks made on the path leading to disclosing p, namely input binders and case clauses. The antecedent $\bar{p}$ can either stand for a channel c, meaning that Q knows c, an input variable x, meaning that the related input is satisfied (i.e., $x = $ some(c)), or a label l, meaning that l is attained.

At each step of the evaluation, the first parameter of $[\![\cdot]\!]$ corresponds to the sub-process of P that has still to be translated, while the second parameter is a logic formula, intuitively carrying the hypothesis on the knowledge Q needs to attain the current point in P. The translation function is structurally defined over processes as explained below.

If P is 0, then there is no location to be attained and thus no constraint is produced. If $P = !P'$ or $P = (\nu c) P'$, then it spontaneously evolves to P', hence Q does not need any knowledge to attain P' and gains no knowledge since no communication is performed. A parallel composition is translated taking the union of the sets into which the components are translated.

Communication actions have instead an impact on the knowledge of Q: inputs represent checks that require knowledge, outputs fulfil those checks, and case clauses determine the flow of control. Whenever such an action $[\![{}^{l}a.P']\!]\varphi$ is reached in the translation, a constraint $\varphi \rightsquigarrow \bar{l}$ is generated: if the attacker attains l, then the security checks on a path to l must be fulfilled, and thus φ

Table 2. The translation from processes to propositional constraints

$$[\![0]\!]\varphi \quad = \emptyset \qquad\qquad\qquad [\![!P]\!]\varphi \quad = [\![P]\!]\varphi$$
$$[\![P_1|P_2]\!]\varphi = [\![P_1]\!]\varphi \cup [\![P_2]\!]\varphi \qquad [\![(\nu c)\,P]\!]\varphi = [\![P]\!]\varphi$$

$$[\![{}^l b.P]\!]\varphi \;\; = [\![P]\!](\varphi \wedge \mathsf{hp}(b)) \cup \mathsf{th}(\varphi, b) \cup \{\varphi \leftsquigarrow \bar{l}\}$$
$$[\![{}^l c!t.P]\!]\varphi = [\![P]\!]\varphi \cup \{\varphi \leftsquigarrow \bar{c}\} \cup \{\varphi \leftsquigarrow \bar{l}\}$$

$$[\![{}^l\mathsf{case}\ x\ \mathsf{of\ some}(y): P_1\ \mathsf{else}\ P_2]\!]\varphi = [\![P_1]\!](\varphi \wedge \bar{x}) \cup [\![P_2]\!](\varphi \wedge \neg\bar{x}) \cup \{\varphi \leftsquigarrow \bar{l}\}$$

$$\mathsf{hp}(c?x) = \bar{c} \qquad\qquad\qquad \mathsf{hp}(\&_q(c_1?x_1,\dots,c_n?x_n)) = \langle\!\langle q \rangle\!\rangle(\bar{c_1},\dots,\bar{c_n})$$

$$\mathsf{th}(\varphi, c?x) = \{(\varphi \wedge \bar{c}) \leftsquigarrow \bar{x}\} \qquad \mathsf{th}(\varphi, \&_q(b_1,\dots,b_n)) = \bigcup_{i=1}^{n} \mathsf{th}(\varphi, b_i)$$

$$\langle\!\langle \forall \rangle\!\rangle(h_1,\dots,h_n) = \bigwedge_{i=1}^{n} h_i \qquad\qquad\qquad \langle\!\langle \exists \rangle\!\rangle(h_1,\dots,h_n) = \bigvee_{i=1}^{n} h_i$$

must evaluate to **tt**. Moreover, the nature of action a determines whether or not other constraints are produced and how the translation proceeds.

Consider a simple input ${}^l c?x.P'$: whenever such action is consumed, it must be that the attacker knows the communication channel c, therefore we translate P' under the hypothesis $\varphi \wedge \bar{c}$. Moreover, if the input is consumed, then x must be bound to $\mathsf{some}(c')$, hence we produce a constraint $(\varphi \wedge \bar{c}) \leftsquigarrow \bar{x}$. These two steps respectively accommodate the hypothesis we need for passing a binder, and the thesis we can establish whenever a binder is passed. In Table 2 functions hp and th take care of formalising this intuition, that seamlessly applies to quality binders, where the hypothesis is augmented accounting for the combinations of inputs that satisfy the binder, as dictated by the quality guard q. The last section of Table 2 shows two cases for q, but any Boolean predicate can be used.

The execution of an output ${}^l c!t$ satisfies all the security checks represented by inputs waiting on c. Therefore, if Q can trigger such output, it obtains the knowledge related to c without having to know the channel directly, and thus a constraint $\varphi \leftsquigarrow \bar{c}$ is generated. It is worthwhile observing that this behaviour is justified by the broadcast semantics, and by the fact that the calculus is limited to testing whether or not something has been received over a given channel, shifting the semantic load on the notion of secure channel. Moreover, note that the asymmetry between input and output is due to the fact that outputs are non-blocking.

A **case** construct is translated by taking the union of the constraints into which the two branches are translated: as the check is governed by the content of the **case** variable x, we record that the then branch is followed only when x is bound to $\mathsf{some}(c)$ by adding a literal $\bar{x}$ to the hypothesis, as we do for inputs, and we add $\neg\bar{x}$ if the else branch is followed.

The set of constraints $[\![P]\!]\mathbf{tt}$ computed according to Table 2 can be normalised so as to produce a compact representation of system P. Whenever two rules $\varphi \leftsquigarrow \bar{p}$ and $\varphi' \leftsquigarrow \bar{p}$ are in $[\![P]\!]\mathbf{tt}$, they are replaced with a single rule $(\varphi \vee \varphi') \leftsquigarrow \bar{p}$.

This simplification is intuitively sound since if φ leads to obtain p and φ' leads to obtain p, then p is available to the attacker under the condition that $\varphi \vee \varphi'$ is known. In the following, we assume to deal with sets of constraints in such format.

4.2 Attacker Model: Lucky Attackers and Insiders

A rule $\varphi \leftsquigarrow \overline{p}$ in $[\![P]\!]$tt describes how Q can attain p playing according to the rules of the system, namely fulfilling the checks described by φ. Nonetheless, when p is a channel, an attacker can always try to obtain it directly, for instance guessing some cryptographic keys. In order to account for this possibility, we enrich each rule $\varphi \leftsquigarrow \overline{c}$ by replacing the consequent with the disjunction $g_c \vee \varphi$, where literal g_c (for "guess c") represents the possibility of learning c directly, incurring the corresponding cost. Finally, for each channel c such that no rule $\varphi \leftsquigarrow \overline{c}$ is in $[\![P]\!]$tt, we add to $[\![P]\!]$tt a constraint $g_c \leftsquigarrow \overline{c}$, expressing that Q has no option but guessing the channel.

It is worthwhile observing how resorting to propositional logic integrates with the under-approximating nature of the analysis: a channel can either be learnt or not, and its cost contribute or not to the cost of an attack. This means that we do not keep track of the number of attempts made to guess some information, and always assume that guessing c is successful whenever g_c is found to be true. When looking for optimal combinations of channels with respect to the cost structure, we will then count the cost of those channels that Q must guess in order to attain the label of interest, thus obtaining an under-approximation of the cost of running the attack.

Finally, notice how the cost map allows modelling insiders: by decreasing the cost of guessing a given piece of information we can model an attacker who has access to part of the secret, for instance to the rules according to which a random password is generated or to its first letter.

Example. The translation of our example returns a set containing the following constraints, augmented as explained above:

$$\dfrac{\overline{1}}{\overline{\mathsf{id} \wedge \mathsf{pwd}} \leftsquigarrow \overline{2}} \qquad \dfrac{\overline{\mathsf{id}} \leftsquigarrow \overline{x_{id}}}{g_{\mathsf{access}} \vee (\overline{\mathsf{id} \wedge \mathsf{pwd}}) \leftsquigarrow \overline{\mathsf{access}}} \qquad \dfrac{\overline{\mathsf{pwd}} \leftsquigarrow \overline{x_p}}{g_{\mathsf{id}} \leftsquigarrow \overline{\mathsf{id}}}$$

$$\underbrace{\dfrac{\dfrac{\overline{3}}{\overline{\mathsf{id}} \leftsquigarrow \overline{x'_{id}}}}{\dfrac{\overline{\mathsf{mail}} \leftsquigarrow \overline{x_m}}{\dfrac{\overline{\mathsf{pin}} \leftsquigarrow \overline{x_c}}{\overline{\mathsf{id} \wedge (\mathsf{mail} \vee \mathsf{pin})} \leftsquigarrow \overline{4}}}}_{\varphi} \qquad \begin{array}{c} \varphi \wedge \overline{x_m} \leftsquigarrow \overline{5} \\[4pt] \varphi \wedge \neg \overline{x_m} \leftsquigarrow \overline{6} \\[4pt] \varphi \wedge (\neg \overline{x_m}) \wedge \overline{x_c} \leftsquigarrow \overline{7} \\[4pt] g_{\mathsf{pwd}} \vee (\varphi \wedge \overline{x_m}) \vee (\varphi \wedge (\neg \overline{x_m}) \wedge \overline{x_c}) \leftsquigarrow \overline{\mathsf{pwd}} \end{array} \qquad \begin{array}{c} g_{\mathsf{mail}} \leftsquigarrow \overline{\mathsf{mail}} \\[4pt] g_{\mathsf{pin}} \leftsquigarrow \overline{\mathsf{pin}} \end{array}$$

where the only way for Q to know id, mail, pin is to guess them. Observe that the capability of using the password channel is obtained either by satisfying the recovery mechanism or by guessing pwd. For the sake of conciseness, we have omitted the conjunct tt in all the constraints.

5   Computing Optimal Assignments via SMT

In order to compute the set of sets of channels $\delta(l)$ that allow reaching l incurring minimal costs, we need to solve an optimisation problem subject to the Boolean constraints $[\![P]\!]$tt, where $\leftsquigarrow$ can be freely interpreted as the propositional backward implication $\Leftarrow$. There exist various techniques to cope with such problems, each suitable for particular choices of cost sets and objective functions. In the following, we show how to exploit an SMT solver to tackle the problem in its most general form. We limit to mention here that Pseudo-Boolean optimisation or Answer Set Programming with weighted rules are efficient and elegant alternatives for dealing with the monoid $(\mathbb{Z}, +)$ and linear objective functions.

The problem. In a nutshell, our task reduces to compute a satisfying assignment M of the propositional formula

$$\psi = \bar{l} \wedge \bigwedge_{(\varphi \leftsquigarrow \bar{p}) \in [\![P]\!]\text{tt}} (\varphi \Leftarrow \bar{p})$$

namely, we assume that l is reached and we look for the consequences (i.e., implicants of $\bar{l}$). In particular, we are interested in all the assignments M that satisfy ψ, denoted $M \models \psi$, and are minimal with respect to a function of the literals g_i's representing the need for guessing channels:

$$f(g_1, \ldots, g_n) = (g_1 \cdot \text{cost}(c_1)) \oplus \cdots \oplus (g_n \cdot \text{cost}(c_n))$$

where the cost of obtaining a channel contributes to the total cost of the attack only if Q decides to guess the channel, incurring the corresponding cost, $g \cdot \text{cost}(c)$ standing for if g then $\text{cost}(c)$ else $\bot$ (recall that $\oplus$ is assumed to be monotone and $\bot$ its neutral element). If no solution is found, i.e. ψ is unsatisfiable, then the program point indicated by l is not reachable.

Denoting M a satisfying assignment of ψ, we write $\delta(M)$ for the set of literals that are true in M. Eventually, it might be that there exists a number of assignments with minimal costs, and thus $\delta(l)$ is defined as

$$\delta(l) = \{\delta(M) \mid M \models \psi \wedge \text{minimal}(M)\}$$

and finally we shall take as result of the analysis the security level σ minimal among those onto which α maps the sets of channels in $\delta(l)$, or their greatest lower bound in case they are incomparable (recall that Σ is a lattice).

An SMT-based algorithm. Such an optimisation problem can be tackled by computing assignments for a list $\pi_1, \ldots, \pi_n$ of SMT problems, where π_i is a more constrained version of π_{i-1} that requires to improve on the cost of the current solution. The initial problem π consists of the propositional constraints ψ and of the objective function f, whose value is stored in variable goal. Then, while the problem is satisfiable, we improve on the cost of the current assignment by asserting new constraints which tighten the value of goal, until unsatisfiability is

Data: The problem $\pi \equiv \psi \wedge (\text{goal} := f(g_1, \ldots, g_n))$
Result: the set $\mathcal{M}$ of pairs (assignment,cost) such that the assignment is
        minimal w.r.t. f

$\mathcal{M} \leftarrow \emptyset$;
while π *satisfiable* **do**
   | $M \leftarrow \text{get-model}(\pi)$;
   | $k \leftarrow M(\text{goal})$;
   | **forall the** $(M', k') \in \mathcal{M} \mid k \sqsubset_{\mathcal{K}} k'$ **do**   // M outperforms M'
   | | $\mathcal{M} \leftarrow \mathcal{M} \setminus \{(M', k')\}$
   | **end**
   | $\mathcal{M} \leftarrow \mathcal{M} \cup \{(M, k)\}$;
   | $\pi \leftarrow \pi \wedge \neg(\bigwedge_{i=1}^{n}(\overline{c_i} = M(\overline{c_i}))) \wedge \neg(\text{goal} \sqsupseteq_{\mathcal{K}} k)$;
end

Algorithm 1. The SMT-based solving procedure

reported. As for the cost set (comparing and combining costs), SMT solvers offer native support for numeric costs and common mathematical functions, while
more complex cost sets have to be encoded manually.

    Algorithm 1 displays the pseudo-code of the procedure. In particular, observe
that when a new problem π_i is generated, additional constraints are asserted
that ask for (i) a different assignment and (ii) a non-greater cost: the former
condition speeds up the search, while the latter explores the cost frontier.

    The termination of the algorithm is ensured by the finiteness of possible as-
signments to the propositional variables of the π_i's, whose propositional structure
does not change throughout the loop, and by the fact that the same assignment
cannot occur twice as solution due to the new constraints we generate in each
iteration: at most, we need to solve as many π_i's as models of ψ (ALL-SAT).
The correctness of the procedure stems from the fact that when unsatisfiability is
claimed, by construction of the π_i's there cannot exist further assignments that
comply with the cost constraints. Finally, observe that the Boolean satisfiability problem is NP-complete, but in the last decade solvers have been developed
that can handle instances with millions of variables, and are increasingly used
in software verification. Our implementation is based on Microsoft Z3.

Example. Consider the login system discussed in Sect. 2, and assume to work in
the cost set $(\mathbb{Z}, +)$. The engineering of a sensible cost map is a delicate task that
involves cryptographic arguments. Due to space constraint we make here the
simplistic assumption that costs to channels are given by the number of bits to
be guessed: $\text{cost(pin)} = 28$ (7 digits, 4 bits each) and $\text{cost(pwd)} = 56$ (8 symbols,
7 bit per ASCII symbol). We assume that the user id is known (the target e-
mail itself, for instance), and that the password of the third-party mailbox is
comparable to pwd (as the constraints put by Microsoft are customary also to
other e-mail providers). Finally, we disregard channel access as it is only used
after the label of interest is reached. The problem is thus to minimise

$$f(g_{\text{id}}, g_{\text{pwd}}, g_{\text{mail}}, g_{\text{pin}}) = g_{\text{id}} \cdot \text{cost(id)} + g_{\text{pwd}} \cdot \text{cost(pwd)} + g_{\text{pin}} \cdot \text{cost(pin)} + g_{\text{mail}} \cdot \text{cost(mail)}$$

under the constraints given by ψ where label 2 is asserted. Instructed with such input, our procedure finds that the formula is satisfiable and the single cheapest assignment is $M = [g_{\mathsf{id}} \mapsto \mathsf{tt}, g_{\mathsf{pwd}} \mapsto \mathsf{ff}, g_{\mathsf{mail}} \mapsto \mathsf{ff}, g_{\mathsf{pin}} \mapsto \mathsf{tt}]$, with cost given by $\mathsf{cost}(\mathsf{id}) + \mathsf{cost}(\mathsf{pin}) = 28$, and entailing $\delta(2) = \{\{\mathsf{id}, \mathsf{pin}\}\}$.

As for the desired security levels, we observed in Sect. 3 that $\gamma(2) = \gamma(5) = \gamma(7) = \mathsf{restricted}$ should hold, for we want the account to be equally protected on all the paths leading to granting access. As the cost for accessing an account in normal condition is 56, it is reasonable to set

$$\alpha(\{c_1, \ldots, c_n\}) = \begin{cases} \mathsf{restricted} & \text{if } \sum_{i=1}^n c_i \geq 56 \\ \mathsf{unrestricted} & \text{otherwise} \end{cases}$$

We would like to verify that $\mathsf{restricted} \sqsubseteq_\Sigma \alpha(\{\mathsf{id}, \mathsf{pin}\})$, which is false since $\mathsf{cost}(\mathsf{id}) + \mathsf{cost}(\mathsf{pin}) = 28$. It is thus the case that the implementation potentially guarantees less protection than the amount required by the specification, and therefore we shall issue a warning to the designer of the system.

Obviously, costs are central in determining the outcome of the analysis. For example, we could consider to choose pwd from a password dictionary, for it is unrealistic to assume randomly generated bits: the size of such dictionaries is usually less than the number of sequences of 7 digits, and thus with this cost map the analysis might say that the recovery mechanism offers enough protection. Likewise, a limit to the number of attempts can equalise the protection.

Finally, it is worthwhile noticing that the framework can be exploited to measure the *distance* between the implementation and the specification, and not only there qualitative compliance.

5.1   Motivating Complex Cost Sets

So far we have worked with an example in the cost set $(\mathbb{Z}, +)$, for it is natively encoded into SMT solvers and matches a first intuition of the notion of cost. More realistic numeric considerations can be formalised in the increasingly popular frameworks for the *quantification of information leakage*, e.g. [15], obtaining more robust definitions of function α. Nonetheless, it is not always the case that we are able to describe with numbers the security provided by channels: sometimes the techniques used to ensure security are even incomparable.

Observe that Algorithm 1 is already equipped to cope with the more general problem of optimising on partially ordered cost sets. An interesting case of non-linear cost sets is offered by the study of security in Cyber-Physical Systems, where components combine both software and physical features. In particular, in such systems an attack could require to assemble cyber actions with physical tampering [16], whose costs can either be comparable or not depending on the nature of the quantities we are interested in (for instance, energy and memory are not directly comparable).

In general, three elements characterise the problem and push for the comprehensive SMT-based approach: the non-linearity of the cost set, its symbolic nature, and the non-linearity of the objective function.

A mundane approach to password recovery. Yahoo!Mail password recovery mechanism differs from the one provided by *Microsoft account* in that it is (also) possible to recover a password by answering two personal questions like "What is your mother's maiden name?". It is unclear how to quantify the difficulty of such questions in terms of numbers. Nonetheless, it is simpler for an attacker to get hold of such secrets than guessing a randomly generated pin [17].

A symbolic quantification of the two paths leading to logging into the mailbox can then be modelled in the cost set ($\{\mathsf{cheap}, \mathsf{expensive}\}, \oplus$), where the cost of answering a question is cheap and the cost of guessing the password is $\mathsf{expensive}$. As for the monoid operator, a suggestion is to use $\max(\cdot, \cdot)$, since asking one, two, or three questions will annoy an attacker but does not really make their task much harder.

The SMT implementation of this example requires to encode the cost structure, that is, declaring its elements and defining the ordering relation as well as the monoid operator. Running the analysis in this cost set, we verified the existence of a cheap path leading to authenticating, namely the path that exploits the question-based recovery mechanism. The framework thus suggests that such option should not be allowed, otherwise we would not provide uniform security on all paths guarding the protected region.

6   Conclusion

In the design of software, physical, and cyber-physical systems, security is often perceived as a qualitative need, but can only be attained quantitatively. Especially when physical components are involved, it is simply impossible to predict and confront any possible attack. Even if it were possible, it would be unrealistic to have an unlimited budget to implement security mechanisms.

The protection analysis we presented has both the merit of automatically inferring the attacks to which a system is subject, among those accountable for in the framework, and to estimate the effort required by a lucky attacker for bypassing the protection mechanisms in place. Hence, the approach enables to identify potential weak paths and compare desired with actual protection. Moreover, the framework allows reasoning with symbolic and non-linearly ordered cost structures, as it is often more natural and informative to describe the relationships between different protection mechanisms instead of assigning them absolute numbers. We showed how the analysis applies to real scenarios giving meaningful insights on the problem of password recovery. Finally, the SMT-based optimisation technique proposed for computing the analysis is exploitable in all the contexts where propositional models have to be ranked.

Future developments include extending the approach beyond Boolean considerations about guessing capabilities, as they intuitively integrate with a probabilistic view of the world. On the practical side we aim at a stand-alone version of the SMT-based solution engine, so as to boost its applicability to other problems.

Acknowledgement. This work is supported by the IDEA4CPS project, granted by the Danish Research Foundations for Basic Research (DNRF86-10).

References

1. Amoroso, E.: Fundamentals of Computer Security Technology. Prentice-Hall (1994)
2. Nielson, H.R., Nielson, F., Vigo, R.: A Calculus for Quality. In: Păsăreanu, C.S., Salaün, G. (eds.) FACS 2012. LNCS, vol. 7684, pp. 188–204. Springer, Heidelberg (2013)
3. Mödersheim, S., Viganò, L.: Secure Pseudonymous Channels. In: Backes, M., Ning, P. (eds.) ESORICS 2009. LNCS, vol. 5789, pp. 337–354. Springer, Heidelberg (2009)
4. Paulson, L.C.: The inductive approach to verifying cryptographic protocols. Journal of Computer Security 6(1-2), 85–128 (1998)
5. Weidenbach, C.: Towards an automatic analysis of security protocols in first-order logic. In: Ganzinger, H. (ed.) CADE 1999. LNCS (LNAI), vol. 1632, pp. 314–328. Springer, Heidelberg (1999)
6. Riis Nielson, H., Nielson, F.: Flow Logic: A Multi-paradigmatic Approach to Static Analysis. In: Mogensen, T.Æ., Schmidt, D.A., Sudborough, I.H. (eds.) The Essence of Computation. LNCS, vol. 2566, pp. 223–244. Springer, Heidelberg (2002)
7. Blanchet, B.: Automatic verification of correspondences for security protocols. Journal of Computer Security 17(4), 363–434 (2009)
8. de Moura, L., Bjørner, N.: Satisfiability modulo theories: introduction and applications. Communications of the ACM 54(9), 69–77 (2011)
9. Nieuwenhuis, R., Oliveras, A.: On SAT Modulo Theories and Optimization Problems. In: Biere, A., Gomes, C.P. (eds.) SAT 2006. LNCS, vol. 4121, pp. 156–169. Springer, Heidelberg (2006)
10. Cimatti, A., Franzén, A., Griggio, A., Sebastiani, R., Stenico, C.: Satisfiability Modulo the Theory of Costs: Foundations and Applications. In: Esparza, J., Majumdar, R. (eds.) TACAS 2010. LNCS, vol. 6015, pp. 99–113. Springer, Heidelberg (2010)
11. Meadows, C.: A cost-based framework for analysis of denial of service in networks. Journal of Computer Security 9(1), 143–164 (2001)
12. Dillig, I., Dillig, T., McMillan, K., Aiken, A.: Minimum Satisfying Assignments for SMT. In: Madhusudan, P., Seshia, S.A. (eds.) CAV 2012. LNCS, vol. 7358, pp. 394–409. Springer, Heidelberg (2012)
13. The MITRE Corporation: Common Weakness Enumeration. Weak Password Recovery Mechanism for Forgotten Password (ID:640), http://cwe.mitre.org
14. Open Web Application Security Project: Choosing and Using Security Questions Cheat Sheet, http://www.owasp.org
15. Alvim, M.S., Chatzikokolakis, K., Palamidessi, C., Smith, G.: Measuring Information Leakage Using Generalized Gain Functions. In: 25th IEEE Computer Security Foundations Symposium (CSF 2012), pp. 265–279. IEEE (2012)
16. Vigo, R.: The Cyber-Physical Attacker. In: Ortmeier, F., Daniel, P. (eds.) SAFECOMP 2012 Workshops. LNCS, vol. 7613, pp. 347–356. Springer, Heidelberg (2012)
17. Griffith, V., Jakobsson, M.: Messin' with Texas Deriving Mother's Maiden Names Using Public Records. In: Ioannidis, J., Keromytis, A.D., Yung, M. (eds.) ACNS 2005. LNCS, vol. 3531, pp. 91–103. Springer, Heidelberg (2005)
18. Nielson, F., Nielson, H.R., Hansen, R.R.: Validating firewalls using flow logics. Theoretical Computer Science 283(2), 381–418 (2002)

A   Broadcast Semantics and Correctness Statements

The semantics of Table 4 is based on the transition relation $P \Longrightarrow P'$, which is enabled by combining a local transition $\xrightarrow{\lambda}$ with the structural congruence defined in Table 3.

The semantics models asynchronous broadcast communication, and makes use of a label $\lambda ::= \tau \mid c_1!c_2$ to record whether or not a broadcast is available in the system. Output is thus a non-blocking action, and when it is performed the broadcast is recorded on the arrow. When a process guarded by a binder receives an output, the broadcast remains available to other processes willing to input. This behaviour is encoded in rules (In-ff) and (In-tt), where we distinguish the case in which a binder has not received enough input, and thus keeps waiting, from the case in which a binder is satisfied and thus the computation may proceed. These rules rely on two auxiliary relations, one defining how an output affects a binder, and one describing when a binder is satisfied (enough inputs have been received), displayed in the third and fourth section of Table 4, respectively, and originally introduced in [2].

The semantics is instrumental to phrase the correctness of the analysis:

$$\text{if } \quad P|Q \Longrightarrow^* C[^l P'] \quad \text{then} \quad \exists C \in \delta(l) \text{ s.t. } C \subseteq \mathsf{fn}(Q)$$

i.e., for all the executions in which Q can drive P to l, the analysis provides a set of channels that under-approximates the knowledge required by Q.

Technically, it seems convenient to organise a formal proof in two steps. First, if $P|Q$ reaches l then $P|H[\mathsf{fn}(Q)]$ reaches l, where process H is the hardest attacker possible and is parametrised on the knowledge of Q. H can be thought as the (infinite) process executing all possible actions on $\mathsf{fn}(Q)$, and the proof simply argues that whatever Q can, H can (Lemma 1). A similar approach is explained in detail in [18].

Finally, the second step shows that if $P|H[C']$ reaches l, then there must be a set $C \in \delta(l)$ such that $C \subseteq C'$ (Theorem 1).

Definition 1 (Hardest attacker). *Let* $\mathcal{N} = \{c_1, \ldots, c_n\}$ *be a finite set of names.* $H[\mathcal{N}]$ *is the process that does all possible sequence of output actions on* $\mathcal{N}$: $H[\mathcal{N}] \triangleq (\nu d)\,(!(c_1!d)) \mid \ldots \mid (!(c_n!d))$.

Table 3. The structural congruence of the calculus

$P \equiv P$	$P_1 \equiv P_2 \Rightarrow P_2 \equiv P_1$	$P_1 \equiv P_2 \wedge P_2 \equiv P_3 \Rightarrow P_1 \equiv P_3$
$P \mid 0 \equiv P$	$P_1 \mid P_2 \equiv P_2 \mid P_1$	$P_1 \mid (P_2 \mid P_3) \equiv (P_1 \mid P_2) \mid P_3$
$(\nu c)\,P \equiv P$ if $c \notin \mathsf{fn}(P)$	$(\nu c_1)\,(\nu c_2)\,P \equiv (\nu c_2)\,(\nu c_1)\,P$	$(\nu c)\,(P_1 \mid P_2) \equiv ((\nu c)\,P_1) \mid P_2$ if $c \notin \mathsf{fn}(P_2)$
$!P \equiv P \mid !P$	$P_1 \equiv P_2 \Rightarrow C[P_1] \equiv C[P_2]$	

Table 4. The transition rules of the calculus

$$\frac{P_1 \equiv (\nu \vec{c})\, P_2 \quad P_2 \xrightarrow{\lambda} P_3}{P_1 \Longrightarrow P_3} \;\; \text{(Sys)}$$

$$^l c_1!c_2.P \xrightarrow{c_1!c_2} P \;\; \text{(Out)}$$

$$\frac{P_1 \xrightarrow{c_1!c_2} P_1' \quad c_1!c_2 \vdash b \to b' \quad b' ::_{\text{ff}} \theta}{P_1 \mid {}^l b.P_2 \xrightarrow{c_1!c_2} P_1' \mid {}^l b'.P_2} \;\; \text{(In-ff)} \qquad \frac{P_1 \xrightarrow{c_1!c_2} P_1' \quad c_1!c_2 \vdash b \to b' \quad b' ::_{\text{tt}} \theta}{P_1 \mid {}^l b.P_2 \xrightarrow{c_1!c_2} P_1' \mid P_2\theta} \;\; \text{(In-tt)}$$

$$^l \text{case some}(c) \text{ of some}(y) : P_1 \text{ else } P_2 \xrightarrow{\tau} P_1[c/y] \;\; \text{(Then)}$$

$$^l \text{case none of some}(y) : P_1 \text{ else } P_2 \xrightarrow{\tau} P_2 \;\; \text{(Else)}$$

$$\frac{P \xrightarrow{\tau} P'}{(\nu c)\, P \xrightarrow{\tau} (\nu c)\, P'} \;\; \text{(Res-tau)} \qquad \frac{P \xrightarrow{c_1!c_2} P'}{(\nu c)\, P \xrightarrow{c_1!c_2} (\nu c)\, P'} \;\; \text{if } c \neq c_1 \wedge c \neq c_2 \;\; \text{(Res-out)}$$

$$\frac{P_1 \xrightarrow{\tau} P_1'}{P_1 | P_2 \xrightarrow{\tau} P_1' | P_2} \;\; \text{(Par-tau)} \qquad \frac{P_1 \xrightarrow{c_1!c_2} P_1'}{P_1 | P_2 \xrightarrow{c_1!c_2} P_1' | P_2} \;\; \text{if } P_2 = !P_2' \vee P_2 = {}^l c_1'!c_2' P_2' \;\; \text{(Par-out)}$$

$$c_1!c_2 \vdash c_1?x \to [\text{some}(c_2)/x] \qquad c_1!c_2 \vdash c_3?x \to c_3?x \;\; \text{if } c_1 \neq c_3$$

$$\frac{c_1!c_2 \vdash b_1 \to b_1' \quad \cdots \quad c_1!c_2 \vdash b_n \to b_n'}{c_1!c_2 \vdash \&_q(b_1, \ldots, b_n) \to \&_q(b_1', \ldots, b_n')}$$

$$c?x ::_{\text{ff}} [\text{none}/x] \qquad [\text{some}(c)/x] ::_{\text{tt}} [\text{some}(c)/x]$$

$$\frac{b_1 ::_{v_1} \theta_1 \quad \cdots \quad b_n ::_{v_n} \theta_n}{\&_q(b_1, \ldots, b_n) ::_v \theta_n \cdots \theta_1} \qquad \{\!\{q\}\!\}(v_1, \ldots, v_n) = v$$

Lemma 1. *Let* P, Q *be processes. If* $P|Q \Longrightarrow^* C[{}^l P']$ *then* $P|H[\text{fn}(Q)] \Longrightarrow^* C[{}^l P']$.

Proof. By induction on the length of the derivation sequence.

Lemma 2. *Let* P *be a process and* $\mathcal{N}$ *a set of names. If* $P|H[\mathcal{N}] \Longrightarrow^* C[{}^l P']$, *then, for all processes* R *with* $R \equiv C[{}^l P']$ *and for all contexts* C', $P|H[\mathcal{N}] \Longrightarrow^* C'[R']$.

Proof. By induction on the shape of the inference tree for the step $R \equiv C[{}^l P']$.

Theorem 1 (Correctness of the protection analysis). *Let* P *be a process and* $\mathcal{N}$ *a set of names. If* $P|H[\mathcal{N}] \Longrightarrow^* C[{}^l P']$, *then there exists* $\mathcal{N}' \in \delta(l)$ *such that* $\mathcal{N}' \subseteq \mathcal{N}$.

Proof. By induction on the length of the derivation sequence, exploiting Lemma 2 in the inductive step.

Metrics for Differential Privacy in Concurrent Systems[*]

Lili Xu[1,3,4,5], Konstantinos Chatzikokolakis[2,3], and Huimin Lin[4]

[1] INRIA, Paris, France
[2] CNRS, Paris, France
[3] Ecole Polytechnique, Paris, France
[4] Institute of Software, Chinese Academy of Sciences, Beijing, China
[5] Graduate University, Chinese Academy of Sciences, Beijing, China

Abstract. Originally proposed for privacy protection in the context of statistical databases, differential privacy is now widely adopted in various models of computation. In this paper we investigate techniques for proving differential privacy in the context of concurrent systems. Our motivation stems from the work of Tschantz et al., who proposed a verification method based on proving the existence of a stratified family between states, that can track the privacy leakage, ensuring that it does not exceed a given leakage budget. We improve this technique by investigating a state property which is more permissive and still implies differential privacy. We consider two pseudometrics on probabilistic automata: The first one is essentially a reformulation of the notion proposed by Tschantz et al. The second one is a more liberal variant, relaxing the relation between them by integrating the notion of amortisation, which results into a more parsimonious use of the privacy budget. We show that the metrical closeness of automata guarantees the preservation of differential privacy, which makes the two metrics suitable for verification. Moreover we show that process combinators are non-expansive in this pseudometric framework. We apply the pseudometric framework to reason about the degree of differential privacy of protocols by the example of the Dining Cryptographers Protocol with biased coins.

1 Introduction

Differential privacy [14] was originally proposed for privacy protection in the context of statistical databases, but nowadays it is becoming increasingly popular in many other fields, ranging from programming languages [24] to social networks [23] and geolocation [20]. One of the reasons of its success is its independence from side knowledge, which makes it robust to attacks based on combining various sources of information.

In the original definition, a query mechanism $\mathcal{A}$ is ϵ-differentially private if for any two databases u_1 and u_2 which differ only for one individual (one row), and any property Z, the probability distributions of $\mathcal{A}(u_1), \mathcal{A}(u_2)$ differ on Z at most by e^ϵ, namely, $\Pr[\mathcal{A}(u_1) \in Z] \leq e^\epsilon \cdot \Pr[\mathcal{A}(u_2) \in Z]$. This means that the presence (or the data) of an individual cannot be revealed by querying the database. In [7], the principle of

[*] This work has been partially supported by the project ANR-12-IS02-001 PACE, by the project ANR-11-IS02-0002 LOCALI, by the INRIA Large Scale Initiative CAPPRIS and by the National Natural Science Foundation of China (Grant No.60833001).

E. Ábrahám and C. Palamidessi (Eds.), FORTE 2014, LNCS 8461, pp. 199–215, 2014.
© IFIP International Federation for Information Processing 2014

differential privacy has been formally extended to measure the degree of protection of secrets in more general settings.

In this paper we deal with the problem of verifying differential privacy properties for concurrent systems, modeled as probabilistic automata admitting both nondeterministic and probabilistic behavior. In such systems, reasoning about the probabilities requires *solving* the nondeterminism first, and to such purpose the usual technique is to consider functions, called *schedulers*, which select the next step based on the history of the computation. However, in our context, as well as in security in general, we need to restrict the power of the schedulers and make them unable to distinguish between secrets in the histories, or otherwise they would plainly reveal them by their choice of the step. See for instance [6,8,2] for a discussion on this issue. Thus we consider a restricted class of schedulers, called *admissible schedulers*, following the definition of [2]. Admissibility is introduced to deal with bisimulation-like notions in security contexts: Two bisimilar processes are typically considered to be indistinguishable, yet an unrestricted scheduler could trivially separate them.

The property of differential privacy requires that the observations generated by two different secret values be probabilistically similar. In standard concurrent systems the notion of similarity is usually formalized as an equivalence, preferably preserved under composition, i.e., a congruence. We mention in particular trace equivalence and bisimulation. The first is often used for its simplicity, but in general is not compositional [17]. The second one is a congruence and it is appealing for its proof technique. Process equivalences have been extensively used to formalize security properties like secrecy [1] and noninterference [15,25,26].

In this paper we focus on metrics suitable for verifying differential privacy. Namely, metrics for which the distance between two processes determines an upper bound on the ratio of the probabilities of the respective observables. We start by considering the framework proposed by Tschantz et al. [27], which was explicitly designed for the purpose of verifying differential privacy. Their verification technique is based on proving the existence of an indexed family of bijections between states. The parameter of the starting states, representing the privacy budget, determines the level of differential privacy of the system, which decreases over time by subtracting the absolute difference of probabilities in each step during mutual simulation. Once the balance reaches zero, processes must behave exactly the same. We reformulate this notion in the form of a pseudometric, showing some novel properties as a distance relation.

The above technique is sound, but has a rather rigid budget management. The main goal of this paper is to make the technique more permissive by identifying a pseudometric that is more relaxed and still implies an upper bound on the privacy leakage.

In particular, the pseudometric we propose is based on a thriftier use of the privacy budget, which is inspired by the notion of *amortisation* used in some quantitative bisimulations [18,10]. The idea is that, when constructing the bijections between states, the differences among the probabilities of related states are kept with their sign, and added with their sign through each step. In this way, successive differences can compensate (amortise) each other, and rather than always being consumed, the privacy budget may also be refurbished. In [18] the idea of amortisation is applied on a set of cost-based actions. The quantitative feature considered here is discrete probability distributions over states, which is shown to benefit from the theory of amortisation as well.

Furthermore, there is a soundness criterion on the distance notion for probabilistic concurrent systems defined in [13]. It says that 0-distance in a pseudometric is expected to fully characterise bisimilarity. We show that 0-distance in the two pseudometrics implies bisimilarity while the converse does not hold. Although the pseudometrics do not thoroughly satisfy the criterion, we prove that several process combinators including parallel composition are non-expansive in the pseudometrics. Non-expansiveness gives a desirable property that when close processes are placed in the same context, the resulting processes are still close in the distance. This can be viewed as an analogue of the congruence properties of bisimulation. Finally, we illustrate the verification technique of differential privacy using the example of the Dining Cryptographers Problem(DCP) with biased coins.

More related Work. Verification of differential privacy has become an active area of research. Among the approaches based on formal methods, we mention those based on type-systems [24,16] and logical formulations [3].

In a previous paper [28], one of the authors has developed a compositional method for proving differential privacy in a probabilistic process calculus. The technique there is rather different from the ones presented in paper: the idea is based on decomposing a process in simpler processes, computing the level of privacy of these, and combining them to obtain the level of privacy of the original program.

A line of one very interesting approach related to ours in spirit - considering pseudometrics on probabilistic automata - includes the work by Desharnais et al. [13] and Deng et al. [11]. They both use the metric à la Kantorovich proposed in [13], which represents a cornerstone in the area of bisimulation metrics. It would be attractive to see how the Kantorovich metric can be adapted to reason about differential privacy.

Finally, among several formalizations of the notion of information protection based on probability theory, we mention some rather popular approaches, mainly based on information theory, in particular, to consider different notions of entropy depending on the kind of adversary, and to express the leakage of information in terms of the notion of mutual information. We name a few works also discussed in the models of probabilistic automata and process algebra: Boreale [4] establishs a framework for quantifying information leakage using absolute leakage, and introduces a notion of rate of leakage. Deng et al. [12] use the notion of relative entropy to measure the degree of anonymity. Compositional methods based on Bayes risk method are discussed by Braun et al. [5]. A metric for probabilistic processes based on the Jensen-Shannon divergence is proposed in [22] for measuring information flow in reactive processes. Unlike the information-theoretical approach, differential privacy provides strong privacy guarantees independently from side knowledge. However, progress for differential privacy has been relatively new and going slowly. It would be interesting to see how the issues stressed and the reasoning techniques developed there can be adapted for differential privacy.

Contribution. The main contributions of this paper can be summarized as follows:

- We reformulate the notion of approximate similarity proposed in [27] in terms of a pseudometric and we study the properties of the distance relation (in Section 3).

- We propose the second pseudometric which is more liberal than the former one, in the sense that the total differences of probabilities get amortised during the mutual simulation. We show that the level of differential privacy is continuous with respect to the metric, which says that if every two processes running on two adjacent secrets of a system are close in the metric then the system is differentially private, making the metric suitable for verification (in Section 4).
- We show that 0-distance in the pseudometrics implies bisimilarity (in Section 5).
- We present the non-expansiveness property in the pseudometrics for CCS_p operators in a probabilistic variant of Milner's CCS [21] (in Section 6).
- We use the pseudometric framework to show that the Dining Cryptographers protocol with probability-p biased coins is $|\ln \frac{p}{1-p}|$-differentially private. (in Section 7).

The rest of the Paper. In the next section we recall some preliminary notions about probabilistic automata, differential privacy and pseudometrics. Section 8 concludes. Long proofs can be found in the appendix.

2   Preliminaries

2.1   Probabilistic Automata

Given a set X, we denote by $Disc(X)$ the set of discrete sub-probability measures over X; the support of a measure μ is defined as $supp(\mu) = \{x \in X | \mu(x) > 0\}$. A *probabilistic automaton* (henceforth PA) $\mathcal{A}$ is a tuple $(S, \overline{s}, A, D)$ where S is a finite set of *states*, $\overline{s} \in S$ is the *start state*, A is a finite set of action *labels*, and $D \subseteq S \times A \times Disc(S)$ is a *transition relation*. We write $s \xrightarrow{a} \mu$ for $(s, a, \mu) \in D$, and we denote by $act(d)$ the action of the transition $d \in D$. A PA $\mathcal{A}$ is *fully probabilistic* if from each state of $\mathcal{A}$ there is at most one transition available.

An *execution* α of a PA is a (possibly infinite) sequence $s_0 a_1 s_1 a_2 s_2 \ldots$ of alternating states and labels, such that for each $i : s_i \xrightarrow{a_{i+1}} \mu_{i+1}$ and $\mu_{i+1}(s_{i+1}) > 0$. We use $lstate(\alpha)$ to denote the last state of a finite execution α. We use $Exec^*(\mathcal{A})$ and $Exec(\mathcal{A})$ to represent the set of finite and all executions of $\mathcal{A}$, respectively. A *scheduler* of a PA $\mathcal{A} = (S, \overline{s}, A, D)$ is a function $\zeta : Exec^*(\mathcal{A}) \mapsto D$ such that $\zeta(\alpha) = s \xrightarrow{a} \mu \in D$ implies that $s = lstate(\alpha)$. The idea is that a scheduler selects a transition among the ones available in D, basing its decision on the history of the execution. The *execution tree* of $\mathcal{A}$ with respect to the scheduler ζ, denoted by $\mathcal{A}_\zeta$, is a fully probabilistic automaton $(S', \overline{s}', A', D')$ such that $S' \subseteq Exec^*(\mathcal{A})$, $\overline{s}' = \overline{s}$, $A' = A$, and $\alpha \xrightarrow{a} \nu \in D'$ if and only if $\zeta(\alpha) = lstate(\alpha) \xrightarrow{a} \mu$ for some μ and $\nu(\alpha a s) = \mu(s)$. Intuitively, $\mathcal{A}_\zeta$ is produced by unfolding the executions of $\mathcal{A}$ and resolving all non-deterministic choices using ζ. Note that $\mathcal{A}_\zeta$ is a simple and fully probabilistic automaton. We use α with primes and indices to range over states in an execution tree.

A *trace* is a sequence of labels in $A^* \cup A^\omega$ obtained from executions by removing states. We use $[]$ to represent the empty trace, and $\frown$ to concatenate two traces. A state α of $\mathcal{A}_\zeta$ induces a probability measure over traces as follows. The basic measurable events are the cones of finite traces, where the cone of a finite trace t, denoted by C_t, is the set $\{t' \in A^* \cup A^\omega | t \leq t'\}$, where $\leq$ is the standard prefix preorder on sequences.

The probability of a cone C_t induced by state α, denoted by $\Pr_\zeta[\alpha \rhd t]$, is defined recursively as follows.

$$\Pr_\zeta[\alpha \rhd t] = \begin{cases} 1 & \text{if } t = [\,], \\ 0 & \text{if } t = a^\frown t' \text{ and } act(\zeta(\alpha)) \neq a, \\ \sum_{s_i \in supp(\mu)} \mu(s_i)\Pr_\zeta[\alpha as_i \rhd t'] \\ & \text{if } t = a^\frown t' \text{ and } \zeta(\alpha) = s \xrightarrow{a} \mu. \end{cases} \tag{1}$$

Admissible schedulers. We consider a restricted class of schedulers, called *admissible schedulers*, following the definition of [2]. Essentially this definition requires that whenever given two *adjacent* states s, s', namely, differing only for the choice for some secret value, then the choice made by the scheduler on s and s' should be consistent, i.e. the scheduler should not be able to make a different choice on the basis of the secret. Note that in [27] scheduling is not an issue since non-determinism is not allowed.

More precisely, in [2] admissibility is achieved by introducing tags for transitions. Admissible schedulers are viewed as entities that have access to a system through a screen with buttons, where each button represents one (current) available option, i.e. an enabled tag. A scheduler ζ is admissible if for all finite executions having the same sequence of screens, ζ decides the same tagged transition for them.

Pseudometrics on states. A pseudometric[1] on S is a function $m : S^2 \to \mathbb{R}$ satisfying the following properties: $m(s, s) = 0$ (reflexivity), $m(s, t) = m(t, s)$ (symmetry) and $m(s, t) \leq m(s, u) + m(u, t)$ (triangle inequality). We define $m_1 \preceq m_2$ iff $\forall s, t :$ $m_1(s, t) \geq m_2(s, t)$ (note that the order is reversed).

2.2 Differential Privacy

Differential privacy [14] was originally defined in the context of statistical databases, by requiring that a mechanism (i.e. a probabilistic query) gives similar answers on *adjacent* databases, that is those differing on a single row. More precisely, a mechanism $\mathcal{K}$ satisfies ϵ-*differential privacy* iff for all adjacent databases x, x': $\Pr[\mathcal{K}(x) \in Z] \leq e^\epsilon \cdot \Pr[\mathcal{K}(x') \in Z]$ for all $Z \subseteq range(\mathcal{K})$. Differential privacy imposes looser restrictions on non-adjacent secrets, which is considered as another merit of it.

In this paper, we study concurrent systems taking a secret as input and producing an observable trace as output. Let U be a set of secrets and $\sim$ an adjacency relation on U, where $u \sim u'$ denotes the fact that two close secrets u, u' should not be easily distinguished by the adversary after seeing observable traces. A *concurrent system* $\mathcal{A}$ is a mapping of secrets to probabilistic automata, where $\mathcal{A}(u), u \in U$ is the automaton modelling the behaviour of the system when running on u. Differential privacy can be directly adapted to this context:

Definition 1 (Differential Privacy). *A concurrent system* $\mathcal{A}$ *satisfies* ϵ-differential privacy *(DP) iff for any* $u \sim u'$, *any finite trace* t *and any admissible scheduler* ζ:

$$\Pr_\zeta[\mathcal{A}(u) \rhd t] \leq e^\epsilon \cdot \Pr_\zeta[\mathcal{A}(u') \rhd t]$$

---

[1] Unlike a metric, points in a pseudometric need not be distinguishable; that is, one may have $m(s, t) = 0$ for distinct values $s \neq t$.

3 The Accumulative Pseudometric

In this section, we present the first pseudometric based on a reformulation of the relation family proposed in [27]. We reformulate their notion in the form of an approximate bisimulation relation, named *accumulative bisimulation*, and then use it to construct a pseudometric on the state space.

We start by defining an approximate lifting operation that lifts a relation over states to a relation over distributions. Intuitively, we use a parameter ϵ to represent the total privacy leakage budget. A parameter c ranging over $[0, \epsilon]$, starting from 0, records the current amount of leakage and increasing over time by adding the maximum absolute difference of probabilities, denoted by σ, in each step during mutual simulation. Once c reaches the budget bound ϵ, processes must behave exactly the same. Since the total bound is ϵ, only a total of ϵ privacy can be leaked, a fact that will be used later to verify differential privacy. We use D to simply differentiate notions of this section from the following sections.

Definition 2. *Let $\epsilon \geqslant 0$, $c \in [0, \epsilon]$, $\mathcal{R} \subseteq S \times S \times [0, \epsilon]$. The D-approximate lifting of $\mathcal{R}$ up to c, denoted by $\mathcal{L}^D(\mathcal{R}, c)$, is the relation on $Disc(S)$ defined as:*

$$\mu \mathcal{L}^D(\mathcal{R}, c) \mu' \quad \textit{iff} \quad \exists \ \textit{bijection} \ \beta : supp(\mu) \to supp(\mu') \ \textit{such that}$$

$$\forall s \in supp(\mu) : (s, \beta(s), c + \sigma) \in \mathcal{R} \quad \textit{where} \quad \sigma = \max_{s \in supp(\mu)} \left| \ln \frac{\mu(s)}{\mu'(\beta(s))} \right|$$

This lifting allows us to define an approximate bisimulation relation:

Definition 3 (Accumulative bisimulation). *A relation $\mathcal{R} \subseteq S \times S \times [0, \epsilon]$ is a ϵ-accumulative bisimulation iff for all $(s, t, c) \in \mathcal{R}$:*

1. $s \xrightarrow{a} \mu$ *implies* $t \xrightarrow{a} \mu'$ *with* $\mu \mathcal{L}^D(\mathcal{R}, c) \mu'$
2. $t \xrightarrow{a} \mu'$ *implies* $s \xrightarrow{a} \mu$ *with* $\mu \mathcal{L}^D(\mathcal{R}, c) \mu'$

We can now define a pseudometric based on accumulative bisimulation as:

$$m^D(s, t) = \min\{\epsilon \mid (s, t, 0) \in \mathcal{R} \ \text{for some} \ \epsilon\text{-accumulative bisimulation} \ \mathcal{R}\}$$

Proposition 1. m^D *is a pseudometric, that is:*

1. *(reflexivity)* $m^D(s, s) = 0$
2. *(symmetry)* $m^D(s_1, s_2) = m^D(s_2, s_1)$
3. *(triangle inequality)* $m^D(s_1, s_3) \leq m^D(s_1, s_2) + m^D(s_2, s_3)$

Proof Sketch. The proof proceeds by showing for each clause respectively that: 1. $Id_S = \{(s, s, 0) \mid s \in S\}$ is a 0-accumulative bisimulation; 2. Assume that $(s_1, s_2, 0)$ is in a ϵ-accumulative bisimulation $\mathcal{R}$, then $\mathcal{R}' = \{(s'_2, s'_1, c) \mid (s'_1, s'_2, c) \in \mathcal{R}\}$ is a ϵ-accumulative bisimulation; 3. Assume that $(s_1, s_2, 0)$ is in the ϵ_1-accumulative bisimulation $\mathcal{R}_1 \subseteq S \times S \times [0, \epsilon_1]$, $(s_2, s_3, 0)$ is in the ϵ_2-accumulative bisimulation $\mathcal{R}_2 \subseteq S \times S \times [0, \epsilon_2]$. Their relational composition $\mathcal{R}_1 \mathcal{R}_2 \subseteq S \times S \times [0, \epsilon_1 + \epsilon_2]$:

$$\{(s'_1, s'_3, c) \mid \exists s'_2, c_1, c_2.(s'_1, s'_2, c_1) \in \mathcal{R}_1 \wedge (s'_2, s'_3, c_2) \in \mathcal{R}_2 \wedge c \leq c_1 + c_2\}$$

is a $\epsilon_1 + \epsilon_2$-accumulative bisimulation. □

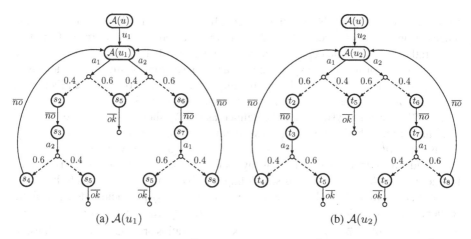

(a) $\mathcal{A}(u_1)$ (b) $\mathcal{A}(u_2)$

Fig. 1. A PIN-checking system: $m^D(\mathcal{A}(u_1), \mathcal{A}(u_2)) = \infty$, $m^A(\mathcal{A}(u_1), \mathcal{A}(u_2)) = \ln \frac{9}{4}$

Verification of differential privacy using m^D. As already shown in [27], the closeness of processes in the relation family implies a level of differential privacy. We here restate this result in terms of the metric m^D.

Lemma 1. *Given a PA $\mathcal{A}$, let $\mathcal{R}$ be a ϵ-accumulative bisimulation, $c \in [0, \epsilon]$, let ζ be an admissible scheduler, t be a finite trace, α_1, α_2 two finite executions of $\mathcal{A}$. If $(lstate(\alpha_1), lstate(\alpha_2), c) \in \mathcal{R}$, then*

$$\frac{1}{e^{\epsilon-c}} \le \frac{\Pr_\zeta[\alpha_1 \rhd t]}{\Pr_\zeta[\alpha_2 \rhd t]} \le e^{\epsilon-c}$$

The above lemma shows that in a ϵ-accumulative bisimulation, two states related by a current leakage amount c, produce distributions over the same trace that only deviate by a factor $(\epsilon - c)$ representing the remaining amount of leakage. Then it is easy to get that the level of differential privacy is continuous with respect to m^D.

Theorem 1. *A concurrent system $\mathcal{A}$ is ϵ-differentially private if $m^D(\mathcal{A}(u), \mathcal{A}(u')) \le \epsilon$ for all $u \sim u'$.*

4   The Amortised Pseudometric

As shown in the previous section, m^D is useful for verifying differential privacy. However, a drawback of this metric is that the definition of accumulative bisimulation is too restrictive: first, the amount of leakage is only accumulated, independently from whether the difference in probabilities is negative or positive. Moreover, the accumulation is the same for all branches, and equal to the worst branch, although the actual difference on some branch might be small. As a consequence, m^D is inapplicable in several systems, as shown by the following toy example.

Example 1. Consider a PIN-checking system $\mathcal{A}(u)$ in which the PIN variable u is designated from two secret codes u_1 and u_2. In order to protect the secrecy of the two PINs, rather than announcing to a user deterministically that whether the password he enters is correct or wrong, the system makes a response probabilistically. The idea is to give a positive answer with a higher probability when the password and the PIN match, and to give a negative answer with a higher probability otherwise.

The PIN-checking system could be defined as the PA shown in Fig. 1. We use label a_i to model the behavior that the password entered by a user is u_i, where $i \in \{1, 2\}$. We use label $\overline{ok}$ and $\overline{no}$ to represent a positive and a negative answer, respectively.

Consider an admissible scheduler always choosing for $\mathcal{A}(u_1)$ the a_1-branch (the case for the a_2-branch is similar), thus scheduling for $\mathcal{A}(u_2)$ also the a_1-branch. It is easy to see that the ratio of probabilities for $\mathcal{A}(u_1)$ and $\mathcal{A}(u_2)$ producing the same finite sequences $(a_1\overline{no}\,a_2\,\overline{no})^*$ is $(\frac{0.4 \times 0.6}{0.6 \times 0.4})^* = 1$. For the rest sequences $(a_1\overline{no}\,a_2\,\overline{no})^* a_1\overline{ok}$ and $(a_1\overline{no}\,a_2\,\overline{no})^* a_1\overline{no}\,a_2\,\overline{ok}$, we can check that the ratios are bounded by $\frac{9}{4}$. Thus, $\mathcal{A}$ satisfies $\ln\frac{9}{4}$-differential privacy. However, we can not find an accumulative bisimulation with a bounded ϵ between $\mathcal{A}(u_1)$ and $\mathcal{A}(u_2)$. The problem lies in that the leakage amount is always accumulated by adding the absolute differences during cyclic simulations, resulting in a convergence to ∞.

In order to obtain a more relaxed metric, we employ the *amortised bisimulation* relation of [18,10]. The main intuition behind this notion is that the privacy leakage amount in each simulation step may be either reduced due to a negative difference of probabilities, or increased due to a positive difference. Hence, the long-term budget gets amortised, in contrast to the accumulative bisimulation in which the budget is always consumed. We start by defining the corresponding lifting, using A to represent amortised bisimulation-based notions. Note that the current leakage c ranges over $[-\epsilon, \epsilon]$.

Definition 4. *Let* $\epsilon \geqslant 0$, $c \in [-\epsilon, \epsilon]$, $\mathcal{R} \subseteq S \times S \times [-\epsilon, \epsilon]$. *The A-approximate lifting of* $\mathcal{R}$ *up to* c, *denoted by* $\mathcal{L}^A(\mathcal{R}, c)$, *is a relation on* $Disc(S)$ *defined as:*

$$\mu \mathcal{L}^A(\mathcal{R}, c)\mu' \quad iff \quad \exists\, bijection\ \beta : supp(\mu) \to supp(\mu')\ such\ that$$

$$\forall s \in supp(\mu) : (s, \beta(s), c + \ln\frac{\mu(s)}{\mu'(\beta(s))}) \in \mathcal{R}$$

Note that if $\ln\frac{\mu(s)}{\mu'(\beta(s))}$ is positive, then after this mutual step, the current leakage for s and $\beta(s)$ gets increased, otherwise decreased. We are now ready to define amortised bisimulation.

Definition 5 (Amortised bisimulation). *A relation* $\mathcal{R} \subseteq S \times S \times [-\epsilon, \epsilon]$ *is a* ϵ-*amortised bisimulation iff for all* $(s, t, c) \in \mathcal{R}$:

1. $s \xrightarrow{a} \mu$ *implies* $t \xrightarrow{a} \mu'$ *with* $\mu\mathcal{L}^A(\mathcal{R}, c)\mu'$
2. $t \xrightarrow{a} \mu'$ *implies* $s \xrightarrow{a} \mu$ *with* $\mu\mathcal{L}^A(\mathcal{R}, c)\mu'$

Similarly to the previous section, we can finally define a pseudometric on states as:

$$m^A(s, t) = \min\{\epsilon \mid (s, t, 0) \in \mathcal{R} \text{ for some } \epsilon\text{-amortised bisimulation } \mathcal{R}\}$$

Proposition 2. m^A *is a pseudometric.*

Proof Sketch. The proof proceeds by showing that: 1. $Id_S = \{(s, s, 0) | s \in S\}$ is a 0-amortised bisimulation; 2. Assume that $(s_1, s_2, 0)$ is in a ϵ-amortised bisimulation $\mathcal{R}$, then $\mathcal{R}' = \{(s'_2, s'_1, c) \,|\, (s'_1, s'_2, -c) \in \mathcal{R}\}$ is a ϵ-amortised bisimulation; 3. Let $(s_1, s_2, 0)$ be in the ϵ_1-amortised bisimulation $\mathcal{R}_1 \subseteq S \times S \times [-\epsilon_1, \epsilon_1]$, $(s_2, s_3, 0)$ be in the ϵ_2-amortised bisimulation $\mathcal{R}_2 \subseteq S \times S \times [-\epsilon_2, \epsilon_2]$. Their relational composition $\mathcal{R}_1 \mathcal{R}_2 \subseteq S \times S \times [-\epsilon_1 - \epsilon_2, \epsilon_1 + \epsilon_2]$:

$$\{(s'_1, s'_3, c) | \exists s'_2, c_1, c_2.(s'_1, s'_2, c_1) \in \mathcal{R}_1 \wedge (s'_2, s'_3, c_2) \in \mathcal{R}_2 \wedge c_1 + c_2 = c\}$$

is a $\epsilon_1 + \epsilon_2$-amortised bisimulation.   □

Verification of differential privacy using m^A. We now show that m^A can be used to verify differential privacy.

Lemma 2. *Given a PA $\mathcal{A}$, let $\mathcal{R}$ be a ϵ-amortised bisimulation, $c \in [-\epsilon, \epsilon]$, let ζ be an admissible scheduler, t be a finite trace, α_1, α_2 two finite executions of $\mathcal{A}$. If $(lstate(\alpha_1), lstate(\alpha_2), c) \in \mathcal{R}$, then*

$$\frac{1}{e^{\epsilon+c}} \le \frac{\Pr_\zeta[\alpha_1 \rhd t]}{\Pr_\zeta[\alpha_2 \rhd t]} \le e^{\epsilon-c}$$

Note that there is a subtle difference between Lemmas 1 and 2, in that the denominator in the left-hand bound is $e^{\epsilon+c}$ instead of $e^{\epsilon-c}$. This comes from the amortised nature of $\mathcal{R}$. We can now show that differential privacy is continuous with respect to m^A as well.

Theorem 2. *A concurrent system $\mathcal{A}$ is ϵ-differentially private if $m^A(\mathcal{A}(u), \mathcal{A}(u')) \le \epsilon$ for all $u \sim u'$.*

Proof Sketch. Since $m^A(\mathcal{A}(u), \mathcal{A}(u')) \le \epsilon$ for all $u \sim u'$, by the definition of m^A, there exists a ϵ-amortised bisimulation $\mathcal{R}$ such that $(\mathcal{A}(u), \mathcal{A}(u'), 0) \in \mathcal{R}$. By Lemma 2, for any admissible scheduler ζ, any finite trace t:

$$\frac{1}{e^{\epsilon}} \le \frac{\Pr_\zeta[\mathcal{A}(u) \rhd t]}{\Pr_\zeta[\mathcal{A}(u') \rhd t]} \le e^{\epsilon}$$

Thus, we obtain that $\mathcal{A}$ is ϵ-differentially private.   □

Example 2 (Example 1 revisited). Consider again the concurrent system shown in Fig. 1. Let S and T denote the state space of $\mathcal{A}(u_1)$ and $\mathcal{A}(u_2)$, respectively. Let $\mathcal{R} \subseteq S \times T \times [\ln \frac{4}{9}, \ln \frac{9}{4}]$. It is straightforward to check according to Def. 5 that the following relation is an amortised bisimulation between $\mathcal{A}(u_1)$ and $\mathcal{A}(u_2)$.

$$\mathcal{R} = \{ \ (\mathcal{A}(u_1), \mathcal{A}(u_2), 0),$$
$$(s_2, t_2, \ln \tfrac{2}{3}), (s_5, t_5, \ln \tfrac{3}{2}), (s_3, t_3, \ln \tfrac{2}{3}), (s_4, t_4, 0), (s_5, t_5, \ln \tfrac{4}{9}),$$
$$(s_6, t_6, \ln \tfrac{3}{2}), (s_5, t_5, \ln \tfrac{2}{3}), (s_7, t_7, \ln \tfrac{3}{2}), (s_8, t_8, 0), (s_5, t_5, \ln \tfrac{9}{4}) \ \}$$

Thus $m^A(\mathcal{A}(u_1), \mathcal{A}(u_2)) \le \ln \frac{9}{4}$. By Theorem 2, $\mathcal{A}$ is $\ln \frac{9}{4}$-differentially private.

5 Comparing the Two Pseudometrics

In this section, we formally compare the two metrics, showing that our pseudometric is indeed more liberal than the first one. Moreover,we investigate whether they can fully characterise bisimilarity. We show that m^D and m^A only imply bisimilarity, while the converse direction does not hold because of the strong requirement of the bijections in their definitions.

We show that m^A is bounded by m^D. Note the converse does not hold, since Examples 1 and 2 already show the cases in which m^D is infinite while m^A is finite.

Lemma 3. $m^D \preceq m^A$.

Proof Sketch. Let $\mathcal{R}^D \subseteq S \times S \times [0, \epsilon]$ be the ϵ-accumulative bisimulation such that $(s, t, 0) \in \mathcal{R}^D$. It is sufficient to show that the relation $\mathcal{R}^A \subseteq S \times S \times [-\epsilon, \epsilon]$ defined on the basis of $\mathcal{R}^D$ as follows is a ϵ-amortised bisimulation.

$$(s', t', c^A) \in \mathcal{R}^A \text{ iff } \exists c^D.(s', t', c^D) \in \mathcal{R}^D \wedge |c^A| \leq c^D$$

Relations with probabilistic bisimilarity. We adopt the notion of probabilistic bisimilarity which was first defined in [19]. An equivalence relation over S can be lifted to a relation over distributions over S by stating that two distributions are equivalent if they assign the same probability to the same equivalence class.

Formally, let $\mathcal{R} \subseteq S \times S$ be an equivalence relation. Two probability distributions μ_1 and μ_2 are $\mathcal{R}$-equivalent, written $\mu_1 \mathcal{L}(\mathcal{R}) \mu_2$, iff for every equivalence class $E \in S/\mathcal{R}$ we have $\mu_1(E) = \mu_2(E)$, in which $\mu_i(E) = \sum_{s \in E} \mu_i(s)$, $i = 1, 2$.

Definition 6. *An equivalence relation $\mathcal{R} \subseteq S \times S$ is a* strong bisimulation *iff for all* $(s, t) \in \mathcal{R}$, $s \xrightarrow{a} \mu$ *implies* $t \xrightarrow{a} \mu'$ *with* $\mu \mathcal{L}(\mathcal{R}) \mu'$[2]. *We write* $s \sim t$ *whenever there is a strong bisimulation that relates them.* $\sim$ *is the maximum strong bisimulation, namely* strong bisimilarity.

Proposition 3. *The following hold:*

- $m^D(s, t) = 0 \Rightarrow s \sim t$
- $m^A(s, t) = 0 \Rightarrow s \sim t$

The proofs are achieved by showing that the relation $\mathcal{R}$ induced by 0 distance in m^A (or m^D), namely, $(s, t) \in \mathcal{R}$ iff $m^A(s, t) = 0$, is a strong bisimulation.

6 Process Algebra

Process algebras provide the link to the desired compositional reasoning about approximate equality in such a pseudometric framework. We would like process operators to be *non-expansive* in the pseudometrics, which allows us to estimate the degree of differential privacy of a complex system from its components. In this section we consider a simple process calculus whose semantics is given by probabilistic automata. We define

---

[2] The converse is implied by the symmetry of the equivalence relation $\mathcal{R}$.

$$\text{ACT} \quad \frac{}{\alpha.P \xrightarrow{\alpha} \delta(P)} \qquad\qquad \text{PROB} \quad \frac{}{\bigoplus_{i \in I} p_i \, P_i \xrightarrow{\tau} \sum_i p_i \, P_i}$$

$$\text{SUM1} \quad \frac{P \xrightarrow{\alpha} \mu}{P + Q \xrightarrow{\alpha} \mu} \qquad\qquad \text{PAR1} \quad \frac{P \xrightarrow{\alpha} \mu}{P \,|\, Q \xrightarrow{\alpha} \mu \,|\, Q}$$

$$\text{COM} \quad \frac{P \xrightarrow{a} \delta(P') \quad Q \xrightarrow{\bar{a}} \delta(Q')}{P \,|\, Q \xrightarrow{\tau} \delta(P' \,|\, Q')} \qquad \text{RES} \quad \frac{P \xrightarrow{\alpha} \mu \quad \alpha \neq a, \bar{a}}{(\nu a)P \xrightarrow{\alpha} (\nu a)\mu}$$

Fig. 2. The semantics of CCS_p. SUM1 and PAR1 have corresponding right rules SUM2 and PAR2, omitted for simplicity.

prefixing, non-deterministic choice, probabilistic choice, restriction and parallel composition constructors for the process calculus, and show that they are non-expansive in the sense that when neighboring processes are placed in the same context, the resulting processes are still neighboring.

The syntax of CCS_p is:

$$\begin{aligned} \alpha \quad &::= \quad a \mid \bar{a} \mid \tau & \text{prefixes} \\ P, Q \quad &::= \quad \alpha.P \mid P \,|\, Q \mid P + Q \mid \bigoplus_{i \in 1..n} p_i P_i \mid (\nu a)P \mid \mathbf{0} & \text{processes} \end{aligned}$$

Here $\bigoplus_{i \in 1..n} p_i P_i$ stands for a probabilistic choice constructor, where the p_i's represent positive probabilities, i.e., they satisfy $p_i \in (0, 1]$ and $\sum_{i \in 1..n} p_i = 1$. It may be occasionally written as $p_1 P_1 \oplus \cdots \oplus p_n P_n$. The rest constructors are the standard ones in Milner's CCS [21].

The semantics of a CCS_p term is a probabilistic automaton defined according to the rules in Fig. 2. We write $s \xrightarrow{a} \mu$ when (s, a, μ) is a transition of the probabilistic automaton. We also denote by $\mu | Q$ the measure μ' such that $\mu'(P|Q) = \mu(P)$ for all processes P and $\mu'(R) = 0$ if R is not of the form $P|Q$. Similarly $(\nu a)\mu = \mu'$ such that $\mu'((\nu a)P) = \mu(P)$. A transition of the form $P \xrightarrow{a} \delta(P')$, i.e. a transition having for target a Dirac measure, corresponds to a transition of a non-probabilistic automaton.

Proposition 4. *If* $m(P, Q) \leq \epsilon$, *where* $m \in \{m^D, m^A\}$, *then*

1. $m(a.P, a.Q) \leq \epsilon$
2. $m(pR \oplus (1 - p)P, pR \oplus (1 - p)Q) \leq \epsilon$
3. $m(R + P, R + Q) \leq \epsilon$
4. $m((\nu a)P, (\nu a)Q) \leq \epsilon$
5. $m(R \,|\, P, R \,|\, Q) \leq \epsilon$.

Proof sketch. The proof proceeds by finding a ϵ-accumulative (resp. amortised) bisimulation relation witnessing their distance in m not greater than ϵ. Let $\mathcal{R}$ be a ϵ-accumulative (resp. amortised) bisimulation relation witnessing $m(P, Q) \leq \epsilon$. Define

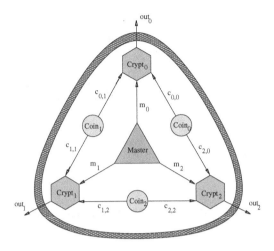

Fig. 3. Chaum's system for the Dining Cryptographers

the relation $Id_S = \{(s, s, 0)|s \in S\}$. We construct for each clause a relation $\mathcal{R}'$ as follows and show that it is a ϵ-accumulative (resp. amortised) bisimulation relation.

1. $\mathcal{R}' = \{(a.P, a.Q, 0)\} \cup \mathcal{R}$,
2. $\mathcal{R}' = \{(pR \oplus (1-p)P, pR \oplus (1-p)Q, 0)\} \cup \mathcal{R} \cup Id_R$,
3. $\mathcal{R}' = \{(R + P, R + Q, 0)\} \cup \mathcal{R} \cup Id_R$,
4. $\mathcal{R}' = \{((\nu a)P', (\nu a)Q', c) \mid (P', Q', c) \in \mathcal{R}\}$,
5. $\mathcal{R}' = \{(R' \mid P', R' \mid Q', c) \mid (P', Q', c) \in \mathcal{R}\} \cup Id_R$.

7   An Application to the Dining Cryptographers Protocol

In this section we use the pseudometric method to reason about the degree of differential privacy of the Dining Cryptographers Protocol [9] with biased coins. In particular, we show that with probability-p biased coins, the degree of differential privacy in the case of three cryptographers is $|\ln \frac{p}{1-p}|$. This result can also be generalized to the case of n cryptographers.

The problem of the Dining Cryptographers is the following: Three cryptographers dine together. After the dinner, the bill has to be paid by either one of them or by another agent called the master. The master decides who will pay and then informs each of them separately whether he has to pay or not. The cryptographers would like to find out whether the payer is the master or one of them. However, in the latter case, they wish to keep the payer anonymous.

The Dining Cryptographers Protocol (DCP) solves the above problem as follows: each cryptographer tosses a fair coin which is visible to himself and his neighbor to the left. Each cryptographer checks his own coin and the one to his right and, if he is not paying, announces "agree" if the two coins are the same and "disagree" otherwise. However, the paying cryptographer says the opposite. It can be proved that the master is paying if and only if the number of disagrees is even [9].

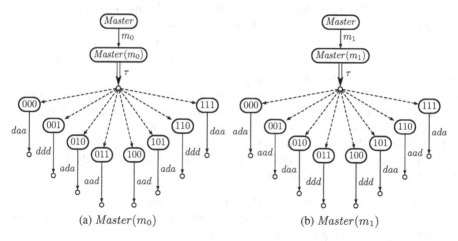

Fig. 4. The probabilistic automata of the Dining cryptographers

The graph shown in Fig. 3 illustrates the dinner-table and the allocation of the coins between the three cryptographers. We consider the coins which are probability-p biased, i.e., producing 0 (for "head") with probability p, and 1 (for "tail") with $1 - p$. We consider the final announcement in the order of $out_0\, out_1\, out_2$, with $out_i \in \{a, d\}$ (a for "agree" and d for "disagree", $i \in \{0, 1, 2\}$) announced by $Crytp_i$. For example, if $Crytp_0$ is designated to pay, $Coin_0\, Coin_1\, Coin_2 = 010$, then $out_0\, out_1\, out_2 = ada$.

We are interested in the case when one of the cryptographers is paying, since that is the case in which they want to keep the payer anonymous. We use $Master(m_i)$ to denote the system in which $Crytp_i$ is designated to pay. To show that the DCP is differentially private, both pseudometrics introduced before can be used. In this problem, it suffices to find between $Master(m_i)$'s bounded distances in the accumulative pseudometric m^D, more precisely, bounded accumulative bisimulation relations.

Proposition 5. *A DCP with three cryptographers and with probability-p biased coins is $|\ln \frac{p}{1-p}|$-differentially private.*

Proof. Fig. 4 shows two probabilistic automata $Master(m_0)$ and $Master(m_1)$ when $Crytp_0$ and $Crytp_1$ are paying respectively. Basically they are probabilistic distributions over all possible outcomes $Coin_0\, Coin_1\, Coin_2$ (i.e. inner states) produced by the three-coins toss, followed by an announcement determined by each outcome. For simplicity initial τ transitions are merged harmlessly. Let $b_0 b_1 b_2$ and $c_0 c_1 c_2$ represent two inner states of $Master(m_0)$ and $Master(m_1)$ respectively. There exists a bijection function f between them:

$$c_0 c_1 c_2 = f(b_0 b_1 b_2) = b_0 (b_1 \oplus 1) b_2$$

where $\oplus$ represents the addition modulo 2 (xor), such that the announcement of $b_0 b_1 b_2$ can be shown equal to the one of $c_0 c_1 c_2$.

Note that, the probability of reaching an inner state $b_0 b_1 b_2$ from $Master(m_0)$ is $p^i (1 - p)^{(3-i)}$, where $i \in \{0, 1, 2, 3\}$ is the number of 0 in $\{b_0, b_1, b_2\}$. Because

$c_0 = b_0, c_1 = b_1 \oplus 1, c_2 = b_2$, the ratio between the probabilities of reaching $b_0 b_1 b_2$ from $Master(m_0)$ and $c_0 c_1 c_2$ from $Master(m_1)$ differs at most by $|\ln \frac{p}{1-p}|$. It is easy to see that $\{(Master(m_0), Master(m_1), 0)\} \cup \{ (b_0 b_1 b_2, f(b_0 b_1 b_2), |\ln \frac{p}{1-p}|) \mid b_0, b_1, b_2 \in \{0, 1\} \}$ forms a $|\ln \frac{p}{1-p}|$-accumulative bisimulation relation. Thus $m^D(Master(m_0), Master(m_1)) \leq |\ln \frac{p}{1-p}|$.

Similarly, we consider the probabilistic automata $Master(m_2)$ when $Crytp_2$ is paying (though omitted in Fig. 4). Let $e_0 e_1 e_2$ represent one of its inner states. We can also find a bijection f' between $c_0 c_1 c_2$ and $e_0 e_1 e_2$: $e_0 e_1 e_2 = f'(c_0 c_1 c_2) = c_0 c_1(c_2 \oplus 1)$, and a bijection f'' between $b_0 b_1 b_2$ and $e_0 e_1 e_2$: $e_0 e_1 e_2 = f''(b_0 b_1 b_2) = (b_0 \oplus 1) b_1 b_2$ such that they output same announcements, The rest proceeds as above. By Theorem 1, the DCP is $|\ln \frac{p}{1-p}|$-differentially private.   □

The above proposition can be extended to the case of n dining cryptographers where $n \geq 3$. We assume that the n cryptographers are fully connected, i.e., that a coin exists between every pair of cryptographers. Let c_{kl} $(k, l \in Z, k, l \in [0, n-1], k < l)$ be the coin linking two cryptographers $Crytp_k$ and $Crytp_l$. In this case the output of $Crytp_i$ would be $out_i = c_{0i} \oplus c_{1i} \oplus \cdots c_{i(n-1)} \oplus pay(i)$, where $pay(i) = 1$ if $Crytp_i$ pays and 0 otherwise.

Proposition 6. *A DCP with n fully connected cryptographers and with probability-p biased coins is $|\ln \frac{p}{1-p}|$-differentially private.*

We can see that the more the coins are biased, the worse the privacy gets. If the coins are fair, namely, $p = 1 - p = \frac{1}{2}$, then the DCP is 0-differentially private, in which case the privacy is well protected. With the help of the pseudometric method, we get a general proposition about the degree of differential privacy of DCP. Moreover, it is obtained through some local information, rather than by computing globally the summations of probabilities for each trace.

8   Conclusion and Future Work

We have investigated two pseudometrics on probabilistic automata: the first one is a reformulation of the notion proposed in [27], the second one is designed in the sense that the total privacy leakage bound gets amortised. Each of them establishs a framework for the formal verification of differential privacy for concurrent systems. Namely, the closer processes are in the pseudometrics, the higher level of differential privacy they can preserve. We have showed that our pseudometric is more liberal than the former one. They both impliy strong bisimilarity, and the typical process algebra operators are non-expansive with respect to the distance in the pseudometrics. We have used the pseudometric verification method to learn that: A Dining Cryptographers protocol with probability-p biased coins is $|\ln \frac{p}{1-p}|$-differentially private.

In this paper we have mainly focused on developing a basic framework for the formal verification of differential privacy for concurrent systems. In the future we plan to develop more realistic case-studies and applications. Another interesting direction, which is also our ongoing work, is to investigate a new pseudometric, adapted from the metric à la Kantorovich proposed in [13], see whether it can fully characterise bisimilarity, and moreover, release the bijection requirement in the definition of the quantitative bisimulations considered in this paper.

Acknowledgements. The authors wish to thank Catuscia Palamidessi, Frank D. Valencia and the anonymous reviewers for providing constructive comments and recommendations on an earlier version of this paper.

References

1. Abadi, M., Gordon, A.D.: A calculus for cryptographic protocols: The spi calculus. Inf. and Comp. 148(1), 1–70 (1999)
2. Andrés, M.E., Palamidessi, C., Sokolova, A., Rossum, P.V.: Information Hiding in Probabilistic Concurrent Systems. TCS 412(28), 3072–3089 (2011)
3. Barthe, G., Köpf, B., Olmedo, F., Béguelin, S.Z.: Probabilistic relational reasoning for differential privacy. In: Proc. of POPL. ACM (2012)
4. Boreale, M.: Quantifying information leakage in process calculi. In: Bugliesi, M., Preneel, B., Sassone, V., Wegener, I. (eds.) ICALP 2006. LNCS, vol. 4052, pp. 119–131. Springer, Heidelberg (2006)
5. Braun, C., Chatzikokolakis, K., Palamidessi, C.: Compositional methods for information-hiding. In: Amadio, R.M. (ed.) FOSSACS 2008. LNCS, vol. 4962, pp. 443–457. Springer, Heidelberg (2008)
6. Canetti, R., Cheung, L., Kaynar, D., Liskov, M., Lynch, N., Pereira, O., Segala, R.: Task-structured probabilistic i/o automata. In: Proc. of WODES (2006)
7. Chatzikokolakis, K., Andrés, M.E., Bordenabe, N.E., Palamidessi, C.: Broadening the scope of differential privacy using metrics. In: De Cristofaro, E., Wright, M. (eds.) PETS 2013. LNCS, vol. 7981, pp. 82–102. Springer, Heidelberg (2013)
8. Chatzikokolakis, K., Palamidessi, C.: Making random choices invisible to the scheduler. In: Caires, L., Vasconcelos, V.T. (eds.) CONCUR 2007. LNCS, vol. 4703, pp. 42–58. Springer, Heidelberg (2007)
9. Chaum, D.: The dining cryptographers problem: Unconditional sender and recipient untraceability. Journal of Cryptology 1, 65–75 (1988)
10. de Frutos-Escrig, D., Rosa-Velardo, F., Gregorio-Rodríguez, C.: New bisimulation semantics for distributed systems. In: Derrick, J., Vain, J. (eds.) FORTE 2007. LNCS, vol. 4574, pp. 143–159. Springer, Heidelberg (2007)
11. Deng, Y., Chothia, T., Palamidessi, C., Pang, J.: Metrics for action-labelled quantitative transition systems. In: Proc. of QAPL. ENTCS, vol. 153, pp. 79–96. Elsevier (2006)
12. Deng, Y., Pang, J., Wu, P.: Measuring anonymity with relative entropy. In: Dimitrakos, T., Martinelli, F., Ryan, P.Y.A., Schneider, S. (eds.) FAST 2006. LNCS, vol. 4691, pp. 65–79. Springer, Heidelberg (2007)
13. Desharnais, J., Jagadeesan, R., Gupta, V., Panangaden, P.: The metric analogue of weak bisimulation for probabilistic processes. In: Proc. of LICS, pp. 413–422. IEEE (2002)
14. Dwork, C.: Differential privacy. In: Bugliesi, M., Preneel, B., Sassone, V., Wegener, I. (eds.) ICALP 2006. LNCS, vol. 4052, pp. 1–12. Springer, Heidelberg (2006)
15. Focardi, R., Gorrieri, R.: Classification of security properties (part i: Information flow). In: Focardi, R., Gorrieri, R. (eds.) FOSAD 2000. LNCS, vol. 2171, pp. 331–396. Springer, Heidelberg (2001)
16. Gaboardi, M., Haeberlen, A., Hsu, J., Narayan, A., Pierce, B.C.: Linear dependent types for differential privacy. In: POPL, pp. 357–370 (2013)

17. Jou, C.-C., Smolka, S.: Equivalences, congruences, and complete axiomatizations for probabilistic processes. In: Baeten, J.C.M., Klop, J.W. (eds.) CONCUR 1990. LNCS, vol. 458, pp. 367–383. Springer, Heidelberg (1990)
18. Kiehn, A., Arun-Kumar, S.: Amortised bisimulations. In: Wang, F. (ed.) FORTE 2005. LNCS, vol. 3731, pp. 320–334. Springer, Heidelberg (2005)
19. Larsen, K.G., Skou, A.: Bisimulation through probabilistic testing. Inf. and Comp. 94(1), 1–28 (1991)
20. Machanavajjhala, A., Kifer, D., Abowd, J.M., Gehrke, J., Vilhuber, L.: Privacy: Theory meets practice on the map. In: Proc. of ICDE, pp. 277–286. IEEE (2008)
21. Milner, R.: Communication and Concurrency. Series in Comp. Sci. Prentice Hall (1989)
22. Mu, C.: Measuring information flow in reactive processes. In: Qing, S., Mitchell, C.J., Wang, G. (eds.) ICICS 2009. LNCS, vol. 5927, pp. 211–225. Springer, Heidelberg (2009)
23. Narayanan, A., Shmatikov, V.: De-anonymizing social networks. In: Proc. of S&P, pp. 173–187. IEEE (2009)
24. Reed, J., Pierce, B.C.: Distance makes the types grow stronger: a calculus for differential privacy. In: Proc. of ICFP, pp. 157–168. ACM (2010)
25. Ryan, P.Y.A., Schneider, S.A.: Process algebra and non-interference. Journal of Computer Security 9(1/2), 75–103 (2001)
26. Smith, G.: Probabilistic noninterference through weak probabilistic bisimulation. In: CSFW, pp. 3–13 (2003)
27. Tschantz, M.C., Kaynar, D., Datta, A.: Formal verification of differential privacy for interactive systems (extended abstract). ENTCS 276, 61–79 (2011)
28. Xu, L.: Modular reasoning about differential privacy in a probabilistic process calculus. In: Palamidessi, C., Ryan, M.D. (eds.) TGC 2012. LNCS, vol. 8191, pp. 198–212. Springer, Heidelberg (2013)

A   Appendix

A.1   Proof of Lemma 2

Proof. We prove by induction on the length of trace t: $|t|$.

1. $|t| = 0$: According to equation (1), for any ζ, $\Pr_\zeta[\alpha_1 \rhd t] = \Pr_\zeta[\alpha_2 \rhd t] = 1$.
2. IH: For any two executions α_1 and α_2 of $\mathcal{A}$, let $s_1 = lstate(\alpha_1)$ and $s_2 = lstate(\alpha_2)$. $(s_1, s_2, c) \in \mathcal{R}$ implies that for any admissible scheduler ζ, trace t' where $|t'| \leq L$: $\frac{1}{e^{\epsilon+c}} \leq \frac{\Pr_\zeta[\alpha_1 \rhd t']}{\Pr_\zeta[\alpha_2 \rhd t']} \leq e^{\epsilon-c}$.
3. We have to show that for any admissible scheduler ζ, trace t with $|t| = L + 1$, $(s_1, s_2, c) \in \mathcal{R}$ implies $\frac{1}{e^{\epsilon+c}} \leq \frac{\Pr_\zeta[\alpha_1 \rhd t]}{\Pr_\zeta[\alpha_2 \rhd t]} \leq e^{\epsilon-c}$.
   Assume that $t = a^\frown t'$. We prove first the right-hand part $\Pr_\zeta[\alpha_1 \rhd t] \leq e^{\epsilon-c} * \Pr_\zeta[\alpha_2 \rhd t]$. According to equation (1), two cases must be considered:
   - Case $act(\zeta(\alpha_1)) \neq a$. Then $\Pr_\zeta[\alpha_1 \rhd t] = 0$. Since ζ is admissible, it schedules for α_2 a transition consistent with α_1, namely, not a transition labeled by a either. Thus $\Pr_\zeta[\alpha_2 \rhd t] = 0$, the inequality is satisfied.
   - Case $\zeta(\alpha_1) = s_1 \xrightarrow{a} \mu_1$. So, $\Pr_\zeta[\alpha_1 \rhd t] = \sum_{s_i \in supp(\mu_1)} \mu_1(s_i)\Pr_\zeta[\alpha_1 a s_i \rhd t']$. Since $(s_1, s_2, c) \in \mathcal{R}$, there must be also a transition from s_2 such that $s_2 \xrightarrow{a} \mu_2$ and $\mu_1 \mathcal{L}^A(\mathcal{R}, c)\mu_2$. Since ζ is admissible, $\zeta(\alpha_2) = s_2 \xrightarrow{a} \mu_2$. We use t_i to range over elements in $supp(\mu_2)$. Thus, $\Pr_\zeta[\alpha_2 \rhd t] = \sum_{t_i \in supp(\mu_2)} \mu_2(t_i) \cdot$

$\Pr_\varsigma[\alpha_2 at_i \rhd t']$. Since $\mu_1 \mathcal{L}^A(\mathcal{R}, c)\mu_2$, there is a bijection $\beta : supp(\mu_1) \longrightarrow supp(\mu_2)$, s.t. for any $s_i \in supp(\mu_1)$, there is a state $t_i \in supp(\mu_2)$, $t_i = \beta(s_i)$ and $(s_i, t_i, c + \ln \mu_1(s_i) - \ln \mu_2(t_i)) \in \mathcal{R}$. Apply the inductive hypothesis to $\alpha_1 a s_i, \alpha_2 a t_i$ and t', we get that:

$$\Pr_\varsigma[\alpha_1 as_i \rhd t'] \le e^{\epsilon - (c + \ln \mu_1(s_i) - \ln \mu_2(t_i))} * \Pr_\varsigma[\alpha_2 at_i \rhd t'] \tag{2}$$

Thus,

$$\Pr_\varsigma[\alpha_1 \rhd t] \tag{3}$$

$$= \sum_{s_i \in supp(\mu_1)} \mu_1(s_i)\Pr_\varsigma[\alpha_1 as_i \rhd t'] \tag{4}$$

$$\le \sum_{s_i \in supp(\mu_1)} \mu_1(s_i)e^{\epsilon - (c + \ln \mu_1(s_i) - \ln \mu_2(\beta(s_i)))}\Pr_\varsigma[\alpha_2 a\beta(s_i) \rhd t'] \tag{5}$$

$$= \sum_{s_i \in supp(\mu_1)} \mu_1(s_i) * \frac{\mu_2(\beta(s_i))}{\mu_1(s_i)} * e^{\epsilon - c} * \Pr_\varsigma[\alpha_2 a\beta(s_i) \rhd t'] \tag{6}$$

$$= \sum_{t_i \in supp(\mu_2)} \mu_2(t_i) * e^{\epsilon - c} * \Pr_\varsigma[\alpha_2 at_i \rhd t'] \tag{7}$$

$$= e^{\epsilon - c} \sum_{t_i \in supp(\mu_2)} \mu_2(t_i)\Pr_\varsigma[\alpha_2 at_i \rhd t'] \tag{8}$$

$$= e^{\epsilon - c} * \Pr_\varsigma[\alpha_2 \rhd t] \tag{9}$$

which completes the proof of right-hand part. Lines (4) and (9) follow from the equation (1). Line (5) follow from the inductive hypothesis, i.e. Line (2).
For the left-hand part $\Pr_\varsigma[\alpha_2 \rhd t] \le e^{\epsilon + c} * \Pr_\varsigma[\alpha_1 \rhd t]$, exchange the roles of s_1 and s_2, use β^{-1} instead of β, and all the rest is analogous. $\quad\square$

A.2 Proof of Proposition 6

Proof sketch. The proof proceeds analogously to the case of three cryptographers. To find an accumulative bisimulation relation between every two instances of the DCP $Master(m_i)$ and $Master(m_j)$, $(i, j) \in Z, i, j \in [0, n-1], i < j)$, we point out here mainly the bijection function between their inner states. Let $b_{12}b_{13} \cdots b_{(n-1)n}$ and $c_{12}c_{13} \cdots c_{(n-1)n}$ represent the inner states of $Master(m_i)$ and $Master(m_j)$ respectively, where the subscript (kl), $(k, l \in \mathcal{Z}, k, l \in [0, n-1], k < l)$, indicates the coin linking two cryptographers $Crytp_k$ and $Crytp_l$. There exists a bijection function f between them defined as: $c_{12}c_{13} \cdots c_{(n-1)n} = f(b_{12}b_{13} \cdots b_{(n-1)n})$, precisely,

$$c_{kl} = \begin{cases} b_{kl} \oplus 1 & \text{if } kl = ij, \\ b_{kl} & \text{otherwise.} \end{cases}$$

We can check that the bijective states defined in this way produce the same announcement in $Master(m_i)$ and $Master(m_j)$. Moreover, only the coin (ij) is different, the ratio between the probability mass of every bijective states is at most $|\ln \frac{p}{1-p}|$. $\quad\square$

Dimming Relations for the Efficient Analysis of Concurrent Systems via Action Abstraction

Rocco De Nicola[1], Giulio Iacobelli[2], and Mirco Tribastone[2]

[1] IMT — Institute for Advanced Studies Lucca, Italy
rocco.denicola@imtlucca.it
[2] Electronics and Computer Science
University of Southampton, United Kingdom
{g.iacobelli,m.tribastone}@soton.ac.uk

Abstract. We study models of concurrency based on labelled transition systems where abstractions are induced by a partition of the action set. We introduce *dimming relations* which are able to relate two models if they can mimic each other by using actions from the same partition block. Moreover, we discuss the necessary requirements for guaranteeing compositional verification. We show how our new relations and results can be exploited when seemingly heterogeneous systems exhibit analogous behaviours manifested via different actions. Dimming relations make the models more homogeneous by collapsing such distinct actions into the same partition block. With our examples, we show how these abstractions may considerably reduce the state-space size, in some cases from exponential to polynomial complexity.

1 Introduction

Behavioural relations are powerful techniques to reason about models based on labelled transition systems. The classic notion of bisimulation relates two states P and Q such that any action performed by P can be matched by the same action from Q (and vice versa). Weak bisimulation exploits the fact that some behaviour is abstracted away by hiding the identity of certain actions that can be considered uninteresting at some desired level of detail [1]. Alternatively, in some situations, by exploiting specific structural properties, e.g. symmetries [2], it is possible to study the properties of a given model by considering another one with a smaller state-space size, thus reducing the cost of the analysis.

We propose an approach that lies between ignoring actions and accounting for their similarities. We study behavioural relations that take a coarse-grained view of a model, based on partitioning the set of actions that it can exhibit. Our first notion relates P and Q whenever Q is able to match a given action a performed by P *with any action* in the same partition block of a (and vice versa). We call this *dimmed bisimulation* to highlight that, based on the action partition, the modeller is able to see and reason about the original system at different levels of detail and thus with different levels of accuracy. Clearly, dimmed bisimulation equivalence is less discriminating than bisimilarity, whenever the partition over

E. Ábrahám and C. Palamidessi (Eds.), FORTE 2014, LNCS 8461, pp. 216–231, 2014.
© IFIP International Federation for Information Processing 2014

the actions is nontrivial. For instance, using standard process algebraic notation, let us consider $a_1.0 + a_2.0$: a simple process that offers a choice between two actions, a_1 and a_2, and then stops. This will be dimmed bisimilar to $a_1.0$ if both a_1 and a_2 belong to the same partition block; evidently, $a_1.0+a_2.0$ is not bisimilar to $a_1.0$. This simple example shows that it is possible to obtain a more compact description when the modeller is content with reasoning at the level of partition representatives instead of considering detailed concrete actions. Indeed, we will present more substantial examples where the effect of this abstraction will be more significant. To provide some intuition behind this approach, let $\parallel$ denote a generic parallel operator and consider $a_1.0 \parallel a_2.0 \parallel \cdots \parallel a_n.0$, e.g., a model of n independent threads of execution, each performing a distinct computation a_i, $1 \leq i \leq n$, and then stopping. The state space size of this (concrete) system is 2^n; however, allowing all a_i to be actions of the same partition block permits a dramatic reduction of the (abstract) state space to only $n+1$ states, where each of them tracks the number of processes that have not become inert (0) yet.

An analogous state-space reduction could have been obtained by assuming that the actions in the same partition block represent unnecessary detail in the model. Thus, in $a_1.0 + a_2.0$ one would replace a_1 and a_2 with *internal* τ actions, yielding $\tau.0+\tau.0$, which is bisimilar to $\tau.0$. However, there are two major drawbacks with this approach. Firstly, in such a reduced form it is not possible to keep track of the concrete actions from which the internal ones are originated. Secondly, sometimes this abstraction may not be possible, for instance when a_1 and a_2 are intended to be used for synchronising with other processes.

More closely related to our behavioural relations is turning one action, say a_2, into another one. For instance, identification of $a_1.0+a_2.0$ with $a_1.0$ can be done by using $(a_1.0+a_2.0)[f]$ where f is the relabelling function such that $f(a_1) = a_1$ and $f(a_2) = a_1$. Indeed, we provide a characterisation of dimmed bisimulation based on the existence of an appropriate f such that $P[f]$ is bisimilar, in the classical sense, to $Q[f]$. Thus, dimmed bisimulation is able to relate processes that behave bisimilarly after an appropriate relabelling of their actions.

A highly desirable property of any behavioural relation for process algebra is establishing that it is preserved by its operators. Here we study a CSP-like process algebra (see, e.g., [3]) where the parallel operator is parameterised by a synchronisation action set. We find that dimmed bisimilarity is preserved only if certain syntactic conditions are met. For instance, it is preserved by parallel composition under *singleton coherence*, i.e., if non-trivial partition blocks contain only actions that are performed independently and not used for synchronisation.

Unfortunately, the singleton coherence restriction rules out the possibility of compositional reasoning for models of practical interest. For instance, using again the simple example discussed above, $a_1.0 + a_2.0$ could not be placed in any context where both a_1 and a_2 are synchronisation actions. However, this represents a typical modelling pattern whereby a process is able to offer two (or more) different options to the environment. In order to deal with situations of this kind, we introduce *dimmed simulation* (whereby, analogously to the classic notion of simulation, any action performed by P can be matched by Q with any other action in the same partition block, but not vice versa). We will see that *dimmed similarity* is preserved by parallel composition under the much more generous assumption of *block coherence*, essentially requiring that a whole partition block must be included in a synchronisation set if this contains an action of the partition block.

We will apply our results to a number of models which prototypically show typical patterns of communication in distributed systems, where *heterogeneity* is expressed as analogous behaviour with distinct actions. We will study a simple model of fork/join mechanism. This can be relevant, for instance, to capture certain aspects of novel programming paradigms such as MapReduce (see, e.g., [4]). Here, a distinct action type is used for each worker thread to signal that it has finished work. Second, we study a producer/consumer system mediated by a buffer (e.g., [5]), where the existence of different classes of items is captured by having the buffer expose distinct pairs of *put* and *get* actions for each item class. Finally, we consider Milner's *cyclers* model [1], a benchmark in the process algebra literature. In all these cases, the state-space size of such models grows exponentially with the number of components in the model. Our dimming relations allow us to analyse systems after making them more *homogeneous*, by offering a coarser-grained view, as induced by action partitioning. Obviously, the modeller has to be satisfied by the provided abstract view. For example, she may be content with ensuring that the fork/join model only captures that *some* sub-tasks have been fulfilled by *some* threads; or that an action *put* enables an action *get* in any buffer place, without necessarily wanting to know *which* specific thread has completed or which specific item class has been handled. In some of our examples, it turns out that it is possible to obtain dimmed (bi-)similar processes with state-space sizes of polynomial, rather than exponential, complexity.

Paper outline. After introducing our CSP-like process algebra, Section 2 discusses dimmed bisimulation and studies compositionality and its characterisation in terms of action relabelling. Section 3 applies our results to the case studies. Section 4 introduces dimmed simulation. Section 5 discusses related work, while Section 6 briefly concludes. Unless otherwise stated, all proofs can be found in the technical report available at http://eprints.imtlucca.it/1655/.

2   Dimmed Bisimulation

We carry out our investigation in the context of a process algebra with CSP-style semantics. However, with appropriate changes our ideas of dimmed relations carry over to other synchronisation operators such as the binary one in CCS [1].

Definition 1 (Process Algebra Syntax). *Let $\mathcal{A}$ be a set of actions and $\mathcal{L} = \mathcal{A} \cup \{\tau\}$, with $\tau \notin \mathcal{A}$, be the set of labels. Our process algebra has the syntax*

$$P ::= \mathbf{0} \mid a.P \mid P + P \mid K \mid P[f] \mid P \parallel_L P \mid P/L$$

$$\frac{}{a.P \xrightarrow{a} P} \qquad \frac{P \xrightarrow{a} P'}{P+Q \xrightarrow{a} P'} \qquad \frac{Q \xrightarrow{a} Q'}{P+Q \xrightarrow{a} Q'} \qquad \frac{P \xrightarrow{a} P'}{K \xrightarrow{a} P'} \, K \triangleq P$$

$$\frac{P \xrightarrow{a} P'}{P[f] \xrightarrow{f(a)} P'[f]} \qquad \frac{P \xrightarrow{a} P'}{P/L \xrightarrow{a} P'/L} \, a \notin L \qquad \frac{P \xrightarrow{a} P'}{P/L \xrightarrow{\tau} P'/L} \, a \in L$$

$$\frac{P \xrightarrow{a} P'}{P \parallel_L Q \xrightarrow{a} P' \parallel_L Q} a \notin L \qquad \frac{Q \xrightarrow{a} Q'}{P \parallel_L Q \xrightarrow{a} P \parallel_L Q'} a \notin L \qquad \frac{P \xrightarrow{a} P' \quad Q \xrightarrow{a} Q'}{P \parallel_L Q \xrightarrow{a} P' \parallel_L Q'} a \in L$$

Fig. 1. Process algebra semantics

where $a \in \mathcal{L}$, $K \in \mathcal{K}$, with $\mathcal{K}$ the set of constants and $K \triangleq P$, $f : \mathcal{L} \to \mathcal{L}$ is a relabelling function with $f(\tau) = \tau$, and $L \subseteq \mathcal{A}$. Let $\mathcal{P}$ be the set of processes, that is the set of terms generated by the grammar above.

We use standard syntax, thus: τ is the internal action; $\mathbf{0}$ is the inert process, that does nothing; $a.P$ denotes *prefixing*, which can perform an a-action and become P; $P + P$ offers a *choice* between behaviours; K is a *constant*, for recursion; $P[f]$ is a process to which a *relabelling* of its actions is applied (where τ cannot be relabelled); $P \parallel_L P$ is the generalised *parallel* operator, whereby the two operands are required to synchronise only over the actions that are in the set L; P/L models *hiding*, whereby an action performed by P is made internal if it is in L.[1] These rules are captured by the operational semantics in Fig. 1.

Notation 1 *Throughout the paper, we let $\mathfrak{F} = \{\mathcal{F}_1, \ldots, \mathcal{F}_m\}$ denote a partition of $\mathcal{A}$. If $a \in \mathcal{A}$ we let $[a]_{\mathfrak{F}}$ denote the partition block $\mathcal{F}_i$ such that $a \in \mathcal{F}_i$; when $\mathfrak{F}$ is clear from the context, we omit the subscript and simply write $[a]$. We extend the notation $[\cdot]$ to τ by setting $[\tau] = \{\tau\}$.*

Definition 2. *Let $\mathfrak{F}$ be a partition of $\mathcal{A}$. We say that $P \xrightarrow{[a]} P'$ iff there exists $b \in [a]$ such that $P \xrightarrow{b} P'$.*

According to this definition and to the previous notation, if $P \xrightarrow{\tau} P'$ then we write $P \xrightarrow{[\tau]} P'$. Intuitively, Definition 2 gives us the *dimmed behaviour* of a process P: if it can make a *concrete* action b then we say that it can make an *abstract* action $[a]$, which essentially stands for saying that "P can make at least one of the actions of the partition block to which b belongs." Our notion of dimmed bisimulation allows processes to match each other's actions so long as they are in the same partition block.

Definition 3 (Dimmed Bisimulation). *Given a partition $\mathfrak{F}$, a binary relation $\mathcal{R}$ over $\mathcal{P}$ is an $\mathfrak{F}$-dimmed bisimulation iff whenever $(P, Q) \in \mathcal{R}$ and $a \in \mathcal{L}$:*

- *if $P \xrightarrow{[a]} P'$ then $Q \xrightarrow{[a]} Q'$ and $(P', Q') \in \mathcal{R}$;*

---

[1] Our notions naturally extend to weak variants.

– if $Q \xrightarrow{[a]} Q'$ then $P \xrightarrow{[a]} P'$ and $(P', Q') \in \mathcal{R}$.

Two processes P, Q are $\mathfrak{F}$-dimmed bisimilar, written $P \sim_{\mathfrak{F}} Q$, iff there exists an $\mathfrak{F}$-dimmed bisimulation that relates them.

Let us stress that the classic notion of bisimulation, hereafter denoted by $\sim$, can be recovered by choosing $\mathfrak{F}$ as the trivial singleton partition (which yields $[a] = \{a\}$ for all $a \in \mathcal{A}$). With an appropriate choice of the action partition, it is possible to find dimmed bisimilar processes that are easier to analyse. For instance, using again the simple process presented in Section 1, it holds that $a_1.0 + a_2.0 \sim_{\mathfrak{F}} a_1.0$ (and also that $a_1.0 + a_2.0 \sim_{\mathfrak{F}} a_2.0$) if $\{a_1, a_2\} \in \mathfrak{F}$. This is because $\mathcal{R} = \{(a_1.0 + a_2.0, a_1.0), (0, 0)\}$ is an $\mathfrak{F}$-dimmed bisimulation. For instance, both $a_1.0 + a_2.0 \xrightarrow{a_1} 0$ and $a_1.0 + a_2.0 \xrightarrow{a_2} 0$ imply that $a_1.0 + a_2.0 \xrightarrow{[a_1]} 0$ and $a_1.0 \xrightarrow{[a_1]} 0$ since $a_1.0 \xrightarrow{a_1} 0$. Please notice that, in this particular case, the dimmed bisimilar process has the same number of states, but fewer transitions. Later we will provide examples where also the number of states will be reduced.

As expected, similarly to classical bisimulation, the following holds.

Theorem 1. *For any partition $\mathfrak{F}$, the relation $\sim_{\mathfrak{F}}$*

a) is an equivalence relation;
b) is the largest $\mathfrak{F}$-dimmed bisimulation;
c) satisfies the following property: $P \sim_{\mathfrak{F}} Q$ iff, for any $a \in \mathcal{L}$,

– if $P \xrightarrow{[a]} P'$ then $Q \xrightarrow{[a]} Q'$ and $P' \sim_{\mathfrak{F}} Q'$;
– if $Q \xrightarrow{[a]} Q'$ then $P \xrightarrow{[a]} P'$ and $P' \sim_{\mathfrak{F}} Q'$.

Let us observe that, with $\{a_1, a_2\} \in \mathfrak{F}$, it is also possible to establish the relation $a_1.0 + a_2.0 \sim_{\mathfrak{F}} a_1.0 + a_1.0$. This intuitively suggests that dimmed bisimulation can be understood as a form of relabelling that turns actions of a partition block into possibly distinct actions within the same partition block. Indeed, in this simple case we have that $(a_1.0 + a_2.0)[f] \sim (a_1.0 + a_1.0)[f]$ for f such that $f(a_1) = a_1$ and $f(a_2) = a_1$.

Dimmed bisimulation can be characterised in terms of actions relabelling. We start with identifying functions that relabel within the same block of $\mathfrak{F}$.

Definition 4. *A relabelling function $f : \mathcal{L} \to \mathcal{L}$ is said to be partition-preserving (pp) for $\mathfrak{F}$ iff for each $\mathcal{F} \in \mathfrak{F}$ and for each $a \in \mathcal{F}$ it holds that $f(a) \in \mathcal{F}$.*

Theorem 2 (Characterisation of Dimmed Bisimulation via relabelling).
Given a partition $\mathfrak{F}$, $P \sim_{\mathfrak{F}} Q$ iff there exists a pp-function f for $\mathfrak{F}$ such that $P[f] \sim Q[f]$.

We now study whether dimmed bisimulation is preserved by the operators of our process algebra. For hiding and parallel composition, that are parameterised by an action set L, we need to impose syntactic restrictions on the set L, which we call *block coherence* and *singleton coherence*, respectively. Roughly speaking, block coherence requires that an element of $\mathfrak{F}$ is either completely in the action set L, or completely outside. Singleton coherence, instead, requires that each action belonging to the action set L cannot be aggregated with other actions.

Definition 5. *Given a partition $\mathfrak{F}$ and $L \subseteq \mathcal{A}$, we say that L is*

- block coherent *with $\mathfrak{F}$ iff $\forall \mathcal{F} \in \mathfrak{F}$ such that $\mathcal{F} \cap L \neq \emptyset$ we have $\mathcal{F} \subseteq L$.*
- singleton coherent *with $\mathfrak{F}$ iff $\forall \mathcal{F} \in \mathfrak{F}$ such that $\mathcal{F} \cap L \neq \emptyset$ we have $|\mathcal{F}| = 1$.*

For instance, let $\mathfrak{F} = \{\{a_1, a_2\}, \{b\}\}$. Then $\{b\}$ is singleton coherent with $\mathfrak{F}$, whereas $\{a_1, a_2\}$ is not. However, $\{a_1, a_2\}$ is block coherent with $\mathfrak{F}$. Furthermore, every action set L is singleton coherent with the trivial singleton partition of the action set; finally, the empty set is singleton coherent with any $\mathfrak{F}$.

Theorem 3 (Compositionality for Dimmed Bisimulation). *Let P and Q be two processes such that $P \sim_{\mathfrak{F}} Q$. Then it holds that:*

i) $a.P \sim_{\mathfrak{F}} b.Q$ for any a, b such that $[a] = [b]$;
ii) $P + R \sim_{\mathfrak{F}} Q + S$ for any two processes R and S such that $R \sim_{\mathfrak{F}} S$;
iii) $P[g] \sim_{\mathfrak{F}} Q[g]$ for any function g that is partition preserving for $\mathfrak{F}$;
iv) $P/L \sim_{\mathfrak{F}} Q/L$ for L block coherent with $\mathfrak{F}$;
v) $P \parallel_L R \sim_{\mathfrak{F}} Q \parallel_L S$ if $R \sim_{\mathfrak{F}} S$ and L is singleton coherent with $\mathfrak{F}$.

In general, dimmed bisimulation is not preserved if the above syntactical restrictions are not satisfied. To see this, let us take, for instance, processes $a_1.\mathbf{0}$ and $a_2.\mathbf{0}$, and some partition $\mathfrak{F}$ such that $\{a_1, a_2\} \subseteq [a_1]$. Then it holds, that $a_1.\mathbf{0} \sim_{\mathfrak{F}} a_2.\mathbf{0}$. For relabelling, let $b_1 \notin [a_1]$ and define f such as $f(a_1) = b_1$, $f(a_2) = a_2$, and $f(b_1) = b_1$, whence f is not a pp-function. Then, it holds that $a_1.\mathbf{0}[f] \not\sim_{\mathfrak{F}} a_2.\mathbf{0}[f]$. For hiding, $a_1.\mathbf{0}/L \not\sim_{\mathfrak{F}} a_2.\mathbf{0}/L$ if $L = \{a_1\}$. Finally, dimmed bisimulation is not preserved by parallel composition if the action set is not singleton coherent with $\mathfrak{F}$. For instance, $a_1.\mathbf{0} \parallel_{\{a_1\}} a_1.\mathbf{0} \not\sim_{\mathfrak{F}} a_2.\mathbf{0} \parallel_{\{a_1\}} a_1.\mathbf{0}$.

Working with dimmed bisimilar candidates. The following fact establishes a clear relationship between a process P and the process obtained by inserting P in a context making use of a relabelling pp-function. In practice, it allows us to find a nontrivial (i.e., nonidentical) candidate bisimulating process.

Proposition 1. *Let $\mathfrak{F}$ be a partition and f be a pp-function for $\mathfrak{F}$. Then it holds that $P \sim_{\mathfrak{F}} P[f]$.*

Proof. The relation $\{(P', P'[f]) \mid f$ is a pp-function for $\mathfrak{F}\}$ is an $\mathfrak{F}$-dimmed bisimulation. □

Notice that, in general, the state space of P is as large as that of $P[f]$. However, in some cases, it may be easier to find a smaller process by studying how the pp-function f distributes over the process algebra operators.

Proposition 2. *Let f be a pp-function for $\mathfrak{F}$. It holds that*

i) $(P[g])[f] \sim_{\mathfrak{F}} P[f]$ for any function g that is partition preserving for $\mathfrak{F}$;
ii) $(P/L)[f] \sim_{\mathfrak{F}} (P[f])/L$ for L block coherent with $\mathfrak{F}$;
iii) $(P \parallel_L Q)[f] \sim_{\mathfrak{F}} P[f] \parallel_L Q[f]$ if L is singleton coherent with $\mathfrak{F}$.

Interestingly, dimmed bisimilarity behaves rather differently than bisimilarity with respect to distributivity. For instance, in *i)* the information of the pp-function g is lost, while bisimilarity uses function composition $f \circ g$; the analogous statement to *ii)* for bisimilarity requires a similar form of coherence for L, i.e. $a \in L$ iff $f(a) \in L$; finally, *iii)* uses a weaker assumption on f than bisimilarity, for which f must be injective, but has a syntactic restriction on the synchronisation set, unlike bisimilarity. In fact, singleton coherence and partition preservation coincide with requiring that f be injective on the synchronised actions.

Let us also remark that, in general, distributivity may not be preserved when the side conditions are not satisfied. For instance:

- $(a_1.\mathbf{0}[g])[f] \not\sim_{\mathfrak{F}} (a_1.\mathbf{0})[f]$ if $g(a_1) = b$, with $b \notin [a_1]$, and $f(a_1) = a_1$ and $f(b) = b$;
- $((a_1.\mathbf{0}+a_2.\mathbf{0})/\{a_1\})[f] \not\sim_{\mathfrak{F}} ((a_1.\mathbf{0}+a_2.\mathbf{0})[f])/\{a_1\}$ if $f(a_2) = a_1$ and $f(a_1) = a_1$, with $\{a_1, a_2\} \in \mathfrak{F}$;
- $(a_1.\mathbf{0} \parallel_{\{a_1,a_2\}} a_2.\mathbf{0})[f] \not\sim_{\mathfrak{F}} (a_1.\mathbf{0})[f] \parallel_{\{a_1,a_2\}} (a_2.\mathbf{0})[f]$, with the same f as above.

Different levels of dimming. So far, all our results have assumed a given fixed partition of the action set. Now we turn to considering what can be said for models with different levels of dimming, induced by different partitions. In general, for any two partitions, establishing dimmed bisimilarity with one partition does not allow us to infer dimmed bisimilarity for the other. For example, $a_1.\mathbf{0}+a_2.\mathbf{0}+b.\mathbf{0} \sim_{\mathfrak{F}_1} a_1.\mathbf{0}+a_2.\mathbf{0}$ for $\mathfrak{F}_1 = \{\{a_1, b\}, \{a_2\}\}$; but $a_1.\mathbf{0}+a_2.\mathbf{0}+b.\mathbf{0} \not\sim_{\mathfrak{F}_2} a_1.\mathbf{0} + a_2.\mathbf{0}$ if $\mathfrak{F}_2 = \{\{a_1, a_2\}, \{b\}\}$. However, it turns out that the usual partial order based on *partition refinement* captures the intuitive idea that one partition provides a higher level of abstraction than the other. Formally, given two partitions $\mathfrak{F}_1$ and $\mathfrak{F}_2$, one says that $\mathfrak{F}_1$ is a *refinement* of $\mathfrak{F}_2$, written as $\mathfrak{F}_1 \leq \mathfrak{F}_2$, if every element of $\mathfrak{F}_1$ is a subset of an element of $\mathfrak{F}_2$. In this case, it is also said that $\mathfrak{F}_1$ is *finer* than $\mathfrak{F}_2$ and that $\mathfrak{F}_2$ is *coarser* than $\mathfrak{F}_1$.

Proposition 3. *Let $\mathfrak{F}_1$, $\mathfrak{F}_2$ be two partitions of $\mathcal{A}$ such that $\mathfrak{F}_1 \leq \mathfrak{F}_2$ and let P and Q be two processes such that $P \sim_{\mathfrak{F}_1} Q$; then it holds that $P \sim_{\mathfrak{F}_2} Q$.*

Proof. $\mathfrak{F}_1 \leq \mathfrak{F}_2$ entails that $[a]_{\mathfrak{F}_1} \subseteq [a]_{\mathfrak{F}_2}$ for any $a \in \mathcal{A}$. Thus $\mathcal{R} \triangleq \{(P', Q') \mid P' \sim_{\mathfrak{F}_1} Q'\}$ contains (P, Q) and is an $\mathfrak{F}_2$-dimmed bisimulation. $\square$

Let us denote by $\mathfrak{F}_0$ the trivial singleton partition, for which it holds that $\mathfrak{F}_0 \leq \mathfrak{F}$ for any $\mathfrak{F}$. Since $\sim = \sim_{\mathfrak{F}_0}$, as a corollary of the above proposition we have the following.

Corollary 1. $\sim$ *implies* $\sim_{\mathfrak{F}}$ *for any partition $\mathfrak{F}$.*

3   Dimmed Bisimulation at Work

In this section we present how to exploit dimmed bisimulation in three examples of typical modelling patterns of distributed systems. In all cases, Corollary 1 will be used in order to find dimmed bisimilar processes that are much easier to analyse than the original ones. Given some process P, the idea is to first find some Q such that $P \sim_{\mathfrak{F}} Q$; then, using well-known algorithms [6], one reduces Q up to bisimulation into R, from which it holds that $P \sim_{\mathfrak{F}} R$. For instance, the relation $a_1.0 + a_2.0 \sim_{\mathfrak{F}} a_1.0$ can be interpreted as establishing first that $a_1.0 + a_2.0 \sim_{\mathfrak{F}} a_1.0 + a_1.0$, and then observing that $a_1.0 + a_1.0 \sim a_1.0$.

Our first example studies a concurrent system with fork/join synchronisation, which could be used for a high-level model of a MapReduce computing task [4].

Example 1 (A Fork/Join System). Let us consider $\mathcal{A} = \{fork, join\} \cup \{w_i \mid 1 \le i \le n\}$. Our model consists of a master process, denoted by F, which invokes (*fork*) n worker threads. Each worker thread, W_i, performs a distinct type of computation, modelled as a distinct action w_i. Once all threads finish their task, the master process collects the results (*join*) and repeats the cycle invoking the threads again. The model is as follows.

$$F \triangleq fork.join.F \qquad\qquad W_i \triangleq fork.w_i.join.W_i \qquad 1 \le i \le n.$$
$$M := F \parallel_L W_1 \parallel_L \cdots \parallel_L W_n, \qquad L = \{fork, join\}.$$

Model M has a state space size that grows as $2^n + 1$. In addition, it cannot be further minimised up to bisimulation. Dimmed bisimulation, on the other hand, may yield a simpler model which enjoys linear complexity of the state space size. To show this, let us take $\mathfrak{F} = \{\{fork\}, \{join\}, \{w_i \mid 1 \le i \le n\}\}$; that is, let us assume that the modeller wishes to abstract away from the identity of the worker thread that finishes works, but wants nevertheless to observe that *some thread* has completed. Then L is singleton coherent with $\mathfrak{F}$, and we have that $W_i \sim_{\mathfrak{F}} W_1$ for all $1 \le i \le n$. Thus, Theorem 3 yields that $M \sim_{\mathfrak{F}} \bar{M}$, with

$$\bar{M} := F \parallel_L \underbrace{W_1 \parallel_L \cdots \parallel_L W_1}_{n \text{ times}}.$$

Now, $\bar{M}$ still has $2^n + 1$ states, but *it can* be minimised up to bisimulation due to the symmetry among the worker threads, which are now copies of the same process. In this case, it is sufficient to just *count* how many worker threads are performing w_1. More precisely, let us consider the process $\bar{W}_0$ defined as

$$\bar{W}_0 \triangleq fork.\bar{W}_1, \qquad \bar{W}_i \triangleq w_1.\bar{W}_{i+1}, \quad \text{for } 1 \le i \le n, \qquad \bar{W}_{n+1} \triangleq join.\bar{W}_0.$$

Then it holds that $\underbrace{W_1 \parallel_L \cdots \parallel_L W_1}_{n \text{ times}} \sim \bar{W}_0$, from which, by Proposition 1, it follows that $M \sim_{\mathfrak{F}} F \parallel_L \bar{W}_0$. Hence, given a model with $2^n + 1$ states, we were able to construct a dimmed bisimilar one with only $n + 2$ states.

In the above example, nontrivial parts of the action set involve actions which are never synchronised. That is, dimmed bisimulation can be inferred *compositionally*, starting from the simplest concurrent processes, because they are composed together over synchronisation action sets that satisfy singleton coherence.

Table 1. State-space sizes for M and $\bar{M}$ in Example 2 (after minimisation of both processes up to bisimulation), denoted by $|M|$ and $|\bar{M}|$, respectively

n_1	n_2	m_1	m_2	k	$|M|$	$|\bar{M}|$	$|M|/|\bar{M}|$
1	1	1	1	1	48	18	2.67
2	2	2	2	1	243	50	5.06
1	1	1	1	10	1056	99	10.67
2	2	2	2	10	5346	275	19.44
1	1	1	1	100	82416	909	90.67
2	2	2	2	100	417213	2525	165.23
3	3	2	2	100	741744	3535	209.83

By contrast, the following examples can still be related to more compact dimmed bisimilar processes; however, dimmed bisimilarity *cannot* be inferred compositionally because the synchronisation sets are not singleton coherent. Thus a relation must be directly given for the whole composite process. In Section 4 we will, however, show how compositional reasoning on the same examples can be recovered at the cost of establishing only dimmed simulation.

Our second case study is a model of a producer/consumer system where the interaction is mediated by a buffer of finite capacity (see also [5]).

Example 2 (Multi-class Producer/Consumer). For simplicity, let us consider two classes of producers and two classes of users which share the same buffer. Let m_1 (resp., m_2) be the number of producers of the first (resp., second) class; let n_1 and n_2 be the number of consumers. Finally, let k be the buffer capacity.

A class-i producer, for $i = 1, 2$, is modelled by $P_i \triangleq prod_i.put_i.P_i$; here $prod_i$ models an independent action that describes the production of an item, whereas put_i is a synchronisation action to be performed with the buffer: It can be executed only when there is at least one place available in the buffer. In a similar fashion, the model of a class-i consumer is given by $C_i \triangleq get_i.cons_i.C_i$. In this case, get_i is a synchronisation action with the buffer, whereas the (independent) consumption of an item is modelled by action $cons_i$. Finally, a place in the buffer is $B \triangleq put_1.get_1.B + put_2.get_2.B$. Our overall model is

$$M := \big(P_1[m_1] \parallel_\emptyset P_2[m_2]\big) \parallel_{L_1} B[k] \parallel_{L_2} \big(C_1[n_1] \parallel_\emptyset C_2[n_2]\big)$$

where $L_1 = \{put_1, put_2\}$, $L_2 = \{get_1, get_2\}$, and $S[l]$ abbreviates $\underbrace{(S \parallel_\emptyset \cdots \parallel_\emptyset S)}_{l \text{ times}}$.

A reasonable abstraction is not to insist on keeping the two classes of producers (resp. consumers) distinct. Let us thus consider the action partition $\mathfrak{F} = \{L_1, L_2, \{prod_1, prod_2\}, \{cons_1, cons_2\}\}$. It is possible to show that

$$M \sim_{\mathfrak{F}} \bar{M}, \quad \text{with} \quad \bar{M} := P_1[m_1 + m_2] \parallel_{L_1} B_1[k] \parallel_{L_2} C_1[n_1 + n_2].$$

That is, producers and consumers of the second class are dimmed bisimilar to those of the first class; furthermore, a buffer place with two distinct actions is dimmed bisimilar to a buffer with actions of a single representative type.

Table 2. State-space sizes for M_n and $\bar{M}_n$ in Example 3 (after minimisation of both processes up to bisimulation), denoted by $|M_n|$ and $|\bar{M}_n|$, respectively

n	$|M_n|$	$|\bar{M}_n|$	$|M_n|/|\bar{M}_n|$
3	37	35	1.05
9	6913	715	9.67
12	73729	1820	40.51
15	737281	3876	190.22
16	1572865	4845	324.64
17	3342337	5985	558.45

As with Example 1, the state-space reduction achieved can be significant. Indeed, Table 1 compares the state-space sizes of M and $\bar{M}$ (after minimisation of both processes up to bisimulation) for different values of n_1, n_2, m_1, m_2, and k.[2]

Next we discuss a classical example in the process algebra literature.

Example 3 (Milner's Cyclers [1]). Milner's cyclers is a model of a scheduler that allows a set of processes P_1, P_2, ..., P_n to cyclically perform local computations in succession; that is, process P_i cannot start its computation until P_{i-1} has instructed it to do so. The model constants are given by:

$$P_i \triangleq \gamma_i.Q_i + \sum_{j=1, j \neq i}^{n} \gamma_j.P_i \qquad Q_i \triangleq \alpha_i.R_i \qquad R_i \triangleq \gamma_{s_i}.S_i + \beta_i.T_i$$

$$S_i \triangleq \beta_i.P_i + \sum_{j=1, j \neq i, s_i}^{n} \gamma_j.S_i \qquad T_i \triangleq \gamma_{s_i}.P_i \qquad 1 \leq i \leq n,$$

were s_i denotes the successor of process i, i.e., $s_i := i+1$ if $1 \leq i \leq n-1$, and $s_i := 1$ if $i = n$. Action γ_i represents the signal that process i is able to start the computation; its performance is modelled by action α_i; upon completion, the process may signal the start to its successor (hence, to achieve cyclic behaviour R_n will perform action γ_1), or notify the end of the local computation via β_i, in either order. Process S_i describes the state of a cycler which has already started the computation and let the next cycler go. In that state, it may witness some γ_j-action performed by other cyclers; in this case, the cycler ignores this signal and behaves as S_i again. The model is completed by a scheduler, Sc, that will enforce the start of P_1:

$$Sc \triangleq \gamma_1.Sc' \qquad\qquad Sc' \triangleq \sum_{i=1}^{n} \gamma_i.Sc'$$

---

[2] For the derivation of the state spaces of the examples presented in this paper, we used a software tool for a stochastic process algebra [7], which yields a doubly labelled transition system of which we ignored the rate information.

Thus, the overall system is described by $M_n := Sc \parallel_L P_1 \parallel_L \cdots \parallel_L P_n$ with $L = \{\gamma_1, \ldots, \gamma_n\}$.

Let us consider the abstraction whereby the modeller is not interested in the specific identity (i.e., the position in the cycle) of a process performing an action. That is, let us take $\mathfrak{F} = \{\{\alpha_1, \ldots, \alpha_n\}, \{\beta_1, \ldots, \beta_n\}, \{\gamma_1, \ldots, \gamma_n\}\}$ and processes

$$\bar{P} \triangleq \gamma_1.\bar{P} + \gamma_1.\bar{Q} \qquad \bar{Q} \triangleq \alpha_1.\bar{R} \qquad \bar{R} \triangleq \gamma_1.\bar{S} + \beta_1.\bar{T}$$

$$\bar{S} \triangleq \beta_1.\bar{P} + \gamma_1.\bar{S} \qquad \bar{T} \triangleq \gamma_1.\bar{P} \qquad \bar{Sc} \triangleq \gamma_1.\bar{Sc}$$

Let $\bar{M}_n := \bar{Sc} \parallel_L \overbrace{\bar{P} \parallel_L \cdots \parallel_L \bar{P}}^{n \text{ times}}$. Although with this abstraction we loose the circular order, we preserve the feature that local computations must be performed exclusively, i.e., in any state of the system at most one process can perform the corresponding α action. Then, similarly to Example 2, it can be shown that $M_n \sim_{\mathfrak{F}} \bar{M}_n$. Now, $\bar{M}_n$ can be reduced by exploiting the symmetry between the $\bar{P}$ components. The state-space size of Milner's model cannot be reduced up to strong bisimilarity, unlike $\bar{M}_n$ which has polynomial complexity growing as $\binom{n+4}{n}$. Table 2 compares the state spaces for different values of n.

4   Dimmed Simulation

As mentioned, single coherence may be an impediment to compositional reasoning for some interesting models such as Examples 2 and 3. Fortunately, compositional reasoning can still be applied if one uses dimmed *simulation* instead of dimmed bisimulation. In passing, we note that simulation was introduced by Milner much earlier than bisimulation [8], and it has since then been used for establishing interesting properties of systems. For example, in [9] it is argued that "in many cases, neither trace equivalence nor bisimilarity, but similarity is the appropriate abstraction for computer-aided verification."

Definition 6 (Dimmed Simulation). *Given a partition $\mathfrak{F}$, a binary relation $\mathcal{R}$ over $\mathcal{P}$ is an $\mathfrak{F}$-dimmed simulation iff whenever $(P, Q) \in \mathcal{R}$ and $a \in \mathcal{L}$:*

– if $P \xrightarrow{[a]} P'$ then $Q \xrightarrow{[a]} Q'$ and $(P', Q') \in \mathcal{R}$.

For two processes P and Q, we say that Q $\mathfrak{F}$-dimmedly simulates P, written $P \preceq_{\mathfrak{F}} Q$, if there is an $\mathfrak{F}$-dimmed simulation which relates them.

Similarly to dimmed bisimulation, using the trivial singleton partition we recover the standard notion of simulation between processes, hereafter denoted by $\preceq$. We state the next proposition without proof.

Proposition 4. *The following hold:*

i) $\preceq_{\mathfrak{F}}$ is a preorder;
ii) $P \sim_{\mathfrak{F}} Q \implies P \preceq_{\mathfrak{F}} Q \land Q \preceq_{\mathfrak{F}} P$.

Mutatis mutandis, the relationship between dimmed simulation and simulation is the same as the relationship between dimmed bisimulation and bisimulation as discussed in Section 2. That is, Theorem 2 carries over. Further, dimmed similarity is preserved by partition refinement (cf. Proposition 3), thus similarity implies dimmed similarity (cf. Corollary 1). Propositions 1 and 2 hold also for dimmed simulation by point ii) of Proposition 4.

The results of Theorem 3 would carry over as well. However, in the case of dimmed simulation it is possible to relax the assumption on singleton coherency, which is needed for the preservation of dimmed bisimulation by parallel composition. Here, instead, we will just require block coherency, as well as a form of *homogeneity* of the two operands of the parallel composition with respect to the synchronisation set. To formally define this notion, we denote by $Act(P)$ the set of all actions that can be performed by process P; for all $a \in \mathcal{L}$,

$$a \in Act(P) \text{ iff } \exists n \geq 1 : P \xrightarrow{a_1} P_1 \xrightarrow{a_2} \cdots \xrightarrow{a_n} P_n , \; a_n = a.$$

Definition 7 (Homogeneous Processes). *Let P and Q be two processes, $L \subseteq \mathcal{A}$, and $\mathfrak{F}$ a partition. P and Q are said to be* homogeneous *for L with respect to $\mathfrak{F}$ iff*

$$\left| \big(Act(P) \cup Act(Q)\big) \cap [a] \right| \leq 1, \qquad \text{for all } a \in L.$$

Essentially, we require that both P and Q be able to perform at most one of the synchronisation actions belonging to the same element of $\mathfrak{F}$. For instance, let $P \triangleq a_1.\mathbf{0} + a_2.\mathbf{0}$, $Q \triangleq a_1.Q + a_2.Q$, and $\{a_1, a_2\} \in \mathfrak{F}$. Then P and Q are not homogeneous for $L = \{a_1, a_2\}$ in $\mathfrak{F}$. Let us now consider their respectively dimmed similar processes, $\bar{P} \triangleq a_1.\mathbf{0}$ and $\bar{Q} \triangleq a_1.\bar{Q}$. In this case, instead, it holds that $\bar{P}$ and $\bar{Q}$ are homogeneous for L in $\mathfrak{F}$.

Theorem 4 (Compositionality for Dimmed Simulation). *Let P, Q be two processes such that $P \preceq_{\mathfrak{F}} Q$. Then it holds that:*

i) $a.P \preceq_{\mathfrak{F}} b.Q$ for all a, b such that $[a] = [b]$;
ii) $P + R \preceq_{\mathfrak{F}} Q + S$, for any R, S such that $R \preceq_{\mathfrak{F}} S$;
iii) $P[g] \preceq_{\mathfrak{F}} Q[g]$ for any g pp-function for $\mathfrak{F}$;
iv) $P/L \preceq_{\mathfrak{F}} Q/L$ if L is block coherent with $\mathfrak{F}$;
v) $P \parallel_L R \preceq_{\mathfrak{F}} Q \parallel_L S$, for R, S such that $R \preceq_{\mathfrak{F}} S$, if L is block coherent with $\mathfrak{F}$ and Q and S are homogeneous for L with respect to $\mathfrak{F}$.

The conditions required for the last point deserve more explanation. In general, dimmed simulation is not preserved if only L is block coherent with $\mathfrak{F}$ but Q and S *are not* homogeneous for L with $\mathfrak{F}$. To show this take, for instance, $P := a_1.\mathbf{0} + a_2.\mathbf{0}$, $R := P$, $Q := a_1.\mathbf{0}$, and $S := a_2.\mathbf{0}$, with $L = \{a_1, a_2\}$ and $L \in \mathfrak{F}$. Similarly, if the condition of homogeneity is satisfied but L is not block coherent with $\mathfrak{F}$, dimmed simulation may not be preserved either. For instance, take $P := a_1.\mathbf{0}$, $R := P$, $Q := a_2.\mathbf{0}$, $S := Q$, with $L = \{a_1\}$ and $\{a_1, a_2\} \in \mathfrak{F}$. Finally, we wish to point out the fact that homogeneity is to be satisfied only by the simulating process $Q \parallel_L S$. This is why we have preferred a statement in the form of item v) instead of the weaker "$P \preceq_{\mathfrak{F}} Q \implies P \parallel_L R \preceq_{\mathfrak{F}} Q \parallel_L R$ for Q, R homogeneous for L in $\mathfrak{F}$ and L block coherent with $\mathfrak{F}$." Stated in this way, homogeneity for Q and R would imply some form of homogeneity also in the simulated process $P \parallel_L R$. Indeed, R cannot enable two or more alternative synchronisation actions within the same part, thus significantly reducing the class of composite processes $P \parallel_L R$ that can be simulated. This is because, since L must be block coherent with $\mathfrak{F}$, it could in principle contain two actions a_1, a_2 belonging to the same part. But R can enable only one of them, say a_1. Therefore there would be $a_2 \in L$ which is never performed by one of the two operands. This, in turn, would cause a_2 never to be seen at all by $P \parallel_L R$.

Let us apply of dimmed simulation to our previous examples, showing that they can be simplified *compositionally* via $\preceq_{\mathfrak{F}}$ (but not with $\sim_{\mathfrak{F}}$).

Example 2 (continued). It possible to show that $P_2 \sim_{\mathfrak{F}} P_1$. Theorem 3 could be used to show that $P_1[m_1] \parallel_{\emptyset} P_2[m_2] \sim_{\mathfrak{F}} P_1[m_1 + m_2]$. Similarly, it holds that $B[k] \sim_{\mathfrak{F}} B_1[k]$, where $B_1 \triangleq put_1.get_1.B_1$. However, although $(P_1[m_1] \parallel_{\emptyset} P_2[m_2]) \parallel_{L_1} B[k] \sim_{\mathfrak{F}} P_1[m_1 + m_2] \parallel_{L_1} B_1[k]$ does hold, this fact *cannot* be inferred compositionally from Theorem 3 because L_1 is not singleton coherent with $\mathfrak{F}$. Thus, a simpler dimmed bisimilar process to M cannot be obtained by congruence. Instead, a dimmed similar process can indeed be constructed compositionally. Since $\sim_{\mathfrak{F}}$ implies $\preceq_{\mathfrak{F}}$, we have that $P_1[m_1] \parallel_{\emptyset} P_2[m_2] \preceq_{\mathfrak{F}} P_1[m_1 + m_2]$ and $B[k] \preceq_{\mathfrak{F}} B_1[k]$. Now, $P_1[m_1 + m_2]$ and $B_1[k]$ are homogenous for L_1 and L_1 is block coherent with the chosen $\mathfrak{F}$. Hence, item v) of Theorem 4 yields

$$\left(P_1[m_1] \parallel_{\emptyset} P_2[m_2] \right) \parallel_{L_1} B[k] \preceq_{\mathfrak{F}} P_1[m_1 + m_2] \parallel_{L_1} B_1[k].$$

Analogously, it holds that $C_1[n_1] \parallel_{\emptyset} C_2[n_2] \preceq_{\mathfrak{F}} C_1[n_1 + n_2]$. Again, we have that $P_1[m_1 + m_2] \parallel_{L_1} B_1[k]$ and $C_1[n_1 + n_2]$ are homogeneous for L_2 and L_2 is block coherent with $\mathfrak{F}$. Therefore we are able to conclude (compositionally) that

$$M \preceq_{\mathfrak{F}} \bar{M}, \quad \text{with} \quad \bar{M} := P_1[m_1 + m_2] \parallel_{L_1} B_1[k] \parallel_{L_2} C_1[n_1 + n_2].$$

Example 3 (continued). Similarly to the previous example, in Section 3 we discussed that

$$Sc \parallel_L P_1 \parallel_L P_2 \parallel_L P_3 \sim_{\mathfrak{F}} \bar{S}c \parallel_L \bar{P} \parallel_L \bar{P} \parallel_L \bar{P}.$$

However, compositional reasoning was not possible because L is not singleton coherent. Once again, L is instead block coherent for the action partition $\mathfrak{F}$ chosen in this case. Now, it holds that $Sc \preceq_{\mathfrak{F}} \bar{S}c$ and $P_i \preceq_{\mathfrak{F}} \bar{P}$. This implies that the relation $Sc \parallel_L P_1 \parallel_L P_2 \parallel_L P_3 \preceq_{\mathfrak{F}} \bar{S}c \parallel_L \bar{P} \parallel_L \bar{P} \parallel_L \bar{P}$ can indeed be proven by repeatedly using point v) of Theorem 4.

5   Related Work

At the very core of our dimmed relations is an abstraction operated at the level of the transition system generated from a process term, which lifts concrete actions a, b, ..., to elements $[a]$, $[b]$, ..., of a given partition of the action set. As such, this work is in the general context of abstract interpretation [10], where a model approximation can preserve properties of interest, for example expressed as logical formulae (e.g., [11–13]). This framework has also been considered in process algebra as early as in [14], where an approximation based on a preorder on the action set of CCS is studied. Although dimmed bisimilarity is a special case of the *extended bisimilarity* in [14], our approach is novel with respect to the use of such an abstraction. Indeed, [14] focuses on *partial specification*, i.e., replacing a process with another that can perform an *extended* action that can mimic any other concrete one. Partial specification is inherently non-symmetric since the identity of the concrete action is lost, differently from our dimmed relations where we preserve the information on its partition block. More recently, Galpin presented an analogous extension to bisimulation for process algebra for biochemical systems [15]. However, when used for state-space reduction purposes, her notion cannot be compared to our dimmed relations because [15] requires further conditions on the rate parameters in order to have congruence, and to obtain reduced models that can be related stochastically to the original ones.

The present paper is also related to [16], where the authors consider abstract interpretation to reduce infinite branching to finite branching of value-passing LOTOS based on trace semantics to enable model checking.

A large body of literature has also focused on action *refinement*, dual to the notion of action abstraction, where the main idea is that an atomic action is expanded into a process, e.g., a more detailed sequence of actions [17–19].

6 Conclusion

Dimmed behavioural relations permit trading-off between a detailed knowledge of the action types exhibited by a concrete model under study and a potentially more compact description arising from collapsing several actions together.

From a theoretical standpoint, the characterisation in terms of actions relabelling seems to do justice to this classic process algebra operator, which has been often neglected in recent developments of this field (see [20] for a discussion). The property of partition-preservation for a relabelling function presented in this paper is less restrictive than injectivity, as required for standard bisimulation results; yet it permits compositional reasoning for our dimmed relations.

From a more pragmatic standpoint, on a number of modelling patterns of practical interest, we showed that our dimmed relations can be effectively employed for a significantly more efficient (yet more abstract) analysis of heterogeneous systems, when heterogeneity is captured by the presence of analogous but formally distinct behaviours which are told apart by the use of distinct actions.

Future work will be concerned with a thorough investigation of a logical characterisation of dimmed bisimulation and simulation. We expect, however, that a straightforward adaptation of Hennessy-Milner logic should characterise the former; instead, an extension of simulation to *ready simulation* should be characterised by a suitably revised class of *denial formulas*, along the lines of [21].

Acknowledgement. Luca Aceto, Jane Hillston, and Davide Sangiorgi are gratefully acknowledged for very insightful comments on an earlier draft of this paper. Most of this work was done while G.I. and M.T. were at LMU Munich and R.d.N. was visiting; the authors would like to thank Martin Wirsing and his group for the excellent scientific and social atmosphere. This work was partially supported by the DFG project FEMPA and by the EU project QUANTICOL, 600708.

References

1. Milner, R.: A Calculus of Communication Systems. LNCS, vol. 92. Springer, Heidelberg (1980)
2. Bošnački, D., Donaldson, A.F., Leuschel, M., Massart, T.: Efficient Approximate Verification of Promela Models Via Symmetry Markers. In: Namjoshi, K.S., Yoneda, T., Higashino, T., Okamura, Y. (eds.) ATVA 2007. LNCS, vol. 4762, pp. 300–315. Springer, Heidelberg (2007)
3. Roscoe, A.: The Theory and Practice of Concurrency. Prentice Hall (1997)
4. Dean, J., Ghemawat, S.: MapReduce: simplified data processing on large clusters. Commun. ACM 51, 107–113 (2008)
5. Aldini, A., Bernardo, M., Corradini, F.: A Process Algebraic Approach to Software Architecture Design. Springer Publishing Company (2009)
6. Paige, R., Tarjan, R.: Three partition refinement algorithms. SIAM Journal on Computing 16, 973–989 (1987)
7. Tribastone, M., Duguid, A., Gilmore, S.: The PEPA Eclipse Plug-in. Performance Evaluation Review 36, 28–33 (2009)
8. Milner, R.: An algebraic definition of simulation between programs. In: IJCAI, pp. 481–489 (1971)
9. Henzinger, M.R., Henzinger, T.A., Kopke, P.W.: Computing simulations on finite and infinite graphs. In: FOCS, pp. 453–462. IEEE Computer Society (1995)
10. Cousot, P., Cousot, R.: Abstract interpretation: a unified lattice model for static analysis of programs by construction or approximation of fixpoints. In: POPL, pp. 238–252. ACM, New York (1977)
11. Clarke, E.M., Grumberg, O., Long, D.E.: Model checking and abstraction. ACM Trans. Program. Lang. Syst. 16, 1512–1542 (1994)
12. Dams, D., Gerth, R., Grumberg, O.: Abstract interpretation of reactive systems. ACM Trans. Program. Lang. Syst. 19, 253–291 (1997)
13. Fecher, H., Huth, M.: Model checking for action abstraction. In: Logozzo, F., Peled, D.A., Zuck, L.D. (eds.) VMCAI 2008. LNCS, vol. 4905, pp. 112–126. Springer, Heidelberg (2008)
14. Thomsen, B.: An extended bisimulation induced by a preorder on actions. M.Sc. thesis, Aalborg University (1987)
15. Galpin, V.: Equivalences for a biological process algebra. TCS 412, 6058–6082 (2011)
16. Fantechi, A., Gnesi, S., Latella, D.: Towards automatic temporal logic verification of value passing process algebra using abstract interpretation. In: Sassone, V., Montanari, U. (eds.) CONCUR 1996. LNCS, vol. 1119, pp. 563–578. Springer, Heidelberg (1996)

17. Glabbeek, R., Goltz, U.: Equivalence notions for concurrent systems and refinement of actions. In: Kreczmar, A., Mirkowska, G. (eds.) MFCS 1989. LNCS, vol. 379, pp. 237–248. Springer, Heidelberg (1989)
18. Aceto, L., Hennessy, M.: Towards action-refinement in process algebras. Information and Computation 103, 204–269 (1993)
19. Gorrieri, R., Rensink, A., Zamboni, M.A.: Action refinement. In: Handbook of Process Algebra, pp. 1047–1147. Elsevier (2000)
20. Sangiorgi, D.: Introduction to Bisimulation and Coinduction. Cambridge University Press (2011)
21. Bloom, B., Istrail, S., Meyer, A.R.: Bisimulation can't be traced. J. ACM 42, 232–268 (1995)

On the Step Branching Time Closure
of Free-Choice Petri Nets*

Stephan Mennicke, Jens-Wolfhard Schicke-Uffmann, and Ursula Goltz

TU Braunschweig, Germany
{mennicke,goltz}@ips.cs.tu-bs.de, drahflow@gmx.de

Abstract. Free-choice Petri nets constitute a non-trivial subclass of
Petri nets, excelling in simplicity as well as in analyzability. Extensions
of free-choice nets have been investigated and shown to be translatable
back to interleaving-equivalent free-choice nets. In this paper, we investigate extensions of free-choice Petri nets up to step branching time
equivalences. For extended free-choice nets, we achieve a generalization
of the equivalence result by showing that an existing construction respects weak step bisimulation equivalence. The known translation for
behavioral free-choice does not respect step branching time equivalences,
which turns out to be a property inherent to all transformation functions
from this net class into (extended) free-choice Petri nets. By analyzing
the critical structures, we find two subsets of behavioral free-choice nets
that are step branching time equivalent to free-choice nets. Finally, we
provide a discussion concerning the actual closure of free-choice Petri
nets up to step branching time equivalences.

1   Introduction

A well-known abstraction from distributed systems is the model of Petri nets,
arranging the aspects of causally dependent and concurrent actions in a neat
graphical representation. Petri nets stem from the ideas given in the PhD thesis
of C. A. Petri [12]. Petri forced system states to be structured by means of
local states, meeting the concepts of distributed systems, where components are
distributed over several locations. That actions of a single component depend
on local state information only is naturally captured by the firing rule of Petri
nets. In addition, Petri nets offer an intuitive notion of concurrent computation
by the *step firing rule*, a generalization of the firing rule allowing more than one
transition to fire in parallel (or unordered). Hence, system analysis of distributed
systems specified by Petri nets may actually be aware of uncertainties in the
order in which actions occur. Although decidable, many interesting properties
such as *liveness* or *boundedness* of Petri nets are hard in terms of computational
complexity [5].

The Petri net class of *free-choice Petri nets* (FC-nets) is non-trivial w. r. t.
expressive power, while efficient analysis algorithms are provided [4,5]. The core

---

* This work is supported by the DFG (German Research Foundation).

E. Ábrahám and C. Palamidessi (Eds.), FORTE 2014, LNCS 8461, pp. 232–248, 2014.

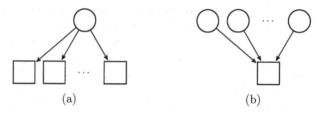

Fig. 1. The two net principles allowed in FC-nets

idea of *free-choice* is that if the system sometimes has a choice between multiple actions, it always has this choice. It is never the case that only some of these actions are available. Choices between actions may be resolved independently of the system state. The simplest implementation in terms of a Petri net class is provided by FC-nets, comprising only those nets in which conflicting transitions have one condition at most. The two basic subnets following from this restriction are depicted in Fig. 1.

The fundamental results leading to efficient analysis algorithms of FC-nets are achieved in the field of *structure theory* [1], where semantic properties shall follow from syntactical ones. For instance, the *Commoner/Hack Criterion* for FC-nets implies liveness, reducing the liveness problem to a semi-structural property, the basis for efficient analysis. For a comprehensive overview on structure theory, we refer to Best and Wimmel [3]. Esparza provides a survey on computational complexity of analysis algorithms for (free-choice) Petri nets [5].

E. Best states that most of the fundamental results from structure theory do not persist, when using a more expressive net class than FC-nets [1]. However, there are Petri net classes exhibiting the basic concept of free-choice to some degree, provoking the desire to relate them to the original FC-nets. *Extended free-choice nets* exhibit free-choice in that transitions sharing one precondition, share all preconditions. Once again, the set of transitions to choose from does not depend on the system state. In contrast to the aforementioned classes, free-choice may also be described by behavioral notions. A Petri net is a *behavioral free-choice net* if in any system state (reachable from the initial state), two conflicting transitions are either enabled or disabled. Hence, whenever the system has the choice of some of these transitions, it can choose between all of them, again independent of the system state. Best and Shields prove all these net classes equivalent by showing transformations from behavioral free-choice nets to extended free-choice nets and from extended free-choice nets to FC-nets to respect a form of interleaving simulation equivalence [2]. However, it is unclear whether the results from structure theory transfer from FC-nets to free-choice related net classes when considering step semantics of Petri net behavior. Such a transfer would help greatly in applying analysis algorithms for FC-nets to distributed systems where step semantics are relevant.

We analyze the class of FC-nets up to step branching time equivalences. The *Linear Time – Branching Time Spectrum* by van Glabbeek provides a lattice of equivalence notions for linear time behavior such as traces, and branching time behavior such as bisimulation [6]. We aim at covering the branching behavior of a system, i. e., we take the decision-making process into account. *Failure equivalence* is one of the weakest branching time equivalences, serving as a separator equivalence. If a transformation from one net class into another is impossible, we show that any transformation respecting at least failure equivalence must fail. On the contrary, we use bisimulation equivalence to prove that a particular transformation is correct. For Petri nets, there are two different approaches in interpreting the equivalence notions by van Glabbeek, (i) interleaving, i. e., one action at a time, and (ii) steps, i. e., independent actions may occur unordered or even in parallel. As distributed systems operate in an asynchronous fashion, the step interpretation is appropriate here. Transformations implementing a form of *busy waiting protocol* are not tolerated. Thus, we incorporate divergence-sensitiveness in the equivalences.

Extended free-choice nets remain equivalent to FC-nets under step branching time equivalences. We generalize the proof by Best and Shields to concurrency-aware equivalences. Unfortunately, the well-known construction from behavioral free-choice nets to extended free-choice nets does not respect step branching time behavior, in general. This property turns out to be inherent to all transformation functions from behavioral to (extended) FC-nets. We tackle this problem by analyzing two subsets of behavioral free-choice nets, both being step branching time equivalent to FC-nets. Finally, we discuss the step branching time closure of FC-nets by *symmetrically asynchronous Petri nets*, a net class occurring in the literature discussion of the difference between synchronous and asynchronous behavior [7]. We prove that FC-nets and symmetrically asynchronous Petri nets are equivalent up to step branching time, linking the closure of the class of FC-nets to the closure of symmetrically asynchronous Petri nets.

In Sect. 2, we introduce the basic notions for this paper. The relation between FC-nets and extended free-choice nets is established in Sect. 3 whereas Sect. 4 discusses relations to behavioral free choice net classes. Sect. 5 discusses symmetrically asynchronous Petri nets and their relation to FC-nets. By Sect. 6, we conclude the paper.

2   Basic Notions

In this section, we provide basic notions necessary to follow the employed theories and results concerning free-choice Petri nets. The state notion of Petri nets is based on multisets, which are sets possibly containing the same element multiple times.

Definition 1 (Multiset). *Let S, S' be non-empty sets. A multiset M over S ($M \in \mathbb{N}^S$) is a function $M : S \to \mathbb{N}$. For two multisets A and B over S, we define (i) $A + B$ to be the multiset over S with $(A+B)(s) = A(s) + B(s)$ for all $s \in S$, (ii) $A - B$ to be the multiset over S with $(A-B)(s) = \max\{0, A(s) - B(s)\}$ for all $s \in S$, (iii) $(A \cap B)$ likewise via $(A \cap B)(s) = \min\{A(s), B(s)\}$, and (iv) $A \leq B$ iff $A(s) \leq B(s)$ for all $s \in S$. The operations (i)–(iii) are generalized to multisets A over S and B over S', resulting in a multiset $(A\,op\,B)$ over $S \cup S'$.*

By $\mathbf{0}_S$ we denote the empty multiset over S. Let $S \supseteq A = \{a_1, \ldots, a_n\}$. Then A denotes the multiset with $A(a_i) = 1$ $(i = 1, \ldots, n)$.

2.1 Petri Nets

In this paper, we consider finite labeled place/transition nets, consisting of two disjoint finite sets P and T, the set of places and the set of transitions, a flow relation F, relating places and transitions, an initial marking, i.e., a multiset over the set of places, and a labeling function for transitions.

Definition 2 (Petri Net). *Let Act with $\tau \notin$ Act be a finite set of actions. A Petri net is a 5-tuple $N = (P, T, F, M_0, l)$ where P and T are disjoint finite sets, $F \subseteq (P \times T) \cup (T \times P)$, M_0 a multiset over P, and $l : T \to \text{Act} \cup \{\tau\}$ a function. If l is injective and $l(T) \subseteq \text{Act}$, then N is plain. If l is injective except for τ, i.e., $\forall t, t' \in T : t \neq t' \wedge l(t) = l(t') \Rightarrow l(t) = \tau$, then N is plain-labeled. For a node $n \in P \cup T$, by ${}^\bullet n := \{x \in P \cup T \,|\, (x, n) \in F\}$ we denote the preset of n and, analogously, by $n^\bullet := \{y \in P \cup T \,|\, (n, y) \in F\}$ the postset of n. The notions for pre- and postset canonically extend to (multi-)sets of nodes.*

We assume plain Petri nets as input models for the transformations we describe throughout the paper, because τ-transitions are reserved for implementation purposes. Transformed nets shall preserve the original net transitions but may make use of additional invisible ones. Thus, we expect transformed nets to be plain-labeled.

Petri nets offer a graphical notation, where places are drawn as circles, transitions as boxes, and the flow relation is represented by directed edges, called *arcs*. A marking M is graphically represented by drawing $M(p)$ black dots in the center of each place p.

Definition 3 (Firing Rule). *Let $N = (P, T, F, M_0, l)$ be a Petri net, $M, M' \in \mathbb{N}^P$, $G \in \mathbb{N}^T$, G non-empty and finite. G is called a step from M to M', denoted $M[G\rangle_N M'$ iff (i) G is enabled under M, denoted $M[G\rangle_N$, meaning that ${}^\bullet G \leq M$, and (ii) $M' = (M - {}^\bullet G) + G^\bullet$.*

If N is clear from the context, we write $M[G\rangle$ instead of $M[G\rangle_N$ (likewise for $M[G\rangle_N M'$). A marking M is *reachable* in $N = (P, T, F, M_0, l)$ if there are markings $M_1, \ldots, M_n$ and a sequence of steps $G_1, \ldots, G_n$ such that $M_{i-1}[G_i\rangle_N M_i$ $(0 < i \leq n)$ and $M = M_n$. The set of all reachable markings together with the step relation $[G\rangle_N$ induces the state graph of a Petri net, called *reachability graph*.

A common semantic requirement on Petri nets is that each place holds at most one token at each reachable marking. Such nets are called *1-safe nets*. For finite Petri nets, this property implies that the reachability graph of a net is finite, thus exhibiting the expressive power of finite automata. For the generality of our results, we use a more expressive class of Petri nets, but maintain an important aspect of safe Petri nets: Two conflicting transitions, i.e., two transitions sharing a place in their preset, may not fire concurrently, i.e., in the same step. This class of nets is called *structural conflict nets* and was first introduced by van Glabeek et al. [9].

Definition 4 (Reachable Markings, 1-safety, Structural Conflict Net).
*Let $N = (P, T, F, M_0, l)$ be a Petri net. The set $[N\rangle$ of reachable markings of N
is defined as the smallest set containing M_0, closed under $[G\rangle_N$, meaning that
if $M \in [N\rangle$ and $M[G\rangle M'$ for any G, then $M' \in [N\rangle$. N is 1-safe iff $M \in [N\rangle$
implies that for all $p \in P : M(p) \leq 1$. The concurrency relation $\smile \subseteq T^2$ is given
by $t \smile u \Leftrightarrow \exists M \in [N\rangle : M[\{t\} + \{u\}\rangle_N$. N is a structural conflict net iff for all
$t, u \in T$ with $t \smile u$ we have $^\bullet t \cap {}^\bullet u = \emptyset$.*

For the remainder of this paper, we assume all nets to be structural conflict nets.

2.2   Semantic Equivalences

The comparison between classes of Petri nets may be performed either by structural equivalences or equivalences capturing certain aspects of the behavior of
the net classes. We concentrate on behavioral equivalences in this paper. For a
comprehensive overview on comparative equivalence notions, see, e. g., [6].

As a basis for the equivalence notions, we introduce three transition relations
for visible and invisible steps, as well as a trace relation. To this end, we divide
the set of transitions of a Petri net N into a set of *observable transitions* $\mathcal{O}(N) :=$
$\{t \in T \mid l(t) \in \mathsf{Act}\}$ and a set of *invisble transitions* $\mathcal{U}(N) := \{t \in T \mid l(t) = \tau\}$.

Definition 5 (Labeled Transition Relation). *Let $N = (P, T, F, M_0, l)$ be
a Petri net over* Act. *(i)* $M \xrightarrow{A}_N M'$ *iff* $\exists G \in \mathbb{N}^{\mathcal{O}(N)} : M[G\rangle M' \wedge l(G) = A$,
(ii) $M \xrightarrow{\tau}_N M'$ *iff* $\exists t \in \mathcal{U}(N) : M[\{t\}\rangle M'$, *and (iii)* $M \xRightarrow{\sigma} M'$ *iff*
$\sigma = a_1 a_2 \dots a_n \in \mathsf{Act}^*$ *and*

$$M \xrightarrow{\tau}{}^*_N \xrightarrow{\{a_1\}}_N \xrightarrow{\tau}{}^*_N \xrightarrow{\{a_2\}}_N \xrightarrow{\tau}{}^*_N \dots \xrightarrow{\tau}{}^*_N \xrightarrow{\{a_n\}}_N \xrightarrow{\tau}{}^*_N M'$$

where $\xrightarrow{\tau}{}^*_N$ *denotes the reflexive and transitive closure of* $\xrightarrow{\tau}_N$.

Again, we drop the subscripted net identifier N when appropriate.

Based on the previously defined transition relation, we are now able to define
our step branching time equivalences. The first equivalence is *step failure equivalence* being the weakest step branching time equivalence we are aware of. It
comprises the trace behavior together with a set of steps, the net is not capable
of after a given trace.

Definition 6 (Step Failure Equivalence). *Let $N = (P, T, F, M_0, l)$ be a Petri
net labeled over* Act, $\sigma \in \mathsf{Act}^*$, *and* $X \subseteq \mathbb{N}^{\mathsf{Act}}$. (σ, X) *is a step failure pair of
N iff* $\exists M : M_0 \xRightarrow{\sigma} M \wedge M \not\xrightarrow{\tau} \wedge \forall A \in X : M \not\xrightarrow{A}$. $\mathcal{F}(N)$ *denotes the set of
all step failure pairs of N. Two Petri nets N_1, N_2 are step failure equivalent,
$N_1 \approx_\mathcal{F} N_2$ iff $\mathcal{F}(N_1) = \mathcal{F}(N_2)$.*

Note that we use a weak (abstracting from τs) version here, as the equivalences
we employ have to handle visible as well as invisible transitions. Furthermore,
step failure equivalence is divergence-sensitive in that any form of divergence
caused by τ-transitions results in exclusion of the corresponding trace from the
set of failure pairs. This is ensured by the requirement that from the reachable
marking M, no τ-transition may be enabled. We will use step failure equivalence

to obtain separation results. Towards the other end of the step branching time spectrum, there is *step bisimilarity*. Again, we employ the weak version enabling us to abstract from τ-transitions.

Definition 7 (Weak Step Bisimilarity). *Let* $N_i = (P_i, T_i, F_i, M_i, l_i)$ *(i =* $1, 2$*) be two Petri nets. A weak step bisimulation between* N_1 *and* N_2 *is a relation* $R \subseteq \mathbb{N}^{P_1} \times \mathbb{N}^{P_2}$ *such that*

1. $(M_1, M_2) \in R$ *and*
2. *if* $(M_1', M_2') \in R$, *then*
   (a) $M_1' \xrightarrow{\tau} M_1'' \Rightarrow \exists M_2'' \in \mathbb{N}^{P_2} : M_2' \xrightarrow{\tau}^* M_2'' \wedge (M_1'', M_2'') \in R$,
   (b) $M_1' \xrightarrow{A} M_1'' \Rightarrow \exists M_2'' \in \mathbb{N}^{P_2} : M_2' \xrightarrow{\tau}^* \xrightarrow{A} \xrightarrow{\tau}^* M_2'' \wedge (M_1'', M_2'') \in R$,
   (c) $M_2' \xrightarrow{\tau} M_2'' \Rightarrow \exists M_1'' \in \mathbb{N}^{P_1} : M_1' \xrightarrow{\tau}^* M_1'' \wedge (M_1'', M_2'') \in R$,
   (d) $M_2' \xrightarrow{A} M_2'' \Rightarrow \exists M_1'' \in \mathbb{N}^{P_1} : M_1' \xrightarrow{\tau}^* \xrightarrow{A} \xrightarrow{\tau}^* M_1'' \wedge (M_1'', M_2'') \in R$.

N_1 *and* N_2 *are* weak step bisimilar, $N_1 \approx_{\mathcal{B}} N_2$ *iff there exists a weak step bisimulation between* N_1 *and* N_2.

If two nets are weak step bisimilar, then they are step failure equivalent. The converse does not hold, in general. Hence, step failure equivalence is coarser than weak step bisimulation thus $N_1 \not\approx_{\mathcal{F}} N_2$ implies $N_1 \not\approx_{\mathcal{B}} N_2$. Therefore, we use step failure equivalence for separation results.

3   Free-Choice and Extended Free-Choice

Free-choice Petri nets (FC-nets) are generalizations of *S-nets* and *T-nets*, both representing net classes providing efficient analysis algorithms, e. g., for liveness or boundedness [1]. FC-nets allow choices between transitions, but only if there is at most one place in the preset of the conflicting transitions (cf. Fig. 1 (a)), and synchronization of places, but only in the way that there is at most one transition in the postset of the synchronized places (cf. Fig. 1 (b)). The conflict pattern refers to restrictions imposed on S-nets, while the synchronization pattern follows restrictions as imposed on T-nets. Hence, every time a conflict occurs, it occurs between the same set of transitions and it is not influenced by the rest of the net.

Definition 8 (Free-Choice Petri Net). *A Petri net* $N = (P, T, F, M_0, l)$ *is a free-choice Petri net (FC-net) iff*
$$\forall p \in P \; \forall t \in T : (p, t) \in F \Rightarrow p^{\bullet} = \{t\} \vee {}^{\bullet}t = \{p\}.$$

FC-nets come with a natural notion of distributed component, called *free-choice cluster*. Given an FC-net $N = (P, T, F, M_0, l)$, the free-choice cluster of a transition $t \in T$ is the *conflict cluster* of t, i.e., $[t] = ({}^{\bullet}t)^{\bullet}$. The set of all conflict clusters and thus free-choice clusters of N, denoted by $\mathcal{C}(N)$, imposes a partitioning on the set of transitions if N is an FC-net. Thus, a free-choice cluster may be seen as a component of a system N. Note that each component has at most one role, either to resolve a conflict between actions or to synchronize

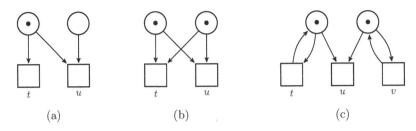

Fig. 2. Three nets that are not FC-nets

parallel components. Each component $C \in \mathcal{C}(N)$ is equipped with interfaces $^\bullet C$ (the set of input places) and $C^\bullet$ (the set of output places). If some of the places of a component belong to the initial marking, these places are initially marked in the component. Hence, FC-nets are expressive enough to describe non-trivial distributed behavior by a combination of locally restricted choices and synchronization. As already motivated, FC-nets excel in a wide range of applications, mostly due to their structural properties implying semantic properties. For a comprehensive overview, we refer to [1,3]. Unfortunately, not every Petri net is an FC-net (cf. Fig. 2). However, if a Petri net is behavioral equivalent to an FC-net, analysis results on the transformed net enables us to (partially) reason about semantic properties of the original net.

The Petri net depicted in Fig. 2 (b) belongs to the class of *extended free-choice nets* (EFC-nets). EFC-nets are characterized by the property that if two transitions share any place in their preset, then they share all preplaces. Thus, these nets exhibit the free-choice property to a certain extent, as conflicting transitions always depend on the same set of places.

Definition 9 (Extended Free-Choice Net). *A Petri net* $N = (P, T, F, M_0, l)$ *is an* extended free-choice net *iff* $\forall t_1, t_2 \in T : {}^\bullet t_1 \cap {}^\bullet t_2 \neq \emptyset \Rightarrow {}^\bullet t_1 = {}^\bullet t_2$.

Furthermore, we observe that the clustering described for FC-net transitions also works in EFC-nets, i.e., $\mathcal{C}(N)$ of an EFC-net N is a partition on the set of transitions of N. Therefore, we call a conflict cluster of an EFC-net *EFC-cluster*. Note that every FC-net is also an EFC-net, but the converse does not hold in general. However, Best and Shields proved that there is a behavioral correspondence by showing that EFC-nets may be transformed into FC-nets, respecting a form of *interleaving simulation* [2].

The core idea of that transformation is to split an EFC-cluster $C \in \mathcal{C}(N)$ into two operational parts, (i) a synchronization of all input places of C and (ii) a choice between all transitions in C. For (i), an unobservable transition is added, consuming one token from each input place of C and producing a token to an additional place p_C. In part (ii), all the transitions in C consume from p_C. An example transformation, namely from the EFC-net in Fig. 2 (b) into the corresponding FC-net is depicted in Fig. 3 (a). Formally, the transformation is defined as follows [2,1].

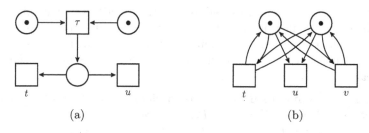

(a)   (b)

Fig. 3. FC-net and EFC-net Constructions

Definition 10 (*FC(N)*). *Let* $N = (P, T, F, M_0, l)$ *be a Petri net. We define* $FC(N) := (P', T', F', M_0, l')$ *where*

$$P' = P \cup \{p_{[u]} \mid [u] \in \mathcal{C}(N)\}$$
$$T' = T \cup \{\tau_{[u]} \mid [u] \in \mathcal{C}(N)\}$$
$$F' = (F \cap (T \times P)) \cup \{(\tau_{[u]}, p_{[u]}) \mid [u] \in \mathcal{C}(N)\} \cup$$
$$\{(p, \tau_{[u]}) \mid [u] \in \mathcal{C}(N), p \in {}^{\bullet}[u]\} \cup \{(p_{[t]}, t) \mid t \in T\}$$
$$l' = l \cup \{(\tau_{[u]}, \tau) \mid [u] \in \mathcal{C}(N)\}.$$

By Best and Shields, $FC(N)$ is an FC-net simulating N if N is an EFC-net [2].

Let us now determine if EFC-nets remain equivalent to FC-nets when considering concurrency-aware equivalences. As we employ structural conflict nets, two transitions may only fire in a step if they do not share any preplace. Furthermore, the transformation defined above preserves conflict clusters in the sense that $\mathcal{C}(N) \subseteq \mathcal{C}(FC(N))$. Hence, if two transitions belonged to a step of N, they are still part of a step of $FC(N)$. Formally, the transformation function FC enjoys the property that an EFC-net N and $FC(N)$ are weak step bisimilar. The weak version of the equivalence is necessary, as FC introduces τ-transitions that do not belong to the original plain EFC-net.

Theorem 1. *Let N be a plain EFC-net. Then $N \approx_B FC(N)$.*

The proof of this theorem relies on the observation that the markings of N are also markings of $FC(N)$. The only difference is that the construction introduces some new places, one per EFC-cluster, that only hold a token if their preceding τ-transition has fired. $R = \{(M_1, M_2) \mid M_1 \in [N\rangle \wedge M_1 \xrightarrow{\tau}{}^{*}_{FC(N)} M_2\}$ is a weak step bisimulation relation between N and $FC(N)$.

Thus, EFC-nets remain equivalent to FC-nets under concurrency-aware equivalences, even by using the well-known transformation. Intuitively, this paves the way for FC-net-based analysis for distributed systems being specified by EFC-nets. In the following section, we try to repeat this result for *behavioral free-choice nets* (BFC-nets). Unfortunately, not all BFC-nets exhibit (step) behavior that may be expressed by an equivalent FC-net.

4   Behavioral Free-Choice

Free-choice may be explored by a behavioral notion. The net in Fig. 2 (c) is neither an FC-net nor an EFC-net. However, in every reachable marking, conflicting transitions t and u as well as u and v are either enabled or disabled. Although not all conflicting transitions depend on exactly the same resources, the initial conflict situation remains invariant. Once again, this meets the intuition of free-choice. This observation is the basis for *behavioral free-choice nets* (BFC-nets).

Definition 11 (Behavioral Free-Choice Net). *A* behavioral free-choice net *(BFC-net) is a Petri net* $N = (P, T, F, M_0, l)$ *where*
$$\forall t, u \in T : {}^\bullet t \cap {}^\bullet u \neq \emptyset \Rightarrow \forall M \in [N\rangle : {}^\bullet t \leq M \Leftrightarrow {}^\bullet u \leq M.$$

Every EFC-net is a BFC-net and thus every FC-net is also a BFC-net. However, for BFC-nets, the conflict clustering does not provide the property that $\mathcal{C}(N)$ partitions the set of transitions, e. g., the net depicted in Fig. 2 (c) has two overlapping conflict clusters, namely $\{t, u\}$ and $\{u, v\}$. By merging those overlapping clusters, we reach a partitioning of the set of transitions, called BFC-clusters where $\langle u \rangle$ denotes the BFC-cluster of u. Thus, transitions in a BFC-cluster do not necessarily share all of their preplaces, e. g., t and v in Fig. 2 (c) belong to the same BFC-cluster but ${}^\bullet t \cap {}^\bullet v = \emptyset$. However, the BFC-net property ensures that, e. g., in Fig. 2 (c), both t and v are enabled as long as u does not fire. In Fig. 4 (a), another BFC-net is depicted. As before, either all transitions of the BFC-cluster $\langle t \rangle$ are enabled or disabled. Thus, without changing the (step) behavior of the BFC-net, we may make each transition t dependent on all places in ${}^\bullet \langle t \rangle$. In order to preserve the markings of the original net, each additional arc is complemented by an arc in the opposite direction. For the net in Fig. 4 (a) we get the EFC-net depicted in Fig. 4 (b). The same implementation idea applied to the BFC-net in Fig. 2 (c) yields the EFC-net depicted in Fig. 3 (b). For BFC-nets, the result of this construction is always an EFC-net that is interleaving branching time equivalent to the original net [1]. Thus, by performing the FC-net construction described in Sect. 3, we get an FC-net that is at least interleaving branching time equivalent to the original BFC-net.

Definition 12 ($EFC(N)$). *Let* $N = (P, T, F, M_0, l)$ *be a Petri net. We define* $EFC(N) := (P, T, F', M_0, l)$ *where*
$$F' := F \cup \{(p, u), (u, p) \mid u \in T, p \in {}^\bullet \langle u \rangle, (p, u) \notin F\}.$$

In Fig. 4, we depicted all intermediate translation steps finally yielding the FC-net depicted in Fig. 4 (c), which is indeed weak step bisimilar to the BFC-net in Fig. 4 (a). Unfortunately, the EFC-net depicted in Fig. 3 (b) is not weak step bisimilar to the net in Fig. 2 (c), as the formerly concurrent transitions t and v are now conflicting. Hence, the proposed construction from the literature does not respect weak step bisimilarity.

In general, there is no transformation from the net in Fig. 2 (c) into a step branching time equivalent (E)FC-net. This is due to the pattern, called *pure M*, the net contains, which has been shown to be stable under step branching time equivalences by van Glabbeek et al. [7]. A pure M is characterized by three distinct transitions, t, u, v with ${}^\bullet t \cap {}^\bullet u \neq \emptyset$, ${}^\bullet u \cap {}^\bullet v \neq \emptyset$, and ${}^\bullet t \cap {}^\bullet v = \emptyset$ such that there is a reachable marking under which all three transitions are enabled. Thus, transitions t and v may fire concurrently while the synchronizing transition u

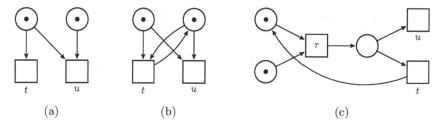

Fig. 4. From BFC-nets to FC-nets

is in conflict with both. In particular, van Glabbeek et al. prove that if a Petri net contains a *pure* M, then every step failure equivalent [8] and thus every *step ready equivalent* [7] Petri net contains a pure M. Hence, every step branching time equivalent Petri net containing the net depicted in Fig. 2 (c) is condemned to contain the same pattern again.

Fortunately, the containment of pure Ms is no necessary condition for a Petri net to be a BFC-net, e.g., the BFC-net in Fig. 4 (a) does not even have three transitions. Therefore, we devise two subclasses of BFC-nets that do not have pure Ms in the following. First, we restrict BFC-nets to those nets that do not have self-loops. Second, we look at the intersection of BFC-nets and so called asymmetric choice nets in which self-loops are allowed. See again [1] for an overview on asymmetric choice nets. Both subclasses turn out to be step branching time equivalent to FC-nets.

4.1   BFC-nets without Self-Loops

In this section, we briefly discuss pure Ms in BFC-nets without self-loops. A self-loop is constituted by a transition t and a place p such that t consumes from and produces to p.

Definition 13 (Self-Loop). *Let $N = (P, T, F, M_0, l)$ be a Petri net. N has a self-loop iff $\exists p \in P : {}^\bullet p \cap p^\bullet \neq \emptyset$.*

If we now consider BFC-nets without any self-loops, we need to reassess our argumentation above on why BFC-nets are not equivalent to FC-nets. Without a self-loop, a pure M is not expressible, because if t or v fired without returning the token to their preplaces they share with u, the overall net would not obey the BFC-net property. Indeed, the construction known from the literature works for BFC-nets without self-loops, proving that BFC-nets without self-loops are step-branching equivalent to (E)FC-nets.

Theorem 2. *Let N be a plain BFC-net without self-loops. Then $EFC(N) \approx_B N$.*

In order to prove that the construction does not change the step behavior of N, it is sufficient to show that $t \smile u$ implies $\langle t \rangle \neq \langle u \rangle$ for all $t, u \in T$. Suppose, there are transitions contradicting this requirement. If there is a reachable marking

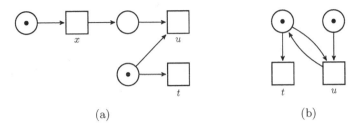

Fig. 5. Two AC-nets having a Partially and Fully Reachable N

enabling t and u, then after firing t, u is enabled while t is not, contradicting that N is a BFC-net. Therefore, the EFC-net construction does not restrict the set of enabled steps from reachable markings. The remaining proof follows the same principles as the proof of Theorem 3, provided in the appendix. Next, we discuss a subclass that allows self-loops in BFC-nets but restricts the class structurally to not contain Ms.

4.2   BFC-nets and Asymmetric Choice

The condition for a Petri net to be an EFC-net may be reformulated in terms of places, yielding exactly the same net class as by Def. 9 [1]. In this definition, a Petri net is an EFC-net iff for all places p and q it holds that $p^\bullet \cap q^\bullet \neq \emptyset$ implies that $p^\bullet = q^\bullet$. In an *asymmetric choice net* (AC-net), this restriction is weakened to an alternative between the two set-inclusions between $p^\bullet$ and $q^\bullet$. Before discussing the combination of BFC-nets and AC-nets, we clarify the relation between AC-nets and FC-nets.

Definition 14 (Asymmetric Choice Net). *A Petri net* $N = (P, T, F, M_0, l)$ *is an* asymmetric choice net *(AC-net) iff*
$$\forall p, q \in P : p^\bullet \cap q^\bullet \neq \emptyset \Rightarrow p^\bullet \subseteq q^\bullet \vee q^\bullet \subseteq p^\bullet.$$

In case $p^\bullet \subseteq q^\bullet$ but $q^\bullet \not\subseteq p^\bullet$, all transitions in $q^\bullet$ are enabled if at least p and q hold tokens. This restriction hardly enforces the concepts of free-choice, as it does not require conflicting transitions to be chosen freely. However, the Petri net depicted in Fig. 2 (a) shows an example AC-net, which may be simulated by an FC-net. We discuss this transformation in Sect. 5. Considering the same net in a larger context, it is unclear whether a token eventually occurs on the second input place of u. The AC-net in Fig. 5 (a) shows an example context. The choice between transitions t and u does only occur if transition x fires in advance. In an adversary scenario, transition x might only fire if transition t has fired, which makes u unable to fire at all. In the literature, such a situation is called *(asymmetric) confusion* [13], which may not be simulated by any FC-net, as choices may never occur conditionally. In general, we characterize such conditional choices by the notion of *partially and fully reachable* Ns. Here, the existence of a subnet like the one in Fig. 2 (a) is expected and two distinct markings, one under which t is enabled and one enabling t and u.

Definition 15 (Partially and Fully Reachable N). *Let* $N = (P, T, F, M_0, l)$ *be a Petri net.* $(t, u) \in T^2$ *is a* partially and fully reachable N *iff* ${}^\bullet t \cap {}^\bullet u \neq \emptyset$, $|{}^\bullet u| > 1$, *and* $\exists M_t, M \in [N\rangle : {}^\bullet t \leq M_t \wedge {}^\bullet u \nleq M_t \wedge {}^\bullet \{t, u\} \leq M$.

Note that this notion does not only characterize asymmetric confusion patterns, but also nets as the one depicted in Fig. 5 (b). Just as in the case of pure Ms, partially and fully reachable Ns are stable w.r.t. step branching time equivalences.

Proposition 1. *Let* N *be a plain Petri net with a partially and fully reachable* N. *Then for all plain-labeled Petri nets* N' *with* $N \approx_\mathcal{F} N'$ *it holds that* N' *has a partially and fully reachable* N.

Proof. Let $N = (P, T, F, M_0, l)$ and (t, u) a partially and fully reachable N of N, i.e., there exist reachable markings M_t and M such that M_t enables t, but not u and M enables both. Thus, there is a σ such that $M_0 \overset{\sigma}{\Longrightarrow} M_t$ and since N is plain, and hence deterministic [14], (1) $(\sigma, X) \in \mathcal{F}(N)$ implies that $\{l(t)\} \notin X$ and there exists (σ, X) with $\{l(u)\} \in X$. From the existence of M we deduce that (2) there is a σ' such that $M_0 \overset{\sigma'}{\Longrightarrow} M$ and (3) $(\sigma', X) \in \mathcal{F}(N)$ implies that $\{l(t)\} \notin X \wedge \{l(u)\} \notin X$. As N is a structural conflict net, (4) there exists $(\sigma', X) \in \mathcal{F}(N)$ such that $\{l(t), l(u)\} \in X$.

Let $N' = (P', T', F', M'_0, l')$ be a Petri net with $N \approx_\mathcal{F} N'$, i.e., $\mathcal{F}(N) = \mathcal{F}(N')$. Therefore, $\mathcal{F}(N')$ obeys (1)–(4). Hence, there exist transitions $t', u' \in T'$ with $l'(t') = l(t)$ and $l'(u') = l(u)$. By (3) and (4), we have that ${}^\bullet t' \cap {}^\bullet u' \neq \emptyset$. By (1), we get that there is a place $p \in {}^\bullet u' \setminus {}^\bullet t'$ thus $|{}^\bullet u'| > 1$. By (1), there is a marking $M_{t'}$ with $M'_0 \overset{\sigma}{\Longrightarrow} M_{t'}$ and ${}^\bullet t' \leq M_{t'} \wedge {}^\bullet u' \nleq M_{t'}$, as otherwise there would be a failure pair $(\sigma, X) \in \mathcal{F}(N')$ with $\{l'(t')\} \in X$. By (2), there is a marking M' with $M'_0 \overset{\sigma'}{\Longrightarrow} M'$ and by (3) ${}^\bullet t' \leq M' \wedge {}^\bullet u' \leq M'$. By (4) $\{t', u'\}$ is no step from M'. Summarizing, N' has a partially and fully reachable N. □

Corollary 1. *There is no transformation function from plain AC-nets to plain-labeled step branching time equivalent FC-nets.*

However, the BFC-net in Fig. 2 (c) does not respect the restrictions as imposed on AC-nets. In general, such structures may not occur in an AC-net and conversely, partially and fully reachable Ns are ruled out in BFC-nets, which paves the way for the following theorem.

Theorem 3. *Let* N *be a plain BFC-net and an AC-net. Then* $EFC(N) \approx_B N$.

Note that Best and Shields already prove that EFC yields an EFC-net for BFC-nets [2]. Concerning the proof of Theorem 3, we benefit from the construction given in Def. 12, adding no more places to the original net. Thus, every marking of N is also a marking of $EFC(N)$. Furthermore, the construction does not change the enabledness condition for transitions, and it does not even increase or decrease formerly existing steps. Thus, the desired weak step bisimulation between N and $EFC(N)$ is $R = \{(M, M) \mid M \in [N\rangle\}$. The proof that R is a weak step bisimulation is provided in the appendix.

5   Symmetric Asynchrony

Throughout the last section, we have seen two subclasses of BFC-nets that are step branching time equivalent to FC-nets. However, BFC-nets do not represent a reasonable basis for the step branching time closure of FC-nets, i. e., there are non-BFC-nets being behaviorally equivalent to FC-nets, e. g., the net depicted in Fig. 2 (a). In this section, we analyze a Petri net class that appears in the context of investigations on synchronous and asynchronous interaction. R. van Glabbeek et al. introduced this class that does not distinguish simultaneous and delayed token removals from more than one place on a behavioral level [7]. Each place of a Petri net is assumed to reside on an individual location. If a transition has only one preplace, it may be assigned to the same location. Two transitions reside on a shared location if they share a preplace that is allowed on the same location. Thus, whenever a transition synchronizes more than one place, i. e., more than one location, it resides on a different location than any of its preplaces. Interaction delays between locations are simulated by an additional τ-transition and place on each arc crossing location borders, an *asynchronous implementation*. A Petri net is symmetrically asynchronous iff it is step failure equivalent to its asynchronous implementation.

Definition 16 (Symmetric Asynchrony [7]). *Let $\mathcal{L}$ be a set of locations and $N = (P, T, F, M_0, l)$ be a Petri net. A (distribution) function $\lambda : (P \cup T) \to \mathcal{L}$ is a symmetric distribution on N when*

$\lambda(p) = \lambda(q)$ *for $p, q \in P$ only if $p = q$,*

$\lambda(t) = \lambda(p)$ *for $t \in T, p \in P$ only if $^\bullet t = \{p\}$ and*

$\lambda(t) = \lambda(u)$ *for $t, u \in T$ only if $t = u$ or $\exists p \in P : \lambda(t) = \lambda(p) = \lambda(u)$,*

$\mathcal{I}_\lambda(N) := (P \cup P_\tau, T \cup T_\tau, F', M_0, l)$ *is the asynchronous implementation (w. r. t. λ) of N iff*

$$P_\tau := \{s_t \mid t \in T, s \in {}^\bullet t, \lambda(s) \neq \lambda(t)\},$$
$$T_\tau := \{t_s \mid t \in T, s \in {}^\bullet t, \lambda(s) \neq \lambda(t)\},$$
$$F' := \{(t, s) \mid t \in T, s \in t^\bullet\} \cup \{(s, t) \mid s \in {}^\bullet t, \lambda(s) = \lambda(t)\} \cup$$
$$\{(s, t_s), (t_s, s_t), (s_t, t) \mid t \in T, s \in {}^\bullet t, \lambda(s) \neq \lambda(t)\},$$
$$l'(t) := \begin{cases} l(t) & \text{if } t \in T \\ \tau & \text{otherwise.} \end{cases}$$

N is symmetrically asynchronous iff there exists a symmetric distribution λ on N such that $N \approx_{\mathcal{F}} \mathcal{I}_\lambda(N)$.

R. van Glabbeek et al. prove that a Petri net is symmetrically asynchronous iff there is a symmetric distribution λ and the Petri net has no *distributed conflict* w. r. t. λ [7]. A Petri net is said to have a distributed conflict w. r. t. λ iff there are two distinct transitions t, u with $^\bullet t \cap {}^\bullet u \neq \emptyset$, $\lambda(t) \neq \lambda(u)$, and there is a reachable marking enabling t. Another characterization of symmetrically asynchronous Petri nets is given in terms of a Petri net pattern, called *partially reachable N* [7], which follows the definition given in Def. 15, leaving out the existence of the marking M (full reachability). All the nets depicted in Fig. 2 have partially reachable Ns, obstructing symmetric asynchrony.

R. van Glabbeek et al. conjecture that there is a strong relation between symmetrically asynchronous nets and FC-nets [8], which we finally prove in the following. Given a symmetrically asynchronous Petri net $N = (P, T, F, M_0, l)$, i. e., there is a symmetrical distribution $\lambda : P \cup T \to \mathcal{L}$ such that N has no distributed conflict w. r. t. λ. We transform N under λ by $FC_{sym}(N) = (P, \hat{T}, \hat{F}, M_0, l)$ where

- $\hat{T} := \{t \in T \mid \forall p \in {}^\bullet t : \forall u \in p^\bullet : \lambda(p) = \lambda(u) \vee u = t\}$ and
- $\hat{F} := F \cap ((P \times \hat{T}) \cup (\hat{T} \times P))$.

This transformation yields an FC-net by removing transitions obstructing the FC-net properties.

Lemma 1. *Let N be a symmetrically asynchronous Petri net. Then, $FC_{sym}(N)$ is an FC-net.*

Proof. Let $N = (P, T, F, M_0, l)$ be a symmetrically asynchronous Petri net and λ the required symmetrical distribution. N has no distributed conflict w. r. t. λ [7], i. e., $\forall t, u \in T \ \forall p \in {}^\bullet t \cap {}^\bullet u : t = u \vee \lambda(p) = \lambda(u) \vee \nexists M \in [N\rangle : {}^\bullet t \leq M$. Let $\hat{N} = FC_{sym}(N)$ with set of transitions $\hat{T}$ and arc relation $\hat{F}$. We show that for all $p \in P$ and all $t \in \hat{T}$, $(p, t) \in \hat{F}$ implies ${}^\bullet t = \{p\}$ or $p^\bullet = \{t\}$. Assume there is a place p and a transition t with $(p, t) \in \hat{F}$, but ${}^\bullet t \neq \{p\}$ and $p^\bullet \neq \{t\}$. Hence, there exists a place $q \neq p$ with $q \in {}^\bullet t$ and a transition $u \in T$ with $t \neq u$ and $u \in p^\bullet$. As λ is symmetrical, p is not co-located with q and t, q is not co-located with u and t, and hence, t is not co-located with u. There are two cases to consider, (1) $\lambda(p) = \lambda(u)$ and (2) $\lambda(p) \neq \lambda(u)$. If (1), then $u \notin \hat{T}$, because by definition of $\hat{T}$, for all transitions in $p^\bullet$, it must hold that they are co-located with p or they are equal to u. But $u \neq t$, $t \in p^\bullet$ and $\lambda(p) \neq \lambda(t)$. If (2), then $u, t \notin \hat{T}$ by definition of $\hat{T}$. In detail, $t \notin \hat{T}$, as there is a transition $u \in p^\bullet$ with $\lambda(p) \neq \lambda(u)$ (by assumption (2)). $u \notin \hat{T}$, as there is a transition, $t \in p^\bullet$, with $\lambda(t) \neq \lambda(p)$ (by λ being symmetrical). Hence, either $\{t\} = p^\bullet$ or t does not even exist. Thus, $FC_{sym}(N)$ is an FC-net.   □

Fortunately, none of the removed transitions takes part in actual behavior, as all of them are dead transitions, i. e., there is no reachable marking enabling them.

Lemma 2. *Let $N = (P, T, F, M_0, l)$ be a symmetrically asynchronous Petri net and $FC_{sym}(N) = (P, \hat{T}, \hat{F}, M_0, l)$. Then for all $t \in T \setminus \hat{T}$ there is no $M \in [N\rangle$ such that $M[\{t\}\rangle$.*

Proof. Assume there is a $t \in T \setminus \hat{T}$ and a marking $M \in [N\rangle$ such that t is enabled under M. By definition of $\hat{T}$, there is a $p \in {}^\bullet t$ and a $u \in p^\bullet$ such that $\lambda(p) \neq \lambda(u)$ and $u \neq t$. But M enabled t, contradicting the assumption that N is symmetrically asynchronous, i. e., N has no distributed conflict.   □

Hence, FC_{sym} yields step branching time equivalent FC-nets.

Theorem 4. *Let N be a plain symmetrically asynchronous Petri net. Then $N \approx_\mathcal{B} FC_{sym}(N)$.*

This theorem directly follows from Lemma 2. As every FC-net is also symmetrically asynchronous, we get the following correspondence between the step branching time closure of FC-nets and of symmetrically asynchronous nets.

Corollary 2. *Let N be a plain Petri net. N is weak step bisimilar to a plain-labeled FC-net iff N is weak step bisimilar to a plain-labeled symmetrically asynchronous Petri net.*

6   Conclusions and Future Work

We provided an overview on well-known free-choice related Petri net classes and their transformations between them. Our goal was to analyze their relations under concurrency-aware equivalences, namely step branching time equivalences. EFC-nets are equivalent to FC-nets while BFC-nets contain critical structures not expressible by any FC-net. We proved that two subclasses of BFC-nets, namely self-loop free BFC-nets and BFC-nets that are also AC-nets, are behaviorally equivalent to FC-nets respecting concurrent steps. Finally, we proved that the closure of step branching time equivalent FC-nets relies on the closure of symmetrically asynchronous Petri nets, a syntactically larger class than FC-nets.

FC-nets come with efficient analysis algorithms that are also useful for the analysis of distributed systems. Positive results in this paper may be used to transport many of the analysis techniques of FC-nets to broader net classes like EFC-nets or BFC-nets. Negative results we pointed to or actually proved, sketch a limit of efficient analyzability, as Best stated that many of the free-choice related results do not hold for net classes beyond free-choice [1].

For future work, we plan to tackle the closure of symmetrically asynchronous Petri nets, i. e., FC-nets (cf. Corollary 2). In [11], partial closure and remaining problematic structures are provided by equating symmetrically asynchronous Petri nets with distributed systems and asking for the class of distributable Petri nets. For another notion of distributed Petri nets related to the aforementioned pure M, such a closure is provided by van Glabbeek et al. in terms of *ST bisimulation*, a strong equivalence taking causality into account [10]. The EFC-net construction presented in this paper adds causality. Thus, a causality-preserving transformation remains to be found if possible.

References

1. Best, E.: Structure theory of petri nets: the free choice hiatus. In: Brauer, W., Reisig, W., Rozenberg, G. (eds.) APN 1986. LNCS, vol. 254, pp. 168–205. Springer, Heidelberg (1987)
2. Best, E., Shields, M.W.: Some equivalence results for free choice nets and simple nets and on the periodicity of live free choice nets. In: Protasi, M., Ausiello, G. (eds.) CAAP 1983. LNCS, vol. 159, pp. 141–154. Springer, Heidelberg (1983)
3. Best, E., Wimmel, H.: Structure theory of petri nets. In: Jensen, K., van der Aalst, W.M.P., Balbo, G., Koutny, M., Wolf, K. (eds.) Transactions on Petri Nets and Other Models of Concurrency VII. LNCS, vol. 7480, pp. 162–224. Springer, Heidelberg (2013)

4. Desel, J., Esparza, J.: Free Choice Petri Nets. Cambridge University Press, New York (1995)
5. Esparza, J.: Decidability and complexity of petri net problems – an introduction. In: Reisig, W., Rozenberg, G. (eds.) APN 1998. LNCS, vol. 1491, pp. 374–428. Springer, Heidelberg (1998)
6. van Glabbeek, R.J.: The linear time - branching time spectrum. In: Baeten, J.C.M., Klop, J.W. (eds.) CONCUR 1990. LNCS, vol. 458, pp. 278–297. Springer, Heidelberg (1990)
7. van Glabbeek, R.J., Goltz, U., Schicke, J.-W.: On synchronous and asynchronous interaction in distributed systems. In: Ochmański, E., Tyszkiewicz, J. (eds.) MFCS 2008. LNCS, vol. 5162, pp. 16–35. Springer, Heidelberg (2008)
8. van Glabbeek, R.J., Goltz, U., Schicke, J.W.: Symmetric and asymmetric asynchronous interaction. In: ICE 2008, Satellite Workshop ICALP 2008. ENTCS, vol. 229, pp. 77–95. Elsevier (2009)
9. van Glabbeek, R.J., Goltz, U., Schicke, J.W.: Abstract processes of place/transition systems. Information Processing Letters 111(13), 626–633 (2011)
10. van Glabbeek, R.J., Goltz, U., Schicke-Uffmann, J.W.: On characterising distributability. LMCS 9(3) (2013)
11. Mennicke, S.: Strong Distributability Criteria for Petri Nets. Master's thesis, TU Braunschweig, Germany (May 2013)
12. Petri, C.A.: Kommunikation mit Automaten. Ph.D. thesis, TU Darmstadt (1962)
13. Rozenberg, G., Thiagarajan, P.: Petri nets: Basic notions, structure, behaviour. In: Rozenberg, G., de Bakker, J.W., de Roever, W.-P. (eds.) Current Trends in Concurrency. LNCS, vol. 224, pp. 585–668. Springer, Heidelberg (1986)
14. Vidal-Naquet, G.: Deterministic languages of petri nets. In: Girault, C., Reisig, W. (eds.) Application and Theory of Petri Nets. Informatik-Fachberichte, vol. 52, pp. 198–202. Springer, Heidelberg (1982)

A   Proof of Theorem 1

Let $N = (P, T, F, M_0, l)$ be a plain EFC-net and $N' = FC(N) = (P', T', F', M_0', l')$. We prove that $R = \{(M_1, M_2) \mid M_1 \in [N\rangle, M_1 \xrightarrow{\tau}{}^*_{N'} M_2\}$ is a bisimulation. Note that $P \subseteq P'$ and $T \subseteq T'$. $(M_0, M_0') \in R$, as $M_0 = M_0'$. Let $(M_1, M_2) \in R$. As N is τ-free, there are three cases to consider:

1. $M_1 \xrightarrow{A}_N M_1'$, i.e., $M_1[G\rangle_N M_1'$ and $l(G) = A$. Note that ${}^\bullet t \cap {}^\bullet t' = \emptyset$ for all $t, t' \in G$ ($t \neq t'$), due to N being a structural conflict net. Existence of marking M_2' with $M_2 \xrightarrow{\tau}{}^*_{N'} \xrightarrow{A}_{N'} \xrightarrow{\tau}{}^*_{N'} M_2'$ and $(M_1', M_2') \in R$ is shown in two cases, (i) $M_2 = M_1$ and (ii) $M_2 \neq M_1$.
   In case (i), $\forall t \in G : \forall p \in {}^\bullet[t] : M_1(p) > 0$ and thus $M_2(p) > 0$. By construction, there are transitions $\tau_{[t]}$ enabled in N' for each $t \in G$, i.e., $M_2[\{\tau_{[t]} \mid t \in G\}\rangle_{N'}$ Hence, $M_2 \xrightarrow{\tau}{}^*_{N'} M_2''$ and $M_2''[G\rangle_{N'}$. Therefore, $M_2 \xrightarrow{\tau}{}^*_{N'} \xrightarrow{A}_{N'} M_2'$. Furthermore, $M_2' = M_1'$, as all outgoing arcs of transitions are preserved. By definition, $(M_1', M_2') \in R$. In case (ii), $M_1 \xrightarrow{\tau}{}^*_{N'} M_2$. Hence, for each $t \in G$ either $M_2[\{t\}\rangle_{N'}$ or $M_2[\tau_{[t]}\rangle_{N'}$. Let $G' = \{\tau_{[t]} \mid t \in G \wedge M_2[\tau_{[t]}\rangle_{N'}\}$. G' is a step from M_2 to M_2'' and by construction, $M_2''[G\rangle_{N'}$. Hence, $M_2'' \xrightarrow{A}_{N'} M_1'$

and $M_2 \xrightarrow{\tau}{}^*_{N'} \xrightarrow{A}_{N'} M_2'$. If $M_2' = M_1'$, $(M_1', M_2') \in R$ is implied. If not, then $M_1' \xrightarrow{\tau}{}^*_{N'} M_2'$, as otherwise, G was no step from M_2'' to M_2'. Thus, $(M_1', M_2') \in R$.

2. $M_2 \xrightarrow{\tau}_{N'} M_2'$. Then $M_1 \xrightarrow{\tau}{}^*_N M_1$ and $(M_1, M_2') \in R$.

3. $M_2 \xrightarrow{A}_{N'} M_2'$, $M_2[G\rangle_{N'} M_2'$ and $l(G) = A$. We need to show that $M_1 \xrightarrow{A}_N M_1'$ and $(M_1', M_2') \in R$. We construct M_1 by reversing τ-transitions in N'. As $(M_1, M_2) \in R$, $M_1 \xrightarrow{\tau}{}^*_{N'} M_2$. By construction, G is enabled under M_2 iff G is enabled under M_1. Hence, there is a marking M_1' such that $M_1 \xrightarrow{A}_N M_1'$. If $M_2' = M_1'$, then the claim is implied. Otherwise, M_2' evolves from M_1' by firing the τ firing sequences we rolled back earlier. By definition, $(M_1', M_2') \in R$.

Hence, R is a weak step bisimulation between N and $FC(N)$. $\square$

B   Proof of Theorem 3

Let $N = (P, T, F, M_0, l)$ be a BFC-AC-net specification and $EFC(N) = N' = (P, T, F', M_0, \hat{l})$. We prove that $R = \{(M, M) \mid M \in [N\rangle\}$ is a weak step bisimulation between N and N'. By definition, $(M_0, M_0) \in R$. Let $(M_1, M_2) \in R$. The cases for τ-steps are obsolete, as N and N' are plain.

1. $M_1 \xrightarrow{A}_N M_1'$, i.e., there is a step G from M_1 to M_1' and $l(G) = A$. As N' is τ-free, we have to give a marking M_2' such that $M_2 \xrightarrow{A}_{N'} M_2'$ and $(M_1', M_2') \in R$. If G is enabled by M_2, then $M_2' = M_1'$ where $M_2[G\rangle M_2'$, as $M_2 = M_1$ and tokens that are consumed due to the construction of N' are reproduced. Additionally, the original outgoing arcs of transitions are preserved. As N is a structural conflict net and due to the construction, for transitions $t_1, t_2 \in G$ it holds that ${}^\bullet t_1 \cap {}^\bullet t_2 = \emptyset$. It remains to be shown that $\hat{G} = G$ is enabled by M_2, i.e., ${}^\bullet\hat{G} \leq M_2$. Let $\hat{t} \in \hat{G}$ with $\hat{t} = t$. The $\hat{t}/\hat{G}$ notation just helps distinguishing between elements of N and N'. As in N', no arcs were removed, it holds that $|{}^\bullet\hat{t}| \geq |{}^\bullet t|$. In case of equality, the claim holds and G may fire under M_2. If $|{}^\bullet\hat{t}| > |{}^\bullet t|$, then there are places $p, q \in P$ and a transition $u \in T$ such that $p \in {}^\bullet t \cap {}^\bullet u$, $q \notin {}^\bullet t$ but $q \in {}^\bullet u$ — due to the fact that N is an AC-net. Hence, in N' there is an additional arc from q to $\hat{t}$. As N is a BFC-net, t is enabled iff u is enabled and hence, $q \in M_1$. Thus, $q \in M_2$. In conclusion ${}^\bullet\hat{t} \leq M_2$ thus ${}^\bullet\hat{G} \leq M_2$, i.e., $\hat{G}$ is enabled by M_2 and may fire, producing a new marking M_2' with the properties described above.

2. $M_2 \xrightarrow{A}_{N'} M_2'$, i.e., there is a step G from M_2 to M_2' and $l(G) = A$. N is τ-free and therefore, we need to give a marking M_1' such that $M_1 \xrightarrow{A}_N M_1'$ and $(M_1', M_2') \in R$. As before, a t in N has less or equal incoming arcs than t in N'. As, $M_2 = M_1$ by definition of R, G is a step from M_1 to a marking M_1'. Every token that is consumed by some t in N', due to the construction of N', is reproduced in N'. In N such tokens are not even consumed by t. The original postsets of transitions are preserved and hence, $M_1[G\rangle_N M_1'$ and $M_2' = M_1'$ thus $(M_1', M_2') \in R$. $\square$

Coinductive Definition of Distances between Processes: Beyond Bisimulation Distances[*]

David Romero-Hernández and David de Frutos Escrig

Dpto. Sistemas Informáticos y Computación
Facultad CC. Matemáticas, Universidad Complutense de Madrid, Spain
dromeroh@pdi.ucm.es, defrutos@sip.ucm.es

Abstract. Bisimulation captures in a coinductive way the equivalence between processes, or trees. Several authors have defined bisimulation distances based on the bisimulation game. However, this approach becomes too local: whenever we have in one of the compared processes a large collection of branches different from those of the other, only the farthest away is taken into account to define the distance. Alternatively, we have developed a more global approach to define these distances, based on the idea of how much we need to modify one of the compared processes to obtain the other. Our original definition only covered finite processes. Instead, now we present here a coinductive approach that extends our distance to infinite but finitary trees, without needing to consider any kind of approximation of infinite trees by their finite projections.

1 Introduction

Bisimulation [16,14,20] is a popular way to define the semantics of processes. Starting from their operational semantics, defined by a transition system, it captures the "natural" behavior of the processes, paying attention to the branching in them, but abstracting away from possible repetitions of equivalent behaviors. Bisimulations are just coinductive proofs of the equivalence between processes, and in fact they became one of the main causes of the popularization of the study of coinduction [20] and coalgebras [19,11,12] in the last years. They can be established in many different ways, in particular by means of the bisimulation game [21], that enlightens the co-character of bisimilarity.

When comparing two processes, the proof of their bisimilarity certainly indicates us that they are equivalent. The problem comes if we receive the information that they are not bisimilar. Then, if we substitute one component by the other, it is expected that the behavior of the full system will change "at least a bit". We want to quantify those deviations; they are formalized by our (new) distance between processes with respect to the bisimulation equivalence.

Recently, several variants of the bisimulation game have been used to define "bisimulation distances" [4,6,8,1]. They develop the seminal ideas in several previous works, such as [5,9,23]. However, as we have already illustrated in [17,18]

---

[*] Partially supported by the Spanish projects STRONGSOFT (TIN2012-39391-C04-04) and PROMETIDOS S2009/TIC-1465.

E. Ábrahám and C. Palamidessi (Eds.), FORTE 2014, LNCS 8461, pp. 249–265, 2014.

by means of several examples, these distances have some "limitations", that we try to remove by means of our new bisimulation distance. We also include in this paper some new examples enlightening the difference between our approach and those based in the bisimulation game.

Whenever we formalize the family of computations of a process we obtain a tree. Therefore, any distance between processes induces a distance between those trees. We have followed this path in the opposite way: let us look for a "natural" notion of distance between trees, and we will turn it into a distance between processes. In [17] we have presented an operational definition of our new *global bisimulation distance* for the particular case of finite trees. Roughly speaking, we define our distance between trees "computing" the costs in order to transform one of the trees into the other. We consider a given distance $\mathbf{d}$ on the alphabet of actions, so that the cost of substituting an action a by another b is given by $\mathbf{d}(a, b)$.

In this paper, we use coinduction to define the distance between processes in which we are interested. Of course, an alternative way to define the distance between infinite trees is to approximate them by their finite projections, and then taking limits. Looking for an "homogeneous" procedure that could capture all these approximations in a compact way, we introduce our coinductive distance as the coinductive "closure" of the finite transformations by means of which we defined our distance between finite processes in [17]. Once we have it, we get all the machinery of coinductive proofs in order to study our distance.

Even if the notion of tree is omnipresent in the field of semantics of processes, there is not a clearly standardized presentation of the different classes of trees in the literature. This is why we start the paper by reminding in Section 2 the definitions on trees and labelled transition systems that we use in the following. In Section 3, we recall the previous work on bisimulation distances and our alternative operational proposal covering mainly finite trees. Section 4 is the core of the paper and presents the coinductive extension of this approach covering also infinite trees. Finally, we conclude with a short section devoted to a discussion on the continuity of the coinductive distance, and the conclusions of the paper.

We strongly acknowledge the detailed reading and the suggestions of the referees of this paper, that have contributed to improve the presentation of this work.

2   Preliminaries

Let us start by recalling the coalgebraic definition of labelled transition systems (lts). As usual, we use them to represent the operational semantics of processes.

Definition 1. *Labelled Transition Systems (lts)*[1] *on a set of actions* $\mathbb{A}$ *and a set of states* N, *are given by a function* $succ : N \to \mathcal{P}(\mathbb{A} \times N)$. *We denote each*

---

[1] Therefore, lts's are just arc-labelled graphs, or more formally coalgebras $succ : N \to LTS(N, \mathbb{A})$ of the functor $LTS(N, \mathbb{A}) := \mathcal{P}(\mathbb{A} \times N)$ on the plain category of sets, *Set.* See for instance [12,20] for much more on coalgebras.

lts by the corresponding pair $(N, succ)$. A lts with initial state $(N, succ, n_0)$, is just a lts $(N, succ)$ where some distinguished (initial) state $n_0 \in N$ is fixed. To simplify our notation, we usually remove the succ component from lts's.

We say that any sequence $n_0 a_1 n_1 \ldots a_k n_k$ with $(a_{i+1}, n_{i+1}) \in succ(n_i) \; \forall i \in \{0 \ldots k - 1\}$, is a path in (N, n_0). We denote the set of paths (or computations) by $Path(N, n_0)$. We say that the system N is *finite state*, if $|N| < \infty$; (N, n_0) is *finite*, if $|Path(N, n_0)| < \infty$; we say that (N, n_0) has only *finite computations*, if there is no infinite path $n_0 a_1 n_1 a_2 n_2 \ldots$. We say that a system N is *finitely branching*, if for all $n \in N$ we have $|succ(n)| < \infty$.

Example 1. (See Fig.1) Two simple finite-state systems that however have infinitely many computations are the following: $N_{1,\infty} = \{n_0\}$, with $succ(n_0) = \{(a, n_0)\}$; $N_{2,\infty} = \{n_0, n_1\}$, with $succ(n_0) = succ(n_1) = \{(a, n_0), (a, n_1)\}$.

Example 2. (See Fig.1) Next three interesting non-finitely branching systems:

1. $N_{\mathbb{N}} = (\mathbb{N}, succ, 0)$ with $\mathbb{A} = \mathbb{N}$, $succ(0) = \{(k, k) \mid k \in \mathbb{N}\}$, $succ(k) = \emptyset$, $\forall k > 0$.
2. $N_2 = \{0\} \cup \{(i, j) \mid i, j \in \mathbb{N}, 1 \leq j \leq i\}$, taking $n_0 = 0$ with $succ(0) = \{(a, (n, 1)) \mid n \in \mathbb{N}\}$ and $succ((i, j)) = \{(a, (i, j + 1))\}$ if $j < i$, while $succ((i, i)) = \emptyset$.
3. $N_2^+ = N_2 \cup \{(\infty, n) \mid n \in \mathbb{N}\}$, changing also the definition of $succ$, taking $succ(0) = \{(a, (x, 1)) \mid x \in \mathbb{N} \cup \{\infty\}\}$ and $succ((\infty, j)) = \{(a, (\infty, j + 1))\}$.

We can define (rooted) trees as a particular class of lts's:

Definition 2. *We say that a system (N, n_0) is (or defines) a tree t if for all $n \in N$ there is a single path $n_0 a_1 n_1 \ldots a_k n_k$ with $n_k = n$. Then, we say that each node n_k is at* level k *in t, and define $Level_k(t) = \{n \in N \mid n$ is at level k in $t\}$. We define the* depth *of t as $depth(t) = sup\{l \in \mathbb{N} \mid Level_l(t) \neq \emptyset\} \in \mathbb{N} \cup \{\infty\}$. We denote by $Trees(\mathbb{A})$ the class of trees on the set $\mathbb{A}$, and by $FTrees(\mathbb{A})$, the subclass of finite state trees.*

Any node $n \in N$ of a tree $t = (N, succ, n_0)$ induces a subtree $t_n = (N_n, succ, n)$, where N_n is the set of nodes $n'_k \in N$ such that there exists a path $n'_0 a_1 n'_1 \ldots a_k n'_k$ with $n'_0 = n$. We decompose any tree t into the formal sum $\sum_{n_{1j} \in Level_1(t)} a_j t_{n_{1j}}$. Since our trees are unordered, by definition, this formal sum is also unordered. The tree $\mathbf{0}$ corresponds to the system $(\{n_0\}, succ_0, n_0)$ with $succ_0(n_0) = \emptyset$, while if $|Level_1(t)| = 1$ we have $t = at'$, which can be reversed to define the tree at' starting from $a \in \mathbb{A}$ and $t' \in Trees(\mathbb{A})$. In a similar way, whenever $Level_1(t) = N_1 \cup N_2$ is a disjoint decomposition of that set, we can write $t = \sum_{n_{1j} \in N_1} a_j t_{n_{1j}} + \sum_{n_{1k} \in N_2} a_k t_{n_{1k}}$, which can be also reversed to define the sum $(+)$ of trees. Note that $+$ becomes commutative by definition.

For any tree $t \in Trees(\mathbb{A})$, we define its *first-level width*, that we will represent by $||t||$, as $||t|| = |Level_1(t)|$. We also define the *first k-levels width of t*, denoted by $||t||_k$, as $||t||_k = max\{||t_n|| \mid n \in \bigcup_{l \leq k} Level_l(t)\}$. *Finitary trees* are just trees that are finitely branching systems, or equivalently, those such that $||t||_k < \infty$, $\forall k \in \mathbb{N}$. We denote by $FyTrees(\mathbb{A})$ the collection of *finitary trees* in $Trees(\mathbb{A})$.

All the systems in Ex.2 are indeed trees. Instead, those in Ex.1 are not trees.

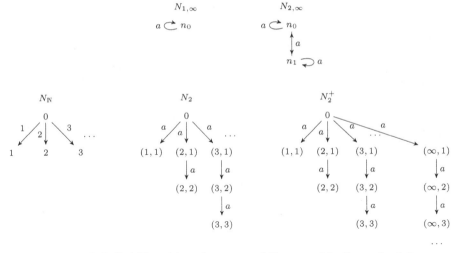

Fig. 1. Labelled Transitions Systems and Trees used in Examples 1-2

Definition 3. *Given a lts with initial state* $(N, succ, n_0)$, *we define its unfolding* $unfold(N)$ *as the tree* $(\overline{N}, \overline{succ}, \overline{n_0})$, *where* $\overline{N} = Path(N, n_0)$, $\overline{succ}(n_0 a_1 \ldots n_k) = \{(a, n_0 a_1 \ldots n_k a n') \mid (a, n') \in succ(n_k)\}$, *and* $\overline{n_0} = n_0$.

Definition 4. *Let* $(N, succ)$ *be a lts. We say that a relation* $\mathcal{R}$ *on* N *is a bisimulation, if for all* $(n, n') \in \mathcal{R}$ *we have*

- $\forall\, (a, n_1) \in succ(n)\ \exists\, (a, n_1') \in succ(n'),\ (n_1, n_1') \in \mathcal{R}$.
- $\forall\, (a, n_2) \in succ(n')\ \exists\, (a, n_2') \in succ(n),\ (n_2', n_2) \in \mathcal{R}$.

We say that n *and* n' *are bisimilar if there exists some bisimulation* $\mathcal{R}$ *such that* $(n, n') \in \mathcal{R}$, *and then we write* $n \sim n'$.

By considering the disjoint union of two systems, we can extend the definition above to relate states from two different systems. In particular, if we consider two *lts* with initial state (or equivalently two trees) we say that $(N, succ, n_0) \sim (N', succ', n_0')$ if and only if there is a bisimulation containing the pair (n_0, n_0'). Usually we will simply write $n_0 \sim n_0'$, and the same in the case of trees, as usual.

The fact that systems are represented by their unfolding is formalized by the following result.

Proposition 1. *For any lts with initial state* $(N, succ, n_0)$, *and its unfolding* $(\overline{N}, \overline{succ}, \overline{n_0})$, *we have* $n_0 \sim \overline{n_0}$.

Definition 5. *Given a tree* $t = (N, succ, n_0)$ *and* $k \in \mathbb{N}$, *we define its k-th cut or projection,* $\pi_k(t)$, *as the restriction of* t *to the nodes in* $\bigcup_{l \leq k} Level_l(t)$:

$$\pi_k(t) = (\pi_k(N), succ_k, n_0),\ where\ \pi_k(N) = \bigcup_{l \leq k} Level_l(t),\ succ_k(n) = succ(n)$$
$$for\ n \in \bigcup_{l < k} Level_l(t),\ and\ succ_k(n) = \emptyset\ if\ n \in Level_k(t).$$

Proposition 2. *For any* $t \in Tree(\mathbb{A})$ *and* $l, k \in \mathbb{N}$ *with* $l \leq k$, *we have* $\pi_l(\pi_k(t)) = \pi_l(t)$. *Any finitary tree is unequivocally defined by its sequence of projections:* $\forall t, t' \in FyTree(\mathbb{A})$ $(\forall k \in \mathbb{N} \; \pi_k(t) \sim \pi_k(t')) \Rightarrow t \sim t'$.

Example 3. The result above becomes false if we consider infinitary trees. For the trees N_2 and N_2^+ in Ex.2, we have $\pi_k(N_2) \sim \pi_k(N_2^+) \; \forall k \in \mathbb{N}$, since the "additional" branch executing a^k provided by N_2^+ can be "absorbed" by the infinitely many such branches that we already have in $\pi_k(N_2)$. Therefore, this is a (well known) counterexample disproving the continuity of bisimilarity wrt the approximations, provided by the projections π_k, if we allow infinitary trees.

As a consequence, we will restrict ourselves to finitely branching processes all along the rest of the paper. It would not be enough to consider instead just image finiteness trees, because our approach considers all the successors of each node in an homogeneous way, without taking care of their labels. Then, problems can appear as soon as a node has infinitely many successors.

3   Classical and Global Bisimulation Distances

We consider domains of actions $(\mathbb{A}, \mathbf{d})$, where $\mathbf{d} : \mathbb{A} \times \mathbb{A} \rightarrow \mathbb{R}^+ \cup \{\infty\}$ is a distance between actions, with $\mathbf{d}(a, b) = \mathbf{d}(b, a)$, $\forall a, b \in \mathbb{A}$, and, as usual, $\mathbf{d}(a, b) = 0 \Leftrightarrow a = b$, and $\mathbf{d}(a, c) + \mathbf{d}(c, b) \geq \mathbf{d}(a, b)$, $\forall a, b, c \in \mathbb{A}$ where $+$ is extended to $\mathbb{R}^+ \cup \{\infty\}$ as usual. Intuitively $\mathbf{d}(a, b) = \infty$ expresses that two actions are absolutely not interchangeable. If the value of a distance $\mathbf{d}(a, b)$ is not specified in our examples, we will assume that $\mathbf{d}(a, b) = \infty$.

The well known bisimulation game [15,22], allows us to characterize the bisimilarity relation. It is played by two players: the attacker ($\mathcal{A}$) and the defender ($\mathcal{D}$). The former executes any fireable transition from one of the compared trees, and the second has to reply it in the other tree. The attacker wins if the defender cannot counteract one of his moves; while the defender wins if he can reply forever.

Theorem 1. *([15,22]) For any* $t, t' \in Trees(\mathbb{A})$ $t \sim t'$ *(resp.* $t \not\sim t'$*) if and only if* $\mathcal{D}$ *(resp.* $\mathcal{A}$*) has a winning strategy for the bisimulation game starting at* (t, t').

Most of the recent approaches to define distances between processes –e.g. [7]– use quantitative versions of the bisimulation game. As in the plain bisimulation game, the defender has to simulate the action played by the attacker, but in this case he can fail to reply an a transition, firing instead some b. However, whenever he cheats the attacker, he has to pay him for the distance $\mathbf{d}(b, a)$. Then, the distance between two trees t and t' (equivalently, between two processes) is defined as the value of that game starting from the roots of t and t'. In the following, we will call "classical" the distances defined following this approach.

Inspired by the notion of amortized bisimulation [13], we have developed a coinductive presentation of the classical bisimulation distances [17]. Instead of giving a definition of the distance between two trees, that requires the use of fix-point theory, we state when an indexed family of relations between trees provides a collection of bounds on the distances between the pairs of trees in them.

As done for instance in [2,8], and thoroughly discussed in [3], when comparing pairs of processes, it is natural to introduce a "discount factor" $\alpha \in (0,1)$. Then, the differences in the k-th level of the compared trees are weighted by α^k, follow-ing the idea that differences in the far future are less important than those in the near. As a consequence, it is possible to obtain finite distances when comparing two processes with "infinitely many differences" between them. However, we will also allow that $\alpha = 1$ to cover the case in which we are not interested in the weighting of those differences.

Definition 6. *(see [17]) Given a domain of actions* $(\mathbb{A}, \mathbf{d})$ *and a discount factor* $\alpha \in (0,1]$*, we say that a family of relations between trees,* $\mathcal{R} \subseteq Trees(\mathbb{A}) \times Trees(\mathbb{A}) \times \mathbb{R}^+$*, is a classical bisimulation distance family (cbdf) for* $\mathbf{d}$ *and* α*, if it satisfies*

$$
\begin{array}{ccc}
t & R_d & t' \\
\forall a \downarrow & \Longrightarrow & \downarrow \exists b \\
t_1 & R_{\frac{d-\mathbf{d}(b,a)}{\alpha}} & t'_1
\end{array}
\quad \wedge \quad
\begin{array}{ccc}
t & R_d & t' \\
\exists a \downarrow & \Longleftarrow & \downarrow \forall b \\
t_1 & R_{\frac{d-\mathbf{d}(b,a)}{\alpha}} & t'_1
\end{array}
$$

where, we take tR_dt' *if and only if* $(t,t',d) \in \mathcal{R}$ *and implicitly, we are assuming that the values* $d - \mathbf{d}(b,a)$ *are nonnegative. We say that* t *and* t' *are at most at classical bisimulation distance* d *for the factor* α*, and then we write* $d_{\mathbf{d}}^\alpha(t,t') \leq d$*, if there is some cbdf* $\mathcal{R}$ *with* tR_dt'*.*

Proposition 3. *(see [17]) The value of the quantitative game –see [7]– defining the "classical" bisimulation distance* $dist_{\mathbf{d}}^\alpha(t,t')$ *is* $\inf(\{d \in \mathbb{R}^+ \mid d_{\mathbf{d}}^\alpha(t,t') \leq d\})$*.*

It is well known that, for finitary trees, this classical bisimulation distance is indeed a quantitative refinement of bisimilarity.

Theorem 2. *For all* t*,* $t' \in FyTrees(\mathbb{A})$ *and any discount factor* $\alpha \in (0,1]$*, we have* $t \sim t'$ *if and only if* $d_{\mathbf{d}}^\alpha(t,t') \leq 0$*, if and only if* $dist_{\mathbf{d}}^\alpha(t,t') = 0$*.*

In spite of this, we consider that in some cases this distance generates values that do not accurately reflect the differences between some pairs of trees.

Example 4. (see Fig. 2) We have a service that allows some access to the bits of our password, once we have identified ourselves in the appropriate way. Let us abstract this service as the tree $t = \sum_{i \in 1..64} a_i$. Now, let us assume that a'_i represents a cracked access to the corresponding position. Then, for each $j \in \{1 \ldots 64\}$ the system represented by the tree $t'_j = (\sum_{i \neq j} a_i) + a'_j$ certainly is wrong, but does not compromise too much the security of the system. Instead, the totally cracked system represented by $t'_{1..64} = \sum_{i \in 1..64} a'_i$ corresponds to a disastrous situation. If we take $\mathbf{d}(a_i, a'_i) = 1$, we obtain $dist_{\mathbf{d}}^1(t'_j, t) = 1$, but also $dist_{\mathbf{d}}^1(t'_{1..64}, t) = 1$.

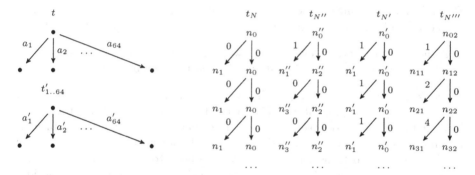

Fig. 2. Trees used in Ex. 4 - Ex.8

The bad behavior of the "classical" bisimulation distance stems from the fact that the quantitative bisimulation game only considers single computations of the compared trees. As a consequence, it cannot capture the differences "accumulated" by repeated use of a system, as illustrated in Ex.4. Later, we will see how our "global" approach copes with this feature in a more satisfactory manner.

In [17], we have presented our operational definitions that allow us to obtain bounds for our new global distances between finite trees. These bounds are given by the cost of any transformation that turns one of the trees into the other. The following definition states which are the valid steps of those transformations and their costs. Roughly, any application of idempotency of $+$ has no cost, while the change of an action a at level k into another b has as cost $\alpha^k \mathbf{d}(b, a)$.

Definition 7. *Given a domain of actions $(\mathbb{A}, \mathbf{d})$ and a discount factor $\alpha \in (0, 1]$, we inductively define the distance steps on $FTrees(\mathbb{A})$ by*

1. $d \geq 0 \Rightarrow (t \leadsto^1_{\alpha,d} t + t \wedge t + t \leadsto^1_{\alpha,d} t)$.   2. $d \geq \mathbf{d}(a, b) \Rightarrow at \leadsto^1_{\alpha,d} bt$.
3. $t \leadsto^1_{\alpha,d} t' \Rightarrow t + t'' \leadsto^1_{\alpha,d} t' + t''$.   4. $t \leadsto^1_{\alpha,d} t' \Rightarrow at \leadsto^1_{\alpha,\alpha d} at'$.

We associate to each distance step its level, that is a natural number. The level of any step generated by 1. or 2. is one; while if the level of the corresponding premise $t \leadsto^1_{\alpha,d} t'$ is k, then the level of a step generated by 3. (resp. 4.) is k (resp. $k+1$). Finally, we define the family of global distance relations $\langle \leadsto_{\alpha,d} \mid d \in \mathbb{R}^+ \rangle$, taking $t \leadsto_{\alpha,d} t'$ if there exists a sequence $\mathcal{S} := t = t^0 \leadsto^1_{\alpha,d_1} t^1 \leadsto^1_{\alpha,d_2} t^2 \leadsto^1_{\alpha,d_3} \cdots \leadsto^1_{\alpha,d_n} t^n = t'$, with $\sum_{i=1}^n d_i = d$.

Therefore, we can see any sequence of distance steps turning t into t' as a sequence of local transformations $t^i \leadsto^1_{\alpha,d_i} t^{i+1}$. Each one of them either changes a single label or duplicates a partial branch at a certain level of t^i.

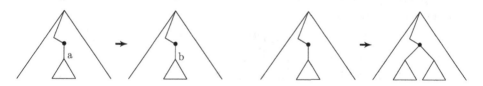

Remark 1. For technical reasons we want that $t \leadsto_{\alpha,d} t$ for any t, and all $d \in \mathbb{R}^+$. This can be obtained by considering the sequence $\mathcal{S} := t \leadsto^1_{\alpha,d} t + t \leadsto^1_{\alpha,0} t$.

Although at the formal level we only work with the relations $\leadsto_{\alpha,d}$, sometimes we also talk about the (global) distance defined by these bounds.

Example 5. Let us consider again the systems in Ex.4. Now, it is immediate to check that $t \leadsto_{1,1} t'_j$ for all $j \in \{1\ldots64\}$. Therefore, in this case, the global bisimulation distance between t and any t'_j coincides with the classical bisimulation distance. However $t \leadsto_{1,64} t'_{1..64}$, but we do not have $t \leadsto_{1,d} t'_{1..64}$ for any $d < 64$: in order to transform t into $t'_{1..64}$, we need to change each a_i into a'_i, paying one unit at each step. Instead, we had $dist^1_d(t, t'_{1..64}) = 1$. We consider that our global distance reflects in a much more accurate way the "intuitive" distance between these trees.

Example 6. We have to pass an examination about a subject with l lessons. A good student would study all of them, thus getting $S = \sum_{1..l} a_l$, which means that he totally knows the subject. At the exam the examiners choose somehow k lessons, and then each student can select a single one to develop. This means that any student that ignores up to k-1 lessons could perfectly pass the exam. These students are represented by $S_I = \sum_{i \notin I} a_i$, where I is the set of lessons that they did not study. Now, at which extend such an student is risky? What happens if the day of the exam he forgets some lesson?. If $|I| = k - 1$, then as soon as he forgets a single lesson he is in risk of failing; instead, if $|I| = 1$ he has definitely much more chances. This is again captured by our global bisimulation distance, but not by the classical one. The situation is similar to that studied in [10], where they wanted to capture how many failures are allowed before a system will fail to satisfy the requirements at its specification.

4   The Coinductive Global Bisimulation Distance

To get a general coinductive definition of our global distance for *FyTrees(*$\mathbb{A}$*)*, we keep the first three rules in Def.7, that allow us to make changes at the first level of the trees. But instead of rule 4, we introduce a coinductive rule that allows us to replace any non trivial subtree t at depth one by another t', getting a distance αd, whenever (t, t', d) is in the family that defines our global distance.

We formalize our definition in two steps. The first one, introduces the rules that produce the steps of the *coinductive transformations* between trees, starting from any family of triples (t, t', d), with t, $t' \in FyTrees(\mathbb{A})$ and $d \in \mathbb{R}^+$.

Definition 8. *Given a domain of actions* $(\mathbb{A}, \mathbf{d})$*, a discount factor* $\alpha \in (0, 1]$ *and a family* $\mathcal{D} \subseteq FyTrees(\mathbb{A}) \times FyTrees(\mathbb{A}) \times \mathbb{R}^+$*, we define the family of relations* $\equiv^{\mathcal{D},\alpha}_d$*, by:*

1. *For all* $d \geq 0$ *we have (i)* $(\sum_{j \in J} a_j t_j) + at + at \equiv^{\mathcal{D},\alpha}_d (\sum_{j \in J} a_j t_j) + at$ *,*
   and (ii) $(\sum_{j \in J} a_j t_j) + at \equiv^{\mathcal{D},\alpha}_d (\sum_{j \in J} a_j t_j) + at + at$*.*
2. $(\sum_{j \in J} a_j t_j) + at \equiv^{\mathcal{D},\alpha}_{\mathbf{d}(a,b)} (\sum_{j \in J} a_j t_j) + bt$*.*

3. For all $(t, t', d) \in \mathcal{D}$ we have $(\sum_{j \in J} a_j t_j) + at \equiv_{ad}^{\mathcal{D}, \alpha} (\sum_{j \in J} a_j t_j) + at'$.

Remark 2. To simplify the notation, we will simply write $\equiv_d$ instead of $\equiv_d^{\mathcal{D}, \alpha}$, whenever $\mathcal{D}$ and α will be clear from the context.

Next, the second one. Inspired by the conditions imposed to bisimulations –that can be seen as "circular proofs" of bisimilarity of all the pairs in them– we introduce the coinductive proof obligations imposed to the families of triples as above, in order to define satisfactory coinductive families of distances.

Definition 9. *Given a domain of actions* $(\mathbb{A}, \mathbf{d})$ *and a discount factor* $\alpha \in (0, 1]$, *we say that a family* $\mathcal{D}$ *is an* α-*coinductive collection of distances* (α-*ccd*) *between finitary trees, if for all* $(t, t', d) \in \mathcal{D}$ *there exists a finite coinductive transformation sequence* $\mathcal{C} := t = t^0 \equiv_{d_1}^{\mathcal{D}, \alpha} t^1 \equiv_{d_2}^{\mathcal{D}, \alpha} \ldots \equiv_{d_n}^{\mathcal{D}, \alpha} t^n = t'$, *with* $d \geq \sum_{j=1}^{n} d_j$. *Then, when there exists an* α-*ccd* $\mathcal{D}$ *with* $(t, t', d) \in \mathcal{D}$, *we will write* $t \equiv_d^\alpha t'$, *and say that tree* t *is at most at distance* d *from tree* t' *wrt* α.

Notation: We say that the steps generated by application of rules 1 and 2 in Def.8 are *first level steps*; while those generated by rule 3 are *coinductive steps*.

Remark 3. The reason because we have introduced the condition $d \geq \sum_{j=1}^{n} d_j$, and not just $d = \sum_{j=1}^{n} d_j$, is in order to guarantee that whenever we have $t \equiv_d^\alpha t'$ and $d \leq d'$ we also have $t \equiv_{d'}^\alpha t'$. In particular, using the trivial sequence $\mathcal{C} := \mathbf{0} = \mathbf{0}$, we can prove that $\mathbf{0} \equiv_d^\alpha \mathbf{0}$ for all $d \in \mathbb{R}^+$. This could not be inferred if we would impose instead the condition $d = \sum_{j=1}^{n} d_j$. In fact, the case of $\mathbf{0}$ is the only one in which we need the inequality in Def. 9, because for any other tree t' we can apply Def. 8.1 twice, by considering any summand at of t'. Instead, in Def. 7 we can apply 7.1 even to $t = \mathbf{0}$, thus we can indeed simply take $d = \sum_{i=1}^{n} d_i$ at the end of the definition.

Remark 4. In order to avoid technical difficulties, the authors defining the classical bisimulation distance usually consider processes without termination. Instead, since we have mainly consider finite trees in [17], we needed to take into account termination. Our Def. 7 does not allow any "unexpected" termination when comparing two trees. If we desire to allow some terminations without necessarily entailing an infinite distance, then two simple extensions are possible. We could either establish a fixed payment f (that however will be weighted by the level at which it occurs), for any unexpected termination, including at any α-ccd $\mathcal{D}$ all the pairs $(t, \mathbf{0}, f)$, and no proof obligation for them. Or instead, we could pay for any lost action, considering a function $lost : Act \to \mathbb{R}^+$. Then, we could introduce tuples $(at + t', \mathbf{0}, d)$ in the α-ccd family $\mathcal{D}$, and for each one of them we need to check that there exist $(t, \mathbf{0}, d_1)$, $(t', \mathbf{0}, d_2) \in \mathcal{D}$ such that $\alpha d_1 + d_2 + lost(a) \leq d$. However, in order to make more understandable the paper, in the following we will not consider any of these extensions.

The next example presents a pair of trees with infinitely many differences, but a finite global bisimulation distance between them.

Example 7. (see Fig. 2) Let us consider the domain of actions $(\mathbb{N}, \mathbf{d})$, where $\mathbf{d}$ is the usual distance for numbers, and the trees $t_N = unfold(N)$ and $t_{N'} = unfold(N')$, with $N = \{n_0, n_1\}$, $succ(n_0) = \{(0, n_0), (0, n_1)\}$ and $succ(n_1) = \emptyset$; and $N' = \{n'_0, n'_1\}$, $succ'(n'_0) = \{(0, n'_0), (1, n'_1)\}$ and $succ'(n'_1) = \emptyset$. Then, we have $t_N \equiv_2^{\mathcal{D}, 1/2} t_{N'}$, using the family $\mathcal{D} = \{(t_N, t_{N'}, 2)\}$. We can prove that this is indeed a $\frac{1}{2}$-ccd, by considering the sequence: $\mathcal{C} := t_N \equiv_1^{1/2} t_{N''} \equiv_1^{1/2} t_{N'}$, where $t_{N''} = unfold(N'')$, with $N'' = \{n''_0, n''_1, n''_2, n''_3\}$, $succ''(n''_0) = \{(1, n''_1), (0, n''_2)\}$, $succ''(n''_1) = \emptyset$, $succ''(n''_2) = \{(0, n''_2), (0, n''_3)\}$ and $succ''(n''_3) = \emptyset$. The first step is obtained by application of rule 2 in Def.8, while the second one is obtained by application of rule 3, using the fact that $2\frac{1}{2} = 1$.

Note how the coinductive procedure "aggregates" the summands that produce the bound for the distance 2 in a single step. In fact, it is not necessary at all to sum any infinite series, as it would be the case if we would obtain that bound as the limit for the distances between the corresponding finite approximations of the two compared processes. Finally, we can observe that no bound $d < 2$ for the distance can be obtained in this way: $t_N \equiv_d^{\mathcal{D}, 1/2} t_{N'}$ does not hold for any $d < 2$, because for any such d we have $d < 1 + d/2$; so that, the check for the condition in Def. 9 would fail.

But, making greater the differences in the example above, we can get pairs of trees that are infinitely far away each other, wrt our global bisimulation distance.

Example 8. (see Fig. 2) Let us consider the tree t_N from Ex.7, and the tree $t_{N'''} = (N''', succ''', n_{0,2})$ with $N''' = \{n_{0,2}\} \cup \{n_{i,j} \mid i \in \mathbb{N} - \{0\}, j \in \{1, 2\}\}$, $succ'''(n_{i,1}) = \emptyset$ and $succ'''(n_{i,2}) = \{(2^i, n_{i+1,1}), (0, n_{i+1,2})\}$. We have $dist_d^{1/2}(t_N, t_{N'''}) = 1$. Instead, $t_N \equiv_d^{1/2} t_{N'''}$ does not hold for any $d \in \mathbb{R}^+$. As a matter of fact, for the finite projections of these two trees, we have $\pi_k(t_N) \equiv_k^{1/2} \pi_k(t_{N'''})$, for all $k \in \mathbb{N}$, but we do not have $\pi_k(t_N) \equiv_d^{1/2} \pi_k(t_{N'''})$, for any $d < k$.

Based on the notion of bisimilarity, our coinductive global bisimulation distance, and the α-ccd used to define it, inherit most of its basic properties, once quantified in the adequate way.

Definition 10. *1. We say that a family $\mathcal{D}$ is triangular-transitivity closed (ttc) (resp. + closed (+c)), if for all $(t, t', d), (t', t'', d') \in \mathcal{D}$, we have $(t, t'', d+d') \in \mathcal{D}$ (resp. $(t + t'', t' + t'', d) \in \mathcal{D}$).*
2. Given a family $\mathcal{D}$, we define its tt-closure as the least family $\mathcal{D}^*$ defined by the clauses i) $\mathcal{D} \subseteq \mathcal{D}^*$; ii) If $(t, t', d), (t', t'', d') \in \mathcal{D}^*$ then $(t, t'', d+d') \in \mathcal{D}^*$.
3. Given a family $\mathcal{D}$, we define its +-closure as the family $\mathcal{D}^+ = \{(t + t'', t' + t'', d) \mid (t, t', d) \in \mathcal{D}\}$.

Proposition 4. *If $\mathcal{D}$ is an α-ccd, then $\mathcal{D}^*$ and $\mathcal{D}^+$ are too.*

As a consequence, we can assume that any ccd is ttc or +c, when convenient.

Corollary 1 (triangular-transitivity). *For any discount factor $\alpha \in (0, 1]$, whenever we have $t \equiv_d^\alpha t'$ and $t' \equiv_{d'}^\alpha t''$, we also have $t \equiv_{d+d'}^\alpha t''$.*

Next, we state the relationship between our global bisimulation distance, bisimilarity and the classical bisimulation distance.

Proposition 5. *1. For $t, t' \in FyTrees(\mathbb{A})$, $\alpha \in (0, 1]$, we have $t \sim t' \Leftrightarrow t \equiv_0^\alpha t'$.*
2. Our global bisimulation distance is greater or equal than the classical one.

Corollary 2. *The topology induced by our global bisimulation distance is strictly finer than that induced by the classical bisimulation distance.*

Proof. It is an immediate consequence of Prop.5.2 and the (counter)Ex.8. Taking $\mathbb{R}^+$ as alphabet, and $2^i/k$ as labels of the edges of $t_{N'''}$, we obtain a family of trees $\{t_{N'''}^k \mid k \in \mathbb{N}\}$. Under the classical distance, any open ball centered in t_N, contains infinitely many trees $t_{N'''}^k$, but none of them is in any such ball for our global distance.

$\square$

Our coinductive definition of the global bisimulation distance generalizes our operational definition for finite trees.

Lemma 1. *Any sequence $\mathcal{S}$ producing $t \leadsto_{\alpha,d} t'$ can be "factorized" into an "structured" sequence $\mathcal{T} := t = t^{0,2} \leadsto_{\alpha,d_{11}} t^{1,1} \leadsto_{\alpha,d_{12}}^1 t^{1,2} \leadsto_{\alpha,d_{21}} \cdots \leadsto_{\alpha,d_{k2}}^1 t^{k,2} \leadsto_{\alpha,d_{(k+1)1}} t^{k+1,1} = t'$, where the $\sum d_{1i} + \sum d_{2i} = d$, and the distance steps $t^{l,1} \leadsto_{\alpha,d_{l2}}^1 t^{l,2}$ in it are exactly all the first level steps in $\mathcal{S}$. So that, no one of the subsequences producing $t^{l,2} \leadsto_{\alpha,d_{(l+1)1}} t^{l+1,1}$ contains any first level step.*

Proposition 6. *Any sequence $\mathcal{S}^l$ producing $t^{l,2} = \sum_{i=1}^m a_i t_i \leadsto_{\alpha,d_{(l+1)1}} t^{l+1,1} = \sum_{i=1}^m a_i t_i'$ can be reordered getting an "ordered" sequence $\mathcal{O} := t^{l,2} = \sum_{i=1}^m a_i t_i \leadsto_{\alpha,d_{(l+1)1}^1} \sum a_i t_i^1 \leadsto_{\alpha,d_{(l+1)1}^2} \sum a_i t_i^2 \leadsto_{\alpha,d_{(l+1)1}^3} \cdots \leadsto_{\alpha,d_{(l+1)1}^m} \sum a_i t_i^m = \sum_{i=1}^m a_i t_i' = t^{l+1,1}$, where $\sum_{j=1}^m d_{(l+1)1}^j = d$, $t_i^j = t_i' \; \forall j \le i$, and $t_i^j = t_i \; \forall j > i$.*

This means that for each $j \in \{1, \ldots, m\}$ $\sum a_i t_i^{j-1} \leadsto_{\alpha,d_{(l+1)1}^j} \sum a_i t_i^j$ corresponds to $a_j t_j \leadsto_{\alpha,d_{(l+1)1}^j} a_j t_j'$, so that the distance steps in the former are exactly those from $\mathcal{S}^l$ working at the corresponding summand $a_j t_j$ of t. As a consequence, for each $j \in \{1, \ldots, m\}$ we also have $t_j \leadsto_{\alpha,(d_{(l+1)1}^j)/\alpha} t_j'$, which is obtained by removing the common prefix a_j from the steps of the subsequence generating $a_j t_j \leadsto_{\alpha,d_{(l+1)1}^j} a_j t_j'$.

Proposition 7. *For $t, t' \in FTrees(\mathbb{A})$, the operational (Def.7) and the coinductive definition of our distance between trees coincide, that means $t \equiv_d^\alpha t' \Leftrightarrow t \leadsto_{\alpha,d} t'$.*

Proof. $\Rightarrow$ | Given an α-ccd relating finite trees with $(t, t', d) \in \mathcal{D}$, we can "unfold" the corresponding sequence, $\mathcal{C}$, checking $t \equiv_d^{\mathcal{D},\alpha} t'$, into a sequence of distance steps, $\mathcal{S}$, proving that $t \leadsto_{\alpha,d} t'$. We proceed by induction on $depth(t)$, as follows.

Let $t^i \equiv_{d_i}^{\mathcal{D},\alpha} t^{i+1}$ be an intermediate step in the coinductive sequence $\mathcal{C}$. If $depth(t^i) = 0$, we will trivially get $t^i \leadsto_{\alpha,d_i} t^{i+1}$. For $depth(t) \ge 1$, we apply rule 3 in Def.8, getting $t^i = t_1^i + a t_1 \equiv_{d_i}^{\mathcal{D},\alpha} t_1^i + a t_1' = t^{i+1}$ for $(t_1, t_1', d_i/\alpha) \in \mathcal{D}$. By

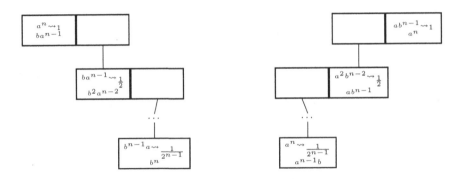

Fig. 3. Arborescent presentation of the operational sequences induced by an α-ccd

applying the induction hypothesis, we get $t_1 \leadsto_{\alpha,d_i/\alpha} t_1'$, and using rules 4 and 3 in Def.7, we obtain the desired result $t^i = t_1^i + at_1 \leadsto_{\alpha,d_i} t_1^i + at_1' = t^{i+1}$.

$\Leftarrow$ | Given a sequence of distance steps, $\mathcal{S}$, proving that $t \leadsto_{\alpha,d} t'$, we can "fold" it into a coinductive sequence, $\mathcal{C}$, checking $t \equiv_d^{\mathcal{D},\alpha} t'$. For each $(t,t',d) \in \mathcal{D}$ we consider the factorization of the sequence $\mathcal{S}$ and its reordering as done in Prop.6. We get $t = \sum_{i \in I_0} a_i t_i \leadsto_{\alpha,d_{02}^i} \sum_{i \in I_0} a_i t_i' \leadsto_{\alpha,d_{11}^1}^1 \sum_{i \in I_1} a_i t_i \leadsto_{\alpha,d_{12}^i}^1$ $\sum_{i \in I_1} a_i t_i' \leadsto_{\alpha,d_{21}^i}^1 \cdots \leadsto_{\alpha,d_{(k+1)2}^i}^1 \sum_{i \in I_{k+1}} a_i t_i' = t'$, where for each sequence $\sum_{i \in I_j} a_i t_i \leadsto_{\alpha,d_{j2}^i} \sum_{i \in I_j} a_i t_i'$ and each $i \in I_j$, we have $t_i \leadsto_{\alpha,d_{j2}^i/\alpha} t_i'$ with $\sum_{i \in I_j} d_{j2}^i = d_{j2}$. Now, applying the induction hypothesis, we have $(t_i, t_i', d_{j2}^i/\alpha) \in \mathcal{D}$, for all $i \in I_j$, so that $\sum a_i t_i \equiv_{\alpha d_1}^{\mathcal{D},\alpha} \sum a_i t_i^1 \equiv_{\alpha d_2}^{\mathcal{D},\alpha} \sum a_i t_i^2 \equiv_{\alpha d_3}^{\mathcal{D},\alpha} \cdots \equiv_{\alpha d_{|I_j|}}^{\mathcal{D},\alpha}$ $\sum a_i t_i^{|I_j|} = \sum a_i t_i'$.

Therefore, each sequence $\sum_{i \in I_j} a_i t_i \leadsto_{\alpha,d_{j2}^i} \sum_{i \in I_j} a_i t_i'$ at the factorization above can be substituted by a sequence of $|I_j|$ valid coinductive steps, getting a total distance $\sum_{j=0}^{k+1} \sum_{i \in I_j} d_{j1}^i + \sum_{j=0}^{k+1} \sum_{k=1}^{|I_j|} \alpha d_k = d$. $\qquad\square$

Next, a pair of examples to illustrate the unfolding and folding procedures.

Example 9. Let us consider the family of trees $\{a^n \mid n \in \mathbb{N}\}$, defined by $a^0 = \mathbf{0}$ and $a^{n+1} = aa^n$. We define b^n in an analogous way. Now, if $\mathbf{d}(a,b) = 1$, we have $a^n \equiv_2^{1/2} b^n \ \forall n \in \mathbb{N}$, using $\mathcal{D} = \{(a^n, b^n, 2) \mid n \in \mathbb{N}\}$, that is shown to be a $\frac{1}{2}$-ccd by considering $\mathbf{0} = \mathbf{0}$ and the sequences $\mathcal{C}^n := a^n = aa^{n-1} \equiv_{1/2 \cdot 2}^{\mathcal{D},1/2}$ $ba^{n-1} \equiv_{1/2 \cdot 2}^{\mathcal{D},1/2} bb^{n-1} = b^n$. Using the notion of unfolding above, we get the operational sequences $\mathcal{S}^n := a^n \leadsto_{\frac{1}{2},1}^1 ba^{n-1} \leadsto_{\frac{1}{2},1/2}^1 b^2 a^{n-2} \leadsto_{\frac{1}{2},1/4}^1 \cdots \leadsto_{\frac{1}{2},\frac{1}{2^{n-1}}}^1$ b^n. If we preserve the structure of the sequences $\mathcal{C}^n$, whose unfolding produce these operational sequences, we can visualize them in a arborescent way –see Fig.3–. The structure reminds that of *B-trees*, where we have nodes containing keys and pointers between them. The last give access to the elements in between the former that are located at nodes at "lower" levels. By means of the (inorder) traversing of the obtained tree we recover the original operational sequences.

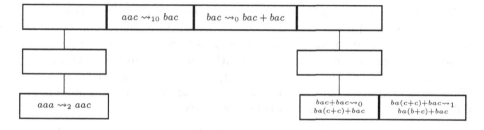

Fig. 4. Arborescent presentation of the operational sequence $\mathcal{S}$ in Ex.10

We are just "pushing the distance steps down" that correspond to "lower" levels, by introducing arcs that "move" the steps to the corresponding level. But whenever we have several steps in a row, that are not first level, then we group all of them introducing a single arc. We proceed in the same way down and down, introducing a "leaf" whenever we arrive to the level of a distance step, and new arcs going down, if there are other steps at the group at lower levels, either before or after the one which generated that leaf.

It is interesting to observe that we can also turn a^n into b^n in the opposite way, which means to use the same $\frac{1}{2}$-ccd, but a different sequence to check that it is indeed a $\frac{1}{2}$-ccd. We take now $\mathcal{C}'^n := a^n = aa^{n-1} \equiv_{1/2\cdot2}^{\mathcal{D},1/2} ab^{n-1} \equiv_1^{\mathcal{D},1/2} bb^{n-1} = b^n$. Its unfolding produces the "symmetric" tree on the right of Fig.3. Certainly, you can also recognize the reversibility of the operational sequences: by reading $\mathcal{C}'^n$ from right to left we recover $\mathcal{C}^n$, simply interchanging the roles of a and b.

Example 10. Taking $\mathbb{A} = \{a, b, c\}$ with $\mathbf{d}(a, c) = 8$, $\mathbf{d}(b, c) = 4$ and $\mathbf{d}(a, b) = 10$, we obtain $aaa \rightsquigarrow_{\frac{1}{2},13} ba(b + c) + bac$, by means of the sequence $\mathcal{S} := aaa \rightsquigarrow_{\frac{1}{2},2}^1$ $aac \rightsquigarrow_{\frac{1}{2},10}^1 bac \rightsquigarrow_{\frac{1}{2},0}^1 bac + bac \rightsquigarrow_{\frac{1}{2},0}^1 ba(c + c) + bac \rightsquigarrow_{\frac{1}{2},1}^1 ba(b + c) + bac$. In Fig.4 we see its arborescent presentation whose folding generates the $\frac{1}{2}$-ccd $\mathcal{D} = \{(aaa, ba(b+c)+bac, 13), (aaa, aac, 2), (aa, ac, 4), (a, c, 8), (bac+bac, ba(b+c) + bac, 1), (ac, a(b + c), 2), (c, (b + c), 4)\}$.

This is a more illustrative example of the general form of these arborescent presentations: we can have several "leaves" together with no arc in between them, when they correspond to several consecutive steps of the sequence at the current level. We can also have "degenerated" nodes, with a single arc down the tree, which corresponds to a subsequence of steps with none at the current level.

Even if Prop.7 only concerns finite trees, it reveals the duality between induction and coinduction, which is particularly interesting in the infinite case.

Example 11. Let us consider the tree $a^\infty = unfold(N_{1,\infty})$, with $N_{1,\infty}$ as in Ex.1. In an analogous way, we obtain the tree b^∞. We have $\pi_n(a^\infty) = a^n$, with a^n as in Ex.9. Therefore, a^∞ can be seen as the limit of its projections, and as we had $a^n \equiv_2^{1/2} b^n$, we have also $a^\infty \equiv_2^{1/2} b^\infty$. This can be proved by means of the (trivial!) collection $\mathcal{D} = \{(a^\infty, b^\infty, 2)\}$. We can check that $\mathcal{D}$ is indeed an $\frac{1}{2}$-ccd using the sequence $\mathcal{C} := a^\infty = aa^\infty \equiv_1^{\mathcal{D},1/2} ba^\infty \equiv_{\frac{1}{2}\cdot2}^{\mathcal{D},1/2} bb^\infty = b^\infty$.

Now, the (infinite!) "unfolding" of C would produce an infinite tree, that would "generate" an "infinite" operational sequence, which (intuitively) "converges" to b^∞, and "gives" us the bound 2 for the distance between a^∞ and b^∞. But our coinductive approach avoids the consideration of these limits. Moreover, the "traversing" of the arborescent presentations of the sequences, needed in many of our coinductive proofs, would produce "nested" infinite sequences much more difficult to cover without the coinductive approach.

Example 12. Let us take $\mathbb{A} = \{a, b, c, d\}$ with $\mathbf{d}(a, b) = 4$, $\mathbf{d}(c, d) = 1$. We can prove $ac^\infty + ad^\infty \equiv_6^{1/2} bc^\infty + bd^\infty$, using $\mathcal{D} = \{(ac^\infty + ad^\infty, bc^\infty + bd^\infty, 6), (c^\infty, d^\infty, 2)\}$, where the second triple in $\mathcal{D}$ is checked as in Ex.11; while for the first one we consider the coinductive sequence $\mathcal{C} := ac^\infty + ad^\infty \equiv_1^{1/2} ac^\infty + ac^\infty \equiv_0^{1/2} ac^\infty \equiv_4^{1/2} bc^\infty \equiv_0^{1/2} bc^\infty + bc^\infty \equiv_1^{1/2} bc^\infty + bd^\infty$.

Anyway, out of the informal level (where it is quite useful!) and the finite case (where it is sound), we will avoid the use of this unfolding in our formal developments. However, the following definition formalizes the use of finite unfolding, getting a generalized characterization of the relations $\equiv_d^\alpha$. It combines our two approaches (inductive, Def.7, and coinductive, Def.8,9) in a more flexible way; now operational steps can be used, not only at the first level of the trees, but also at any lower level.

Definition 11. *We consider the extension of the family of relations* $\langle \leadsto_{\alpha,d}^1 | d \in \mathbb{R}^+ \rangle$ *in Def.7 to FyTrees($\mathbb{A}$). Now, given a family* $\mathcal{D} = \{(t_i, t_i', d_i) \mid i \in I\}$ *with* $t_i, t_i' \in FyTrees(\mathbb{A})$ *and* $d_i \in \mathbb{R}^+$, *we define the family of relations* $\hat{\equiv}_d^{\mathcal{D},\alpha}$, *by:*

1. *$t \leadsto_{\alpha,d}^1 t'$ implies $t \hat{\equiv}_d^{\mathcal{D},\alpha} t'$.*
2. *For all $(t, t', d) \in \mathcal{D}$ we have $(\sum_{j \in J} a_j t_j) + at \hat{\equiv}_{\alpha \cdot d}^{\mathcal{D},\alpha} (\sum_{j \in J} a_j t_j) + at'$.*

Now, we can proceed exactly as in Def.9, using the relations $\hat{\equiv}_d^{\mathcal{D},\alpha}$ *instead of* $\equiv_d^{\mathcal{D},\alpha}$, *getting the family of relations* $\hat{\equiv}_d^\alpha$.

Proposition 8. *For all $d \in \mathbb{R}^+$, $\alpha \in (0, 1]$, the relations $\equiv_d^\alpha$ and $\hat{\equiv}_d^\alpha$ are equal.*

The (simple) proof of this result uses the fact that operational steps not at the first level of the trees, can be "hidden" into nested coinductive steps. However, their explicit use will produce in some cases much shorter and clearer proofs.

5   On the Continuity of the Global Bisimulations Distance

We have proved in Prop.7 the consistency between our inductive and coinductive definitions for finite trees. This can be turned into the limit by considering the coinductive definition and the (finite) projections of infinite processes.

Proposition 9. *For any α-ccd $\mathcal{D}$, the projected family $\pi(\mathcal{D}) = \{(\pi_n(t), \pi_n(t'), d) \mid (t, t', d) \in \mathcal{D}, n \in \mathbb{N}\}$ is an α-ccd that proves $t \equiv_d^\alpha t' \Rightarrow \forall n \in \mathbb{N} \; \pi_n(t) \equiv_d^\alpha \pi_n(t')$.*

Proof. Let $\mathcal{C} := t = t^0 \equiv_{d_1}^{\mathcal{D},\alpha} \ldots \equiv_{d_k}^{\mathcal{D},\alpha} t^k = t'$ be the sequence proving that $(t, t', d) \in \mathcal{D}$ satisfies the condition in order $\mathcal{D}$ to be an α-ccd. Then each projected sequence $\pi_n(\mathcal{C}) := \pi_n(t) = \pi_n(t^0) \equiv_{d_1}^{\pi(\mathcal{D}),\alpha} \ldots \equiv_{d_k}^{\pi(\mathcal{D}),\alpha} \pi_n(t^k) = \pi_n(t')$ proves that $(\pi_n(t), \pi_n(t'), d) \in \pi(\mathcal{D})$ satisfies the condition in order $\pi(\mathcal{D})$ to be an α-ccd. It is clear that the projection under π_n of any first level step in $\mathcal{C}$, is also a valid step in $\pi_n(\mathcal{C})$. Moreover, any coinductive step in $\mathcal{C}$ using $(t_1, t_1', d) \in \mathcal{D}$, can be substituted by the corresponding projected step, that uses $(\pi_{n-1}(t_1), \pi_{n-1}(t_1'), d) \in \pi(\mathcal{D})$.

$\square$

Remark 5. Alternatively, we can consider for each $n \in \mathbb{N}$ a family $\mathcal{D}_n = \pi_n(\mathcal{D}) = \{(\pi_m(t), \pi_m(t'), d) \mid (t, t', d) \in \mathcal{D}, \ m \in \mathbb{N} \wedge m \leq n\}$, using the fact that the subtrees of a projection $\pi_n(t)$ are also projections $\pi_m(t'')$ of subtrees t'' of t, for some $m < n$. These families satisfy $\pi_m(\mathcal{D}) \subseteq \pi_n(\mathcal{D})$, whenever $m \leq n$.

Example 13. Let us consider the trees a^∞ and b^∞ in Ex.11 and the $\frac{1}{2}$-ccd $\mathcal{D} = \{(a^\infty, b^\infty, 2)\}$ that proves $a^\infty \equiv_2^{1/2} b^\infty$, by means of the sequence $\mathcal{C} := a^\infty = aa^\infty \equiv_1^{\mathcal{D},1/2} ba^\infty \equiv_{\frac{1}{2}\cdot 2}^{\mathcal{D},1/2} bb^\infty = b^\infty$. Now for the families $\mathcal{D}_n = \pi_n(\mathcal{D})$ in Remark 5, we have $\mathcal{D}_n = \{(a^m, b^m, 2) \mid m \leq n\}$, which gives us $a^n \equiv_2^{1/2} b^n$ by means of the sequence $\mathcal{C}^n = \pi_n(\mathcal{C}) := a^n = aa^{n-1} \equiv_1^{\mathcal{D}_n,1/2} ba^{n-1} \equiv_{\frac{1}{2}\cdot 2}^{\mathcal{D}_n,1/2} bb^{n-1} = b^n$.

We conjecture that the converse of Prop.9 asserting the continuity of our coinductive distance, is also true. Unfortunately, the proof of this result is being much more complicated than we expected. Our idea, is to use the reasoning in the proof of Prop.9 in the opposite direction and the correspondence between operational and coinductive sequences in the finite case. As far as we have a collection of "uniform"[2] operational sequences $\mathcal{S}^n := \pi_n(t) \leadsto_{\alpha,d} \pi_n(t')$, we could "overlap" all of them getting an infinite tree as that in Fig.3. By "folding" this tree we obtain the coinductive sequence $\mathcal{C}$, proving $t \equiv_d^\alpha t'$. Next we provide a simple example.

Example 14. Let us consider the trees $t = ac^\infty + ad^\infty$ and $t' = bc^\infty + bd^\infty$, as in Ex.12, and the same distance **d** as there. Then we have:

$$\pi_1(t) = a + a \leadsto_{\frac{1}{2},0}^{(1)} a \leadsto_{\frac{1}{2},4}^{(1)} b \leadsto_{\frac{1}{2},0}^{(1)} b + b = \pi_1(t'),$$

$$\pi_2(t) = ac + ad \leadsto_{\frac{1}{2},\frac{1}{2}}^{(2)} ac + ac \leadsto_{\frac{1}{2},0}^{(1)} ac \leadsto_{\frac{1}{2},4}^{(1)} bc \leadsto_{\frac{1}{2},0}^{(1)} bc + bc \leadsto_{\frac{1}{2},\frac{1}{2}}^{(2)} bc + bd = \pi_2(t'),$$

$$\pi_3(t) = acc + add \leadsto_{\frac{1}{2},\frac{1}{2}\cdot 1}^{(2)} acc + acd \leadsto_{\frac{1}{2},\frac{1}{4}\cdot 1}^{(3)} acc + acc \leadsto_{\frac{1}{2},0}^{(1)} acc \leadsto_{\frac{1}{2},4}^{(1)}$$
$$bcc \leadsto_{\frac{1}{2},0}^{(1)} bcc + bcc \leadsto_{\frac{1}{2},\frac{1}{2}\cdot 1}^{(2)} bcc + bdc \leadsto_{\frac{1}{2},\frac{1}{4}\cdot 1}^{(3)} bcc + bdd = \pi_3(t').$$

We have included the superscripts (k) to indicate at which level we apply each transformation step. Each of these sequences can be obtained from the following one by removing the steps marked with $(i + 1)$ and applying π_i.

Now, if we consider the operational sequences, $\mathcal{S}^n$, relating $\pi_n(t)$ and $\pi_n(t')$, for any $n \in \mathbb{N}$, we obtain $\pi_n(t) \leadsto_{\frac{1}{2},d_n} \pi_n(t')$, for some $d_n < 6$. For instance, we

---

[2] Uniformity here means that for any $n, k \in \mathbb{N}$ with $k \geq n$ the steps of all the sequences $\mathcal{S}^k$ corresponding to the first n-levels are always the same.

get $\pi_1(t) \rightsquigarrow_{\frac{1}{2},4} \pi_1(t')$, $\pi_2(t) \rightsquigarrow_{\frac{1}{2},5} \pi_2(t')$ and $\pi_3(t) \rightsquigarrow_{\frac{1}{2},5.5} \pi_3(t')$. The obtained distances form an increasing (but bounded) sequence, since each of the operational sequences expand the former ones, adding new costs caused by the (new) differences at the bottom levels.

Turning these operational sequences into coinductive ones, C^n, as in Prop.7 we obtain the proof of $\pi_n(t) \equiv_6^{1/2} \pi_n(t')$, for all $n \in \mathbb{N}$. Here, it is convenient to use the (same) value 6 at all the cases.

$$C^1 := a + a \equiv_1^{1/2} a + a \equiv_0^{1/2} a \equiv_4^{1/2} b \equiv_0^{1/2} b + b \equiv_1^{1/2} b + b,$$
$$C^2 := ac + ad \equiv_1^{1/2} ac + ac \equiv_0^{1/2} ac \equiv_4^{1/2} bc \equiv_0^{1/2} bc + bc \equiv_1^{1/2} bc + bd,$$
$$C^3 := acc + add \equiv_1^{1/2} acc + acc \equiv_0^{1/2} acc \equiv_4^{1/2} bcc \equiv_0^{1/2} bcc + bcc \equiv_1^{1/2} bcc + bdd.$$

We expect that whenever we have $\pi_n(t) \equiv_d^\alpha \pi_n(t')$ $\forall n \in \mathbb{N}$ there will be a collection of uniform sequences proving these facts. For $t, t' \in FTrees(\mathbb{A})$ with $||t||_n, ||t'||_n \le l$ and $t \rightsquigarrow_{\alpha,d} t'$, we should prove this by means of a sequence S that only uses intermediate trees t'' with $||t''||_n \le f(l,n)$, for a certain function f. But, the existence of such a uniform bound is still to be proved.

6   Conclusions and Future Work

We have presented a coinductive characterization of our global bisimulation distance, that previously we presented in an operational and an algebraic way. So, we extend our distance to the case of infinite trees without needing to introduce any complex notion of limit of our finite transformations generating the distances between finite trees. The coinductive approach makes the work in a much easier way. Our coinductive distances are always "sound" wrt the distances between their respective finite approximations. We expect that the "completeness" result, ending the proof of continuity, will also be true.

Besides the work devoted to complete the proof of the continuity theorem, now we are working in two complementary directions. On the one hand, we will try to apply our coinductive distance in order to define distances for testing, which should state how far away is a process to pass the tests imposed by any specification. On the other hand, we will continue the theoretical study of our coinductive distances. We consider that the results here are very promising, showing a new field of application of coinductive techniques into the study of the semantics of processes. We hope that much more will be shortly coming.

References

1. Černý, P., Henzinger, T.A., Radhakrishna, A.: Quantitative simulation games. In: Manna, Z., Peled, D.A. (eds.) Time for Verification. LNCS, vol. 6200, pp. 42–60. Springer, Heidelberg (2010)
2. Černý, P., Henzinger, T.A., Radhakrishna, A.: Simulation distances. In: Gastin, P., Laroussinie, F. (eds.) CONCUR 2010. LNCS, vol. 6269, pp. 253–268. Springer, Heidelberg (2010)

3. de Alfaro, L., Henzinger, T.A., Majumdar, R.: Discounting the future in systems theory. In: Baeten, J.C.M., Lenstra, J.K., Parrow, J., Woeginger, G.J. (eds.) ICALP 2003. LNCS, vol. 2719, pp. 1022–1037. Springer, Heidelberg (2003)
4. de Alfaro, L., Majumdar, R., Raman, V., Stoelinga, M.: Game relations and metrics. In: LICS 2007, pp. 99–108. IEEE Computer Society (2007)
5. Desharnais, J., Gupta, V., Jagadeesan, R., Panangaden, P.: Metrics for labeled markov systems. In: Baeten, J.C.M., Mauw, S. (eds.) CONCUR 1999. LNCS, vol. 1664, pp. 258–273. Springer, Heidelberg (1999)
6. Desharnais, J., Laviolette, F., Tracol, M.: Approximate analysis of probabilistic processes: Logic, simulation and games. In: QEST 2008, pp. 264–273. IEEE Computer Society (2008)
7. Fahrenberg, U., Legay, A., Thrane, C.R.: The quantitative linear-time–branching-time spectrum. In: FSTTCS 2011. LIPIcs, vol. 13, pp. 103–114. Schloss Dagstuhl - Leibniz-Zentrum für Informatik (2011)
8. Fahrenberg, U., Thrane, C.R., Larsen, K.G.: Distances for weighted transition systems: Games and properties. In: QAPL 2011, pp. 134–147 (2011)
9. Giacalone, A., Jou, C., Smolka, S.A.: Algebraic reasoning for probabilistic concurrent systems. In: Proc. IFIP TC2 Working Conference on Programming Concepts and Methods, pp. 443–458. North-Holland (1990)
10. Henzinger, T.A., Otop, J.: From model checking to model measuring. In: D'Argenio, P.R., Melgratti, H. (eds.) CONCUR 2013 – Concurrency Theory. LNCS, vol. 8052, pp. 273–287. Springer, Heidelberg (2013)
11. Jacobs, B.: Exercises in coalgebraic specification. In: Blackhouse, R., Crole, R.L., Gibbons, J. (eds.) Algebraic and Coalgebraic Methods in the Mathematics of Program Construction. LNCS, vol. 2297, pp. 237–280. Springer, Heidelberg (2002)
12. Jacobs, B.: Introduction to coalgebra. towards mathematics of states and observations (2012), http://www.cs.ru.nl/B.Jacobs/CLG/JacobsCoalgebraIntro.pdf
13. Kiehn, A., Arun-Kumar, S.: Amortised bisimulations. In: Wang, F. (ed.) FORTE 2005. LNCS, vol. 3731, pp. 320–334. Springer, Heidelberg (2005)
14. Milner, R.: Communication and concurrency. Prentice Hall (1989)
15. Nielsen, M., Clausen, C.: Bisimulation, games, and logic. In: Karhumäki, J., Rozenberg, G., Maurer, H.A. (eds.) Results and Trends in Theoretical Computer Science. LNCS, vol. 812, pp. 289–306. Springer, Heidelberg (1994)
16. Park, D.M.R.: Concurrency and automata on infinite sequences. In: Deussen, P. (ed.) GI-TCS 1981. LNCS, vol. 104, pp. 167–183. Springer, Heidelberg (1981)
17. Romero Hernández, D., de Frutos Escrig, D.: Defining distances for all process semantics. In: Giese, H., Rosu, G. (eds.) FMOODS/ FORTE 2012. LNCS, vol. 7273, pp. 169–185. Springer, Heidelberg (2012)
18. Romero Hernández, D., de Frutos Escrig, D.: Distances between processes: A pure algebraic approach. In: Martí-Oliet, N., Palomino, M. (eds.) WADT 2012. LNCS, vol. 7841, pp. 265–282. Springer, Heidelberg (2013)
19. Rutten, J.J.M.M.: Universal coalgebra: a theory of systems. Theor. Comput. Sci. 249(1), 3–80 (2000)
20. Sangiorgi, D.: Advanced topics in bisimulation and coinduction. Cambridge Tracts in Theoretical Computer Science (2011)
21. Stirling, C.: The joys of bisimulation. In: Brim, L., Gruska, J., Zlatuška, J. (eds.) MFCS 1998. LNCS, vol. 1450, pp. 142–151. Springer, Heidelberg (1998)
22. Stirling, C.: Bisimulation, modal logic and model checking games. Logic Journal of the IGPL 7(1), 103–124 (1999)
23. Ying, M., Wirsing, M.: Approximate bisimilarity. In: Rus, T. (ed.) AMAST 2000. LNCS, vol. 1816, pp. 309–322. Springer, Heidelberg (2000)

Mechanizing the Minimization
of Deterministic Generalized Büchi Automata[*]

Souheib Baarir[1,2] and Alexandre Duret-Lutz[3]

[1] Université Paris Ouest Nanterre la Défense, Nanterre, France
[2] Sorbonne Universités, UPMC Univ. Paris 6, UMR 7606, LIP6, Paris, France
souheib.baarir@lip6.fr
[3] LRDE, EPITA, Le Kremlin-Bicêtre, France
adl@lrde.epita.fr

Abstract. Deterministic Büchi automata (DBA) are useful to (prob-abilistic) model checking and synthesis. We survey techniques used to obtain and minimize DBAs for different classes of properties. We extend these techniques to support DBA that have generalized and transition-based acceptance (DTGBA) as they can be even smaller. Our minimiza-tion technique—a reduction to a SAT problem—synthesizes a DTGBA equivalent to the input DTGBA for any given number of states and num-ber of acceptance sets (assuming such automaton exists). We present benchmarks using a framework that implements all these techniques.

1 Introduction

Deterministic Büchi automata (DBA) are used in several domains like proba-bilistic model checking [3] or synthesis of distributed systems [13]. DBAs are commonly obtained from Büchi automata (BA) by applying Safra's construc-tion [20] or, when it works, some powerset-based construction [9]. Since appli-cations are usually more efficient when dealing with small automata, it makes sense to try to minimize these DBA (i.e., find an equivalent DBA such that no smaller equivalent DBA exist). Two techniques can be used depending on the class of the DBA at hand. Weak DBAs (where accepting cycles cannot mix with rejecting cycles) are minimizable almost like finite automata [16]. For the general case, which is NP-complete [21], Ehlers [11] gives a reduction to a SAT problem.

For model checking, several efficient algorithms have been developed to check the emptiness of BAs, but also generalized Büchi automata (GBA) [19], and even transition-based generalized Büchi automata (TGBA) [8]. GBAs have multiple sets of accepting states, while TGBAs have multiple sets of accepting transitions. All these automata types are expressively equivalent, but GBAs and TGBAs are more concise than BAs. Furthermore, TGBAs are naturally obtained from linear-time temporal logic (LTL) formulae [10].

In this paper, we discuss the construction of minimal deterministic transition-based generalized Büchi automata (DTGBA) for which we do not know any

---

[*] This work has been supported by the project ImpRo/ANR-2010-BLAN-0317.

E. Ábrahám and C. Palamidessi (Eds.), FORTE 2014, LNCS 8461, pp. 266–283, 2014.
© IFIP International Federation for Information Processing 2014

general minimization technique. To handle (non-deterministic) TGBA as input, we propose (and implement) two processing chains that convert TGBA into minimal DTGBA. One attempts to determinize transition-based Büchi automata via a powerset construction, the other uses Safra's construction. Although these two determinizations do not work with generalized acceptance, we interpret the resulting automaton as a DTGBA with a single acceptance set and attempt to minimize it using *more* acceptance sets. The minimization technique we propose is a generalization of Ehlers' SAT-based procedure [11] to deal with DTGBA instead of DBA. This way we effectively obtain a minimal DTGBA, even though we use determinization procedures that do not support generalized acceptance.

The paper is organized as follows. Section 2 defines the various types of automata, some conversions between them, and key concepts. Section 3 reviews the hierarchy of recurrence properties and algorithms that exist to determinize or minimize automata in that class. Section 4 shows how to encode the minimization of a DTGBA as a SAT-problem, and then discusses its use. Finally, Section 5 presents results on the minimization of DTGBA obtained from LTL formulae.

2   Preliminaries

Let AP be a finite set of (atomic) propositions, and let $\mathbb{B} = \{\bot, \top\}$ represent Boolean values. An assignment is a function $\ell : \text{AP} \to \mathbb{B}$ that valuates each proposition. $\Sigma = \mathbb{B}^{\text{AP}}$ is the set of all assignments of AP. X^* (resp. X^ω) denotes the set of finite (resp. infinite) sequences over a set X. The empty sequence is denoted ε. A *word* $w \in (\mathbb{B}^{\text{AP}})^\omega$ is an infinite sequence of assignments. A *language* (also called *property*) is a set of words. For any infinite sequence π we denote by $\inf(\pi)$ the set of elements that appear infinitely often in π.

Definition 1 (Labeled Transition System). *An LTS is a tuple $S = \langle \text{AP}, Q, \iota, \delta \rangle$ where AP is a finite set of atomic propositions, Q is a finite set of states, $\iota \in Q$ is the initial state, $\delta \subseteq Q \times \mathbb{B}^{\text{AP}} \times Q$ is the transition relation, labeling each transition by an assignment.*

A run of an LTS is an infinite sequence $\pi = (q_0, \ell_0, q_1)(q_1, \ell_1, q_2)$ $(q_2, \ell_2, q_3) \cdots \in \delta^\omega$ of transitions such that $q_0 = \iota$. For any such run, we denote by $\pi_{|Q} = q_0 q_1 q_2 \cdots \in Q^\omega$ the sequence of states it visits, and we say that π recognizes the word $\ell_0 \ell_1 \ell_2 \cdots \in (\mathbb{B}^{\text{AP}})^\omega$.

A cycle $C = (q_1, \ell_1, q_2)(q_2, \ell_2, q_3) \dots (q_n, \ell_n, q_1)$ is a finite sequence of transitions that forms a loop and visits the finite sequence $C_{|Q} = q_1 \dots q_n$ of states. For notational convenience, we sometime interpret $C_{|Q}$ as a set of states.

As an implementation optimization, and to simplify illustrations, it is practical to use *edges* labeled by Boolean formulae to group *transitions* with same sources and destinations: for instance two *transitions* $(s_1, a\bar{b}, s_2)$ and (s_1, ab, s_2) will be represented by an *edge* from s_1 to s_2 and labeled by the Boolean formula a.

For convenience of notation, we may view the relation δ as a one-argument function $\delta : Q \to 2^{(\mathbb{B}^{\text{AP}} \times Q)}$ with $\delta(q) = \{(\ell, d) \mid (q, \ell, d) \in \delta\}$ or as a two-argument function $\delta : Q \times \mathbb{B}^{\text{AP}} \to 2^Q$ with $\delta(q, \ell) = \{d \mid (q, \ell, d) \in \delta\}$.

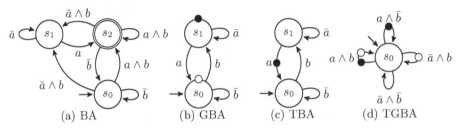

Fig. 1. Minimal deterministic automata recognizing the LTL formula $\mathsf{GF}a \wedge \mathsf{GF}b$

Definition 2 (Deterministic and Complete). *An LTS* $\mathcal{S} = \langle \mathrm{AP}, Q, \iota, \delta \rangle$ *is deterministic iff* $|\delta(q, \ell)| \leq 1$ *for all* $q \in Q$ *and* $\ell \in \mathbb{B}^{\mathrm{AP}}$, *and it is complete iff* $|\delta(q, \ell)| \geq 1$ *for all* q *and* ℓ.

To characterize the infinite runs of an LTS that should be accepted, we consider several variants of Büchi automata that differ by their acceptance condition.

Definition 3 (Büchi-like Automata). *A Büchi-like automaton is a pair* $\mathcal{A} = \langle S, \mathcal{F} \rangle$ *where* S *is an LTS, and* $\mathcal{F}$ *is a finite set whose semantic is defined differently for each type of acceptance. Given a run* π *and a cycle* C:
BA: *for Büchi Automata,* $\mathcal{F} \subseteq Q$, π *is accepted iff* $\inf(\pi_{|Q}) \cap \mathcal{F} \neq \emptyset$, *and* C *is accepting iff* $C_{|Q} \cap \mathcal{F} \neq \emptyset$;
GBA: *for Generalized Büchi Automata,* $\mathcal{F} \subseteq 2^Q$, π *is accepted iff* $\forall F \in \mathcal{F}$, $\inf(\pi_{|Q}) \cap F \neq \emptyset$, *and* C *is accepting iff* $\forall F \in \mathcal{F}$, $C_{|Q} \cap F \neq \emptyset$;
TBA: *for Transition-based Büchi Automata,* $\mathcal{F} \subseteq \delta$, π *is accepted iff* $\inf(\pi) \cap \mathcal{F} \neq \emptyset$, *and* C *is accepting iff* $C \cap \mathcal{F} \neq \emptyset$;
TGBA: *for Transition-based Generalized Büchi Automata,* $\mathcal{F} \subseteq 2^\delta$, π *is accepted iff* $\forall F \in \mathcal{F}$, $\inf(\pi) \cap F \neq \emptyset$, *and* C *is accepting iff* $\forall F \in \mathcal{F}$, $C \cap F \neq \emptyset$.
In all cases the language $\mathcal{L}(\mathcal{A})$ *of an automaton is the set of words recognized by accepting runs of* $\mathcal{A}$. *A cycle is rejecting iff it is not accepting.*
   DBA, DGBA, DTBA, and DTGBA, denote the restrictions of the above types to automata where the associated LTS S *is deterministic.*

As an example, Fig. 1 shows one deterministic and complete automaton of each type. For BA, the states in $\mathcal{F}$ (called accepting states), are traditionally denoted by double circles. For GBA, $\mathcal{F} = \{F_1, F_2, \ldots\}$ is a set of acceptance sets $F_i \subseteq Q$, and each of these F_i is pictured using colored dots on the side of the states it contains (a state may have multiple such dots if it belongs to multiple acceptance sets). For transition-based acceptance (TBA or TGBA), we put those colored dots on the transitions (of course, only one color is used for TBA).

Definition 4 (SCC). *A* strongly connected component *(SCC) of an automaton* $\langle S, \mathcal{F} \rangle$ *is a set of states that are pairwise connected in* S, *and that is maximal with respect to inclusion. An SCC is* accepting *if it contains an accepting cycle, otherwise, it is* rejecting. *An SCC with a single state and no cycle is called* trivial.

Definition 5 (Automaton Typeness). *An automaton $\mathcal{A} = \langle S, \mathcal{F} \rangle$ is said to be β-type if there exists an automaton $\mathcal{B} = \langle S, \mathcal{F}' \rangle$ of acceptance type β such that $\mathscr{L}(\mathcal{A}) = \mathscr{L}(\mathcal{B})$. In other words, $\mathcal{A}$ is β-type if we can change its acceptance set so that it accepts the same language with the same transition structure but with a different type of acceptance condition (the β one).*

For instance any BA $\langle S, \mathcal{F} \rangle$ is GBA-type, because it can be trivially represented as the GBA $\langle S, \{\mathcal{F}\} \rangle$. Any GBA $\langle S, \{F_1, \ldots, F_n\} \rangle$ is TGBA-type, since it is equivalent to the TGBA $\langle S, \{F_1', \ldots, F_n'\} \rangle$ with $F_i = \{(s, \ell, d) \mid (s, \ell, d) \in \delta \wedge s \in F_i\}$ (i.e., the membership of any state to some accepting set F_i is transferred to all its outgoing transitions). Similarly all BA are TBA-type, and all TBA are TGBA-type. These trivial conversions can sometime be used in the opposite direction. For instance a TGBA is "trivially" GBA-type if all the outgoing transitions of each state belong to the same acceptance sets.

Since a TGBA can represent any considered type (BA, GBA, TBA) using the same transition structure, it is often practical to consider only TGBAs and treat the other types as particular cases. For algorithms that cannot deal with generalized acceptance, a TGBA can be *degeneralized* into a TBA or a BA [2]. For instance the TBA of Fig. 1(c) was degeneralized from the TGBA of Fig. 1(d).

Definition 6 (Realizability). *A property (or an automaton) is β-realizable if there exists an automaton with β acceptance that accepts the same language.*

Any Büchi-like automaton is β-realizable for $\beta \in \{\text{BA}, \text{GBA}, \text{TBA}, \text{TGBA}\}$. Furthermore any deterministic Büchi-like automaton is $D\beta$-realizable. However it is well known than not all BAs are DBA-realizable, and this fact holds for the three other types of Büchi acceptance as well.

Definition 7 (Weakness). *An automaton is* inherently weak *if it contains no accepting cycle that has a state in common with a rejecting cycle.*

This notion of *inherent weakness* [5] generalizes the more common notion of weak automaton [4, 6] where states of an SCC should be either all accepting or all non-accepting. Defining $\mathcal{F}$ as the set of states that belong to some accepting cycle will turn any inherently weak automaton into a Weak BA (WBA) [5].

Definition 8 (Minimal-state automaton [17]). *For a language $L \subseteq \Sigma^\omega$, let $\approx_L \subseteq \Sigma^* \times \Sigma^*$ be the right-congruence defined by $u \approx_L v$ iff $u\alpha \in L \iff v\alpha \in L$ for all $\alpha \in \Sigma^\omega$. Let $[\cdot]$ denote the equivalence classes of L, i.e., $[u] = \{v \in \Sigma^* \mid u \approx_L v\}$. The minimal-state automaton of L, denoted $MSA(L)$ is the (complete and deterministic) LTS $\langle AP, \{[u] \mid u \in \Sigma^*\}, [\varepsilon], \delta \rangle$ where $\delta([u], \ell) = [u\ell]$.*

3   Existing Determinization and Minimization Procedures

We now discuss several existing procedures to determinize and minimize Büchi automata. Some of these apply only to specific subclasses of temporal properties.

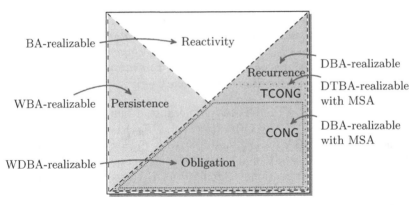

Fig. 2. Hierarchy of temporal properties in relation with subclasses of Büchi BA

Figure 2 shows a classification of temporal properties, using the names from Manna and Pnueli [18], and with an additional couple of interesting subclasses. The whole square represents the entire set of BA-realizable properties, also called *reactivity* properties. This set includes *persistence* properties, which can be realized by weak automata, and *recurrence* properties ,which can be realized by deterministic automata. The intersection of these last two sets defines the *obligation* properties, which can be realized by weak and deterministic automata. The *obligation* class includes the well-known subclasses of *safety* and *guarantee* properties (not depicted here), as well as all their Boolean combinations.

Determinization. Assume that a recurrence property φ is represented by a possibly non-deterministic BA $A_\varphi = \langle T, \mathcal{F} \rangle$, and for which we wish to obtain a DBA $D_\varphi = \langle T', \mathcal{F}' \rangle$. We can consider different procedures depending on the class to which φ belongs.

If φ is known to be an obligation (for most LTL formulae, this can be checked syntactically [6]), then a weak DBA (WDBA) D_φ can be obtained from A_φ in a quite efficient way [9]: T should be determinized by the classical powerset construction to create $T' = \mathcal{P}(T)$, and the set $\mathcal{F}'$ can be computed by selecting one word of each SCC of T' and checking whether it is accepted by A_φ. Dax et al. [9] additionally show that if it is not known whether a property φ is an obligation, this procedure may still be applied but its result D_φ must then be checked for equivalence with A_φ.

The class CONG is defined as the set of languages L which are realizable by a BA automaton whose LTS is $MSA(L)$, this includes all obligations as well as some properties that are not expressible by weak automata. For instance the property specified by the formula $G(a \rightarrow X\neg a) \wedge GF(a)$ is in CONG: it has three equivalence classes $[\varepsilon]$, $[a]$, and $[aa]$, and the corresponding MSA can be used to define the DBA shown in Fig. 3(a).

The formula GFa is not in CONG because its MSA has a single state (the language has no distinguishing prefixes), yet there is no single-state DBA that can recognize GFa. However there exists a 1-state DTBA for this property, shown in Fig. 3(b). We could therefore define the class TCONG of properties that are

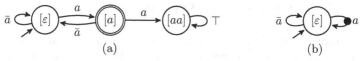

Fig. 3. (a) $G(a \rightarrow X\neg a) \wedge GFa$ specifies a property in CONG: it is realizable by a DBA whose LTS is the MSA of its language. (b) Although GFa is not in CONG, its MSA can serve as a support for an equivalent DTBA.

DTBA-realizable with their MSA as LTS. Note that $GFa \wedge GFb$ whose MSA also has a single state, is not in TCONG: its minimal DTBA is shown in Fig. 1(c).

Dax et al. [9] show that you can apply the classical powerset construction to determinize the LTS of any BA $A_\varphi = \langle T, \mathcal{F} \rangle$ recognizing a property in CONG, and the resulting deterministic LTS $T' = \mathcal{P}(T)$ can be labeled as a DBA $D_\varphi = \langle T', \mathcal{F}' \rangle$ recognizing $\mathscr{L}(A_\varphi)$. The algorithm used to obtain the necessary $\mathcal{F}'$ is more complex than the one used for weak automata as it requires an enumeration of all the elementary cycles in T'. Futhermore, the DBAs obtained this way are not necessary minimal. This construction can be extended straightforwardly to transition-based acceptance; this way we may obtain DTBAs for properties (such as GFa) where the original state-based procedure would not deliver any DBA.

Another determinization procedure, which applies to all recurrence properties, is to use Safra's construction [20] to convert a BA into a deterministic Rabin automaton (DRA). More generally, Schewe and Varghese [22] have recently proposed a determinization algorithm that inputs a TGBA and outputs a DRA. DRA that express recurrence properties are all DBA-type, and Krishnan et al. [15] show how to compute the associated DBAs.

Unfortunately, all these determinization procedures produce only DBA (or DTBA). To our knowledge, there is no determinization procedure that would produce a deterministic automaton with generalized acceptance.

Minimization. Minimizing a DBA, i.e., building a DBA such that no smaller equivalent DBA exist, is in general, an NP-complete problem [21].

However, weak DBAs (i.e., obligation properties) can be minimized using an algorithm identical to those performed on deterministic finite automata: the only requirement is to choose the acceptance of trivial SCCs correctly [16].

For the more general recurrence properties, Ehlers [11] gives an encoding of an equivalent minimal DBA as the solution of a SAT problem. His technique can also be extended straightforwardly to minimize a DTBA.

Until now there were no minimization procedure for generalized Büchi automata. In the next section we show an encoding inspired by Ehlers' [11] for minimizing DTGBAs. For any DTGBA A with n states and m acceptance sets, our encoding attempts to synthesize an equivalent DTGBA with n' states and m' acceptance sets for some given n' or m' (and possibly $m' > m$). By combining this procedure with existing (non-generalized) determinizations, we effectively obtain a minimal DTGBA with multiple acceptance sets, even though we do not know of any determinization procedure that supports generalized acceptance.

4 Synthesis of Equivalent DTGBA

Given a complete DTGBA $R = \langle\langle AP, Q_R, \iota_R, \delta_R\rangle, \mathcal{F}_R\rangle$, and two integers n and m, we would like to construct (when it exists) a complete DTGBA $C = \langle\langle AP, Q_C, \iota_C, \delta_C\rangle, \mathcal{F}_C\rangle$ such that $\mathcal{L}(R) = \mathcal{L}(C)$, $|Q_C| = n$ and $|\mathcal{F}_C| = m$. We call R the *reference* automaton, and C, the *candidate* automaton.

Since C and R are complete and deterministic, any word of Σ^ω has a unique run in R and C, and testing $\mathcal{L}(R) = \mathcal{L}(C)$ can be done by ensuring that each word is accepted by R iff it is accepted by C. In practice, this is checked by ensuring that any cycle of the synchronous product $C \otimes R$ corresponds to cycles that are either accepting in C and R, or rejecting in both.

This observation is used by Ehlers [11] for his SAT encoding. In his case, a cycle in a DBA can be detected as accepting as soon as it visits an accepting state. We use a similar encoding for our setup. However, because of the generalized acceptance condition of DTGBAs, we have to keep track of all the acceptance sets visited by paths of the product to ensure that cycles have the same acceptance status in both C and R.

4.1 Encoding as a SAT Problem

Let $SCC_R \subseteq 2^{Q_R}$ denote the set of non-trivial strongly connected components of R, and let $Acc(q_1', \ell, q_2') = \{A \in \mathcal{F}_R \mid (q_1', \ell, q_2') \in A\}$ be the set of acceptance sets of R that contain the transition $(q_1', \ell, q_2') \in \delta_R$.

We encode C with two sets of variables:

- The variables $\{\langle q_1, \ell, q_2\rangle_{\delta_C} \mid (q_1, q_2) \in Q_C^2, \ell \in \Sigma\}$ encode the existence of transitions $(q_1, \ell, q_2) \in \delta_C$ in the candidate automaton.
- Variables $\{\langle q_1, \ell, A_i, q_2\rangle_{\mathcal{F}_C} \mid (q_1, q_2) \in Q_C^2, \ell \in \Sigma, A_i \in \mathcal{F}_C\}$ encode the membership of these transitions to the acceptance set $A_i \in \mathcal{F}_C$ of C.

For the product $C \otimes R$, we retain the reachable states, and parts of paths that might eventually be completed to become cycles.

- A variable in $\{\langle q, q', q, q', \emptyset, \emptyset\rangle \mid q \in Q_C, q' \in Q_R\}$ encodes the existence of a reachable state (q, q') in $C \otimes R$. The reason we use a sextuplet to encode such a pair is that each (q, q') will serve as a starting point for possible paths.
- A variable in $\{\langle q_1, q_1', q_2, q_2', F, F'\rangle \mid (q_1, q_2) \in Q_C^2, S \in SCC_R, (q_1', q_2') \in S^2, F \subseteq \mathcal{F}_C, F' \subseteq \mathcal{F}_R\}$ denotes that there is a path between (q_1, q_1') and (q_2, q_2') in the product, such that its projection on the candidate automaton visits the acceptance sets $F \subseteq \mathcal{F}_C$, and its projection on the reference automaton visits the acceptance sets $F' \subseteq \mathcal{F}_R$. This set of variables is used to implement the cycle equivalence check, so the only q_1' and q_2' that need to be considered should belong to the same non-trivial SCC of R.

With these variables, the automaton C can be obtained as a solution of the following SAT problem. First, C should be complete (i.e., δ_C is total):

$$\bigwedge_{q_1 \in Q_C, \ell \in \Sigma} \bigvee_{q_2 \in Q_C} \langle q_1, \ell, q_2\rangle_{\delta_C} \tag{1}$$

The initial state of the product exists. Furthermore, if (q_1, q_1') is a state of the product, $(q_1', \ell, q_2') \in \delta_R$ is a transition in the reference automaton, and

$(q_1, \ell, q_2) \in \delta_C$ is a transition in the candidate automaton, then (q_2, q'_2) is a state of the product too:

$$\bigwedge \langle \iota_C, \iota_R, \iota_C, \iota_R, \emptyset, \emptyset \rangle \wedge \bigwedge_{\substack{(q_1,q_2)\in Q_C^2, q'_1\in Q_R, \\ (\ell,q'_2)\in\delta_R(q'_1)}} \langle q_1, q'_1, q_1, q'_1, \emptyset, \emptyset \rangle \wedge \langle q_1, \ell, q_2 \rangle_{\delta_C} \to \langle q_2, q'_2, q_2, q'_2, \emptyset, \emptyset \rangle \quad (2)$$

Any transition of the product augments an existing path, updating the sets F and F' of acceptance sets visited in each automata. Unfortunately, we have to consider all possible subsets $G \in 2^{\mathcal{F}_C}$ of acceptances sets to which the candidate transition (q_2, ℓ, q_3) could belong, and emit a different rule for each possible G.

$$\wedge \bigwedge_{\substack{(q_1,q_2,q_3)\in Q_C^3, \\ (F,G)\in(2^{\mathcal{F}_C})^2, \\ S\in SCC_R, (q'_1,q'_2)\in S^2, \\ F'\in 2^{\mathcal{F}_R}, (\ell,q'_3)\in\delta_R(q'_2)}} \left(\begin{array}{l} \langle q_1, q'_1, q_2, q'_2, F, F' \rangle \\ \wedge \langle q_2, \ell, q_3 \rangle_{\delta_C} \\ \wedge \bigwedge_{A\in G} \langle q_2, \ell, A, q_3 \rangle_{\mathcal{F}_C} \\ \wedge \bigwedge_{A\notin G} \neg \langle q_2, \ell, A, q_3 \rangle_{\mathcal{F}_C} \end{array} \right) \to \begin{array}{l} \langle q_1, q'_1, q_3, q'_3, F\cup G, \\ F'\cup Acc(q'_2, \ell, q'_3) \rangle \end{array} \quad (3)$$

If a path of the product is followed by a transition $(q'_2, \ell, q'_3) \in \delta_R$ and a transition $(q_2, \ell, q_3) \in \delta_C$ that both closes the cycle $(q_3 = q_1 \wedge q'_3 = q'_1)$, but such that this cycle is non-accepting with respect to the reference automaton $(Acc(q'_2, \ell, q'_3) \cup F' \neq \mathcal{F}_R)$, then the cycle formed in the candidate automaton by (q_2, ℓ, q_1) should not be accepting (at least one acceptance set of $\mathcal{F}_C \setminus F$ is missing):

$$\wedge \bigwedge_{\substack{(q_1,q_2)\in Q_C^2, F\in 2^{\mathcal{F}_C}, \\ S\in SCC_R, (q'_1,q'_2)\in S^2, F'\in 2^{\mathcal{F}_R}, \\ (\ell,q'_3)\in\delta_R(q'_2), q'_3=q'_1, \\ Acc(q'_2,\ell,q'_3)\cup F'\neq\mathcal{F}_R}} \langle q_1, q'_1, q_2, q'_2, F, F' \rangle \wedge \langle q_2, \ell, q_1 \rangle_{\delta_C} \to \neg \bigwedge_{A\in\mathcal{F}_C\setminus F} \langle q_2, \ell, A, q_1 \rangle_{\mathcal{F}_C} \quad (4)$$

Conversely, if a path of the product is followed by a transition $(q'_2, \ell, q'_3) \in \delta_R$ and a transition $(q_2, \ell, q_3) \in \delta_C$ that both closes the cycle $(q_3 = q_1 \wedge q'_3 = q'_1)$, but such that this cycle is accepting with respect to the reference automaton $(Acc(q'_2, \ell, q'_3) \cup F' = \mathcal{F}_R)$, then the cycle formed in the candidate automaton by (q_2, ℓ, q_1) should also be accepting ((q_2, ℓ, q_1) should belong at least to all missing acceptance sets $\mathcal{F}_C \setminus F$):

$$\wedge \bigwedge_{\substack{(q_1,q_2)\in Q_C^2, F\in 2^{\mathcal{F}_C}, \\ S\in SCC_R, (q'_1,q'_2)\in S^2, F'\in 2^{\mathcal{F}_R}, \\ (\ell,q'_3)\in\delta_R(q'_2), q'_3=q'_1 \\ Acc(q'_2,\ell,q'_3)\cup F'=\mathcal{F}_R}} \langle q_1, q'_1, q_2, q'_2, F, F' \rangle \wedge \langle q_2, \ell, q_1 \rangle_{\delta_C} \to \bigwedge_{A\in\mathcal{F}_C\setminus F} \langle q_2, \ell, A, q_1 \rangle_{\mathcal{F}_C} \quad (5)$$

Optimizations. As suggested by Ehlers [11], the set of possible solutions can be optionally constrained with some partial symmetry breaking clauses. Assuming $Q_C = \{q_1, ..., q_n\}$ and $\Sigma = \{\ell_0, ..., \ell_{m-1}\}$ we can order the transitions of the solution lexicographically with respect to their source and label, as (q_1, ℓ_0, d_1), (q_1, ℓ_1, d_2), ..., (q_1, ℓ_{m-1}, d_m), (q_2, ℓ_0, d_{m+1}), etc., and constrain the solution so that the destination of the first transition should be chosen between $d_1 \in \{q_1, q_2\}$, the destination of the second between $d_2 \in \{q_1, q_2, q_3\}$, etc.

$$\wedge \bigwedge_{1\leq i\leq |Q|, 0\leq j<|\Sigma|, (i-1)|\Sigma|+j+3\leq k\leq n} \neg \langle q_i, \ell_j, q_k \rangle_{\delta_C} \quad (S)$$

REDUCESTATESDTGBA($R, m = R.\text{nb\_acc\_sets}()$):
   repeat:
      $n \leftarrow R.\text{nb\_states}()$
      $C \leftarrow$ SYNTHESIZEDTGBA($R, n - 1, m$)
      if C **does not exists: return** R
      $R \leftarrow C$

Fig. 4. Given a complete DTGBA A, attempt to build an equivalent smaller one with the same number of acceptance sets

Equations (3)–(5) can be encoded more efficiently when q_1' and q_2' belong to a weak SCC. In that case it is not necessary to remember the history F' of the acceptance sets seen by paths in that SCC, since all paths are either accepting or rejecting. Variables of the form $\langle q_1, q_1', q_2, q_2', F, F' \rangle$ where $F' \in 2^{\mathcal{F}_R}$ can hence be restricted to just $F' = \emptyset$, limiting the number of variables and clauses emitted.

State-based Output. To produce automata with state-based acceptance, it suffices to consider all variables $\langle q, \ell, A_i, q' \rangle_{\mathcal{F}_C}$ that share the same q and A_i as aliases. This way, the DTGBA output is DGBA-type.

4.2   Usage

We call SYNTHESIZEDTGBA(R, n, m) the procedure that:
1. inputs a complete DTGBA R, two integers $n = |Q_C|$ and $m = |\mathcal{F}_C|$,
2. produces a DIMACS file with all the above clauses,
3. calls a SAT solver to solve this problem,
4. builds the resulting DTGBA C if it exists. The construction of this automaton depends only on the value of variables $\{\langle q, \ell, q' \rangle_{\delta_C} \mid (q, q') \in Q_C^2, \ell \in \Sigma\} \cup \{\langle q, \ell, A_i, q' \rangle_{\mathcal{F}_C} \mid (q, q') \in Q_C^2, \ell \in \Sigma, A_i \in \mathcal{F}_C\}$.

Although equation (1) constraints C to be complete, there is no explicit constraint for C to be deterministic. By construction, any word w is accepted in R iff it is accepted by any run that recognizes w in C. In the presence of two transitions $\langle q, \ell, d_1 \rangle_{\delta_C}$ and $\langle q, \ell, d_2 \rangle_{\delta_C}$ when building C, we can safely ignore one of them to ensure determinism.

Minimization: $|\mathcal{F}_C| = |\mathcal{F}_R|$. Given a complete DTGBA $R = \langle\langle AP, Q_R, \iota_R, \delta_R \rangle, \mathcal{F}_R \rangle$, we may use SYNTHESIZEDTGBA in a loop such as the one shown in Fig. 4 to reduce the number of states of the automaton. By default, we keep the same number $m = |\mathcal{F}_R|$ of acceptance sets for the candidate automaton.

Minimization with Generalization: $|\mathcal{F}_C| > |\mathcal{F}_R|$. A greater reduction might be obtained by increasing the number $m = |\mathcal{F}_C|$ of acceptance sets. This can be interpreted as the converse of a degeneralization: instead of augmenting the number of states to reduce the number of acceptance sets, we augment the number of acceptance sets in an attempt to reduce the number of states.

It is however not clear how this increase of m should be done. Figure 5 shows an example of a property that can be expressed by a 4-state DTGBA if $m = 1$, a 2-state DTGBA if $m = 2$ and a 1-state DTGBA if $m = 4$. Interestingly, the smallest DTGBA for $m = 3$ also has two states. Consequently an algorithm

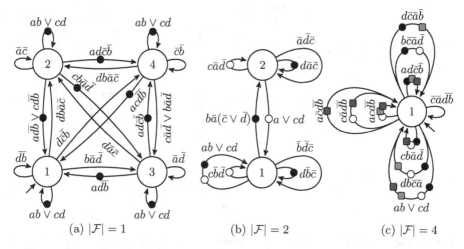

Fig. 5. Examples of minimal DTGBA recognizing $(\mathsf{GF}a \wedge \mathsf{GF}b) \vee (\mathsf{GF}c \wedge \mathsf{GF}d)$

that increments m as long as it reduces the number of states would never reach $m = 4$.

We leave open the problem of finding the smallest m such that no smaller equivalent DTGBA with a larger m can be found. Instead, we use the following heuristic: let m be the number of acceptance set that were "naturally" used to translate the formula φ into a TGBA A_φ (before any degeneralization or determinization). In the case of $(\mathsf{GF}a \wedge \mathsf{GF}b) \vee (\mathsf{GF}c \wedge \mathsf{GF}d)$, each F operator will require one acceptance set during the translation [10], so we would use $m = 4$.

5 Implementation and Experiments

5.1 Implemented Tools

Figure 6 gives an overview of the processing chains we implemented to produce a minimal DTGBA or DTBA. With the exception of 1t12dstar 0.5.1, a tool written by Joachim Klein [14] to convert LTL formulae into deterministic Rabin or Streett automata, all the other white boxes correspond to algorithms that have been implemented in Spot 1.2, and have been integrated in two command-line tools: 1t12tgba at the top of the picture, and dstar2tgba at the bottom.

1t12tgba takes as input an LTL formula and translates it into a TGBA $A = \langle S, \mathcal{F} \rangle$ [10]. If the desired number of acceptance sets m was not supplied on the command-line, we set $m \leftarrow |\mathcal{F}|$ right after this step. We now attempt WDBA minimization [9], if that succeeded, we output a minimal weak DBA (looking for transition-based or generalized acceptance will not reduce it further). Otherwise, we simplify the TGBA using simulation-based reductions [2]. If the resulting TGBA has more than one acceptance set but we plan to build a DTBA (i.e. $m = 1$), we degeneralize it. If the resulting TBA is nondeterministic, we attempt the transition-based variant of Dax et al. [9]'s powerset construction followed by

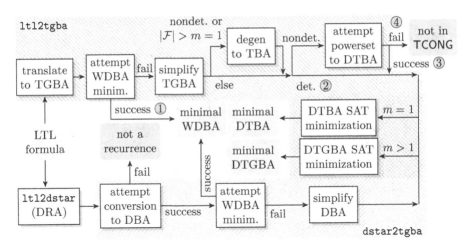

Fig. 6. The two tool chains we use to convert an LTL formula into a DTBA or a DTGBA. $|\mathcal{F}|$ is the number of acceptance condition of the current automaton, while m is the desired number of acceptance sets.

a cycle-enumeration to decide the acceptance of each transition. This procedure works only on a TBA, hence the previous degeneralization is also performed on any nondeterministic TGBA. If this powerset construction fails to produce an equivalent DTBA, it means the input property is not in TCONG. Otherwise the deterministic automaton is sent for SAT-based minimization. We have two procedures implemented: "DTGBA SAT" is the encoding described in Sec. 4.1, while "DTBA SAT" is an adaptation of Ehlers' encoding [11] to transition-based Büchi acceptance and is more-efficient to use when $m = 1$ (see Annex A). Not apparent on this picture, is that these two algorithms can be configured to output automata that are DBA-type or DGBA-type, as discussed in the last paragraph of Sec. 4.1. To solve SAT problems, we use glucose 2.3 [1], which is ranked first in the hard-combinatorial benchmark of the 2013 SAT Competition.

If the automaton could not be determinized by ltl2tgba, the second approach with dstar2tgba is used instead. This approach starts with ltl2dstar to convert the input LTL formula into a deterministic Rabin automaton (DRA). The produced DRA is then converted to a DBA [15] if such a DBA exists, otherwise it means that the formula is not a recurrence. The resulting DBA is turned into a minimal WDBA if it expresses an obligation [9], otherwise it is simplified using simulation-based reduction, before finally proceeding to SAT-based minimization.

5.2   Experiments

To assert the effectiveness of our minimization procedures, we took LTL formulas expressing recurrence properties, and attempted to build a minimal DBA, DTBA, and DTGBA for each of them. The LTL formulae are all those listed by Ehlers [11], and those of Esparza et al. [12] that are DBA-realizable. We also added a few formulas of our own.

For comparison, we also ran Ehlers' DBAminimizer (dated November 2011) [11]: a tool that takes deterministic Rabin automata, as produced by ltl2dstar, and converts them into their minimal DBA by solving a SAT problem with PicoSat (version 957). This tool is named "DBAm..zer" in our tables.

We executed our benchmark on a machine with four Intel Xeon E7-2860 processors and 512GB of memory. We limited each minimization procedure (the entire process of taking an LTL formula or a Rabin automaton into a minimal DBA, including writing the problem to disk, not just the SAT-solving procedure) to 2 hours, and each process to 40GB of memory.

For presentation, we partitioned our set of formulae into four classes, based on which path they would take in ltl2tgba, denoted by the ⊗ marks in Fig. 6.

① Formulae that correspond to obligations properties. On these formulas, the powerset construction can be used to obtain a DBA [9], and this DBA can be minimized in polynomial time [16]. Using a SAT-based minimization in this case would be unreasonable.

② Formulae for which ltl2tgba translator naturally produces deterministic automata, without requiring a powerset construction.

③ Formulae that ltl2tgba can successfully convert into a DTBA by applying a powerset construction.

④ Formulae that ltl2tgba would fail to convert into a DTBA, and for which dstar2tgba is needed.

For size reason, we only present an excerpt of the results for the most interesting classes: ④ (Table 1) and ③ (Table 2).[1]

For each formula we show the size of the DRA constructed by ltl2dstar, the size of the DTBA or DBA built by dstar2tgba before SAT-minimization, and the size of the minimal DBA, DTBA or DTGBA after SAT-minimization. In the case of DTGBA the desired number of acceptance sets m is shown in the second column (this m was computed by running only the translation algorithm of ltl2tgba, and picking $m \leftarrow |\mathcal{F}|$ on the result).

Column "C." indicates whether the produced automata are complete: rejecting sink states are always omitted from the sizes we display, and this explains differences when comparing our tables with other papers that measure complete automata. When $C = 0$, a complete automaton would have one more state.

Cases that took more than 2 hours or 40GB are shown as "(killed)"; an additional "$\leq n$" gives the number of states of the smallest automaton successfully computed. SAT problems requiring more than 2^{31} clauses, the maximum supported by state-of-the-art solvers, are shown as "(intmax)". Cases where the output of the SAT minimization is smaller than the input are shown with a light gray background. Bold numbers show cases where the minimal DTBA is smaller than the minimal DBA (transition-based acceptance was useful) and cases where the minimal DTGBA is smaller than the minimal DTBA (generalized acceptance was useful). Dark gray cells show cases where the tool returned an automaton that was not minimal. For dstar2tgba, it is because glucose

---

[1] Detailed results and instructions to reproduce the benchmark can be found at
http://www.lrde.epita.fr/~adl/forte14/

Table 1. Formulae that we do not know how to determinize other than via DRA

		DRA	DBA	DBAm..zer		minDBA		minDTBA		minDTGBA		
m	C.	$\lvert Q\rvert$	$\lvert Q\rvert$	$\lvert Q\rvert$	time	$\lvert Q\rvert$	time	$\lvert Q\rvert$	time	$\lvert Q\rvert$	$\lvert\mathcal{F}\rvert$	time
$(\bar a \wedge Fa)\,R(\bar b\,R\,XFc)$	2	1	60	24	(killed)		11	1585	7	14	7	1	815
$\bar a \wedge ((Fb\,U\,a)\,W\,Xc)$	2	0	31	20	(killed)		(killed≤15)		(killed≤14)		(killed≤13)		
$(a\,R(b\,R\,Fc))\,W\,XGb$	1	1	31	24	(killed)		(killed≤11)		8	188	8	1	190
$(a\,R\,Fb)\,U\,X\bar c$	2	1	19	13	11	1356	11	2405	10	55	10	1	182
$F(a \wedge Fb)\,W\,Xc$	2	1	25	16	(killed)		(killed≤12)		11	1445	10	2	364
$(F\bar a\,R\,F\bar b)\,W\,G\bar c$	2	1	18	15	5	59	5	14	4	12	4	1	444
$((Fa\,U\,b)\,R\,Fc)\,W\,X\bar c$	3	1	47	32	11	1216	11	1792	9	55	(intmax)		
$G((a \wedge b)\vee Ga \vee F(\bar c \wedge XXc))$	1	1	49	27	(killed)		9	577	7	307	7	1	307
$Ga\,R(F\bar b \wedge (c\,U\,b))$	2	0	10	9	8	13	8	27	6	1	5	2	36
$G(F(\bar a \wedge Fa)\,U\,(b\,U\,Xc))$	3	1	52	35	(killed)		10	1304	7	981	(intmax)		
$GF(a \wedge F(b \wedge Fc))$	3	1	10	10	4	1	4	1	3	1	1	3	156
$G(F\bar a \vee (Fb\,U\,c))$	3	1	29	23	4	1368	4	77	3	76	(intmax)		
$G(F\bar a\,U\,X(F\bar b \wedge Xb))$	3	1	58	37	(killed)		4	480	3	512	(intmax)		
$GF(a \wedge XXXFb)$	2	1	66	6	66	4927	3	0	2	0	1	2	1
$G(G\bar a \vee ((Fb\,U\,c)\,U\,a))$	3	1	20	18	10	174	10	191	9	59	18	1	3183
$X(\bar a \wedge Fa)\,R(a\,M\,Fb)$	2	1	11	11	9	3	9	2	9	2	9	1	10
$X(\bar a \vee G(a \wedge \bar b))\,R\,F(c \wedge Fb)$	2	1	29	18	11	1467	11	1905	10	46	9	2	667
$XF\bar a\,R\,F(b \vee (\bar a \wedge F\bar c))$	3	1	17	12	7	0	7	1	6	0	6	1	101
$X((Fa \wedge XFb)\,R\,XFc)$	3	1	54	34	(killed)		(killed≤13)		10	149	(intmax)		

Table 2. Formulae determinized via the TBA-variant of the procedure of Dax et al. [9]

		DRA	DTBA	DBA	DBAm..zer		minDBA		minDTBA		minDTGBA		
m	C.	$\lvert Q\rvert$	$\lvert Q\rvert$	$\lvert Q\rvert$	$\lvert Q\rvert$	time	$\lvert Q\rvert$	time	$\lvert Q\rvert$	time	$\lvert Q\rvert$	$\lvert\mathcal{F}\rvert$	time
$(a\,U\,X\bar a) \vee$	2	0		10	12			8	3.9	6	0.5	6	1	3.6
$XG(\bar b \wedge XFc)$			10	8	8	8	4.2	8	2.3	6	0.1	6	1	1.7
$F(a \wedge GFb) \vee (Fc \wedge$	5	1		4	5			5	0.0	4	0.0	4	1	1.9
$Fa \wedge F(c \wedge GF\bar b))$			7	6	6	5	0.1	5	0.0	4	0.0	4	1	68.9
$GF(a \leftrightarrow XXb)$	1	1		7	11			6	2.7	4	0.1	4	1	0.1
			9	9	9	6	1.2	6	1.8	4	0.2	4	1	0.2
$GF(a \leftrightarrow XXXb)$	1	1		15	23			(killed≤11)		(killed≤8)		(killed≤8)		
			17	17	17	(killed)		(killed≤11)		(killed≤8)		(killed≤8)		
$(GFb \wedge GFa) \vee$	4	1		5	9			5	2.0	4	0.1	1	4	25.3
$(GFc \wedge GFd)$			13	8	8	5	2.2	5	1.5	4	1.3	1	4	406.0
$X((a\,M\,F((b \wedge c) \vee$	3	1		14	18			(killed≤12)		11	3934.0	10	3	2010.5
$(\bar b \wedge \bar c)))\,W(G\bar c\,U\,b))$			29	22	22	(killed)		(killed≤12)		11	4628.4	22	1	1617.2
$X(a\,R((\bar b \wedge F\bar c)\,M\,X\bar a))$	2	0		10	12			10	4188.5	9	52.7	8	2	13.0
			13	13	13	10	1449.4	10	3424.5	9	52.3	8	2	37.1
$X(G(\bar a\,M\,\bar b) \vee$	1	0		7	8			7	0.2	6	0.1	6	1	0.1
$G(a \vee G\bar a))$			14	13	13	7	1.3	7	1.1	6	0.4	6	1	0.4
$XXG(Fa\,U\,Xb)$	2	1		10	14			8	2.9	6	1.1	5	2	17.5
			21	18	18	8	80.6	8	11.3	6	12.2	5	2	337.0

answers INDETERMINATE when it is not able to solve the problem: dstar2tgba then pessimistically assumes that the problem is unsatisfiable and returns the input automaton.

The couple of cases where we are able to produce a minimal DBA, but DBAminimizer failed, are because we apply more efficient simplification routines on the DBA before it is passed to the SAT-minimization, our encoding takes advantage of SCCs in the reference automaton, and we use a different SAT solver. The cases where we fail to output minimal DBA, but successfully output a DTBA (or even a DTGBA) are due to the fact that DTBA and DTGBA will produce smaller automata, so the last iteration of the algorithm of Fig. 4, the one where the problem is UNSAT (often the more time-consuming problem), is applied to a smaller automaton. Finally bold numbers of the minDTGBA column confirm that using generalized acceptance can actually reduce the size of a DBA or DTBA. Note that useless acceptance sets have been removed from all DTGBA produced [2], so $|\mathcal{F}|$ might be smaller than m.

Table 2 shows an excerpt of class ③: formulae that can be determinized by the powerset construction of Dax et al. [9]. As this construction enumerates all cycles of the determinized automaton to fix its acceptance sets, it is potentially very long. We therefore compare our two approaches: each formula of the table has two result lines, the upper line corresponds to ltl2tgba (with the powerset construction), while the lower line shows results via ltl2dstar (with Safra's construction). In this table, the former approach is almost always the fastest.

These tables show that even if powerset and Safra's construction are only able to deal with a single acceptance set, so force us to degeneralize automata, we can successfully reconstruct minimal DTGBAs with generalized acceptance.

6   Conclusion and Future Work

Deterministic Büchi automata are mandatory in some applications like verification of Markov decision processes, probabilistic model checking, or synthesis of distributed systems from LTL specifications. In these contexts small automata are more than welcome. Furthermore, it is well known that transition-based and generalized acceptance contributes to the conciseness of automata. However, to our knowledge, there did not exist any algorithm to produce minimal and generalized deterministic Büchi automata. Furthermore, we do not know of any determinization algorithm that would build a generalized automaton.

In this paper, we have presented a complete framework with two complete processing chains for determinizing and minimizing transition-based generalized Büchi automata. Even though we construct non-generalized deterministic automata before minimizing them, our SAT-based minimization can be used to produce minimal DTGBA for a given number of acceptance sets m.

Our results show that this SAT-based technique is effective for medium-sized automata. For large automata, SAT-solving is expensive, but it could still be run with a time constraint to produce a smaller (but not necessarily minimal) DTGBA.

In the future we plan to improve our encoding by using more structural information about the reference automaton to reduce the number clauses and variables used, and, hopefully, deal with larger automata. We also need to investigate the problem, mentioned in Section 4.2, of selecting the "best" m for a given automaton, and the possibility to extend Dax et al.'s technique to a class of properties that are realizable by a DTGBA whose LTS is a MSA (this class would contain TCONG).

Other recent algorithms from the literature should also be considered for integration in our setup. For instance our TGBA simplification step of Fig. 6 could be improved using other simulation techniques [21, 7], and an implementation of determinization technique of [22] could also contribute to reducing the size of the automaton that has to be minimized.

References

1. Audemard, G., Simon, L.: Predicting learnt clauses quality in modern SAT solvers. In: IJCAI 2009, pp. 399–404 (July 2009)
2. Babiak, T., Badie, T., Duret-Lutz, A., Křetínský, M., Strejček, J.: Compositional approach to suspension and other improvements to LTL translation. In: Bartocci, E., Ramakrishnan, C.R. (eds.) SPIN 2013. LNCS, vol. 7976, pp. 81–98. Springer, Heidelberg (2013)
3. Baier, C., Katoen, J.-P.: Principles of Model Checking. MIT Press (2008)
4. Bloem, R., Ravi, K., Somenzi, F.: Efficient decision procedures for model checking of linear time logic properties. In: Halbwachs, N., Peled, D.A. (eds.) CAV 1999. LNCS, vol. 1633, pp. 222–235. Springer, Heidelberg (1999)
5. Boigelot, B., Jodogne, S., Wolper, P.: On the use of weak automata for deciding linear arithmetic with integer and real variables. In: Goré, R.P., Leitsch, A., Nipkow, T. (eds.) IJCAR 2001. LNCS (LNAI), vol. 2083, pp. 611–625. Springer, Heidelberg (2001)
6. Černá, I., Pelánek, R.: Relating hierarchy of temporal properties to model checking. In: Rovan, B., Vojtáš, P. (eds.) MFCS 2003. LNCS, vol. 2747, pp. 318–327. Springer, Heidelberg (2003)
7. Clemente, L., Mayr, R.: Advanced automata minimization. In: POPL 2013, pp. 63–74. ACM (2013)
8. Couvreur, J.-M., Duret-Lutz, A., Poitrenaud, D.: On-the-fly emptiness checks for generalized büchi automata. In: Godefroid, P. (ed.) SPIN 2005. LNCS, vol. 3639, pp. 169–184. Springer, Heidelberg (2005)
9. Dax, C., Eisinger, J., Klaedtke, F.: Mechanizing the powerset construction for restricted classes of ω-automata. In: Namjoshi, K.S., Yoneda, T., Higashino, T., Okamura, Y. (eds.) ATVA 2007. LNCS, vol. 4762, pp. 223–236. Springer, Heidelberg (2007)
10. Duret-Lutz, A.: LTL translation improvements in Spot. In: VECoS 2011. British Computer Society (September 2011)
11. Ehlers, R.: Minimising deterministic büchi automata precisely using SAT solving. In: Strichman, O., Szeider, S. (eds.) SAT 2010. LNCS, vol. 6175, pp. 326–332. Springer, Heidelberg (2010)

12. Gaiser, A., Křetínský, J., Esparza, J.: Rabinizer: Small deterministic automata for ltl(**F**,**G**). In: Chakraborty, S., Mukund, M. (eds.) ATVA 2012. LNCS, vol. 7561, pp. 72–76. Springer, Heidelberg (2012)
13. Finkbeiner, B., Schewe, S.: Uniform distributed synthesis. In: LICS 2005, pp. 321–330 (June 2005)
14. Klein, J., Baier, C.: Experiments with deterministic ω-automata for formulas of linear temporal logic. Theoretical Computer Science 363, 182–195 (2005)
15. Krishnan, S.C., Puri, A., Brayton, R.K.: Deterministic ω-automata vis-a-vis deterministic Büchi automata. In: Du, D.-Z., Zhang, X.-S. (eds.) ISAAC 1994. LNCS, vol. 834, pp. 378–386. Springer, Heidelberg (1994)
16. Löding, C.: Efficient minimization of deterministic weak ω-automata. Information Processing Letters 79(3), 105–109 (2001)
17. Maler, O., Staiger, L.: On syntactic congruences for ω-languages. In: Enjalbert, P., Wagner, K.W., Finkel, A. (eds.) STACS 1993. LNCS, vol. 665, pp. 586–594. Springer, Heidelberg (1993)
18. Manna, Z., Pnueli, A.: A hierarchy of temporal properties. In: PODC 1990, pp. 377–410. ACM (1990)
19. Rozier, K.Y., Vardi, M.Y.: A multi-encoding approach for LTL symbolic satisfiability checking. In: Butler, M., Schulte, W. (eds.) FM 2011. LNCS, vol. 6664, pp. 417–431. Springer, Heidelberg (2011)
20. Safra, S.: Complexity of Automata on Infinite Objects. PhD thesis, The Weizmann Institute of Science, Rehovot, Israel (March 1989)
21. Schewe, S.: Beyond hyper-minimisation—minimising DBAs and DPAs is NP-complete. In: FSTTCS 2010. LIPIcs, vol. 8, pp. 400–411. Schloss Dagstuhl LZI (2010)
22. Schewe, S., Varghese, T.: Tight bounds for the determinisation and complementation of generalised büchi automata. In: Chakraborty, S., Mukund, M. (eds.) ATVA 2012. LNCS, vol. 7561, pp. 42–56. Springer, Heidelberg (2012)

A   Synthesis of Equivalent DTBA

This section gives our transition-based adaptation of Ehlers' encoding [11]. After giving a straightforward adaptation of his encoding to deal with DTBA instead of DBA, we list some additional optimizations we applied in our implementation.

From a reference DTBA $R = \langle \langle \Sigma, Q_R, \iota_R, \delta_R \rangle, \mathcal{F}_R \rangle$, we give a set of constraints that ensures a candidate DTBA $C = \langle \langle \Sigma, Q_C, \iota_C, \delta_C \rangle, F_C \rangle$ is equivalent to R.

We encode C with two sets of variables:

- The variables $\{ \langle q_1, \ell, q_2 \rangle_{\delta_C} \mid (q_1, q_2) \in Q_C^2, \ell \in \Sigma \}$ encode the existence of transitions $(q_1, \ell, q_2) \in \delta_C$ in the candidate automaton.
- Variables $\{ \langle q_1, \ell, q_2 \rangle_{\mathcal{F}_C} \mid (q_1, q_2) \in Q_C^2, \ell \in \Sigma \}$ encode the membership of these transitions to the acceptance set $\mathcal{F}_C$.

For the product $C \otimes R$, we retain the reachable states, and parts of paths that might eventually be completed to become cycles.

- A variable in $\{ \langle q, q' \rangle_G \mid q \in Q_C, q' \in Q_R \}$ encodes the existence of a reachable state (q, q') in $C \otimes R$.
- A variable in $\{ \langle q_1, q_1', q_2, q_2' \rangle_C \mid (q_1, q_2) \in Q_C^2, (q_1', q_2') \in Q_R^2 \}$ denotes that there is an acyclic path between (q_1, q_1') and (q_2, q_2') in the product, such that its projection on the candidate automaton C does not visit $\mathcal{F}_C$.

– A variable in $\{\langle q_1, q_1', q_2, q_2' \rangle_R \mid (q_1, q_2) \in Q_C^2, (q_1', q_2') \in Q_R^2\}$ denotes that there is an acyclic path between (q_1, q_1') and (q_2, q_2') in the product, such that its projection on the reference automaton R does not visit $\mathcal{F}_R$.

The problem is encoded as follows. The candidate automaton is complete:

$$\bigwedge_{q_1 \in Q_C, \ell \in \Sigma} \bigvee_{q_2 \in Q_C} \langle q_1, \ell, q_2 \rangle_{\delta_C} \tag{6}$$

The initial state of the product exists. Furthermore if (q_1, q_1') is a state of the product, $(q_1', \ell, q_2') \in \delta_R$ is a transition in the reference automaton, and $(q_1, \ell, q_2) \in \delta_C$ is transition in the candidate automaton, then (q_2, q_2') is a state of the product too:

$$\wedge \quad \langle \iota_C, \iota_R \rangle_G \quad \wedge \bigwedge_{\substack{(q_1, q_2) \in Q_C^2, q_1' \in Q_R \\ (\ell, q_2') \in \delta_R(q_1')}} \langle q_1, q_1' \rangle_G \wedge \langle q_1, \ell, q_2 \rangle_{\delta_C} \to \langle q_2, q_2' \rangle_G \tag{7}$$

Each state of the product corresponds to an empty path that is non-accepting in the reference and in the candidate automata:

$$\wedge \bigwedge_{q_1 \in Q_C, q_1' \in Q_R} \langle q_1, q_1' \rangle_G \to (\langle q_1, q_1', q_1, q_1' \rangle_R \wedge \langle q_1, q_1', q_1, q_1' \rangle_C) \tag{8}$$

Otherwise when one of the two transitions does not close the cycle ($q_3 \neq q_1 \vee q_3' \neq q_1'$), then the non-accepting path is prolonged:

$$\wedge \bigwedge_{\substack{(q_1, q_2, q_3) \in Q_C^3, (q_1', q_2') \in Q_R^2 \\ (\ell, q_3') \in \delta_R(q_2'), (q_2', \ell, q_3') \notin F_R \\ (q_3' \neq q_1') \vee (q_3 \neq q_1)}} \langle q_1, q_1', q_2, q_2' \rangle_R \wedge \langle q_2, \ell, q_3 \rangle_{\delta_C} \to \langle q_1, q_1', q_3, q_3' \rangle_R \tag{9}$$

If a path of the product that is non-accepting with respect to the **reference** automaton, is completed by a **non-accepting** transition (q_2', ℓ, q_3') and a transition (q_2, ℓ, q_3) that both closes the cycle ($q_3 = q_1 \wedge q_3' = q_1'$), then (q_2, ℓ, q_1) is also non-accepting:

$$\wedge \bigwedge_{\substack{(q_1, q_2) \in Q_C^2, (q_1', q_2') \in Q_R^2, \\ (\ell, q_3') \in \delta_R(q_2'), (q_2', \ell, q_3') \notin F_R \\ q_3' = q_1'}} \langle q_1, q_1', q_2, q_2' \rangle_R \wedge \langle q_2, \ell, q_1 \rangle_{\delta_C} \to \neg \langle q_2, \ell, q_1 \rangle_{\mathcal{F}_C} \tag{10}$$

Otherwise when one of the two transitions does not close the cycle ($q_3 \neq q_1 \vee q_3' \neq q_1'$) and the candidate transition (q_2, ℓ, q_3) is non-accepting, then the non-accepting path is prolonged (note that we don't care whether $(q_2', \ell, q_3') \in F_R$ or not):

$$\wedge \bigwedge_{\substack{(q_1, q_2, q_3) \in Q_C^3, (q_1', q_2') \in Q_R^2 \\ (\ell, q_3') \in \delta_R(q_2'), \\ (q_3' \neq q_1') \vee (q_3 \neq q_1)}} \langle q_1, q_1', q_2, q_2' \rangle_C \wedge \langle q_2, \ell, q_3 \rangle_{\delta_C} \wedge \neg \langle q_2, \ell, q_3 \rangle_{\mathcal{F}_C} \to \langle q_1, q_1', q_3, q_3' \rangle_C \tag{11}$$

Conversely, if a path of the product that is non-accepting with respect to the **candidate** automaton, is completed by an **accepting** transition (q_2', ℓ, q_3') and a transition (q_2, ℓ, q_3) that both closes the cycle ($q_3 = q_1 \wedge q_3' = q_1'$), then (q_2, ℓ, q_1) is also accepting:

$$\wedge \bigwedge_{\substack{(q_1,q_2)\in Q_C^2,\, (q_1',q_2')\in Q_R^2, \\ (\ell,q_3')\in\delta_R(q_2'),\, (q_2',\ell,q_3')\in F_R \\ q_3'=q_1'}} \langle q_1,q_1',q_2,q_2'\rangle_C \wedge \langle q_2,\ell,q_1\rangle_{\delta_C} \rightarrow \langle q_2,\ell,q_1\rangle_{\mathcal{F}_C} \quad (12)$$

The symmetry-breaking equation (S) of Section 4 applies here as well.

As we did in our DTGBA encoding of Sec. 4.1, variables of the form $\langle q_1,q_1',q_2,q_2'\rangle_C$ or $\langle q_1,q_1',q_2,q_2'\rangle_R$ should be limited to cases where q_1' and q_2' belong to the same SCC of R, since it is not possible to build a cycle outside an SCC. Furthermore, variables of the form $\langle q_1,q_1',q_1,q_1'\rangle_R$ or $\langle q_1,q_1',q_2,q_2'\rangle_C$ are actually superfluous. Each time we use such a variable in equations (9)–(12), we could replace it by $\langle q_1,q_1'\rangle_G$. Doing so will avoid generating $|Q_C|\times|Q_R|$ variables, and all the clauses generated by equation (8) which is no longer needed.

Formal Verification of Complex Properties on PLC Programs

Dániel Darvas[1], Borja Fernández Adiego[1], András Vörös[2], Tamás Bartha[3], Enrique Blanco Viñuela[1], and Víctor M. González Suárez[4]

[1] CERN, European Organization for Nuclear Research,
Geneva, Switzerland
{bfernand,ddarvas,eblanco}@cern.ch
[2] Budapest University of Technology and Economics,
Budapest, Hungary
vori@mit.bme.hu
[3] Institute for Computer Science and Control, Hungarian Academy of Sciences,
Budapest, Hungary
bartha.tamas@sztaki.mta.hu
[4] University of Oviedo, Gijón, Spain
victor@isa.uniovi.es

Abstract. Formal verification has become a recommended practice in the safety-critical application areas. However, due to the complexity of practical control and safety systems, the state space explosion often prevents the use of formal analysis. In this paper we extend our former verification methodology with effective property preserving reduction techniques. For this purpose we developed general rule-based reductions and a customized version of the Cone of Influence (COI) reduction. Using these methods, the verification of complex requirements formalised with temporal logics (e.g. CTL, LTL) can be orders of magnitude faster. We use the NuSMV model checker on a real-life PLC program from CERN to demonstrate the performance of our reduction techniques.

Keywords: PLC, model checking, automata, temporal logic, reduction, cone of influence, NuSMV.

1 Introduction

At CERN (European Organization for Nuclear Research) large industrial installations, such as cryogenics, HVAC (heating, ventilation, and air conditioning) and vacuum systems rely on PLC (Programmable Logic Controller) based control systems. These systems are critical to CERN's operation and guaranteeing that their behaviours conform to their requirement specifications is of highest importance. Formal verification, and especially model checking is a promising technique to ensure that PLC programs meet their specifications.

The difficulties of bringing model checking techniques to the automation industry are twofold. First, both a formal model of the system to be verified and a formal specification of the verification criteria need to be created. They are

E. Ábrahám and C. Palamidessi (Eds.), FORTE 2014, LNCS 8461, pp. 284–299, 2014.

usually the result of a cooperation between a control engineer and a formal methods expert, with potential for misunderstanding. A second concern is the amount of necessary computation resources. Therefore, the formal models for verifying industrial control systems should be generated automatically, making the verification and validation process less complex and error-prone for the control engineers. The general models created automatically are usually huge for real applications, thus this generation should be extended with reduction techniques.

Our goal is to verify complex requirements coming from the real design and development process. To formalise those requirements, we need to use powerful temporal logic, as the properties to be checked cannot be expressed by simple Boolean logic. Here we target Computation Tree Logic (CTL) and Linear Temporal Logic (LTL) expressions. We proposed previously a methodology for automated modelling and verification of PLC programs [1]. In this paper we focus on reduction techniques making the automated verification of complex properties quicker on real PLC programs. We present general rule-based reductions and a customized version of the cone of influence (COI) reduction tailored to our intermediate models. Experimental verification results on a CERN's real-life ST (Structured Text) [2] program using the NuSMV model checker are also included in the paper.

The rest of the paper is structured as follows: the next part overviews the work related to abstraction techniques applied for PLC verification. Section 2 introduces the general methodology designed to automatically generate formal models out of PLC programs. Section 3 presents the property preserving reduction techniques we apply. Section 4 analyses the proposed techniques showing verification results on a real case study. Finally, Section 5 concludes the paper.

Related Work. Although abstraction and reduction techniques for software verification have previously been studied by other authors, none of them provides a complete workflow to generate and verify PLC programs automatically, especially for programs written in ST language (the most common PLC development language in CERN). In this section, the existing results about reduction techniques applied to PLC systems are discussed.

There were multiple attempts to verify PLC programs using model checking [3–7], but these do not include any specific technique to handle the state space explosion problem automatically, therefore they cannot be applied for our purposes.

In [8] the authors address the problem of state explosion of formal models derived from IL (Instruction List) PLC programs by using an algorithm based on data and interpretation abstraction. Their algorithm has several limitations, e.g. only Boolean variables can be used. In [9], bounded model checking is applied to PLC programs. A simple intermediate model is used to translate PLC programs written in IL language to formal models. Reduction techniques such as constant folding, slicing, and forward expression propagation are employed to optimize the models for bounded model checking. However, this approach can only check reachability, so it does not support the more general properties necessary for our complex requirements. Similarly in [10], a method for verifying PLC programs written in IL using the Counterexample-Guided Abstraction Refinement (CE-GAR) is presented. The limitations of the approach are the same as for other CEGAR approaches: it can handle only safety properties.

As can be seen from the extensive research in this field, the verification of PLC systems is an important task, and our work extends the former results in order to be suitable for real industrial applications and complex properties.

2   Motivation

This section describes the complexity issues of verifying PLC programs. First, we introduce the application environment and the control systems at CERN, then we outline the modelling methodology.

2.1   Application Environment

PLCs are embedded computers applied for industrial control and monitoring tasks. This application domain requires quick and reliable software. Therefore the PLC programs have simple structure and static memory handling, but large number of I/O variables. To have consistent inputs and outputs, they perform a cyclic process called *scan cycle* consisting of three subsequent steps: (1) reading the actual values to the memory, (2) interpreting and executing the implemented PLC program, and (3) assigning the computed values to the real output peripheries. PLCs can be programmed using several different languages [2]. Here we focus ST (Structured Text) language, as it is widely used in CERN. ST is a syntactically Pascal-like, high level language to describe function blocks of controllers (see Fig. 1 for a small ST example). The detailed introduction of the language can be read in [2]. The building elements of ST are functions and function blocks ("stateful functions"), called from the cyclic main program.

At CERN, control systems are developed by using the UNICOS (Unified Industrial Control System) framework [11]. It provides a library of base objects representing common industrial control instrumentation (e.g. sensor, actuators, subsystems). These objects are expressed as function blocks in ST language. The correctness of the UNICOS library and the PLC programs are crucial, as a failure can cause significant damage in the equipment, as well as delay in the experiments. Our main goal is to apply model checking to these baseline objects. The PLC programs have finite set of states and finite variables, therefore model checking is a viable technique for formal verification in this domain.

2.2   Modelling Methodology

In this section, we give a brief overview of our previous approach to generate formal models of PLC programs. Our goal is to be able to handle diverse input and output formalisms, i.e. PLC programs written in different PLC languages and the model formats of various verification tools. Supporting several verification tools means that we can exploit their advantages in terms of simulation facilities, property specification methods, and verification techniques. For this reason, we designed a generic *intermediate model* (IM) [1], representing the behaviour of the verified programs. This model is based on a network of automata[1] representing the control flow graph (CFG) of the PLC program. The IM is a structure $\mathcal{M} = (A, I)$, where A is a set of automata, I is a set of synchronizations. Each automaton is a tuple $A_i = (S, T, V, s_0, V_0)$, where L is a set of states (locations), T is a set of guarded transitions, V is a set of typed variables, l_0 is the initial state and V_0 is the initial value of the variables. A synchronization $I_i = (t, t') \in I$ connects two transitions that should be fired together. We allow maximum one synchronization connected to a transition t.

This IM is similar to the formalism defined in [12], but without clocks for time representation and with slightly different synchronization semantics (see [1] for more details). It provides easy adaptability to a big variety of model checking tools.

Thus, our transformation workflow consists of two main steps: first, the source code of the program is transformed into the IM using the known specialities of the PLC environment (like the scan cycle). The result is essentially a CFG. Next, the IM is translated to the inputs of the verification tools, like NuSMV, UPPAAL or BIP. This approach makes the transformation easy to extend as it decouples the input and output languages. The reader can find further information and more details on this modelling methodology in our report [1].

2.3   Complexity Issues

Our former experiments have shown that the presented modelling approach can be used successfully for transforming ST code to the input languages of various model checker tools. However, verification was seldom successful.

Each base object of the UNICOS library can contain hundreds of variables, not to mention programs consisting of multiple objects. We take as an example an often-used base object of the library that is a behavioural representation of an actuator (e.g. valves, heaters, motors) driven by digital signals. This object is implemented in ST as a function block, calling several other functions. With 60 input variables (of which 13 are parameters and several integers), 62 output variables, and 3 timer instances, this object is representative of other UNICOS objects in terms of size and complexity.

Therefore it is unavoidable to apply advanced algorithms to reduce the task of the model checker. We apply various reduction and abstraction techniques in the different steps of the transformation chain. We designed the intermediate model so that reduction and abstraction techniques are easily applicable on it, and all the model checkers can benefit from the effect of the reductions. The next section is dedicated to these reduction methods. In Section 4, this base object is used to evaluate our reduction techniques.

---

[1] Here we target PLC code without interrupts, thus the CFG can be represented by one single automaton. If interrupts are considered, building the product automaton would not be effective.

3   Reduction Techniques

The requirements to be verified are often complex, containing multiple temporal logic operators and involving a large number of variables, which limits the set of possible reduction techniques. Therefore we have chosen to use property preserving reduction methods. (We also apply non-preserving abstractions for specific purposes such as modelling timers, however, that is not within the scope of this paper.) These algorithms aim at preserving only those behaviours of the system that are relevant from the specification point of view. By using property preserving techniques, the meaning of the model is not modified with regard our assumptions, thus these reductions do not induce any false results that would make the verification much more difficult.

Our reductions are applied to the intermediate model that corresponds to the control flow graph of the PLC program. (Most of these reduction techniques are general for any CFG, not just for the CFGs of PLC programs.) In a PLC the requirements need to be checked only at the beginning and at the end of the PLC cycles, but not in the intermediate states, as the transient values are not written to the physical outputs of the PLC. As a consequence, the order of the variable assignments is not important, as long as the result at the end of the PLC cycle will be the same. Thus, we know that the requirements are only to be checked at specific locations of the CFG.

We do not consider concurrency problems. A PLC code without interrupts is usually single threaded, therefore concurrency problems cannot arise.

In the rest of this section, we present our reductions techniques:

- a new heuristic *cone of influence reduction* algorithm adapted for models representing CFGs (Sect. 3.1),
- heuristic *rule-based reduction* techniques to support the cone of influence algorithm (Sect. 3.2), and
- a *mode selection* method which allows the developer to fine-tune the verification by setting the operational mode to be verified (Sect. 3.3).

3.1   Cone of Influence

Cone of influence (COI) [13] is one of the most powerful property preserving reduction techniques. Its main idea is to identify which part of the model is relevant for the evaluation of the given requirement. The unnecessary parts of the model can be removed without affecting the result. This can help to handle the state space explosion problem.

NuSMV has a built-in cone of influence implementation that can reduce the verification time drastically. However, in some cases we experienced slow verification even when the COI algorithm could theoretically reduce the model size to trivial. By analysing this implementation we found out that this reduction technique could be much more powerful if it were *applied to our intermediate model directly*, where the structure of the CFG is known, before it is transformed to a general state-transition system.

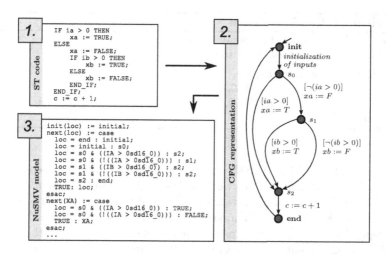

Fig. 1. Example for control flow graph representation of an ST code in NuSMV

In higher level models there is usually more knowledge about the modelled system, therefore the reductions are generally more efficient if they are applied to a higher abstraction level. In this case, the COI algorithm can benefit from the structure information present in the intermediate model, but missing from the generated NuSMV model. Thus, we developed a simple, yet powerful new heuristic cone of influence algorithm, which outperforms the COI method built in NuSMV for our models. To explain the idea behind our approach, first we give an overview of the COI implementation of NuSMV. Afterwards, we introduce our method, and then compare them.

Representing a Control Flow Graph in NuSMV. Before discussing the COI implementation of NuSMV, the method of transforming the CFG represented by the intermediate model to the input language of NuSMV has to be introduced. The input language of NuSMV represents a Mealy machine, whose states comprise the set of possible valuations of every defined state variable [14, 15]. In order to create a NuSMV model corresponding to a control flow graph, a natural way of modelling is to express every variable with a dedicated state variable, and to represent the current location in the CFG with an additional state variable (we call it variable *loc*). This variable *loc* encodes the structure of the CFG along with the guard expressions on its transitions. The example on Fig. 1 shows an extract from a simple ST code, the corresponding CFG and its NuSMV representation.

The COI Implementation of NuSMV. The COI algorithm of NuSMV has no public documentation. However, as this tool is released under the LGPL license, it is possible to analyse its source code.

Algorithm 1. ConeOfInfluence

---

input : $\mathcal{M}$: network of automata, Q: requirement
output : true, iff COI modified the model

$\mathcal{L} \leftarrow$ UnconditionalStates$(\mathcal{M})$;
$D \leftarrow$ NecessaryVariables$(\mathcal{M}, \mathcal{L}, Q)$;
Removal of all variables in $V \setminus D$, with their guards and assignments;
return $V \setminus D \neq \emptyset$;

At the creation of the NuSMV's internal COI model, the dependencies of each variable are computed (function `coiInit`). A variable v *depends on* every variable v' used for the computation of v. (E.g., if the next state of v is defined with a case block in the NuSMV model, all the variables and values will be in the set of dependencies.) Then, a transitive closure is computed for all the variables occurring in the formula to be evaluated. If a variable x is necessary for some reason, all the variables presented in the assignment block of x will be necessary too. Therefore, it is trivial that according to the NuSMV implementation, the variable *loc* is necessary for a variable v, if it is assigned at least once in the CFG, because this assignment is guarded by a location of the CFG. As *loc* is necessary, all the variables in its next-state relation definition will be necessary too which means all variables taking place in guards are necessary. Thus none of the variables used in guards can be eliminated by the COI of NuSMV.

Our COI. We observed that usually it would be possible to reduce the model by removing conditional branches that do not affect the variables in the requirement. In the example shown in Fig. 1, none of the conditional branches is necessary if only variable c is used in the requirement, therefore the variables *ia* and *ib* could be eliminated as well.

Of course, guards can affect the control flow, therefore it is not possible to eliminate all the guards. Here we propose a simple heuristic working well for PLC programs, because of their general properties discussed in this section. The base idea is that there are states (locations) in the CFG that are "unconditional", i.e. all possible executions go through them.

This COI variant consists of three steps (formally: see Algorithm 1):

1. identification of unconditional states,
2. identification of variables influencing the evaluation of the given requirement,
3. elimination of non-necessary variables.

In the following part of this section, these three steps are introduced.

Identification of Unconditional States. The first step of our COI reduction is to identify the set $\mathcal{L}$ of unconditional states. To ensure the correctness of the algorithm, it is necessary that $\mathcal{L}$ does not include conditional states.

To identify the unconditional states, we defined a measure for the states. A *trace* is a list of states $(s_1, s_2, \ldots, s_n)$, where s_1 is the initial state of the automaton, s_n is the end state of the automaton, and there is a transition be-tween each (s_i, s_{i+1}) state pairs. Let $F(s)$ be the fraction of possible traces[2] going through a state s. It is known that all the traces go trough the initial state s_0, therefore $F(s_0) = 1$. For the rest of the states, F can be calculated based on the incoming transitions.

Let $I_T(s) \in 2^T$ depict the set of incoming transitions to state s, and mark the set of outgoing transitions from state s as $O_T(s) \in 2^T$. Let $I_S(t) \in S$ be the source state of transition t. With this notation, the formal definition of $F(s)$ is the following:

$$F(s) := \begin{cases} 1 & \text{if } s = s_0, \\ \sum_{t \in I_T(s)} \frac{F(I_S(t))}{|O_T(I_S(t))|} & \text{otherwise} \end{cases} . \tag{1}$$

After calculating F for each state, it is easy to compute the set of uncondi-tional states: $\mathcal{L} = \{s \in S : F(s) = 1\}$.

Notice, that the intermediate model can contain loops (beside the main loop representing the PLC cycle) due to loops in the input model. In this case, we handle all states in the loop as conditional states (without computing F for them). It has to be noted too that the UNICOS base objects do not contain any loops, and it is also common for other industrial PLC programs.

Identification of Necessary Variables. The goal of the second step is to collect automatically all the variables necessary to evaluate the given requirement (see Algorithm 2). Let D be the set of necessary variables. It is trivial that every variable in the requirement should be in D. After that, for each variable assign-ments that modify a variable in D, the variables in the assignment will also be added to the set D. Furthermore, the guard dependencies should also be added to D, i.e. all the variables that can affect the execution of the analysed variable assignment. If the set of D grew, all the assignments should be checked again.

In the following, we define a function $\mathcal{A}_T: T \to 2^V$, which gives all the variables that can affect the execution of variable assignments on transition t.

First, a supporting function $\mathcal{A}_S: S \to 2^V$ is defined which gives all the variables necessary to determine if state s will be active or not during an execution. This function can benefit from the previously explored unconditional states $\mathcal{L}$, as it is known that no variable is necessary to decide if they can be activated during an execution. Thus, for every state $s \in S$, the function $\mathcal{A}_S(s)$ is the following:

$$\mathcal{A}_S(s) := \begin{cases} \emptyset & \text{if } s \in \mathcal{L} \\ \bigcup_{t \in I_T(s)} \mathcal{A}_T(t) & \text{if } s \notin \mathcal{L} \end{cases} . \tag{2}$$

It means that for the unconditional states, the set of affecting variables is empty, as a consequence of their definition. If a state is not unconditional, the set of variables affecting that this state is active or not is the set of variables affecting the firing of all its incoming transitions.

---

[2] Here we do not consider cycles inside the CFG beside of the cycle corresponding to the main cycle.

For every transition $t \in T$, the function $\mathcal{A}_T(t)$ is the following:

$$\mathcal{A}_T(t) := \mathcal{A}_S\left(I_S(t)\right) \cup \bigcup_{t' \in O_T(I_S(t))} \{variables\ in\ guard\ of\ t'\}. \tag{3}$$

It means that the firing of transition t is affected by the variables that influences its source state $(I_S(t))$ and by the variables in the guard of t. Furthermore, it is also influenced by the variables used in the guard of transitions that can be in conflict with t, i.e. the guard variables of $t' \in O_T(I_S(t))$.

Elimination of Non-necessary Variables. In the second step, the set D of necessary variables is determined. In the last step, all the variables not in D should be deleted. Also, to ensure the syntactical correctness, all the guards and variable assignments containing variables $v \notin D$ should be deleted. They do not affect the evaluation of the requirement, otherwise they should be in set D.

Difference between Our COI and the COI of NuSMV. The main difference between our COI and the COI implementation of NuSMV is in the handling of conditional branches. If there is a conditional branch in the CFG, but the variables in the requirement are not affected by this choice, there is no need for the variables in its guard. This difference can be observed in Fig. 2, which shows the CFG introduced in Fig. 1, after applying the different COIs, and assuming that only variable c is used in the requirement (e.g., $\mathsf{EF}\ c < 0$). The COI of NuSMV can identify that the variables xa and xb are not used to compute c, therefore they will be removed. But the variables ia and ib are used in guards, thus they are kept (see Fig. 2(a)).

Our COI algorithm can detect that because xa and xb are deleted, the ia and ib variables can be deleted too, because those guards do not affect c, i.e. no matter which computation path is executed between locations s_0 and s_2, the assignment of variable c will be the same (see Fig. 2(b)).

Algorithm 2. NecessaryVariables

---

input : $\mathcal{M}$: network of automata, $\mathcal{L}$: set of unconditional states,
          Q: requirement
output : D : set of necessary variables

$D \leftarrow \{variables\ in\ Q\}$;
repeat
    │ **foreach** *variable assignment* $\langle v := Expr \rangle$ *on transition* t **do**
    │ │ **if** $v \in D$ **then**
    │ │ │ // adding assignment and guard dependencies
    │ │ │ $D \leftarrow D \cup \{variables\ in\ Expr\} \cup \mathcal{A}_T(t)$;
until D *is not changed*;
return D;

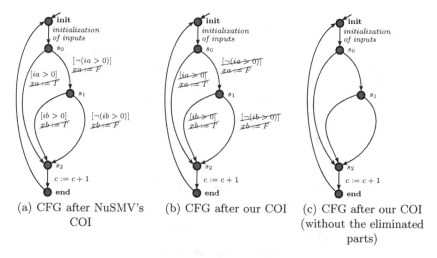

(a) CFG after NuSMV's COI

(b) CFG after our COI

(c) CFG after our COI (without the eliminated parts)

Fig. 2. Example comparing our and the NuSMV's cone of influence algorithm

3.2   General Rule-Based Reductions

Our cone of influence implementation only eliminates variables and the connected variable assignments and guards, without modifying the structure of the CFG. Therefore, the resulting model of the COI often contains empty transitions, unnecessary states, etc. We identified the frequent situations when reduction can be applied and we developed heuristic, rule-based reductions that make the model smaller and easier to verify.

This kind of CFG reductions are not new, they are used for example in numerous compilers to simplify the machine code and to improve the performance. We refer the reader for details to [16].

Similar reductions can be applied for some particularities in the input source codes. For example, in our UNICOS examples it is common to have an array of Boolean values, where some bits are always false. Using simple heuristics, this situation can be identified and instead of creating an unnecessary variable to store that bit, it can be substituted with the constant false value.

All the general reductions presented are defined by a matching pattern and the modification that should be performed, thus they are defined as a set of graph transformations. Our reductions can be categorized as follows:

- **Model simplifications.** The aim of these reductions is to simplify the intermediate model without reducing its potential state space (thus without eliminating states or variables). This group includes elimination of unnecessary variable assignments or transitions, and simplification of logical expressions. These reductions do not reduce the model themselves, we created them to support the other reduction techniques. For example, if the model contains an empty conditional branch (due to for example another

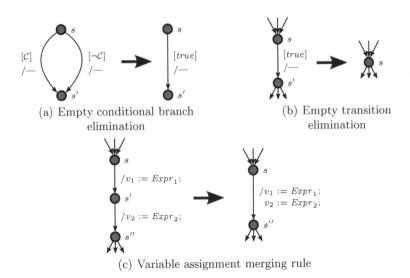

(a) Empty conditional branch elimination

(b) Empty transition elimination

(c) Variable assignment merging rule

Fig. 3. Example reduction rules

reduction), it can be removed without changing the meaning of the model. This rule is illustrated with the Fig. 3(a).

- **Model reductions.** These methods can reduce the potential state space by eliminating states and variables. This group includes heuristics to merge transitions or states, to eliminate variables that have always the same constant value, etc. For example, if a transition has no guard, no synchronization, and no variable assignment (which can be a side effect of the COI reduction), then the two states on the end of the transition can be merged and the transition can be deleted. This rule is illustrated with Fig. 3(b).

- **Domain-specific reductions.** We can benefit from the assumption we made at the beginning of Section 3 that variables are only checked at the end of the PLC cycle. Our two main domain-specific reductions are the following:

  • *Transition merging.* Two consecutive transitions can be merged if they represent a sequence in the CFG and their variable assignments are not in conflict, i.e. their order does not affect each other's value. Formally, $v_a := E_a$ and $v_b := E_b$ are not in conflict if $v_a \notin Vars(E_b)$, $v_b \notin Vars(E_a)$, and $v_a \neq v_b$, where $Vars(E)$ means all variables used in expression E. This can easily be extended to two set of variable assignments, thus it can be reapplied to merged transitions. Fig. 3(c) illustrates this reduction rule.

  • *Variable merging.* Two variables can be merged if they always have the same value at the end of the PLC cycles. While creating two variables for the same purpose can be considered as a bad programming practice, it is a common pattern in the source code of our systems. This feature is used to improve code readability by assigning a meaningful name to a bit of an input array (for example `PFailSafePosition` instead of `ParReg01[8]`).

Traceability. It has to be noted that not all the previously mentioned reduction techniques are property preserving in themselves. For instance, if two variables v and w are merged, thus w will be deleted, the properties containing w are not possible to evaluate. For this reason, we generate a mapping throughout the reductions that contains all the variable substitutions. Based on this mapping, the necessary aliases can be generated for the NuSMV model. For example, an alias w can be added to the model having always the same value as v, as it is known that they always contain the same value at the end of the PLC cycles. Aliases do not modify the size of the state space or the complexity of the model checking.

Workflow. As discussed in the beginning of Section 3.2, the COI algorithm can enable the rule-based reductions. Therefore, after the COI algorithm, all the reduction techniques introduced in this section will be applied, which can enable other reductions or other possible variable removal for the COI algorithm. Therefore we implemented the reductions in an iterative manner. First, the COI is executed. Then, all the possible reductions are applied. If the COI or one of the rule-based reductions was able to reduce the model, all the reductions are executed again. This iterative workflow is described formally in Algorithm 3. (The function Reduce($r, \mathcal{M}$) applies reduction r on the model $\mathcal{M}$ and returns true, iff the reduction modified the model.)

Example. A simple example is shown here illustrating our reduction workflow. If our COI is applied to the Fig. 1 CFG example, then Fig. 2(c) CFG will be obtained. If the reductions presented on Fig. 3(a) and Fig. 3(b) are applied on it, the result will be the simple Fig. 4 CFG.

Algorithm 3. Reductions
---
input : $\mathcal{M}$: model, Q: requirement

bool *changed*;
repeat
  $\quad$ *changed* $\leftarrow$ ConeOfInfluence($\mathcal{M}, Q$);
  $\quad$ **foreach** $r \in \{$*rule-based reductions*$\}$ **do**
  $\quad\quad\mid$ *changed* $\leftarrow$ Reduce($r, \mathcal{M}$) $\vee$ *changed*;
until *changed* = *false*;

Fig. 4. Example CFG after our COI and the reductions

3.3 Mode Selection

Our initial motivation is to verify UNICOS base objects, the basic building modules of the control systems in CERN. Each base object is generic and can be adapted for the specific uses by setting some parameters. Parameters are input variables that are constant during the execution, as they are hard-coded into the PLC application.

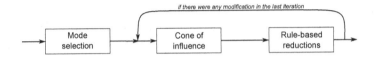

Fig. 5. Overview of the reduction workflow

A significant part of our real requirements have assumptions on the parameters, like "if parameter p_1 is true, then always true that ...". For these requirements, we can use general models and express the parameter configuration in the temporal logic formula, or by adding invariants to the model. However, better performance can be achieved if we encode the configuration in the model itself by replacing the parameter with its constant value. This way, the developers can select the operational mode of the object on which the verification should be performed, i.e. they can fine-tune the verification to their needs. This method is applied only once, before all the other reductions.

The advantages of this method are the following:

- There is no need to create a variable for the fixed parameter as it is substituted with a constant.
- The rule-based reductions can simplify the expressions. For example, if there is a guard $[p_1 \land p_2 \land p_3]$ in the CFG and p_1 is fixed to false, the guard will be always false and can be replaced by a constant false.
- The simplification of the expressions can help the cone of influence reduction to remove the unnecessary variables. E.g., if p_2 and p_3 are only used in the guard $[p_1 \land p_2 \land p_3]$, and p_1 is fixed to false, the variables p_2 and p_3 can be removed. Using the COI in NuSMV or if the fixed parameter is expressed through invariants, this reduction cannot be done.

Now the complete reduction workflow can be summarized. After the transformation of the source code into the intermediate model, the given parameters are fixed to the required values. Then the cone of influence reduction and the

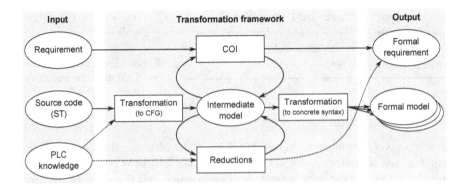

Fig. 6. Overview of the modelling approach

rule-based reductions are performed iteratively (as seen in Fig. 5). It is important to note, that since every reduction rule deletes something from the model
upon firing, they cannot "reduce" the model infinite times, thus the iteration
cycle will stop in finite time. The transformation workflow extended with the
reduction techniques can be seen on Fig. 6.

4   Evaluation

In this section, we show measurement results to evaluate our solution. For the
evaluation we used the base object introduced in Section 2.3. The effect of our
methods on the state space and the run time reduction are introduced. Furthermore, these measurements illustrate, how the different reduction techniques can
complement each other.

State Space. The model generated from the base object is big, as its potential
state space (PSS, the number of possible values of all the variables) contains $3.8 \cdot 10^{239}$ states without any reductions. Fig. 7 shows measurements about the size of
the potential state space without and with our rule-based reductions, and with
different COI reductions using a real-life requirement without mode selection. As
can be seen, NuSMV's cone of influence can reduce the state space significantly,
however our implementation provides much better results. For example, if the
rule-based reductions are enabled, the size of the PSS is $1.2 \cdot 10^{87}$ with NuSMV's
COI, and $4.3 \cdot 10^{26}$ with our own COI implementation.

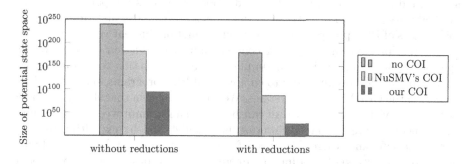

Fig. 7. Measurements comparing the different COI solutions

Verification Run Time. The difference between the COI implementations can
also be observed on the run time of the verification. Table 1 shows verification
run time measurements and measurements about the internal BDD (binary decision diagram) data structures of NuSMV that represent the state space. In these
cases, three different real-life requirements were evaluated. Req. 1 is an LTL expression with form of $G(\alpha \ U \ \beta)$, Req. 2 and 3 are CTL safety expressions ($AG(\alpha)$),
Req. 4 is a complex LTL expression ($G((\alpha \wedge X(\beta \ U \ \gamma)) \rightarrow X(\beta \ U \ \delta))$) describing

a real requirement coming from the developers. In the requirements the Greek letters represent Boolean logical expressions containing multiple (usually 1–5) variables. Without our reductions (even if NuSMV's COI is used), none of them could be executed in a day, thus these reductions are inevitable. These measurements show that by using our COI implementation, the verification run time can be reduced by 1–3 orders of magnitude compared to the COI of NuSMV. The same reduction can be observed in the number of allocated BDD nodes (#Node). The reduction in the peak number of live BDD nodes (#PNode) is smaller, but significant. These measurements show the efficiency of our method.

Table 1. Requirement evaluation measurements

	no reduct.+	our reductions + NuSMV COI			our reductions + our COI		
Req.	NuSMV COI	Runtime	#PNode	#Node	Runtime	#PNode	#Node
1	—	896 s	$8.8 \cdot 10^5$	$1.8 \cdot 10^8$	2.5 s	$2.2 \cdot 10^5$	$1.1 \cdot 10^6$
2	—	1,250 s	$9.9 \cdot 10^5$	$8.8 \cdot 10^8$	19.0 s	$4.6 \cdot 10^5$	$1.4 \cdot 10^7$
3	—	19,300 s	$3.4 \cdot 10^6$	$1.6 \cdot 10^{10}$	1,440 s	$1.3 \cdot 10^6$	$1.6 \cdot 10^9$
4	—	649 s	$9.0 \cdot 10^5$	$5.5 \cdot 10^8$	2.3 s	$2.2 \cdot 10^5$	$9.2 \cdot 10^5$

5   Conclusion and Future Work

This paper presents a solution to make the formal verification of real PLC programs possible by extending automatic model generation with property preserving reduction techniques. These reduction techniques are part of a general methodology based on an intermediate model suitable for transforming the formal models of PLC programs into the input format of different verification tools.

Our results show that by using cone of influence reduction (tailored to our specific application domain) and simple rule-based reduction techniques allows us to apply model checking even to complex real PLC programs, such as the base objects of the CERN's control systems. We have also shown that the effectiveness of the cone of influence algorithm can be significantly improved by performing the reductions directly on the intermediate model, and by exploiting relevant domain-specific knowledge. Moreover, further fine-tuning can be obtained with our proposed method of handling parameter configurations for operational mode selection, by adapting the model to the scenario to be checked.

Our future plans comprise the integration of the tool and methodology in the UNICOS development process. In addition, extending and optimizing the abstraction techniques are ongoing work.

References

1. Darvas, D., Fernández, B., Blanco, E.: Transforming PLC programs into formal models for verification purposes. Internal note, CERN (2013),
http://cds.cern.ch/record/1629275/files/CERN-ACC-NOTE-2013-0040.pdf

2. IEC 61131: Programming languages for programmable logic controllers (2013)
3. Rausch, M., Krogh, B.: Formal verification of PLC programs. In: Proc. of the American Control Conference, pp. 234–238 (1998)
4. Bauer, N., Engell, S., Huuck, R., Lohmann, S., Lukoschus, B., Remelhe, M., Stursberg, O.: Verification of PLC programs given as sequential function charts. In: Ehrig, H., Damm, W., Desel, J., Große-Rhode, M., Reif, W., Schnieder, E., Westkämper, E. (eds.) INT 2004. LNCS, vol. 3147, pp. 517–540. Springer, Heidelberg (2004)
5. Canet, G., Couffin, S., Lesage, J.J., Petit, A., Schnoebelen, P.: Towards the automatic verification of PLC programs written in Instruction List. In: Proc. of Int. Conf. on Systems, Man, and Cybernetics 2000, pp. 2449–2454. Argos Press (2000)
6. Pavlović, O., Ehrich, H.D.: Model checking PLC software written in function block diagram. In: International Conference on Software Testing, pp. 439–448 (2010)
7. Soliman, D., Frey, G.: Verification and validation of safety applications based on PLCopen safety function blocks. Control Engineering Practice 19(9), 929–946 (2011)
8. Gourcuff, V., de Smet, O., Faure, J.M.: Improving large-sized PLC programs verification using abstractions. In: 17th IFAC World Congress (2008)
9. Lange, T., Neuhäußer, M., Noll, T.: Speeding up the safety verification of programmable logic controller code. In: Bertacco, V., Legay, A. (eds.) HVC 2013. LNCS, vol. 8244, pp. 44–60. Springer, Heidelberg (2013)
10. Biallas, S., Brauer, J., Kowalewski, S.: Counterexample-guided abstraction refinement for PLCs. In: Proc. of 5th International Workshop on Systems Software Verification, pp. 2–12. USENIX Association (2010)
11. Blanco, E., et al.: UNICOS evolution: CPC version 6. In: 12th ICALEPCS (2011)
12. Behrmann, G., David, A., Larsen, K.G.: A tutorial on UPPAAL. In: Bernardo, M., Corradini, F. (eds.) SFM-RT 2004. LNCS, vol. 3185, pp. 200–236. Springer, Heidelberg (2004)
13. Clarke, E.M., Grumberg, O., Peled, D.A.: Model Checking. The MIT Press (1999)
14. Cavada, R., Cimatti, A., Jochim, C.A., Keighren, G., Olivetti, E., Pistore, M., Roveri, M., Tchaltsev, A.: NuSMV 2.5 User Manual. FBK-irst (2011)
15. Cimatti, A., Clarke, E., Giunchiglia, E., Giunchiglia, F., Pistore, M., Roveri, M., Sebastiani, R., Tacchella, A.: NuSMV 2: An opensource tool for symbolic model checking. In: Brinksma, E., Larsen, K.G. (eds.) CAV 2002. LNCS, vol. 2404, pp. 359–364. Springer, Heidelberg (2002)
16. Cooper, K.D., Torczon, L.: Engineering a Compiler, 2nd edn. Morgan Kaufmann Publishers Inc. (2012)

Author Index